COMPOSING A CIVIC LIFE

COMPOSING A CIVIC LIFE
A Rhetoric and Readings for Inquiry and Action

SECOND EDITION

MICHAEL BERNDT

Normandale Community College

AMY MUSE

University of St. Thomas

PEARSON
Longman

New York San Francisco Boston
London Toronto Sydney Tokyo Singapore Madrid
Mexico City Munich Paris Cape Town Hong Kong Montreal

Executive Editor: Lynn M. Huddon
Senior Marketing Manager: Sandra McGuire
Senior Supplements Editor: Donna Campion
Production Manager: Denise Phillip
Project Coordination, Text Design, and Electronic Page Makeup: Electronic Publishing
    Services Inc., NYC
Senior Design Manager/Cover Designer: Nancy Danahy
Cover Photo: © National Geographic/Getty Images, Inc.
Photo Researcher: Julie Tesser
Senior Manufacturing Buyer: Dennis J. Para
Printer and Binder: R. R. Donnelley and Sons
Cover Printer: Phoenix Color Corporation

For permission to use copyrighted material, grateful acknowledgment is made to the copyright
holders on pp. 569–572, which are hereby made part of this copyright page.

Library of Congress Cataloging-in-Publication Data

Berndt, Michael
    Composing a civic life : a rhetoric and readings for inquiry and action / Michael Berndt;
Amy Muse.-- 2nd ed.
        p. cm.
    Includes bibliographical references and index.
    ISBN 0-321-41359-8
    1. Readers--Community life. 2. Community life--Problems, exercises, etc. 3. English
language--Rhetoric--Problems, exercises, etc. 4. Report writing--Problems, exercises, etc. 5.
College readers. I. Muse, Amy. II. Title.
PE1127.S6B47 2006
808'.0427--dc22

                                                        2006002935

Visit us at www.ablongman.com/berndt

ISBN 0-321-41359-8

1 2 3 4 5 6 7 8 9 10——DOC——09 08 07 06

To Mike Carls, my American government teacher,
for modeling good teaching and a dedicated civic life.

To Suzanne, my wife, for offering
encouragement and time.

To Reid, who was born at the project's beginning,
and Paige, who was born at the end,
for putting all things into perspective.

Michael Berndt

To my parents, Bill and Marlene Muse,
for setting the example of a life engaged in
and enriched by community and learning.

Amy Muse

To our students—past, present, and future—who inspire us
with their curiosity and empathy.

Brief Contents

Detailed Contents

4 Arguing: Action as Inquiry 119

5   Writing in Communities: Academic Research and Social Action 156

6 The Family as Community 195

10 Communities of Faith 462

Preface

We wrote the first edition of *Composing a Civic Life* between 1999 and 2002; during that period we witnessed a broad calling for civic engagement. Social, religious, and political leaders were urging Americans to become more engaged in their communities. Scholars and activist writers such as Robert Putnam, Jedediah Purdy, and Paul Rogat Loeb were calling citizens to strengthen community ties. Politicians and community leaders including Al Gore, Sam Nunn, Ervin Duggan, and Colin Powell were calling citizens to renew America's social contract by volunteering or participating in community affairs. Since that time, we have seen many examples of increased civic engagement, from the expansion of organizations such as Moveon.org and True Majority to the renewed civic mission of high schools and universities.

At the same time, we have grown to better appreciate the challenges citizens face in becoming more engaged. After the initial wave of political excitement and citizen action, we discovered—as have many in generations before us—the real difficulties of finding common ground with those who do not share our views. In the last four years, we have watched the country grow seemingly more, not less divided. In *The Impossible Will Take a Little While: A Citizen's Guide to Hope in a Time of Fear* (2005), Paul Loeb expresses well the anxieties that many of us have experienced in recent years:

> We live in a difficult time, fraught with uncertainty and risk. From terrorist threats, foreign military ventures of questionable purpose, and mushrooming white collar crime, to skyrocketing health care costs, mounting national debt, and an economy that appears rigged for the benefit of the greedy and ruthless, the world can at times seem overwhelming, beyond our control.

Colleges, like many other facets of our society, have become sites for these concerns. We see students challenge the right of professors to express their political views. We see rises in classroom incivility and academic dishonesty, while legislators demand greater accountability from educators. We see more emphasis on grades and standardized testing than on individual learning, while we see less investment from professors and students in the public life of their colleges.

How we respond to these challenges can make the writing classroom a model of rigorous, ethical inquiry and action, one that could set a standard for work we do in other classes and communities. This hope is based on several assumptions about students and instructors.

FOR STUDENTS

Students, we believe that you have a genuine desire to learn and to participate more actively in your communities. We believe this in spite of the pressure on you to focus on individual success in the form of well-paying jobs after graduation. We also believe that you can rise to the intellectual level of whatever material you are given, and that the quality of your thinking and writing will improve if you are given meaningful, challenging material with which to work. We also realize, however, that many of you will find it difficult to present your views where you could be challenged or where you could be made to feel uncomfortable. Growth involves some serious exploration of your values and existing ideas. In this class and in others, we ask that you put forth a good faith effort and give critical attention both to what you are being taught and to your own reaction to those ideas. If you find certain conversations uncomfortable, ask yourself why. The measure of your learning is not the accumulation of pleasurable experiences but a growing awareness of the possibilities of both your own life story and of those in your communities.

TO INSTRUCTORS

Instructors, we believe that you come into the classroom with energy, commitment, and expertise. The last thing we have wanted is to discourage you from using those strengths. Instead of writing a text so comprehensive that you feel like a supplement in your own classroom, we have favored an interactive approach that sets up you, your students, and the text as more equal partners in the creation of classroom knowledge. For example, much of the writing instruction is set up as a series of inquiries. We provide just enough instruction to set up individual or in-class exercises. These exercises encourage students to work with you in creating classroom knowledge, providing a framework where we can work as fellow inquirers. We also have sought to add opportunities for you to help students learn actively, drawing out their preconceptions about writing and community issues so that they can begin to argue and inquire with a better sense of their existing values and beliefs. For this interactive process to work, however, we encourage you to communicate actively with your students, opening up your own ideas about learning to write and why you are all engaging in classroom activities.

To realize this vision of the writing classroom and of learning critical thinking, reading, and writing in the context of civic lives, we have updated many of the text's current features and added new ones.

UPDATED FEATURES

- *A first-week unit on citizenship that introduces the book's main subjects.* The first chapter continues to offer an interactive series of short inquiries designed to raise larger questions about citizenship and community life. We have new questions that explore the implications of relocating naturalization services under the Department of Homeland Security and the new Congressional law requiring some schools to teach the U.S. Constitution. We have also added an optional bridge to Chapter 7, "The Higher Education Community," for instructors who want their initial inquiry into citizenship to focus on the immediate context of the college campus and the writing classroom.

- *A wider approach to critical thinking and reading.* Because we believe writing and reading are interrelated skills, we have tried to better integrate them into our discussions of critical reading and the writing process—emphasizing, for instance, the importance of learning to read as writers. We also have provided more advice on how to read a wider variety of texts effectively, including print and electronic media.

- *An accessible, adaptive writing process.* We continue to present the writing process as a series of interconnected steps that push writers to look both inward and outward. We have learned, however, to spend more time asking students to conceptualize the writing process and drawing out their perceptions about writing that can make their processes less effective.

- *A fresh, common-sense approach to research.* We use questions of how to develop a just society to frame inquiry as both an individual and communal exploration. We then ask students to put their ideas about a just society into dialogue with Ursula Le Guin's "The Ones Who Walk Away from Omelas" to model the way our inquiries participate in larger conversations. Finally, we use the hope for a just society as a running example in our introduction of primary and secondary research methods. Our hope is to provide a meaningful context for introducing methods of library, media, and field research that encourages the kind of inquiry into their lives' purpose that is often lacking in their other communities.

- *Writing instruction based on the genres of public debate.* We have expanded our discussion of the genres of public debate to include Web logs, or blogs, and to showcase ways students have sought to communicate their ideas outside the usual range of letters, editorials, posters, and zines.

NEW FEATURES

- *New readings throughout the book.* Based on feedback from students and instructors, we have added new readings in most chapters while preserving those readings that work particularly well. For example, we have kept Susan B. Anthony's "Women's Right to Vote" and the Black Panthers' "Ten Point Plan," which effectively show how these writers extended both the principles and the language of the Declaration of Independence to secure civic rights for women and African Americans, respectively. We have added lively and challenging readings such as one of Barbara Ehren-reich's essays on religious fundamentalism; Mark Edmundson's contro-versial *Harper's* essay "The Uses of a Liberal Education: As 'Lite' Entertainment for Bored College Students"; and a chapter of Barrie Jean Borich's memoir *My Lesbian Husband.* As usual, we have sought readings from a variety of genres and have included new editorials by David Brooks and Stanley Fish; song lyrics from Peter Mayer; a cartoon by Tom Tomor-row; letters to the editor in response to Benjamin Barber's "Jihad vs. McWorld"; and pamphlets and posters.

• *Updated case studies that engage contemporary debates.* Five of the six case studies are new to this edition and involve students in debating issues that are still in progress, such as attitudes toward same-sex marriage, the idea that students should create an Academic Bill of Rights for themselves, rea-sons why women are put at the center (and often made the battleground) of the so-called "clash of civilizations" between modern and fundamen-talist cultures, and how blogs are affecting journalism and political action.

• *Capstone learning projects.* At the end of each case study, we have added a Continuing the Case Study project that uses simulations and other interactive projects to act on what is learned through the case study readings and class discussion. For example, the capstone pro-ject in Chapter 7, "The Higher Education Community," has students imagine they serve on their college's judicial board, the group that hears cases in which students have been charged with violating the institution's code of conduct. This simulation, which asks them to try a case on disorderly conduct, can deepen our understanding of the college community by studying instances when the social contract between students and colleges has broken down. In other case stud-ies students get the opportunity to become legislators who debate whether we should have a federal Marriage Protection Amendment, scientific researchers who measure their impact on the Earth, and social analysts who use the Social Change Wheel to understand the civil rights movement.

CONTINUING FEATURES

• *An approach to arguing that emphasizes inquiry.* The strategies of arguing well are presented as a natural expression of our empathy, our capacity to anticipate and shape how people respond to our ideas. Because arguing strategies can be used unethically, to discourage critical thinking and break down community ties, we treat arguing as inquiry, our effort to test our ideas by introducing them into the conversations going on around us.

- *A multidisciplinary approach to the research essay.* To apply the more general principles of inquiry and argument to work in academic disciplines—such as history, sociology, biology, or business—we take readers through the process of writing a research paper. Using the stories of several different students, we help students discover a research question, set up a research plan, and write up the results in a format appropriate to different academic disciplines. Because these disciplines have their own standards for good research and research papers, we include exercises to help students discover and compare those standards for themselves. Learning to be a savvy college writer means learning how to identify and meet an instructor's expectations, regardless of the discipline.

- *Emphasis on historical viewpoints.* Examining social issues in historical perspective can deepen our understanding of how those issues originated and whether they are truly unique to our time. For that reason, we continue to include historical case studies such as the role of faith communities in the civil rights movement in Chapter 10, "Communities of Faith."

- *Dialogue boxes to encourage critical thinking and reading as writers.* In each chapter you will find two types of dialogue boxes. Stop and Think boxes prompt students to connect what they are reading to other issues and to their own experiences. Writing Style boxes offer additional writing tips, as well as discussion of the conventions of academic and public writing. These style boxes connect the writing instruction of the beginning chapters with the readings, asking students to think about the readings as crafted texts.

- *An Instructor's Manual.* This manual, available to qualified adopters of this book, assists instructors in using the unique features of this Second Edition, provides suggestions for building syllabi, and offers different assignment sequences.

While we have been in the process of revising this book, the United States has been embroiled in a war on terrorism that involves the entire world community. The need for critical thinking and civic education is more urgent than ever. We hope you will continue the conversation with us.

ACKNOWLEDGMENTS

Over the six years we have been developing and redeveloping this book, we have accumulated many debts it is now our pleasure to acknowledge. The project began as a response to the University of Minnesota's freshman writing courses on citizenship and public ethics. For help in conceiving the project and crafting the manuscript, we thank our colleagues from the University of Minnesota, especially Tim Gustafson, Ilene Alexander, Lillian Bridwell-Bowles,

Patrick Bruch, Anne Carter, Pat Crain, Elaine Cullen, Eric Daigre, Piyali Nath Dalal, Tom Reynolds, John Wallace, and Jonathan Cullick. We are also grateful to students in three semesters of classes who gave us honest feedback on what works and what does not.

We have found allies in our other scholarly communities, as well. At the University of St. Thomas, Tom Connery, Dean of the College of Arts and Sciences, and Michael Mikolajczak, chair of the English department, have been warm supporters, and colleagues Andy Scheiber, Marty Warren, Bob Miller, Ellen Kennedy, Greg Robinson-Riegler, and Kanishka Chowdhury have shown particular interest in the project by asking challenging questions and offering smart reading suggestions. We also want to thank Mike Klein of the Justice and Peace Studies department for the use of his Social Change Wheel exercise in the civil rights movement case study in Chapter 10. At Normandale Community College, Kari Fisher, Gail Cywinski, Jack Miller, Linda Tetzlaff, and David Pates kindly lent us their attention as we talked through ideas. Paula Backscheider and Richard Graves of Auburn University supported the project from its inception; and Keith Abney, Cal Poly-San Luis Obispo, cheerfully answered e-mails on questions of teaching ethics from the point of view of a philosopher.

Ideas for the Second Edition were tested and developed in a workshop at Coastal Carolina University in August 2005. Many thanks for this opportunity go to Daniel Ennis, Associate Dean; Shannon Stewart, Director of First Year Composition; and the excellent workshop attendees: Julia Ross, Ellen Arnold, Sara Sobata, Tom Clancy, Sally Purcell, Grant Collins, Molly Howard, Brandon Evans, Cliff Saunders, Rebecca Hamill, and Scott Pleasant.

In the Twin Cities we have been fortunate to have a number of communities that serve as our models of civic life. We would like especially to thank D'Ann Urbaniak Lesch and all the folks at the Jane Addams School for Democracy in St. Paul, and Chris Nevin and the teachers and students at Abraham Lincoln International High School in Minneapolis, where questions about citizenship were honed. And here and beyond we are always grateful for the interest, sustenance, and good ideas of friends and family, including Van and Lori Muse, Larry Lindeman and Ellen Muse-Lindeman, and Sarah Spencer. Doug Phillips and Suzanne Berndt deserve paragraphs of their own.

In the Longman community, we would like to thank Sandy Lindelof, who was our local representative and an early and enthusiastic proponent of the project. Sandy introduced us to our editor, Lynn Huddon. Lynn's expertise, experience, and patience have guided us through this process and made this a better book. We would also like to acknowledge Nicole Solano, Editorial Assistant; Denise Phillip, Production Manager; Lisa Kinne, Project Editor; and Teresa Ward, who worked with us on both editions of the Instructor's Manual. Our tireless permissions editors, Natalie Giboney and Julie Tesser, have endured our many revisions with remarkable forbearance and good humor.

Finally, we would like to thank the reviewers whose enthusiasm and strong responses, both positive and negative, showed how deeply instructors feel about civics as a part of writing instruction: Jesse T. Airaudi, Baylor University; Martha Brooks, John Tyler Community College; Robin Hardin, Cape Fear Community College; A. F. Mareck, Michigan Technological University; and Ruth Ray, Wayne State University.

Michael Berndt
Amy Muse
December 2005

CHAPTER 1

What Does It Mean to Be a Citizen?

An idea is a feat of association.
—Robert Frost

▓ **GETTING STARTED** ▓ Picturing Citizenship

When you hear the question "What does it mean to be a citizen?" what ideas come first to your mind? If you imagine concepts such as freedom or duty or actions such as voting, try to visualize them; are there objects, persons, or events that help you picture these ideas? Hold one of those images in your mind, then take out a piece of clean paper and draw that image in the paper's center.

Some images, such as flags, will be easy to draw, but others, such as a group of people living together in harmony, will not, so you might symbolize that idea with two stick figures holding hands. The image does not have to be drawn well, but it should be kept relatively small to give you room on the paper for further drawing. As you introduce yourself to your classmates, describe what image you drew and why. Then compare the images; are there significant differences or similarities?

FIRST INQUIRY: USING MIND MAPS TO ASSESS WHAT YOU KNOW ABOUT CITIZENSHIP

The pictures you drew in the Getting Started exercise are the first step in creating a Mind Map of citizenship. Created by Tony Buzan and based on the notebooks of great thinkers such as Leonardo da Vinci, Mind Maps help us create and examine our ideas. Writers begin with a central image and expand outward, writing down additional words or images that they associate with the central image. From these new words and images, writers can see new connections, creating more ideas and expanding the map further.

While Mind Maps can be used in a variety of ways, from planning an activity to taking class notes, the map of citizenship included below demonstrates how writers can use maps to brainstorm, or generate ideas, about citizenship. Created by several freshmen at the University of Minnesota, this Mind Map represents only one of thousands of possible maps. As you analyze it, describe how the Mind Map helped you create or examine ideas about citizenship. Then assess whether the map achieves three common goals of brainstorming: 1) to assess what we already know, 2) to alert us to what we do not know, and 3) to suggest directions for further inquiry.

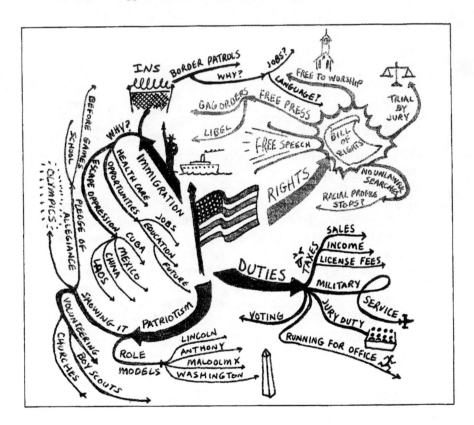

As you examined the Mind Map, did you think of other ideas or images associated with citizenship? Now assess your own ideas about citizenship by creating your own Mind Map.

▓ **EXERCISE 1.1** ▓ Creating Your Own Mind Map

1. *Place the paper with your image of citizenship in front of you.* Starting a Mind Map with a picture or symbol encourages creativity because we associ-

ate many ideas and feelings with visual images. Placing the image in the center of your paper will free you to expand in any direction.

2. *Write down any words suggested by the image.* In different locations around the central image, write down any words, phrases, or images inspired by the central image. You should not second-guess any of your ideas by worrying about what others will think. Next, connect the words and images to your central image with arrows that point outward from the center. These arrows can help you organize your thoughts by showing the direction of your thinking.

3. *Continue expanding on the secondary words and images.* Using each new word, phrase, or image as your starting point, expand your ideas, connecting those ideas with new arrows. As you expand outward, include specific ideas and examples that clarify the elements in your map. A completed Mind Map often resembles a spider's web because each new word or image suggests additional ideas that radiate outward from it. Finish your Mind Map only when you have exhausted your ideas. Even though you may not use every item in a Mind Map, having an abundance of ideas can offer more possible directions for further inquiry.

Once you have finished your Mind Map, meet in small groups and compare your ideas. Do some of your words and images parallel those of your classmates? Do other words or images suggest conflicting ideas about citizenship? As a follow-up exercise, you might do a class Mind Map, beginning with the most commonly used image from the Getting Started exercise.

SECOND INQUIRY: DICTIONARY DEFINITIONS

Your Mind Maps may have suggested many common ideas among your classmates. At the same time, the maps may have highlighted differences in your definitions of citizenship that are hard to reconcile. One student may associate citizenship with social protests while another may associate it with law, order, and social harmony. One student may see citizenship primarily as our civil rights, while another may focus on our civic duties. To reconcile these differences, we might turn to an outside authority such as a dictionary. Consulting a dictionary about unfamiliar words becomes natural for college students; perhaps you even looked up the words *citizen* and *citizenship* in the dictionary before beginning your Mind Map.

Dictionaries guide readers on a word's pronunciation and usage and trace its etymology (its earliest introduction into the language). Dictionaries also provide several features useful to understanding a word's meaning. Each dictionary's editorial board identifies the alternative meanings of a word, using numbers to differentiate them and letters to note differences within a particular meaning. Some dictionaries even provide examples, called *citations*, of how the word is used in a sentence. *The Oxford English Dictionary,* for example, provides citations from writers of different historical periods, showing how a word can gain new meanings over time. Finally, dictionaries occasionally provide synonyms, which are words with similar meaning. To further explore how dictionaries work, try the following exercise:

▨ EXERCISE 1.2 ▨ Comparing Dictionary Definitions

Look up the words *citizen* and *citizenship* in your own dictionary, compare them with the following definitions, and then—either individually or in small groups—respond to the following questions.

1. There are a number of differences in the dictionary definitions. The variety might be a result of writing for different audiences. Who might be the probable audiences and what might be the likely purposes for each definition, based on each definition's features?

2. Consider your needs as a college writer. Which of the dictionary definitions would be most useful to you, and why?

3. To communicate their ideas effectively, writers choose precisely worded statements over vague, generally worded statements. Do the dictionary definitions help to clarify your ideas of citizenship by giving you more precisely worded descriptions?

Urdang, Laurence, ed. *The American Century Dictionary*. New York: Warner Books, 1995.

> **cit·i·zen** /sit′əzən/ *n.* member of a country, state, city, etc. —**cit′i-zen·ry** /-rē/ *n.*; **cit′i-zen·ship′** *n.* [OFr, rel. to CITY]

Webster's Ninth New Collegiate Dictionary. Springfield: Merriam-Webster Inc., 1988.

> **cit·i·zen** \'sit-ə-zən *also* -sən\ *n* [ME *citizein,* fr. AF *citezein,* alter. of OF *citeien,* fr. *cité* city] (14c) **1** : an inhabitant of a city or town; *esp* : one entitled to the rights and privileges of a freeman **2 a** : a member of a state **b** : a native or naturalized person who owes allegiance to a government and is entitled to protection from it **3** : a civilian as distinguished from a specialized servant of the state — **cit·i·zen·ly** \-zən-lē *also* -sən-\ *adj*
> **syn** CITIZEN, SUBJECT, NATIONAL mean a person owing allegiance to and entitled to the protection of a sovereign state. CITIZEN is preferred for one owing allegiance to a state in which sovereign power is retained by the people and sharing in the political rights of those people; SUBJECT implies allegiance to a personal sovereign such as a monarch; NATIONAL designates one who may claim the protection of a state and applies esp. to one living or traveling outside that state.
> **cit·i·zen·ess** \-zə-nəs *also* -sə-\ *n* (1796) : a female citizen
> **cit·i·zen·ry** \-zən-rē *also* -sən-\ *n, pl* **-ries** (1819) : a whole body of citizens
> **citizen's arrest** *n* (1952) : an arrest made not by a law officer but by a citizen who derives his authority from the fact that he is a citizen
> **citizens band** *n* (1965) : a range of radio-wave frequencies that in the U.S. is allocated officially for private radio communications
> **cit·i·zen·ship** \'sit-ə-zən-ˌship\ *n* (1611) **1** : the status of being a citizen **2 a** : membership in a community (as a college) **b** : the quality of an individual's response to membership in a community

The Oxford English Dictionary. 2nd ed. Oxford: Clarendon Press, 1989.

citizen ('sɪtɪzən). Forms: 4 citisein, -sain, -ecyn(e, citesayne, -ceyn, -zeyn, citizein, 4–5 citeseyn, -zein(e, 4–6 -sen, 5 cita-, citiesyn, cetisen, cyterane (Sc.), -eyn, -ein, sitesyn, sytisin, (setsayne), 5–6 citesyn, -zen, 6 cyterzyn, cityzen, -sen, cittesen, cytiezin, cytyzyn, 7 cittizen, 6-cittizen. [ME. *citisein*, etc., a. Anglo-Fr. *citeseyn*, -zein, *sithezein*, altered form of OF. *citeain*, *citehain*, *citein*, *citeen*, *citien*, *citain*, later *citeyen*, *citoyen*:—L. type *civitātān-um, f. *civitāt-em* city (cf. *oppidān-um*, *villān-um*): Romanic type *civitatāno*, *-dano*, whence P: *ciutaaan*, Sp. *ciudadano*, Pg. *ciudadāo*; and P: *ciptaaan*, It. *cittadano*, now *cittadino*. OF. *cite(n̄ain*. The intercalation of *s*(z) in Anglo-Fr. *citesain* has not been explained: association with *dainzain* denizen, which was often an equivalent term, has been suggested.

The suggestion that *z* was a mistaken reading of *y*, meaning *y*, on the part of a 13th or 14th c. scribe or scribes, is in every respect untenable.]

1. An inhabitant of a city or (often) of a town; esp. one possessing civic rights and privileges, a burgess or freeman of a city.

c1314 *Guy Warw.* (A.) 5503 þe citiseins of þat cite wel often god þonkeden he. c1330 *Arth. & Merl.* 5000 To London...thai come. The citizins fair in hem nome. 1382 Wyclif *Acts* xxl. 39, I am a man...of Tarsus, a citeseyn or burgeys, of a citee not unknown. c1400 *Destr. Troy* 3263 [MS. after 1500] Sum of the Citizens assemblit with all. *Ibid.* 11879 Citavins. 1480 Caxton *Chron. Eng.* ccvi. 187 The cyterzyns of london. c1480 *Pol. Poems* (1859) I. 281 He thonckyd the cetisence of thayre fidelite. 1513 *Aen. 4 Hen. VIII.* c. 9. §2 Citezens of Cities and Burgeys of boroughes and Townes. 1556 *Chron. Gr. Friars* (1852) 16 The kynge (Hen. VI.) came to London, & there was warchippfully reseved of the citesenis in whytt gownes & redde whoddes. 1596 Shaks. *Tam. Shr.* iv. ii. 95 Pisa renowned for graue Citizens. c1674 Clarendon *Hist. Reb.* (1704) III. xv. 472 You, the Knights, Citizens, and Burgesses, of the House of Commons. a1699 Lady Halkett *Autobiog.* (1875) 20 Furnished with an honest Citrisen. 1782 Cowper *Gilpin* 1 John Gilpin was a citizen Of credit and renown. 1841 Macaulay *Hist. Eng.* I. 352 The chiefs of the mercantile interest are no longer citizens. They avoid, they almost contemn, municipal honours and duties.

b. Used also as feminine. (Cf. CITIZENESS.)

1605 *Lond. Prodigal* III. i. 143, I'll have thee go like a citizen, in a guarded gown and a French hood. 1655 *Francion* vi. 20 She who was the most antient of the two Citizens.

c. A townsman, as opposed to a countryman.

1324 Barclay *Cyt. & Uplondyshm. Prol.*, Faustus accused and blamed cyterzyns, Amyntas blamed the rurall men ageyne. 1845 S. Austin *Ranke's Hist. Ref.* II. 209 Both citizens and peasants are tired of it. 1860 Ruskin *Mod. Paint.* V. i. i. 4 The words 'countryman...villager', still signify a rude and untaught person, as opposed to the words 'townsman' and 'citizen'.

d. A civilian as distinguished from a soldier; in earlier times also distinguished from a member of the landed nobility or gentry. Johnson says 'a man of trade, not a gentleman'.

1607 Shaks. *Cor.* III. iii. 53 When he speakes not like a Citizen You finde him like a Soldier. 1871 [see CITIZENHOOD].

e. With reference to the 'heavenly city', the New Jerusalem.

1340 Hampole *Pr. Consc.* 8925 þis ceté of heven...ilka citesayne þat wonned þare. 1526 *Pilgr. Perf.* (W. de W. 1531) I b. Amonge y⁻ citezyns of heuen. 2665 Boyle *Occas. Refl.* v. x. (1675) 338 A Citizen of the Heavenly Jerusalem, and but a Stranger and a Sojourner here.

2. A member of a state, an enfranchised inhabitant of a country, as opposed to an alien; in *U.S.*, a person, native or naturalized, who has the privilege of voting for public offices, and is entitled to full protection in the exercise of private rights.

138. Wyclif *Sel. Wks.* II. 69 [He] clevede to oon of þe citizeins of þat countre. 1538 Starkey *England* 46 The nombur of cytyzyns, in euery communalite, cyte, or cuntrey. 1633 Massinger *Guardian* v. iv. To saue one citizen is a greater prise Than to have killed in war ten enemies. 1752 Hume *Ess. & Treat.* (1777) I. 281 A too great disproportion among the citizens weakens any state. a1799 Washington (Webster), If the citizens of the United States should not be free and happy, the fault will be entirely their own. 1843 *Penny Cycl.* XXVI. 137 A pledge, both to American citizens and foreign states. 1875 Jowett *Plato* (ed. 2) V. 79 The object of our laws is to make the citizens as friendly and happy as possible. 1884 Gladstone in *Standard* 29 Feb. 2/4 A nation where every capable citizen was enfranchised. *Mod.* Arrest of an American citizen.

b. as a title, representing Fr. *citoyen*, which at the Revolution took the place of *Monsieur*.

1795 *Argus Dec.* 26 Letter from the Minister for Foreign Affairs to Citizen Miot. 1799 *Med. Jrnl.* I. 155 He was called to the female citizen (= *citoyenne*) Dangeville, whom he found in a miserable situation. 1801 *Ibid.* V. 359 Such.

Citizen Mayor, are the motives of the propositions which the Committee have the honour of laying before you. 1837 Carlyle *Fr. Rev.* III. ii. 1.

c. *phr.* **citizen of the world**: one who is at home, and claims his rights, everywhere; a cosmopolitan; also, **citizen of nature**. (Cf. Cicero *De Leg.* i. xxiii. 61 *civem totius mundi*.)

1474 Caxton *Chesse* 31 Helde hym bourgeys and cytezeyn of the world. 1625 Bacon *Ess. Goodness, etc.* (Arb.) 207 If a Man be Gracious, and Courteous to Strangers, it sheweth, he is a Citizen of the World. 1760 Goldsm. (*title*), The Citizen of the World; or, Letters from a Chinese Philosopher. 1762–71 H. Walpole *Vertue's Anecd. Paint.* (1786) III. 148 An original genius, a citizen of nature.

3. *transf.* Inhabitant, occupant, denizen. (Of men, beasts, things personified.)

c1384 Chaucer *H. Fame* 930 (Fairf. MS.) In this Region certeyn Duelleth many a Citezeyn Of which that seketh Doun Plato These ben euvrysch bestes. 1508 Fisher *Wks.* (1876) 235 Who ben the cytezyns of this regyon, truly none other but deuylles. 1593 Shaks. *Lucr.* 465 His hand...Rude ram, to batter such an ivory wall!—May feel her heart—poor citizen!—distress'd Wounding itself to death. 1603 Dekker *Griss'l* (1841) 5 Let's ring a hunter's peal...in the ears Of our swift forest citizens. c1630 Drumm. of Hawth. *Poems* I. xxvi. *Wks.* (1711) 5 A citizen of Thetis christal floods.

4. *adj.* = CITIZENISH, city-bred. *nonce-use.*

1611 Shaks. *Cymb.* iv. ii. 8. I am not well: But not so Citizen a wanton. as To seeme to dye, etc sicke.

5. *attrib.* and *Comb.*, chiefly *appositive*, as **citizen-king**, **-magistrate**, **-prince**, **-soldier**, **-sovereign**; also, **citizen-life**; **citizen-like** adj. **Citizens' Advice Bureau**, any of a network of local offices where members of the public may obtain free and impartial advice, esp. when experiencing difficulties with authorities or other individuals; **citizen's arrest** *Law* (orig. *U.S.*), an arrest carried out without a warrant by a private citizen (allowable in certain cases); **Citizens(') Band** orig. *U.S.*, a short-wave band made available for private radio communication; abbrev. *C.B.*

1830 Hobhouse in T. Juste *S. Van de' Weyer* (1871) App. iii. 168 He [Leopold] may do very well for a 'citizen-king. 1852 Hr. Martineau *Hist. Peace* (1877) III. iv. xiii. 113 All eyes were fixed on the citizen-king [Louis Philippe]. 1874 Mahaffy *Soc. Life Greece* viii. 254 *Citizen life was too precious to be poured out in wrath. 1598 Florio *Cittadinesco*, *Citizen-like. 1847 Emerson *Repr. Men, Plato Wks.* (Bohn) I. 309 He [Socrates] affected a good many citizen-like traits. 1837–9 Hallam *Hist. Lit.* I. iii. 159 A republican government that was rapidly giving way before the *citizen-prince. 1939 *Times* 5 Oct. 11/1 The Queen...visited Branches of the *Citizens' Advice Bureau of the Charity Organisation Society at Fulham, Chelsea, Battersea and Clapham. 1969 *Guardian* 29 July 5/5 There is already a citizens' advice bureau just down the road. 1984 *Metro (Auckland)* Mar. 103/2 A phone call to the central Citizens' Advice Bureau soon put me in touch with them all. 1941 *Rep. Cases Supreme Court Calif.* XVI. 659 Defendant concedes that he intended to make a *citizen's arrest – upon a charge of perjury. 1978 *Daily Tel.* 9 Nov. 1/7 A citizen's arrest...ended the nationwide hunt... He pinned her arms behind her and said: 'I am taking no chances on you, lady. I am making a citizen's arrest.' 1986 *Guardian* 20 Aug. 1/5 Joseph Hanson...was detained after a private detective made a citizen's arrest on a double-decker bus. 1948 *Radio & TV News* Dec. 44 (*heading*) *Citizens Band oscillator. *Ibid.* 44/3 It has been possible to obtain greater output at higher efficiencies with less heating power in cathode type than in filamentary types at the Citizens Band frequency. 1958 *Ibid.* Nov. 37/1 There are many needs for radio, in delivery vehicles, on farms, and in small business. The Citizens Band has been a convenient catch-all for these groups. *Ibid.* 38/2 Under Citizens Band rules power was limited and eligibility requirements were simple. 1976 Perkowski & Stral *Joy of CB* ii. 13 As originally established in 1948, there were three classes of Citizens Band licenses available. 1981 *Times* 4 Mar. 16/3 The messy compromise which Ms Whitelaw...announced over the introduction of Citizens Band radio was in the end forced on the Government. 1843 Prescott *Mexico* (1850) II. 310 The *citizen-soldiers of Villa Rica.

Hence **citizen** *v.*, to address as 'citizen'.

1871 *Daily News* 19 Apr. 5 Now the sentinel 'citizens' me, and I 'citizen' him.

citizenship ('sɪtɪzənʃɪp). [f. as CITIZEN + -SHIP.] The position or status of being a citizen, with its rights and privileges.

1611 Cotgr., *Citoyennerie*, a Citizenship, the freedome of a Citie. a1792 Br. Horne *Occas. Serm.* 158 (T.) Our citizenship, as saith the apostle, is in heaven. a1832 Sir J. Sinclair · *Corr* II. 13 General laws, relative to naturalization and citizenship. 1864 *City Chamberlain to Garibaldi* in *Times* 21 Apr., The City of London invites you to-day to accept the highest honour at her disposal, placing your distinguished name upon the list of worthies inscribed upon the roll of honorary citizenship. 1869 Seeley *Lect. & Ess.* i. 9 The Italian allies...had not yet been admitted to the Roman citizenship. 1881 N. T. (*Rev. Vers.*) *Phil.* iii. 20 Our citizenship [Wyclif living, 16th c. ov. conversation] is in heaven.

Black's Law Dictionary. 6th ed. St. Paul: West Publishing, 1990.

Citizen. One who, under the Constitution and laws of the United States, or of a particular state, is a member of the political community, owing allegiance and being entitled to the enjoyment of full civil rights. All persons born or naturalized in the United States, and subject to the jurisdiction thereof, are citizens of the United States and of the state wherein they reside. U.S.Const., 14th Amend. See Citizenship.

"Citizens" are members of a political community who, in their associated capacity, have established or submitted themselves to the dominion of a government for the promotion of their general welfare and the protection of their individual as well as collective rights. Herriott v. City of Seattle, 81 Wash.2d 48, 500 P.2d 101, 109.

The term may include or apply to children of alien parents born in United States, Von Schwerdtner v. Piper, D.C.Md., 23 F.2d 862, 863; U. S. v. Minoru Yasui, D.C.Or., 48 F.Supp. 40, 54; children of American citizens born outside United States, Haaland v. Attorney General of United States, D.C.Md., 42 F.Supp. 13, 22; Indians, United States v. Hester, C.C.A.Okl., 137 F.2d 145, 147; National Banks, American Surety Co. v. Bank of California, C.C.A.Or., 133 F.2d 160, 162; nonresident who has qualified as administratrix of estate of deceased resident, Hunt v. Noll, C.C.A.Tenn., 112 F.2d 288, 289. However, neither the United States nor a state is a citizen for purposes of diversity jurisdiction. Jizemerjian v. Dept. of Air Force, 457 F.Supp. 820. On the other hand, municipalities and other local governments are deemed to be citizens. Rieser v. District of Columbia, 563 F.2d 462. A corporation is not a citizen for purposes of privileges and immunities clause of the Fourteenth Amendment. D. D. B. Realty Corp. v. Merrill, 232 F.Supp. 629, 637.

Citizenship. The status of being a citizen. There are four ways to acquire citizenship: by birth in the United States, by birth in U.S. territories, by birth outside the U.S. to U.S. parents, and by naturalization. See Corporate citizenship; Diversity of citizenship; Dual citizenship; Federal citizenship; Naturalization; Jus sanguinis; Jus soli.

The dictionary definitions give us more ideas to associate with citizenship, such as being an inhabitant of a city. They may also give us a clearer idea of what citizen and citizenship mean by providing more precisely worded descriptions. For example, we may not have differentiated between "native" and "naturalized" citizens in our understanding of citizenship. Nevertheless, the different dictionaries, like the preceding Mind Maps, still define the words in slightly different ways. For example, the first meaning given for *citizen* in the *American Century Dictionary* does not mention entitlement to civic rights or privileges, as do the others. If dictionaries are supposed to be our authorities for a word's meanings, why don't they all define words in exactly the same way?

The most obvious answer for the differences between the dictionaries is that, like any form of written communication, each has its own *purpose* and *audience*. For example, the range of the *American Century Dictionary* is broad but each entry is brief; it is also inexpensive, appealing to general readers who want a guide useful for looking up unknown words but who do not need to distinguish among a word's different senses. *The Oxford English Dictionary*, on the other hand, has a different purpose and audience. Proposed by the Philological Society in England in 1857, the dictionary took more than seventy years to complete and occupies twelve large volumes. The second edition, which came out in 1989, defines more than half a million words and occupies twenty volumes. The dictionary is so large because its purpose is to demonstrate, through the use of citations, the full range of the word's various meanings. Because the cost of producing such an exhaustive work is high, few general readers can afford to buy it. Consequently, its audience tends to be researchers and library patrons.

Dictionaries such as *Webster's Ninth New Collegiate Dictionary* are more common for college students, who may need a rigorous but affordable guide. Finally, some dictionaries, such as *Black's Law Dictionary*, are specialized for a particular audience. The use of precise legal language (e.g., "All persons born or naturalized in the United States, and subject to the jurisdiction thereof") and the references to relevant court cases (e.g., *Herriott v. City of Seattle*) make the definitions more useful to lawyers, law students, and legal scholars.

Dictionary definitions are not the only writing situations shaped by the writer's purpose and audience. All forms of writing, from personal diaries to business memos, are shaped by the writer's subject, purpose, audience, and the situation within which it is being written. This is an important point to consider. You will communicate more effectively if you know what restrictions your subject will place on your writing, what goals you have for writing about the subject, what expectations your audience will bring to the essay, and what conditions of your time and place will affect how you can write. As a follow-up exercise, you might list different writing types or situations, and then discuss how the writer's subject, purpose, audience, and situation shape each of these examples.

STOP AND THINK

TIME TO BRING IN THE COLLEGE COMMUNITY?

In the first two inquiries, you explored citizenship in its most general sense. You may have noted, however, that your Mind Map and dictionary definitions tended to define citizenship in the context of nation states, or countries. The remaining inquiries in this chapter continue exploring citizenship in that context, asking you to examine the process for acquiring U.S. citizenship, excerpts from the U.S. Constitution, citizenship-related advertisements and cartoons from U.S. magazines,

continued on next page

and narratives of living in the United States. The insights you gain about citizenship will inform your work in the other chapters.

Your classroom also offers you a community, however, one that may concern you more at present than the national community. At this point, you might continue your study of citizenship by shifting from national citizenship to citizenship in your classroom. One of the central purposes of educational institutions in this country has been to prepare students to be good citizens. You can study your college's mission statement; your course's learning objectives, classroom policies, writing assignments; and stories of past writing experiences to answer several questions relevant to composing a civic life. How does writing fit into your school's vision of an educated individual? How will your classroom cultivate a purposeful community? How do critical thinking, critical reading, and writing relate to informed, effective citizenship? The value of this inquiry is to make you more aware of what knowledge, attitudes, or skills you need to develop to be a stronger writer and citizen.

THIRD INQUIRY: OFFICIAL DOCUMENTS

Dictionary definitions describe how English speakers and writers use concepts such as citizenship. To learn how these concepts are defined in the context of American political and social institutions, we might examine official documents. Official documents such as laws, court opinions, and organization policies—even mission statements, press releases, and the published speeches of public officials—offer definitions closely tied to the visions and practices of actual businesses, government agencies, and public interest groups. In this section we will examine two sets of documents fundamental to American citizenship: the U.S. Citizenship and Immigration Services (USCIS) naturalization requirements, and the Constitution of the United States.

U.S. Citizenship and Immigration Services Naturalization Requirements

According to the U.S. Citizenship and Immigration Services (USCIS), around 849,807 immigrants arrived legally in the United States in 2000. Many of these immigrants apply for U.S. citizenship. The Immigration and Nationality Act (INA) of 1952 and its many amendments serve as the basis for existing immigration law. Because the law is complex, the USCIS offers guides to assist immigrants in applying for citizenship. A candidate for citizenship must satisfy residency requirements, complete the application process, get fingerprinted, go through an interview, and demonstrate basic understanding of the English language and of American history and government. The process outlined in those guides has been simplified in this chapter to illustrate some of the ideas about citizenship that form the basis of the process. After you complete each stage, consider the follow-up questions individually or in groups.

In order to even apply to become a U.S. citizen, a candidate must first pass several naturalization requirements. A candidate for citizenship must

- Be at least eighteen years old.
- Have been "lawfully admitted for permanent residence" according to immigration laws, which means that the person has been registered as an immigrant and has filled out certain forms (for census and tax purposes, for example); this is in contrast to a person who arrives as an "illegal alien" and does not have registration papers (who is, in other words, "undocumented").
- Have been a lawful resident for at least five years and have been physically present in the U.S. for at least thirty months out of those previous five years.
- Have resided in a state or district for at least three months.

In short, the person must be an adult who has entered the country through the standard legal channels and has lived here most of the last five years. In small groups or as a class, consider the following questions:

1. Why do you think it is so important for citizenship candidates to be lawful residents for at least five years?
2. Why must they have stayed in one state or district for three months?
3. What do these requirements suggest about the USCIS definition of citizenship?

If candidates meet the above requirements, they must still meet additional eligibility criteria. Complete part ten of the Request for Naturalization form (Form N-400), which appears on pages 10–11; as you answer the questions, consider what these criteria have to do with U.S. citizenship.

Unlike the first set of criteria, the eligibility factors relating to political party involvement, military service, and personal moral character seem less clear. For example, section D—designed to assess what the USCIS calls *good moral character*—may seem insufficient for assessing a candidate's character. A candidate might meet the criteria and still be a poor citizen morally. In addition, Question 22 might seem an invasion of individual privacy. Should the government be able to learn, for example, if you are an alcoholic? Keep these larger questions in mind as you complete the next stage of the application process: the United States history and government exam.

The U.S. history and government exam consists of twenty questions chosen randomly from a set list. Because candidates respond to questions orally or in writing, USCIS officers can assess another eligibility requirement, the candidates' ability to speak, read, write, and understand the English language. On page 12 are twenty questions selected randomly from samples provided by the USCIS to help candidates prepare for the exam.

Part 10. Additional Questions

Please answer questions 1 through 14. If you answer "Yes" to any of these questions, include a written explanation with this form. Your written explanation should (1) explain why your answer was "Yes," and (2) provide any additional information that helps to explain your answer.

- //- -

B. Affiliations

8. a. Have you **EVER** been a member of or associated with any organization, association, fund, foundation, party, club, society, or similar group in the United States or in any other place? ☐ Yes ☐ No

b. If you answered "Yes," list the name of each group below. If you need more space, attach the names of the other group(s) on a separate sheet of paper.

Name of Group	Name of Group
1.	6.
2.	7.
3.	8.
4.	9.
5.	10.

9. Have you **EVER** been a member of or in any way associated *(either directly or indirectly)* with:

   a. The Communist Party? ☐ Yes ☐ No

   b. Any other totalitarian party? ☐ Yes ☐ No

   c. A terrorist organization? ☐ Yes ☐ No

10. Have you **EVER** advocated *(either directly or indirectly)* the overthrow of any government by force or violence? ☐ Yes ☐ No

11. Have you **EVER** persecuted *(either directly or indirectly)* any person because of race, religion, national origin, membership in a particular social group, or political opinion? ☐ Yes ☐ No

- //- -

D. Good Moral Character

For the purposes of this application, you must answer "Yes" to the following questions, if applicable, even if your records were sealed or otherwise cleared or if anyone, including a judge, law enforcement officer, or attorney, told you that you no longer have a record.

15. Have you **EVER** committed a crime or offense for which you were NOT arrested? ☐ Yes ☐ No

16. Have you **EVER** been arrested, cited, or detained by any law enforcement officer (including INS and military officers) for any reason? ☐ Yes ☐ No

17. Have you **EVER** been charged with committing any crime or offense? ☐ Yes ☐ No

18. Have you **EVER** been convicted of a crime or offense? ☐ Yes ☐ No

19. Have you **EVER** been placed in an alternative sentencing or a rehabilitative program (for example: diversion, deferred prosecution, withheld adjudication, deferred adjudication)? ☐ Yes ☐ No

20. Have you **EVER** received a suspended sentence, been placed on probation, or been paroled? ☐ Yes ☐ No

21. Have you **EVER** been in jail or prison? ☐ Yes ☐ No

Part 10. Additional Questions *(Continued)*

Write your INS "A"- number here:

A _ _ _ _ _ _ _ _ _

If you answered "Yes" to any of questions 15 through 21, complete the following table. If you need more space, use a separate sheet of paper to give the same information.

Why were you arrested, cited, detained, or charged?	Date arrested, cited, detained, or charged *(Month/Day/Year)*	Where were you arrested, cited, detained or charged? *(City, State, Country)*	Outcome or disposition of the arrest, citation, detention or charge *(No charges filed, charges dismissed, jail, probation, etc.)*

Answer questions 22 through 33. If you answer "Yes" to any of these questions, attach (1) your written explanation why your answer was "Yes," and (2) any additional information or documentation that helps explain your answer.

22. Have you **EVER**:

   a. been a habitual drunkard? ☐ Yes ☐ No

   b. been a prostitute, or procured anyone for prostitution? ☐ Yes ☐ No

   c. sold or smuggled controlled substances, illegal drugs or narcotics? ☐ Yes ☐ No

   d. been married to more than one person at the same time? ☐ Yes ☐ No

   e. helped anyone enter or try to enter the United States illegally? ☐ Yes ☐ No

   f. gambled illegally or received income from illegal gambling? ☐ Yes ☐ No

   g. failed to support your dependents or to pay alimony? ☐ Yes ☐ No

23. Have you **EVER** given false or misleading information to any U.S. government official while applying for any immigration benefit or to prevent deportation, exclusion, or removal? ☐ Yes ☐ No

24. Have you **EVER** lied to any U.S. government official to gain entry or admission into the United States? ☐ Yes ☐ No

F. Military Service

29. Have you **EVER** served in the U.S. Armed Forces? ☐ Yes ☐ No

30. Have you **EVER** left the United States to avoid being drafted into the U.S. Armed Forces? ☐ Yes ☐ No

31. Have you **EVER** applied for any kind of exemption from military service in the U.S. Armed Forces? ☐ Yes ☐ No

32. Have you **EVER** deserted from the U.S. Armed Forces? ☐ Yes ☐ No

H. Oath Requirements *(See Part 14 for the text of the oath)*

Answer questions 34 through 39. If you answer "No" to any of these questions, attach (1) your written explanation why the answer was "No" and (2) any additional information or documentation that helps to explain your answer.

34. Do you support the Constitution and form of government of the United States? ☐ Yes ☐ No

35. Do you understand the full Oath of Allegiance to the United States? ☐ Yes ☐ No

36. Are you willing to take the full Oath of Allegiance to the United States? ☐ Yes ☐ No

37. If the law requires it, are you willing to bear arms on behalf of the United States? ☐ Yes ☐ No

38. If the law requires it, are you willing to perform noncombatant services in the U.S. Armed Forces? ☐ Yes ☐ No

39. If the law requires it, are you willing to perform work of national importance under civilian direction? ☐ Yes ☐ No

1. What are the colors of the American flag?
2. How many states are there in the union?
3. Can the Constitution be changed?
4. For how long do we elect the president?
5. How many branches are there in the American government?
6. How many senators are there in Congress?
7. What is the Bill of Rights?
8. Who said, "Give me liberty or give me death?"
9. Which countries were our enemies during World War II?
10. Who elects the President of the United States?
11. Why did the Pilgrims come to America?
12. Who wrote "The Star-Spangled Banner"?
13. Who was the main writer of the Declaration of Independence?
14. What special group advises the president?
15. What is the minimum voting age in the United States?
16. When was the Declaration of Independence adopted?
17. What kind of government does the United States have?
18. In what year was the Constitution written?
19. Where is the White House located?
20. What is the introduction to the Constitution called?

After you have answered the questions, check your answers at the end of the chapter. To pass this portion of the test, candidates need to get twelve or more correct. The exam can give each of us insight into our own knowledge of U.S. history and government; when joined with the other naturalization requirements, it can also tell us something about how Congress, which establishes naturalization laws, defines citizenship. If you recall that all of the dictionary definitions of citizenship refer to membership in a community, you can see that the naturalization requirements make assumptions about the nature of our national community.

A community is usually defined as a group of people living in the same place and sharing the same institutions, but the definitions also carry the sense of having common rights and claims that bond individual members together. Reread the naturalization requirements and U.S. history and government exam; then consider the following questions.

1. Do these requirements assume a common set of values? How would you describe these values? Should the U.S. government set minimum moral standards for naturalization candidates? What might be the social consequences of not setting such standards?

2. Do these requirements assume a common U.S. history, or a view of what is most important in U.S. history? Could Question 11, asking why the Pilgrims came to America, be replaced with "Why did the Spanish conquistadors come to the Americas?" Assuming that USCIS officers must select those questions they consider most important for U.S. history—because they can ask only twenty questions in all—would the new question suggest a new version of U.S. history?

3. Should USCIS officers require citizens to demonstrate competence in English? What is the value to a community of having a common language?

4. Do these requirements assume a common political ideology (a set of ideas about how a society should be run)? Should a candidate who believes in a different political ideology, such as communism, be allowed to gain U.S. citizenship?

5. The Homeland Security Act of 2002 relocated the former Immigration and Naturalization Service into the Department of Homeland Security (DHS). The mission of the DHS is to "prevent and deter terrorist attacks and protect against and respond to threats and hazards to the nation." Its mission is also to "ensure safe and secure borders, welcome lawful immigrants and visitors, and promote the free-flow of commerce." Although securing our borders is presented next to welcoming lawful immigrants, do you see potential tension between these different duties?

6. Should USCIS officers require citizens to take an oath of allegiance? Many immigrants who are naturalized continue to maintain familial and political ties with their countries of origin. Do you see any benefits or drawbacks to citizens having dual loyalties?

In answering the above questions, you may discover that not everyone has the same ideas about the nature of our national political community. Disagreements on issues of public ethics, which we will explore in later chapters, are often based on just such competing ideas. For example, the conflict in states such as California over bilingual education—teaching students in more than one language—involves larger disagreements over the place of non-English languages in the United States. As you read the next official source of ideas on citizenship, the U.S. Constitution, consider how it does or does not anticipate the issues raised in the above questions.

The U.S. Constitution

The United States existed for just over ten years without a written constitution. The Constitution was written in 1787 because the previous effort at constitutional government, the Articles of Confederation, failed to adequately define the power and responsibility of the federal government and its relationship with the states. Under a federal system, power is shared between a national government and state governments, with each having clearly established powers. Although citizens are subject to both national and state laws, their rights and powers are also recognized in the Constitution. As you will discover in later chapters, American society has often struggled to balance the competing interests of the national government, individual states, and individual citizens.

The U.S. Constitution is made up of a preamble, a statement of the document's purpose; seven articles outlining the makeup, responsibilities, and procedures of the government; and twenty-seven amendments, or changes, that have been made to those articles. Here is an index of the Constitution:

I. Preamble
II. Article One: The Legislative Branch
III. Article Two: The Executive Branch
IV. Article Three: The Judicial Branch
V. Article Four: Relations Between the States
VI. Article Five: The Amendment Process
VII. Article Six: General Provisions, Supremacy of the Constitution
VIII. Article Seven: Ratification Process
IX. Amendments

Included below are selected passages from the U.S. Constitution; the complete text can be accessed from the National Archives Web site. After you've read the selections, consider the questions that follow.

The Constitution of the United States

We the People of the United States, in Order to form a more perfect Union, establish Justice, insure domestic Tranquillity, provide for the common defence, promote the general Welfare, and secure the Blessings of Liberty to ourselves and our Posterity, do ordain and establish this Constitution for the United States of America.

Article. I.

Section. 1.
All legislative Powers herein granted shall be vested in a Congress of the United States, which shall consist of a Senate and House of Representatives.

Section. 2.
The House of Representatives shall be composed of Members chosen every second Year by the People of the several States, and the Electors in each State shall have the Qualifications requisite for Electors of the most numerous Branch of the State Legislature.

No Person shall be a Representative who shall not have attained to the age of twenty five Years, and been seven Years a Citizen of the United States, and who shall not, when elected, be an Inhabitant of that State in which he shall be chosen.

Representatives and direct Taxes shall be apportioned among the several States which may be included within this Union, according to their respective Numbers, which shall be determined by adding to the whole Number of free Persons, including those bound to Service for a Term of Years, and excluding Indians not taxed, three fifths of all other Persons. The actual Enumeration shall be made within three Years after the first Meeting of the Congress of the United States, and within every subsequent Term of ten Years, in such Manner as they shall by Law direct. The Number of Representatives shall not exceed one for every thirty Thousand, but each State shall have at Least one Representative; and until such enumeration shall be made, the State of New Hampshire shall be entitled to chuse three, Massachusetts eight, Rhode-Island and Providence Plantations one, Connecticut five, New-York six, New Jersey four, Pennsylvania eight, Delaware one, Maryland six, Virginia ten, North Carolina five, South Carolina five, and Georgia three.

Article. IV.

Section. 1.

Full Faith and Credit shall be given in each State to the public Acts, Records, and judicial Proceedings of every other State. And the Congress may by general Laws prescribe the Manner in which such Acts, Records and Proceedings shall be proved, and the Effect thereof.

Section. 2.

The Citizens of each State shall be entitled to all Privileges and Immunities of Citizens in the several States.

A Person charged in any State with Treason, Felony, or other Crime, who shall flee from Justice, and be found in another State, shall on Demand of the executive Authority of the State from which he fled, be delivered up, to be removed to the State having Jurisdiction of the Crime.

No Person held to Service or Labour in one State, under the Laws thereof, escaping into another, shall, in Consequence of any Law or Regulation therein, be discharged from such Service or Labour, but shall be delivered up on Claim of the Party to whom such Service or Labour may be due.

Section. 3.

New States may be admitted by the Congress into this Union; but no new State shall be formed or erected within the Jurisdiction of any other State; nor any State be formed by the Junction of two or more States, or Parts of States, without the Consent of the Legislatures of the States concerned as well as of the Congress.

The Congress shall have Power to dispose of and make all needful Rules and Regulations respecting the Territory or other Property belonging to the United States; and nothing in this Constitution shall be so construed as to Prejudice any Claims of the United States, or of any particular State.

Section. 4.

The United States shall guarantee to every State in this Union a Republican Form of Government, and shall protect each of them against Invasion; and on Application of the Legislature, or of the Executive (when the Legislature cannot be convened) against domestic Violence.

Article. V.

The Congress, whenever two thirds of both Houses shall deem it necessary, shall propose Amendments to this Constitution, or, on the Application of the Legislatures of two thirds of the several States, shall call a Convention for proposing Amendments, which, in either Case, shall be valid to all Intents and Purposes, as Part of this Constitution, when ratified by the Legislatures of three fourths of the several States, or by Conventions in three fourths thereof, as the one or the other Mode of Ratification may be proposed by the Congress; Provided that no Amendment which may be made prior to the Year One thousand eight hundred and eight shall in any Manner affect the first and fourth Clauses in the Ninth Section of the first Article; and that no State, without its Consent, shall be deprived of its equal Suffrage in the Senate.

Article. VI.

All Debts contracted and Engagements entered into, before the Adoption of this Constitution, shall be as valid against the United States under this Constitution, as under the Confederation.

This Constitution, and the Laws of the United States which shall be made in Pursuance thereof; and all Treaties made, or which shall be made, under the Authority of the United States, shall be the supreme Law of the Land; and the Judges in every State shall be bound thereby, any Thing in the Constitution or Laws of any state to the Contrary notwithstanding.

Amendments

[Note: The first ten amendments to the Constitution, the Bill of Rights, were proposed to Congress on September 25, 1789, and ratified on December 15, 1791. (Originally there were twelve amendments proposed; the first two, in regard to compensating members of Congress and the number of constituents for each representative, were not ratified. Numbers 3–12 became the first ten amendments.)]

Amendment I.

Congress shall make no law respecting an establishment of religion, or prohibiting the free exercise thereof; or abridging the freedom of speech, or of the press; or the right of the people peaceably to assemble, and to petition the Government for a redress of grievances.

Amendment II.

A well regulated Militia, being necessary to the security of a free State, the right of the people to keep and bear Arms, shall not be infringed.

Amendment III.

No Soldier shall, in time of peace be quartered in any house, without the consent of the Owner, nor in time of war, but in a manner to be prescribed by law.

Amendment IV.

The right of the people to be secure in their persons, houses, papers, and effects, against unreasonable searches and seizures, shall not be violated, and no Warrants shall issue, but upon probable cause, supported by Oath or affirmation, and particularly describing the place to be searched, and the persons or things to be seized.

Amendment V.

No person shall be held to answer for a capital, or otherwise infamous crime, unless on a presentment or indictment of a Grand Jury, except in cases arising in the land or naval forces, or in the Militia, when in actual service in time of War or public danger; nor shall any person be subject for the same offence to be twice put in jeopardy of life or limb; nor shall be compelled in any criminal case to be a witness against himself, nor be deprived of life, liberty, or property, without due process of law; nor shall private property be taken for public use, without just compensation.

Amendment VI.

In all criminal prosecutions, the accused shall enjoy the right to a speedy and public trial, by an impartial jury of the State and district wherein the crime shall have been committed, which district shall have been previously ascertained by law, and to be informed of the nature and cause of the accusation; to be confronted with the witnesses against him; to have compulsory process for obtaining witnesses in his favor, and to have the Assistance of Counsel for his defence.

Amendment VII.

In Suits at common law, where the value in controversy shall exceed twenty dollars, the right of trial by jury shall be preserved, and no fact tried by a jury, shall be otherwise re-examined in any Court of the United States, than according to the rules of the common law.

Amendment VIII.

Excessive bail shall not be required, nor excessive fines imposed, nor cruel and unusual punishments inflicted.

Amendment IX.

The enumeration in the Constitution, of certain rights, shall not be construed to deny or disparage others retained by the people.

Amendment X.

The powers not delegated to the United States by the Constitution, nor prohibited by it to the States, are reserved to the States respectively, or to the people.

Amendment XIII.

Section 1.
Neither slavery nor involuntary servitude, except as a punishment for crime whereof the party shall have been duly convicted, shall exist within the United States, or any place subject to their jurisdiction.

Section 2.
Congress shall have power to enforce this article by appropriate legislation.
    [Passed by Congress January 31, 1865. Ratified December 6, 1865.]

Amendment XIV.

Section. 1.
All persons born or naturalized in the United States and subject to the jurisdiction thereof, are citizens of the United States and of the State wherein they reside. No State shall make or enforce any law which shall abridge the privileges or immunities of citizens of the United States; nor shall any State deprive any person of life, liberty, or property, without due process of law; nor deny to any person within its jurisdiction the equal protection of the laws.

Section. 2.
Representatives shall be apportioned among the several States according to their respective numbers, counting the whole number of persons in each State, excluding Indians not taxed. But when the right to vote at any election for the choice of electors for President and Vice President of the United States, Representatives in Congress, the Executive and Judicial officers of a State, or the members of the Legislature thereof, is denied to any of the male inhabitants of such State, being twenty-one years of age, and citizens of the United States, or in any way abridged, except for participation in rebellion, or other crime, the basis of representation therein shall be reduced in the proportion which the number of such male citizens shall bear to the whole number of male citizens twenty-one years of age in such State.

Section. 3.
No person shall be a Senator or Representative in Congress, or elector of President and Vice President, or hold any office, civil or military, under the United States, or under any State, who, having previously taken an oath, as a member of Congress, or as an officer of the United States, or as a member of any State legislature, or as an executive or judicial officer of any State, to support the Constitution of the United States, shall have engaged in insurrection or rebellion against the same, or given aid or comfort to the enemies thereof. But Congress may by a vote of two-thirds of each House, remove such disability.

Section. 4.

The validity of the public debt of the United States, authorized by law, including debts incurred for payment of pensions and bounties for services in suppressing insurrection or rebellion, shall not be questioned. But neither the United States nor any State shall assume or pay any debt or obligation incurred in aid of insurrection or rebellion against the United States, or any claim for the loss or emancipation of any slave; but all such debts, obligations and claims shall be held illegal and void.

Section. 5.

The Congress shall have power to enforce, by appropriate legislation, the provisions of this article.

[Passed by Congress June 13, 1866. Ratified July 9, 1868.]

Amendment XV.

Section. 1.

The right of citizens of the United States to vote shall not be denied or abridged by the United States or by any State on account of race, color, or previous condition of servitude.

Section. 2.

The Congress shall have power to enforce this article by appropriate legislation.

[Passed by Congress February 26, 1869. Ratified February 4, 1870.]

Amendment XIX.

Section. 1.

The right of citizens of the United States to vote shall not be denied or abridged by the United States or any State on account of sex.

Section. 2.

Congress shall have power to enforce this article by appropriate legislation.

[Passed by Congress June 4, 1919. Ratified August 18, 1920.]

Amendment XXVI.

[Note: Amendment 14, section 2, of the Constitution was modified by Section 1 of the 26th amendment.]

Section. 1.

The rights of citizens of the United States, who are eighteen years of age or older, to vote shall not be denied or abridged by the United States or by any State on account of age.

Section. 2.

The Congress shall have power to enforce this article by appropriate legislation.

[Passed by Congress March 23, 1971. Ratified July 1, 1971.]

Here are some questions that may help you reflect on what you have read. The questions encourage you to consider the Constitution as a written document and to recall the other documents on citizenship that you have studied so far.

1. What impressions of American citizenship do you get from the Constitution? How do these impressions compare with those you got from your Mind Map, the dictionary definitions, and the USCIS naturalization requirements?

2. The majority of the Constitution deals with the makeup, procedures, and authority of the federal government. Is this what you expected when you began reading the Constitution? Why do you think the rights of individual citizens were not addressed until the amendments?

3. How would you describe the language of the Constitution? Consider the kinds of words used, the words' specificity or vagueness, the length and complexity of the sentences, and so on. Does this language fit the authors' purpose and audience?

4. Under the Tenth Amendment to the Constitution, the power to determine what schools will teach resides in the states. In 2004, however, Congress passed a mandate, authored by West Virginia Senator Robert Byrd, requiring all schools that receive federal money from the Department of Education to teach the U.S. Constitution on September 17, Constitution Day and Citizenship Day. Do you think a required day to study the Constitution makes sense? What suggestions do you have for how the document should be taught meaningfully to students?

While the U.S. Constitution provides the framework for the citizens' relation to their government, it is only one of many laws defining how citizens ought to live. There are rules for driving automobiles, for operating a business, for running political campaigns. There are laws protecting individuals within families, protecting groups within society, and for taking affirmative action against past injustices. Take a few minutes to brainstorm other laws that define what individuals can or cannot do as citizens. You might also consult your library, the Internet, or government agencies to examine the laws themselves.

Then, consider the fact that all of these laws are written. What advantages do written laws offer for a community? Are there disadvantages? Finally, create a list of other instances where writing helps to define your communities or the issues your community is facing. How significant is writing to citizens' lives?

FOURTH INQUIRY: VISUAL MESSAGES

In addition to government documents, you might examine the many messages about citizenship that circulate in our communities. Advertisements, public service messages, works of art, flags, memorials, the credos and mission statements of civic organizations—citizens are exposed to thousands of messages every day, each of which seeks to affect how we view our community membership. These messages may complicate—or oversimplify—the definitions of citizenship that we find in official documents.

Many of these messages are conveyed to us using visual means. Recognizing that these messages attempt to shape our understanding of citizenship, we can learn how to read them and respond to them thoughtfully. In Chapter 4, you will study how writers seek to persuade us using written and visual texts. To get some initial practice analyzing visual texts, examine the following messages. The first is an advertisement for a consumer affairs organization that appeared in *U.S. News & World Report* May 27, 2002 (p. 22). The second is a cartoon that appeared in *The New Yorker* October 15, 2001 (p. 23). Here are some questions to help you begin your analysis.

1. What is the central message of each visual text? What associations does each piece make between being a good citizen and being a consumer? Note when the pieces were published; e.g., the cartoon appeared one month after the September 11, 2001 attacks. Why is this significant?
2. Who is the audience for these messages? What do you know about *U.S. News & World Report* and the *New Yorker*? Why would these particular images be printed in those individual magazines?
3. Read the two images side by side, as if they were in a conversation with one another, each conveying a message to you. In what ways could the cartoon be read as a critique of or commentary upon the advertisement?
4. Do you think the pieces are effective? Why or why not?
5. Do you think the pieces are ethical? Why or why not?

Your analysis of the visual texts may have illustrated just how complex these messages can be. They often use sophisticated strategies to communicate, and they raise important question about what it means to be a "good" citizen. To continue your inquiry into how visual messages shape our understanding of citizenship, bring additional examples into your classroom: more advertisements or public service announcements from magazines and billboards, for instance, or even bumper stickers and T-shirts.

...to make your own food choices. At least according to the food police and government bureaucrats who have proposed "fat taxes" on foods they don't want you to eat. Now the trial lawyers are threatening class-action lawsuits against restaurants for serving America's favorite foods and drinks.

We think they're going too far.

It's your food. It's your drink. It's your freedom.
Find out more about attacks on your favorite foods and drinks at:

ConsumerFreedom.com

Reprinted with permission from The Center for Consumer Freedom.

"*This isn't for me—it's for the economy.*"

FIFTH INQUIRY: NARRATIVES OF CITIZENSHIP

In the preceding sections, you inquired further into the definition of citizenship. The definitions you examined, however, are collective and general; they do not illustrate how individual citizens experience their citizenship. For example, the Fourteenth Amendment guarantees citizens "equal protection of the laws," but our history has repeatedly shown that some groups—whether because of race, class, gender, age, sexual orientation, or ability—have not experienced the same privileges and immunities as other citizens. To learn about citizenship as it is lived by individuals, we can turn to their stories.

In this section, you will find three narratives from citizens of different historical periods. The insights these writers provide about their civic lives are tied to the narrative as a form of writing. Unlike dictionary definitions and legal documents, narratives can teach us about citizenship in unique ways. Narratives can

- *Dramatize ideas.* Writers can show a character's actions and the consequences, encouraging readers to discover the writer's ideas or arguments for themselves.
- *Show us other viewpoints.* We can better appreciate how individual citizens think or feel by seeing, for ourselves, how they interpret events around them.
- *Appeal to our emotions.* Using vivid descriptions of people, places, and events, writers can inspire us, encourage us to empathize, even anger us into taking action.
- *Generate interest.* Stories intrigue us as human beings. Writers can catch and hold our attention by appealing to our imaginations.

As you read the following narratives, underline lines or passages that illustrate the qualities outlined above. In addition, explore other ways in which these narratives, as forms of writing, teach you about citizenship. Then, after you have read the narratives, read the suggestions for writing your own narrative of citizenship.

Eva Paus
Reflections of a New U.S. Citizen

Dr. Eva Paus is currently the Director of the Center for Global Initiatives and a Professor of Economics at Mount Holyoke College. Dr. Paus grew up in Germany and became a U.S. citizen on March 14, 2002. This account of her experience going through the naturalization process appeared as an editorial in the Sunday Republican *(May 5, 2002).*

On March 14, I became a U.S. citizen. Together with 390 others from many different countries I took the pledge of allegiance in Boston's historic Faneuil Hall. It was a crisp, beautiful morning. The atmosphere was solemn but expectant. Some struggled to contain their joy; others were a bit apprehensive, as if doubtful of their newly accorded status until they could actually hold the Certificate of Naturalization in their hands. As I sat there on the ground floor of this impressive building waiting for the ceremonies to begin, my family beaming down from the balconies and the busts of Founding Fathers peering at me somewhat quizzically from the back of the stage, I found myself thinking about citizenship in the United States — what it would mean to me; what it ought to mean to all of us.

In front of me was the famous life-size painting of Daniel Webster, pleading with his Senate colleagues for "liberty and union, now and forever." I felt surrounded, and inspired, by a history of impassioned advocacy and principled dissent. I thought of the arguments against the injustices of British colonialism that Samuel Adams had raised in this very place more than 200 years ago. And my memory played over the stories of other figures of the Revolutionary period, stories that I had learned only recently as preparation for my "citizenship interview." Out of this background, a definition of citizenship began to emerge, to be sure one premised on placing country before self; these men were, after all, devoted patriots. But I was struck also by their devotion not just to country but to ideas, indeed, their willingness to actively criticize and even to revolt against "their country" when Britain ceased to deserve their loyalty.

Then, the judge arrived, and an official of the Immigration and Naturalization Service called the meeting to order. Undoubtedly, each of the nearly 400 people around me had somewhat different reasons for wanting to become a U.S. citizen. But I wondered how many of them noticed, how different were the conceptions of citizenship presented to us during the proceedings, and how far they diverged from the sort of citizenship that Samuel Adams or Daniel Webster might have described had they had been given a place on the program.

The first official message came from the INS. To be in Faneuil Hall that day, each aspiring citizen had to have passed an oral examination with an INS official.

One of the questions in the study guide for the interview asks the respondent to name one benefit of being a citizen of the United States. The suggested answer is "to obtain Federal Government jobs, to travel with a U.S. passport, or to petition for close relatives to come to the United States to live."

5   The second message came from Magistrate Judge Marianne Bowler who presided over the ceremony. She impressed upon us the importance of exercising our most fundamental rights and responsibilities as citizens, namely to vote and to accept the call for jury duty.

And the third interpretation came from President George W. Bush. In a letter we found on our chairs, the President called upon us to respect each human being and to be "citizens building communities of service and a nation of character."

Potential economic benefits, participation in elections and the trial process, and responsibility to our fellow human beings and communities are indeed important benefits and obligations of U.S. citizenship. Yet each of these definitions seemed in its way more limited and limiting than the notion of citizenship I had hoped to hear celebrated — a notion embracing each citizen's responsibility to promote liberty and justice for all, to dissent when dissent is called for — an active, critical citizenship worthy of the founders of the Republic.

These reflections were not the only ones I had that morning. I thought also of the twists of fate that had led me to acquire citizenship in a country that had interned my father in an Idaho P.O.W. camp for German soldiers after WWII. Like me, he had had to study the political system of the United States and to pass a test. But in his case, as he left Camp Rupert for home in 1946, his satisfactory performance was his ticket out of the country, not a way to stay in.

My parents' generation had not been raised to scrutinize and question institutions of authority. They had been taught to obey and to follow. My generation of Germans, born in the late 40s and 50s, were not raised to question either. But the reality of the Holocaust and the War prompted many of us to face uncomfortable questions about citizenship and government.

10   Maybe, on that sunny morning in Faneuil Hall, we did not hear about the importance of a more active citizenship because liberty and justice and the right to dissent are to be taken for granted. But I don't think so. We live in a country where most people know more about the Simpsons than the Constitution and at a time when some regard dissent as the nemesis, rather than the essence, of democracy. We may hope that the tragic events of September 11th have turned Americans from a decades-long preoccupation with personal well-being toward a new public spiritedness. Certainly, in some ways, that appears to be true. But when the Minority Leader of the U.S. Senate can demand angrily to know how one of his colleagues can dare to voice even the mildest criticism of the President's anti-terrorism policies, when global inequality continues to grow and hundreds of millions of people in the world live in desperate poverty, all seemingly beyond the consciousness of most Americans, then there is still much work to be done to redefine, redirect, and revitalize our ideas of citizenship, not just at home, but in an interdependent world.

■ **QUESTIONS FOR FURTHER INQUIRY** ■

1. What is Paus's definition of citizenship? Why does she look to past Americans such as Daniel Webster and Samuel Adams for inspiration?

2. In paragraph seven, Paus summarizes the messages of citizenship given to her by the INS, the magistrate judge, and President George W. Bush. Explain why these definitions are more "limited and limiting" than her own definition of citizenship. Do you agree with her? Why or why not?

3. In the last paragraph, Paus describes the current status of citizenship in our country: "We live in a country where most people know more about the Simpsons than the Constitution and at a time when some regard dissent as the nemesis, rather than the essence, of democracy." To test this idea in your college community, you might formulate a survey and ask 50 of your fellow students questions about contemporary TV programs and key parts of the U.S. Constitution. Are they truly uninformed about the basic structure of their country's government?

Benjamin Franklin
from *Autobiography*

■ ■

Benjamin Franklin (1706–1790) worked as a printer in Philadelphia, where he became deeply involved in the civic life of that city and the developing nation. Later in life, he served in the Continental Congress, on the committee to draft the Declaration of Independence, and as America's ambassador to France. A great believer in living a civic life, he set up one of the earliest libraries, organized a fire company, updated the U.S. Post Office, helped found the American Philosophical Society, and invented the Franklin stove and the lightning rod. The following passages are excerpted from his Autobiography *(The Library of America, 1993), which he worked on from 1771 until his death in 1790, when it was left unfinished.*

It was about this time that I conceiv'd the bold and arduous Project of arriving at moral Perfection. I wish'd to live without committing any Fault at any time; I would conquer all that either Natural Inclination, Custom, or Company might lead me into. As I knew, or thought I knew, what was right and wrong, I did not see why I might not *always* do the one and avoid the other. But I soon found I had undertaken a Task of more Difficulty than I had imagined: While my Care was employ'd in guarding against one Fault, I was often surpriz'd by another. Habit took the Advantage of Inattention. Inclination was sometimes too strong for Reason. I concluded at length, that the mere speculative Conviction that it was our Interest to be compleatly virtuous, was not sufficient to prevent our Slipping, and that the contrary Habits must be broken and good Ones acquired and established, before we can have any Dependance on a steady uniform Rectitude of Conduct. For this purpose I therefore contriv'd the following Method.—

In the various Enumerations of the moral Virtues I had met with in my Reading, I found the Catalogue more or less numerous, as different Writers included more or fewer Ideas under the same Name. Temperance, for Example, was by some confin'd to Eating & Drinking, while by others it was extended to mean the moderating every other Pleasure, Appetite, Inclination or Passion, bodily or mental, even to our Avarice & Ambition. I propos'd to myself, for the sake of Clearness, to use rather more Names with fewer Ideas annex'd to each, than a few Names with more Ideas; and I included under Thirteen Names of Virtues all that at that time occurr'd to me as necessary or desirable, and annex'd to each a short Precept, which fully express'd the Extent I gave to its Meaning.—

These Names of Virtues with their Precepts were

1. TEMPERANCE.
   Eat not to Dulness.
   Drink not to Elevation.

2. SILENCE.
   Speak not but what may benefit others or your self. Avoid trifling Conversation.

3. ORDER.
   Let all your Things have their Places. Let each Part of your Business have its Time.

4. RESOLUTION.
   Resolve to perform what you ought. Perform without fail what you resolve.

5. FRUGALITY.
   Make no Expence but to do good to others or yourself: i.e. Waste nothing.

6. INDUSTRY.
   Lose no Time.—Be always employ'd in something useful.—Cut off all unnecessary Actions.—

7. SINCERITY.
   Use no hurtful Deceit.
   Think innocently and justly; and, if you speak, speak accordingly.

8. JUSTICE.
   Wrong none, by doing Injuries or omitting the Benefits that are your Duty.

9. MODERATION.
   Avoid Extreams. Forbear resenting Injuries so much as you think they deserve.

10. CLEANLINESS
    Tolerate no Uncleanness in Body, Cloaths or Habitation.—

11. TRANQUILITY
    Be not disturbed at Trifles, or at Accidents common or unavoidable.

12. CHASTITY.
Rarely use Venery but for Health or Offspring; Never to Dulness, Weakness, or the Injury of your own or another's Peace or Reputation.——
13. HUMILITY.
Imitate Jesus and Socrates.——

My intention being to acquire the *Habitude* of all these Virtues, I judg'd it would be well not to distract my Attention by attempting the whole at once, but to fix it on one of them at a time, and when I should be Master of that, then to proceed to another, and so on till I should have gone thro' the thirteen. And as the previous Acquisition of some might facilitate the Acquisition of certain others, I arrang'd them with that View as they stand above. *Temperance* first, as it tends to procure that Coolness & Clearness of Head, which is so necessary where constant Vigilance was to be kept up, and Guard maintained, against the unremitting Attraction of ancient Habits, and the Force of perpetual Temptations. This being acquir'd & establish'd, *Silence* would be more easy, and my Desire being to gain Knowledge at the same time that I improv'd in Virtue, and considering that in Conversation it was obtain'd rather by the Use of the Ears than of the Tongue, & therefore wishing to break a Habit I was getting into of Prattling, Punning & Joking, which only made me acceptable to trifling Company, I gave *Silence* the second Place. This, and the next, *Order*, I expected would allow me more Time for attending to my Project and my Studies; RESOLUTION once become habitual, would keep me firm in my Endeavours to obtain all the subsequent Virtues; *Frugality* & *Industry*, by freeing me from my remaining Debt, & producing Affluence & Independance would make more easy the Practice of *Sincerity* and *Justice*, &c. &c.. Conceiving then that agreeable to the Advice of Pythagoras in his Golden Verses,* daily Examination would be necessary, I contriv'd the following Method for conducting that Examination.

**Let not the stealing God of Sleep surprize,*
Nor creep in Slumbers on thy weary Eyes,
Ere ev'ry Action of the former Day,
Strictly *thou dost, and* righteously *survey.*
With Rev'rence at thy own Tribunal stand,
And answer justly to thy own Demand.
Where have I been? In what have I transgrest?
What Good or Ill has this Day's Life exprest?
Where have I fail'd in what I ought to do?
In what to GOD, *to Man, or to myself I owe?*
Inquire severe whate'er from first to last,
From Morning's Dawn till Ev'nings Gloom has past.
If Evil were thy Deeds, repenting mourn,
And let thy Soul with strong Remorse be torn:
If Good, the Good with Peace of Mind repay,
And to thy secret Self with Pleasure say,
Rejoice, my Heart, for all went well to Day.

5   I made a little Book in which I allotted a Page for each of the Virtues. I rul'd each Page with red Ink so as to have seven Columns, one for each Day of the Week, marking each Column with a Letter for the Day. I cross'd these Columns with thirteen red Lines, marking the Beginning of each Line with the first Letter of one of the Virtues, on which Line & in its proper Column I might mark by a little black Spot every Fault I found upon Examination, to have been committed respecting that Virtue upon that Day.

Form of the Pages

TEMPERANCE.							
Eat not to Dulness. *Drink not to Elevation.*							
	S	M	T	W	T	F	S
T							
S	● ●	●			●		
O	●	●	●		●	●	●
R			●				
F		●					
I			●				
S							
J							
M							
Cl.							
T							
Ch							
H							

I determined to give a Week's strict Attention to each of the Virtues successively. Thus in the first Week my great Guard was to avoid every the least Offence against Temperance, leaving the other Virtues to their ordinary Chance, only marking every Evening the Faults of the Day. Thus if in the first Week I could keep my first Line marked T clear of Spots, I suppos'd the Habit of that Virtue so much strengthen'd and its opposite weaken'd, that I might venture extending my Attention to include the next, and for the following Week keep both Lines clear of Spots. Proceeding thus to the last, I could go thro' a Course compleat in Thirteen Weeks, and four Courses in a Year.—And like him who having a Garden to weed, does not attempt to eradicate all the bad Herbs at once, which would exceed his Reach and his Strength, but works on one of the Beds at a time, & having accomplish'd the first proceeds to a second; so I should have, (I hoped) the encouraging Pleasure of seeing on my Pages the Progress I made in Virtue, by clearing successively my Lines of their Spots, till in the End by a Number of Courses, I should be happy in viewing a clean Book after a thirteen Weeks daily Examination.

This my little Book had for its Motto these Lines from Addison's *Cato;*

Here will I hold: If there is a Pow'r above us,
(And that there is, all Nature cries aloud
Thro' all her Works) he must delight in Virtue,
And that which he delights in must be happy.

Another from Cicero.

O Vite Philosophia Dux! O Virtutum indagatrix, expultrixque vitiorum! Unus dies bene, &
ex preceptis tuis actus, peccanti immortalitati est anteponendus.[1]

Another from the Proverbs of Solomon speaking of Wisdom or Virtue;

Length of Days is in her right hand, and in her Left Hand Riches and Honours; Her Ways
are Ways of Pleasantness, and all her Paths are Peace. III, 16, 17.

And conceiving God to be the Fountain of Wisdom, I thought it right and necessary to solicit his Assistance for obtaining it; to this End I form'd the following little Prayer, which was prefix'd to my Tables of Examination; for daily Use.

O Powerful Goodness! bountiful Father! merciful Guide! Increase in me that Wisdom which
discovers my truest Interests; Strengthen my Resolutions to perform what that Wisdom dic-
tates. Accept my kind Offices to thy other Children, as the only Return in my Power for thy
continual Favours to me.

10   I us'd also sometimes a little Prayer which I took from Thomson's *Poems,* viz

Father of Light and Life, that Good supreme,
O teach me what is good, teach me thy self!
Save me from Folly, Vanity and Vice,
From every low Pursuit, and fill my Soul
With Knowledge, conscious Peace, & Virtue pure,
Sacred, substantial, neverfading Bliss!

The Precept of *Order* requiring that *every Part of my Business should have its*
allotted Time, one Page in my little Book contain'd the following Scheme of Employment for the Twenty-four Hours of a natural Day,

---

[1] *A paraphrased translation (with several lines omitted): "O, Philosophy, guide of life! O teacher of virtue and*
corrector of vice. One day of virtue is better than an eternity of vice." Tusculan Disputations *5.2.5*

The Morning Question, What Good shall I do this Day?	5	Rise, wash, and address *Powerful Goodness*; contrive Day's Business and take the Resolution of the Day; prosecute the present Study; and breakfast.—
	6	
	7	
	8	
	9	Work.
	10	
	11	
	12	Read, or overlook my Accounts, and dine.
	1	
	2	
	3	Work.
	4	
	5	
	6	
Evening Question, What Good have I done to day?	7	Put Things in their Places, Supper, Musick, or Diversion, or Conversation, Examination of the Day.
	8	
	9	
	10	
	11	
	12	
	1	Sleep.—
	2	
	3	
	4	

I enter'd upon the Execution of this Plan for Self Examination, and continu'd it with occasional Intermissions for some time. I was surpriz'd to find myself so much fuller of Faults than I had imagined, but I had the Satisfaction of seeing them diminish. To avoid the Trouble of renewing now & then my little Book, which by scraping out the Marks on the Paper of old Faults to make room for new Ones in a new Course, became full of Holes: I transferr'd my Tables & Precepts to the Ivory Leaves of a Memorandum Book, on which the Lines were drawn with red Ink that made a durable Stain, and on those Lines I mark'd my Faults with a black Lead Pencil, which Marks I could easily wipe out with a wet Sponge. After a while I went thro' one Course only in a Year, and afterwards only one in several Years; till at length I omitted them entirely, being employ'd in Voyages & Business abroad with a Multiplicity of Affairs, that interfered. But I always carried my little Book with me. My Scheme of ORDER, gave me the most Trouble, and I found, that tho' it might be practicable where a Man's Business was such as to leave him the Disposition of his Time, that of a Journey-man Printer for instance, it was not possible to be exactly observ'd by a Master, who must mix with the World, and often receive People of Business at their own Hours.—*Order* too, with regard to Places for Things, Papers, &c. I found extreamly difficult to acquire. I had not been early accustomed to it, & having an exceeding good Memory, I was not so sensible of the Inconvenience attending Want of Method. This Article therefore cost me so much painful Attention & my Faults in it vex'd me so much, and I made so little

Progress in Amendment, & had such frequent Relapses, that I was almost ready to give up the Attempt, and content my self with a faulty Character in that respect. Like the Man who in buying an Ax of a Smith my Neighbour, desired to have the whole of its Surface as bright as the Edge; the Smith consented to grind it bright for him if he would turn the Wheel. He turn'd while the Smith press'd the broad Face of the Ax hard & heavily on the Stone, which made the Turning of it very fatiguing. The Man came every now & then from the Wheel to see how the Work went on; and at length would take his Ax as it was without farther Grinding. No, says the Smith, Turn on, turn on; we shall have it bright by and by; as yet' tis only speckled. Yes, says the Man; but—*I think I like a speckled Ax best.*—And I believe this may have been the Case with many who having for want of some such Means as I employ'd found the Difficulty of obtaining good, & breaking bad Habits, in other Points of Vice & Virtue, have given up the Struggle, & concluded that *a speckled Ax was best.* For something that pretended to be Reason was every now and then suggesting to me, that such extream Nicety as I exacted of my self might be a kind of Foppery in Morals, which if it were known would make me ridiculous; that a perfect Character might be attended with the Inconvenience of being envied and hated; and that a benevolent Man should allow a few Faults in himself, to keep his Friends in Countenance. In Truth I found myself incorrigible with respect to *Order;* and now I am grown old, and my Memory bad, I feel very sensibly the want of it. But on the whole, tho' I never arrived at the Perfection I had been so ambitious of obtaining, but fell far short of it, yet I was by the Endeavour made a better and a happier Man than I otherwise should have been, if I had not attempted it; As those who aim at perfect Writing by imitating the engraved Copies, tho' they never reach the wish'd for Excellence of those Copies, their Hand is mended by the Endeavour, and is tolerable while it continues fair & legible.—

And it may be well my Posterity should be informed, that to this little Artifice, with the Blessing of God, their Ancestor ow'd the constant Felicity of his Life down to his 79th Year in which this is written. What Reverses may attend the Remainder is in the Hand of Providence: But if they arrive the Reflection on past Happiness enjoy'd ought to help his Bearing them with more Resignation. To *Temperance* he ascribes his long-continu'd Health, & what is still left to him of a good Constitution. To *Industry* and *Frugality* the early Easiness of his Circumstances, & Acquisition of his Fortune, with all that Knowledge which enabled him to be an useful Citizen, and obtain'd for him some Degree of Reputation among the Learned. To *Sincerity* & *Justice* the Confidence of his Country, and the honourable Employs it conferr'd upon him. And to the joint Influence of the whole Mass of the Virtues, even in their imperfect State he was able to acquire them, all that Evenness of Temper, & that Chearfulness in Conversation which makes his Company still sought for, & agreable even to his younger Acquaintance. I hope therefore that some of my Descendants may follow the Example & reap the Benefit.—

It will be remark'd that, tho' my Scheme was not wholly without Religion there was in it no Mark of any of the distinguishing Tenets of any particular Sect.—I had purposely avoided them; for being fully persuaded of the Utility and Excellency of my Method, and that it might be serviceable to People in all Religions, and intending some time or other to publish it, I would not have any thing in it that should prejudice any one of any Sect against it.—I purposed writing a little Comment on each Virtue, in which I would have shown the Advantages of possessing it, & the Mischiefs attending its opposite Vice; and I should have called my Book the ART *of Virtue*, because it would have shown the *Means & Manner* of obtaining Virtue; which would have distinguish'd it from the mere Exhortation to be good, that does not instruct & indicate the Means; but is like the Apostle's Man of verbal Charity, who only, without showing to the Naked & the Hungry *how* or where they might get Cloaths or Victuals, exhorted them to be fed & clothed. *James* II, 15, 16.—

15   But it so happened that my Intention of writing & publishing this Comment was never fulfilled. I did indeed, from time to time put down short Hints of the Sentiments, Reasonings, &c. to be made use of in it; some of which I have still by me: But the necessary close Attention to private Business in the earlier part of Life, and public Business since, have occasioned my postponing it. For it being connected in my Mind with a *great and extensive Project* that required the whole Man to execute, and which an unforeseen Succession of Employs prevented my attending to, it has hitherto remain'd unfinish'd.—

In this Piece it was my Design to explain and enforce this Doctrine, that vicious Actions are not hurtful because they are forbidden, but forbidden because they are hurtful, the Nature of Man alone consider'd: That it was therefore every ones Interest to be virtuous, who wish'd to be happy even in this World. And I should from this Circumstance, there being always in the World a Number of rich Merchants, Nobility, States and Princes, who have need of honest Instruments for the Management of their Affairs, and such being so rare, have endeavoured to convince young Persons, that no Qualities were so likely to make a poor Man's Fortune as those of Probity & Integrity.

My List of Virtues contain'd at first but twelve: But a Quaker Friend having kindly inform'd me that I was generally thought proud; that my Pride show'd itself frequently in Conversation; that I was not content with being in the right when discussing any Point, but was overbearing & rather insolent; of which he convinc'd me by mentioning several Instances;—I determined endeavouring to cure myself if I could of this Vice or Folly among the rest, and I added *Humility* to my List, giving an extensive Meaning to the Word.—I cannot boast of much Success in acquiring the *Reality* of this Virtue; but I had a good deal with regard to the *Appearance* of it.—I made it a Rule to forbear all direct Contradiction to the Sentiments of others, and all positive Assertion of my own. I even forbid myself agreable to the old Laws of our Junto,[2] the Use of every Word or

---

[2]*Junto was an organization that Franklin, a printer, formed in 1727 with a group of other tradesman in Philadelphia. In his biography* Franklin of Philadelphia *(Harvard UP, 1986), Esmond Wright describes it as "part mutual aid society, part social fraternity, part academy. Its organization was modeled on Mather's neighborhood Benefit Societies, but it was touched also by Masonic principles: it was intended to be secret and exclusive. The questions the members set themselves included 'queries on any point of Morals, Politics or Natural Philosophy,' but the real motivation was self-improvement, the 'wish to do good' that would also bring them advantages, or even profit" (37–38).*

Expression in the Language that imported a fix'd Opinion; such as *certainly, undoubtedly,* &c. and I adopted instead of them, *I conceive, I apprehend,* or *I imagine* a thing to be so or so, or it so appears to me at present.—When another asserted something that I thought an Error, I deny'd my self the Pleasure of contradicting him abruptly, and of showing immediately some Absurdity in his Proposition; and in answering I began by observing that in certain Cases or Circumstances his Opinion would be right, but that in the present case there *appear'd* or *seem'd* to me some Difference, &c. I soon found the Advantage of this Change in my Manners. The Conversations I engag'd in went on more pleasantly. The modest way in which I propos'd my Opinions, procur'd them a readier Reception and less Contradiction; I had less Mortification when I was found to be in the wrong, and I more easily prevail'd with others to give up their Mistakes & join with me when I happen'd to be in the right. And this Mode, which I at first put on, with some violence to natural Inclination, became at length so easy & so habitual to me, that perhaps for these Fifty Years past no one has ever heard a dogmatical Expression escape me. And to this Habit (after my Character of Integrity) I think it principally owing, that I had early so much Weight with my Fellow Citizens, when I proposed new Institutions, or Alterations in the old; and so much Influence in public Councils when I became a Member. For I was but a bad Speaker, never eloquent, subject to much Hesitation in my choice of Words, hardly correct in Language, and yet I generally carried my Points.—

In reality there is perhaps no one of our natural Passions so hard to subdue as *Pride.* Disguise it, struggle with it, beat it down, stifle it, mortify it as much as one pleases, it is still alive, and will every now and then peep out and show itself. You will see it perhaps often in this History. For even if I could conceive that I had compleatly overcome it, I should probably be proud of my Humility.—

Thus far written at Passy 1784

▓ QUESTIONS FOR FURTHER INQUIRY ▓

1. Americans often identify Franklin as one who achieved the American Dream: he became wealthy and powerful in local and state governments. How does his search for moral perfection fit with achieving the American Dream?

2. Working from the details Franklin gives us about the way he lives his life, what does he value as both a private person and as a public citizen? How much do you think he distinguishes between the two? What might be his definition of citizenship?

3. Franklin's ideas about living a successful, moral life still influence the plans of many self-improvement advocates. Create your own written plan for successful living, live by it for at least a week, and then compare your plan and your experiences with Franklin's. Did you become a better person when following your plan? Will you continue to follow it in the future?

WRITING STYLE

CRAFTING A PERSONA

In Chapter 4, you will learn how to craft your persona, the image your writing projects to others of your ability as a thinker, writer, and researcher; your attitude towards your subject and readers; and your personality. Franklin presents a very distinctive persona in his *Autobiography*.

At one point in his narrative, he says that while he may not have acquired genuine humility, he had succeeded "a good deal with regard to the *Appearance* of it." To guard against complaints that the *Autobiography* is a boastful record of his many accomplishments, Franklin works hard to create the appearance of humility in his writing. He records his mistakes and failures as well as his successes and he often pokes fun at himself. For example, in the beginning of the *Autobiography*, he lists his reasons for writing about his life. The last of his reasons, he states, is to "gratify my own Vanity. Indeed I scarce ever heard or saw the introductory Words, *Without Vanity I may say*, etc. but some vain thing immediately followed. Most People dislike Vanity in others whatever Share they have of it themselves, but I give it fair Quarter wherever I meet with it . . . ." In what other ways does Franklin seek to create a more humble persona?

Review your own writing. What kind of persona do you think it shows to readers? What features of your writing would lead them to this conclusion? How might you change your persona to meet new writing situations, e.g., a cover letter for a job application, a letter to a friend, or a research paper?

Ralph Ellison
Prologue from *Invisible Man*

Ralph Ellison was born in Oklahoma in 1914. In 1933, he won a state scholarship to study music at the Tuskegee Institute; while there he met Richard Wright who encouraged him to become a writer. Ellison moved to New York where he eventually worked for the WPA's federal Writer's Project. His novel Invisible Man *(1952) won the 1953 National Book Award. Considered a classic of American literature,* Invisible Man *follows an African-American antihero's efforts to define himself and his place in American society. In a 1955 interview for* The Paris Review, *Ralph Ellison offered this explanation for why he writes:*

> I feel that with my decision to devote myself to the novel I took on one of the responsibilities inherited by those who practice the craft in the United States: that of describing for all that fragment of the huge diverse American experience which I know best, and which offers me the possibility of contributing not only to the growth of the literature but to the shaping of the culture as I should like it to be.

Literary critics in the 1960s often criticized Ellison for not trying more actively to shape American culture. Specifically, they criticized his unwillingness to use his fiction to protest against racism. In "The World and the Jug" (in two parts, 1963 and 1964), he responded that "protest is an element of all art, though it does not necessarily take the form of speaking for a political or social program."

Prologue

I am an invisible man. No, I am not a spook like those who haunted Edgar Allan Poe; nor am I one of your Hollywood-movie ectoplasms. I am a man of substance, of flesh and bone, fiber and liquids—and I might even be said to possess a mind. I am invisible, understand, simply because people refuse to see me. Like the bodiless heads you see sometimes in circus sideshows, it is as though I have been surrounded by mirrors of hard, distorting glass. When they approach me they see only my surroundings, themselves, or figments of their imagination—indeed, everything and anything except me.

Nor is my invisibility exactly a matter of a biochemical accident to my epidermis. That invisibility to which I refer occurs because of a peculiar disposition of the eyes of those with whom I come in contact. A matter of the construction of their *inner* eyes, those eyes with which they look through their physical eyes upon reality. I am not complaining, nor am I protesting either. It is sometimes advantageous to be unseen, although it is most often rather wearing on the nerves. Then too, you're constantly being bumped against by those of poor vision. Or again, you often doubt if you really exist. You wonder whether you aren't simply a phantom in other people's minds. Say, a figure in a nightmare which the sleeper tries with all his strength to destroy. It's when you feel like this that, out of resentment, you begin to bump people back. And, let me confess, you feel that way most of the time. You ache with the need to convince yourself that you do exist in the real world, that you're a part of all the sound and anguish, and you strike out with your fists, you curse and you swear to make them recognize you. And, alas, it's seldom successful.

One night I accidentally bumped into a man, and perhaps because of the near darkness he saw me and called me an insulting name. I sprang at him, seized his coat lapels and demanded that he apologize. He was a tall blond man, and as my face came close to his he looked insolently out of his blue eyes and cursed me, his breath hot in my face as he struggled. I pulled his chin down sharp upon the crown of my head, butting him as I had seen the West Indians do, and I felt his flesh tear and the blood gush out, and I yelled, "Apologize! Apologize!" But he continued to curse and struggle, and I butted him again and again until he went down heavily, on his knees, profusely bleeding. I kicked him repeatedly, in a frenzy because he still uttered insults though his lips were frothy with blood. Oh yes, I kicked him! And in my outrage I got out my knife and prepared to slit his throat, right there beneath the lamplight in the deserted street, holding him in the collar with one hand, and opening the knife with my teeth—when it occurred to me that the man had not *seen* me, actually; that he, as far as he knew, was in the midst of a walking nightmare! And I stopped the blade, slicing the air as I pushed him away, letting him fall back to the street. I stared at him hard as the lights of a car stabbed through the darkness. He lay there, moaning on the asphalt; a man almost killed by a phantom. It unnerved me. I was both disgusted and ashamed. I was like a drunken man myself, wavering about on weakened legs. Then I was amused: Something in this man's thick head had sprung out and beaten him within an inch of his life. I began to laugh at this crazy discovery. Would he have awakened at the point of death? Would Death himself have freed him for wakeful living? But I didn't linger. I ran away into the dark, laughing so hard I feared I might rupture myself. The next day I saw his picture in the *Daily News*, beneath a caption stating that he had been "mugged." Poor fool, poor blind fool, I thought with sincere compassion, mugged by an invisible man!

Most of the time (although I do not choose as I once did to deny the violence of my days by ignoring it) I am not so overtly violent. I remember that I am invisible and walk softly so as not to awaken the sleeping ones. Sometimes it is best not to awaken them; there are few things in the world as dangerous as sleepwalkers. I learned in time though that it is possible to carry on a fight against them without their realizing it. For instance, I have been carrying on a fight with Monopolated Light & Power for some time now. I use their service and pay them nothing at all, and they don't know it. Oh, they suspect that power is being drained off, but they don't know where. All they know is that according to the master meter back there in their power station a hell of a lot of free current is disappearing somewhere into the jungle of Harlem. The joke, of course, is that I don't live in Harlem but in a border area. Several years ago (before I discovered the advantages of being invisible) I went through the routine process of buying service and paying their outrageous rates. But no more. I gave up all that, along with my apartment, and my old way of life: That way based upon the fallacious assumption that I, like other men, was visible. Now, aware of my invisibility, I live rent-free in a building rented strictly to whites, in a section of the basement that was shut off and forgotten during the nineteenth century, which I discovered when I was trying to escape in the night from Ras the Destroyer. But that's getting too far ahead of the story, almost to the end, although the end is in the beginning and lies far ahead.

5   The point now is that I found a home—or a hole in the ground, as you will. Now don't jump to the conclusion that because I call my home a "hole" it is damp and cold like a grave; there are cold holes and warm holes. Mine is a warm hole. And remember, a bear retires to his hole for the winter and lives until spring; then he comes strolling out like the Easter chick breaking from its shell. I say all this to assure you that it is incorrect to assume that, because I'm invisible and live in a hole, I am dead. I am neither dead nor in a state of suspended animation. Call me Jack-the-Bear, for I am in a state of hibernation.

My hole is warm and full of light. Yes, *full* of light. I doubt if there is a brighter spot in all New York than this hole of mine, and I do not exclude Broadway. Or the Empire State Building on a photographer's dream night. But that is taking advantage of you. Those two spots are among the darkest of our whole civilization—pardon me, our whole *culture* (an important distinction, I've heard)—which might sound like a hoax, or a contradiction, but that (by contradiction, I mean) is how the world moves: Not like an arrow, but a boomerang. (Beware of those who speak of the *spiral* of history; they are preparing a boomerang. Keep a steel helmet handy.) I know; I have been boomeranged across my head so much that I now can see the darkness of lightness. And I love light. Perhaps you'll think it strange that an invisible man should need light, desire light, love light. But maybe it is exactly because I *am* invisible. Light confirms my reality, gives birth to my form. A beautiful girl once told me of a recurring nightmare in which she lay in the center of a large dark room and felt her face expand until it filled the whole room, becoming a formless mass while her eyes ran in bilious jelly up the chimney. And so it is with me. Without light I am not only invisible, but formless as well; and to be unaware of one's form is to live a death. I myself, after existing some twenty years, did not become alive until I discovered my invisibility.

That is why I fight my battle with Monopolated Light & Power. The deeper reason, I mean: It allows me to feel my vital aliveness. I also fight them for taking so much of my money before I learned to protect myself. In my hole in the basement there are exactly 1,369 lights. I've wired the entire ceiling, every inch of it. And not with fluorescent bulbs, but with the older, more-expensive-to-operate kind, the filament type. An act of sabotage, you know. I've already begun to wire the wall. A junk man I know, a man of vision, has supplied me with wire and sockets. Nothing, storm or flood, must get in the way of our need for light and ever more and brighter light. The truth is the light and light is the truth. When I finish all four walls, then I'll start on the floor. Just how that will go, I don't know. Yet when you have lived invisible as long as I have you develop a certain ingenuity. I'll solve the problem. And maybe I'll invent a gadget to place my coffee pot on the fire while I lie in bed, and even invent a gadget to warm my bed—like the fellow I saw in one of the picture magazines who made himself a gadget to warm his shoes! Though invisible, I am in the great American tradition of tinkers. That makes me kin to Ford, Edison and Franklin. Call me, since I have a theory and a concept, a "thinker-tinker." Yes, I'll warm my shoes; they need it, they're usually full of holes. I'll do that and more. . . .

Please, a definition: A hibernation is a covert preparation for a more overt action. . . .

Meanwhile I enjoy my life with the compliments of Monopolated Light & Power. Since you never recognize me even when in closest contact with me, and since, no doubt, you'll hardly believe that I exist, it won't matter if you know that I tapped a power line leading into the building and ran it into my hole in the ground. Before that I lived in the darkness into which I was chased, but now I see. I've illuminated the blackness of my invisibility—and vice versa. And so I play the invisible music of my isolation. The last statement doesn't seem just right, does it? But it is; you hear this music simply because music is heard and seldom seen, except by musicians. Could this compulsion to put invisibility down in black and white be thus an urge to make music of invisibility? But I am an orator, a rabble rouser—Am? I *was,* and perhaps shall be again. Who knows? All sickness is not unto death, neither is invisibility.

10   I can hear you say, "What a horrible, irresponsible bastard!" And you're right. I leap to agree with you. I am one of the most irresponsible beings that ever lived. Irresponsibility is part of my invisibility; any way you face it, it is a denial. But to whom can I be responsible, and why should I be, when you refuse to see me? And wait until I reveal how truly irresponsible I am. Responsibility rests upon recognition, and recognition is a form of agreement. Take the man whom I almost killed: Who was responsible for that near murder—I? I don't think so, and I refuse it. I won't buy it. You can't give it to me. *He* bumped *me, he* insulted *me.* Shouldn't he, for his own personal safety, have recognized my hysteria, my "danger potential"? He, let us say, was lost in a dream world. But didn't *he* control that dream world—which, alas, is only too real!—and didn't *he* rule me out of it? And if he had yelled for a policeman, wouldn't *I* have been taken for the offending one? Yes, yes, yes! Let me agree with you, I was the irresponsible one; for I should have used my knife to protect the higher interests of society. Some day that kind of foolishness will cause us tragic trouble. All dreamers and sleepwalkers must pay the price, and even the invisible victim is responsible for the fate of all. But I shirked that responsibility; I became too snarled in the incompatible notions that buzzed within my brain. I was a coward . . .

But what did *I* do to be so blue? Bear with me.

▓ QUESTIONS FOR FURTHER INQUIRY ▓

1. Ellison's narrator admits, "I am one of the most irresponsible beings that ever lived. Irresponsibility is part of my invisibility; any way you face it, it is a denial. But to whom can I be responsible, and why should I be, when you refuse to see me?" What are the consequences to a democratic society if certain groups or individuals are marginalized?

2. Compare this narrative to the Black Panthers' "Ten Point Plan" in Chapter 4. How do their responses to injustice differ? Is the Black Panthers' response better or worse than the invisible man's?

3. In a 1955 interview for *The Paris Review,* Ralph Ellison argues that "One function of serious literature is to deal with the moral core of a given society. Well, in the United States the Negro and his status have always stood for that moral concern. He symbolizes among other things the human and social possibility of equality." What is the prospect for equality represented in this narrative? What are the prospects now, more than four decades later?

WRITING STYLE

WRITING AS A PERFORMANCE ART

Ellison's wonderful "music of invisibility" should remind us that writing can be a performance. When readers begin a written work, they are agreeing to be led by the writer. This gesture puts responsibility on the writer to perform well, giving readers what they want and need. Everything we select from our ideas to our specific words shapes the readers' experience.

In practical terms, this might mean withholding information to create some suspense. It might mean including the actual speech of interesting characters. It might even mean mixing realistic and fantastic situations, such as a basement room with 1,369 lights in it. The point is that writers' imaginations can be infinitely creative if they can learn to expand their ideas about what makes a proper essay.

To help themselves get into a role, actors often exaggerate some feature of their characters. For example, if an actor needs to play a wily, slithering character, she might practice by pretending to be a snake. Then, she can tone it down to where she exhibits the qualities she wants without the exaggeration. This exercise is good for writers as well. Identify some quality you want to emphasize in your own writing. Perhaps you want to project an angry tone or make your readers laugh. Exaggerate that quality; have fun with it. Then, if you need to, you can tone down your performance to make it fit your subject, purpose, audience, and situation. Hopefully, enough of that quality will remain to enliven your writing style.

WRITING YOUR OWN NARRATIVE OF CITIZENSHIP

Like dictionary definitions and legal documents, narratives follow their own writing conventions, strategies of presentation that, over time, readers have come to expect. When writers violate these conventions, they usually do so strategically. In other words, they discover those strategies that will help them most effectively achieve their purpose. Here are several strategies common in narratives:

- *Focus on a main idea or dominant impression.* Knowing what idea, attitude, or feeling you want to communicate through your story can help you decide which parts of the story to emphasize. Ralph Ellison includes many details in his story, but they all contribute to his main point: The invisible man is not recognized by the white citizens of the United States and New York City. Although he does not directly comment on what this means in terms of social justice, racial equality, or the place of African Americans in our national community, his details dramatize these issues, letting us develop those insights for ourselves.

- *Organize events for effect.* As long as you provide clear transitions, your plot (the sequence of events that make up your story) can begin and end just about anywhere. What strategy you choose depends on the point you want to convey to your readers. You could start at the beginning and move to the end; you could drop readers into the action, pause to give background information, and then return to the action; or you could, as Ellison does to his narrator, begin at the end and then return to the beginning to explain how the ending situation came about.

- *Choose a perspective that complements your purpose.* Individuals see the same events in different ways. Writers can use this fact to achieve their purpose. They might tell a story from their own perspective, from the perspective of another participant, or even from the perspective of an objective narrator, someone not involved in the story's events. For instance, Benjamin Franklin tells the story of his rise to wealth and prominence as an example for others to follow. At the same time, telling his own story lets him include the doubts he felt and the mistakes he made along the way; this strategy gives his rags-to-riches story a more human quality.

- *Use specific details, sensory descriptions, and actual dialog.* Writers can make their stories seem more real for readers by using specific details. For example, Eva Paus describes both her impressive physical surroundings and the feelings of those waiting to take the oath of citizenship. Details such as "my family beaming down from the balconies and the busts of Founding Fathers peering at me somewhat quizzically from the back of the stage" emphasize the atmosphere of anticipation and solemnity.

Narratives offer extraordinary opportunities for communicating our ideas of citizenship as it is lived. As you write your own citizenship narratives, go back to the qualities that narratives offer. Does your narrative dramatize or show your ideas, expose readers to particular viewpoints, appeal to their emotions, and engage their imaginations?

ASSESSING THE PROGRESS OF OUR INQUIRIES

Before turning to the final chapter exercises, we should assess how far we have come in answering the central question of this chapter: What does it mean to be a citizen? Past students have made the following observations in answering this question:

- *Being a citizen means having both a private and public life.* Even if we don't participate actively in politics or follow social issues, our communities' laws, values, and beliefs shape our private lives. Private citizens can shape a community's laws, values and beliefs by getting involved. Benjamin Franklin affected the quality of his public life by becoming a party leader in the Pennsylvania Assembly and later serving in the Continental Congress.

- *Being a citizen means testing our ideas and values against experience.* Americans may believe, in principle, that they have an obligation to help poorer countries. Eva Paus recognized, however, that Americans are often oblivious to the millions of human beings currently living in poverty. This awareness encouraged her to get involved with global education on her campus. Students need opportunities to develop a deeper sense of their responsibilities as global citizens.

- *Writing can help us think through our ideas about citizenship.* In writing about what citizenship means we can find the words that clarify our own ideas. In writing about his daily activities and long-term goals, Benjamin Franklin gained insights into his own responsibility as a citizen of Philadelphia and the new United States. Shaping his thoughts throughout his life into a narrative helped him to see the importance of critically examining his own choices and effecting change in the community around him.

- *Writing can let us share our ideas about citizenship with others.* Although Ralph Ellison's story is fictional, it lets him show what citizens can experience when they aren't acknowledged as full members of the community. Because Ellison's character was seen only as a threatening abstraction, he struggled to be seen as a real individual. However, by writing this story, Ellison makes the community's racism real for other citizens. Reading Ellison's narrative encourages us to rethink our own ideas about race, identity, and the kind of community we want to build in America.

In the first chapter, thinking, reading, and writing represent both opportunities to ask questions (inquiry) and to exchange ideas (action). In the chapters that follow, we will expand this process of inquiry and action to some of the most pressing questions facing our communities. Through these questions, we will explore our civic lives, our experiences as members of various communities. This exploration will also cultivate within us what the ancient Greek philosopher Socrates called the *examined life.* The civic life is an examined life when we consciously consider the choices we make in our education, our friendships, our government, and our planet. Socrates once told his students, "the unexamined life is not worth living." While we might not go that far, we do believe that an examined life is better for ourselves and our communities.

In Chapter 2, we will explore the examined life further by learning the strategies for thinking, reading, and writing critically that make such a life possible. Because our private and public lives are intertwined, these strategies will help us to live more thoughtful lives, and they will also serve as civic skills, tools we can use to participate more effectively in the community.

Chapters 3 and 4 take inquiry and action to a more rigorous level, one consistent with the kind of work you will do as college students. As we have already discovered in Chapter 1, inquiry can be a form of action: performing research using dictionaries, government documents, and personal narratives actively challenges our thinking, and the act of research is itself a form of social action. In the same way, presenting our ideas to others can be a form of inquiry. The responses we get push us to reshape or refine these ideas.

Finally, Chapter 5 helps us recognize that inquiry and action occur within specific social conditions. Our ability to research and argue is influenced by the parameters set within a classroom; our access to libraries, research facilities, and experts; and the routes available to us for communicating with the larger public. These conditions will become real for us as we work through the writing assignments in each chapter.

PROJECTS FOR INQUIRY AND ACTION

1. Tell a personal story that illustrates a point you want to make about what citizenship means to you. Use the story to set up a further discussion of your point or integrate your comments within the story itself.

2. Compare and contrast experiences as a member of different communities. These communities might be national, international, local, or unofficial, such as a political organization, a student group, a religious group, or a social club. Your community might also be defined by a shared ethnic identity, sexual identity, class, or subculture. Whatever communities you decide to compare, show us with relevant, specific examples what it is like to be a member of more than one community. Do these communities complement one another? Do they conflict? Do they encourage you to be a different person within each group?

3. Analyze a recent event to show how it exemplifies some point about citizenship. In writing your analysis, use specific details from the event and specific discussion of how those details illustrate your point.

4. Pick a social issue that interests you, then look around campus for any groups or resources that would help you research the issue and advocate a particular position. Write a guide to other students explaining how they can use campus resources to participate in public debate over the issue you selected.

5. Talk with your instructors, examine the syllabi from your courses, and review the classes you need for your degree: are there opportunities for you to do coursework that also benefits other communities? Write an essay that shows how students within your major can also be good citizens.

6. Prepare an extended etymology of the word *citizenship* to show how the term's meaning has been shaped over time. You might also write an essay that compares your own experiences as a citizen with a definition from the dictionary or official government documents.

7. Prepare your own Code of Citizenship that outlines the principles of participation in a particular community. Then, explain in detail why you created each principle.

Answers to the U.S. History and Government Exam

The complete list of one hundred questions that the U.S. Citizenship and Immigration Services uses as part of the U.S. citizenship exam can be found at http://uscis.gov/graphics/services/natz/100q.pdf. The USCIS Web site also includes an interactive self-test visitors can use to test their knowledge of U.S. history and government.

1. Red, white, blue
2. 50
3. Yes
4. Four years
5. 3
6. 100
7. The first 10 amendments
8. Patrick Henry
9. Germany, Italy, Japan
10. The Electoral College
11. For religious freedom
12. Francis Scott Key
13. Thomas Jefferson
14. The cabinet
15. 18
16. July 4, 1776
17. Republican
18. 1787
19. Washington, D.C. (1600 Pennsylvania Avenue, NW)
20. The Preamble

CHAPTER 2

Critical Literacy: The Skills to Live an Examined Life

Thought is activism, discussion is activism, education is activism every bit as much as licking stamps at campaign headquarters.
—*Paul Rogat Loeb,* Soul of a Citizen

GETTING STARTED Critical Thinking as Examining Life

Read the following story. Imagine you have received it as e-mail from a friend:

Don't forget to look!!!
   This is really scary . . .
   According to an article by Dr. Beverly Clark, in the Journal of the United Medical Association (JUMA), the mystery behind a recent spate of deaths has been solved.
   If you haven't already heard about it in the news, here is what happened.
   3 women in Chicago turned up at hospitals over a 5 day period, all with the same symptoms. Fever, chills, and vomiting, followed by muscular collapse, paralysis, and finally, death. There were no outward signs of trauma. Autopsy results showed toxicity in the blood. These women did not know each other and seemed to have nothing in common. It was discovered, however, that they had all visited the same restaurant (Big Chappies, at Blare Airport), within days of their deaths.
   The health department descended on the restaurant, shutting it down. The food, water, and air conditioning were all inspected and tested, to no avail. The big break came when a waitress at the restaurant was rushed to the hospital with similar symptoms. She told doctors that she had been on vacation, and had only went to the restaurant to pick up her check. She did not eat or drink while she was there, but had used the restroom. That is when one toxicologist, remembering an article he had read, drove out to the restaurant, went into the restroom, and lifted the toilet seat. Under the seat, out of normal view, was a small spider.
   The spider was captured and brought back to the lab, where it was determined to be the South American Blush Spider (*arachnius gluteus*), so named because of its reddened flesh color. This spider's venom is extremely toxic, but can take several days to take effect. They live in

cold, dark, damp climates, and toilet rims provide just the right atmosphere. Several days later a lawyer from Los Angeles showed up at a hospital emergency room. Before his death, he told the doctor that he had been away on business, had taken a flight from New York, changing planes in Chicago before returning home. He did not visit Big Chappies while there. He did, as did all of the other victims, have what was determined to be a puncture wound on his right buttock. Investigators discovered that the flight he was on had originated in South America. The Civilian Aeronautics Board (CAB) ordered an immediate inspection of the toilets of all flights from South America, and discovered the Blush spider's nests on 4 different planes! It is now believed that these spiders can be anywhere in the country.

So please, before you use a public toilet, lift the seat to check for spiders. It can save your life!

And please pass this on to everyone you care about.

If you received this warning, would you believe it or not? How would you respond? Why?

Reread the message carefully, answer the following questions, and then discuss your answers with the class.

1. What words or phrases make this message seem credible? Underline them. Which words or phrases stand out to you as suspicious and unreliable? Draw a squiggly line underneath them. What can this message tell you about establishing credibility as a writer?

2. Have you ever received a message such as this? If so, write down what you remember about it. What are the common traits of messages such as this one? What strategies would you use to verify the truth of this message?

3. What consequences might there be in uncritically believing this warning and passing it along to others? What if this warning had been about suspicious individuals who may have contaminated your city's water supply?

Messages such as this warning against poisonous toilet spiders pop up frequently on our computers these days. Because they are often labeled "Urgent!" or "Important!" many people respond to them before thinking carefully and checking them for accuracy. This particular warning is a well-known urban legend, a fictional story that masquerades as a true account and gets circulated throughout our communities. We tend to believe urban legends even when they are not true because they prey on our real fears, whether about poisonous spiders, children getting abducted, or car-jackers lurking at gas stations. You can read more about this urban legend at Snopes.com, a Web site dedicated to researching and debunking urban legends: http://www.snopes.com/horrors/insects/buttspdr.htm.

Critical thinking and close reading—the skills you just used to evaluate the urban legend—are civic skills. As Paul Rogat Loeb states in the opening quotation, thinking, talking, and educating ourselves and others are activities just as important to our civic lives as campaigning or voting. They are essential elements of *critical literacy*. The term *literacy* means our ability to read and write. *Critical literacy* takes those abilities further: reading carefully to understand; writing to think. As critically literate people, we think, read, and write with greater awareness, precision, and complexity. We need critical literacy not just for success in college, but for a genuine, vital democracy. Citizens need to be able to distinguish worthy information from deceptive advertising, biased media reports, slanted political rhetoric, get-rich-quick schemes, pseudo-academic studies, and hoaxes such as the urban legend above.

Becoming critically literate, however, means more than just protecting ourselves from misinformation. It also means attending to our own roles as speakers and writers, paying attention to the impact our thoughts and words have on others. In other words, we need to be aware of our ethical responsibilities as communicators and to develop what philosophers call a *moral imagination*. Critical literacy helps us to imagine greater futures and to relate to others and know ourselves in deeper ways. In short, it helps us live an examined life.

Critical thinking, then, is an approach to life, not just a tool for academic work. In our daily lives as well as in our academic studies we are faced with situations that ask us to think carefully and act wisely. Critical thinkers are those who meet these situations with sharp powers of discrimination, active imaginations, and the ability to empathize with others.

For instance, critical thinkers tend to:

- **Ask questions.** They even question their own assumptions and beliefs, wanting to know why they think what they think.
- **Look at issues from multiple perspectives.** They can put themselves in the place of others and recognize that individuals with different opinions can be equally sincere but may be basing their opinions on different beliefs, values, or experiences.
- **Uncover hidden assumptions and prejudices.** In order to understand arguments, they go under them to reveal the underlying values and beliefs. People tend to assume that their values and beliefs are natural and shared by others, and thus may not even be aware of how these assumptions shape their viewpoints.
- **Refuse to oversimplify situations.** They see that situations are generally more complicated than they may appear, and so they examine the contexts—social, cultural, historical, personal—in which the situations occur.
- **Research to expand their perspectives.** They seek more information from sources such as printed materials, broadcast media, and other people. Instead of reaching decisions by consulting their own feelings only, they reach out and consult the ideas of others. Instead of blindly accept-

ing information, they approach it from different perspectives and analyze where it is coming from.

Throughout this chapter, we use Thomas Jefferson's Declaration of Independence as a text for practicing critical literacy. First, we provide you with exercises to read and respond to the Declaration; and then, in the second part of the chapter, we describe the process Jefferson used in drafting the Declaration. You can compare his writing process to the one you are beginning to develop.

FIRST INQUIRY: CRITICAL READING AS ACTIVE CONVERSATION

Books are to be called for and supplied on the assumption that the process of reading is not a half-sleep; but in the highest sense an exercise, a gymnastic struggle; that the reader is to do something for himself.

—*Walt Whitman*

What really knocks me out is a book that, when you're all done reading it, you wish the author that wrote it was a terrific friend of yours and you could call him up on the phone whenever you felt like it.

—*Holden Caulfield*, The Catcher in the Rye

When you read other parts of this textbook, you probably did not think much about *how* you read it. Concentrating on the book's ideas, you may have taken for granted the process by which you experienced those ideas. Yet reading is a fascinating process. Reading opens new subjects to us, connects us to other beings, and frees us to enter new worlds. Reading is a powerful tool for expanding the boundaries of our private and public lives. But what is *critical reading?*

Usually we think of critical reading as defensive or practical. We read other people's claims skeptically, to defend ourselves against the exaggerated promises of advertisers and propaganda writers. We might also read carefully, using the practical tools of critical reading to retain more information from written sources, such as textbooks. Both of these definitions share the assumption that readers have responsibilities toward themselves and the texts they are reading. In this sense, critical reading is like engaging writers in a conversation. Without our participation, a written work is nothing but ink and paper. When we read, we bring the work's ideas to life in our minds; consequently, we are obliged to read carefully, recreating the writer's ideas with accuracy. At the same time, we are obliged to reflect on what we read. The writer's ideas will become part of our knowledge, part of who we are, so we should make sure that what we retain is truly valuable. Critical reading, like critical thinking, is part of living an examined life.

Critical reading takes longer than simply reading, but it has several advantages. First, it saves us time by focusing our attention. If you have ever read to the bottom of a page, only to discover you do not remember what you just read, then you can appreciate the importance of reading actively. Second, critical reading makes our research more efficient. If you have ever had to page through a book or reread an article to find some quote you vaguely remember, then you can appreciate the value of underlining passages and taking notes. Third, critical reading helps us get more from the reading experience. If you have spent hours reading works that you cannot remember a week later, then you can appreciate techniques such as previewing, summarizing, and responding.

Try developing your own critical reading practice using Thomas Jefferson's Declaration of Independence. The Declaration is a significant historical document and a model of clear and elegant prose. Its reputation is so strong that we continue to quote its famous lines "We hold these truths to be self-evident" with awe and respect. If you can engage thoughtfully in conversation with such a revered text, you can learn to read any text critically.

1. The first step of critical reading is drawing out and being aware of your previous knowledge, what you bring to the experience. To that end, write down what you already know about the Declaration of Independence before you begin reading. What expectations, attitudes, or ideas do you have?

2. Read the first paragraph and stop. Describe *how* you read it.

3. Go back and read it again. Do you notice yourself doing anything differently now that you are thinking about how you read?

4. Read the entire text and write down how closely the actual text met your expectations. Do you still have the same attitudes toward the text? Then, discuss what you wrote with your classmates and what strategies you used to read effectively.

The Declaration of Independence

IN CONGRESS, July 4, 1776.

The unanimous Declaration of the thirteen united States of America.

When in the Course of human events, it becomes necessary for one people to dissolve the political bands which have connected them with another, and to assume among the powers of the earth, the separate and equal station to which the Laws of Nature and of Nature's God entitle them, a decent respect to the opinions of mankind requires that they should declare the causes which impel them to the separation.

We hold these truths to be self-evident, that all men are created equal, that they are endowed by their Creator with certain unalienable Rights, that among these are Life, Liberty and the pursuit of Happiness. —That to secure these rights, Governments are instituted among Men, deriving their just powers from the consent of the governed, —That whenever any Form of Government becomes destructive of these ends, it is the Right of the People to alter or to abolish it, and to institute new Government, laying its foundation on such principles and organizing its powers in such form, as to them shall seem most likely to effect their Safety and Happiness. Prudence, indeed, will dictate that Governments long established should not be changed for light and transient causes; and accordingly all experience hath shewn, that mankind are more disposed to suffer, while evils are sufferable, than to right themselves by abolishing the forms to which they are accustomed. But when a long train of abuses and usurpations, pursuing invariably the same Object evinces a design to reduce them under absolute Despotism, it is their right, it is their duty, to throw off such Government, and to provide new Guards for their future security. —Such has been the patient sufferance of these Colonies; and such is now the necessity which constrains them to alter their former Systems of Government. The history of the present King of Great Britain is a history of repeated injuries and usurpations, all having in direct object the establishment of an absolute Tyranny over these States. To prove this, let Facts be submitted to a candid world.

He has refused his Assent to Laws, the most wholesome and necessary for the public good.

He has forbidden his Governors to pass Laws of immediate and pressing importance, unless suspended in their operation till his Assent should be obtained; and when so suspended, he has utterly neglected to attend to them.

He has refused to pass other Laws for the accommodation of large districts of people, unless those people would relinquish the right of Representation in the Legislature, a right inestimable to them and formidable to tyrants only.

He has called together legislative bodies at places unusual, uncomfortable, and distant from the depository of their public Records, for the sole purpose of fatiguing them into compliance with his measures.

He has dissolved Representative Houses repeatedly, for opposing with manly firmness his invasions on the rights of the people.

He has refused for a long time, after such dissolutions, to cause others to be elected; whereby the Legislative powers, incapable of Annihilation, have returned to the People at large for their exercise; the State remaining in the mean time exposed to all the dangers of invasion from without, and convulsions within.

He has endeavoured to prevent the population of these States; for that purpose obstructing the Laws for Naturalization of Foreigners; refusing to pass others to encourage their migrations hither, and raising the conditions of new Appropriations of Lands.

He has obstructed the Administration of Justice, by refusing his Assent to Laws for establishing Judiciary powers.

He has made Judges dependent on his Will alone, for the tenure of their offices, and the amount and payment of their salaries.

He has erected a multitude of New Offices, and sent hither swarms of Officers to harrass our people, and eat out their substance.

He has kept among us, in times of peace, Standing Armies without the Consent of our legislatures.

He has affected to render the Military independent of and superior to the Civil power.

He has combined with others to subject us to a jurisdiction foreign to our constitution, and unacknowledged by our laws; giving his Assent to their Acts of pretended Legislation:

For Quartering large bodies of armed troops among us:

For protecting them, by a mock Trial, from punishment for any Murders which they should commit on the Inhabitants of these States:

For cutting off our Trade with all parts of the world:

For imposing Taxes on us without our Consent:

For depriving us in many cases, of the benefits of Trial by Jury:

For transporting us beyond Seas to be tried for pretended offences:

For abolishing the free System of English Laws in a neighbouring Province, establishing therein an Arbitrary government, and enlarging its Boundaries so as to render it at once an example and fit instrument for introducing the same absolute rule into these Colonies:

For taking away our Charters, abolishing our most valuable Laws, and altering fundamentally the Forms of our Governments:

For suspending our own Legislatures, and declaring themselves invested with power to legislate for us in all cases whatsoever.

He has abdicated Government here, by declaring us out of his Protection and waging War against us.

He has plundered our seas, ravaged our Coasts, burnt our towns, and destroyed the lives of our people.

He is at this time transporting large Armies of foreign Mercenaries to compleat the works of death, desolation and tyranny, already begun with circumstances of Cruelty & perfidy scarcely paralleled in the most barbarous ages, and totally unworthy the Head of a civilized nation.

He has constrained our fellow Citizens taken Captive on the high Seas to bear Arms against their Country, to become the executioners of their friends and Brethren, or to fall themselves by their Hands.

He has excited domestic insurrections amongst us, and has endeavoured to bring on the inhabitants of our frontiers, the merciless Indian Savages, whose known rule of warfare, is an undistinguished destruction of all ages, sexes and conditions.

In every stage of these Oppressions We have Petitioned for Redress in the most humble terms: Our repeated Petitions have been answered only by repeated injury. A Prince whose character is thus marked by every act which may define a Tyrant is unfit to be the ruler of a free people.

Nor have We been wanting in attentions to our British brethren. We have warned them from time to time of attempts by their legislature to extend an unwarrantable jurisdiction over us. We have reminded them of the circumstances of our emigration and settlement here. We have appealed to their native justice and magnanimity, and we have conjured them by the ties of our common kindred to disavow these usurpations, which, would inevitably interrupt our connections and correspondence. They too have been deaf to the voice of justice and of consanguinity. We must, therefore, acquiesce in the necessity, which denounces our Separation, and hold them, as we hold the rest of mankind, Enemies in War, in Peace Friends.

We, therefore, the Representatives of the United States of America, in General Congress, Assembled, appealing to the Supreme Judge of the world for the rectitude of our intentions, do, in the Name, and by Authority of the good People of these Colonies, solemnly publish and declare, That these United Colonies are, and of Right ought to be Free and Independent States; that they are Absolved from all Allegiance to the British Crown, and that all political connection between them and the State of Great Britain, is and ought to be totally dissolved; and that as Free and Independent States, they have full Power to levy War, conclude Peace, contract Alliances, establish Commerce, and to do all other Acts and Things which Independent States may of right do. And for the support of this Declaration, with a firm reliance on the protection of divine Providence, we mutually pledge to each other our Lives, our Fortunes and our sacred Honor.

You may discover in talking to your classmates that you all had different experiences reading the Declaration; these differences illustrate *how actively we participate in the creation of the works we read.* We bring our own values, beliefs, experiences, and interests into conversation with the authors'. Similarly, we bring different reading skill levels and strategies to these texts. Compare the strategies your class discussed with the following list created by our students.

Good critical readers tend to:

- **Preview the whole piece.** *Create a mental picture of the work as a whole and form expectations about its content and its historical and social context.* Test these expectations as you read. This will encourage you to read the work itself more actively.

    1. Give the reading a once-over. Read the title, the table of contents, any subheadings or section titles within the body, and any pictures, graphs, or other visual aids and illustrations.

2. Examine the author's biographical information, the place of publication (e.g., academic journal, popular magazine, etc.), and any bibliographic information (such as the date of publication).

3. Skim the first few paragraphs for the thesis or a statement of the author's purpose, the introductory and concluding paragraphs for the overall argument, and the summary on the book's jacket (if it has one).

4. Look for textual clues. Are there subheadings? Are some words listed in bold or italics, or printed in the margin? How does the text give you clues as to what is most important to remember?

- **Read interactively.** *Dig into the writing physically, ask questions, and connect ideas while you read.* This will help you get more out of the reading experience. The strategies focus your attention, encourage you to record your ideas while reading, and even help you articulate your own arguments.

  1. Circle unfamiliar words or concepts and look them up in a dictionary or encyclopedia.

  2. Mark the writer's definitions of key terms and evidence of his or her assumptions.

  3. Underline key points, striking passages, or interesting arguments. What you underline will vary with your purpose for reading a work (e.g., if you are looking for good writing techniques or ideas about a particular subject).

  4. Annotate the text by jotting notes in the margins that record your response to the piece, such as "good," "no way," or "proof?" You can also note references to other works or events (such as "sounds like Orwell" or "compare with *Fight Club*"), your own rebuttals, and the like.

- **Internalize the writer's ideas.** *Outline the content and the structure of the writer's argument in order to better understand and retain it.* You will sharpen your understanding of a text, preserve an accurate record of the writer's ideas for later use, and gain ideas for your own writing.

  1. Paraphrase the writer's main idea, or thesis. Sometimes the thesis is actually written in the essay—usually in the first few paragraphs—and sometimes it is implied, meaning it isn't actually stated but everything in the essay leads readers to realize that main idea. To ensure you have internalized that idea and will be able to remember it, you should paraphrase it. In other words, you should write the thesis using your own words. If it takes you several sentences to identify the author's main idea, that is fine.

  2. Summarize the work. A summary is generally a short overview of the author's thesis and the main supporting arguments or ideas. To

write a summary, go back through your annotations, identify the main supporting ideas—those that served as the main idea of a particular chapter, section, or cluster of paragraphs—and paraphrase them in a smooth, coherent paragraph. More advice on writing summaries can be found in Chapter 4.

3. Take note of topic sentences that announce central ideas, and transition words that signal connections between ideas.

4. Reflect on how the *form* is affecting your response to the content. Pay attention to the conventions of the genre in which the author is writing. If it were written in a different genre, would it affect you differently?

• **Go beyond the text.** *Respond to the text and use it to develop your own ideas.* The real work of critical reading is done in our own creative response to what we read. We need to go beyond underlined passages, one-word comments, and questions to more sustained conversations with the writer's ideas. The nature of this conversation can vary, depending on what qualities or ideas in the text attract our attention. The following prompts encourage a wide range of creative responses.

1. Can you extend the author's main argument, applying it to new subjects?

2. What might be the consequences of public policies based on the author's ideas?

3. Can you find personal experiences to support and to challenge the author's main argument?

4. What do the author's arguments say about his or her values and beliefs?

5. Who might disagree with the author's arguments and why?

6. How would people from a different time period view the author's arguments?

7. How would people of a different culture view the author's arguments?

8. Can you imagine situations in which the author's main argument would be unethical?

9. Why had people not made the author's arguments before?

Not all of these prompts will apply to particular texts; they are, rather, general frameworks for seeing an author's ideas from different perspectives. Trying several different prompts on the same text can encourage new ways of seeing the same material.

Overall, good critical readers tend to *read as writers*. They read with an awareness of how the form affects their response to the content. In other words, they take note of *how the piece was written,* how the writer's choices affect their reading experience. This also gives them ideas for how to develop their own writing. When you are reading other writers' work you are building a repertoire of possibilities for your own writing projects. The various organizational patterns, arguments, and stylistic choices of authors can be retained as options for your own work.

SECOND INQUIRY: USING A WRITER'S NOTEBOOK TO CONNECT THINKING, READING, AND WRITING

I write entirely to find out what is on my mind, what I'm thinking, what I'm looking at, what I'm seeing, and what it means.

—*Joan Didion, "Why I Write"*

What sort of diary should I like mine to be? Something loose knit and yet not slovenly, so elastic that it will embrace any thing, solemn, slight or beautiful that comes into my mind. I should like it to resemble some deep old desk, or capacious hold-all, in which one flings a mass of odds and ends without looking them through.

—*Virginia Woolf,* A Writer's Diary

The thinking, reading, and writing we have done so far have often overlapped; we used one civic skill to help us master another. For example, consider the complex ways these skills interact in reading critically:

- As we read a text, we relate the author's ideas to our experiences and to other texts. Reading provides us with new ideas and challenges our current ways of thinking.

- To help our reading, we annotate the text, paraphrase the author's ideas, and write critical responses. Writing focuses our attention and helps us remember more; it also encourages good critical thinking.

- If we want to respond more extensively, we might use brainstorming strategies such as Mind Maps to generate ideas. In this case, we would write to actually start our thinking.

- At the same time, we write our ideas down to remember them. We might even reread them later and consider them more critically, expanding or clarifying our ideas further.

In each of these examples, we use one skill to help us perform another; the skills are interconnected. One of the best—and easiest—ways to appreciate the ways thinking, reading, and writing assist one another is to keep a writer's notebook. A notebook is a place where you can exercise these skills and record your efforts for later use. The notebook itself does not have to be anything formal: a spiral notebook, a sketchbook, or perhaps a bound journal with an inspiring cover. The notebooks of Leonardo Da Vinci, for example, are made up of more than 5,000 pages, many of which are notes written on loose-leaf paper. One sample page is shown on page 58.

As we can see from the sample page, Da Vinci brought together words and pictures, often without any formal order. In working through his many inquiries on art, physics, health, or engineering, he created a method in his notebooks that worked for him. In our own notebooks, we can write down great quotations, notes from our reading, or questions we would like to answer. We can paste in cartoons, news clippings, or photographs. We can plan out our projects, reflect on the day's experiences, or draw our own pictures. The whole point of the notebook is to provide ourselves with a place where we can work on our thoughts or record interesting ideas. Notebooks should inspire our creative and analytical thinking by giving our minds material on which to work. How we construct these notebooks will ultimately depend on what strategies help us think, read, and write most effectively. Another, different example from one of the authors' notebooks appears on page 59.

As this example illustrates, writers' notebooks vary. People do not read, think, or write in the same ways, so their notebooks will reflect those differences. Those who are visually oriented, for instance, might have notebooks with a lot of pictures, Mind Maps, and drawings. Those who are technologically savvy might create personal Web logs that serve as notebooks, where they can post statements, pictures, or questions; link up to interesting Web sites; or host online discussions. However these notebooks are created, they provide writers with a record of their learning and of their interests at a given time. Professor Susan Miller informs us that past writers often thought of keeping a notebook as "making a portable memory" or an "index of yourself."

Keeping a writer's notebook as you go through your composition course and through college can help you experience the way your thinking, reading, and writing develop. These skills usually develop slowly, yet your experience at college will shape them strongly. Having a record of your progress can help you recognize the ways you will be changed by this experience. You may also find that keeping a writer's notebook will benefit your writing by inspiring you to write, by giving you ideas to write about, and by preserving your thinking, reading, and writing for later use.

Here is a way to get started: In your writer's notebook, write down one hundred questions you want to know the answer to. They can range from abstract to concrete, serious to trivial: "What's the meaning of life?" "Why is the sky blue?" "What should I major in?" "What is a comma splice?" "Are the mind and the brain identical?" At first, the questions will come easily, but it is important to keep thinking of and writing down questions even when you think you cannot think of any more. One hundred questions is a lot, but it will push you to consider more than you might have if you settled for the first twenty at the top of your head. It will also push you out of the mindset that only certain questions are appropriate ones to explore in writing. It is fine if a number of the questions are variants of one another; in fact, it is expected, for you are drawn to particular subjects and themes.

A Page from Leonardo Da Vinci's Notebooks

When you are in the habit of using your writer's notebook to record ideas and questions, you will create a reservoir of writing ideas, so that when you need a research question or paper topic, you will be ready to go.

Asking questions is one of the strongest signs of our curiosity. The practice of asking questions cultivates the inquiring mind. It exercises our creativity, because asking questions encourages us to see things from new or various perspectives. When you get into the habit of asking and writing down ques-

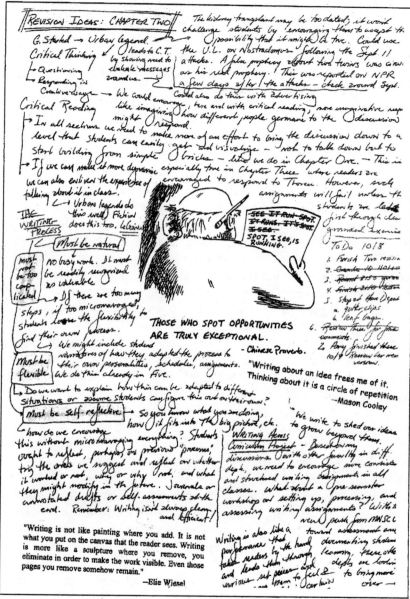

A Page from One of the Authors' Notebooks

tions, you will find it easier to bring them up for closer examination in academic assignments. In that way, college assignments become exercises in investigating the questions you want most to answer. Perhaps most important at this time in your life, asking questions can help you direct your education. Rather than passively accepting the expectations of others, you should embrace the possibilities open to you as a student. Exploring the questions you are most interested in helps you to command and shape your education.

THIRD INQUIRY: DEVELOPING YOUR WRITING PROCESS

We may be bored by the phrase 'the writing process,' but it is a wonderful process. When you have written some inspired draft, it has found a home *outside* you—*on paper*. Having that draft *outside* your head gives the brain new perspective. Your brain, behind your eyes, looks at what you've written. It sees ways to deepen or to contradict the text. Let it. Let the brain do this wonderful work.

—*Carol Bly*, Beyond the Writers' Workshop

You may not consider yourself a "writer" in any classic sense. You may not see yourself as a warbling poet, a slick and savvy copy writer, or a tormented soul hunched over an old, clackety typewriter. But all college students are writers; writing is an essential part of the college experience. You will write to demonstrate your knowledge, to record your inquiries, and to develop your mind, learning how to think with more rigor, focus, and subtlety.

Of course, having to write does not make writing seem less daunting. How does one get from the jumble of half-baked ideas and vague intentions to a clear, focused document that communicates our insights to others? The answer is to see writing as a process. If we try to create a perfect piece of writing the first time, we will be daunted; we will stare dumbly at our computer screens, we will procrastinate, we will curse the instructor who brought this writing assignment into our lives. On the other hand, if we break up a writing project into smaller, more manageable steps, we can empower ourselves. We can give ourselves specific, achievable goals; we can better visualize where we are in the project; we can better manage our time; and we can build momentum as we complete steps successfully.

Before we discuss what these steps might look like, we should pause to reflect on how we imagine our current writing process. We all go through a process of some sort, even if we wait to begin an assignment until the night before it is due. Some processes are better than others, however, either because the resulting product is stronger, the process is less stressful, or we learn more about our subjects and ourselves along the way. To reflect on your current writing process, you might begin by picturing how you complete a writing assignment. If you were to draw it, what would it look like? Take a minute to picture your writing process and draw it in your writer's notebook.

Perhaps your process resembles a timeline, like this student's.

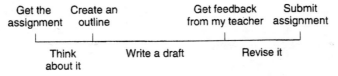

Many student writers initially experience the process of writing as a linear process, with a short period of brainstorming and perhaps outlining ideas, a long period of writing, followed by a briefer period of revision before handing in the essay. Other students may overextend the easier stages and compress the more difficult stages, as this cartoon of another student's writing process suggests:

Experienced writers will often visualize their process in less linear ways. They will focus on their growing understanding more than on the mechanical steps through which they proceed.

"Writing is not like painting where you add. It is not what you put on the canvas that the readers sees. Writing is more like a sculpture where you remove, you eliminate in order to make the work visible. Even those pages you remove somehow remain."

—Elie Wiesel

How writers visualize writing has implications for how they go through the process. For example, Elie Wiesel has described writing as a process of sculpting, eliminating material until his work becomes clear and visible; this suggests a writing process that emphasizes creating a lot of ideas and then analyzing them until a clear main point emerges.

Read the following descriptions from other writers. What kind of image would you draw to fit their descriptions? What does each writer emphasize in his or her process?

> I cannot start a story or chapter without knowing how it ends . . . . Of course, it rarely ends that way.
>
> —Kazuo Ishiguro

> Writing a first draft is very much like watching a Polaroid develop. You can't—and, in fact, you're not supposed to—know exactly what the picture is going to look like until it has finished developing.
>
> —Anne Lamott

> It has always been my practice to cast a long paragraph in a single mould, to try it by my ear, to deposit it in my memory, but to suspend the action of the pen till I had given the last polish to my work.
>
> —Edward Gibbon

Even though these images suggest different ways of imagining a writing process, they all tend to see the writing process as cyclical, or *recursive,* rather than linear; the writers continually return to the same materials, rethinking their subject and how they present it. They visualize the process as one of continually digging deeper or of refining their material, rather than of correcting mistakes.

To explain this process more clearly and encourage you to develop a recursive writing process for yourself, we have broken the writing instruction in this inquiry into three general stages:

1. Conceiving
2. Clarifying
3. Crafting

Here is an overview of the activities writers go through in each stage:

1. **Conceiving:** This stage is made up of three intertwining steps: planning, prewriting, and drafting.
   - *Planning:* Writers explore their writing situation.
   - *Prewriting:* Writers generate ideas and discover their focus.
   - *Drafting:* Writers explore and expand upon those ideas and discover the essay's focus and direction.

2. **Clarifying:** This stage is made up of three intertwining steps—re-seeing, reviewing, and revising.
   - *Re-seeing:* Writers take time to evaluate their initial ideas and opinions, and to re-envision the work as a whole.
   - *Reviewing:* Writers test their work on readers to see how effectively they have communicated their ideas and intentions.
   - *Revising:* Writers reshape their work with a clearer understanding of their purpose and audience: what they want to say and how they want to say it to readers.

3. **Crafting:** This stage is made up of two intertwining steps—editing and proofreading.
   - *Editing:* Writers reread their work, revising for clarity, smoothness, and style.
   - *Proofreading:* Writers reread their work to ensure proper spelling and usage, and to polish the final work.

As we go through this process, keep the following points in mind.

First, *the writing process is as much intellectual revision as writing revision.* Much of our thinking relies on language; our ideas take shape through words. As we revise our writing, we improve the clarity, strength, and sophistication of our ideas.

Second, *writing processes are not absolutes.* Although our writing will be better if we develop it through a process, the process itself will vary between individuals and between writing situations. To illustrate this point, we will examine, at each stage of the writing process, the process Thomas Jefferson used to write the Declaration of Independence. Although his writing process parallels the one described here, he altered, shortened, or collapsed different steps to fit his situation. As a beginning writer, you might give each stage a good faith effort. Then, in future writing assignments, you can adapt the process to your own style—not necessarily what is easiest for you, but what lets you produce a quality final draft most effectively.

Third, although we've laid it out here as a sequence of steps, *the process is not really linear.* In real writing situations, we do not completely "finish" one step and move to the next. Instead, we return frequently to earlier steps, each time engaging our ideas and clarifying and refining them.

Finally, *the writing process asks us to look both inward and outward.* As we go through each step, we think critically about our subject and about our own values and beliefs. In an intensive way, we live an examined life when we write. We also look outward to our audience, crafting our writing to reach them most effectively. In this way, writing is activism; it can help us to forge relationships with others in our community, seek ways to resolve disagreements, and forward our common interests.

Conceiving: The Early Stage of Writing

Imagine yourself sitting in front of an empty computer screen or a blank sheet of paper. Your assignment is to write a six-page essay with an innovative thesis, an easy-to-follow structure, smooth transitions, and vivid details. Not knowing quite how to begin, you had procrastinated until now, the night before it is due. You have twelve hours left. Begin.

Does such a task seem insurmountable?

It may seem less time consuming to begin directly with a final draft—conceiving, clarifying, and crafting as you go along. You will probably discover, however, that the time you waste trying to start, to generate clear and polished thoughts, and to unify ideas that do not fit together naturally will nearly equal what you would have spent in planning, prewriting, and drafting. In addition, by taking the time to work through these early stages in the writing process, your essay will likely avoid the faults common in essays written at the last minute. It will avoid the bland introductions, the vague theses, and the wandering structure—a patchwork of ideas held loosely together with transition words. It will also avoid the irrelevant details, the bits of rejected sentences that the writer forgot to erase, and the conclusion that trails off at the end into an incoherent whimper or tacks on a simplistic platitude.

Taking time early in the process to understand your writing situation will make the entire project easier and less stressful; it will also improve the quality of your work dramatically.

Planning: Exploring Your Writing Situation

Jefferson's Writing Situation

Realizing that their efforts at compromise had failed, the Congress of the American colonies decided on June 11, 1776 to declare independence from Great Britain. To prepare a draft of that declaration, they formed a committee that consisted of Thomas Jefferson, Benjamin Franklin, John Adams, Roger Sherman, and Robert R. Livingston. Since Jefferson was known as an excellent writer and was from the key political state of Virginia, he was delegated the task of writing the first draft. He knew that not all of the colonies believed that declaring independence was wise; therefore, this document he was about to draft had to convince the rest of the Congress to form a united front, as well as announce to the English government that the colonies were declaring themselves independent.

When Jefferson was assigned to write the Declaration of Independence, he was given his subject, the purposes of his document, and American and British audiences who each held different values and beliefs. To successfully achieve his purposes with these audiences, he had first to understand his writing situation. When we too get a writing assignment, we should take a moment to understand what is expected of us. Whether we write for instructors or the public, knowing our audience's expectations, both for what we should write about and how we should write about it, can help us reach such readers more successfully. Here are some questions we should always know the answers to, even before we begin writing.

- When are the drafts and final essay due?
- Does the essay have a designated subject matter or topic?
- Does it have to be written in a particular genre or format (e.g., a critical essay, a lab report, a narrative)? If so, what are the conventions of that genre that we will need to follow?
- Has the essay's purpose been established by the instructor (e.g., a narrative that shows readers what it means to live as a member of a particular community)? If not, what might be our purpose (e.g., to inform, to persuade, to entertain, or all three)?
- Has the instructor issued other instructions (e.g., include at least four sources, include a separate title page)?
- Will the essay be written to audiences outside of class? If so, how will they need to be addressed?
- How will the work be evaluated (e.g., more weight on a clear focus than on correct spelling)?

You might also talk to your instructor more generally about the assignment, and you might request to see models of successful work, not to mimic them but to better visualize the sort of product that is expected of you. What topics have students chosen in the past? Why did the instructor choose to give this particular assignment? The more you know, the more effectively you can meet readers' expectations.

Prewriting: Generating Ideas

Jefferson's Prewriting

Because he was busy with congressional matters during the day, Jefferson set aside the early morning and late evening hours for writing the Declaration of Independence. He was in Philadelphia and did not have time to go home to his study in Virginia on the weekends, so he wrote in his room on an eighteenth-century version of a "laptop"—a portable lap desk that he had had made to his specifications.

When he began drafting the Declaration, Jefferson had already been thinking about the ideas in it. For years he had been reading works about human rights and recording his thoughts in his notebook. Among the authors he had read were English philosopher John Locke, who advocated for the rights of individuals, and Scottish philosopher Francis Hutcheson, who emphasized group values. You can see some of their ideas competing in Jefferson's work.

Because writing is a creative endeavor, much of the process of writing consists of generating ideas. We need to generate ideas at all stages of the writing process; for instance, to get started we generate ideas for essay topics. Later, we write to explore new perspectives on our subject and to clarify our thinking. We also write to work through problems we encounter with our writing; for example, we might try several different methods to explain a difficult concept before we find one we like. You will remember that in Chapter 1 we used brainstorming techniques to discover what we know and how well we know it, to open new avenues for inquiry, and to find a way into an essay (e.g., whether we want to tell a story or analyze a current event). At each stage of writing you can use a range of strategies to help yourself find the ideas or the clarity you need for that specific stage. Learning how to use a number of strategies allows you to choose the one you need in the particular situation, just as knowing how to work with a number of tools allows you to select the most effective one for the job. For example, listing ideas would work if you had only the back of your checkbook to write on, and freewriting ideas on a computer would work if the ideas are coming to you faster than you can handwrite them.

The primary goal of the stage of prewriting is to generate a critical mass of ideas and, out of that mass, to find a focus for your piece of writing. The term *prewriting* is somewhat of a misnomer, because you write to generate those ideas and find that focus: you write in preparation for writing. Below is a list of common strategies for generating ideas; these are often also called *invention strategies*. We encourage you to try all of the invention strategies in order to discover which work best for you under particular conditions and at different stages in the writing process. We also urge you to push your brainstorming or idea generating. Often we see students obediently going through the process because they have to, but abandoning it after only a cursory effort and moving on to the drafting stage before they have had a chance to really let the invention strategies work. Keep working with the strategy until you feel you have a lot to say and a sense of direction for your piece of writing.

- **Talking.** Talk with others about your topic, and work out and test your ideas with them. You can use a tape recorder in order to preserve any great insights.

  Talking is a natural, comfortable way to discover ideas; it can, however, distract you from getting started if the talking wanders from the subject into regular conversation.

- **Freewriting.** Write your initial idea or topic at the top of a blank page. Then write, without stopping or lifting your pen, for ten minutes. Do not stop to edit yourself; keep writing even if you run out of things to say. This helps you dislodge ideas and discover new ones.

  Freewriting has the advantage of pushing you to discover insights you might not have thought of otherwise; it has the disadvantage of producing a lot of work that is less focused, so you often have more material to toss out.

- **Reading.** Read about your topics on the Internet, in magazines, newspapers, and books. You will deepen your knowledge of the subject and also discover connections to other subjects, which will give you ideas for fresh angles for writing.

  Reading is one of the most useful modes of generating ideas; however, it has the disadvantage of being time-consuming and it can encourage procrastination by keeping you from deciding upon a point of focus.

- **Questioning.** Ask yourself the journalist's questions (who, what, when, where, why, and how) as well as "what is the significance of this issue?" and "who would care?"

  A formal strategy of questioning can help you to develop a good sense of purpose and appropriate audience, as well as to be thorough in your coverage. Sticking too closely to just the questions can keep you from exploring and deepening your project, however.

- **Listing.** Write your topic at the top of a sheet of paper, and then make a list of your thoughts about it—directions you might take it, related ideas, and such. These do not have to be full sentences, just a few words. Or, if you have no topic yet, write your assignment guidelines at the top of the page and list all the possible topics you can think of. Listing works by free association, so do not stop to edit yourself, even if some of your ideas sound stupid.

  As with freewriting, listing is useful for dislodging ideas when you feel you have no ideas. Its disadvantage is that, because it does not make you articulate your ideas in full sentences, it does not make you develop your ideas as full thoughts; thus, you can be left with somewhat disjointed ideas.

- **Mapping** or **Treeing.** These strategies give you a visual representation of your ideas, and can help you structure them and connect them. Write your topic or main idea in the center of the page. Make a Mind Map of it, following the instructions in Chapter 1. Or, to use the treeing strategy, draw a line extending from that center idea, and write a related idea on that line or branch, and then ideas related to that branch as various extended twigs. Continue in this way, connecting ideas to the trunk or various branches. You might draw the lines and write the ideas in different colors or different styles.

  Mapping techniques have the advantage of allowing you to visualize the whole of your project and provide clear relationships between the various parts; they have the disadvantage of sometimes taking longer to produce, and, because they produce images rather than sentences, you do not generate as much immediately useable text to incorporate into your writing project.

- **Outlining.** Start with your main point or working thesis. Then list and detail the various points you want to make to support that thesis. The outline can be made in paragraphs, Roman numerals, bullet points—whatever works best for you. The point is for you to be able to get a sense of the whole essay, the point you want to make, and some sense of how you will get there.

  Outlines have the advantage of getting you quickly organized and allowing you to experiment with arranging your ideas before you attempt to work out a full draft; they have the disadvantage of occasionally encouraging you to narrow your thoughts and settle on a format too quickly. For this reason, outlining is a strategy that often works best after you have already thought through your project and are ready to organize and structure your argument's main points. Many writers find that outlining works well *after* they have completed a draft, because it helps them re-see what they have written and organize points more clearly and logically.

Drafting

> ### Jefferson's Drafting
> The Library of Congress still has Jefferson's "official Rough Draught" of the Declaration of Independence. This is the draft he took to Franklin and Adams for their comments. Although Jefferson called it a rough draft, it was carefully thought out, and evidence indicates that it was not by any means his *first* draft; he wrote and rewrote it to clarify his thinking. Like all writers, Jefferson began his drafting from his own thinking. We see earlier versions of his argument in documents he had written previously, such as "A Summary View of the Rights of British America" and the preamble to the Virginia Constitution. In the draft of the Declaration of Independence, Jefferson tried to work out his thoughts on human rights and to find the words that would capture his vision of the new independent United States. Later, in the revision stages, he reshaped paragraphs and points of the Declaration to meet the needs of the specific audiences.

Up to this point, you wrote, talked, read, or researched to generate ideas, a critical mass of material that would impel you forward into the next stage of the writing process: drafting. The goal of drafting is to give this material a focus and shape. Of course, this task is not easy. Your materials hold so many possibilities that you may feel as though any essay you write must explode into a thousand different directions at once. Unfortunately, essays do not unfold this way for readers, who receive your ideas linearly, sentence by sentence and paragraph by paragraph. If you tried to write your final essay at this early stage you would likely wander from point to point, repeat your ideas, or lead readers down intellectual dead ends. To effectively communicate your ideas to readers, you need to focus those ideas and give to them a shape that readers will recognize.

Sometimes you finish prewriting with a clear *working thesis,* that is, a recognizable sense of what you want to communicate to your readers. Often, however, you still need to figure out what you think about your topic and what you want to focus on; in this case you might write an *inquiry draft* or *zero draft.* This is a more focused stage of freewriting in which you dive in and write about your subject without a clear sense yet of where it will lead you. You do not worry about introductions, organization, or grammar. You do not worry that you are repeating yourself or developing ideas in a mishmash fashion. You let the act of writing help you discover what you want to say about the topic. Of course, bells will not go off and confetti will not fall from the ceiling when you happen across a good working thesis. As you write, be alert to any statements about your topic that excite you, that you could write about for several more pages; chances are, you have a good candidate for your working thesis. Remember that any mass of prewriting could probably lead you to dozens of different theses.

Another way you'll know you have a potentially good working thesis is if it helps you to get an intellectual handle on the material. You will not only get a sense of direction, you will also be able to visualize what shape the essay will take. For example, a thesis such as "The Big Mac is, layer for layer, the finest sandwich ever created" suggests analysis. The writer will analyze each layer of the Big Mac to show why it is so wonderful. The structure, then, might move from two all-beef patties, special sauce, lettuce, and cheese to pickles, onions, and a sesame-seed bun. On the other hand, a thesis such as "Preparing a Big Mac requires skill and grace under pressure" promises to explain an activity. The thesis suggests the writer will organize chronologically from beginning to end: from heating the two pucks of beef to lathering on the sauce to wrapping it all up in a box. In both examples, the writer could use the thesis to visualize, or to see in his or her mind, what the essay might look like. The thesis and structure are intertwined; the structure is how you will lead readers to see the truth of your thesis.

To fully develop the visualization suggested by your working thesis, you might try the invention strategy of *outlining.* Imagine the thesis as the destination you want your readers to reach. You have a general sense of direction from your visualization, but if you want to lead other people to your destination, you will need to offer more explicit directions. Outlining pushes you to be explicit, clarifying the purpose of each step and how it helps readers to see the truth of your thesis. In other words, outlining pushes you to be more intellectually honest. At the same time, outlines encourage creativity. They are quick and relatively painless to create, so you can play around with different strategies, as you might map out different routes, imagining which would be most the interesting or practical for your guests.

Having a working thesis and some idea of the structure does make drafting the actual essay easier. Where you go from here may vary, however, because the drafting process itself varies from writer to writer. The precise content, direction, shape, and tone of each essay you write will differ, but each will have a main point or thesis of some sort, and each piece of writing will have a beginning, a middle, and an end. Writers, in many creative and varied ways, lead readers into their writing, make an impression or an argument, and escort them out of the writing. Understanding the function and particular qualities of each of these parts of an essay will help you create the most appropriate and effective ways of communicating your thoughts to your readers.

Beginning Your Essay: Introductions

Introductions are essential to any piece of writing because they establish subject matter, focus, direction, pace, argument, point of view, tone, and persona. Readers depend heavily upon introductions to draw them into the essay, provide them with information, and give them direction as to the content, the author's perspective, and significance of what is to come in the rest of the essay. The introduction is the make-or-break point of many essays, for it is the point at which readers will decide whether they want to read on or to toss the paper aside; they tend to prejudge the whole essay based on their impressions of the introduction.

For these reasons, an introduction can be daunting to write, especially if you think you have to know everything from your subject matter to tone and point of view, all at once. However, you do not need to enter your draft with a completed introduction. The process of working out your introduction will help you focus, organize your thoughts, determine your direction, and get you involved in and excited about your argument; and the process of working out your entire draft will help you develop your introduction. Many professional writers first sketch out a working introduction that guides them through their drafting process. This is meant to be a crutch to help them get going. Then, after they have completed the draft and have a better idea of what they want to say, they return to the opening and carefully craft an introduction that leads readers meaningfully into the essay.

To figure out what strategy will best lead readers into your essay, consider your subject matter, your thesis, and how you want to present yourself to and converse with your readers. You have many choices for beginning a piece of writing, which include but are not limited to the following:

- Pose a question.
- Present dialogue between characters or figures.
- Tell an anecdote or story, or relate a case study.
- Describe a scene, event, or item.
- Offer a statistic or fact (generally a surprising or startling one).
- Quote a text or person.
- Provide background or contextual material to prepare readers for your thesis.

Note the ways the various authors in this book introduce their works. Skim through one community chapter, reading only the introductions. Which ones stand out to you? Why? In which essays is the thesis not placed in the introduction? What effect(s) does this have on you as a reader? What does the author do instead to draw you in and prepare you for the essay to follow?

Developing Your Essay: Body Paragraphs

The body of your essay is where you do most of the explicit work of leading readers to see the truth of your thesis. That is, the body paragraphs develop and support your thesis, whether the thesis has been formally announced in the introduction, will be revealed later, or remains implied throughout. In most—but not all—cases, each body paragraph will focus on explaining one aspect, or supporting point, of the thesis, which will be announced in the topic sentence of the paragraph. Each paragraph will provide evidence to support the thesis, and transitions will connect the paragraphs to one another and will advance the thesis throughout the essay.

Topic sentences hold a paragraph together. They are the main points to which all of the other sentences in the paragraph are connected. While you are drafting, topic sentences help you organize your thoughts; then, in the finished product, they provide guidance and direction for the readers. As Stephen King says in *On Writing,* "Topic-sentence-followed-by-support-and-description insists that the writer organize his/her thoughts, and it also provides good insurance against wandering away from the topic."

Topic sentences are generally either the first or last sentence in a paragraph. At the beginning of a paragraph, topic sentences announce the paragraph's topic or point. Because we indent or add white space to indicate the beginnings of new paragraphs, the reader's eye is drawn to the beginnings of paragraphs; therefore, the first sentence of a paragraph carries a lot of weight and can be a good spot to place your strongest claims. However, you can also organize the paragraph by introducing readers to examples that let them recognize an overall point for themselves. This point gets reinforced in a topic sentence that closes the paragraph.

Body paragraphs provide the evidence that supports your thesis. As you will learn in Chapter 4, each paragraph should contain reasoning and/or specific evidence to explain or prove the claim that is stated in the topic sentence of the paragraph. Depending upon your purpose and audience, you might supply evidence from:

- Your own logical reasoning.
- Your or others' personal experience.
- Observations and experiments.
- Research studies and the professional opinions of authorities and experts.
- Data and statistics.

If you receive a comment that your paper lacks depth, it does not mean that you are a shallow person and incapable of thinking deeply; it probably means that your paper lacks support. The support you provide for each claim is the real core or the substance of your argument; without it you are just asserting a claim and asking readers to believe you.

Transitions create continuity, or flow, between one idea and the next. They do this by showing the relationship between the point you just made and the point you are about to make. For instance, "furthermore" tells the reader you are continuing to develop the point you just made, adding evidence to it; but "however" suggests that you are about to move in a different direction, probably disagreeing with a previous point. You can find whole lists of transitional words and phrases in writing handbooks. Providing smooth transitions that clearly show the relationship between the supporting points of your thesis will advance the thesis step by step. Transitions also provide the flow that is essential to readability and enjoyment and keep an essay from sounding choppy.

Transitional paragraphs can help you signal a move from one idea to the next. You can also use an entire paragraph to provide a transition. For example, when you are moving from one fairly complex point to another, just a phrase or sentence may not provide enough direction for readers, and you may want to use a paragraph to wrap up the first point, signal your move, and prepare readers for the next point.

Ending Your Essay: Conclusions

Conclusions are the paragraph or paragraphs that wrap up the loose ends of your essay. They are memorable when readers are led smoothly out of your argument but are motivated to continue thinking about it and learning from the essay's insights. Think of enlarging the world of your essay as you narrow it to a close: the audience should feel a sense of closure, but should also feel that they can continue the conversation on this topic beyond your essay.

Student writers have often been taught to reiterate their thesis statements in the concluding paragraph. Academic essay assignments in lower-division undergraduate courses are generally short enough, however, that readers have not had time to forget your introduction and thesis, so mere reiteration can be condescending or just plain boring—for you as well as the reader. Do reaffirm your thesis, restating your main point in a fresh way, but then go beyond it. To conclude in the most appropriate and effective manner for your specific writing project, consider your subject matter, the tone and seriousness of your argument, your specific audience, and, most important, your purpose—what you want readers to do as a result of reading your essay. As with introductions, you have a number of choices for how to do this, which include but are not limited to the following:

- Circle back to your introduction: its opening anecdote, story, quotation, dialogue, or question.
- Present the implications of your argument in a wider context.
- Pose a question that has arisen as a result of your thesis.
- Make a suggestion to readers as to where to go next, what action they can take.
- Make a connection with readers by noting ways your argument might affect them personally.

Note the ways the various authors in this book conclude their works. As you did with the introductions, skim through one community chapter reading only the conclusions. Which ones do you find most effective, and why? What is the effect they have on you as a reader? What do the authors do to give you a sense of closure? What do they do to let you make your own conclusions and to continue the work of the essay on your own?

Clarifying: The Middle Stage of Writing

Peer-Reviewing Jefferson's Draft

After working out the first draft, Jefferson presented his "original Rough Draught" to Franklin and Adams. (See a copy of it on the following page.) Both were trusted readers, experienced writers, and statesmen, and they had the good of the overall document foremost in their minds. Both of them read and wrote their suggestions for revision on Jefferson's draft; Jefferson then took those suggestions and incorporated them into a clean copy for the whole committee. Members Sherman and Livingston made minor suggestions, which he also incorporated. Historians have noted that forty-seven alterations, three new paragraphs among them, were made to the document before it was presented to the Congress for their revisions on June 28, 1776.

When we have completed a first draft of our work, we enter a middle stage of the writing process in which we look inside ourselves and outside to readers to deepen and clarify our thoughts. This happens long before we attempt to make stylistic improvements or correct grammar. As writer Carol Bly observes, this stage is more *psychological* than it is artistic because we are closely examining our own ideas and convictions. We want to intensify and develop those ideas for ourselves before we submit them to critique. Thus, in *re-seeing* we reacquaint ourselves with what we have written and evaluate how well it expresses what we really want to say. Then, by *reviewing* we discover how effectively our draft is engaging readers and communicating our intentions, and by *revising* we reshape the whole piece with new attention to our own intentions and our readers' needs and desires.

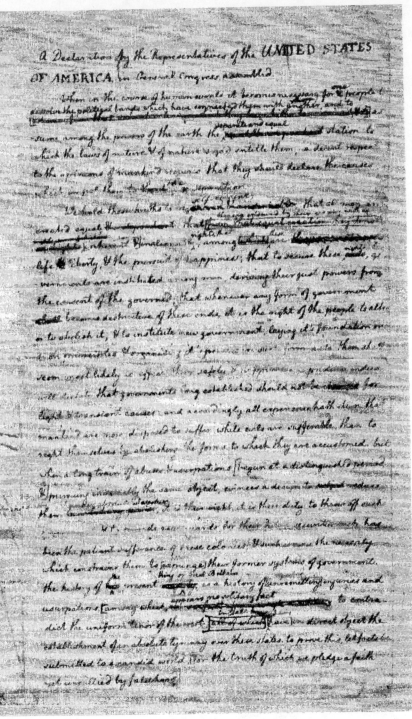

Jefferson's "Original Rough Draught" of the Declaration of Independence

Re-seeing: Rethinking Your Premises

[E]xperienced writers describe their primary objective when revising as finding the form or shape of their argument. Although the metaphors vary, the experienced writers often use structural expressions such as "finding a framework," "a pattern," or "a design" for their argument. When questioned about this emphasis, the experienced writers responded that since their first drafts are usually scattered attempts to define their territory, their objective in the second draft is to begin observing general patterns of development and deciding what should be included and what excluded.

—Nancy Sommers, "Revision Strategies of Student Writers
and Experienced Adult Writers"

Whereas most student writers tend to view the revision process as a matter of *correcting*, experienced writers tend to view it as a time to sit back and *re-see* the work in its entirety and to *rethink* the premises of the thesis and the overall shape of the piece. This can sound overwhelming to student writers because it is more time-consuming than merely correcting errors, and few students have had training and experience in substantive revision. Rethinking the premises of your thesis may well mean changing your mind, and consequently changing your thesis and the entire direction of your paper. Sometimes this will be the case. At other times, you will just refine what you already have in draft form.

First, allow yourself to take a step back and re-see the whole. Reread your draft. Reacquaint yourself with what you have written. One reason for doing this is that writers often continue to think about their subjects, consciously or unconsciously, after the draft is completed. As a result, the essay you have in your mind is sometimes clearer and more developed than the essay you have on paper. Rereading the draft reacquaints you with what you had actually written.

Rethink the premises of your argument. To deepen and refine your initial ideas, when you make claims, ask yourself whether you truly believe what you have said. Are you just going along with what everyone else says, or are you repeating things you have heard of but not really experienced for yourself? What values, beliefs, or assumptions lie *underneath* what you have said? What are you not saying yet? It may be something you have not discovered yet, or it may be something you are afraid you cannot say, because it is an unpopular idea. Grant yourself the courage to rethink your thoughts, to complicate them, and to change them.

Visualize the overall shape of the piece of writing. As you read the entire piece again and again, is there an image or phrase that stands out to you, that seems to work like a magnet to hold the essay together? Often such images and phrases, your best insights, are buried in the body of the paper because they were discoveries you made in the process of drafting. Find those insights, excavate them, and move them to more prominent sections of the paper. One of those insights might make a better thesis than your working thesis, for instance. It may even give you a great title. Reading for these magnetic words or phrases will help you to find the framework, pattern, or design that Sommers refers to in the passage quoted above.

Reviewing: Getting Feedback from Readers

Feedback from someone I'm close to gives me confidence, or at least it gives me time to improve. Imagine that you are getting ready for a party and there is a person at your house who can check you out and assure you that you look wonderful or, conversely, that you actually do look a tiny tiny tiny bit heavier than usual in this one particular dress or suit or that red makes you look just a bit like you have sarcoptic mange. Of course you are disappointed for a moment, but then you are grateful that you are still in the privacy of your own home and there is time to change.

— *Anne Lamott,* Bird by Bird: Some Instructions on Writing and Life

Writing is about forging a connection of minds through language. If you want to communicate effectively you need to know, at various points in the writing process, whether your language is successfully conveying your ideas. While you let your mind and body recover from the drafting and re-seeing processes, you can give your work to trusted others to read to see how they respond to your ideas and whether those ideas are understandable and engaging. Feedback can come from many different sources. Here are just a few suggestions:

- Make an appointment and discuss the draft with your instructor.
- Work with a tutor in your school's writing center.
- Give it to your parents to read. They can often provide good insights, and you will create an opportunity to reconnect with them now that you are in college.
- Find trusted classmates or friends who have already had composition courses or who are taking the class with you.
- Visit your old high-school English teacher. They are usually overworked, but they know how to give feedback and might appreciate the respect you are showing for their expertise.

As you pass around your drafts, keep several points in mind. First, let your readers see the assignment sheet. If they do not know the context in which you are writing and your intended audience, they may give you misleading advice. Second, encourage them to respond to the larger issues; the goal is not to correct spelling errors or mechanical problems, but to discover whether you have made your points as clear and substantive and appealing as they can be. Third, encourage them to give feedback freely. You are the one who must ultimately decide what advice to take or leave. Many of your readers will be, like you, learning how to think and talk about writing. If they worry about misleading you, they will not want to discuss the larger revision issues.

Admittedly, working with others can be difficult, and the process of subjecting your work to the critique of others can be psychologically painful because we tend to see our writing as an intimate extension of ourselves. Like most authors, Thomas Jefferson was also sensitive to changes made to his writing.

Historians tell us that evidently Jefferson sat in Congress and fumed while his text was cut and changed. He wrote later that during the revising Ben Franklin sat next to him and tried to comfort him by telling him the story of a young hatmaker who had made an advertising sign that first read "John Thompson, Hatter, makes and sells hats for ready money." After he asked his friends to critique it for him, however, the sign was reduced to just the words "John Thompson," and a picture of a hat.

Jefferson held a grudge about the group's revision for years, insisting that his original draft was better. He even sent copies of both versions to his friends for them to judge whether his was not the stronger version. Ultimately, though, he was proud of his work on this important document. For the epitaph on his gravestone, he composed a list of his greatest accomplishments: "Author of the Declaration of Independence [and] of the Statute of Virginia for religious toleration & Father of the University of Virginia." (Interestingly, he omitted President of the United States.)

As Anne Lamott stated above, a trusted reader can save us from later embarrassment, frustration, or even failure. In order to be a trusted reader yourself, use your critical reading strategies to converse with the author's work. As with any essay you read, read interactively, responding in the margins and marking the text when you find passages that are striking, vivid, persuasive, vague, ineffective, and so on. In addition, keep in mind that your goal is to help the author develop his or her *own* thoughts as clearly and precisely as possible. While reviewing the work can provide a great opportunity to argue about the subject—pushing the author to think more deeply and clearly about his or her views—you should not, as a reviewer of the writing, try to change the author's views to your own.

And, to get feedback on the specific criteria on which you will be evaluated, ask pointed questions about the piece of writing. Here are some basic questions and suggestions that pertain to most essays; revise them and add others as needed for your specific writing situation.

- Look at the assignment and evaluation criteria. Does the essay fulfill the assignment? Does it meet all the requirements imposed by the instructor?
- Look at the thesis. When you read the draft, what one thing draws everything in the essay together? Write out this main point or thesis in your own words. Is it clear, concrete, and intriguing? Is the thesis not simply repeated but actually developed and enhanced throughout the body of the essay?
- Look at the introduction. Is the choice of an introduction strategy the most compelling and accurate one for the author's purposes? Does the

introduction clearly set up the argument and lead you into it? Do you feel well prepared for the essay that will follow, and engaged so that you *want* to read?

- Look at the structure of the argument. Remember that essays are like guided tours or classroom lectures; authors need to lead readers clearly from one point to the next to see the truth of the thesis. Does the author need to reorganize the order of the argument's points? Does the author need to focus on clearer and more precise topic sentences? Do transitions explain the relationship between various points and guide readers more explicitly from point to point?

- Look at the evidence given as support for the argument. The argument will be stronger if readers can see the argument's truth for themselves. Has the author sufficiently developed the supporting arguments, using specific details, so that you can visualize for yourself his or her point? Is the support that is given relevant to the overall thesis? Are there holes or weaknesses that leave you confused as to how the author came to his or her conclusion? Is more evidence or explanation needed to make the argument clearer or more compelling?

- Look at the conclusion. By the conclusion, has the thesis been effectively developed? Does its truth now seem self-evident? How does the author leave you? Does he or she provide closure? Does the author connect with readers in the conclusion? Does the conclusion encourage you to continue thinking about the subject beyond the author's thesis?

As you learned in the previous section, writing can help us think through our ideas about a piece of writing. The same is true for readers; they can use the writing of comments to you to clarify their feedback. At the same time, readers should not stop with writing a response. They should also talk with the writer. Talking, as another form of brainstorming, will help both reader and writer to discover new ideas that could help the writer revise.

Once you have gotten responses from your various readers, bring them together in your writer's notebook by summarizing them. What were the most common concerns? What aspects of the draft did they most like or dislike? Did their paraphrases of your thesis match what you intended? Summarizing their comments can help you internalize your readers' views. You can now use their insights and advice to help you revise.

Revising: Reshaping Your Work

Revising Jefferson's Declaration

From July 2 through July 4, the Congress debated Jefferson's draft and made a large number of changes. Some were stylistic; for instance, they changed "We hold these truths to be sacred and undeniable" to the now-familiar and resonant "We hold these truths to be self-evident." Such revisions resulted in a smoother, more polished draft.

Two large changes were made to Jefferson's content. After the "He has" phrases in the body of the document, Jefferson had directed a paragraph toward the English people, the "British brethren," criticizing them for not supporting the colonies. Congress softened that paragraph substantially, not wanting to incur the wrath of the Britons, many of whom were relatives and friends.

Jefferson also included, as the last of the "He has" phrases, a sharp indictment of George III for waging "cruel war against human nature itself"—that is, for permitting the slave trade. A slave owner himself, Jefferson was highly ambivalent about the institution of slavery and wanted to phase it out. However, purely in terms of argumentation, George III was not to blame for the colonies' use of slaves; many of the colonies were still willingly participating in and/or benefiting from the slave trade. It is often the case that a writer must relinquish a cherished idea or statement because it does not fit smoothly into the thesis of the essay. (Of course, the Continental Congress also deleted the paragraph because they knew not all the colonies would agree to sign the Declaration if they would have to give up slavery. Congress needed everyone to sign for them to become the *United* States. These changes also illustrate the ethical decisions that are bound up with argumentation and writing.)

Throughout this revision process you have looked inward to your increasingly clear sense what you want to say and how you want to say it and outward to your readers' advice. Now you can take your insights and their advice and reshape your essay with a heightened sense of *audience.* Student writers often find the idea of shaping their work for a specific audience to be at best a hassle and at worst a censoring of their own expression. However, there is an important distinction to make between changing your *content* for readers—having controversial stances suppressed or being coerced into saying the same thing everyone else is saying—and revising your *form,* in which your stance becomes more firmly and clearly communicated as a result of making your thesis more straightforward and precise, reordering paragraphs, or clarifying sentence structure. The latter, not the former, is what instructors are almost always requesting when they ask for revision.

Reshaping with readers in mind reminds us that writing is an ethical act as well as an intellectual act. Revising gives us a chance to pay close attention to being clear, engaging, and honest at each point of the essay, from its introduction through its conclusion. For instance, the thesis is a promise or commitment you make to your readers. You give your word that, over the course of your essay, you will *show* the truth of your thesis to your readers; it is assumed, then, that your thesis should require demonstration. Your readers will find your thesis more effective and interesting if they can learn from it and if there is room for disagreement and discussion, as opposed to a thesis that presents a fact that does not need proving, an obvious statement, or a merely subjective judgment.

Although it is conventional in academic essays to announce the thesis at the end of the introductory paragraph, you can also do so in a separate introductory paragraph, as a turning point in the middle of your essay, or as a revelation at the end of your essay. Consider where your readers will need that information most and where they will respond to it best. Wherever you place your thesis, however, it is an ending of sorts: it is what you have resolved (however tentatively) about your argument. The rest of the essay serves as a space for you to show the readers how you came to that conclusion.

As you revise the body of the essay, particularize your argument by adding details and qualifying your points. When you come to claims, ask whether they are *really* and *always* true, or whether they are *somewhat* and *sometimes* true. If they are only true under certain circumstances, then admit that, and name the circumstances. This process will make you a subtle, more generous thinker and communicator as well as a better, more precise writer.

Of course, making these decisions is generally much easier if we know who our readers are. Our understanding of the audience's needs and expectations is often intuitive—we make reasonable guesses as to what will best teach them, inspire them, or persuade them. Nevertheless, we should consciously attend in the revision process to how much we think our audience knows or cares about our subject, where the common ground is between us and them, and what values or beliefs we share with them that we can draw upon in addressing them.

Crafting: The Later Stage of Writing

Writing is a recursive process; this means that you continually return to the beginning of the piece and work through the stages of the process again, each time tightening your focus and adding the knowledge you have gained from your last time through the process. At the crafting stage you are ready to adopt the mindset of an artisan, looking to the sentences and words themselves— the style, precision, and grace of your language. The care you give these items reveals the seriousness and professionalism of your work.

At this crafting stage, think first of editing for clarity, style, and grace of expression, and then proofreading for correctness. Grammar is more an aid to communication than a series of hard and fast rules that indicate whether or not an essay is "correct." This stage is when your writing handbook will be of most use to you. Now that you've got a deepened draft, your writing handbook will help you shape and refine it because it provides advice on improving your style of expression as well as instruction on correct usage of grammar, punctuation, and mechanics. Work closely with it and look things up as you have questions.

Editing

Although you may think that editing means skimming an essay to catch mistakes in spelling and punctuation, you should see it as an opportunity to further refine your thinking by reflecting carefully on the words and sentences that convey that thinking. At this stage, writers can focus on the clarity, grace, and style of their expression. They can check whether their words are clear and precise. They can check whether their sentences are clearly structured and easy to follow, varied in length, reach an appropriate level of complexity for readers, and emphasize the more important information. They can also make sure their tone and diction, or word choice, communicate effectively with a desired audience. Some of these qualities, such as clarity and precision, are essential to all good writing; other qualities, such as tone, will vary with different purposes and readers.

The following strategies instruct you on editing your own work, taking you step by step through different editing tasks.

- Repeating the same sentence structure and length can make writing sound choppy. Read your sentences aloud to see if your writing is falling into such a pattern.
- Look in the style section of your writing handbook for advice on sentence structure and variety. Experiment with combining sentences or varying the structure of sentences both to convey your thoughts precisely and to engage readers.
- Check to see that your title accurately conveys the focus of your essay and will attract your readers' interest.
- Rewrite the introduction to reflect what you discovered while drafting (rather than what you first thought you would write about). Lead readers methodically into the essay, and, in many cases, into your thesis.
- Rewrite the last sentences of your conclusion so that you lead readers out of your essay clearly and powerfully.
- When you are working with source materials, read carefully to make sure all of your quotations and paraphrases are accurate, and that you have cited all of the sources you have used and have provided precise page numbers or URLs for Web pages. Also make sure that you have documented all sources fully according to the style manual that has been assigned, e.g., MLA or APA. (See Chapter 5 for more information on using quotations and citing and documenting sources.)

Proofreading

Proofreading is the final step in preparing your writing for submission. It is the time at which you polish your text and ready it for presentation. This involves correcting the spelling, punctuation, and mechanics (such as apostrophe use), and formatting the essay according to your audience's expectations. This stage should not be hurried through because even minor matters such as uncorrected typos and apostrophe errors indicate carelessness and can affect how seriously readers take your ideas.

- Because you are familiar with the words and rhythm of the essay it is easy for your eyes to miss errors, words left out, etc. Try reading the essay aloud *backward*, beginning by reading the last sentence, then the one before it, and so on.

- Read through carefully and correct typos. Watch for missing words and word errors that the spell checker program does not catch because the words are not misspelled (such as *where* and *were*, or *woman* and *women*), and words that were left out. Reading aloud will help you catch these errors.

- Read for common grammatical errors such as run-on sentences, comma splices, or sentence fragments. Double-check that the sentence you split in half while editing does not get left as a sentence and a sentence fragment, and that the words you bracketed to come back to later do not remain bracketed.

- Read for mechanical errors involving usage of commas, semicolons, and apostrophes. Pay particular attention to the correct use of apostrophes to indicate possession (e.g., the dog's bone or the dogs' bone), and the incorrect use of apostrophes with plural nouns (e.g., the dog's ran down the street together). If you are unsure of what to do in a particular situation, consult your handbook for an example.

- Correct uses of commonly confused words such as it's/its, your/you're, there/their/they're, to/too/two; as well as effect vs. affect, and conscious vs. conscience.

- Correct uses of common misspellings or misunderstandings of words such as "could of" for "could've," the contraction of "could have."

- Overall, know your own weak points and check for them. What aspects of grammar or mechanics have you consistently been corrected on or consistently been confused about? Consult your handbook, instructor, or a writing center tutor for guidance.

- Ready the presentation of the text for submission. Double-check your format. How are you to do the page numbering, heading, title, margins, font size, and such?

- Ready the whole package for submission. Are you supposed to include earlier drafts or other work with it? Are you supposed to submit the essay in a folder? Are you supposed to staple the pages together, or to use a paper clip?

CONTINUING THE INQUIRY: CRITICAL LITERACY AND CITIZENSHIP

The Critical Compromise of the Declaration of Independence

Representatives of the American colonies struggled to decide on the details of the Declaration of Independence. Jefferson especially could not understand why Congress could keep slavery to preserve the colonies' "greater good":

their union. Historians have argued that we could just as easily have had a smaller version of the Civil War at this time, and indeed the founders were planting the seeds of that war in this critical compromise. Susan B. Anthony and the Black Panthers show in their critiques (printed in Chapter 4) that all the universal goods and rights proclaimed in the Declaration were not being experienced by many Americans.

This final inquiry encourages you to practice critical thinking, reading, and writing in an environment of democratic collaboration. Many situations today require us to compose and revise documents with others; nearly all governmental, institutional, educational, and business work includes some collaborative writing. Working with other writers can be hard on egos, and, significantly, hard on ideals. We all need to learn when and how to negotiate and compromise, and when and how to concede smaller points to win larger ones.

As an exercise in democratic collaboration, you might discuss whether the country needs to officially apologize for the past enslavement of African Americans. In recent years, American leaders have issued apologies and offered reparations for the country's past human rights violations. In 1988, Ronald Reagan formally apologized to Japanese Americans for their internment in U.S. prison camps during World War II, offering $20,000 to each Japanese American who had been interned. In 1993, the U.S. Congress officially apologized to native Hawaiians for overthrowing the Kingdom of Hawaii. In 1997, Bill Clinton apologized to survivors of the Tuskegee syphilis experiment, offering $10 million to the surviving victims and their families. In 2000, Kevin Gover, Assistant Secretary-Indian Affairs, Department of the Interior, apologized for the agency's history of inhumane treatment of Native Americans. In the same year, Ohio Democrat Tony Hall introduced a resolution calling for the U.S. government to apologize for the slavery of African Americans. In the following exercise, discuss whether we need an official, written apology for slavery, and whether we need to offer reparations for it.

1. Divide into several small groups of four to five people. Discuss whether we should have an official, written apology for the history of slavery in the United States; and, furthermore, if we should make reparations to African Americans for the years of slavery.

   a. If you decided the United States should apologize, draft the apology (just one good paragraph will do for this assignment) and a plan for any reparations, along with your reasons justifying it.

   b. If you decide the country should not apologize, write a memo (again, a paragraph is fine) stating why there should be no official apology or reparations, along with your reasoning justifying it.

2. Each group then reads its document aloud and passes around a written copy of it. Then, the entire class can debate these documents and

collaborate on drafting one good paragraph that communicates the class's opinion whether there should be an official apology, and if so, what it should look like, and if not, why not.

In nearly every case, the members of the class will represent a number of opinions—not just for or against opinions, but a full spectrum of nuanced responses. For example, some may want an apology but no reparations; other may want reparations but only a certain amount. Your task is to give everyone a chance to air their views and to find a way to incorporate as many views as possible, into the final document. Afterward, reflect on the process of writing collaboratively. What worked well? What was particularly difficult? Did anything new arise as a result of working collaboratively?

PROJECTS FOR INQUIRY AND ACTION

1. Reflect in your notebook on the work you have done over the course of this chapter. How have you sensed yourself becoming a more critical thinker? How might your thinking, reading, and writing critically help you to develop an examined life?

2. Do you think that all people read in the same way? In what ways might our different experiences affect the ways we read a text? For instance, do women read differently from men? You might begin your inquiry with Jonathan Culler's essay "Reading as a Woman" and Pat Schweikert's essay "Reading Ourselves." (See the bibliography for where to find these essays.) Compare their theories to your own experience, and discuss with others how they read.

3. Why are you here in college? What does "higher education" mean to you?

4. What connections are there between liberty and education?

5. What is the relevance of the Declaration of Independence today? Does it still speak to us individually and as a nation? If so, how? If not, how and why not?

6. Citizens composed the United States, in part, through writing: the Declaration of Independence and the Constitution provided cohesion for the colonies. Do we still construct our national identity through writing today? If so, how? If we no longer construct our national identity through writing, why do we not? How do we construct our identity, then, if not through writing?

7. What kind of world are we constructing through our writing? What values would you like to see our country (or some other community) develop? How, realistically, could you help in the construction?

CHAPTER 3

Researching: Inquiry as Action

For apart from inquiry, apart from the praxis [practice or action],
individuals cannot be truly human. Knowledge emerges only through
invention and re-invention, through the restless, impatient, continuing,
hopeful inquiry human beings pursue in the world, and with each other.
—*Paulo Freire*, Pedagogy of the Oppressed

▓ **GETTING STARTED** ▓ Inquiring in Our Communities

In his book *Why Read?*, professor Mark Edmundson claims that the purpose of
education is "to give people an enhanced opportunity to decide how they should
live their lives." Our lives, however, are usually not lived in isolation. They are
embedded in various overlapping communities that shape who we are and what
we think. When we think about how we should live, therefore, it is not just a
private and individual question but public and communal as well.

Imagine that you and your classmates are the subjects of an extreme reality
TV show: Classtaways. You are taken to a desert island and are left there for one
year, during which time you are to form a community. You have no communication
with the outside world. All your basic needs of food and water are taken care of.
This is your opportunity to do things right, to create an ideal and just society. To
build the society on common ground, you will need to answer the following
questions:

1. What is the *purpose* of your community? What will you do for the next year?
2. How will you allocate your resources? (Food and water will be available, but
   you have to decide how to ration and distribute them.)
3. How will you organize yourselves? For instance, how will you divide the labor
   of building housing, sanitation, and so on, and how will you govern yourselves?
4. How will you deal with conflict?

Before you discuss these questions as a group, you might explore them
individually using these four methods of inquiry:

- *Think*. Take some time to reflect on the questions. You might take a
  walk, stare out the window, or shoot hoops as you think.

- *Talk.* Discuss the question with at least two other people—e.g., your friends, minister, parents, teachers, or people you see each day on the bus.
- *Read.* Seek answers to the question from government textbooks, survival manuals, magazine articles on leadership or group building, newspapers, Web sites—from any printed source.
- *Write.* In your notebook, record your experiences thinking, talking with others, and reading. Then, expand your thoughts using the invention strategies you learned in Chapter 2, such as freewriting and mapping.

After you have tried these different methods of inquiry, discuss your discoveries with your entire class. Summarize the possibilities in a master document. Then, discuss your experiences with the different methods. Try using the following questions to guide your discussion:

1. Did the different methods of inquiry provoke different answers to the question? If so, in what ways?
2. Which methods of inquiry gave you the most insight? Why?
3. Which methods of inquiry were the most enjoyable to pursue? Why?

When students in our classes discussed how it felt to work with various methods of inquiry, they expressed different preferences. You too will find some methods more enjoyable, informative, or enlightening than others.

You might prefer *talking* because it allows you to connect with others while you learn. For instance, you could have had a conversation with your grandmother from Indiana, a lifelong fan of the nineteenth-century utopian community of New Harmony. Her admiration of their communal projects and consensus building led her to emphasize these traits in your family.

You might prefer *reading* because it allows you to explore the question at your leisure, without having to respond to someone else's statements. For instance, you could have read books about utopian communities such as Thomas More's *Utopia* or group survivor situations such as William Golding's *Lord of the Flies*. You might have extracted several thoughtful quotes to share with your class.

You might find *writing* most useful because it allows you to build on the ideas you have in front of you. For instance, you could have created your own constitution, a system of government and a set of laws, to guide you in your creation of an ideal society.

In each of these instances, our students found themselves more engaged in the process of inquiry when they could draw from a variety of research methods. They also found new opportunities to connect with others both in doing their research and in sharing their results. As Brazilian educator Paulo Freire says in the opening quotation, inquiry is an essential part of being human. When we reflect on the events, people, and issues surrounding us, we shape our sense of the world, defining who we are as members of different communities. In this sense inquiry is also a form of social action, the action of an examining citizen. By getting us to talk with other people and read other people's thoughts, inquiry connects us with citizens who are conducting searches of their own.

Inquiry, in other words, is not just for research papers. Inquiry, or research, is a natural response to the questions that come up in our lives. We research when figuring out which school to attend, what scholarships to apply for, what buses to take, and what MP3 player to buy. Even when we are not focused on some specific task, such as building an island utopia, we research to enrich our lives. We research to understand the natural world, to explore our spirituality, or to discover our family history. Researching, then, is a process of discovery that helps us understand a situation, a text, or a person more clearly and fully. In short, researching is a way of thinking through issues, of examining life, and of connecting with others.

You have already been researching in your work with this book. In Chapter 1 you worked through methods of inquiry in order to develop answers to your questions about the meanings of citizenship: you consulted reference works, examined legal and historical documents, and read narratives of people's lived experiences. The methodical process you followed and the variety of sources you consulted allowed you to gradually deepen your understanding of citizenship. You discovered that our citizenship extends far beyond our basic duties of voting, paying taxes, and obeying laws. It extends to living an examined life. In Chapter 2, you began to experience what it means to live an examined life when you critically read and responded to others' words, and developed your own writing process to think through issues, articulate your perspective, and solve problems. Essential to this examining process is the writer's notebook, which gives you a space in which you can explore the questions that most fascinate you.

Developing an inquiring mindset and learning how to ask the questions that inspire innovation and unlock mysteries are critical to academic success and to advancement in our world. This chapter's exercises guide us through methods of inquiry that will help us to test, complicate, and thereby deepen the questions we ask, the answers we discover, and the actions we take in the world. It takes our natural curiosity, our inborn inclination to inquire, and gives it *greater structure* and *discipline* by introducing new methods for inquiring and by making those methods we already know more sophisticated.

FIRST INQUIRY: USING CRITICAL READING AND WRITING AS A CATALYST FOR INQUIRY

The starting point for inquiries is often ourselves. We begin with our curiosity and concern, our experiences and prior knowledge. We write to examine those rigorously and ascertain what our thoughts and feelings are. When we begin an inquiry and write about our own views, it may feel as if we are acting entirely on our own. However, we are actually responding to things we have read and experienced. Thus, our process of inquiry builds on what we have learned.

At the same time, our inquiries also take us out of ourselves to other people who ponder the same questions we do. When we read and respond to their works, we create conversation. As in face-to-face conversations, we join our thoughts with others' and seek to advance knowledge on a particular subject. Writers converse over time and across cultures, interacting with people they will never meet but who explore the same ideas and contribute to the same discussions. As active inquirers we have an ethical obligation to search out other people's discoveries, and to acknowledge the contributions they have made to our thinking. In addition, we have an ethical obligation to examine closely those contributions, so our choice to follow them is really an informed and thoughtful one.

We may not often think of literature as the starting place for an academic investigation, but imaginative writing can spark our own imaginations, help us to see a situation in fresh ways, and formulate questions that can lead us into inquiry and action. (For example, see the Stop and Think box in Chapter 9 on "The Value of Poetry to Civic Dialogues.")

In the Getting Started experiment you were asked to plan an ideal society. What we asked you to do, however, has been done many times before. Architects and urban planners, geographers and bioengineers, psychologists, philosophers, and novelists have imagined such societies. We see their visions in contemporary planned communities such as Celebration, Florida; nineteenth-century utopian societies such as Brook Farm or Amana Colonies; and imaginative works including Plato's *Republic,* Elizabeth Gaskell's *Cranford,* B. F. Skinner's *Walden Two,* and Charlotte Perkins Gilman's *Herland,* as well as in movies such as *Mosquito Coast* and television shows such as *Star Trek* and *The X-Files.*

Utopian societies rarely seem to last, however; nearly all the imaginative accounts show the community falling from high hopes and noble actions into disorder, conflict, or violence. Perhaps factions arise among community members, the technology fails on which the community's prosperity is based, or members lose the fervor that brought them together. These imaginative accounts seem to suggest that while people may want to create ideal communities, working consciously to improve societies, they will usually find a way to muck it up. The central fear that these works seem to reiterate is that human beings may be unable to create a happy and just society.

Ursula Le Guin's classic short story "The Ones Who Walk Away from Omelas" serves as the catalyst for developing this chapter's inquiry into community. As you read, relate the story's ideas to your conceptions of an ideal community.

Ursula Le Guin
The Ones Who Walk Away from Omelas

Ursula Le Guin is a prolific author of novels, essays, poems, and children's books. She is best known as a science fiction writer, although her novels such as The Left Hand of Darkness, *(1969) and* The Dispossessed *(1974) have appealed to many different audiences, challenging their consciences. "The Ones Who Walk Away from Omelas" won the Hugo Award for best short story in 1974.*

With a clamor of bells that set the swallows soaring, the Festival of Summer came to the city. Omelas, bright-towered by the sea. The rigging of the boats in harbor sparkled with flags. In the streets between houses with red roofs and painted walls, between old moss-grown gardens and under avenues of trees, past great parks and public buildings, processions moved. Some were decorous: old people in long stiff robes of mauve and grey, grave master work men, quiet, merry women carrying their babies and chatting as they walked. In other streets the music beat faster, a shimmering of gong and tambourine, and the people went dancing, the procession was a dance. Children dodged in and out, their high calls rising like the swallows' crossing flights over the music and the singing. All the processions wound towards the north side of the city, where on the great water-meadow called the Green Fields boys and girls, naked in the bright air, with mud-stained feet and ankles and long, lithe arms, exercised their restive horses before the race. The horses wore no gear at all but a halter without bit. Their manes were braided with streamers of silver, gold, and green. They flared their nostrils and pranced and boasted to one another; they were vastly excited, the horse being the only animal who has adopted our ceremonies as his own. Far off to the north and west the mountains stood up half encircling Omelas on her bay. The air of morning was so clear that the snow still crowning the Eighteen Peaks burned with white-gold fire across the miles of sunlit air, under the dark blue of the sky. There was just enough wind to make the banners that marked the racecourse snap and flutter now and then. In the silence of the broad green meadows one could hear the music winding through the city streets, farther and nearer and ever approaching, a cheerful faint sweetness of the air that from time to time trembled and gathered together and broke out into the great joyous clanging of the bells.

Joyous! How is one to tell about joy? How describe the citizens of Omelas?

They were not simple folk, you see, though they were happy. But we do not say the words of cheer much any more. All smiles have become archaic. Given a description such as this one tends to make certain assumptions. Given a description such as this one tends to look next for the King, mounted on a splendid stallion and surrounded by his noble knights, or perhaps in a golden litter borne by great-muscled slaves. But there was no king. They did not use swords, or keep slaves. They were not barbarians. I do not know the rules and laws of their society, but I suspect that they were singularly few. As they did without monarchy and slavery, so they also got on without the stock exchange, the advertisement, the secret police, and the bomb. Yet I repeat that these were not simple folk, not dulcet shepherds, noble savages, bland utopians. They were not less complex than us. The trouble is that we have a bad habit, encouraged by pedants and sophisticates, of considering happiness as something rather stupid. Only pain is intellectual, only evil interesting. This is the treason of the artist: a refusal to admit the banality of evil and the terrible boredom of pain. If you can't lick 'em, join 'em. If it hurts, repeat it. But to praise despair is to condemn delight, to embrace violence is to lose hold of everything else. We have almost lost hold; we can no longer describe a happy man, nor make any celebration of joy. How can I tell you about the people of Omelas? They were not naïve and happy children—though their children were, in fact, happy. They were mature, intelligent, passionate adults whose lives were not wretched. O miracle! but I wish I could describe it better. I wish I could convince you. Omelas sounds in my words like a city in a fairy tale, long ago and far away, once upon a time. Perhaps it would be best if you imagined it as your own fancy bids, assuming it will rise to the occasion, for certainly I cannot suit you all. For instance, how about technology? I think that there would be no cars or helicopters in and above the streets; this follows from the fact that the people of Omelas are happy people. Happiness is based on a just discrimination of what is necessary, what is neither necessary nor destructive, and what is destructive. In the middle category, however—that of the unnecessary but undestructive, that of comfort, luxury, exuberance, etc.—they could perfectly well have central heating, subway trains, washing machines, and all kinds of marvelous devices not yet invented here, floating light-sources, fuelless power, a cure for the common cold. Or they could have none of that: it doesn't matter. As you like it. I incline to think that people from towns up and down the coast have been coming in to Omelas during the last days before the Festival on very fast little trains and double-decked trams and that the train station of Omelas is actually the handsomest building in town, though plainer than the magnificent Farmers' Market. But even granted trains, I fear that Omelas so far strikes some of you as goody-goody. Smiles, bells, parades, horses, bleh. If so, please add an orgy. If an orgy would help, don't hesitate. Let us not, however, have temples from which issue beautiful nude priests and priestesses already half in ecstasy and ready to copulate with any man or woman, lover or stranger, who desires union with the deep godhead of the blood, although that was my first idea. But really it would be better not to have any temples in Omelas—at least, not manned temples. Religion yes, clergy no. Surely the beautiful nudes can just wander about, offering themselves like divine soufflés to the hunger of the needy and the rapture of the flesh. Let them join the processions. Let tambourines be struck above the copulations, and the glory of desire be proclaimed upon the gongs, and (a not unimportant point) let the offspring of these delightful rituals be beloved and looked after by all. One thing I know there is none of in Omelas is guilt. But what else should there be? I thought at first there were no drugs, but that is puritanical. For those who like it, the faint insistent sweetness of *drooz* may perfume the ways of the city, *drooz* which first brings a great lightness and brilliance to the mind and limbs, and then after some hours a dreamy languor, and wonderful visions at last of the very arcana and inmost secrets of the Universe, as well as exciting the pleasure of sex beyond all belief; and it is not habit-forming. For more modest tastes I think there ought to be beer. What else, what else belongs in the joyous city? The sense of victory, surely, the celebration of courage. But as we did without clergy, let us do without soldiers. The joy built upon successful slaughter is not the right kind of joy; it will not do; it is fearful and it is trivial. A boundless and generous contentment, a magnanimous triumph felt not against some outer enemy but in communion with the finest and fairest in the souls of all men everywhere and the splendor of the world's summer: this is what swells the hearts of the people of Omelas, and the victory they celebrate is that of life. I really don't think many of them need to take *drooz*.

Most of the processions have reached the Green Fields by now. A marvelous smell of cooking goes forth from the red and blue tents of the provisioners. The faces of small children are amiably sticky; in the benign grey beard of a man a couple of crumbs of rich pastry are entangled. The youths and girls have mounted their horses and are beginning to group around the starting line of the course. An old woman, small, fat, and laughing, is passing out flowers from a basket, and tall young men wear her flowers in their shining hair. A child of nine or ten sits at the edge of the crowd, alone, playing on a wooden flute. People pause to listen, and they smile, but they do not speak to him, for he never ceases playing and never sees them, his dark eyes wholly rapt in the sweet, thin magic of the tune.

5 He finishes, and slowly lowers his hands holding the wooden flute.

As if that little private silence were the signal, all at once a trumpet sounds from the pavillion near the starting line: imperious, melancholy, piercing. The horses rear on their slender legs, and some of them neigh in answer. Sober-faced, the young riders stroke the horses' necks and soothe them, whispering, "Quiet, quiet, there my beauty, my hope. . . ." They begin to form in rank along the starting line. The crowds along the racecourse are like a field of grass and flowers in the wind. The Festival of Summer has begun.

Do you believe? Do you accept the festival, the city, the joy? No? Then let me describe one more thing.

In a basement under one of the beautiful public buildings of Omelas, or perhaps in the cellar of one of its spacious private homes, there is a room. It has one locked door, and no window. A little light seeps in dustily between cracks in the boards, secondhand from a cobwebbed window somewhere across the cellar. In one corner of the little room a couple of mops, with stiff, clotted, foul-smelling heads, stand near a rusty bucket. The floor is dirt, a little damp to the touch, as cellar dirt usually is. The room is about three paces long and two wide: a mere broom closet or disused tool room. In the room a child is sitting. It could be a boy or a girl. It looks about six, but actually is nearly ten. It is feeble-minded. Perhaps it was born defective, or perhaps it has become imbecile through fear, malnutrition, and neglect. It picks its nose and occasionally fumbles vaguely with its toes or genitals, as it sits hunched in the corner farthest from the bucket and the two mops. It is afraid of the mops. It finds them horrible. It shuts its eyes, but it knows the mops are still standing there; and the door is locked; and nobody will come. The door is always locked; and nobody ever comes, except that sometimes—the child has no understanding of time or interval—sometimes the door rattles terribly and opens, and a person, or several people, are there. One of them may come in and kick the child to make it stand up. The others never come close, but peer in at it with frightened, disgusted eyes. The food bowl and the water jug are hastily filled, the door is locked, the eyes disappear. The people at the door never say anything, but the child, who has not always lived in the tool room, and can remember sunlight and its mother's voice, sometimes speaks. "I will be good," it says. "Please let me out. I will be good!" They never answer. The child used to scream for help at night, and cry a good deal, but now it only makes a kind of whining, "eh-haa, eh-haa," and it speaks less and less often. It is so thin there are no calves to its legs; its belly protrudes; it lives on a half-bowl of corn meal and grease a day. It is naked. Its buttocks and thighs are a mass of festered sores, as it sits in its own excrement continually.

They all know it is there, all the people of Omelas. Some of them have come to see it, others are content merely to know it is there. They all know that it has to be there. Some of them understand why, and some do not, but they all understand that their happiness, the beauty of their city, the tenderness of their friendships, the health of their children, the wisdom of their scholars, the skill of their makers, even the abundance of their harvest and the kindly weathers of their skies, depend wholly on this child's abominable misery.

10   This is usually explained to children when they are between eight and twelve, whenever they seem capable of understanding; and most of those who come to see the child are young people, though often enough an adult comes, or comes back, to see the child. No matter how well the matter has been explained to them, these young spectators are always shocked and sickened at the sight. They feel disgust, which they had thought themselves superior to. They feel anger, outrage, impotence, despite all the explanations. They would like to do something for the child. But there is nothing they can do. If the child were brought up into the sunlight out of that vile place, if it were cleaned and fed and comforted, that would be a good thing, indeed; but if it were done, in that day and hour all the prosperity and beauty and delight of Omelas would wither and be destroyed. Those are the terms. To exchange all the goodness and grace of every life in Omelas for that single, small improvement: to throw away the happiness of thousands for the chance of the happiness of one: that would be to let guilt within the walls indeed.

The terms are strict and absolute; there may not even be a kind word spoken to the child.

Often the young people go home in tears, or in a tearless rage, when they have seen the child and faced this terrible paradox. They may brood over it for weeks or years. But as time goes on they begin to realize that even if the child could be released, it would not get much good of its freedom: a little vague pleasure of warmth and food, no doubt, but little more. It is too degraded and imbecile to know any real joy. It has been afraid too long ever to be free of fear. Its habits are too uncouth for it to respond to humane treatment. Indeed, after so long it would probably be wretched without walls about it to protect it, and darkness for its eyes, and its own excrement to sit in. Their tears at the bitter injustice dry when they begin to perceive the terrible justice of reality and to accept it. Yet it is their tears and anger, the trying of their generosity and the acceptance of their helplessness, which are perhaps the true source of the splendor of their lives. Theirs is no vapid, irresponsible happiness. They know that they, like the child, are not free. They know compassion. It is the existence of the child, and their knowledge of its existence, that makes possible the nobility of their architecture, the poignancy of their music, the profundity of their science. It is because of the child that they are so gentle with children. They know that if the wretched one were not there snivelling in the dark, the other one, the flute-player, could make no joyful music as the young riders line up in their beauty for the race in the sunlight of the first morning of summer.

Now do you believe in them? Are they not more credible? But there is one more thing to tell, and this is quite incredible.

At times one of the adolescent girls or boys who go to see the child does not go home to weep or rage, does not, in fact, go home at all. Sometimes also a man or woman much older falls silent for a day or two, and then leaves home. These people go out into the street, and walk down the street alone. They keep walking, and walk straight out of the city of Omelas, through the beautiful gates. They keep walking across the farmlands of Omelas. Each one goes alone, youth or girl, man or woman. Night falls; the traveler must pass down village streets, between the houses with yellow-lit windows, and on out into the darkness of the fields. Each alone, they go west or north, towards the mountains. They go on. They leave Omelas, they walk ahead into the darkness, and they do not come back. The place they go towards is a place even less imaginable to most of us than the city of happiness. I cannot describe it at all. It is possible that it does not exist. But they seem to know where they are going, the ones who walk away from Omelas.

Now put the ideas you gathered in the Getting Started exercise into dialogue with Le Guin's story, in order to clarify and deepen your vision of an ideal community.

▓ EXERCISE 3.1 ▓   Writing to Develop an Inquiry

1. Based on the information you gathered, what are the similarities and differences you see between Le Guin's Omelas and your plan for an island society?

2. In the story, Le Guin's narrator asks readers, "Do you believe? Do you accept the festival, the city, the joy?" Do you think Le Guin's joyful Omelas is possible without imagining that equally intense suffering must be behind it? Do you think your own plan for an island utopia is possible?

3. What experiences, readings, or conversations have led you to accept or reject Le Guin's utopian society and/or your own? In other words, how did you reach your decision on whether these communities are possible?

4. Discuss your community with other members of your class. How many of you share the same conceptions of an ideal community? For instance, how many of you would insist that *equality* or *happiness* be an essential element of your society? How were your conceptions of community affected by Le Guin's story?

If you wanted to continue exploring utopian societies and what they reveal about us, what would you do? You might read more; the philosopher William James' essay "The Moral Philosopher and the Moral Life" was an inspiration for Le Guin's story. Instead, you might join a group on campus, such as Students for a Just Society, or seek out an online community such as The Well. Or, on a larger scale, you might begin noticing connections between policy decisions and living conditions by tracking the actions of your local, state, and/or national legislators. These activities could grow to become quite ambitious. The second inquiry of this chapter encourages you to meet this challenge with a research plan, a written guide to focus your inquiry.

Nearly all writers, from scholars to poets, agree that you will aid your creativity by planning the process of your projects. The planning process is not only a matter of efficiency and thoroughness, it is an intellectual process that makes us refine our questions before we even begin consulting resources. It helps us consider creative and alternative ways of finding information so that we are not limited to the most obvious sources.

SECOND INQUIRY: DEVELOPING A RESEARCH PLAN

All research plans begin with questions and are intended to help writers visualize what kind of research they want to do, how they want to do it, and where they will go for information. For example, when you defined an ideal community, what related questions did it raise for you? What did it make you curious to know more about? The first step for the plan is to focus your larger question into one that interests you in particular. For instance, a few types of questions that might come out of reading Le Guin could include:

- Should we seek to alleviate the suffering of every person in our community?
- Must some people lose for others to win? What are the consequences for a society built on winning?
- How do groups influence us to act in ways that contradict our own values and judgments?
- How is it best to protest a law that I think is unjust? Should I quietly live my own life as a model of resistance to it, or actively protest the law and try to get it changed?
- How does science fiction as a genre affect readers differently from other genres of fiction?

The question should be a true expression of your curiosity. Do not worry yet about having to phrase it in the form it would take as your "research question" in an academic research paper. If you are working on such a project, you can refine and revise the question later, as you discover the project's direction. Begin with what intrigues you most—with what you really want to know—and leave yourself open to finding things you might not have considered otherwise.

What kind of research do you want to do? Define what kind of search this will be. For example, Neil Postman, who was a professor of communications at New York University, makes an important distinction among a search primarily for information, one for knowledge, and one for wisdom. Sometimes, when your issue is not well known to your readers, you will want first to gather information and let others know about it—a sort of fact-finding mission. Perhaps you want to inform readers about the range of people who are forming intentional communities to counter the values of mainstream society. At other times, when an issue is discussed but is not well understood, or needs to be looked at more closely and carefully, you will want to use your inquiry to create new knowledge—to sort through information, analyze a situation, and explain it. Maybe perceptions of these intentional communities have been skewed—they have been pegged as anti-social and dangerous—and we need to investigate what draws people to them. At still other times, especially when it seems that a situation has been misunderstood and people are acting thoughtlessly, you will want to find the wisdom in a situation—to assess and judge it and advise others on courses of action. It may be that living out of mainstream society—"dropping out" or "walking away from Omelas"—is the way to undermine a consumer culture that puts so much stock in the material possessions that people's minds and hearts are ignored. In some projects, of course, you will want to do all of this. In our so-called information age, too often the "news" or "knowledge" we are presented with is nothing more than unexamined information, and we have to learn how to interpret and understand it. In rigorous and ethical inquiry, we examine the sources and contexts of information and seek to generate from it knowledge and, even more, wisdom. This inquiry is always grounded in the context of our examined life, in what concerns us.

How do you want to conduct your research? This is a question about methodology. Your methods will need to match your goals and questions. Think about how you will find your best answers to your questions. Do you think your best answers will come from *quantitative* research (that is, answers that can be expressed in terms of quantity, or numbers, such as statistics), or from *qualitative* research (that is, answers that can be expressed in terms of their qualities, or individual characteristics, such as narratives of people's experiences)? Do you want to focus on reading textual sources from electronic or print media? Do you want to search in historical archives? Or to interview people and get their opinions on a subject?

Where will you go for information? Where, physically, should you search for information? Some projects may start and end in the college library, but others will need you to research in other places and ways. Consider where the conversations around your questions take place, both in terms of the settings of such conversations (e.g., your hometown city council meetings, sports bars, an Internet chat room) and the general contexts for such conversations (e.g., formal religious debates, teenagers' casual conversations, cyberspace). When you answer those questions, determine where you might go to educate yourself. What kinds of sources would probably be most useful and reliable? Try the following exercise to help you focus your question and frame your inquiry.

▦ EXERCISE 3.2 ▦ Developing a Research Plan

1. In your writer's notebook, write down what you already know about your subject, and list any questions you would like to have answered. Choose a question that you like and feel capable of answering. Freewrite on why the question concerns you, why you are obsessing about it, and how it affects you or others you care about. What experience do you have with the questions that you could draw upon?

2. What kind of inquiry will this primarily be? A search for information, knowledge, or wisdom? Why? If it is a combination of kinds, which will need to predominate, and why?

3. How do you want to conduct your research? Will it be mostly quantitative or qualitative? What kind of material will you need to find, and how will you keep track of it?

4. In what settings and contexts does your question get explored? Where are you most likely to find information that will help you examine and explore this question and begin to develop some answers to it?

All of this planning helps you to frame your inquiry. With your plan in hand, you can begin what is generally thought of as the inquiry itself: the search for those sources that can help you answer your questions and support your views. You will probably feel more creative and more confident when you can choose from a range of strategies for inquiring effectively and ethically, and you know how to select the best one(s) for your needs. The third inquiry introduces you to basic research methods that will help you to generate and test answers to your questions. While we have arranged them in order from electronic and printed textual sources to out-in-the-field sources, this is not necessarily the order you will follow for all your inquiries; for example, in some cases library research will follow experimentation or field research rather than precede it.

THIRD INQUIRY: INQUIRING EFFECTIVELY USING RESEARCH METHODS

When we research we have a number of methods available to use, each of which will be most useful in particular circumstances and communities. We need to become familiar with a range of methods, when to use them, and how to use them rigorously and ethically. This means we want to research in a way that uncovers information thoroughly and accurately, and that builds alliances rather than excludes others or robs them of their dignity, their confidence, or their knowledge. To do this conscientiously we need to learn the conventions of inquiry for particular communities and situations. In this next section, we present each of the most basic research methods. We also discuss under what circumstances we might choose that method, and we offer strategies students have discovered to use that method effectively. Finally, we invite you to experiment with the method and discuss its merits and challenges with your classmates.

Becoming Information Literate: Researching Electronic, Print, and Broadcast Media

We often think of the intellectual work of researching as simply the reading of the information we find. However, a large part of the intellectual work of researching lies in the actual searching itself; the sheer abundance of information in our age demands that we become information literate. We must learn the skills needed to find material pertinent to our needs and discern what will hold value for our inquiries. *Information literacy* is the new term used to describe how our perspectives on and practices of researching have changed. Researching is a much wider field of endeavor than it used to be. We now need to be conversant with new forms of technology and in using electronic sources as well as traditional print resources. But this is not just a matter of knowing how to operate the latest machines or software programs. Some principles of information literacy include:

- Knowing how to find and use the latest electronic sources
- Knowing how to interpret and skeptically evaluate sources, including statistics
- Critically reflecting on the social and cultural contexts of information
- Knowing how to publish work of our own using the media channels and technologies available to us

In sum, acquiring information literacy means not just learning a skill, but learning how to access information in a democratic society, how to read critically for yourself, and how to obtain the materials you need to live your life well. One of the ideals of the American Revolution was that people would be able to govern themselves. So that we can advance our knowledge as citizens, we want to take advantage of the resources available to us, and use our freedom responsibly.

Different communities and societies come up with ways to manage and organize their information and make it accessible to others. Today we have the Internet as one of our primary sources for gathering and disseminating information. From our computer terminals we can enter a whole world of information. What we find through that terminal, though, depends upon how well we can access the various storehouses of information. One dimension of becoming information literate is learning to visualize how the various channels of information are entered. For instance, simply searching the general World Wide Web will not bring us to databases of articles and books and many of the materials that will be most useful for our academic studies. For those, we need to enter sites through specific portals. Other materials are available only on subscription-based listservs or on CD-ROM technology that needs to be accessed from a Web site or library.

Researching on the World Wide Web

We begin this discussion of basic research methods with those that use your computer to do research. As teachers and library lovers we of course encourage you to work in your library. However, your library's catalog is most likely accessed through the Web, and you will need knowledge of how to use the Web in order to use the catalog. In addition, you can often use your time more efficiently by searching from your computer terminal first, then going to your library with a list of call numbers and specific titles.

Using the World Wide Web for research allows you, from one location, to do a fairly thorough review of the published material on your subject. It is a good method for fast inquiry, too; it is the fastest form of inquiry we have right now. You can find information on just about any topic and can get up-to-the-minute discoveries, whereas most printed research takes a year or more from writing to publication. Much of what you will find is just surface material, rather than in-depth knowledge, however. On a subject such as Le Guin and utopian communities, for example, you might find Le Guin's own Web site, quotations from her works, or a utopian project put together by Mr. Cooper's ninth grade social studies class. Still, you can generally find an overview of your topic almost immediately.

The Internet may also be our most democratic form of information distribution. You can find information from all kinds of sources, professional and credentialed and otherwise, that can give you a wider range of voices than can often be found in print media. Not all of these voices are reliable, however. In addition to the Ursula Le Guin fan club and Web sites of utopian communities, you might find sites by cults, white supremacists, or wackos. For this reason you should examine material you have found on the Web carefully.

How do you find information online? By using a search engine, you can connect to the Web sites of organizations, institutions, corporations, offices of the government; some listserv and USENET discussions, and individuals' professional and personal Web sites, among other sources. There are a number of them, e.g., Google and Yahoo!. Information sites such as About.com and Wikipedia are fine for initial inquiry and for quick overviews on a subject. However, when you are searching for material to use as evidence of conversation on a topic, these are not strong sources because most of the pieces are unsigned. They are the equivalent of an encyclopedia; they can provide general grounding on a subject, but you should move beyond them to get involved in specific discussions.

Searching the Internet is done either by subject-based or keyword-based inquiries. The subject-based searches, on engines such as Yahoo!, are best when you do not know yet exactly what you are looking for, but just know the general subject area. You can search through the given categories of subject headings and try to focus your search.

When you know more clearly what your issue or topic is, the most effective method for generating material through Internet search engines is by using keywords. Keywords are the words or phrases used most often when people converse about your topic. Try conducting a search for "utopian community," for instance; you might find advertisements for vacation spots, Web sites for religious communities, philosophers' societies, and organizations on both the left and right of the political spectrum; academic discourses; blogs; political manifestos; book clubs; chat rooms and online journals; and a host of other sources, some of which will be useful and others not.

Consider what keywords you will use before you conduct your search. Write down all the words that come up when you think of that issue, of what concerns you have about it, and/or what interests you most about it. What "key" words or phrases keep coming up? Write down synonyms of your keywords, too; for instance, people interested in developing utopian communities often use the term "intentional community" or consider themselves part of the movement for "communitarianism."

Most search engines use the Boolean system of search logic in which placing an AND between keywords will bring up only references with both words, an OR will bring up references with either word, and a NOT will bring up the references with the first word but not the second. You can also truncate words by using a question mark or an asterisk, depending upon the specific search engine. Truncating a word indicates that the search engine should pull up all the variations on the word; for example, vot? or vot* will bring up vote, voter, voting, etc. (Some search engines or databases have different rules. For instance, Yahoo! uses + and − signs rather than AND and OR. Read the searching tips for each search engine or database; this is often found under labels of "advanced search" or "help.")

As you become a skillful researcher you will develop a set of practices that work well for you. If you work online on a home computer, keep track of the best sites for your inquiries by bookmarking them for easy reference. You might also bookmark a collection of reference sites such as these so you can reach them quickly:

The Internet Public Library: http://www.ipl.org

Librarians' Index to the Internet: http://www.lii.org

The Voice of the Shuttle: Web Page for Humanities Research:
   http://vos.ucsb.edu

The Library of Congress http://www.lcweb.loc.gov

The National Archives and Records Administration http://www.nara.gov

Merriam-Webster Dictionary http://www.m-w.com

New Encyclopedia Britannica www.britannica.com

Public information research sites: http://Refdesk.com and
http://libraryspot.com

▩ EXERCISE 3.3 ▩ Using the World Wide Web for Research

1. Choose an issue or topic of interest to you and conduct a search on the Web, tracing your topic through at least three search engines. Record in your notebook what kinds of material you find in each place, especially the sites found on one search engine but not another.

2. Report back to your class what resources are available on your topic, and from what different kinds of sources. Compare the kinds and quality of material you found. How much of it is substantive and useful?

3. Compare your experiences of inquiring on the Web. What do you like and dislike about it? In what ways is it easy and in what ways is it challenging? In what ways is it enlightening and in what ways is it banal or even offensive?

If you want to discuss a subject in more depth and detail than is often found in public chat rooms, you will probably want to subscribe to a listserv that discusses that subject, whether it is conceptions of a utopian society or economics or Picasso. And if you want to find articles from newspapers, magazines, or academic journals, you will need to enter a database, which is where most of them are cataloged. Your school's library will most likely subscribe to several databases, and you will probably need to enter the databases through your college's or public library's Web site. Go to their address and look for a listing of magazine or journal databases.

The various databases contain different kinds of information. For instance, the Lexis-Nexis Academic Universe includes abstracts and many full-text articles on a wide range of subjects from general news to legal and political matters, and health and medical information. Through it you can also find online texts of about fifty U.S. newspapers, including campus newspapers; transcripts of many radio and TV programs, especially NPR, PBS, and CNN; Associated Press news stories; Congressional records (voting records, bills on the House and Senate floor, ways to contact members of Congress); legal information; state and country profiles; and biographical information. Other databases include Expanded Academic Index, Newspaper Index, Ethnic Newswatch, Alternative Press Index, and the AP (Associated Press) Photo Archive, just to name a very few. There are also specialized databases for nearly every discipline, such as business, agriculture, literature, psychology, history, physics, physiology, and education. Ask your librarians which databases would be most useful for your inquiry.

Many full-text articles are available through online databases, but they are not the majority, and you do not want to limit yourself to only those articles you can get online. When you find an article of interest to you, you will need to write down the periodical title, volume and/or date, and page numbers, because you will then need to find the title in your library's online catalog. The database will not always tell you whether your library carries the periodical. When you enter your library's catalog online, look up the periodical title (*not* the article title), and note whether the library carries the periodical itself and the specific volume number you need, and, if so, where in the library you can locate and read it (e.g., in current periodicals, the bound periodicals, or in microforms or on CD-ROM). For example, if you wanted to find the article "The Virtues of Idleness" by Mark Slouka, from *Harper's* magazine (November 2004), you would do a title search in your library's catalog under "Harper's." If your library does not carry the periodical you seek, talk to your librarian, because you can often order articles through Interlibrary Loan (ILL) and sometimes you can receive them electronically and quickly.

▓ EXERCISE 3.4 ▓ Finding Articles in Databases

1. From your library's Web page, search in four databases for journals and other kinds of information on utopian communities or a topic of your choice. Choose a variety of databases, if you can.

2. Determine which articles you can read in your own library, where they are located, and which you will need to order from Interlibrary Loan.

3. Compare your findings with those of your classmates. Discuss the different kinds of material found in the different databases. Under what circumstances would you use particular databases for your research? Which ones do you think you will use most often in your major field?

Researching in the Library

Not all of your sources will be available via electronic media, and at some point you will need to get into the library itself to read materials and ask questions of the experts: the librarians. Your academic work will require you at some time to become familiar with how to access materials in a library system, and your professors will expect you to be familiar with the books and journals in your field of study; it is the way you enter the conversation of your field. In fact, professors and students often do not have the same expectations. Students think the Internet is sufficient for research; professors think it is dubious at best. (See the following Stop and Think box for more on Internet research.) When the material you need will probably be found in books and more serious magazines, newspapers, and journals, the library is your best resource. Published printed materials are still our most consistently reliable form of information, as most of them have to go through a more rigorous process of review before they are published. Your institution's library (and your local public library) is also the repository for all kinds of local information that will not be available elsewhere, such as locally produced and published materials, pamphlets, letters, news items, and historical and rare materials.

Maybe you want to read Hannah Arendt's argument about the banality of evil; or find a copy of Shirley Jackson's short story "The Lottery," which describes a society not unlike Omelas; or Jack Kerouac's *On the Road* for a Beat perspective on getting out of mainstream society and examining life; or read the archives of the local utopian society that built a commune in your hometown in the 1880s; or look at the sociological research into current utopian societies. Where would you search for them?

You want to get acquainted with all aspects of your library and the resources it has to offer you. Begin with a library tour. There are almost always tours scheduled at the beginning of semesters and you can also usually arrange for one at any time during the term if you ask. In addition, get instruction on the catalog system; libraries often have short, guided sessions for this, too. Learning your library's cataloging system, whether Library of Congress, Dewey Decimal System, or both, is essential.

Walk around the library and familiarize yourself with the stacks (the areas where books are shelved), including the folio and quarto size books, which are oversized and often shelved in a separate section. What are the common call numbers for the books in your fields of interest? Where are they located in the library stacks? Where are the current periodicals shelved? The bound periodicals (those prior to the current year)? Reference works (including those available on CD-ROM)? The visual arts, including video and audio recordings? Investigate the special collections department to see what local or rare materials and collections are housed there.

When navigating your library, keep in mind the following tips:

- Look up your materials in the catalog first. Do not wander around the stacks trying to find sources without call numbers. It will take forever. However, when you do have time, wander around the stacks and browse. You will find interesting things you might not ever have discovered otherwise. In both cases you will be using your time wisely.

- Have three or four alternatives when you head to the stacks to find a book, because a book is often not there exactly when you need it. Because books are cataloged by subject matter, browse the books in the same section as the book you seek to see what else has been written on the subject.

- When you are looking for good sources, check the bibliography of the books and articles you have found. You will see some names repeatedly cited; these are often recognized authorities on the topic and you will want to consult their work.

▓ EXERCISE 3.5 ▓ Inquiring in Your Library

1. Learn the library and its cataloging system. Paste a map of the library in your notebook, and make a list of the kinds of resources available there.

2. Using the library's catalog, explore an issue of interest to you. Find at least four different sources of information on it that will require you to visit different sections of the library and locate different kinds of materials, e.g., a reference work, a book, a periodical, and another work, perhaps a dissertation or film or government document or rare manuscript.

3. Discuss with your class the resources in the library, what is available on your topic and from what different kinds of sources, the best study areas, and other interesting things you have found. Generate a list of suggestions for improving the library, especially things that were confusing or needlessly complicated. You could compile these into a whole class list and give them to a librarian.

Throughout your research process, consult your reference librarians. They are terrific resources. They can help you refine your searches and think of sources you may not have thought of. And if your school does not have a book or article you are looking for, they can show you how to order a copy through Interlibrary Loan.

So, what do you do with the all the information you find through electronic and print media resources? You pull the best sources into a critical conversation on your topic by evaluating each one carefully, reading critically as you learned in Chapter 2, considering the source, the timeliness, the credentials of the author, and the tone and attitude of the author. To develop your ability to pull disparate ideas together, create a formal conversation in which, for each source, you have to answer some basic questions (in addition to the critical reading questions):

- What is the author's main point?
- How do the author's ideas relate to each of your other sources?
- How do they relate to your own ideas, values, and beliefs on this subject?

Sources on the Internet should be read with particular skepticism because there are no standards that an author has to meet to have his or her work published there. When you pull up a Web site, look at its address. Note the differences among the sites whose addresses end in .com (commercial establishment), .edu (educational institution), .gov (governmental organization), .org (generally nonprofit organization), or .mil (military organization). The information on .com sites should be read with special care and skepticism because they are generally trying to sell you something. Check the date of publication of your sources, and the dates of statistics, figures, graphs, and such that they use. When you are trying to decide whether to trust a source, pay attention to the author's credentials, especially in relation to the subject matter. If a Web site does not list an author's name or credentials, you might need to look at it more skeptically. But not everyone will be famous or have impressive credentials to their names; do not dismiss a source simply because the author is not well known. Consider whether the issue is addressed in a thoughtful manner and whether its arguments are validated by other sources. For instance, does the source provide and consider more than one perspective on the subject? Does the author appear to be in conversation with other sources by citing and documenting other studies?

Gathering information and discovering the conversation on a topic makes us aware of the other people who are working or have worked on these same issues. When we're working with others' ideas and words, we should be concerned about plagiarism. Plagiarism, the passing off of someone else's work (including their words and ideas) as your own, is considered unethical in our culture, especially in academic culture. You know from your own experience that researching material and thinking critically is hard work. We believe in giving people credit for the hard work they do and the things they discover; and we also care about individual intellectual property and consider that people, in a sense, "own" their ideas. This is why plagiarism is considered unethical, because you are stealing someone else's hard work and not giving him or her the credit for it. In most academic settings plagiarism is grounds for failure of the assignment, failure of the course, or, in the most egregious cases, expulsion from the school. It is a hard charge to recover from; it is hard to be trusted again if it is known you have cheated. Talk with your instructor whenever you have questions or doubts about the ways you are working with your sources.

Most students' plagiarism in unintentional, a result of careless note taking or of copying out passages that are part paraphrase and part direct quotation, without the quotation marks to indicate which is which. Consequently, the distinction between the source's words and ideas and the writer's own words and ideas gets blurred in the writer's essay. Therefore, avoid plagiarism or carelessness and inaccuracy by learning how to take notes clearly and carefully.

STOP**AND**THINK

THE ETHICS OF ONLINE RESEARCH

One of the most remarkable aspects of the World Wide Web is that so much material is shared freely. The ease of getting this information and its plentitude, however, create potential problems for researchers and writers. First, the Web can encourage the attitude that you do not need to respect the intellectual property rights of people who create online documents. The fact that you can surf around in relative anonymity, that you can easily buy essays from paper mills such as School Sucks (www.schoolsucks.com) and Evil House of Cheat (www.CheatHouse.com), that many documents do not have authors' names, and that many of these documents do not cite their own sources rigorously may encourage you to take ideas without acknowledging their source.

Web search engines can also create problems for researchers and writers because most of them make little distinction between good and poor quality information, between peer-reviewed research and company advertising, and between original research and a bunch of Web links. Students who rely too heavily on Web research can produce shallow essays that paraphrase information from sites that have themselves paraphrased information from other sites, and so on. You no longer know whether the information is accurate and unbiased. The ease of cutting and pasting information from Web pages might tempt you to plagiarize (presenting someone else's ideas as your own) or to quote too much and too often. The ease of getting information can also give you a false sense of the difficulties of research, discouraging you from putting in the time to read critically, to summarize and synthesize your source information, and to analyze that information or conduct your own field research. Finally, the process of research, clicking rapidly from one site to another, can undermine your sense of how a particular issue is being discussed; you may lack the background knowledge provided by more in-depth studies. The result may be a fragmented Frankenstein essay made up of bits of information stitched together from many different sites.

All of these concerns can be addressed, but they require awareness of the limitations of online research and an ethical commitment on your part to the standards of good research. We encourage you to discuss this in more detail with your instructor.

Researching with Broadcast Media

Being information literate also means knowing how the broadcast media operate. Knowing when stations or media outlets are owned by individuals or, increasingly, corporations that have ties to other corporations will help you to discern the outlets' possible biases and priorities. What counts as "news" on the news programs? What subjects do not get covered in the mainstream media? How many perspectives, and which perspectives, are given air time? You can get more information on media literacy from the Media Literacy Online Project at the University of Oregon http://interact.uoregon.edu/MediaLit/HomePage. In addition, "media watchdog" Web sites work to hold the media accountable for their reporting. One conservative site is the Media Research Center at www.mediaresearch.org. A liberal choice is the organization FAIR: Fairness and Accuracy in Reporting, at http://www.fair.org/. These sites, because they represent a spectrum of political perspectives, reveal how our ideas of what is fair and accurate are based on our own experiences, contexts, and ideological stances.

You may want to consult broadcast media for your research when your inquiry needs to go beyond or outside the bounds of published written texts. This will be the case when others have not yet analyzed and written about your subject, when your issue is particularly timely, or when your issue emerges from contemporary popular culture that is transmitted through these media more than others.

Part of the research into broadcast media can be conducted just as you would a search for any print materials. A number of transcripts of television and radio programs (particularly news programs) are available through TV and radio stations' Web sites and databases such as Lexis-Nexis. However, you can also conduct research by watching or listening to TV or radio programs and recording your discoveries. One common method for doing so is called a *content analysis.*

To do a content analysis, decide first what your purpose will be—what you will be looking at, and looking for. For example, you might watch prime-time TV shows to discover whether they provide us with any examples of ideal communities that can help us live our lives more ethically. You will look for specific examples that teach you about your question; e.g., what kinds of communities do you find on *The Simpsons, The O.C.,* or *Desperate Housewives?* Watch or listen to particular programs over a set period of time and record the elements you are looking for. Designing a chart for your content analysis will remind you to collect the same information each time, because the most important aspect of doing this effectively is recording data precisely. Details matter in this analysis. Note carefully exactly what you see and hear. Do not exaggerate just to get the result you want. Others will need to rely on your findings, so you need to be sure to be especially vigilant, accurate, and honest.

▓ EXERCISE 3.6 ▓ Inquiring in Broadcast Media

1. Determine your purpose and how you will carry out your experiment, i.e., which shows you will watch or listen to, what exactly you will be looking for, and how long your project will last. Draw up a chart that covers all of the elements you want to record. Form a hypothesis; what do you expect to find?

2. Each week (or day, if you choose a daily program), tune into your program and faithfully record all of the details in your chart. At this point, do not worry about analyzing what you are finding; just record all of the information, whether or not it fulfills your expectations.

3. At the end of the project period, bring your chart to class and discuss your findings with your classmates. Discuss the experience of conducting a content analysis as well as the information you found. In what ways is it enjoyable and in what ways is it challenging research? How did the analysis affect the way you watch TV or listen to the radio? Are you more aware now when you watch or listen to any program? What are you more aware of? What do you notice that you did not before?

By researching in broadcast media we start to notice the effect such media have on our lives, and can enter those conversations. Because more people get their news (and often their knowledge and wisdom, too) from broadcast media, particularly TV, than from any other source, it has been the focus of scrutiny and often of blame for the destructive and unappealing aspects of our society. (For more on this subject, see Tony Earley's story "Somehow Form a Family" in Chapter 6 and Jake Mulholland and Adrienne Martin's essay "Tune Out" in Chapter 11.)

Getting the Lived Experience: Inquiring Through Field Research

There is research you do by sitting at computer terminals, watching TV and films, listening to the radio, and combing through libraries; it includes a lot of reading of text and processing words and images. Then there is research you do out in the field, by talking with people and observing their behavior. This section discusses the nature of field research and how its ethical concerns and researcher preparation vary from text-based forms of inquiry. Then we introduce you to three basic methods of field research: observing, interviewing, and surveying, and offer an exercise at the end that you can practice individually or with your class.

You may want to conduct field research in circumstances where you will be inquiring into a subject that is not yet heavily talked about or documented in written sources, or that is happening on a local level and has not had much, or any, written investigation or formal analysis. In addition, you may quite often find that the best sources of information on a subject are those who are directly experiencing it—for example, those who are living in intentional communities, working for social justice organizations, or organizing Socratic cafes. This can personalize your research and allow you to get more meaningfully involved in it because you will be meeting the people who are living it.

In field research we should remind ourselves not to go into the situation with an argument already decided, but to go in open-minded, and open-eyed, as the most interesting findings will likely come from mundane, everyday details. You might not see these details if you go into the research with a thesis already decided. Good field research takes time: you must work on others' schedules; be there, present, watching, talking; and be patient. You do have time to do some field research for term papers; you just need to plan your project carefully. We provide examples of student field research in Chapter 5.

Whereas much of the ethics of text-based research concerns plagiarism, the ethics of field research concerns working directly with people, their words, their actions, and treating them honestly, openly, and respectfully. With text-based research, the works you encounter are already interpreted by others; with field research, you are the interpreter of your subjects' words and therefore you want to be as accurate and unbiased as you can to avoid distorting their perspective.

The preparation for text-based research and field research is different as well. The process of searching textual materials can be more forgiving. If you are not as organized as you would like, if you missed something the first time you searched, you can reread the books, articles, Web sites, and transcripts. It is not so easy with live subjects, who may find it annoying or insulting. (This does not mean you cannot return to people for fact-checking, for follow-up to your projects, to deepen what you've found, and to stay in contact with them as friends. Those are all important and rewarding parts of this research methodology.) "Conversation" is not always used figuratively in field research. You are often conducting a live conversation and should follow the etiquette necessary for any situation in which you work with people.

Observation

We begin the field research methods with observation, because, as Kristine Hansen points out in *A Rhetoric for the Social Sciences*, "observing is really the basis of all methods" of research. Observing ourselves and others is a core part of an examined life. Probably the first way you learned to inquire into how one should live in community with others, for instance, was by observing your parents' and friends' lives. We observe informally all the time, including when we're using other methods such as reading materials and interviewing and surveying people. We have learned about formal observation from anthropologists, who conduct ethnographic research when they write (*-graphy*) about people (*ethno-*).

You might want to work for a utopian society for a few weeks. You can perform an *unobtrusive observation* by attending meetings or watching people on the street or other open setting. You can also do this by attending theater performances, lectures, protests, political rallies, or meetings and taking careful notes about what transpires there. Or you can perform a *participant observation*, as Margaret Talbot did for her essay "A Mighty Fortress," which you can read in Chapter 6. In this kind of observation you actually participate in the environment, interacting with others in the particular situation you observe. You especially want to do this when you will gain the greatest under-standing of the situation by experiencing it or living it yourself, rather than just observing others doing so. You also can perform a *structured observation* by setting up an environment and watching people who know they are part of an observation experiment. You can do this "live," by observing and taking notes in the setting, or can videotape the situation and take notes on it later.

Whatever form of observation you conduct, take close and extensive notes. You can write out questions you want to answer through your observation so that you can focus your attention. But do not be limited by these questions and do not disregard contradictory behavior. And record your own responses as well. Observe yourself in the situation and take notes, as objectively and in as much detail as you can, of your own reactions without interpreting or judg-ing. Ethnographers use the term *thick description* to describe the practice of taking very detailed notes of everything you observe, as Talbot did with the kind of toys the Scheibner children played with, and the expressions on their faces when discussing religion or dating or household chores. In *The Inter-pretation of Cultures*, anthropologist Clifford Geertz argues that observing in close detail is a way toward understanding others: "We must . . . descend into detail, past the misleading tags, past the metaphysical types, past the empty similarities to grasp firmly the essential character of not only the various cul-tures but the various sorts of individuals within each culture, if we wish to encounter humanity face to face."

When you are taking notes, do not sort through the information while you are recording it—that is, do not categorize or judge or interpret it, just write down everything you see and hear and experience. Anthropologists make a dis-tinction between *realistic details* and *status details*. Realistic details are plain and simple recordings of description that do not advance our understanding or reveal meaning about the person or object or event. Status details reveal habits and morals, or inform us as to themes, relationships, and such. (See the opening para-graph of Talbot's "A Mighty Fortress" for an excellent use of status details.)

Interviewing

In other cases you will want to conduct an interview for your research. Inter-views are generally good for getting the words of an authority on a subject, or for getting the personal opinion of people affected by a certain situation. You can get individuals' perspectives firsthand and, if you maintain a safe and trust-worthy space, can ask the questions that do not get asked by mainstream media sources. Interviews are also a way of sharing information and building com-munity. You are not just taking information from your sources, you are hav-ing a conversation with them.

You could talk with a local community leader who argues that we should live apart from mainstream society. You could also talk with the leader of a local political party who argues we need to live side by side and meet face to face to air our differences. In any case, you will want to prepare well in advance, because you are asking the person or persons to give up some of their time for you. Interviewing is also a very personal form of research. While it has the potential for deep insight, it can also cause hurt feelings or misunderstandings.

Determine your purpose and make sure you are interviewing the best person or persons for the perspective or knowledge you need. Contact the person, explain your project, ask whether he or she has the information you need, and request permission to talk with him or her for a certain amount of time (e.g., a few minutes, or half an hour). If the subject is willing, make an appointment. *Ask at this time, when you are making the appointment, if the subject will allow you to tape record the interview.* Do not insist on it, however, if the person is uncomfortable with it.

If you can, do background reading on the person and the subject matter, so that you can ask more substantial questions and not have to take up a lot of the interview time asking basic questions. Prepare a list of clear questions before the interview, and be familiar with them so you do not have to look down at your questions often.

But do not be afraid to ask "stupid" questions. Do not assume you know how the person you are interviewing will define a term or see a situation, even if it seems obvious. Ask for an explanation; you may be surprised at what you hear.

Above all, *listen.* This may seem like a silly reminder, but often we get nervous and forget just to have a conversation with the interview subject and to listen to what she or he is saying. Do not be so tied to your prepared questions that you hold onto them even if the interview takes a new and interesting direction. Write down the main details of the interview in your notebook while you are there. Put quotation marks around exact words so that you can represent them accurately later. Do not be afraid to ask the person to repeat something so that you can get it all down in your notes. (In fact, do not be afraid to call back later if you need to check the accuracy of a quote; experts especially will appreciate your desire to represent them fairly and precisely.)

Immediately after the interview, take time to go through your notes and fill in information you were not able to get down during the interview. Record the parts of the conversation you might have missed, and go over your quoted material to fill in any gaps. Also, this is the time to note the context for the interview, the environment in which it took place, the tone of the conversation. Record your own response to the interview.

Send a thank-you note afterward. It is the polite thing to do, and it will make contact smoother if you need to talk to the person again. Often you will want to provide the person with a copy of your finished or published interview or essay. This is courteous, and it keeps you honest because you will be especially careful to represent your interview accurately if you know the interviewee is going to read it.

STOP AND THINK

LARRY KING ON ASKING QUESTIONS IN INTERVIEWS

The secret to a successful interview is asking good questions, the ones that will invite your interview subject to speak openly. Watch and listen to skilled interviewers such as Barbara Walters, Ray Suarez, Terry Gross, or Larry King. What kinds of questions do they ask, and how do they ask them? How do they approach asking sensitive questions?

In *How to Talk to Anyone, Anytime, Anywhere*, Larry King writes:

> I have never been afraid to ask what others might consider a dumb question, if it's one I think my viewers will be curious about . . . . I asked President Bush during the 1992 campaign, "Do you dislike Bill Clinton?" Many professional journalists would argue that the question didn't have a thing to do with the campaign, yet the case could be made that it had everything to do with it because it brought out the human element—one man's attitude toward another—in a person who held the highest office in the land.
>
> We're human beings, even those who become president, and that was a question the human beings watching on TV would ask, so I asked it.
>
> I asked Richard Nixon, "When you drive by the Watergate, do you feel weird?" The last time I interviewed President Reagan, I asked him what it was like to be shot. Maybe a reporter would ask him something else about John Hinckley's attempt on his life on March 30, 1981, but I bet a lot of people wondered just what I did.

One special kind of interview is an *oral history*. Usually in an oral history you are interviewing ordinary people rather than experts, and are asking them for their personal experiences with a particular historical event, or for stories of their life in a particular region or time period. These can be truly valuable and meaningful forms of knowledge. For your own personal purposes, you might want to interview your grandparents or other older relatives or friends, or other special people in your life. It is a great way to get to know them better and to discover aspects about their lives and about earlier eras, as well. Because you want to preserve their words as much as possible, it may be best to record these on audio or video tape, in which case you will need to get permission, probably written permission. You will also probably need to make this person or persons feel more at ease, and assure them that their story is worth hearing.

Edward Ives, in *The Tape-Recorded Interview: A manual for field workers in folklore and oral history*, recommends beginning the interview by speaking into the microphone yourself, recording your name and the date and the name of the person you are interviewing and the subject of the interview. Then you can ask the person if he or she will give you permission to interview, and if so, then it is recorded on tape. As in any interview, listen carefully, let the person talk, ask questions that you have prepared but be flexible enough to follow interesting subjects that come up. About one hour is usually sufficient, as you do not want to wear out the interviewee; if you find that there is much more to be said, you can make an appointment for another session or so. As always, send a thank-you note, and send a copy of your interview when it is finished—the print copy or tape.

Surveys

In some inquiries you will want responses from a number of people, so you may want to conduct a survey. This is particularly effective when your inquiry will not be answered by reading other people's research, or when you have very specific information you need to gather, especially local, very current, or personal information, in order to answer questions, make a decision, or develop a program. You might, for example, survey people who live in an intentional community, to see what it is that draws them to that life; or survey people in your neighborhood to see if there is enough interest in developing a communal area on the old school lot for playing and gardening. Surveys, especially when they are written rather than oral, can be the best way to learn people's real attitudes or practices, because people will tend to be more truthful if they believe their answers will remain anonymous.

Like interviews, surveys can be very sensitive forms of research, so you want to prepare carefully before approaching people. First, determine your purpose: what do you want to find out with this survey, what do you want to do with the information you gather? Then decide who would be best to survey. What kinds of people? What age or ethnicity or neighborhood or gender or occupation or interest group? How many people will you need to survey to get a good sampling? Can you find them by just walking around or going to a certain location, or will you need to set up a survey-taking time and invite people? You can also do surveys in your composition or other courses, as you tend to have a captive and interested audience who can also provide feedback on the effectiveness of the survey.

Then draw up your list of questions. Spend time crafting these, as they matter most of all to the success of your project. Consider the formality of your inquiry: if it is more informal and you know the people well, you can be somewhat more casual in your phrasing of the questions, as you can assume shared knowledge and concerns.

What kind of questions should you ask? This depends on what kind of information you need. You can write quantitative *fixed-response* questions, where the survey-taker is given the question and a selection of answers from which to choose. Multiple-choice and true/false questions fall under this category. This kind of question allows you to control the responses and get a more focused outcome. For example:

How often, in any given year, do you volunteer at an organization that is working toward a more equitable society?

1. Nearly every day.
2. About once a week.
3. Maybe once a month.
4. A few times a year.
5. Never.

Or you can write qualitative *open-ended* questions, in which the survey-taker is free to construct his or her own answer to the question. This kind of question allows you to get a fuller, more specific and personalized response. For example:

What does it mean to you to be able to volunteer your free time to work toward a more equitable society?

Ask yourself whether it is more important to get a range of personal responses, or to be able to group responses into distinguishable categories, perhaps for the sake of taking specific action on an issue. Some fixed-response questions can be too restrictive (which may force people to choose answers they wouldn't normally and not give you their candid, individual answers to the question), while some open-ended questions can keep you from getting any overlap or focus from respondents. Therefore, you may want a combination of questions.

You may want to begin the survey with demographic questions (asking them about their age, race, nationality, gender, occupation, income, education, political affiliation, religion, specific group memberships, and so forth), depending on what you want to measure. Usually these questions can be fixed; you can just ask participants to check off answers in boxes.

STOP AND THINK

ROBERT PUTNAM ON CRAFTING QUESTIONS FOR SURVEYS

In his book *Bowling Alone: The Collapse and Revival of American Community,* Robert Putnam relies heavily on evidence from surveys. Although surveys certainly have their limitations, which he acknowledges, they can provide us with information that we get no other way. For instance, Putnam found that "A well-designed poll can provide a useful snapshot of opinions and behavior. Even better, a series of comparable surveys can yield a kind of social time-lapse photography. Just as one snapshot a day from a single camera pointed unvaryingly at the same garden patch can yield a marvelous movie of botanical birth and growth, so a single survey question, if repeated regularly, can produce a striking image of social change. Moreover, if the question has been formulated deftly enough, it can encompass a more diverse and changing social landscape than the study of any single organization."

Be aware of how you ask the questions. For instance, are you assuming that your survey takers are just like you—that they share your race and ethnicity, gender, class, educational background, taste, and such? Are you unintentionally setting up an us-vs.-them situation if you refer to white men, or children, or African Americans, or Muslims as "them" in a question? Are your questions phrased in a way that leads the survey-takers toward one particular answer?

Most of all, your subjects must be able to trust you. When you ask people to answer personal questions about their intimate lives, their opinions or prejudices, their criminal backgrounds—anything that could be held against them—you have a strict obligation to preserve their anonymity. You need to set up the survey questions, environment, and interpretation in such a way that will maintain confidentiality.

▓ EXERCISE 3.7 ▓ Practicing Field Research Techniques

Do some brainstorming on a research question that you and your classmates want to explore, one that will accommodate a variety of research methods. Divide the class into groups who want most to conduct an observation, an interview, or a survey. The individuals in each group can conduct their own individual studies, or groups could plan one together. You may find it educational to have three groups, each of which begins with the same research question, and to compare the different kinds of answers you get when using different research methods.

1. In each case, set your purpose and goals first and then follow the guidelines above for conducting observations, interviews, and surveys.

2. Record your own responses to your field research. Observe yourself as a researcher and take notes, as objectively and in as much detail as you can, of your own reactions without interpreting or judging.

3. Discuss your findings with your class. What different kinds of responses did you get from your different kinds of methods? What kinds of conclusions can you draw? Make sure to discuss the experience of doing the field research. How did you feel? What did you think? How did people respond to you? Did you feel self-conscious? Did you encounter any difficult intellectual or ethical dilemmas? If so, how did you address or resolve them? What was particularly interesting or difficult or surprising about the process? In what ways was it enjoyable and in what ways was it challenging research?

Your field research may be a one-time venture into interviewing or surveying or observing people or events; in other words, you may contact people solely for your immediate researching purposes and may not have future contact with them. However, your field research may develop out of—or may lead into—your work in a service-learning course or from other experience as a participant in a community program. Often field research, because it tends to involve us more personally than does textual research, can make us want to continue working with communities or individuals, or with certain ongoing projects or causes, even if we don't have a particular assignment.

STOP AND THINK

ETHICS OF FIELD RESEARCH

If you are working with human subjects you may need to submit a formal proposal to your college's Institutional Review Board for the Protection of Human Participants (IRB) stating that you will receive the informed consent of your participants and that your study will not cause harm to them. Your IRB can give you full information about the ethics of your research. It is often a lengthy process requiring a lot of paperwork, so if you are doing field research for a school project you will want to get started early.

It is self-evidently important not to harm others in the course of your research. However, go beyond the basics prescribed by your IRB. Go beyond informed consent. Do not use people. Especially when you are conducting research in communities, share the project with those you are interviewing or surveying, and discuss it with them. For years, it was assumed that university-affiliated researchers were those with the knowledge, and community members were information for studies, or were there to be taught the knowledge of the researchers. University researchers have gone into communities and gathered information, often without ever getting to know the people of the community, and without sharing the analyzing and decision-making power with them. Find ways to get yourself and others involved so that you can avoid simply taking information from the community or individuals.

WEAVING TOGETHER INQUIRY AND ACTION IN COMMUNITY-BASED SERVICE LEARNING

At the opening of this chapter we emphasized that inquiry is a form of social action. All inquiry contributes to our education and the action we take in the world. Some inquiry connects directly with action and is itself a form of action. As students you can participate in what are often called *service learning* activities through your institution and make your academic inquiry directly connect with and have an impact on local communities.

Community-based service learning is an experiential approach to education that integrates classroom theory with real-world experience and reflective practice; it takes classroom reading, thinking, and writing and puts it into conversation with real-world situations. It is based on the philosophy that we learn by doing. Students, instead of being passively lectured to, take responsibility for their own learning and learn in interaction with others. Professors, instead of being the sole bearers of knowledge, are also the facilitators of knowledge and learn alongside their students. Because you learn as much—or more—from the community members as they do from you, many educators prefer the term *community learning* to service learning, to avoid the implication that those in the campus community are doing those in the local community a one-way service.

Community-based service learning programs are guided by the belief that institutions of higher education should be preparing students for their whole civic lives, not just their professions (although community learning experience is excellent for developing leadership skills and gaining contacts for future internships and jobs). Through community experience you tend to gain a deeper understanding of civic life and participation because you are actually working with others on specific projects rather than just reading about them in theory.

How does it work? Students and faculty members generally spend part of their semester hours off campus working with the members of a nonprofit community organization, or with students in a school. This collaboration is a way for the campus and local communities to share their resources and to learn from one another's experiences. Service learning gives you the opportunity to research and get involved in issues that might seem too huge to tackle if you were considering doing so all by yourself. When you conduct field research through your service learning, you are doing so in conjunction with community members, and your inquiring can be aimed not just at gathering the information you need, but toward strengthening ties between people in the various communities.

Service learning can also be an excellent mode of inquiry because it allows you to experience how research changes you, the researcher. You discover what you really think by acting on your beliefs every day. You build models based on your real-world experience and compare them with the theories you read in the classroom. Reflective writing is therefore a critical component of service learning. The experience of working in the community is intellectually, politically, and personally challenging and sometimes frustrating or distressing, and you need the space and time to think through your experiences and express them to others. Recording your thoughts in a journal allows you to see how, over time, the community work contributes to your personal, intellectual, and civic development. It helps you gain an awareness of your whole environment, in and out of college. Though it is often difficult, it can be the most rewarding part of your college education.

In English department courses, especially composition courses, service learning opportunities often involve tutoring adults or children in developing English literacy skills, and sometimes in test preparation. This is a good opportunity for you to reflect on your own literacy, its meaning to you, and its place in your world. And, importantly, you can reflect critically upon the ways we educate people—our educational strategies and priorities. In this situation you will be both a teacher and a learner. Teaching others helps us become more aware of how we ourselves have been taught.

Many colleges and universities now have offices dedicated to service learning. Ask on your campus how you can get involved. If you are interested in getting involved in service learning, you will want to prepare first. Before you go out into the community, consider why you want to do so, and what you expect the experience to be like, to do for you, and to do for those you will be working with. In short, examine your motives, because most communities are not interested in having someone come in who wants to "save" them, even if the person means well. Try this class exercise, adapted from one developed by the organization Campus Compact, as a way of discussing attitudes toward community service.

▓ EXERCISE 3.8 ▓ Examining Our Motives

1. Designate one wall of the classroom as the "continuum." (The blackboard wall is good for this.) At one end, write "charitable volunteer"; at the other end, write "radical social activist." Have everyone in class choose a spot along the wall, according to where you would place yourself along the continuum, and stand there.

2. Let each person discuss why he or she chose that specific spot. Discuss what the words "charitable volunteer" and "radical social activist" mean to you. What do they imply about the attitudes toward and purposes of the action you will perform in the community?

3. Ask those at each end to describe the people at the other end. On what points do you agree and disagree?

   Often those who are at one end of the spectrum find it difficult to understand those at the other end, because they have contradictory approaches to solving the same problems. What are your assumptions about the work you will be doing? What do you believe is the best way to achieve a just society? Do you think of yourself, for instance, as trying to help individuals one by one, or are you trying to change an entire system? How will this affect the way you approach service learning activities?

CONCLUSION: INQUIRY AS ARGUMENT

As you inquire you are developing an argument, a way of seeing the situation or issue that you are inquiring into. Chapter 4 introduces you to a number of strategies for recognizing and developing that argument and presenting it to an audience. We argue to learn; in fact, presenting your argument to others becomes another form of inquiry, a way of thinking itself.

▓ PROJECTS FOR INQUIRY AND ACTION ▓

1. In what ways do you now notice yourself "inquiring" more consciously in everyday life? Do you notice a difference if you or other people do *not* research the issues you discuss and debate?

2. What does *inquiry* have to do with *citizenship*? Do you need research skills and knowledge to be a productive, reflective citizen? If so, what kinds of skills and knowledge do you need? Write out all the ways you can imagine inquiry—however you conceive of that right now—being part of a citizen's life. Describe specific scenarios from your own life and others' experiences.

3. As you start to pursue a specific major field or academic discipline, do some research for yourself to see how interested you are in the way that discipline thinks about and creates "knowledge." For instance, what is the history of your discipline? When did it become an academic discipline included in college curricula? What changes has it gone through? Why are you interested in it? What about the way that people in that discipline "think" is interesting to you, or matches the way you think? What are the methods of inquiry in your discipline? Why are these methods considered the most reliable and desirable?

4. How can you get involved in community service learning on your campus? Investigate what resources exist for you.

CHAPTER 4

Arguing: Action As Inquiry

What democracy requires is public debate, not information. Of course it needs information too, but the kind of information it needs can be generated only by vigorous popular debate. We do not know what we need to know until we ask the right questions, and we can identify the right questions only by subjecting our own ideas about the world to the test of public controversy . . . . When we get into arguments that focus and fully engage our attention, we become avid seekers of relevant information. Otherwise, we take in information passively—if we take it in at all.
—*Christopher Lasch,* Revolt of the Elites

▒ GETTING STARTED ▒   Arguing in Our Communities

In Chapter 3 you learned how to use available sources to envision an ideal community. This section asks you to consider a more concrete version of that question, one that will put your ideals into action: "What can we do to improve our communities?" In your writer's notebook, write down five specific suggestions you would like to see your local or national communities implement to improve the quality of their citizens' lives. Here are a few suggestions from previous students:

- Encourage civic-mindedness by requiring one year of military or civil service for all students as they come out of high school.
- We need to enrich our spiritual lives. We should encourage each other to go to church. It doesn't matter what religion, just go.
- Prisoners should have more opportunities to work while in prison. The state's profits from the prisoners' labor can be used to pay for the prisons and prisoners can learn a useful trade.

After you have written down your suggestions, get into small groups and try to convince the other group members that your suggestions are the most practical, ethical, or effective. Each group should use its debates to reduce the members' recommendations to a list of three that they can then present to the rest of the class. The class can then debate the merits of each list. After the debates, answer the following questions in your writer's notebook:

1. How did participants try to convince others that some arguments were more practical, ethical, or effective?
2. How did their persuasive efforts work on others in the class? Did their efforts encourage or discourage critical thinking?
3. Did you learn something more about these subjects through the debates? Why or why not?

The eighteenth-century satirist Jonathan Swift once said that arguments are the "worst sort of conversation." You might agree with Swift if the debates you helped to create in the Getting Started exercise went like these examples we have witnessed in our classes:

- A student was silenced when several others accused him of sucking up to the instructor. He had been participating in class discussion actively, but after the accusation he withdrew, fearing his participation would be viewed as insincere.

- Students stubbornly avoided debate, prefacing every sentence with "I think" or "This is just my opinion." As a result, no one felt challenged enough to critique other positions or defend their own. Instead, the students congratulated themselves on their tolerance for other people's opinions.

- Two students tried to railroad consensus by arguing that the other side's position contradicted biblical teachings. Not wanting to get into a discussion of religious beliefs, most people stopped talking.

On each of these occasions, students afterwards expressed dissatisfaction with the debates; the debates, they said, were entertaining but not very instructive.

If we accept Christopher Lasch's view of arguing, expressed in the opening quotation, then the above examples do indeed represent the worst sorts of conversation. Lasch defines arguments as engaged conversations that push us to think more deeply and critically about issues that affect our communities. Citizens present their views on issues so that others can bring their own values, beliefs, and experiences into dialogue with them. The hope is that such conversations push all participants to clarify their ideas, to account for disagreements, and to discover intelligent, practical solutions to social issues. In this sense, arguing becomes a form of active inquiry.

Students in the above examples discouraged such conversations by turning them into quarrels or shutting them down. The arguers attacked other students' characters to discredit their views, they framed their arguments as opinions to avoid controversy, or they suppressed opposition by making the other arguers uncomfortable. None of these examples encouraged active inquiry. The purpose of arguments, Lasch would argue, is not to harm the other arguer or to win only but to achieve mutual understanding, compromise, a willing consensus, or at least a deeper knowledge of other views. Arguments such as these become the *best* sorts of conversation for achieving democratic solutions to our communities' problems.

If we wish to learn from our arguments or to think through community problems, then we need to learn how to inquire through arguing. The Getting Started exercise showed that you already know how to argue. This chapter builds upon that knowledge, encouraging you to adopt an arguing-to-inquire mindset and to internalize strategies that will make your arguments more rigorous and ethical.

FIRST INQUIRY: WHAT IS ARGUING TO INQUIRE?

Disagreements are an inevitable result of community life. They develop around different political, economic, or religious beliefs. They develop between members of different nations, regions, cultures, generations, sexes, and sexual orientations. Even members of the same community view common issues through their own unique values, experiences, and visions of community life. All of these opportunities for disagreement can create conflict, testing our ability as members to live together in harmony.

How we deal with these disagreements says a lot about our communities. If we fight, cheat, or threaten each other, we create a very different quality of life than if we compromise, build agreement, or submit to acceptable laws. In situations where we want to learn or where our choices really matter, we need ways of arguing that push us to clarify our views, test our opinions, and strengthen community ties.

We learned in Chapter 3 to begin an inquiry by asking questions. Not only is this a natural way to begin, but questions can free us from the temptation to research only to prove what we already believe. Because most questions do not presume only one answer, we can consult many different views. We need to consider each of these views sincerely and rigorously if we are to inquire ethically. This does not mean we should agree with everyone's views. Rather, we should try to understand why, for example, someone would promote vegetarianism, private gun ownership, affirmative action, or any number of views similar or different from our own. Understanding *why* people would argue particular positions on some social issue helps us go under their arguments, appreciating the experiences, values, beliefs, visions, or missions that have pushed them to adopt those positions.

When we read an argument, especially one we disagree with, we are often tempted to judge it immediately. Students in our classes have often responded to readings by saying, "This essay is boring," "That arguer is such an idiot," or "This writer kicks butt." While responses such as these can be a good place to start critical thinking, they should not represent the end of our response.

This is especially true if we want to create communities that treat disagreements as opportunities to learn, not as occasions to bully our neighbors.

Taking the time to understand what arguers are saying and why they are saying it encourages us to inquire more deeply into the conversations circulating around particular social issues. Instead of exchanging arguments and criticizing one another only, arguers seek to go "under" each other's arguments to understand why they disagree and how they might proceed despite their differences. For example, people opposing handgun ownership might criticize organizations such as the National Rifle Association (NRA) for supporting handgun ownership. Calling NRA members Dirty Harry wannabes, however, would not forward the debate. What would is trying to understand how supporters view gun ownership, the government's role in legislating personal safety, and so on. Going under other people's arguments can also make us more effective respondents. Instead of responding to their arguments only, we can challenge the very beliefs and visions that support those arguments, encouraging a more rigorous conversation. For example, instead of simply battering handgun advocates' arguments with arguments of their own, opponents to handgun ownership could challenge the very vision of gun ownership on which the supporters' arguments are based.

Summarizing an Argument

To reach this deeper response to other people's arguments, we first need to understand thoroughly what an arguer is saying. We can develop this level of understanding when faced with written arguments by summarizing them. A summary is usually a short paragraph that presents the thesis and main supporting points of a work. It condenses the work's content so other readers can learn what the original writer is arguing and how that argument is supported. Summaries have value for readers because the readers get a sense of the work before they read it, and summaries have value for writers because the writers must master the original work's ideas enough to teach them to others. Here is an example summary of Jefferson's Declaration of Independence:

> The Declaration justifies the colonies' decision to break off from England. First, it presents the assumptions on which the colonies' argument is based, namely, that people have the inherent rights to live, to be free, to shape their own destinies, and to throw off any government that limits these rights. Second, it presents the many ways England has imposed on the colonists' rights. Third, it argues that England has continually rejected the colonists' efforts to correct these impositions, and therefore the colonists are forced to declare their independence.

We might summarize Jefferson's argument in the Declaration differently, adding or reducing the number of details depending on how thoroughly we want readers to understand Jefferson's work. Yet, regardless of how long our summaries are, we should keep several points in mind if we want to learn from writing them. First, we should write the summary in our own words. Translating an arguer's ideas into language we feel comfortable with pushes us to better grasp those ideas. As a result, we will understand them more fully and remember them longer.

Second, we should focus on the significant points. To give readers some sense of how the writer's argument develops, so they can better comprehend the argument as a whole, we should exclude any details or examples that might distract us from the main points. We should also revise the summary so it comes together as a clear, unified paragraph. In the above example, we can see how Jefferson's argument proceeds because the summary writer organizes the paragraph logically. The writer reinforces this organization by using transition words such as *first, second,* and so on.

Analyzing an Argument

After writing the summary, readers are in a better position to analyze what they have read. To analyze is to take something apart to understand how it works. In this case, however, the goal is not to tear an argument apart so we can criticize it, saying it is poorly written, unconvincing, or immoral (although an argument might be all three). Rather, we analyze the argument to explain where the arguer is coming from and why he or she uses particular strategies to convince us. In other words, we summarize to understand *what* an arguer is saying; we analyze to understand *why* he or she says it.

Unlike summaries, analyses of a work take no particular form. We could write multi-paragraph essays or record insights in our writer's notebooks. In any case, we should keep several points in mind as we analyze a written argument. First, we need to examine the text as writers. Usually, we respond to an arguer's ideas, not paying much attention to how those ideas are presented. Yet, if we really want to understand what values and beliefs shape an arguer's viewpoint, then we need to look at the writing itself. The arguer is usually not available to us to explain why they argue a particular viewpoint, so we have to infer their values and beliefs from the writing itself. We do this by identifying distinguishing features of a written argument, asking questions about those features, and speculating on why the arguer chose those features over others.

In the next section of this chapter, we will discuss different arguing strategies. Knowing how arguers seek to persuade readers can help us identify the strategies they use on us. For example, in the Declaration, Jefferson lists England's transgressions against America. He might have listed three or four examples, instead of almost thirty. A good analyzer would ask what this writing decision says about Jefferson's views of England, its relationship with the American colonies, and the situation in which he was writing. A good analyzer would ask questions about all of an argument's distinguishing features. He or she would assume those features were chosen by the writer deliberately, and, as a result, those choices express the writer's values, beliefs, and purposes for arguing.

Of course, the Declaration—and any text, for that matter—probably will not tell us why the arguer has shaped his or her text in a particular way, but we can speculate based on what we know about writing, arguing, and human nature. We can also speculate based on the arguer's biography, time, place, circumstances, and audience. Because written works usually come out of specific writing situations, we can understand them more fully if we know more about those situations. For example, we can make an educated guess why Jefferson listed so many British transgressions. We know that many Americans felt strong political, social, even familial ties to England. Perhaps one of Jefferson's motives was to persuade these reluctant colonists to become revolutionaries by overwhelming them with evidence. Formulating possible explanations, such as this one, for why Jefferson supported American independence can help us understand his values and beliefs, making our responses to the Declaration more rigorous.

In the following exercise, we can examine two such responses, one by Susan B. Anthony and the other by the Black Panthers organization. Each writer responds to the Declaration, arguing that its promises of life, liberty, and an equal chance at happiness were not being extended to all citizens. At the same time, each writer uses Jefferson's own arguments in making her or his own argument.

▓ EXERCISE 4.1 ▓ Critically Responding to the Declaration of Independence

1. Read the declarations by Susan B. Anthony and the Black Panthers and summarize each of them in your writer's notebook so that readers who have not read the declarations will have a general understanding of what each writer is arguing.

2. Analyze each declaration and write your analyses in your writer's notebook. Writing can be a tool for generating thoughts as well as expressing them, so try to push each analysis to two pages. To help you learn about the background of these writers and of their writing situations, follow the inquiry strategies suggested in Chapter 3.

3. Once you have finished writing your own analyses, compare them with your classmates'. Then discuss the following questions:

   a. Did you find it hard to resist attacking the writers' arguments?

   b. Did you learn more about the declarations by taking the time to summarize and analyze them, instead of jumping to evaluation?

   c. Did you learn persuasive strategies from the works that you can use in your own arguments?

Susan B. Anthony
Women's Right to Vote

Susan B. Anthony (1820–1906) was an early activist, participating in the anti-slavery and temperance movements. Along with Elizabeth Cady Stanton, she joined the women's rights movement in 1852, and eventually became president of the National American Woman Suffrage Association. Beginning in 1868, she published a newspaper, The Revolution, *from Rochester, New York; its masthead read, "Men their rights, and nothing more; women, their rights, and nothing less," and had the aim of establishing "justice for all."*

In 1872, a presidential election year, she decided to test the Fourteenth Amendment to the Constitution. The first section of that Amendment states that "all persons born or naturalized in the United States" are citizens, and are therefore entitled to equal protection under the law. It was written primarily to secure citizenship rights for African Americans after the Civil War, but Anthony took the opportunity to challenge its argument. Anthony, three of her sisters, and other women attempted to register and cast their votes, but were arrested. In 1873, before her trial, Anthony traveled around, giving a speech that has come to be called "Women's Right to Vote." The full text can be found in Elizabeth Cady Stanton, Susan B. Anthony, and Matilda Joslyn Gage, eds., History of Woman Suffrage, *Vol. 2 (Salem, NH: Ayer, 1985) 630–47.*

Women gained the right to vote by the Nineteenth Amendment in 1920, fourteen years after Anthony's death.

I stand before you under indictment for the alleged crime of having voted at the last presidential election, without having a lawful right to vote. It shall be my work this evening to prove to you that in thus doing, I not only committed no crime, but instead simply exercised my citizen's rights, guaranteed to me and all United States citizens by the National Constitution beyond the power of any State to deny.

Our democratic-republican government is based on the idea of the natural right of every individual member thereof to a voice and a vote in making and executing the laws. We assert the province of government to be to secure the people in the enjoyment of their inalienable rights. We throw to the winds the old dogma that government can give rights. No one denies that before governments were organized each individual possessed the right to protect his own life, liberty and property. When 100 to 1,000,000 people enter into a free government they do not barter away their natural rights; they simply pledge themselves to protect each other in the enjoyment of them through prescribed judicial and legislative tribunals. They agree to abandon the methods of brute force in the adjustment of their differences and adopt those of civilization. . . . The Declaration of Independence, the United

States Constitution, the constitutions of the several States and the organic laws of the Territories, all alike propose to *protect* the people in the exercise of their God-given rights. Not one of them pretends to bestow rights.

> All men are created equal, and endowed by their Creator with certain inalienable rights. Among these are life, liberty and the pursuit of happiness. To secure these, governments are instituted among men, deriving their just powers from the consent of the governed.

Here is no shadow of government authority over rights, or exclusion of any class from their full and equal enjoyment. Here is pronounced the right of all men, and "consequently," as the Quaker preacher said, "of all women," to a voice in the government. And here, in this first paragraph of the Declaration, is the assertion of the natural right of all to the ballot; for how can "the consent of the governed" be given, if the right to vote be denied? . . . The women, dissatisfied as they are with this form of government, that enforces taxation without representation—that compels them to obey laws to which they never have given their consent—that imprisons and hangs them without a trial by a jury of their peers—that robs them, in marriage, of the custody of their own persons, wages, and children—are this half of the people who are left wholly at the mercy of the other half, in direct violation of the spirit and letter of the declarations of the framers of this government, every one of which was based on the immutable principle of equal rights to all. By these declarations, kings, popes, priests, aristocrats, all were alike dethroned and placed on a common level, politically, with the lowliest born subject or serf. By them, too, men, as such, were deprived of their divine right to rule and placed on a political level with women. By the practice of these declarations all class and caste distinctions would be abolished, and slave, serf, plebeian, wife, woman, all alike rise from their subject position to the broader platform of equality.

The preamble of the Federal Constitution says:

> We, the people of the United States, in order to form a more perfect union, establish justice, insure domestic tranquility, provide for the common defence, promote the general welfare and secure the blessings of liberty to ourselves and our posterity, do ordain and establish this Constitution for the United States of America.

5   It was we, the people, not we, the white male citizens, nor we, the male citizens; but we, the whole people, who formed this Union. We formed it not to give the blessings of liberty but to secure them; not to the half of ourselves and the half of our posterity, but to the whole people—women as well as men. It is downright mockery to talk to women of their enjoyment of the blessings of liberty while they are denied the only means of securing them provided by this democratic-republican government—the ballot. . . .

For any State to make sex a qualification, which must ever result in the disfranchisement of one entire half of the people, is to pass a bill of attainder, an ex post facto law, and is therefore a violation of the supreme law of the land. By it the blessings of liberty are forever withheld from women and their female posterity. For them, this government has no just powers derived from the consent of the governed. For them this government is not a democracy; it is not a republic. It is the most odious aristocracy ever established on the face of the globe. An oligarchy of wealth, where the rich govern the poor; an oligarchy of learning, where the educated govern the ignorant; or even an oligarchy of race, where the Saxon rules the African, might be endured; but this oligarchy of sex which makes father, brothers, husband, sons, the oligarchs over the mother and sisters, the wife and daughters of every household; which ordains all men sovereigns, all women subjects—carries discord and rebellion into every home of the nation. . . .

It is urged that the use of the masculine pronouns *he, his* and *him* in all the constitutions and laws, is proof that only men were meant to be included in their provisions. If you insist on this version of the letter of the law, we shall insist that you be consistent and accept the other horn of the dilemma, which would compel you to exempt women from taxation for the support of the government and from penalties for the violation of laws. There is no *she* or *her* or *hers* in the tax laws, and this is equally true of all the criminal laws.

Take for example, the civil rights law which I am charged with having violated; not only are all the pronouns in it masculine, but everybody knows that it was intended expressly to hinder the rebel men from voting. It reads, "If any person shall knowingly vote without *his* having a lawful right." . . . I insist if government officials may thus manipulate the pronouns to tax, fine, imprison and hang women, it is their duty to thus change them in order to protect us in our right to vote. . . .

Though the words persons, people, inhabitants, electors, citizens, are all used indiscriminately in the national and State constitutions, there was always a conflict of opinion, prior to the war, as to whether they were synonymous terms, but whatever room there was for doubt, under the old regime, the adoption of the Fourteenth Amendment settled that question forever in its first sentence:

> All persons born or naturalized in the United States, and subject to the jurisdiction thereof, are citizens of the United States, and of the State wherein they reside.

10   The second settles the equal status of all citizens:

> No State shall make or enforce any law which shall abridge the privileges or immunities of citizens of the United States; nor shall any State deprive any person of life, liberty or property without due process of law, or deny to any person within its jurisdiction the equal protection of the laws.

The only question left to be settled now is: Are women persons? I scarcely believe any of our opponents will have the hardihood to say they are not. Being persons, then, women are citizens, and no State has a right to make any new law, or to enforce any old law, which shall abridge their privileges or immunities. Hence, every discrimination against women in the constitutions and laws of the several States is today null and void, precisely as is every one against negroes.

Is the right to vote one of the privileges or immunities of citizens? I think the disfranchised ex-rebels and ex-State prisoners all will agree that it is not only one of them, but the one without which all the others are nothing. Seek first the kingdom of the ballot and all things else shall be added, is the political injunction. . . .

However much the doctors of the law may disagree as to whether people and citizens, in the original Constitution, were one and the same, or whether the privileges and immunities in the Fourteenth Amendment include the right of suffrage, the question of the citizen's right to vote is forever settled by the Fifteenth Amendment. "The right of citizens of the United States to vote shall not be denied or abridged by the United States, or by any State, on account of race, color or previous condition of servitude." How can the State deny or abridge the right of the citizen, if the citizen does not possess it? There is no escape from the conclusion that to vote is the citizen's right, and the specifications of race, color or previous condition of servitude can in no way impair the force of that emphatic assertion that the citizen's right to vote shall not be denied or abridged. . . . If, however, you will insist that the Fifteenth Amendment's emphatic interdiction against robbing United States citizens of their suffrage "on account of race, color or previous condition of servitude," is a recognition of the right of either the United States or any State to deprive them of the ballot for any or all other reasons, I will prove to you that the class of citizens for whom I now plead are, by all the principles of our government and many of the laws of the States, included under the term "previous conditions of servitude."

Consider first married women and their legal status. What is servitude? "The condition of a slave." What is a slave? "A person who is robbed of the proceeds of his labor; a person who is subject to the will of another." By the laws of Georgia, South Carolina and all the States of the South, the negro had no right to the custody and control of his person. He belonged to his master. If he were disobedient, the master had the right to use correction. If the negro did not like the correction and ran away, the master had the right to use coercion to bring him back. By the laws of almost every State in this Union today, North as well as South, the married woman has no right to the custody and control of her person. The wife belongs to the husband; and if she refuse obedience he may use moderate correction, and if she do not like his moderate correction and leave his "bed and board," the husband may use moderate coercion to bring her back. The little word "moderate," you see, is the saving clause for the wife, and would doubtless be overstepped should her offended husband administer his correction with the "cat-o'-nine-tails," or accomplish his coercion with blood-hounds.

Again the slave had no right to the earnings of his hands, they belonged to his master; no right to the custody of his children, they belonged to his master; no right to sue or be sued, or to testify in the courts. If he committed a crime, it was the master who must sue or be sued. In many of the States there has been special legislation, giving married women the right to property inherited or received by bequest, or earned by the pursuit of any avocation outside the home; also giving them the right to sue and be sued in matters pertaining to such separate property; but not a single State of this Union has ever secured the wife in the enjoyment of her right to equal ownership of the joint earnings of the marriage copartnership. And since, in the nature of things, the vast majority of married women never earn a dollar by work outside their families, or inherit a dollar from their fathers, it follows that from the day of their marriage to the day of the death of their husbands not one of them ever has a dollar, except it shall please her husband to let her have it. . . .

15   Is anything further needed to prove woman's condition of servitude sufficient to entitle her to the guarantees of the Fifteenth Amendment? Is there a man who will not agree with me that to talk of freedom without the ballot is mockery to the women of this republic, precisely as New England's orator, Wendell Phillips, at the close of the late war declared it to be to the newly emancipated black man? I admit that, prior to the rebellion, by common consent, the right to enslave, as well as to disfranchise both native and foreign born persons, was conceded to the States. But the one grand principle settled by the war and the reconstruction legislation, is the supremacy of the national government to protect the citizens of the United States in their right to freedom and the elective franchise, against any and every interference on the part of the several States; and again and again have the American people asserted the triumph of this principle by their overwhelming majorities for Lincoln and Grant.

The one issue of the last two presidential elections was whether the Fourteenth and Fifteenth Amendments should be considered the irrevocable will of the people; and the decision was that they should be, and that it is not only the right, but the duty of the national government to protect all United States citizens in the full enjoyment and free exercise of their privileges and immunities against the attempt of any State to deny or abridge. . . .

It is upon this just interpretation of the United States Constitution that our National Woman Suffrage Association, which celebrates the twenty-fifth anniversary of the woman's rights movement next May in New York City, has based all its arguments and action since the passage of these amendments. We no longer petition legislature or Congress to give us the right to vote, but appeal to women everywhere to exercise their too long neglected "citizen's right." We appeal to the inspectors of election to receive the votes of all United States citizens, as it is their duty to do. We appeal to United States commissioners and marshals to arrest, as is their duty, the inspectors who reject the votes of United States citizens, and leave alone those who perform their duties and accept these votes. We ask the juries to return verdicts of "not guilty" in the cases of law-abiding United States citizens who cast their votes, and inspectors of election who receive and count them.

We ask the judges to render unprejudiced opinions of the law, and wherever there is room for doubt to give the benefit to the side of liberty and equal rights for women, remembering that, as Sumner says, "The true rule of interpretation under our National Constitution, especially since its amendments, is that anything *for* human rights is constitutional, everything *against* human rights unconstitutional." It is on this line that we propose to fight our battle for the ballot—peaceably but nevertheless persistently—until we achieve complete triumph and all United States citizens, men and women alike, are recognized as equals in the government.

The Black Panthers
Ten Point Plan

The Black Panther Party was a revolutionary political organization formed in 1966 in the midst of the civil rights movement, soon after the assassination of Malcolm X and the riots in Watts (Los Angeles) in protest to the police beating of a black man. Led by Huey P. Newton, Bobby Seale, and David Hilliard, the Black Panthers fought for black liberation. In contrast to the nonviolent civil disobedience of Martin Luther King, Jr. and the Southern Christian Leadership Conference, whose methods they considered too slow, submissive, and ineffective, the Black Panther Party was committed to a more revolutionary agenda: immediately for blacks to arm themselves against their oppressors, and ultimately to change the structure of inequality in the United States. They also set up local Survival Programs in major American cities to provide services to poor and African-American community members, most famously the Free Breakfast for Children Program. The Ten Point Plan was their manifesto for the end to African-American oppression. You can read more about it at their Web site: http://www.blackpanther.org/.

---

1. **WE WANT FREEDOM. WE WANT POWER TO DETERMINE THE DESTINY OF OUR BLACK AND OPPRESSED COMMUNITIES.** We believe that Black and oppressed people will not be free until we are able to determine our destinies in our own communities ourselves, by fully controlling all the institutions which exist in our communities.

2. **WE WANT FULL EMPLOYMENT FOR OUR PEOPLE.** We believe that the federal government is responsible and obligated to give every person employment or a guaranteed income. We believe that if the American businessmen will not give full employment, then the technology and means of production should be taken from the businessmen and placed in the community so that the people of the community can organize and employ all of its people and give a high standard of living.

3. **WE WANT AN END TO THE ROBBERY BY THE CAPITALISTS OF OUR BLACK AND OPPRESSED COMMUNITIES.** We believe that this racist government has robbed us and now we are demanding the overdue debt of forty acres and two mules. Forty acres and two mules were promised 100 years ago as restitution for slave labor and mass murder of Black people. We will accept the payment in currency which will be distributed to our many communities. The American racist has taken part in the slaughter of our fifty million Black people. Therefore, we feel this is a modest demand that we make.

4. **WE WANT DECENT HOUSING, FIT FOR THE SHELTER OF HUMAN BEINGS.** We believe that if the landlords will not give decent housing to our Black and oppressed communities, then housing and the land should be made

into cooperatives so that the people in our communities, with government aid, can build and make decent housing for the people.

5. **WE WANT DECENT EDUCATION FOR OUR PEOPLE THAT EXPOSES THE TRUE NATURE OF THIS DECADENT AMERICAN SOCIETY. WE WANT EDUCATION THAT TEACHES US OUR TRUE HISTORY AND OUR ROLE IN THE PRESENT-DAY SOCIETY.** We believe in an educational system that will give to our people a knowledge of the self. If you do not have knowledge of yourself and your position in the society and in the world, then you will have little chance to know anything else.

6. **WE WANT COMPLETELY FREE HEALTH CARE FOR ALL BLACK AND OPPRESSED PEOPLE.** We believe that the government must provide, free of charge, for the people, health facilities which will not only treat our illnesses, most of which have come about as a result of our oppression, but which will also develop preventive medical programs to guarantee our future survival. We believe that mass health education and research programs must be developed to give all Black and oppressed people access to advanced scientific and medical information, so we may provide ourselves with proper medical attention and care.

7. **WE WANT AN IMMEDIATE END TO POLICE BRUTALITY AND MURDER OF BLACK PEOPLE, OTHER PEOPLE OF COLOR, ALL OPPRESSED PEOPLE INSIDE THE UNITED STATES.** We believe that the racist and fascist government of the United States uses its domestic enforcement agencies to carry out its program of oppression against black people, other people of color and poor people inside the United States. We believe it is our right, therefore, to defend ourselves against such armed forces and that all Black and oppressed people should be armed for self defense of our homes and communities against these fascist police forces.

8. **WE WANT AN IMMEDIATE END TO ALL WARS OF AGGRESSION.** We believe that the various conflicts which exist around the world stem directly from the aggressive desire of the United States' ruling circle and government to force its domination upon the oppressed people of the world. We believe that if the United States government or its lackeys do not cease these aggressive wars it is the right of the people to defend themselves by any means necessary against their aggressors.

9. **WE WANT FREEDOM FOR ALL BLACK AND OPPRESSED PEOPLE NOW HELD IN U. S. FEDERAL, STATE, COUNTY, CITY AND MILITARY PRISONS AND JAILS. WE WANT TRIALS BY A JURY OF PEERS FOR ALL PERSONS CHARGED WITH SO-CALLED CRIMES UNDER THE LAWS OF THIS COUNTRY.** We believe that the many Black and poor oppressed people now held in United States prisons and jails have not received fair and impartial trials under a racist and fascist judicial system and should be free from incarceration. We believe in the ultimate elimination of all wretched, inhuman penal institutions, because the masses of men and women imprisoned inside the United States or by the United States military are the victims of oppressive conditions which are the real cause of their imprisonment. We believe that when persons are brought to trial they must be guaranteed, by the United States, juries of their peers, attorneys of their choice and freedom from imprisonment while awaiting trial.

10. **WE WANT LAND, BREAD, HOUSING, EDUCATION, CLOTHING, JUS-
TICE, PEACE AND PEOPLE'S COMMUNITY CONTROL OF MODERN
TECHNOLOGY.** When, in the course of human events, it becomes necessary
for one people to dissolve the political bonds which have connected them with
another, and to assume, among the powers of the earth, the separate and equal
station to which the laws of nature and nature's God entitle them, a decent respect
to the opinions of mankind requires that they should declare the causes which
impel them to the separation.

We hold these truths to be self-evident, that all men are created equal; that they
are endowed by their Creator with certain unalienable rights; that among these are
life, liberty, and the pursuit of happiness. That to secure these rights, governments
are instituted among men, deriving their just powers from the consent of the governed; that, whenever any form of government becomes destructive of these ends, it
is the right of the people to alter or to abolish it, and to institute a new government,
laying its foundation on such principles, and organizing its powers in such form as
to them shall seem most likely to effect their safety and happiness. Prudence, indeed,
will dictate that governments long established should not be changed for light and
transient causes; and, accordingly, all experience hath shown that mankind are most
disposed to suffer, while evils are sufferable, than to right themselves by abolishing
the forms to which they are accustomed. But, when a long train of abuses and usurpa-
tion, pursuing invariably the same object, evinces a design to reduce them under
absolute despotism, it is their right, it is their duty, to throw off such government,
and to provide new guards for their future security.

As Anthony's and the Black Panthers' responses demonstrate, arguing does
not mean simply attacking or dismissing an opposing viewpoint. Each of their
texts celebrates the ideals that are proclaimed in the Declaration of Independence, even as they critique the way those ideals have been realized in American
society. Their responses also demonstrate that arguers use a variety of different
strategies to communicate their ideas. Anthony's and the Black Panthers' arguments are radically different in the kinds of arguments they make and in how
they make them. Each writer was sensitive to what their audiences did or did
not want to hear and what appeals and stylistic choices would most move them.

In the Second Inquiry, we will discuss how to make our own arguments
more convincing, by learning how to assess opportunities to inquire by arguing. An arguing-to-inquire mindset means finding appeals that powerfully
affect our audiences while promoting rigorous, ethical conversations. We call
this mindset the arguing mind.

SECOND INQUIRY: DEVELOPING AN ARGUING MIND

Just as disciplined curiosity can help us develop an inquiring mind, so we can
train our empathy to help us develop an arguing mind. According to psy-

chologist William Ickes, empathy is our capacity to infer the thoughts and feelings of others by drawing on close observations, on our memories, and on our knowledge of the people around us. This ability to imaginatively share in the experiences of others is what binds communities together. Aside from consciousness itself, Ickes argues, it "may be the greatest achievement of which the mind is capable" (10).

Of course, our powers of empathy are limited. While we cannot actually read other people's minds, our work in the book so far suggests that we can make credible inferences. In the previous exercise, for example, we used textual clues in Anthony's and the Black Panthers' declarations, information we gathered about the writers' historical and social situations, and our general knowledge and wisdom to infer what the writers believed. We used our empathic imaginations to understand and connect with citizens of two different generations.

In addition to understanding the arguments of others, we also use empathy to anticipate how our audience will respond to arguments of our own. For example, the students who silenced a classmate during one Getting Started exercise used empathy. Based on their knowledge of human behavior, they anticipated that calling him a "suck up" would make him self-conscious, effectively shutting down his participation. Unfortunately, as this example illustrates, empathy can be used unethically, to identify and manipulate the fears of others in order to secure compliance or shut down discussion. We can see this tendency in the worst examples of peer pressure, advertising, and political propaganda.

The arguing mind, however, draws on empathy to promote inquiry. Arguers try to "read" their audience and situation to discern what strategies will be most effective. The goal is to push those involved to defend their views and to respond more rigorously in turn. In other words, the more effectively everyone argues, the more powerfully each participant can inquire. Of course, arguers must balance effectiveness with appropriateness. Many strategies of persuasion are effective but unethical; threatening physical violence is a case in point.

Most communities have their own written or unwritten guidelines for civil, or respectful, arguing. In Chapter 5, we will investigate the standards of civil arguing in academic communities. Here, however, we might begin by identifying some general guidelines for civil arguing in the classroom. As you complete the following exercise, remember that arguing minds seek to use the opportunities afforded by disagreement to inquire, and in the process, they try to preserve the ties that bind members together.

▓ **EXERCISE 4.2** ▓   The Principles of Civil Arguing

1. To help you set guidelines for arguing in the classroom, get into small groups and discuss what makes arguments good or bad (use the goals of promoting inquiry and community as your standards of evaluation).

2. Then, from your observations generalize a list of five principles you would like to see the class observe when conversing about readings, papers, and so on.

3. After each group has made its list, discuss them as a class. Compile them into an overall class list.

4. Each time your class argues, bring out the list and listen for moments when the conversation seems to violate those principles. After the conversation is over, you can then discuss those infractions and why they happened. Do they represent examples of unethical arguing, principles that are too strict, or even conversations where inquiry is not an appropriate goal?

STOP**AND**THINK

DEBORAH TANNEN AND THE ARGUMENT CULTURE

In her 1998 book *The Argument Culture: Moving from Debate to Dialogue*, linguistics professor Deborah Tannen demonstrates that arguing in our culture is based on a Western adversarial model, especially in education and in fields such as law, journalism, and politics. According to this model, social issues have only two sides, with supporters of each attacking the other side, hoping that their view will win out. We need only look at public debates on abortion, gun control, or the death penalty to see the prevalence of this model.

Unfortunately, this kind of public debate "becomes a model for behavior and sets the tone for how individuals experience their relationships to other people and to the society we live in" (280). In other words, citizens learn to oversimplify issues and to criticize different views in their private and public lives.

Tannen suggests we supplement this style of arguing with nonconfrontational alternatives drawn from other cultures and from our own imaginations. We could inquire further into this suggestion by talking to others and by brainstorming. How can we rigorously explore ideas without using an adversarial model? How can we improve the adversarial model to avoid the attacking attitude common to it now?

From previous discussions on civil arguing, two principles have emerged that seem central to the arguing mind. First, arguers need to put their ideas out into the public. We cannot learn through debate unless we express our views to others. Unfortunately, we often assume that everything we argue is a direct and lasting representation of who we are and what we stand for. We forget that the point of arguing to inquire is to learn. No one is born having the wisest views on all issues. If we discover that our views are inaccurate, or if we modify our views as we gather additional information, knowledge, or wisdom, then we ought to celebrate. We are living an examined life.

Second, arguers need to challenge others directly. Arguers frequently present their evidence and persuasive claims only to be met by other arguers presenting evidence and claims of their own. Unless the evidence and claims directly challenge each other, then the arguers talk past one another. They do not seek to shake up each other's ideas or beliefs. For example, a student who thinks the best way to address cheating in college is to toughen penalties is not necessarily talking to a student who thinks cheating is an over-exaggerated issue. To really inquire, they would need to first address the second student's argument. Only if the first student demonstrates that cheating is a genuine problem will the second student be ready to discuss ways to solve it.

Of course, a diverse society such as America's maintains its unity by respecting differences of opinion. This does not mean, however, that we should not use disagreements as opportunities to set up conversations. In other words, if we really wish to be active citizens living examined lives, then we need to seek out opportunities to argue and to frame our arguments in ways that challenge all participants' views. The alternative is to embrace a talk-show mindset in which we accept the truth of all opinions equally, simply because they are opinions.

Because arguments occur in specific places and times, and involve specific people, we need to first learn how to assess opportunities to argue. In Chapter 2, we learned how to assess writing situations; many of those same questions apply here as well. For example, asking ourselves how our audience thinks and feels about our subject can suggest effective arguing strategies. Asking ourselves about the historical and social background of an opportunity can help us decide if this is a good time and place to inquire through arguing. The more rigorously we understand a situation, the more effectively we can prepare to argue within it. Of course, we often don't know everything about our situation, so we must use our imaginations and draw from our own experiences. To begin to habituate yourself to assessing opportunities to argue, try the following exercise.

■ EXERCISE 4.3 ■ Assessing Opportunities to Argue

1. Read the initial readings or case study in one of the book's chapters. You might practice your summarizing skills by writing short summaries of each reading.

2. In your writer's notebook, list at least three places in the readings where you would like to respond. Perhaps you agree or disagree with a writer's ideas, or perhaps you want to qualify them. Your goal is to identify opportunities where you might respond with your own arguments.

3. Next, assess how you might argue to inquire by asking questions; you might refer to the questions listed in "Exploring your Writing Situation" in Chapter 2. Finally, discuss your results with others in the class. Do they agree with your assessments? Are your three places good opportunities to learn by arguing?

In addition to assessing opportunities to argue, we also need to frame our arguments so they participate in existing conversations. Framing an argument is much like framing a research question. To get into an issue, we seek a frame of reference, a way of seeing the issue that allows us to define what kind of research we want to do. The same process occurs in arguing. We need to decide what kind of an argument we want to make. Here are four common places where people disagree, and consequently, where people can argue:

- *Definitions*   As we learned in Chapter 1, definitions often vary with different audiences and purposes. Because the way we define something can shape our responses to it, arguments often form around the appropriate definition of a word or concept. For example, many of the disagreements over family policies in the United States hinge on conflicting definitions of the family.

- *Facts*   Sometimes citizens argue over whether a thing or issue exists or over whether an event has occurred. Environmental groups, business owners, and government officials have argued vigorously in recent years whether the planet is facing an environmental crisis. Some say a phenomenon such as global warming exists; others say it merely reflects natural changes in the Earth's temperature. Participants in this conversation will not discuss solutions until they agree that a problem exists.

- *Evaluations*   When we argue whether a movie is good or bad, a policy is practical or impractical, or a particular action is moral or immoral, we are evaluating. Framing an evaluative argument often means setting up criteria we then use to assess the excellence or morality of a particular thing, issue, or event. For example, determining whether the Internet is good or bad, moral or immoral for American democracy depends on what criteria we use to make that assessment. We might assess the Internet by its ability to offer information or by its ability to encourage face-to-face interaction among community members. Either set of criteria would produce a different evaluation.

- *Actions*   Even if we agree on the facts and an evaluation of those facts, we may disagree on whether to respond and how. For example, most of us would agree that poverty exists in the U.S. and that it is socially and morally bad. However, we may not agree on the best way to respond. Should we promote more employment by encouraging the development of businesses? Should we offer government-sponsored relief programs, or should we do nothing at all as a nation, relying instead on individuals and private charities?

Of course, many arguments will contain different types of arguments. For example, a citizen offering a solution to urban sprawl must first establish that urban sprawl is a problem. Then, he or she can advocate a particular action.

Once we know what kind of an argument we want to make, we can consult those people or written works with whom we want to argue. In other words, we can focus on those people or works that more directly support or contend the argument we have framed. In this way, we force ourselves to account for their views, promoting in our own arguments a more rigorous discussion. To practice framing arguments, try the following exercise:

▓ EXERCISE 4.4 ▓   Framing Our Arguments

1. Taking the opportunities you discovered in Exercise 4.3, brainstorm in your writer's notebook what kinds of argument you want to make. Do you want to argue over facts, definitions, evaluations, or actions, or do you want to combine them?

2. Review the initial readings or case study works you read in Exercise 4.3. Which of these works makes arguments that seem in direct conversation with the kinds of arguments you have framed?

Once we have a clearer sense of the arguments we want to make and the conversations we want to join, we need to consider the strategies we will use to make those arguments more rigorous. This is the subject of the next inquiry.

THIRD INQUIRY: ARGUING EFFECTIVELY

Chapter 2 reminds us that writing is not just self-expression; it is communication with the goal of affecting readers in real ways. Because of our ability to empathize with readers, we can anticipate, in a limited way, how they will be affected by the arguing strategies we use to persuade them. When we appeal to evidence, reason, our credibility as researchers or writers, and to readers' emotions, we already have some sense of how readers will probably respond. Knowing more about these arguing strategies can help us employ them more effectively and more ethically.

Four points about these strategies should be considered before we proceed. First, you already possess the ability to use these arguing strategies. Learning the subtleties of emotional or visual appeals, for example, would be difficult if our cultural upbringing had not already taught us how. We have appealed to sympathy to avoid punishment, we have appealed to reason to get our curfews extended, and we have acted appropriately to persuade our employers that we can handle our jobs. In a thousand different instances, we demonstrate our ability to use these appeals. Learning more about them can help us craft these appeals in more savvy and ethical ways.

Second, persuasion is not an exact science. Although these appeals are presented in a particular order, we do not apply them to our writing methodically.

Rather, we consider what strategies we will use as part of our initial assessment of the arguing opportunity. We also consider types of appeals as we write, and we sharpen our appeals as we revise. Writing persuasively is tied intimately to writing itself, as much a concern through the writing process as clarity, preciseness, or coherence.

Third, different types of appeals often work together. Although these strategies are taught individually, they often complement one another in actual writing. For example, a story might serve as evidence of a claim, but the story might also elicit emotions that encourage readers to accept the claim's truth. On the other hand, examining the types of appeals individually can sensitize us to those times when different appeals might conflict, as when a story serves as good evidence, but prompts emotions damaging to the writer's credibility.

Fourth, whether our appeals are effective and ethical often depends on the writing situation. For example, appealing to church doctrine as evidence of a claim might be both effective and ethical in a religious community, but it might be considered a *fallacy* in a scientific community, a breach of that community's standards for rigorous and ethical arguing.

Usually we think of fallacies as errors in our reasoning, but this view assumes a rationalist perspective. Rationalism is the belief that logic and evidence alone are reliable guides for assessing the truth of a claim. Most academic disciplines base their research methods and arguing standards on rationalism. However, not all communities follow this model, and many of the arguments we participate in will make use of nonrational appeals. As a result, we should know how to detect and use them appropriately. In addition, identifying a fallacy as a violation of an arguer's good faith agreement to inquire rigorously and ethically reminds us of our obligation to learn a community's arguing standards. To test the truth of this fourth point, and of the other three points, try the following exercise as a class:

EXERCISE 4.5   Discovering Types of Appeals

1. Below are three opportunities to inquire through arguing. Choose one of these opportunities as a class and imagine yourself in that situation. Then, in small groups brainstorm what types of appeals or arguing strategies you would use to convince your audience.

   a. The Council to Promote Stronger Families (CPSF) wants you to create a Web site designed to promote family values. What strategies or kinds of appeals can you make to convince Americans to view families as married, heterosexual couples with children? Now, create a Web site that will compete with the CPSF's, convincing Americans to reject the organization's definition of the American family, arguing instead that individuals have the right to establish their own definitions of family. What kinds of appeals would you use in each situation?

   b. Try to convince your parents that they should give you $10,000 (assuming they have it) and let you travel around Europe for a year. What kinds of appeals would you use to persuade them?

   c. Using the case study you read for exercises 4.3 and 4.4, brainstorm the kinds of appeals you would use to persuade a given audience. (The case studies allow you to frame the issue in different ways and arguing strategies come out of particular arguing situations; consequently, you will first need to narrow the case study's issue to a more specific opportunity, similar to the first opportunity above. That example originates from the federal Marriage Protection Amendment case study in Chapter 6.)

2. Next, share your group's ideas with the class. Write the different appeals on the blackboard and categorize them according to the kinds of appeal they make (e.g., to reason, to the emotions, and so on). Then, discuss further whether you think particular appeals are especially effective or potentially unethical.

The above exercise should have demonstrated that we already have an intuitive sense of how to argue. It should have also demonstrated that we can turn to a variety of appeals to support our arguments. What follows is a further inquiry into the more common types. As you may discover, however, our use of these strategies is more subtle and imaginative than these categories can capture.

Appealing to Evidence

In Chapter 3, we learned how to gather information to answer our questions and to develop knowledge and wisdom. The information we gather usually leads us toward particular answers to the questions we have posed. This information is evidence. Normally, we think of evidence as something that we need to prove our points to others. This is true, but when we weave our arguments in with the facts, observations, experimental data, or opinions of knowledgeable people, we are also discovering the truth of these claims for ourselves. The more rigorously we can use evidence as an argumentative strategy, the more sure we can be in our own knowledge and wisdom.

The different research methods we learned in Chapter 3 provide us with different kinds of evidence. The first kind, *quantitative,* allows us to generalize about larger populations. Such evidence can come from surveys, experiments, or observations that quantify, or count, particular phenomena. For example, census data on American families might provide evidence about the number of families that divorce, have children, or contain two working parents. At the same time, such evidence would not help us to understand what going through a divorce, having children, or sharing household responsibilities is like. For that kind of inquiry, we would need to gather evidence on individuals' experiences; in other words, we would need *qualitative* evidence.

Qualitative evidence can come from personal narratives, interviews, interpretations of written documents, or observations of individual behavior. Such evidence is rich in details allowing us to support subtle claims about particular phenomena. For example, Margaret Talbot's interviews with and observations of one American family in Chapter 6 help us understand what it is like to live by conservative religious principles in a secular society. On the other hand, Talbot's research would not support general claims about *all* American families. She would first have to show, using statistics, that the family she studied is representative of many or all American families. Because each evidence type has its own unique strengths and limitations, arguers often draw from both quantitative and qualitative evidence to verify the truth of their claims.

▓ EXERCISE 4.6 ▓ Assessing Appeals to Evidence

To explore how evidence is used to support arguments, isolate appeals to evidence from your list of persuasive strategies or locate ten appeals to evidence in the case study readings. Write down the claim the writer is trying to prove, then write down the evidence he or she uses to support that claim. Consider statistics; statements by authorities or experts; historical, cultural, or physical facts; arguers' personal experiences; other people's experiences (e.g., interviews, summarized observations); and so on. For each of your ten examples, answer the following questions:

1. Do the authors have enough evidence to support their claim?
2. How does this evidence work to convince you?
3. How do they present the evidence? (e.g., Do they put the evidence or claim first?)

Then, discuss these questions with others in the class. How do we know when we have enough evidence, or what kind of evidence we ought to use? In how many ways can we present evidence in a work?

Scottish philosopher David Hume once said, "a wise man proportions his belief to the evidence." This statement is a useful guide for deciding how much evidence we need to support our claims. The more difficult it is for us to accept the truth of a particular claim, the more we would need to surround it with evidence. Consider the following examples, taken from previous discussions. Does each arguer provide enough evidence to support his or her claim?

> . . . all too many marriages today end in divorce, and to most Americans that is a tragedy. But in "liberal marriage," there can never be any real expectation of permanence. In a society in which the liberal understanding of marriage becomes the law of the land, divorce would not only be the norm rather than the exception, but the institution of marriage would disappear altogether.

* * *

Going to Europe would be an educational experience. My friend John went to Italy with his architecture class. He said he learned more about structure and design in two weeks than he did in two semesters at college.

The first example, from Rick Santorum's "The Meaning of Family" in Chapter 6, is a claim without any evidence. For many of his readers such a claim would need no evidence; it is an obvious truth that fits in with their own sense of liberals and of American society. For other readers, however, it is a highly biased statement, representing many unexamined assumptions, such as the belief that marriage would end altogether if homosexuals as well as heterosexuals were permitted to marry. Opponents to Santorum's claim would also consider it a fallacy, an *unsubstantiated claim* that tries to pass itself off as self-evident. Santorum's piece is excerpted from his book *It Takes a Family: Conservatism and the Common Good,* which is aimed at a conservative audience that may already agree with his ideas. They would not necessarily demand support for his claim. On the other hand, to strengthen his own conviction, and to challenge those who might oppose his views, he could have provided evidence showing that broadening the definition of marriage in some areas has caused a weakening of marriage vows in general.

The second example, from a student eager to travel in Europe, appeals to qualitative evidence. The student cites a friend's experience to support his claim that traveling in Europe would be educational. While the student's example exhibits the strength of qualitative evidence—for example, his parents can visualize the student's friend touring Italy and learning about architecture—it lacks the strength of quantitative evidence. One example is not enough to support the general conclusion that everyone who travels to Europe will have an educational experience, especially because the friend went only for two weeks and never left Italy. Once again, it depends on the situation. For some parents, a single example such as this one might be sufficient. For others, many examples, supported by other forms of evidence, might be necessary.

In the second example, the student might even be accused of a fallacy, of offering *misleading evidence,* if he or she withheld the example of two friends who went to Europe, learned absolutely nothing, and even got into trouble with local officials. Ignoring evidence that disagrees with our claims, presenting evidence in ways that oversimplify complex issues, or misrepresenting evidence by taking it out of its original context are all examples of this fallacy because they diminish the rigor and fair-mindedness of our inquiry.

Here are a few additional suggestions from previous students about ways to appeal to evidence rigorously and ethically.

- Readers probably will not change their beliefs just because we tell them to, no matter how strongly we assert our claims. We need to prove, through evidence, any claims they might disagree with. We can learn which claims are most controversial by reading other works on our subject.

- If we don't have evidence to support a claim—because we think it is self-evident or because we cannot find any—we should acknowledge that fact; lacking evidence does not necessarily mean that our claim is wrong. Besides, if we are honest and straightforward, readers will think better of us as arguers.
- We should make our assumptions clear and explicit. Defining our terms and exposing beliefs and values that are relevant to our arguments will help readers understand where we are coming from. Even if they do not agree with those assumptions, they will appreciate our effort to be open and sincere.
- If we cop a condescending attitude toward our subject or our readers, we will encourage those who disagree with us to respond in the same way. If we stay positive, even when we disagree, we can encourage inquiry and preserve community ties.
- We should be aware of the limitations of our writing situation. If we are writing an editorial, for example, we do not have the space to include extensive evidence. If we still want to be rigorous and ethical, we may have to reframe our argument to something smaller and more manageable.

Appealing to Reason

When we tell other arguers to be "reasonable" or to talk "rationally," we usually mean that they should be more *cautious* in what they say, more *dispassionate* in how they say it, and more *self-conscious* in how they carry on the conversation. All of these qualities suggest that appeals to reason are appeals to clear away the clutter, to put aside any thoughts or feelings that might bias our decisions. These qualities also suggest we would, as reasonable arguers, pay attention to the way we make our decisions, in other words, to the patterns of thought we follow to make sense of information and to create knowledge or wisdom. We would have to determine whether we followed these patterns conscientiously.

In this section, we will look more closely at three common patterns of thought: deduction, induction, and analogy. Because these patterns are central to the way we think about ourselves and about the world, we will focus on how to appeal to them more rigorously and methodically.

First, to think *deductively* means to affirm the truth of a specific claim because it fits with larger claims we already accept as true. For example, we see deductive thinking when meteorologists use theories about pressure systems to predict the local weather on any given night. We see it when people criticize some particular action such as driving without a seat belt because it violates common sense. We also see it when religious leaders condemn a social practice such as prostitution because it offends a community's moral principles. Whether we apply general claims about the physical world, human behaviors, or community moral standards, the pattern of our thinking is similar. We assert the truth of a specific claim (e.g., "I must take composition to graduate") by appealing to a larger claim (e.g., "All students at this college must take composition to graduate").

Second, to think *inductively* means to form larger claims by appealing to a number of specific claims. The scientific theories, points of common sense, and moral principles we apply in deductive thinking are often formed through the accumulation of experience and inductive reasoning. If a physics professor asks us to drop a ball and measure its velocity twenty times, he or she is asking us to confirm laws of the physical world, such as gravity. If we get bitten every time we try to pet the neighbor's dog, we can probably assume it will bite us the next time as well. Finally, if we continually hurt others by telling lies, we might conclude that we should not lie anymore (assuming we do not want to hurt others). As these examples illustrate, the reliability of our general claims varies, depending on how many specific examples we accumulate and how carefully we generalize from the examples.

Finally, to think *analogically* means to make sense of something we do not know by comparing it to something we do know. We often use analogies to explain a complicated or abstract concept; we compare the unfamiliar, abstract concept to something concrete and familiar to our audience. In Chapter 9, for instance, David W. Orr's essay "Saving Future Generations from Global Warming" compares global warming to slavery. At first these two things seem too dissimilar to be analogous, but this strange pairing actually hooks the readers' interest. Readers want to know just how global warming and slavery might be related. Orr then develops the analogy by comparing our rationalizations for dismissing the dangers of global warming to earlier generations' justifications for continuing the practice of slavery, which now seem embarrassingly self-serving and indefensible.

Analogies often take the form of metaphors. Writers will use metaphors to describe physical phenomena (e.g., "Mitochondria are the *powerhouses* of the cell"). They use them to visualize complex processes (e.g., "According to Adam Smith, individuals seeking their own economic good are led by *an invisible hand* to benefit their society"). They even use them to reach a moral judgment (e.g., "In the essay 'Lifeboat Ethics,' researcher Garrett Hardin compares our planet to *a lifeboat* with limited space; if we try to save everyone, everyone will sink"). Hardin rejects an older metaphor—that of Earth as a spaceship—and substitutes for it his new one, Earth as a lifeboat. This new metaphor enables him to make his argument more persuasively. If readers find the metaphor itself persuasive, they are likely to find the entire argument persuasive. Comparisons of all kinds are very common in our arguing, formal and informal. Even arguing itself is talked about through analogies. Whether we talk about arguing as combat, with generals strategizing and going on the offensive, or as diplomacy, with representatives seeking compromise, we still conceive of it in terms of analogy.

▓ EXERCISE 4.7 ▓ Assessing Appeals to Reason

To explore how appeals to reason are used to tie claims or evidence into exist-ing knowledge, pull out examples from your list of persuasive strategies or locate ten appeals to reason in the readings. Write down each example, discuss what patterns of thought it follows and then answer the following questions:

1. Is this appeal to reason convincing? Why or why not?
2. Is it sufficiently careful, rigorous, and systematic to convince members of an academic or civic community?
3. In what ways could the appeal be strengthened, to make the truth of the claim it supports more certain?

Here are three additional examples of different appeals to reason, taken from previous classroom discussions. Each represents one of the common patterns of thought discussed above. As you read them, answer the above questions.

People grow by experiencing new things. I will have all kinds of new experi-ences in Europe. I could really grow as a person from this trip.

* * *

Going to Europe would be an educational experience. My friend John went to Italy with his architecture class. He said he learned more about structure and design in two weeks than he did in two semesters at college.

* * *

As one step on behalf of law and order—and on behalf of opportunity as well—the President has initiated the "Weed and Seed" program—to "weed out" criminals and "seed" neighborhoods with programs that address root causes of crime.

In the first example, the writer is appealing to deductive reasoning. The first statement, "People grow by learning about and experiencing new things," is a gen-eralization, a statement expressing the common belief that people mature as human beings by exposing themselves to new experiences. If we accept it as true, then it follows that the arguer, who will learn about and experience new things in Europe, will also grow as a person. In this case, the arguer is asserting the truth of a partic-ular claim—he or she will grow by experiencing new things in Europe—by appeal-ing to the general claim that people grow by experiencing new things.

Of course, we could probably find many examples where people learn about or experience new things but fail to grow. This would suggest that the general statement is not absolutely true, at least not true in the same sense as statements such as "All triangles have three sides" or "All human beings are mor-tal." Most of the general statements we make in life will not be absolutely true; rather, they will be more or less probable. Whether our audience accepts our general claim as probable or improbable, likely or unlikely, will depend on their own experiences. If their experiences have suggested to them that the general claim is often true, they may be willing to accept that the particular claim is true as well. Part of living an examined life is testing our generalized knowledge of the world against lived experience, all of those particular situations where our generalizations may or may not apply. To always assume that our general knowledge is true, especially when dealing with human behavior, is to fall into *dogmatism,* a fallacy in which beliefs are never subjected to examination.

Previous students have come up with several suggestions for improving the rigor and ethical appropriateness of appeals to deductive reasoning.

- Readers might be more willing to accept a general claim, and therefore a particular claim that appeals to it, if that general claim is clearly and precisely worded. For instance, the word *things* in the first example is vague; does it mean any kind of experience such as walking around the block or significant experiences such as traveling to a new country?

- We should qualify our general claims to express how much faith we have in their truth. We might use words such as *often, sometimes, frequently, may, could, in some cases,* and so on to state that our general claim does not apply to all particular claims. For example, we could rewrite the general claim in the first example as "People often grow by learning about and experiencing new things" or "Many people grow by learning about and experiencing new things" if we feel pretty confident in its truth.

- We should make sure our particular claim is really an example of our general claim. For example, if we had already seen everything we planned to visit in Europe, then our claim that visiting Europe would help us grow cannot appeal to our general claim. After all, the things we plan to see would no longer be new to us.

We have already seen the second example, which illustrates an appeal to inductive reasoning, in the Appealing to Evidence section. This example demonstrates an important point about appeals to reason and evidence: They usually work together. In this case, the arguer is drawing on other particular examples to arrive at the general claim "Going to Europe would be an educational experience." This claim is much like the general claim in the previous example: "People grow by experiencing new things." Their similarity suggests another important point: We as human beings usually arrive at general knowledge and wisdom inductively, by generalizing from many particular instances. We then apply this knowledge and wisdom deductively, testing its truth against more particular instances.

Of course, the example of inductive reasoning we have here is weak. To move from one example where a student learned something in Europe to the general claim that everyone going to Europe would have an educational experience is to commit a *hasty generalization* fallacy, meaning we assert a conclusion that is not supported by enough evidence. We might also be guilty of this fallacy if we jumped to a conclusion that is not even suggested by the particular instances we have gathered together. For example, if many students in a course failed, we might assume they did not work very hard. However, the same particular instances, the students failing, might suggest different conclusions. Perhaps the course was very difficult, the instructor taught badly, or the time of day discouraged learning.

Rigorous arguers look closely at any patterns suggested by evidence so the general claims they reach genuinely represent what was going on in the individual instances. Here are additional suggestions offered by previous students.

- If we want readers to believe our general claims, we should show them our evidence. For example, scientists who write reports on their research usually include the raw data so readers can see for themselves whether the scientists reached the correct conclusions.

- We should qualify the conclusions we reach according to how many particular examples we have drawn together and how confident we feel in our inductive reasoning. Using words such as *always, never, all, none, certainly,* or *absolutely* may commit us to a fallacy if our evidence doesn't support such sweeping generalizations.

The last example, from former Vice President Dan Quayle's 1992 speech at the Commonwealth Club of California, illustrates an appeal to analogous reasoning. In this case, Quayle is alluding to someone else's analogy, but his other statements suggest this is an analogy he supports. Something we know about—or at least we can visualize—lawn care, is used as a metaphor for explaining social policy in inner cities. In this case, former President George Bush's program implies that we can create uniform prosperity in inner cities if we remove those people we do not want, the criminals, and encourage those who we do want—the hard-working, honest citizens—by offering them incentive programs designed to eliminate their poverty. Just as weeds seek to choke off the grass, so criminals seek to destroy the efforts of good people to improve their communities.

Analogies such as the one Quayle refers to are hard to create because no two things are exactly the same. Quayle's supporters might believe that this analogy works because they see criminals as different from regular citizens. Criminals are individuals who decide to violate the laws and disrupt their communities. To prevent the rest from being victimized, these criminals must be removed. On the other hand, readers who do not support Quayle's values and beliefs, might accuse him of committing a *false analogy* fallacy, asserting similarities between subjects that are really different. If these critics of Quayle believe that criminals are not essentially different from law-abiding citizens, but are themselves victims of poverty and despair, then they would not accept the "weed and seed" metaphor as accurate.

Philosopher Mark Johnson argues that moral decision-making is essentially imaginative. We use imaginative structures such as analogies as frameworks to make sense of the world around us and to act in ethical ways. Do we see criminals as undernourished grass or noxious weeds? How we answer that question might determine whether we build more prisons or more schools, more court houses or drug rehabilitation programs. Or, do we abandon this analogy altogether, seeking alternative ways we can get a handle on the complex problems facing inner cities.

Previous students have offered several suggestions for improving the rigor and ethical appropriateness of appeals to analogy.

- An analogy is not the same as evidence. Just because you call social programs *seeds* does not mean they will actually work in "growing" better communities.

- We should work out the consequences of our analogies before we use them. If we call criminals *weeds* does that mean we should rip them out of their communities and kill them? Explaining how far we want our analogies to apply—saying criminals are only weeds because they prey on innocent community members—will set limits to readers' imaginations.

- We should be sensitive to the emotions or ideas readers might associate with the words or images we want to use as analogies. For example, if we say criminals are *pond scum,* then we will encourage readers to think and feel about criminals negatively. If we say criminals are *lost sheep,* then we will encourage very different thoughts and feelings. The important point is that in both cases, we have provided no evidence to suggest why readers should think one way or another; the analogies themselves shape our thinking.

You can read more about ways people use definitions to frame debates in George Lakoff's essay "What's in a Word?" in the Chapter 6 case study on same-sex marriage.

Although we already follow patterns of deductive, inductive, and analogous thinking, we can improve our appeals to reason by exercising the suggestions offered above. Included below are four statements on which we can practice. After you read them, discuss how they might be rewritten to represent more cautious, dispassionate, self-conscious reasoning.

1. Hillary Clinton is a "high priestess of feminism and a manipulator." You can't trust her.

2. A 1991 Roper survey revealed that 119 people, out of 6000 questioned, reported experiencing these five indicators of an alien abduction experience: 1) unusual lights in their room, 2) missing time, 3) paralysis, 4) levitation, 5) unexplainable scars on their bodies. If these results are extrapolated to the entire U.S. population, then more than 5 million people have experienced alien abduction. Surely the number of people who have experienced such similar events confirms the truth that aliens are among us.

3. The human mind is a *tabula rasa*, a blank slate on which experience writes.

4. "I don't recall exactly how the idea came to me, but after I rejected Prozac as the means to become a successful teacher of Generation X, I got another idea. If one option was to chemically change my personality with a drug to be more outgoing, entertaining, and nurturing, then the opposite approach would be to consciously alter my behavior and actually *manipulate my environment.* There seemed little doubt that the system was actually pushing me in that direction. It suddenly became clear to me that being a good teacher didn't seem to really matter in the system of rewards and punishments teachers faced; excellence wasn't really the point. It was becoming increasingly clear that the real point was whether you kept students sufficiently amused and entertained."

STOP**AND**THINK

MICHAEL SHERMER AND SKEPTICISM

Michael Shermer, the author of *Why People Believe Weird Things* (1997) and director of the Skeptics Society, defines a skeptic as "one who questions the validity of a particular claim by calling for evidence to prove or disprove it" (17). Skeptics base their beliefs on observation and on clear inductive and deductive reasoning. They also test their knowledge against further observations. Unfortunately, this rational approach to creating knowledge is often short-circuited by the limits of our research tools, by mistakes in our reasoning, or by misunderstandings on what makes for reliable knowledge. Shermer offers several reasons why people believe in alien abductions, ghosts, psychic predictions, and other "weird things" that fail to meet skeptics' criteria for reliable knowledge:

- Our desire for simple, easily understood answers often pushes us to oversimplify complex issues. We need to remember that many issues do not have easy, simple answers; we need to think critically about them.

- We often form a possible solution to an issue and seek evidence to prove it, instead of also seeking evidence to disprove it.

- We frequently mistake rumors for true stories. Just because most of us have heard that alligators roam New York sewers does not mean it is true.

- We tend to remember those instances that confirm our beliefs and to forget those that reject our beliefs. For example, if a psychic makes one correct prediction out of five guesses, we should not forget the four predictions that she or he got wrong.

Because critical thinking is so difficult and people make mistakes all the time, Shermer suggests we adopt an inquiring attitude. We should question other people's claims, not to ridicule them, but to better understand the world around us.

Appealing to Character

Evidence and reason appeal strongly to us today but we also value an arguer's character, those intellectual and moral qualities that distinguish the individual arguer and serve as the basis of his or her reputation. Our character can be established in two ways when we argue: by the history of our actions and by the image we present of ourselves in writing and speaking.

The first way, called our *situated character*, refers to our reputation at a given time and within a given community. The history of what we have said or done within a particular community reveals to its members the kind of person we are. For example, your writing, your participation in class discussion, even your actions during outside conferences have shaped your instructor's and classmates' views on your ability, your seriousness, and your credibility as a critical thinker. You can change your reputation only by changing your behavior, letting community members accumulate a new history of your actions.

The second way, called our *invented character*, refers to our *persona*, the image we project of ourselves by how we write. When we read an essay, we not only digest the content, we also form an opinion of the writer—the writer's knowledge of the subject and his or her ability as a thinker and communicator. This opinion often influences how seriously we consider the writer's ideas. Fortunately, we usually have the leisure to craft our writing carefully, presenting the best possible image of ourselves.

Of course, dismissing someone's argument because of their character, whether situated or invented, can be unethical, what rhetoricians call an *ad hominem* fallacy. This fallacy, which means "to the person," refers to our tendency to dismiss an arguer's claim by dismissing the arguer. Perhaps a writer is known for expressing biased opinions. Perhaps a writer frequently misspells words, adopts a condescending tone toward readers, or uses too many complex words and ideas. Dismissing a speech or written work for these reasons is unethical; critical thinkers believe arguments should be evaluated on their own merit and not on the arguer's alone. Nevertheless, we often make such judgments in our daily lives, and we ought to guard against them both as readers and writers. While we cannot easily change our situated characters, we can practice strategies that improve our invented characters. Because the people who read our arguments probably don't know us very well, our invented characters become quite important.

▓ EXERCISE 4.8 ▓ Assessing Appeals to Character

To explore how situated and invented characters affect our persuasiveness as arguers, review your list of persuasive strategies. Brainstorm additional ways you could impress your audience with your competence, sincerity, or fair-mindedness.

Alternatively, locate two works in the readings where you had a strong positive or negative reaction to the writer. Then, explain why you reacted so strongly. Often our response is intuitive—we are not aware of the reasoning process we went through to reach our conclusions—so we need to analyze the readings closely. Identify five strategies the two writers used that strengthened or weakened their character in your eyes.

Based on previous discussions, here are several strategies for improving our invented characters. Of course, which strategies we use will depend on our writing situation.

- We need to know our subject. We show our credibility by engaging others who have written on the subject, by using specific details, and by carefully explaining how our evidence supports our claims.
- We should acknowledge other people's views. Arguers who dismiss or ignore alternative viewpoints can appear manipulative, as if they are hiding the truth. Showing we appreciate where other people are coming from, even if we disagree with them, will make us appear fair-minded.
- If we appeal to the values and beliefs of our readers, we show that we are one of them. For example, politicians express rural values when talking with farmers, even if they never grew up on a farm. Of course, drawing on the audience's values and beliefs may backfire if the connection we are trying to make with them is insincere. The best way to decide if we should appeal to shared values and experiences is to put ourselves in the audience's position. How would we view someone making such appeals?
- We should express a tone appropriate to our subject and audience. Experts in business communication such as Andrew Carnegie suggest we show a positive attitude even if we disagree with readers. This tone will encourage the audience to hear our arguments more readily than if we were dismissive of or hostile to their views.

Appealing to Emotions

French mathematician Blaise Pascal once wrote, "The heart has its reasons, which reason does not understand." Pascal's suggestion, that humans are sometimes driven by emotions, might seem an unhappy description of our tendency to act irrationally, against the better judgment of cool, objective reasoning. This view, however, assumes that reason and emotion are separate and opposed. It also assumes that reason alone is the proper guide to our actions.

Recent research in neurology indicates that emotions and reasoning are intimately connected. Antonio Damasio, a professor of neurology at the University of Iowa College of Medicine, suggests we modify Pascal's quote to read "The organism has some reasons that reason must utilize" (200). Damasio argues that when we are faced with a decision, our emotions direct us in considering our options. Some courses of action may be supported within the individual by negative or positive feelings; these feelings act as aversions or incentives that limit the number of choices the individual must consider. To recognize this idea, we might read Ursula Le Guin's "The Ones Who Walk Away from Omelas" in Chapter 3. Even though the Omelans' decision to base the joy of thousands on the misery of one child may seem a logical choice— the happiness of many requires the suffering of only one—most of us would probably feel a strong emotional aversion to such a decision.

Knowing the role emotion plays in our decision-making process can sensitize us to its positive or negative effects. To explore this idea, and to discover ways we can appeal to readers' emotions in effective and ethical ways, try the following exercise.

EXERCISE 4.9 ▦ Assessing Appeals to Emotions

To explore how emotional appeals are used to support arguments, review your list of persuasive strategies or locate five examples in the readings where writers try to persuade their audience by encouraging an emotional response. Write these examples down in your writer's notebook and then share them with your classmates. Consider the following questions as you discuss them:

1. What kind of an emotional response is the writer encouraging?
2. How is the writer able to encourage an emotional response?
3. Does this emotional appeal assist or diminish readers' critical thinking? In other words, is it ethical?

Here are three examples from previous discussions, followed by several suggestions for how to use emotional appeals effectively. Do they support Damasio's argument that emotions play an intimate role in reasoning?

Families are the people for whom it matters if you have a cold, are feuding with your mate or training a new puppy. Family members use magnets to fasten the newspaper clippings about your bowling team on the refrigerator door. They save your drawings and homemade pottery. They like to hear stories about when you were young . . . . Whether or not they are biologically related to each other, the people who do these things are family.

*   *   *

All the students in my program are getting international experience. If you don't let me go too, I'll never be able to compete against them in the job market.

*   *   *

Give me money to go to Europe or I will never speak to you again."

In the first example, from Mary Pipher's "Beliefs About Families" in *The Shelter of Each Other* in Chapter 6, readers are encouraged to broaden their definitions of family to include those people with whom they share their experiences, both trivial and important. To persuade her audience, Pipher uses emotional examples such as "training a new puppy." These examples arouse positive feelings, encouraging us to accept her argument. If she relied only on these emotional images to convince us, she might be accused of committing a *sentimental appeal* fallacy, using emotions such as nostalgia to encourage an uncritical response. Emotions can help us reason more constructively, but we need reason and evidence as well to help ensure that we are not being manipulated by the writer.

The second example calls on parents to think of their child's future. The arguer tries to get their consent by arguing that other parents are helping their children. If the arguer's parents truly love their child, and are concerned about his or her welfare, they will join the crowd. In other words, the arguer is appealing to the parents' fear that their child might fall behind in the world. If the arguer appealed only to this emotion, he or she would be committing a *bandwagon* fallacy, persuading readers to agree to an idea because everyone else does. The example might be acceptable if the arguer provided evidence that candidates in his or her field do indeed need international experience. Emotions can connect us to others. Just as appeals to common sense testify to the shared experiences of community members, so emotional appeals testify to our shared emotional needs. However, if we use these needs to compel acceptance of our ideas at the expense of evidence and reason, then we argue unethically.

The third example might seem rather weak as an argument. To threaten the audience with silence in order to compel their agreement is to commit a fallacy; *scare tactics,* direct or indirect threats to our audience, discourage readers from thinking critically about the subject and from considering alternative viewpoints. Emotions can move us to take action. As writers, however, we should exercise the emotional intelligence to be aware of our feelings toward our subject and audience. We can move our readers to act, but in communities where willing consensus is valued, we should seek to move our readers by evidence, reason, a credible persona, and emotional appeals appropriate to that community's arguing standards. If we try to win by threats or unethical appeals to emotions, we only undermine our own credibility.

Here are additional suggestions offered by previous students:

- We should assess the situation to see if emotional appeals are appropriate. Is the subject an emotional one for readers? Would expressing your emotions on the subject help or hurt your purpose? Is emotion appropriate in the genre in which you are writing (e.g., in a science report)?

- We can establish common ground with our readers by acknowledging any emotional attitudes toward the subject that exist out there. Readers may respect us more if we acknowledge how they feel about the subject, especially if we plan to argue against their views.

- We can evoke emotions such as sympathy or pity or anger by choosing scenes or events that will really resonate with them and then describing them in concrete detail. However, we should remember to appeal also to evidence and reason, in case we risk committing a sentimental appeal fallacy.

- We should evoke emotions by paying careful attention to our language use, especially our word choice. This strategy is difficult to use well without alienating readers so it should be used cautiously. For example, consider the very different emotional responses created by using either of the following pairs of words in an abortion debate: baby/fetus, kill/abort, remove/rip apart.

Appealing to Visual Arguments

Visual arguments are all around us. The obvious and most recurrent form they take is in advertising, but we find visual arguments in photojournalism, art, illustrations, TV news programs, cartoons, maps, charts, bar graphs—wherever images are used to demonstrate a point or persuade an audience. Visual arguments are effective because they impact us much more quickly than words do, and they tend to stick with us, to linger in our minds long after we have seen them. This means we should be aware of how visual arguments work, both so we can read them critically and so we can create them effectively.

We often think of photojournalism as presenting us with objective, real images, rather than carefully developed arguments. To analyze the visual arguments present in photojournalism, compare the two family images in Chapter 6. Gigi Kaeser's photograph *Love Makes a Family* and Jeff Riedel's photograph for *The New York Times Magazine* represent two versions of the American family. Each photo asks us to accept this family as legitimate. How does each photographer set up the photograph to claim such legitimacy? As you study them, use the following questions to guide your analysis.

1. Identify the photograph's "thesis" or "message." To identify this, consider what impression it immediately makes on you, what it makes you feel or think. What point does it seem to be making?

2. What seems to be the point of view of the photographer? What vision does he or she have of this American family? Look closely for subtle hints that might not be obvious on your first few viewings of the photo. Notice the background, the setting, and all of the individuals' positions and facial expressions.

3. What seems to be the point of view of the subjects of the photographs? What do their facial expressions and positions convey to you? What do they seem to be thinking?

4. Notice how the textual elements are also part of the argument. What are the "key words" used in the headline and the copy? How do they capture our attention quickly and strike a chord with readers? How does the message of the text—the title and subtitle—of each photograph work with or against the message of the image? Are they complementary; i.e., does the image illustrate the text's argument, or the

text explain the image? Or are they contrasting; i.e., do the image and text seem to give contradictory messages, perhaps to reveal the difference between the appearance and reality of an issue?

Because visual arguments, especially advertisements, are aimed at us on a daily basis and affect the way we choose to live our lives, we need to get in the habit of viewing them critically and with awareness of their goals. Knowing how visual arguments work can also help us use them more effectively in our own work. Although visual arguments work on audiences more immediately than written ones, developing a visual argument follows much the same process as developing a written one. Here are several suggestions for creating your own visual arguments:

- Assess your situation. What is the subject matter, who is the audience, and what is your purpose? Are visual elements appropriate?
- How will you use the visual argument to achieve your purpose? For instance, will it illustrate your point? Will it serve as the primary argument itself and be explained by your text?
- What kind of appeal should the image have? Should it appeal to logic or emotion? Should it strengthen your reputation?
- What kind of image will be most effective? Do you want to use a graph, a table, a photograph, a graphic image, or a work of art?
- How can you avoid misleading or manipulating your audience with your images? Are your graphs, tables, or maps current and accurate? What are the implications of your images; will they convey the message you want and only that message?

Use the previous guidelines to help you complete the following exercise. It gives you an opportunity to practice constructing visual arguments by creating your own print advertisement.

EXERCISE 4.10 ▦ Creating Visual Arguments: Adbusters

Adbusters, a Vancouver-based satire magazine, develops spoofs of famous ads in order to make arguments about the ethics of advertising. Their Web site gives you step-by-step advice on how to develop an ad of your own.

1. Go to the *Adbusters* Web site at http://adbusters.org/spoofads/printad/ and follow their instructions.
2. When you have finished your advertisements, present them to one another and test their effectiveness.
3. Assess your skill at reading the arguments in one another's advertisements.

CONCLUSION: ARGUMENT AS INQUIRY

In Chapter 3, you learned that an inquiring mind seeks information, knowledge, and wisdom. The arguing mind has the same goals, but whereas inquirers ask questions and exercise disciplined research methods, arguers respond to the ideas of others critically and argue their insights rigorously. In other words, they test out possible answers to their questions by actively arguing with others. Yet, because such arguments often create new questions, and the questions we ask often originate from our existing values and beliefs, we should think of inquiring and arguing as interwoven, complementary aspects of the same thoughtful mind.

▓ PROJECTS FOR INQUIRY AND ACTION ▓

1. To reinforce your willingness to pause and understand another person's viewpoint, try analyzing an argument you disagree with; this argument might appear in an essay, book, speech, editorial, or Web site. Try not to criticize the arguer's ideas but to objectively summarize what they believe and then explain, based on your analysis of the work itself, what values and beliefs would push the arguer to hold his or her viewpoint.

2. Write a letter to the editor for your local or campus newspaper recommending an action on an issue that interests you (see Chapter 5 for advice on writing letters to the editor). At the end of the letter, invite responses. Then, collect any responses you get and analyze the kind of conversation you started. How did they respond? What aspects of your letter did they respond to? (If you do not get any responses, you can complete this exercise by discussing why.)

3. Take an issue that means a lot to you and analyze your own reasons why you believe what you believe. What values, beliefs, and experiences have shaped your views on this issue?

4. Over the span of a week, watch different talk shows and news programs that encourage debate and dialogue (e.g., *Crossfire* and *Meet the Press*). Take notes on the participants' arguing styles and strategies. Which styles and strategies seem to most encourage inquiry (i.e., from which do you learn the most)? Which seem most persuasive? Are those styles and strategies that you found most persuasive the same as those that promoted inquiry?

CHAPTER 5

Writing in Communities:
Academic Research and Social Action

> Civic participation is a formula for human happiness, both private and
> public. It is more than a slogan to be intoned or even a duty to be self-
> imposed; it is a delight to be savored as the essential quality of life that
> makes democracy an authentic reality. It will be a pleasure for students
> to fulfill themselves by applying the principles of justice in a democratic,
> community forum—complete with debate, dialogue, advocacy, assertion,
> and implementation.
>
> —*Ralph Nader,* Practicing Democracy

▓ GETTING STARTED ▓   Critical Literacy and Civic Participation

In this opening section, you can use your critical literacy skills—thinking, reading,
writing, researching, and arguing—to investigate a case study from this book or
a current situation that affects the people in your class. After you have read the
case study or researched the current situation, outline, on the blackboard, the main
concerns involved in this situation. What happened or is happening? What are the
stakes for those involved? Why should or shouldn't you get involved?

Next to your outline, brainstorm a list of projects that you could undertake as
students and citizens to investigate this situation and get involved. Push to develop
a range of possibilities, no matter how remote they might seem at the moment.

Finally, discuss the following questions as a class:

1. What channels of action and communication are open to you?
2. In what communities could you communicate your ideas?
3. How could you use your knowledge and skills to act?
4. How and why might these actions be fulfilling and pleasurable?

As members of various private and public communities, you can use
your critical literacy skills to create and share your knowledge with

others. Unfortunately, college students are not always encouraged to participate fully in academic or public conversations, even though they pay tuition and possess legal citizenship. You usually need some degree of training and expertise to participate in these communities, but you can begin to develop these qualities right now. You can conduct substantive research, investigate the conventions of academic and public writing, and participate in public debate. Even as beginning writers, you have more power and more opportunities than you might think.

The authors experienced students' potential while developing the second edition of this book. On August 29, 2005, Hurricane Katrina made landfall near Buras-Triumph, Louisiana. Within hours, sections of the levees protecting New Orleans, Louisiana collapsed. Residents of the city had been ordered to evacuate, but many either ignored the warnings or did not have the means to leave. Hundreds of people were drowned in the flooding or died from the breakdown of health services. Reports of looting and lawlessness, later found to be exaggerated, saturated the news media. According to Homeland Security Secretary Michael Chertoff, Hurricane Katrina was one of the worst catastrophes in our nation's history.

We and our students anxiously watched the television, read the newspapers, shared e-mail postings, and discussed our feelings in class. We wanted to act as students and citizens to better understand the situation and to reach out to others. Students on our campuses responded to the disaster in many ways. They:

- Researched the levees around New Orleans to understand how the storm so easily overwhelmed the work of the U.S. Army Corps of Engineers.
- Researched hurricanes and tropical storms.
- Asked professors to modify existing assignments to allow them to explore events in New Orleans in more depth.
- Initiated a Red Cross fund-raiser through their Student Senate.
- Donated money directly to recovery efforts and collected food and clothing for New Orleans refugees being routed to Minnesota.
- Wrote letters to local and campus newspapers expressing dismay over the breakdown of law and order in New Orleans following the floods.
- Read blogs that pointed out the effects of race and class on who was saved and when.
- Held informal discussion groups around TVs, as they watched events unfold in New Orleans.
- Joined an e-mail petition criticizing the Federal Emergency Management Agency's slow response to the New Orleans disaster.
- Listened to discussions on local and national radio talk shows.
- Organized times for reflective writing, discussion, or group prayer for the victims.

This chapter encourages you to pursue projects such as those listed above so you can realize your own potential for academic and civic participation. As an undergraduate writer in a college classroom, you are a member of an apprenticeship community, one "in training" to join academic, professional, and civic communities. To that end, you are learning to think critically, read carefully, and write clearly and effectively. You are also learning to research issues and develop sound arguments. These skills will get a workout as you learn how to compose works common to academic and civic communities.

FIRST INQUIRY: WRITING IN AN ACADEMIC COMMUNITY

In the first section of this chapter, you will learn how to develop a research paper. The research paper was chosen because it is one of the most common genres in academic communities, and it is the primary vehicle for developing the skills of inquiry and argument necessary to do college-level work. This is true whether you analyze U.S.-Middle East politics, verify the results of studies on frog populations, or research the historical context of William Shakespeare's *Macbeth*. Learning to develop a researched argument is also good for your career and civic life because the higher-level thinking, organization, and analysis it teaches improve your ability to participate effectively in those communities.

Re-seeing the Research Paper

Reflect for a moment on your past experiences with writing research papers. What does the term *research paper* bring to mind for you? What kinds of topics do you generally consider appropriate for a research paper?

Previous students, when asked these questions, often described research papers as "boring," "tedious," or "a lot of busywork in the library." These students also tended to list the same subjects over and over: abortion, capital punishment, euthanasia, marijuana legalization, or gun control. These subjects are certainly important, challenging the bonds of our communities in real ways, but the students who selected them often did so because they believed that such issues were the only research topics available to them.

In Chapters 3 and 4, we learned that inquiring and arguing can be broad, pulling together many interests from our public and private lives. We should bring this same active, inquiring mindset to academic research, asking questions and developing projects that connect with our real interests and life experiences.

For example, here are a few research projects students in our classes have pursued. We will refer to these projects throughout the chapter to illustrate different aspects of the research process.

- Janette researched the history of tattooing and body piercing to understand why her daughter had tattooed her arms and stuck steel rods through her nose, lip, and belly button. Her essay compared contemporary body mutilation practices in the United States with those in other cultures; her goal was to look at these practices in a larger historical and social context.

- Rick could not decide if he should go into mechanical, electrical, or chemical engineering so he wrote an essay that helped other students match one of these areas to their interests, lifestyle, and career goals. To research the subject, he read career literature and interviewed guidance counselors and two engineers from each field.

- Mia wanted to know why people hold religious beliefs. She looked at the research of psychologists to discover what emotional, physical, and psychological needs religions fulfill. Her research paper summarized psychologists' current understanding of this phenomena and suggested areas where they could do additional research.

- Rico, a student in wildlife biology, set up an experiment to test the effects of road salt run-off on local swamp lands. Working with composition and biology instructors, he tested different concentrations of salt water on plants, recorded the different levels of growth over thirty days, and then wrote up his results in a six-page research report.

- Abby compared samples of neighborhood graffiti with popular works of modern art. She used art historians' definitions of art to assess whether graffiti can be seen as a legitimate form of public art.

- At three professional football games, Jake and Robert observed and categorized the behaviors of ten randomly selected fans who were all drinking beer. Drawing together quantitative and qualitative evidence, they argued that these fans tended to cheer and jeer more actively, even as their actual awareness of the game diminished. Their results were written up in an essay that appealed to general readers.

The above examples are meant to show that students should not feel compelled to write only on particular topics and only in one particular style. Even professional researchers explore a variety of subjects and write in a variety of styles, as the next exercise should demonstrate.

EXERCISE 5.1 ▦ Comparing Research Papers

What are the different ways research can be presented? With your class, analyze several research papers. Here are a few examples from this book:

- In Chapter 6, Margaret Talbot's "A Mighty Fortress" offers a substantive, researched essay written for the popular audience of *The New York Times Magazine.*

- In Chapter 8, James L. Watson's "China's Big Mac Attack" is a carefully researched article that explains the complex concept of globalization to the academic audience of the journal *Foreign Affairs.*

- In Chapter 11, "Why We Blog," co-written by Bonnie Nardi, Diane Schiano, Michelle Gumbrecht, and Luke Swartz, is a researched report developed through interviews and published in the academic journal *Communications of the ACM* [Association for Computing Machinery].

As you analyze these essays, use the following questions to guide your discussion.

1. What do the authors' essays have in common as research papers? Do you notice the authors adhering to certain conventions and formulas?
2. In what ways do their essays differ? How would you compare their structures, their ways of presenting research, or the authors' relationship with the audience?
3. How do these essays compare with your existing ideas of research papers? What conventions are consistent or different?

As the above projects and essays hopefully demonstrate, research papers need not be tedious exercises in collecting and regurgitating the ideas of others. Research really can be a meaningful experience if it begins with our genuine interests and concerns. In Chapter 2, you were encouraged to write down one hundred questions to which you would like to know the answer. Many of these questions could serve as excellent research projects if you shed the idea of a typical research topic. For example, Mia was raised as an agnostic, someone who actively questions the existence of a supreme being. Many of her friends, however, were deeply religious. A natural question for her was why? She was inspired to begin her project because the initial question mattered to her; it would help her understand, at least from a psychologist's perspective, why her friends believed.

In addition to being meaningful, research ought to be active. In Chapter 3, we learned that when writers begin an inquiry they often join ongoing conversations. As an apprentice researcher, you might feel inadequate to the task of building on or critiquing the conversations of academics and professional researchers. This is a natural feeling; you have only begun to develop the knowledge and skills needed to become a full and active member of these communities. Nevertheless, this does not mean you should embrace the other extreme, cutting and pasting ideas into a dull, passive summary. Consider the examples of these other students.

- Abby does not have a degree in art history, yet she tested her understanding of modern art by applying definitions of it to a new subject, graffiti. The project not only helped her better understand the difficulty of defining modern art, it also gave her new appreciation for the graffiti covering her neighborhood.
- Rico did not know the first thing about testing the effects of salt on plants. Even after he got help from a biology professor, he ran into several problems with his experimental method. Nevertheless, the experi-

ence taught him a lot about setting up scientific experiments and writing research reports.

• Professional social scientists would have found several problems with the methods Jake and Robert used to observe the effects of alcohol consumption on fan participation. However, Jake and Robert set up their research project in good faith, trying to be rigorous and methodical within the limits of time and money imposed upon them. The experience taught them better ways to conduct observations, and they learned how to make their research accessible to general readers.

In each of these examples, the writers engaged the works of other researchers. Abby looked up definitions of modern art, Rico followed the methods described in other research reports, and Jake and Robert used their experiment to test previous social scientists' results. In each case, the students took action. On a level appropriate to their knowledge, expertise, time, and resources, they questioned, built upon, or added to the knowledge of various communities. At the same time, they exercised their academic and civic skills.

As you plan out your own research projects, consider ways you can respond more actively.

• *You might apply current ideas to new subjects.* One student applied the definition of a subculture to video gamers, defining them as a unique community.

• *You might bring together different viewpoints in new ways.* One student created a dialogue between advocates of creationism and evolution; she wanted to show that these different groups will not be able to really talk until they agree on some basic facts and definitions.

• *You might add to existing research, even if in a small way.* One student interviewed three women who had had abortions; he discovered that the emotional and psychological pain of the procedures had lingered for them, and the clinics these women had visited had not prepared them sufficiently to deal with this pain.

Even if your project does not contribute significantly to academic conversations, it will, in an inspiring way, fulfill your primary purpose—to learn how to research, argue, and write a research paper.

As you work through the next section, keep this wider understanding of the research paper in mind. You may have to modify your project to fit the limits imposed by your writing situation, but you can still start with a question that excites you, one that will inspire you throughout the project.

Forming a Research Question

In Chapter 3, we learned that research often begins with questions. We learned that questions can make the writing process easier by narrowing our topic's scope. We also learned that questions can give us an ending point to the research process. Our work is finished when we have sufficiently answered the question we posed.

For instance, Rick's first research question was a disaster because it tried to cover too much material, and it offered no end to his research. He had posed the question "Which engineering field is the best?" When he began his research, his interviewees each told him not only that their engineering field was the best, but that other engineering fields were peopled with dregs and engineering school drop outs. None of his sources gave him the kind of definitive information he needed to compare and rank engineering fields. To make his project work, Rick needed to reshape his question. Eventually, he came up with "What interests, lifestyle preferences, and career goals should a person interested in mechanical, electrical, or chemical engineering have?" This new question not only limited the scope of his research project, it also helped him end the project. As soon as he had gathered enough evidence to answer this question adequately, he wrote his essay.

A research question can also keep our research honest by encouraging us to consult a variety of sources, not just those that confirm our existing values and beliefs. A well-phrased question does not imply one particular answer or viewpoint; it invites us to test many possible answers against one another and against our own experiences. At the same time, however, our question can imply the kind of project we do to answer it.

For example, by asking how road salt run-off from city streets might affect local swamps, Rico committed himself to one of two science projects. He might consult other studies on salt's effects on plants and generalize to his own local community, or he might set up and conduct his own experiment. He had to choose the latter because no one had published a study of salt's effects on the particular marsh plants in his area. He then had to decide whether to write a scientific research report for specialists in his field or a general essay his fellow citizens could understand and appreciate.

On the other hand, Abby's question "Is the graffiti in my neighborhood art?" permitted her to explore a variety of projects. She could, like an anthropologist, analyze the social purpose of graffiti; does it satisfy the same cultural needs as other works of public art? She could, like a legal scholar, analyze the legal status of graffiti; how is graffiti different from other forms of public art, especially those works of art that really tick people off? Abby could even look at the aesthetic qualities of graffiti to see if they match various definitions of art (e.g., a pleasing unity of expression). When she chose the latter project, she then committed herself to specific research methods. For instance, she had to take lots of photographs of graffiti so she could show the works' aesthetic qualities to her readers.

As Rico's and Abby's experiences suggest, the kind of research project you do will depend in part on the writing situation. Within academic communities, inquiries tend to get divided along disciplinary lines. Biologists, psychologists, literary scholars, historians, business scholars, and so on all approach community issues from their own perspectives, asking questions and practicing research methods that are unique to their fields. They then write up their results in specific formats and styles, publish in particular journals, and evaluate each other's work according to their own intellectual and ethical standards. Learning to write within a particular community empowers you to communicate effectively with its members.

At the same time, the aim of your higher education is not to adopt one way of thinking only, but to practice the variety of ways we can inquire and act. Learning some of the expectations of different academic disciplines can help you write more effectively in a variety of classes, recognize the strengths and limitations of different disciplinary perspectives, and approach issues from multiple perspectives. Even when you want to violate the expectations of a particular community for your own purposes, knowing why they have these expectations can help you anticipate your readers' responses.

In Chapter 4 you explored standards of civil or acceptable arguing. The following exercise asks you to explore the standards academic disciplines use to evaluate civil or acceptable ways to inquire and argue.

▒ EXERCISE 5.2 ▒ Inquiring and Arguing in Academic Communities

You might try this exercise individually, interviewing professors from two or three different disciplines to see how they would respond to your research topic. You might also try this exercise as a class, each member interviewing different professors on how they would respond to a common topic such as violence, children, or emotion. Use the following questions to guide your interviews:

1. Would scholars in your discipline address this topic? What kinds of questions would they ask?
2. What research methods do scholars use in your discipline? How would they research this topic?
3. How would the results of the scholars' research be presented? Who are the different audiences to whom they would write or speak?
4. What are the guidelines for arguing ethically in this discipline? Are some strategies, such as appealing to emotion, discouraged?

In class, have each person go to the board and write down the discipline and some specific answers they got to their questions. Then, as a class, look at the findings and discuss the similarities and differences. What conventions seem fairly standard across all academic disciplines?

Researching the conventions of different disciplines is wise for beginning writers because instructors will appeal to their field's conventions, or the standard ways of presenting writing, when evaluating your work. Consequently, if you want to succeed, you need to actively discover the conventions of each academic community for which you will write.

Planning the Research Project

In Chapter 3, you learned to think through your inquiries, visualizing as much as possible what you wanted to research, why it was important to you, what methods you wanted to use, what audiences you wanted to reach, and how long you had to inquire. In academic communities, this plan is often formalized into a proposal, a detailed account of a research project. Proposals are valuable because they force researchers to clarify what they are going to do and to test how feasible their methods are given the limits of resources, including money and time. As an apprentice researcher, you might simply think through your project by writing in your writer's notebook. As you read through the following suggestions and examples, consider what general truths are being shown about the research process.

Research the Writing Situation

First, researchers need to get some sense of the writing situation. As you discovered in the previous section, the kind of question you ask will push you toward a particular discipline, each with its own set of conventions. These conventions developed over time to help researchers succeed. For example, scientists often number the steps in their methodology to make each step easier to distinguish from the others. This convention helps the scientists to verify a researcher's results by replicating his or her experiment. Mastering conventions such as this one will make you a savvier participant in your academic community. In addition, your instructor may wish to set limits that will affect how you complete your project. For example, he or she might want one kind of research only, a certain number of sources in your bibliography, or a particular documentation style such as MLA. To be successful, you should also ask your instructor to explain what he or she will be looking for in the research papers. You might use the writing situation assessment questions listed in Chapter 2 to guide your inquiry.

When Jake and Robert planned their research project, they realized that the method they needed to use to create credible evidence—in this case, observation—did not fit with the lighthearted paper they wanted to write. Consequently, they had to come up with a hybrid—a serious research project described in a casual, conversational style. You can see another example of this hybrid approach in the essay "Tune Out," in Chapter 11. In both cases, the researchers first had to learn the conventions of these different writing situations so their efforts to go against them would not confuse or irritate their readers.

Set the Scope of Your Research

Second, researchers need to clarify what it is they want to research. In addition to writing and revising your research question, you should write out, in your writer's notebook, how you think this question will define the scope and ending point of your research. For example, after brainstorming on just one graffiti selection, Abby realized that she could not cover all the different aesthetic qualities of the graffiti in her neighborhood (it was too diverse), nor could she afford to take dozens of pictures. She decided right away to limit her selections to five. In addition, she decided to focus on one different aesthetic quality with each selection. Had she discussed all she wanted to with each selection, she figured she would never have finished. As Abby's example illustrates, you may need to set additional limits to your project, in addition to those already imposed by your discipline and your writing instructor. Writing out the scope and end of your project in your notebook can help you make these decisions before you get too involved in the research itself.

Clarify Your Purpose

The third step you should take in planning your research project is to remind yourself why you want to answer your research question. Writing about what you hope to learn and teach your readers can give you a clearer sense of your purpose. For example, Janette's purpose was to regain her sanity in light of her daughter's many tattoos and piercings. She sometimes lost that focus while researching, because she became fascinated with all the bizarre body mutilation rituals that humans practice. When she wrote her essay, however, she tried to show how normal such practices were in their respective societies. Emphasizing that normalcy not only kept her research paper focused, it helped her maintain perspective even when her daughter, a few days before the final draft was due, came home with a chain connecting her lips.

Define Your Methods

The fourth step you should take in planning your research project is to write out a more detailed narrative of your research methods. If you plan to do library research, prepare a bibliography of your sources. If you plan to do a survey, identify how many respondents you will need, where you will conduct the survey, and what specific questions you will ask. If you plan to conduct an experiment using people, consult your college's Institutional Review Board for the Protection of Human Participants. Whatever your research methods, take the time to think through how you will answer your research question and whether your methods are appropriate and practical. For example, when Mia did her initial search for literature explaining why people hold religious beliefs, she said she almost swallowed her tongue. There were way too many books and articles on her subject. She decided to focus primarily on what psychologists had written in the last ten years. This decision let her get through all the readings on time and discuss them in greater depth in her paper. Working out your research method in more detail can also help you anticipate any problems and propose alternative methods or sources of information.

Set Your Schedule

The last step is to work out a schedule for finishing your research. Your instructor will give you some of your deadlines, but you may need to set your own to ensure you are not underestimating how long your work will take. For example, Rico's experiment on the effects of salt water on plants would take six weeks to complete. It would take that long for his plants to germinate and grow. Having thought about it ahead of time, he was able to negotiate new due dates to turn in his work. Jake and Robert did not plan ahead. When the first draft of their research paper was due, they still had two more football games to attend. Consequently, they lost points on their final grades. If instructors are not willing to work with you on the schedule for your project, you may need to adjust your research question or methods. It is better to know this ahead of time, if only to save you anxiety during the research process.

Based on the above examples, we might make two points about planning the research process. First, the more detailed you can make your plan, the easier it will be to get started and to see potential problems. When Janette first narrated her research method, she did not go into detail. She said she planned to go to her local public library to get some books. She also planned to interview some of her daughter's friends who had gotten their bodies tattooed or pierced. When Janette implemented her plan, however, she discovered that her public library did not carry books on the body mutilation rituals of other cultures. Janette might have saved herself the trip had she thought more carefully about what resources would most help her project. Eventually, she browsed a university library catalog from her home computer, prepared a bibliography of possible sources, and then went to the library, saving herself time and grief by going into more details on her research plan.

Another point we might make about planning the research process is that these plans are often educated guesses as to what sources and methods will be most useful. You need to remain flexible, always considering alternative methods you might use or alternative sources you might turn to get the information you need. When Janette asked her daughter's friends why they had gotten tattoos, they did not reply much beyond, "Because they're cool," "Seemed like fun," or "Whatever." Janette decided to use books on the history of tattooing to explain why Americans get tattoos, instead of relying on her daughter's articulate friends. Whenever you do research, remember that things will go wrong—books you need will be checked out, people will not return your surveys, weather will prevent you from observing people's behaviors. This is why you need to plan and start researching early, so you can adjust your methods or select alternative ones when the unanticipated happens. Keep these two points in mind as you complete the following exercise.

▓ EXERCISE 5.3 ▓ Writing Up Your Research Plan

To set up your own research process and to test the advice given above, complete the following steps in your writer's notebook.

1. *Get some sense of the writing situation.* What parameters is your instructor setting for the research paper (e.g., particular methods, formats, page lengths, due dates)?
2. *Clarify what you want to research.* Can you narrow your research question or the scope of your essay to make it manageable within the limits of your writing situation?
3. *Explain why you want to pursue this research project.* What do you hope this information will do for you and for your community? How will those concerns shape the final research paper?
4. *Write a detailed narrative of your research methods.* How will you answer your research question? Why are you choosing some research methods over others?
5. *Work out a schedule for completing the project.* Can you complete your project within the due dates set by your instructor? What problems do you anticipate possibly having, and how will you address them?

After you have completed planning your research project, share your plans with other members in the class. Try to raise concerns with the clarity, appropriateness, or practicality of each other's projects.

Understanding the Conversation on Your Subject

You have many different research methods available to you, from analyzing written texts to observing human behavior. These methods will create different research experiences. For example, with some methods, you will actually craft your research paper as you conduct the research. Once Abby had photographed samples of local graffiti, she began analyzing them, testing the samples' qualities against various definitions of art. She was able to work these analyses directly into her essay, refining her insights as she revised her drafts. Other research methods, however, may require you to complete all the research before writing the paper. Rico was able to write up the methodology section in his scientific research report while planning his project, but he could not write up the results or discussion sections until he had collected all of his data.

Most research projects also require that you acknowledge and participate in the conversations already begun around your subject. You have been learning how to do this in the previous chapters. In Chapter 2, you learned how to read works critically, conversing with writers by underlining, annotating, and commenting on their ideas. In Chapter 3, you learned to research ethically, taking careful note of where you found information. Then, in Chapter 4, you learned to summarize and analyze arguments, seeking to understand the writers' underlying values and beliefs. The next step is to use writing to clarify your views *as they emerge from your conversation with other writers*. When we read the works of other writers, our ideas about our topic change. Our ideas might be challenged, strengthened, qualified, or even reversed. We can use writing to preserve a record of those changes. We can also use writing to help us think through those changes, clarifying what other writers tell us and how their ideas relate to our research question, to our own views, and to the views of other participants in the conversation.

▓ EXERCISE 5.4 ▓   Telling the Story of Your Research

We learned in Chapter 1 that good narratives focus events around a main idea or dominant impression. We can apply this idea to our research by writing a story of our progress in answering our research question. As you read each of your books, articles, Web sites, and so on, answer the following questions in your writer's notebook:

1. What are the main ideas in this work?
2. How does this work help you answer your research question?
3. How do this work's ideas relate to your own at this point?
4. How do this work's ideas relate to those of other works you have read?

As you answer these questions with each source, you will begin to create a narrative of your thinking on this topic. Patterns will emerge of the conversation as you see it. Some writers will agree or disagree; some of their points will match or contradict one another. When you start to get a sense of the conversation, you might create a Mind Map of it, starting with your tentative thesis in the middle and drawing in the ideas of other writers around it. Depending on where you locate those writers you can show, visually, who agrees or disagrees with you, who qualifies your arguments, and who argues points unconnected with your thesis. The goal here is to clarify for yourself how your argument fits into the ongoing conversation.

As you work on this exercise, remember to assume the role of a skeptic. In Chapter 4, you learned that skeptics test the truth of their ideas against evidence and the ideas of other researchers. Often we form research questions with some idea of what we already believe. As you research, try to find evidence and ideas that challenge your tentative thesis. If your views on your topic change as a result of the research process, remember that changing our views is part of living an examined life.

Writing the Research Paper

In Exercises 5.1 and 5.2 you compared the formats researchers in different academic fields use to report the results of their research. Some disciplines use pre-established formats to report their results while others use a thesis-driven format, letting the writer's thesis direct the shape of the essay. When you commit to the research conventions of a particular field, you also commit, to some extent, to the field's writing conventions. These conventions assist researchers in working through their methods and sharing their results with others in their field. In other words, you should think of writing a research paper as a continuation of your research; you are putting your arguments into a community in order to stimulate further discussion. Trying to follow the conventions of your readers' community will encourage them to take your work more seriously, even though, as an apprentice, you are still learning what those conventions are.

For example, Rico learned that researchers in biology follow a pre-established format. Their essays usually begin with an abstract (a short summary of the project and results) and a clear, detailed title. Then, the researcher's question and his or her tentative thesis (called a hypothesis) are introduced, the method of the experiment is described in painstaking detail, and the experiment's results, the raw data, are presented, often in a table or graph format. Finally, the importance of the results is discussed and the initial hypothesis confirmed, denied, or modified. The writing itself tends to be simple, clear, and direct. Although Rico thought these conventions made his paper sound boring and overly formal, he recognized that readers of his work would not be interested in the pleasure of the reading experience, but in the knowledge he created through his experiment. To access that knowledge, they needed everything in the essay to be clear, straightforward, and highly organized.

Rick, on the other hand, let his thesis direct the shape of his essay. Because he was exploring three different engineering fields, he created three different sections, each one covering a different field. Within each field he further divided the essay into sections addressing how that field would appeal to people's interests, lifestyle, and career goals. At the same time, he realized that he needed to energize his essay if he wanted people to get excited about engineering. So, he shaped the sections on interests, lifestyle, and career goals into small stories, drawing on the qualitative evidence he had gathered from his interviews. His goal was to help readers see for themselves what it would mean to live the life of a mechanical, electrical or chemical engineer.

Rico's and Rick's experiences should remind us of two points made in earlier chapters. First, we can make the writing process easier if we try to envision the essay as a whole. For Rico, this was easy; the format was already set, but for Rick, imagining three separate sections, each covering the same three types of information, made his twelve-page research paper easier to write. He could work on specific parts while seeing how all those parts fit together.

Second, we should always keep our audience in mind as we write. If our purpose is to win our audience's agreement, we might be tempted to hold back evidence contrary to our thesis or to use appeals that violate the ethical standards of academic communities. Of course, trying to win agreement may or may not promote further inquiry. If we seek to promote inquiry, however, we should use all our relevant evidence and reasoning to assist readers in seeing for themselves the truth of our conclusions.

▓ EXERCISE 5.5 ▓ Asking Questions to Revise

As you learned in Chapter 2, writers must look inward and outward when revising. They look inward to clarify their ideas, and they look outward to ensure they are communicating those ideas effectively. Ernest Hemingway once said, "The most essential gift for a good writer is a built-in shock-proof shit-detector." Consider these questions your own detectors for writing a research paper. Ask them continuously as you read your drafts out loud.

1. Have you tried to express your own honest views throughout? Are there any places where you felt false, writing only what you thought others wanted to hear?
2. Have you clarified your arguments by defining your terms, explaining complex ideas, and providing plenty of examples?
3. Do you provide enough evidence for your readers to see the truth of your claims for themselves?
4. Have you reasoned carefully and ethically? Are there any places where you have fudged your thinking?
5. Does your essay seek to foster community? Does it engage readers as companions in your search for knowledge and wisdom?

Detecting those moments when your writing slips from clarity, from rigor or from grace will help you revise your research paper into a more effective instrument for promoting inquiry and community with your readers. At the same time, you should remember the community of other writers you conversed with during the research process. They too should be acknowledged in the research paper.

Citing and Documenting Sources

In *Beyond the Writers' Workshop*, Carol Bly writes, "Civilization is partly about noticing and appreciating what other people are doing" (111). To encourage the kind of ethical inquiry central to strong academic communities, we need to notice and appreciate the work of other researchers, acknowledging it when we present our own. We can do this by citing their ideas in our writing. For example, in the previous statement, Bly taught us, the authors, to see documenting in a fresh way, as a civic duty. We wished to acknowledge her contribution by mentioning, or citing, her work in our text. This activity of citing and documenting sources not only promotes community in academia, it helps define it. Research papers are one of the primary ways scholars learn about one another and about their work.

Citing and documenting our sources also moves the work in our respective disciplines forward. First, it encourages more rigorous inquiry. Other readers can locate and check our sources, seeing if we have represented other people's ideas accurately and ethically. As an apprentice researcher, you should cite and document your sources so your instructor can verify that you are indeed mastering the skills of research. Second, citing and documenting sources encourages further inquiry by offering additional research opportunities. Someone reading your research paper might be inspired by an idea you borrowed from another source. Knowing the source you borrowed from would help the reader begin a new research project or develop a broader understanding of your topic.

Citing and documenting sources is useful and ethical, but not all the information we get from them needs to be acknowledged. Facts such as the boiling point of water, the circumference of the Earth, or the founder of Amway do not need to be cited or documented if readers consider them "common knowledge." Common knowledge refers to those facts or bits of information that most people know simply by living as members of a particular community. Even when you have to look up common knowledge, such as who the eighteenth president of the United States was, you do not necessarily have to cite and document it. Had Bly told us simply to cite and document sources that contribute to our thinking, we probably would not have cited her work because the idea is common knowledge to anyone who teaches writing.

If Bly's advice had been new to you, however, would you have needed to acknowledge it? Knowing when to cite and document other people's ideas is not easy, especially when you are an apprentice researcher for whom most of the information you gather is brand new. The Modern Language Association's *Handbook for Writers of Research Papers* gives this advice: "You must indicate the sources of any appropriated material that readers might otherwise mistake for your own." If you are still in doubt, go ahead and cite it; instructors probably will not penalize you just for being conscientious. Another way to decide whether to cite and document a source is if you *want* readers to know the source of particular ideas. Here are a few situations when citing and documenting a source is appropriate:

- If you want to strengthen the persuasiveness of your claims by showing that other professional researchers agree with you.
- If you want readers to verify your research or to consult your sources on their own.
- If you want to identify the other researchers with whom you have been conversing throughout the research process.

One of your strongest contributions as a writer will be telling your audience *how to read* the sources, and how to understand the larger conversation of which they are a part. Remember that your readers have not necessarily read everything that you have, and no one understands the situation in quite the way that you do. Thus, instead of simply inserting a direct quotation from your source to support one of your claims, provide context for the quotation and explain what it means to your overall argument. Put yourself into conversation with the various voices and opinions from your source materials so that you can move beyond simply agreeing or disagreeing with a source, or citing a source as authority.

Using Other Writers' Words and Ideas

We can incorporate other people's words and ideas in two ways, by directly quoting from their works or by paraphrasing, expressing their ideas in our own words. Generally speaking, it is better to paraphrase, because, while we still acknowledge the work of the source, we preserve the flow of our writing by maintaining our own voice. Paraphrasing is also preferable because, in using our own language, we show readers that we understand the other writer's ideas. In some situations, however, direct quotations are preferable, especially when:

- The original writer's words are especially precise, colorful, or eloquently phrased.
- The exact words are needed to convey the writer's meaning, specific tone, or context for the discussion.
- It would be particularly persuasive to hear the voice of a recognized authority or someone who has experience on the subject.

Make sure to put quotation marks around the author's or speaker's words to distinguish them from your own words, and to cite your source according to the conventions of your writing community, whether parenthetically or in footnotes or endnotes.

When you paraphrase, you put the content of what you have read into your own words, while keeping the sense of the original. If you use any of the original words or phrases, put quotation marks around them. Remember that you will still need to cite your source and document it in your bibliography, even if you never quote directly from it.

It takes a lot of work to incorporate other people's words and ideas smoothly and accurately into your own. It is one of the biggest reasons research papers generally take longer to compose than other essays. However, it will make your thinking and, in the end, your paper, far more sophisticated than if you simply drop in direct quotations here and there.

Incorporating Sources

You want to guide your readers through your argument, and you are responsible for helping them understand the sources in the context of the larger conversation on the topic. Therefore, introduce all your sources, whether you use them in the form of a direct quotation, paraphrase, or summary.

Take, for example, this passage from Margaret Talbot's "A Mighty Fortress":

> In their 1999 book, *Blinded by Might*, Cal Thomas, a conservative columnist, and Ed Dobson, a Baptist minister, offered a similar analysis, arguing that "religious conservatives have heard sermons that man's ways are not God's ways . . . . In politics they have fused the two, causing damage to both church and state."

Note how Talbot helps her readers understand how to read this source by:

- Introducing the source by title (in this case, a book) and authors.
- Providing brief introductions to the authors' views and positions.
- Helping readers interpret the comments in conversation with her own thoughts and those of other sources.

She does this by:

- Weaving their words into her own sentence.
- Providing a transition from a point she'd made previously from another source ("offered a similar analysis").
- Revealing the tone of the original statement ("arguing" suggest a neutral, professional tone).
- Providing ellipses to show where she has cut out some words to make the quotation briefer and clearer. We use ellipses, three spaced periods (. . .), leaving a space before the first period and after the third period, to indicate words cut from the middle of a sentence. Talbot uses four spaced periods, which indicates that she has eliminated words between the first and second sentences.

(Note: Talbot is writing for a popular magazine that does not require that she provide a bibliography or cite sources parenthetically or in footnotes. In most academic situations you will be required to provide page numbers and other information in the body of your paper or in footnotes, and again on a formal bibliography or Works Cited page.)

Bibliographies and Documentation

Research papers in academia include bibliographies, called Works Cited pages in MLA style and References pages in APA style. Each source in your paper must appear on that final bibliography, and the entry must be complete and accurate. Likewise, the page numbers you give in the text of your paper must match the page numbers on which the material will be found when readers follow your lead and look up these sources for themselves. It is a time-consuming process that demands careful attention, but it is crucial.

For every direct quotation, and for every piece of evidence that you provide in paraphrase or summary, provide the source in the body of your paper and again in your bibliography. Different professional fields have different conventions for citing and documenting sources. Here we will discuss two of the most common: those developed by the Modern Language Association (MLA) and the American Psychological Association (APA). More detailed information and guidance can be found in the writers' manuals published by each organization, as well as at their Web sites, www.mla.org and www.apa.org.

MLA documentation is used in many humanities fields, including English literature, other modern languages, and rhetoric and composition. It is the convention you will probably be asked to follow for your composition courses. It has two main steps. The first is citing the author's name or source's title and page number parenthetically within the body of the paper. The second step is providing full bibliographic information for each source that appears in the text on a Works Cited list at the end of the paper.

Incorporating authors and titles into the body of your sentences is a good practice as it keeps the parenthetical notes short and unobtrusive. Sometimes a parenthetical note would be cumbersome, for instance, when you want to refer to an interview or survey, or the source is an organization rather than a person, or the source is a Web site or a document with a long title. Whenever it would be smoother to mention the source in the body of your essay, do so. The point of the notes is to quickly and accurately identify sources so that readers can find them readily on the Works Cited page and then track them down for future use. The Works Cited page is a separate page, included at the end of your paper, on which you list all the sources you have cited in a parenthetical note in your paper, whether you quoted, paraphrased, or summarized. Unlike some bibliographies, when using MLA documentation you do not list sources you read and gathered general knowledge from but do not actually cite in the paper. (Holly Van De Venter's essay, printed following, uses MLA documentation style.)

In many of the social sciences (including political science, psychology, sociology, anthropology, and education) you will be asked to use APA conventions in citing and documenting your research papers. APA style has two main steps: citing sources by author's name, publication date, and page number parenthetically within the body of the paper, and then providing full bibliographic information for each source that appears in the text on a References page at the end of the paper. Authors' first names are not given, only their initials. ("Why We Blog" by Bonnie Nardi, et al., in Chapter 11, is written using APA conventions.)

Writers often struggle with balancing their own and others' words. For example, we too often either report on others' works by stringing together a lot of quotations with just a topic sentence here and there of our own argument holding the quotations together; or by writing our own essay and simply dropping in a quotation occasionally to back up a claim. There is no magic proportion or number of citations or sources, and how many you use will vary from project to project, but do consider at what points you need more support or others' words, and at what points you need to step forward and lead in the argument.

Research Process in Action: One Student's Story

Here we present Holly Van De Venter's research paper for her first-year composition course at the University of Minnesota. Her marginal comments give us insight into how she decided upon her topic, how she chose her sources, and how she developed her argument.

Van De Venter 1

Choosing a topic:
When deciding upon a topic, I thought about my life and what I would like to change, improve upon, or complete in the future. Then, I came up with reasons why these topics were important to me. To narrow down the topics, I decided on a choice that not only I cared about, but a topic that others could relate to, and perhaps take action on.

Holly Van De Venter

EngC 1014

Dr. Muse

November 16, 2000

Educating the New America

As a nation made up of immigrants, the United States has always been a melting pot of people, languages, ideas, and customs. As we reflect on our country at the close of the year 2000, we must ask ourselves if we are providing a welcoming environment and if we represent and respect the changing face of American society today. Our country is no longer a white, middle-class population; we are a diverse nation and in states such as California, there is no longer a majority ethnic group. Instead of celebrating and exploring the different ways of life, many people are closing their doors, locking the windows, and shutting the curtains on the new society, the real America.

I believe that one way to foster a new generation, open and accepting to all ways of life, is to teach a foreign language in the primary grades. These children will gain people skills, learn about a different culture, and be more accepting to change. We will give our children not only a

Van De Venter 2

new perspective on the world, but a skill for life: the ability to communicate with others. As the world becomes more global, our students will have a better chance to succeed in the job market, and American diplomats will better understand the people they are trying to help. The benefits of a multilingual nation will be seen through early childhood development, a better understanding of America's demographic makeup, and more success in the global world.

> The thesis was the hardest part because I wanted it to accomplish something.

As a democratic society, we should give everyone an equal chance to succeed. Many studies have been done that show the benefits on brain development when children are challenged to learn two languages concurrently. Studies published in the Bilingual Educational Series: 5 conclude that bilingual students showed a higher level of intelligence than monolingual students. Specifically, in the Pearl and Lambert study of 1962, it proved that with the bilingual child "wider experiences in two cultures have given him advantages . . . . It has left him with a greater mental flexibility, a superiority in concept formation, and a more diversified set of mental abilities" (Ramirez et al. 38). Because the language centers of the brain are still forming in children, learning a second language concurrently with English stimulates thinking from a new angle.

> **Searching for information:**
> I first looked on Internet search engines such as infoseek.com and yahoo.com with numerous sets of keywords, using different combinations of related search topics. This was used as general background, to help me become more familiar with the topic. I also checked out popular news Web sites, such as CNN.com and abcnews.com to see if there had been any recent reporting on my topic.

While the positive effects on the brain are well documented, we cannot overlook the many positive psychological effects on the mind that one can gain also. As our nation becomes more diverse, it will be necessary to understand the different cultures, so we are able to work together without conflict. It is almost impossible to work

Van De Venter 3

together if you don't understand where other points of view are coming from. As found on the Center for Multilingual and Multicultural Research web page, Sabine Ulibarri said:

> In the beginning was the Word. And the
> Word was made flesh. It was so in the beginning
> and it is so today. The language, the Word, carries
> within it the history, the culture, the traditions,
> the very life of a people, the flesh. We cannot even
> conceive of a people without a language, or a
> language without a people. The two are one and
> the same. To know one is to know the other.

We must remember that how one person views his past, largely determines how he views his future. Today, many children do not have any knowledge of their family tree, and are taught even less about their country's history. Implementing foreign language programs would help the students gain insight about the struggles and victories their ancestors had. A Spanish language curriculum would not only include learning the words and sentence structure, but also include lessons about the history, holiday festivals, music, and traditional foods in the Spanish culture. For a Spanish immigrant in that class, he would learn of his heritage and be given a firm foundation for growth and success. His self-confidence would rise because he would be proud of his past, and would look to achieve more in the future. The students who were born in the United States or who do not have any exposure to another culture, would benefit by realizing that there are many ways of life, and that one way of doing something is not the only way. As

My Struggles: Incorporating all the sources I wanted to use was at times difficult. I had several points I wanted to stick to, but had other information that I thought was useful and interesting that didn't really pertain to the thesis. You have to narrow down and decide what you will include and what you won't.

Van De Venter 4

stated in the <u>Memphis Business Journal</u>, Barbara Williams, an elementary foreign language teacher at Christ the King Lutheran School in Memphis says, "We have a Spanish festival to increase awareness of the many Spanish cultures. We want them to know that tacos are not Spanish food but Mexican food, and that all Spanish-speaking people are not Mexican" (qtd. in Greer 27).

The main reason we must change people's way of thinking is evident in the following graph. America's demographic makeup will change dramatically in the next fifty years. How we educate now will determine how our nation will grow in the future. This mix of people will allow us to offer a rich, multicultural, melting-pot experience to the young generation, but we must accept the challenge of educating in a new era.

Choosing sources: When looking at general Web sites, I was skeptical of the information when it didn't contain an author's name or publication information. Because my essay was on education, I trusted resources such as ERIC (Educational Resources Information Center) and the NCBE (National Clearinghouse for Bilingual Education), both of which have been funded in part by grants from the Department of Education. I also found articles in reliable magazines, and when choosing books, I looked at the author's credentials.

Table 5.1

U.S. Population by Ethnicity (in percents)

	2000	2050
White, non-Hispanic	71.5%	52.8%
Hispanic	11.7%	24.3%
Black/African American	12.2%	13.2%
Asian & Pacific Islander	3.8%	8.9%
American Indian, Eskimo, Aleut	0.7%	0.8%

Source: Lundholm-Leary, Kathryn. <u>Biliteracy for a Global Society: An Idea Book on Dual Language Education</u>. George Washington University. August 2000: 11.

Van De Venter 5

In this global job market, American companies are finding it hard to communicate and compete in this fast-paced world. We have been called elitists, isolationists, and tongue-tied because so many corporations do not have competent businesspeople who fluently speak foreign languages. As a result, it has reduced our competitiveness in the business world. Millions of dollars have been lost in business deals where the language has been interpreted wrong.

Because America is the world's democracy leader, giving support to those countries that strive for independence, we have often been in the position of negotiating peace treaties between two warring nations. America could gain the respect of the two parties involved first-hand by showing the ability to work together through face-to-face negotiations instead of through interpreters. With knowledge of the history and culture of a nation, the diplomats would be more understanding and able to see both sides of the argument. Knowledge of the past would help us make better plans for the future.

I acknowledge the fact that adding foreign language programs can be costly. One main reason the American educational system does not place learning a foreign language high on its priorities list, is because many schools feel that the money would be better spent elsewhere. With technology becoming more and more important, many districts have focused their budget on computer upgrades and new software programs. However, some schools across

Van De Venter 6

the nation are implementing these programs on their own. Paul Nikol co-founded the "Foreign Languages in the Community" program because he and others realized that U.S. students are woefully behind in foreign language competency. "We are the only modern industrial nation that doesn't place importance on learning foreign languages and learning them in the primary grades. Here we're isolationists, in a sense, and we're not preparing our kids for the millennium" ("Two Languages 17"). Nine years ago, Nikol teamed with two other teachers to develop a program to educate students in the Spanish language. The school district did give administrative approval, but couldn't afford to hire new teachers. So Nikol turned to high school students to teach classes. Not only do they get to practice and become more proficient in the language, but they get to learn teaching skills and possibly find a career path. Because of many volunteers, the students are reaping the benefits of this program, and it's basically costing the school system nothing.

Transitions, I learned, are necessary and a must to have a paper that smoothly moves from one idea to another. You can't just jump from one idea to the next, or your reader will wonder what happened.

Another argument against teaching multiple languages in the primary grades is that it would lead to segregation between the different minorities, and that students would fall behind in their English language learning. By including all races in language classes, the children are able to interact with each other and learn from their peers. This kind of learning is beneficial because they

Van De Venter 7

are able to understand the benefits of working together. As
proved in numerous studies, the fear of losing English
proficiency is an unfounded claim. The vocabulary of the
English language is actually expanded with exposure to
another language.

While walking through campus at the University of
Minnesota, I hear many different languages spoken around
me. I am amazed at the diverse background and knowledge
these students have. I was shocked at how different the
world is because I really had no background or history on
any other cultures. Sure, I could take a language class to
learn about another way of life, but I would only be playing
catch-up. Instead of always lagging behind, struggling to
become equal, let's instruct our children in a way so that
they are given a head start in the world.

Our society cannot keep educating our children as
though they live in a white, solely English-speaking country.
It is time we open our eyes to the changing face of America.
Instead of hiding from our shortcomings, let's realize that
we can take suggestions for improvements from others. We
must remember that we have much to offer the world, but
there is much we can learn from the world also. Instead of
giving our children limitations, let's give them opportunities
to branch out and explore new ideas, encourage them in
different ways of thinking, and support the many different
cultures that make America what it is today.

My writer's handbook
was a lifesaver. It
helped me on docu-
mentation, word
usage, and ideas on
how to successfully
end my paper.

Van De Venter 8

Works Cited

Center for Multilingual Multicultural Research. University
of Southern California. 7 Nov. 2000. <http://www-
bcf.usc.edu/~cmmr/BEResources.html>.

Greer, Jason. "Foreign languages increasingly added to
elementary schools." *Memphis Business Journal.* 21
Jan. 2000: 27.

Lundholm-Leary, Kathryn. *Biliteracy for a Global Society:
An Idea Book on Dual Language Education.* George
Washington University. Aug. 2000: 11. 20 Nov. 2000.
<http://www.ncbe.gwu.edu/ncbepubs/ideabook/dual/
biliteracy.pdf>.

Ramirez, Manuel, et al. *Bilingual Education Series: 5.*
Center for Applied Linguistics: 38.

"Two Languages Come Early." *NEA Today.* May 1999: 17.

SECOND INQUIRY: WRITING IN CIVIC COMMUNITIES

This next part of the chapter provides you with ways to take your researched argument public. There, you can learn some of the more common genres of public debate, including letters to the editor, pamphlets, and Web pages. You will probably discover that many of the conventions of classroom writing will have to be modified to meet the requirements of these new genres. However, the deeper understanding and more effective arguments you create by writing a researched argument paper will make your other types of writing much more effective.

In Chapter 3 you learned that inquiry can be a form of social action, yet citizens do not necessarily stop at researching the issues, nor do students necessarily stop with writing academic research papers. Consider the following examples from history; they represent only a few of the countless times people have acted on their understanding of a particular issue:

- On December 1, 1955, Rosa Parks refused to give up her seat to a white man on a Montgomery, Alabama bus. She challenged the segregation order in court but lost, so she and others organized a boycott of Montgomery buses that lasted 382 days. Their actions led eventually to the U.S. Supreme Court decision to outlaw segregation on city buses.

- On February 27, 1973, American Indian Movement activists and local Oglala Lakota people occupied a trading post and Catholic church in Wounded Knee, South Dakota. Hoping to attract media attention and voice their grievances, they were instead surrounded by federal agents. The two groups exchanged gunfire during the seventy-one–day standoff.

- On October 25, 1997, fourteen-year-old Adam Chestnut of Toronto, Ohio, participated in the annual Make a Difference Day by collecting used clothing from the people on his paper route. He collected fifty bags of clothing and received an award of $2000, given on his behalf to a Goodwill Industries Rehabilitation Center.

- On April 5, 1999, members of the Animal Liberation Front broke into two University of Minnesota buildings, setting more than one hundred research animals free and damaging around three million dollars in computers and research equipment. They claimed that these animals were being abused; representatives for the university said the loss of the animals would seriously impede research on Alzheimer's and Parkinson's diseases.

- On November 30, 1999, approximately 50,000 people from around the world convened in Seattle, Washington, to disrupt a meeting of the World Trade Organization (WTO). Many of the protesters were college students; they joined labor union members, environmentalists, and supporters of Third World development in protesting the WTO's record of human rights, environmental protection, and fair trade practices. Most of the protests were peaceful, but isolated skirmishes resulted in hundreds of arrests and injuries. The actions in Seattle prepared the way for protests in New York City, Philadelphia, Calgary, Quebec, Los Angeles, and Minneapolis.

The above examples represent a wide range of responses to social issues, from peaceful civil disobedience to violence. Are these acts equally appropriate responses? How would you evaluate the ethical correctness of these acts as they have been described? You may want to research some of these incidents further to get a fuller understanding of the surrounding circumstances before deciding. Is it ever ethical to break the laws or to commit acts of violence? Could you provide guidelines to help citizens decide when such actions are appropriate?

In truth, some of these examples involve complex ethical questions about the propriety of breaking the law and of using violence that should be discussed. The examples should also remind us that social action can bring positive and negative consequences; therefore, we should make ethical considerations part of our decision how to act.

Of course, ethics is already part of our decision to get involved in the first place. Whether we further research a community issue, write a letter to our Congressperson, or protest against some public policy, we are choosing to act by our own values and beliefs. We are making a moral decision. According to Ralph

Nader, an advocate for civic participation, college students are uniquely positioned to advocate democratic solutions to social problems. At the peak of their idealism, they have the energy and commitment to act on their values and beliefs.

Students also represent a powerful education community—16.5 million members in 2004—with access to libraries, expert faculty, laboratories, student organizations, and common places where they can meet and organize. To discover these resources for yourself, you might tour your own campus and identify resources available to students interested in public issues. You might also pick a particular issue that interests you and investigate opportunities for researching and advocating it further.

Student Participation in Public Debate

Within your own writing classroom, you have many opportunities to participate in public debate. As a form of social action, writing is particularly effective. Writers have time to craft their messages carefully, and they can reach a wide audience. Indeed, we usually learn what issues are significant and being discussed in public through the media, including text-based media forms such as newspapers, magazines, pamphlets, and posters. In fact, the media often form the conduit through which we exchange opinions and the place where these opinions meet. To see this, try conducting the following exercise.

EXERCISE 5.6 ▓ Noticing Conversations in the Public Sphere

Follow local and national events in a newspaper for one week. Then answer the following questions:

1. What events were covered during the week? Which ones received priority in terms of their placement within the paper and the depth and extent of the journalists' coverage? Why do you suppose those particular stories received greater coverage?

2. What are the different types of articles written in the newspaper? Can you group these types into categories depending on who writes them, where they are located in the paper, and how they are written?

3. How do these different types of articles shape our awareness of public issues? To get a different perspective, you might watch television news for the same week. Do these programs cover the same events? How is the coverage similar or different? What do newspapers offer that television news does not?

Newspaper editorials, Web sites, and pamphlets are common forms of public writing, yet they probably differ from the essays you have written in the classroom, especially the academic research paper. Professional researchers do publish their research in academic journals, as you discovered earlier in this chapter, and they follow many of the same conventions you do in your own research papers. They must investigate what subjects people want to read about, conduct research appropriate to their fields, and follow a writing process involving peer review. Nevertheless, the work of professional researchers is typically grander in scope and more rigorous in research methods because these professionals have more training, time, and resources.

To prepare his article "Jihad vs. McWorld" for publication in *The Atlantic* magazine, Benjamin Barber put in years of research. He had also selected a topic that people wanted to learn more about. After his article was published, it was widely discussed and increased Barber's fame as a scholar. He used this opportunity to further encourage global awareness by expanding his article into a book, also titled *Jihad vs. McWorld.*

As an apprentice in a writing community, you probably do not have the same degree of access to academic journals or to mainstream media sources. At the same time, you may feel the need to share your values and beliefs with an audience wider than your classroom. A number of opportunities exist for public writing by students. For instance, Holly Van De Venter reworked the results of her research into a letter to the president of the North Dakota Education Association.

Holly Van De Venter

394 Territorial Hall

417 Walnut St. SE

Minneapolis, MN 55455

December 14, 2000

Max Laird

NDEA

PO Box 5055

Bismarck, ND 58502

Dear Max Laird:

I am writing as a North Dakota high school graduate, concerned about the future of education and the economic well-being of our state. I propose that the State of North Dakota require schools to teach a foreign language in the primary grades. The foreign language curriculum should not only teach verb usage and sentence structure, but also include lessons about the history and traditional celebrations.

The biggest benefit in implementing a foreign language program would be the positive change in our society. America's demographic make-up is becoming more diverse every day. We need to expose our children to different ways of life, teach them about different cultures, and help them realize that the United States is no longer a solely English-speaking country. North Dakota has seen an increase in its immigrant population, and teaching young children about their culture would lead to a higher respect for and understanding of each culture's uniqueness.

It is clearly evident that the business world has changed dramatically in the last two decades. This global marketplace requires that we be able to communicate with all countries efficiently to fully realize all the gains from trade. As you can see, teaching foreign languages would not only give our students better communication and people skills, but a head start for any career. These real-world skills would give our graduates a better chance to succeed.

I am fully aware of North Dakota's declining population. One way to attract newcomers to the state and convince people to stay is with a strong education system. Parents want their children to have a strong academic background so they will be prepared for the challenges ahead. This would be a great new opportunity for our children, giving them insight into the changing face of America.

5   I urge you to consider and discuss implementing foreign language programs with your colleagues, and to make it a priority in your upcoming meetings. I ask that the NDEA lobby school administrators and teachers for support, and take a proposal to the ND State Legislature to get funding for elementary foreign language programs. I would appreciate a response and any ideas that you may have on this subject. This call for action comes only with the concern of the students in mind, and the belief that we need to promote our state's educational excellence and build upon it with new programs for the future.

Sincerely,

Holly Van De Venter

If you compare Van De Venter's earlier academic research paper with this letter, you can see that she needed to rewrite her research results to meet the conventions of this form of public writing. To write for the public, you too will need to learn the conventions of public writing, just as you learned the conventions of writing in your classroom. These conventions may develop as a result of the genres' publishing constraints. For example, newspaper stories usually have short paragraphs because the stories are printed in narrow columns on the newspaper page. Long paragraphs would make the columns look too dense and unreadable. Sometimes these conventions develop to help writers better reach their audience. Pamphlets, for instance, are usually brief, visually appealing, and well organized. This format allows people to read the pamphlet quickly.

At the same time, you should also exercise your imagination. In delivering your message, you should strive for clarity, but you can sharpen your work's persuasiveness by using the argumentative strategies outlined in Chapter 4. For example, Van De Venter ends her letter to Max Laird by affirming their common goal of improving education in North Dakota. This strategy sets a tone of cooperation instead of criticism. You can also exercise your imagination by finding new sources and strategies for getting out your message. The growing importance of the Internet, for instance, has new created writing opportunities. You could share your view in a chat room dedicated to your issue, you could e-mail fellow citizens, or you could create your own blog or Web site, linking your arguments with other sites that share your views. In the next section, we will examine several genres of public writing and how readers can decide which genre will be most effective.

The Genres of Public Debate

As with any writing project, our first task is to analyze the writing situation. Public writing, however, is more sensitive than classroom writing to the effects of time and place. For example, a poster might fail to reach its audience if a city ordinance forbids displaying posters in public or if the issue being presented is no longer being discussed by the public. To decide if the genres of public debate are appropriate for expressing your message, and to decide which genre will be most effective, answer the following questions. Then, as you read through brief descriptions of the public writing genres, select those genres which best match your answers to the questions.

- Is this issue or event new to the public?
- Is this issue currently being discussed by the public?
- Where would people interested in this issue, and capable of putting your ideas into action, be likely to encounter your message?
- Because you may need to narrow the scope of your research, what aspects of the subject will most interest and move the public?

- Which argumentative strategies would persuade your audience most effectively?
- What ethical concerns do you have in communicating your message to the public?

News Articles

News articles appear in newspapers, magazines, and news-oriented Web sites. They inform the public about current events and issues that affect the community. They are written primarily by professional journalists, so you may need to try local or college newspapers or organization newsletters to get your articles published. You may even want to create a print or online newsletter of your own.

News articles are a good choice for public writing if:

- You want to inform the public of an issue or event that has not received enough attention. News articles provide valuable information by answering the journalist's basic questions: who, what, where, when, why, and how.
- The issue or event you want to cover represents a current concern for the community.
- You want to reach a wider audience, especially if that audience reads the paper or magazine in which you want to publish the article.

News articles are not the best choice, however, if:

- You want to advocate a particular viewpoint or action. News articles try to remain objective, reporting only on the issues or events themselves and not on what the community ought to do about them.
- You want to analyze your event or issue in depth. While some news articles do go into great depth on a given subject, most cover only the basic information, aiming at those readers who read the articles while commuting, eating, or waiting for a bus.
- The readers of the publication are not in a position to address the issue you raise.

You can find an example of a news article in Chapter 11's case study on blogging; there you will find Lev Grossman's *Time* magazine article "Meet Joe Blog" and a Writing Style box on how to write news articles yourself.

Editorials and Opinion Pieces

Editorials and opinion pieces also appear in newspapers, magazines, blogs, and Web sites, and like news articles they contain detailed facts. Unlike news articles, however, the writers express strong opinions about the events or issues; their purpose is to stimulate public discussion or affect policy, practice, or people's views. The writers are usually professional journalists or editors, so you may need to try local, college, or organization newspapers, or try Web sites that encourage public opinion.

Editorials and opinion pieces are good choices for public writing if:

- You want to advocate a position or course of action on an issue being publicly debated, especially if news articles ran previously in the newspaper or magazine in which you want to publish the piece.
- You want to reach a wide audience, especially if that audience reads the paper or magazine in which you want to publish the article.

Editorials and opinion pieces are not the best choices, however, if:

- You want to avoid controversy. Editorials and opinion pieces express strong views in order to stimulate public debate, not avoid it.
- The readers of the publication are not in a position to respond to your position or to follow your recommended actions.
- You want to advocate your position in depth. While some opinion pieces do go into great depth on a given subject, most run only several paragraphs, focusing on one or two significant points.

You can find examples of editorials and opinion pieces throughout the readings chapters. You will find advice on how to write them yourself in Chapter 8's case study on the "Jihad vs. McWorld" clash of civilizations; there you will find David Brooks' editorial "All Cultures Are Not Equal" from the *New York Times*.

Letters to the Editor

Like news articles and editorials, letters to the editor are common features of newspapers and magazines, but unlike the former genres, letters to the editor are written by readers, not professional journalists. Letters give readers the opportunity to express their views about current issues or about ideas expressed in previous news articles, editorials, or opinion pieces. The space allotted for letters to the editor is limited, however, so writers must compete with other citizens to get their letters accepted.

A letter to the editor is a good choice for public writing if:

- You want to advocate a position or course of action on an issue, or if you want continue a public debate begun by previous news articles, editorials, opinion pieces, or other letters.
- You want to reach a wide audience, especially if that audience reads the paper or magazine in which you want to publish the article.
- You do not have the time to craft a long opinion piece. Letters are usually 150 words or less so writers must get directly to their point.

Letters to the editor are not a good choice, however, if:

- You want to avoid controversy. Letters to the editor encourage others to respond because they express strong opinions.
- You do not address issues relevant to the publication's readers. If your letter does not address an issue currently being covered, the editor probably will not publish the piece.
- You want to advocate your position in depth. Letters that run more than 150 words may either be rejected or edited.

You can find examples of letters to the editor in the Chapter 8 case study; there you will find letters responding to Benjamin Barber's article "Jihad vs. McWorld" and advice on how to write your own letters to the editor.

Letters to Public Officials

Not all of the genres of public debate need to be published. Citizens concerned about a particular social issue can write directly to their representatives in government. While elections and public opinion polls give government representatives some sense of their constituents' opinions, direct letters are often very effective. Representatives recognize that citizens concerned enough to write will probably take the time to vote for or against them in the next election. Because letters to public officials seek to create a one-on-one relationship with the official, writers need to prepare more extensively for their letters to be effective.

A letter to a public official is a good choice for public writing if:

- You want to advocate a specific action or a perspective on an issue that may lead to future actions.
- Your issue can be positively affected by the individual office, governmental body, or political organization to which you write.
- Your opinion matters to the official because you are a constituent, a customer, or a supporter of their cause.

A letter to a public official is not the best choice, however, if:

- The issue is outside their jurisdiction.
- You want to reach a wider audience. Many public officials have their letters read by staff members who compile the information into summaries.
- You want to advocate your position in depth. Because public officials receive so many letters, your letter stands a better chance of being read if it is short and to the point.

Holly Van De Venter's letter in this chapter is an example of a letter to a public official that you can use as a guideline for writing your own letters.

The same conditions that help writers decide whether to write to public officials apply to writing to private individuals. Like government representatives, companies and organizations depend on patronage or public support; consequently, they usually take letters and other forms of public expression seriously.

Pamphlets and Posters

Like other genres, the conventions of pamphlets and posters have evolved to fill specific communication needs. Pamphlets are distributed to people passing on the street, or they are left in public places such as libraries, subways, or college student centers. Posters are placed on lamp posts, in hallways, even on the sidewalk—wherever people's eyes rest as they are traveling. To get these people to take a pamphlet or examine a poster, writers must grab their attention. Consequently, pamphlets and posters rely heavily on visual elements to enliven, clarify and argue their points.

Pamphlets and posters are good choices for public writing if:

- You want to reach a wide audience, especially if the event or issue is related to the location where you display the pamphlets and posters. For example, a pamphlet protesting animal research would be more effective in front of an animal research facility.
- Your issue is readily identifiable and your message is easily understood. Because people spend only minutes looking at a pamphlet or poster, they need to receive and understand your message quickly.
- You have visual elements to complement your argument. People will read your poster or pamphlet if their eyes are drawn to interesting or powerful graphics.
- They complement other forms of direct action such as boycotts, picketing, or rallies. They can then explain to observers why you are engaging in direct action.

Pamphlets and posters are not the best choices, however, if:

- You want to avoid controversy. People reading the posters or accepting the pamphlets may argue with you, tear down your posters, or ask you to leave the area.
- You do not address issues relevant to the people who read your posters or pamphlets. To reach people who can act on your recommendations, you may need to research where your audience would most likely see the writing.
- You want to advocate your position in depth. To hold your readers' attention, you need to deliver your message very quickly, often in less than a minute.
- The place where you want to present the pamphlets or posters does not permit the public display of private messages.

You can learn more about pamphlets in Chapter 6's Writing Style box on Creating a Pamphlet, which refers you to the Family Research Council's pamphlet *The Slippery Slope of Same-Sex Marriage* and gives you advice on making your own pamphlet. Chapter 7's case study on academic freedom includes two informational posters from NoIndoctrination.org and Students for Academic Freedom.

The Internet: Web Sites and Blogs

The Internet provides tremendous opportunities to communicate with people around the world. You can post documents, commentary, or links to an existing Web site or blog. You can also put out inquiries, share information, and form coalitions with other Web site or blog creators.

A Web site or blog is a good choice for public writing if:

- You want to reach a wide audience, even in a short amount of time. Unlike pamphlets or posters, however, readers must come to the site or blog to get your message. To get around this limitation, writers might use pamphlets or posters to introduce issues discussed in more depth on a Web site or blog.
- You want to alert people about an issue that other media forms have not covered.
- You want to encourage arguments as opportunities to better understand an issue. Blogs are often written as thinking laboratories where writers can present and get feedback on ideas that they then revise further.
- You want to advocate your position in depth. Web sites allow you to publish documents of considerable length, but to keep readers' attention you may need to make the work visually accessible, using bullet points, hypertext links, and pictures.
- You want to exercise your personality. Web sites and blogs invite edgy, unrestrained writing voices that would otherwise undermine a traditional journalist's reputation for objectivity.

Web sites and blogs are not the best choices, however, if:

- You cannot advertise the site to your audience. Simply posting a document on the Web or starting up a blog will not guarantee others will find it.
- You cannot write in HTML (hypertext markup language), the computer code that allows writers to create Web sites. Fortunately, programs such as Adobe PageMill and Microsoft FrontPage permit computer-programming novices to create their own Web pages. Additionally, several companies provide very user-friendly platforms for blogs that almost any citizen can learn.
- You do not have time to maintain your site or blog. Blog software can be particularly demanding, requiring weekly entries to keep the site's material from getting archived.

In Chapter 11's case study, you can find an example of a blog entry that gives advice on writing your own blogs.

The Internet: E-mail, Chat Rooms, and Electronic Mailing Lists

The Internet also encourages other forms of public writing, some of which are synchronous (chat rooms are often done in real time) or asynchronous (you usually have to wait to get a reply to an e-mail or to queries on an electronic mailing list, often called a listserv). These electronic forms can give you access to a wide audience, especially of readers who share an interest in the same subjects or issues. The personal nature of e-mails and chat rooms can also encourage people to respond more readily than Web sites.

E-mail, chat rooms, and electronic mailing lists are good choices for public writing if:

- You want to reach citizens from all over the world interested in discussing your issue.
- You want to encourage arguments as opportunities to better understand an issue. The diversity of perspectives can help you better understand your own values and beliefs.
- You want to alert people to an issue that other media forms have not covered, you want to draw information or advice from experts in a particular area, or you want to recruit others to effect social change.

Newsgroups, chat rooms, or listservs are not the best choices, however, if:

- You want to avoid controversy. There is a greater degree of anonymity when communicating online, so people who disagree with you may be less civil than if they talked with you face-to-face. Many electronic mailing lists have moderators, however, who can edit out spam and inappropriate responses.
- Your audience is not in a position to act on your suggestions. Unless the electronic forum has local participants, it is wiser not to present them with local community problems unless they could actually help.
- You want to advocate your position in depth. Participants in chat rooms and electronic mailing lists generally prefer messages no longer than a paragraph or two, especially if they receive many other messages and e-mails.
- Your issue is irrelevant or inappropriate for particular audiences. For example, many college-sponsored electronic mailing lists are created to facilitate research. Members may view calls to social action as spam no matter how just the cause.

Other electronic devices, such as text messaging, can be used to communicate with a wider public. Text messaging chain letters apparently contributed to the resignation of Joseph Estrada, former president of the Philippines. They also provided residents of New Orleans with a means of contacting loved ones during Hurricane Katrina.

Zines

Zines, short for fanzines, are low-budget, self-produced magazines on a variety of topics that allow writers and artists an outlet for their ideas away from the mainstream media. They are much more personal and idiosyncratic than commercial magazines are, and vary widely in terms of quality and quantity. They tend to be focused on one topic or area of interest, whether that is pinball, motherhood, skateboarding, peaceful alternatives to war, organic gardening, or underground music. You can find them photocopied and distributed around your campus or town, or posted on the Web, and they get known mainly by word of mouth. Some that started life as local zines, such as *Bust, Hip Mama,* and *Punk Planet,* have developed into larger-scale magazines with a national following. Although zines rarely speak to large audiences, they are one of the best ways for students to enter the public sphere of debate on topics of particular interest, because instead of having to convince someone else to publish your work, you can create and publish it on your own and distribute it where you want people to read it.

You can find a resource guide for creating and publishing your own zine, as well as recommendations for good zines, at *The Zine and E-zine Resource Guide* site: http://www.zinebook.com/.

▨ PROJECTS FOR INQUIRY AND ACTION ▨

1. Take a moment to reflect upon the research paper you developed. What excited you most about the project? What did you learn from doing it—both about the subject matter or issue you were exploring, and about the process of researching, developing the argument, and writing the paper?

2. If you had "world enough and time," what would you do with your research project? How could you publish the knowledge in it, whether as a research paper or in one of the genres of public debate?

3. How can you imagine yourself changing or in some way making a difference in the situation you are concerned about? What, realistically, would you have to do? How could you get others involved, too?

4. Envision launching a zine, whether by yourself or with a group of friends or classmates. What subject would you focus on? What is not being talked about enough? How would you present your zine—in paper, online, or both? Where and to whom would you initially distribute it, and why?

CHAPTER 6

The Family as Community

> The family is the natural and fundamental group unit of society and is
> entitled to protection by society and the State.
> —*United Nations' Universal Declaration of Human Rights*

> Families are the basic units of society and our most valuable resource.
> Healthy, well-functioning families provide members of all ages with
> rewarding, caring relationships, and with essential mutual support which
> is sustaining throughout the life course. Families are the major producers
> and consumers of goods and services. They make a central contribution
> to the nation's present and future workforce and enhance the quality of
> our society. Conversely, society has a critical effect on families.
> Therefore, it is essential that family policy makers recognize the
> reciprocal influences that families and society have upon each other.
> —*Policy Statement from the National Council on Family Relations*

▓ GETTING STARTED ▓ How Do We See the Family?

1. Write down all of your ideas related to the "traditional family." What images or sets of behaviors do you think are characteristic of families? How would you describe the typical American family? Is your image of a family similar to or different from the typical family? Why?

2. Now examine the families represented in the photographs on pages 211–212. In what ways do these families seem very traditional? In what ways do they differ from and challenge traditional media images of the American family?

3. As a follow-up exercise, collect images of families portrayed in the media, including everything from advertisements to TV shows. What are the consistencies and differences in these images?

O f the many communities to which we belong, the family is continuously identified as the most basic and formative influence on our lives. Yet these "basic units of society" have also been influenced by the same historical and cultural forces that have affected larger communities. We have worried about the breakdown of the traditional family, the evolution of new family structures, the decline of personal responsibility, or the effects of changing economic and social conditions.

Often we look back to earlier generations, imagining that families then were stronger, more stable, and happier than they are now. However, Stephanie Coontz explains in *The Way We Never Were: American Families and the Nostalgia Trap* that "like most visions of a 'golden age,' the 'traditional family'" usually described by people as an ideal "evaporates on closer examination. It is an ahistorical amalgam of structures, values, and behaviors that never co-existed in the same time and place." Extended families with grandparents at home (Grandpa and Grandma Walton) never co-existed with the nuclear family of children and stay-at-home mom (of *Leave it to Beaver* or *The Brady Bunch*).

Whether we celebrate or criticize the current state of American families, we tend to express the same expectations for what families can provide: affection, companionship, preparation for life, and financial, emotional, and spiritual support. The readings in this chapter explore different types of families, assessing their ability to provide for these expectations.

The case study on legislating the definition of family comes from growing concern about broadening our legal definition of marriage to include same-sex couples. In 1996, Congress passed the Defense of Marriage Act (DOMA) and President Clinton signed it into law. The DOMA defined marriage as a legal union between one man and one woman, and it stated that no state was legally bound to recognize a same-sex marriage performed legally in another state. Forty-three states have laws that bar the recognition of same-sex marriages. However, all states' constitutions are required to follow the federal Constitution. In the 2004 election year, members of the House of Representatives and the Senate introduced resolutions to amend the Constitution to ensure uniformity throughout the land.

The United States Constitution was designed to make amending it a long and difficult process, and therefore one that has to be taken very seriously. A bill must pass both houses of Congress with a two-thirds majority. Then it goes on to the states, where it must be approved by three-fourths of the state legislatures.

On July 14, 2004, the Senate voted on a procedural motion to debate the Marriage Protection Amendment (S.J. Res 40) which would have led to an eventual vote on the amendment. The effort failed, however, because sixty votes were needed to bring the amendment to a vote. Forty-eight Senators voted in favor and fifty opposed. On Thursday, September 30, 2004, the House of Representatives voted on the Marriage Protection Amendment, H.J. Res. 106. A two-thirds majority is required to pass an amendment. The MPA received a simple majority with a vote of 227 to 186.

However, the issue of same-sex marriage continues to be debated. On January 24, 2005, Sen. Wayne Allard, R-Colo., re-introduced the federal marriage amendment in the Senate, and twenty-four Republican senators joined Allard in introducing the amendment. They designated the joint resolution S.J. Res. 1, indicating the constitutional amendment was a priority for the Republican leadership in the Senate.

Linguist George Lakoff (author of "What's in a Word?" included in the case study) says that "we can see why the issue of same-sex marriage is so volatile. What is at stake is more than the material benefits of marriage and the use of the word. At stake is one's identity and most central values. This is not just about same-sex couples. It is about which values will dominate in our society."

Mary Pipher
Beliefs About Families

Mary Pipher is a clinical psychologist who works in Lincoln, Nebraska. She is the author of the bestselling book, Reviving Ophelia: Saving the Selves of Adolescent Girls *(1994), that seeks to save teenaged girls from destructive media culture. "Beliefs About Families" is taken from her more recent book* The Shelter of Each Other: Rebuilding Our Families *(New York: Putnam, 1996) in which she examines the lack of community that is now common in families and suggests ways to remedy it.*

When I speak of families, I usually mean biological families. There is a power in blood ties that cannot be denied. But in our fragmented, chaotic culture, many people don't have biological families nearby. For many people, friends become family. Family is a collection of people who pool resources and help each other over the long haul. Families love one another even when that requires sacrifice. Family means that if you disagree, you still stay together.

Families are the people for whom it matters if you have a cold, are feuding with your mate or training a new puppy. Family members use magnets to fasten the newspaper clippings about your bowling team on the refrigerator door. They save your drawings and homemade pottery. They like to hear stories about when you were young. They'll help you can tomatoes or change the oil in your car. They're the people who will come visit you in the hospital, will talk to you when you call with "a dark night of the soul" and will loan you money to pay the rent if you lose your job. Whether or not they are biologically related to each other, the people who do these things are family.

If you are very lucky, family is the group you were born into. But some are not that lucky. When Janet was in college, her parents were killed in a car wreck. In her early twenties she married, but three years later she lost her husband to leukemia. She has one sister, who calls mainly when she's suicidal or needs money. Janet is a congresswoman in a western state, a hard worker and an idealist. Her family consists of the men, women and children she's grown to depend on in the twenty-five years she's lived in her community. Except for her beloved dog, nobody lives with her. But she brings the cinnamon rolls to one family's Thanksgiving dinner and has a Mexican fiesta for families at her house on New Year's Eve. She attends Bar Mitzvahs, weddings, school concerts and soccer matches. She told me with great pride, "When I sprained my ankle skiing last year, three families brought me meals."

I think of Morgan, a jazz musician who long ago left his small town and rigid, judgmental family. He had many memories of his father whipping him with a belt or making him sleep in the cold. Once he said to me, "I was eighteen years old before anyone ever told me I had something to offer." Indeed he does. He plays the violin beautifully. He teaches improvisation and jazz violin and organizes jazz events for his town. His family is the family of musicians and music lovers that he has built around him over the years.

5   If you are very unlucky, you come from a nuclear family that didn't care for you. Curtis, who as a boy was regularly beaten by his father, lied about his age so that he could join the Navy at sixteen. Years later he wrote his parents and asked if he could return home for Christmas. They didn't answer his letter. When I saw him in therapy, I encouraged him to look for a new family, among his cousins and friends from the Navy. Sometimes cutoffs, tragic as they are, are unavoidable.

I think of Anita, who never knew her father and whose mother abandoned her when she was seven. Anita was raised by an aunt and uncle, whom she loved very much. As an adult she tracked down her mother and tried to establish a relationship, but her mother wasn't interested. At least Anita was able to find other family members to love her. She had a family in her aunt and uncle.

Family need not be traditional or biological. But what family offers is not easily replicated. Let me share a Sioux word, *tiospaye,* which means the people with whom one lives. The tiospaye is probably closer to a kibbutz than to any other Western institution. The tiospaye gives children multiple parents, aunts, uncles and grandparents. It offers children a corrective factor for problems in their nuclear families. If parents are difficult, there are other adults around to soften and diffuse the situation. Until the 1930s, when the tiospaye began to fall apart with sale of land, migration and alcoholism, there was not much mental illness among the Sioux. When all adults were responsible for all children, people grew up healthy.

What tiospaye offers and what biological family offers is a place that all members can belong to regardless of merit. Everyone is included regardless of health, likability or prestige. What's most valuable about such institutions is that people are in by virtue of being born into the group. People are in even if they've committed a crime, been a difficult person, become physically or mentally disabled or are unemployed and broke. That ascribed status was what Robert Frost valued when he wrote that home "was something you somehow hadn't to deserve."

Many people do not have access to either a supportive biological family or a tiospaye. They make do with a "formed family." Others simply prefer a community of friends to their biological families. The problem with formed families is they often have less staying power. They might not take you in, give you money if you lose a job or visit you in a rest home if you are paralyzed in a car crash. My father had a stroke and lost most of his sight and speech. Family members were the people who invited him to visit and helped him through the long tough years after his stroke. Of course, there are formed families who do this. With the AIDS crisis, many gays have supported their friends through terrible times. Often immigrants will help each other in this new country. And there are families who don't stick together in crisis. But generally blood is thicker than water. Families come through when they must.

10   Another problem with formed families is that not everyone has the skills to be included in that kind of family. Friendship isn't a product that can be obtained for cash. People need friends today more than ever, but friends are

harder to make in a world where people are busy, moving and isolated. Some people don't have the skills. They are shy, abrasive or dull. Crack babies have a hard time making friends, as do people with Alzheimer's. Formed families can leave many people out.

From my point of view the issue isn't biology. Rather the issues are commitment and inclusiveness. I don't think for most of us it has to be either/or. A person can have both a strong network of friends and a strong family. It is important to define family broadly so that all kinds of families, such as single-parent families, multigenerational families, foster families and the families of gays are included. But I agree with David Blankenberg's conclusion in his book *Rebuilding the Nest:* "Even with all the problems of nuclear families, I will support it as an institution until something better comes along."

Americans hold two parallel versions of the family—the idealized version and the dysfunctional version. The idealized version portrays families as wellsprings of love and happiness, loyal, wholesome, and true. This is the version we see in *Leave It to Beaver* or *Father Knows Best.* The dysfunctional version depicts families as disturbed and disturbing and suggests that salvation lies in extricating oneself from all the ties that bind. Both versions have had their eras. In the 1950s the idealized version was at its zenith. Extolling family was in response to the Depression and war, which separated families. People who had been wrenched away from home missed their families and thought of them with great longing. They idealized how close and warm they had been.

In the 1990s the dysfunctional version of family seems the most influential. This belief system goes along with the culture of narcissism, which sells people the idea that families get in the way of individual fulfillment. Currently, many Americans are deeply mistrustful of their own and other people's families. Pop psychology presents families as pathology-producing. Talk shows make families look like hotbeds of sin and sickness. Day after day people testify about the diverse forms of emotional abuse that they suffered in their families. Movies and television often portray families as useless impediments.

In our culture, after a certain age, children no longer have permission to love their parents. We define adulthood as breaking away, disagreeing and making up new rules. Just when teenagers most need their parents, they are encouraged to distance from them. A friend told me of walking with her son in a shopping mall. They passed some of his friends and she noticed that suddenly he was ten feet behind, trying hard not to be seen with her. She said, "I felt like I was drooling and wearing purple plaid polyester." Later her son told her that he enjoyed being with her, but that his friends all hated their parents and he would be teased if anyone knew he loved her. He said, "I'm confused about this. Am I supposed to hate you?"

15   This socialized antipathy toward families is unusual. Most cultures revere and respect family. In Vietnam, for example, the tender word for lover is "sibling." In the Kuma tribe of Papua, New Guinea, family members are valued above all others. Siblings are seen as alter egos, essential parts of the self. The Kuma believe that

mates can be replaced, but not family members. Many Native American tribes regard family members as connected to the self. To be without family is to be dead.

From the Greeks, to Descartes, to Freud and Ayn Rand, Westerners have valued the independent ego. But Americans are the most extreme. Our founders were rebels who couldn't tolerate oppression. When they formed a new government they emphasized rights and freedoms. Laws protected private property and individual rights. Responsibility for the common good was not mandated.

American values concerning independence may have worked better when we lived in small communities surrounded by endless space. But we have run out of space and our outlaws live among us. At one time the outlaw mentality was mitigated by a strong sense of community. Now the values of community have been superseded by other values.

We have pushed the concept of individual rights to the limits. Our laws let adults sell children harmful products. But laws are not our main problem. People have always been governed more by community values than by laws. Ethics, rather than laws, determine most of our behavior. Unwritten rules of civility—for taking turns, not cutting in lines, holding doors open for others and lowering our voices in theaters—organize civic life. Unfortunately, those rules of civility seem to be crumbling in America. We are becoming a nation of people who get angry when anyone gets in our way.

Rudeness is everywhere in our culture. Howard Stern, G. Gordon Liddy and Newt Gingrich are rude. It's not surprising our children copy them. Phil Donahue and Jay Leno interrupt and children learn to interrupt. A young man I know was recently injured on a volleyball court. The player who hurt him didn't apologize or offer to help him get to an emergency room. An official told him to get off the floor because he was messing it up with his blood and holding up the game. I recently saw an old man hesitate at a busy intersection. Behind him drivers swore and honked. He looked scared and confused as he turned into traffic and almost wrecked his car. At a festival a man stood in front of the stage, refusing to sit down when people yelled out that they couldn't see. Finally another man wrestled him to the ground. All around were the omnipresent calls of "Fuck you." Over coffee a local politician told me she would no longer attend town meetings. She said, "People get out of control and insult me and each other. There's no dialogue; it's all insults and accusations."

20   We have a crisis in meaning in our culture. The crisis comes from our isolation from each other, from the values we learn in a culture of consumption and from the fuzzy, self-help message that the only commitment is to the self and the only important question is—Am I happy? We learn that we are number one and that our own immediate needs are the most important ones. The crisis comes from the message that products satisfy and that happiness can be purchased.

We live in a money-driven culture. But the bottom line is not the only line, or even the best line for us to hold. A culture organized around profits instead of people is not user friendly to families. We all suffer from existential flu, as we search for meaning in a culture that values money, not meaning. Everyone I know wants to do good work. But right now we have an enormous gap between doing what's meaningful and doing what is reimbursed.

▦ QUESTIONS FOR INQUIRY AND ACTION ▦

1. The early years of college are often difficult for students who seek to establish new relationships—often in a new city, state, or country—while trying to maintain relationships with their families at home. How have you tried to both form new families and preserve your existing ones? Have you run into difficulties? What can you do to overcome these difficulties?

2. Pipher presents several stories of individuals living in troubled biological families. Why does she use these stories, and how do they affect you as a reader? Could she use other forms of evidence, and would they work in the same ways?

3. Pipher says that modern families are frequently depicted in the media as dysfunctional burdens individuals must overcome to find self-fulfillment. Look through your local television guide and circle all of the shows that depict dysfunctional families. Then, using a different colored ink, circle all the shows depicting idealized or uplifting families. How do the number of shows compare? Finally, watch sample shows depicting each type of family and make observations in your writer's notebook. Do these shows fit Pipher's descriptions of them?

4. Pipher blames the breakdown of American families on a culture of consumption, rudeness, and narcissism (self-love). How can we work toward a more meaningful, community-based society? Think of one act you can perform that would move us toward a more civil society, one that would strengthen families. Perform that act and then reflect on the consequences in your writer's notebook. Did you make a positive difference in someone else's life?

Tony Earley
Somehow Form a Family
▦ ▦

Tony Earley teaches writing at Vanderbilt University in Nashville. He is the author of a collection of short stories, Here We Are in Paradise *(1994), and the best-selling novel* Jim the Boy *(2000). "Somehow Form a Family" is the first essay in his book of the same title,* Somehow Form a Family: Stories That Are Mostly True *(Chapel Hill, NC: Algonquin Books, 2001).*

In July 1969, I looked a lot like Opie in the second or third season of *The Andy Griffith Show.* I was a small boy with a big head. I wore blue jeans with the cuffs turned up and horizontally striped pullover shirts. I was the brother in a father-mother-brother-sister family. We lived in a four-room house at the edge of the country, at the foot of the mountains, outside a small town in North Carolina, but it could have been anywhere.

On one side of us lived Mr. and Mrs. White. They were old and rich. Their driveway was paved. Mrs. White was the president of the town garden club. When she came to visit Mama she brought her own ashtray. Mr. White was almost deaf. When he watched the news on television, it sounded like thunder in the distance. The Whites had an aluminum travel trailer in which you could see your reflection. One summer they hitched it to their Chrysler and pulled it all the way to Alaska.

On the other side of us lived Mack and Joan. They had just graduated from college. I thought Joan was beautiful, and still do. Mack had a bass boat and a three-tray tackle box in which lurked a bristling school of lures. On the other side of Mack and Joan lived Mrs. Taylor, who was old, and on the other side of Mrs. Taylor lived Mr. and Mrs. Frady, who had a fierce dog. My sister, Shelly, and I called it the Frady dog. The Frady dog lived a long and bitter life. It did not die until well after I had a driver's license.

On the far side of the Whites lived Mr. and Mrs. John Harris; Mr. and Mrs. Burlon Harris lived beyond them. John and Burlon were first cousins. John was a teacher who in the summers fixed lawn mowers, including ours, in a building behind his house. Burlon reminded me of Mr. Greenjeans on *Captain Kangaroo*. He kept horses and let us play in his barn. Shelly once commandeered one of his cats and brought it home to live with us. Burlon did not mind; he asked her if she wanted another one. We rode our bicycles toward Mr. Harris's house as if pulled there by gravity. We did not ride in the other direction; the Frady dog sat in its yard and watched for us.

5   In July 1969, we did not have much money, but in the hierarchy of southern poor, we were the good kind, the kind you would not mind living on your road. We were clean. Our clothes were clean. My parents worked. We went to church. Easter mornings, Mama stood us in front of the yellowbell bush and took our picture. We had meat at every meal—chicken and cube steak and pork chops and ham—and plenty of milk to drink. We were not trashy. Mrs. White would not sit with her ashtray in the kitchen of trashy people. Trashy people lived in the two houses around the curve past Mr. Harris's. When Daddy drove by those houses we could see that the kids in the yard had dirty faces. They were usually jabbing at something with a stick. Shelly and I were not allowed to ride our bicycles around the curve.

I knew we were poor only because our television was black and white. It was an old Admiral, built in the 1950s, with brass knobs the size of baseballs. Its cabinet was perfectly square, a cube of steel with a painted-on mahogany grain. Hoss on *Bonanza* could not have picked it up by himself. It was a formidable object, but its vertical hold was shot. We gathered around it the night Neil Armstrong walked on the moon, but we could not tell what was happening. The picture flipped up and down. We turned off the lights in the living room so we could see better. We listened to Walter Cronkite. In the distance we could hear Mr. White's color TV rumbling. We changed the channel and listened to Huntley and Brinkley. We could hear the scratchy radio transmissions coming down out of space, but we could not see anything. Daddy got behind the TV with a flashlight. He said, "Is that better? Is that better?" but it never was. Mama said, "Just be thankful you've got a television."

After the Eagle had landed but before the astronauts opened the door and came out, Mack knocked on the door and asked us if we wanted to look at the moon. He was an engineer for a power company and had set up his surveyor's transit in the backyard. Daddy and Shelly and I went with him. We left Mama sitting in the living room in the blue light of the TV. She said she did not want to miss anything. The moon, as I remember it, was full, although I have since learned that it wasn't. I remember that a galaxy of lightning bugs blinked against the black pine trees that grew between our yard and that of the Whites. Mack pointed the transit at the sky. Daddy held me up so I could see. The moon inside the instrument was startlingly bright; the man in the moon was clearly visible, although the men on the moon weren't. "You can't see them or anything," Mack said, which I already knew. I said, "I know that." I wasn't stupid and did not like to be talked to as if I were. Daddy put me down. He and Mack stood for a while and talked. Daddy smoked a cigarette. In the bright yard Shelly chased lightning bugs. She did not run, but instead jumped slowly, her feet together. I realized that she was pretending to walk on the moon, pretending that she was weightless. The moon was so bright, it cast a shadow at her feet. I remember these things for sure. I am tempted to say that she was beautiful in the moon-light, and I'm sure she was, but that isn't something I remember noticing that night, only a thing I need to say now.

Eight, maybe nine months later, Shelly and I rode the bus home from school. It was a Thursday, Mama's day off, Easter time. The cherry tree in the garden separating our driveway from that of the Whites was in brilliant, full bloom. We could hear it buzzing from the road. One of us checked the mailbox. We looked up the driveway at our house. Something was wrong with it, but we couldn't tell what. Daddy was adding four rooms on to the house, and we were used to it appearing large and unfinished. We stood in the driveway and stared. Black tar paper was tacked to the outside walls of the new part, but the old part was still covered with white asbestos shingles. In the coming summer, Daddy and a crew of brick masons would finish transforming the house into a split-level ranch style, remarkably similar to the one in which the Bradys would live. I loved the words *split-level ranch-style.* To me they meant "rich."

Shelly and I spotted what was wrong at the same time. A giant television antenna had attached itself to the roof of our house. It was shiny and tall as a young tree. It looked dangerous, as if it would bite, like a praying mantis. The antenna slowly began to turn, as if it had noticed us. Shelly and I looked quickly at each other, our mouths wide open, and then back at the antenna. We sprinted up the driveway.

10   In the living room, on the spot occupied by the Admiral that morning, sat a magnificent new color TV, a Zenith, with a twenty-one-inch screen. Its cabinet was made of real wood. *Gomer Pyle, U.S.M.C.* was on. I will never forget that. Gomer Pyle and Sergeant Carter were the first two people I ever saw on a color television. The olive green and khaki of their uniforms was dazzling. Above them was the blue sky of California. The sky in California seemed bluer than the sky in North Carolina.

We said, "Is that ours?"

Mama said, "I'm going to kill your daddy." He had charged the TV without telling her. Two men from Sterchi's Furniture had showed up at the house that morning with the TV on a truck. They climbed onto the roof and planted the antenna.

We said, "Can we keep it?"

Mama said, "I don't know," but I noticed she had written the numbers of the stations we could get on the dial of the Channel Master, the small box which controlled the direction the antenna pointed. Mama would never have written on anything she planned on taking back to the store.

15   The dial of the Channel Master was marked like a compass. Channel 3 in Charlotte lay to the east; Channel 13 in Asheville lay to the west. Channel 7 in Spartanburg and Channel 4 in Greenville rested side by side below them in the south. For years these cities would mark the outside edges of the world as I knew it. Shelly reached out and turned the dial. Mama smacked her on the hand. Gomer grew fuzzy and disappeared. I said, "Mama, she broke it." When the dial stopped turning, Mama carefully turned it back to the south. Gomer reappeared, resurrected. Jim Nabors probably never looked better to anyone, in his whole life, than he did to us right then.

Mama sat us down on the couch and laid down the law. Mama always laid down the law when she was upset. We were not to touch the TV. We could not turn it on, nor could we change the channel. Under no circumstances were we to touch the Channel Master. The Channel Master was very expensive. And if we so much as looked at the knobs that controlled the color, she would whip us. It had taken her all afternoon to get the color just right.

We lived in a split-level ranch-style house, with two maple trees and a rose bush in the front yard, outside a town that could have been named Springfield. We had a color TV. We had a Channel Master antenna that turned slowly on top of our house until it found and pulled from the sky electromagnetic waves for our nuclear family.

We watched *Hee-Haw*, starring Buck Owens and Roy Clark; we watched *All in the Family, The Mary Tyler Moore Show, The Bob Newhart Show, The Carol Burnett Show*, and *Mannix*, starring Mike Connors with Gail Fisher as Peggy; we watched *Gunsmoke* and *Bonanza*, even after Adam left and Hoss died and Little Joe's hair turned gray; we watched *Adam-12* and *Kojak, McCloud, Colombo*, and *Hawaii Five-O*; we watched *Cannon*, a Quinn Martin production and *Barnaby Jones*, a Quinn Martin production, which co-starred Miss America and Uncle Jed from *The Beverly Hillbillies*. Daddy finished the new part of the house and moved out soon thereafter. He rented a trailer in town and took the old Admiral out of the basement with him. We watched *Mutual of Omaha's Wild Kingdom* and *The Wonderful World of Disney*. After school we watched *Gomer Pyle, U.S.M.C., The Beverly Hillbillies, Gilligan's Island*, and *The Andy Griffith Show*. Upstairs, we had rooms of our own. Mama stopped taking us to church.

On Friday nights we watched *The Partridge Family, The Brady Bunch, Room 222, The Odd Couple*, and *Love American Style*. Daddy came to visit on Saturdays. We watched *The Little Rascals* on Channel 3 with Fred Kirby, the singing cowboy, and his sidekick, Uncle Jim. We watched *The Little Rascals* on Channel 4 with Monty Dupuy, the weatherman, and his sidekick, Doohickey. Mornings, before school, we watched *The Three Stooges* with Mr. Bill on Channel 13. Mr. Bill worked alone. The school year Daddy moved out, Mr. Bill showed Bible story cartoons instead of *The Three Stooges.* That year, we went to school angry.

20   After each of Daddy's visits, Mama said he was getting better. Shelly and I tried to imagine living with the Bradys but realized we would not fit in. They were richer and more popular at school. They did not have Southern accents. One Saturday Daddy brought me a set of golf clubs, which I had asked for but did not expect to get. It was raining that day. I took the clubs out in the yard and very quickly realized that golf was harder than it looked on television. I went back inside and wiped the mud and water off the clubs with Bounty paper towels, the quicker picker upper. Upstairs I heard Mama say, "Do you think he's stupid?" I spread the golf clubs on the floor around me. I tuned in *Shock Theater* on Channel 13 and turned it up loud.

Shelly had a crush on Bobby Brady; I had a crush on Jan. Jan had braces, I had braces. Jan had glasses, I had glasses. Their daddy was an architect. Our daddy lived in a trailer in town with a poster of Wile E. Coyote and the Road Runner on the living room wall. The Coyote held the Road Runner firmly by the neck. The caption on the poster said, "Beep, Beep your ass." I lay in bed at night and imagined being married to Jan Brady but having an affair with Marsha. I wondered how we would tell Jan, what Marsha and I would do then, where we would go. Greg Brady beat me up. I shook his hand and told him I deserved it. Alice refused to speak to me. During this time Mrs. White died. I heard the ambulance in the middle of the night. It sounded like the one on *Emergency.* I opened the door to Mama's room to see if she was OK. She was embarrassed because our dog barked and barked.

Rhoda left *The Mary Tyler Moore Show.* Maude and George Jefferson left *All in the Family;* Florida, Maude's maid, left *Maude.* Daddy moved back in. He watched the news during supper, the TV as loud as Mr. White's. We were not allowed to talk during the news. This was the law. After the news we watched *Rhoda* or *Maude* or *Good Times.* Daddy decided that cutting the grass should be my job. We had a big yard. I decided that I didn't want to do anything he said. Mr. White remarried. The new Mrs. White's daughter died of cancer. The new Mrs. White dug up every flower the old Mrs. White had planted; she cut down every tree and shrub, including the cherry tree in the garden between our driveways. Mama said the new Mrs. White broke her heart. Mr. White mowed and mowed and mowed their grass until it was smooth as a golf course. Mack and Joan paved their driveway.

What I'm trying to say is this: we lived in a split-level ranch-style house; we had a Zenith in the living room and a Channel Master attached to the roof. But Shelly and I fought like Thelma and J.J. on *Good Times.* I wanted to live in Hawaii and work for Steve McGarrett. No bad guy ever got away from McGarrett, except the Chinese master spy Wo Fat. Shelly said McGarrett would never give me a job. In all things Shelly was on Daddy's side; I lined up on Mama's. Friday evenings, when Daddy got home from work, I sneaked outside to snoop around in the glove compartment of his car. I pretended I had a search warrant, that I was Danno on a big case. Shelly reported my snooping to Daddy. I was trying to be a good son.

Every Saturday, before he went to work, Daddy left word that I was to cut the grass before he got home. I stayed in bed until lunch. Shelly came into my room and said, "You better get up." I flipped her the bird. She said, "I'm telling." I got up in time to watch professional wrestling on Channel 3. I hated the bad guys. They did not fight fair. They hid brass knuckles in their trunks and beat the good guys until they bled. They won too often. Mama brought me tomato and onion sandwiches. I could hear Mack on one side and Mr. White on the other mowing their grass. I could hear John Harris and Mr. Frady and Mrs. Taylor's daughter, Lucille, mowing grass. Lucille lived in Charlotte, but came home on weekends just to mow Mrs. Taylor's grass. We had the shaggiest lawn on the road. After wrestling, I watched the *Game of the Week* on Channel 4. Carl Yaztremski of the Boston Red Sox was my favorite baseball player. He had forearms like fenceposts. Nobody messed with him. I listened over the lawn mowers for the sound of Daddy's Volkswagen. Mama came in the living room and said, "Son, maybe you should mow some of the grass before your daddy gets home. You know what's going to happen." I knew what was going to happen. I knew that eventually he would make me mow the grass. I knew that when I was through, Mack would come through the pine trees laughing. He would say, "Charles, I swear that is the laziest boy I have ever seen." Mack had a Snapper Comet riding mower, on which he sat like a king. I never saw him on it that I did not want to bean him with a rock. Daddy would shake his head and say, "Mack, dead lice wouldn't fall off that boy." Every Saturday night we ate out at Scoggin's Seafood and Steak House. *Hee-Haw* came on at seven; *All in the Family* came on at eight.

25   And then Shelly and I were in high school. We watched *M*A*S*H** and *Lou Grant, Love Boat* and *Fantasy Island*. We watched *Dynasty* and *Dallas*. Opie was Richie Cunningham on *Happy Days*. Ben Cartwright showed up in a black bathrobe on *Battlestar Galactica*. The Channel Master stopped working, but no one bothered to have it fixed. The antenna was left immobile on the roof in a compromised position: we could almost get most of the channels. One summer Mack built a pool in his backyard. Joan lay in a bikini beside the pool in the sun. The next summer Mack built a fence. This was during the late seventies. Shelly lay in her room with the lights turned off and listened to *Dark Side of the Moon*. On Friday nights she asked me to go out with her and her friends. I always said no. I did not want to miss *The Rockford Files*.

In those days Shelly and I watched *Guiding Light* when we got home from school. It was our soap. I remember that Ed Bauer's beautiful wife Rita left him because he was boring. Shelly said I reminded her of Ed Bauer. She wore her hair like Farrah Fawcett Majors on *Charlie's Angels*. After *Guiding Light* I changed the channel and watched *Star Trek*. I could not stay awake in school. I went to sleep during homeroom. During the day I woke up only long enough to change classes and eat lunch. I watched *Star Trek* when I got home as if it were beamed to our house by God. I did not want to be Captain Kirk, or any of the main characters. I just wanted to go with them. I wanted to wear a red jersey and walk the long, anonymous halls of the Starship Enterprise as it disappeared into space. One day *Star Trek* was preempted by an *ABC After School Special.* I tried to kick the screen out of the TV. I was wearing sneakers, so the glass would not break. Shelly hid in Mama and Daddy's room. I said, "Five-O. Open up." Then I kicked the door off the hinges.

Our family doctor thought I had narcolepsy. He sent me to a neurologist in Charlotte. Mama and Daddy went with me. In Charlotte, an EEG technician attached wires to my head. A small, round amber light glowed high up in the corner of the examination room. I watched the light until I went to sleep. The neurologist said that the EEG looked normal, but that he would talk to us more about the results in a few minutes. He led us to a private waiting room. It was small and bare and paneled with wood. In it were four chairs. Most of one wall was taken up by a darkened glass. I could not see what was on the other side of it. I studied our reflection. Mama and Daddy were trying to pretend that the glass wasn't there. I said, "Pa, when we get back to the Ponderosa, do you want me to round up those steers on the lower forty?"

Daddy said, "What?"

I said, "Damnit, Jim. I'm a doctor."

30 Daddy said, "What are you talking about?"

Mama said, "Be quiet. They're watching us."

Shelly died on Christmas Eve morning when I was a freshman in college. She had wrecked Mama's car. That night I stayed up late and watched the Pope deliver the Christmas mass from the Vatican. There was nothing else on. Daddy moved out again. My college almost shut down during the week *The Thorn Birds* was broadcast. Professors rescheduled papers and exams. In the basement of my dorm twenty-five nineteen-year-old guys shouted at the TV when the Richard Chamberlain character told the Rachel Ward character he loved God more than he loved her. At age nineteen, it was impossible to love God more than Rachel Ward. My best friend, a guy from Kenya, talked me into switching from *Guiding Light* to *General Hospital.* This was during the glory days of *General Hospital* when Luke and Scorpio roomed together on the Haunted Star. Laura was supposedly dead, but Luke knew in his heart she was still alive; every time he was by himself he heard a Christopher Cross song.

Going home was strange, as if the Mayberry I expected had become Mayberry, R.F.D. Shelly was gone. Daddy was gone. The second Mrs. White died, then Mr. White went away to a nursing home. The Fradys had moved away. John Harris had a heart attack and stopped fixing lawn mowers. Mama mowed our grass by herself with a rider. I stopped going to see Burlon Harris because he teared up every time he tried to talk about Shelly. Mack and Joan had a son named Timmy. Mack and Joan got a divorce. Mack moved to a farm out in the country; Joan moved to town.

Daddy fell in love with Mama my senior year and moved back in. The Zenith began slowly dying. Its picture narrowed into a greenly tinted slit. It stared like a diseased eye into the living room where Mama and Daddy sat. They turned off the lights so they could see better. I became a newspaper reporter. With my first Christmas bonus, I bought myself a television, a nineteen-inch GE. With my second Christmas bonus I bought Mama and Daddy one. They hooked it up to cable. When I visited them on Thursdays we watched *The Cosby Show, Family Ties, Cheers, Night Court,* and *Hill Street Blues.* Daddy gave up on broadcast TV when NBC cancelled *Hill Street Blues* and replaced it with *L.A. Law.* Now he mostly watches the Discovery Channel. Mama calls it the "airplanes and animals channel." They are in the eighteenth year of their new life together. I bear them no grudges. They were very young when I knew them best.

35   In grad school I switched back to *Guiding Light.* I had known Ed Bauer longer than I had known all but a few of my friends. It pleased me to see him in Springfield every afternoon, trying to do good. I watched *The Andy Griffith Show* twice a day. I could glance at Opie and tell you what year the episode was filmed. I watched the Gulf War from a stool in a bar.

Eventually I married a woman who grew up in a family that watched television only on special occasions—when Billie Jean King played Bobby Riggs, when Diana married Prince Charles. My wife was a student in a seminary. She did not want to meet Ed Bauer, nor could I explain, without sounding pathetic, why Ed Bauer was important to me. The first winter we were married I watched the winter Olympics huddled beneath a blanket in the frigid basement of the house we had rented. This was in a closed-down steel town near Pittsburgh, during the time I contemplated jumping from a bridge into the Ohio River. My wife asked the seminary community to pray for me. Ann B. Davis, who played Alice on *The Brady Bunch* was a member of that community. One day I saw her in the cafeteria at school. She looked much the same as when she played Alice, except that her hair was white, and she wore small, gold glasses. I didn't talk to her. I had heard that she didn't like talking about *The Brady Bunch,* and I could not think of anything to say to her about the world in which we actually lived. I sat in the cafeteria and stared at her as much as I could without anyone noticing. I don't know if she prayed for me or not, but I like to think that she did. I wanted to tell her that I grew up in a split-level ranch-style house outside a small town that could have been named Springfield, but that something had gone wrong inside it. I wanted to tell her that years ago Alice had been important to me, that my sister and I had looked to Alice for something we could not name, and had at least seen a picture of what love looked like. I wanted to tell her that no one in my family ever raised their voice while the television was on, that late at night even a bad television show could keep me from hearing the silence inside my own heart. I wanted to tell her that Ed Bauer and I were still alive, that both of us had always wanted to do what was right. Ann B. Davis stood, walked over to the trash can, and emptied her tray. She walked out of the cafeteria and into a small, gray town near Pittsburgh. I wanted her to *be* Alice. I wanted her to smile as if she loved me. I wanted her to say, "Buck up, kiddo, everything's going to be all right." And what I'm trying to tell you now is this: I grew up in a split-level ranch-style house outside a town that could have been anywhere. I grew up in front of a television. I would have believed her.

▓ QUESTIONS FOR INQUIRY AND ACTION ▓

1. Earley's title invokes *The Brady Bunch*, but what else does the title "somehow form a family" reveal about his story?

2. What does Earley tell us directly about his family, and what does he imply? Why is the television so important to his description?

3. Make your own list of the television shows you watched growing up. What would the list tell us about the events going on in your life? What shows affected you most, and why? What has been the lasting effect of television shows on your life?

4. In what ways do you feel connected with others through a specific television show or special event? Survey others your age on the most important moments on television in the past five years. How many do you all agree on? How does television help you form a community?

WRITING STYLE

SHOWING, NOT TELLING

Most books of writing advise aspiring authors: "Show, don't tell." They recommend this because writing is more powerful and affecting when readers can see examples rather than just receive explanation. Writers often "show" by providing lots of precise details and by using dialogue to reveal character and advance the plot.

Tony Earley's story "Somehow Form a Family" contends that he grew up in front of a television and that it shielded him from the emotional trauma of watching his parents quarrel and separate and get back together again. Television allowed him to escape and to imagine himself a different person in different lives. Rather than tell us this directly, Earley shows us indirectly by providing list after list of the television shows he watched during the difficult eras of his life and mentioning his connections with certain shows and characters.

For example, here is one of the passages:

On Friday nights we watched *The Partridge Family, The Brady Bunch, Room 222, The Odd Couple,* and *Love, American Style.* Daddy came to visit on Saturdays. We watched *The Little Rascals* on Channel 3 with Fred Kirby, the singing cowboy, and his sidekick, Uncle Jim. We watched *The Little Rascals* on Channel 4 with Monty Dupuy, the weatherman, and his sidekick, Doohickey. Mornings, before school, we watched *The Three Stooges* with Mr. Bill on Channel 13. Mr. Bill worked alone. The school year Daddy moved out, Mr. Bill showed Bible story cartoons instead of *The Three Stooges.* That year, we went to school angry.

Earley seems to break the "show, don't tell" rule, for he does tell us what he watched and what happened in his life, yet he shows us all of this suggestively: he depends on the names of the TV shows to carry connotations to an audience he assumes knows these shows and their characters. He does not explicate or directly connect his observations of life to the TV shows, but we understand the connections. Do you find this style of storytelling effective? Why or why not?

Gigi Kaeser
Love Makes a Family

Gigi Kaeser, an early childhood educator as well as a photographer, is the co-founder and co-director of Family Diversity Projects, a nonprofit organization that creates photo-text exhibits of families. Family Diversity Projects makes the exhibits available to schools, libraries, community centers, and workplaces. You can find out more about the FDP at their Web site: http://www.lovemakesafamily. org/index.php. This photograph appears on the cover of the brochure for the photo-text exhibit "Love Makes a Family" and is also the cover photo for the companion book Love Makes a Family *(University of Massachusetts Press, 1999).*

Jeff Riedel
Inward Christian Soldiers

Jeff Riedel is a photographer for The New York Times Magazine *who does a lot of fashion photography as well as photojournalism. His portrait of the Scheibner family appeared on the cover of* The New York Times Magazine *on February 27, 2000.*

▨ QUESTIONS FOR INQUIRY AND ACTION ▨

1. In Chapter 4 you will find an exercise that asks you to analyze these photographs in terms of their implied definitions of family.

2. Discuss your impressions of each of the photographs in relation to the various views on family expressed by the readings in this chapter. How are these photographs in conversation with the readings?

3. Research the work of Kaeser and Riedel. How do these photographs compare with other work that they have done? How do they describe themselves as photographers? What do they think their tasks or goals are? Have they commented on either of these particular photos?

4. Take your own or a friend's camera and shoot your own pictures of families. How would you stage your photographs? What impressions or arguments do you want the pictures to make?

Margaret Talbot
A Mighty Fortress
▨ ▨

Veteran journalist Margaret Talbot has been an editor at large for Lingua Franca *and writer for* The New Republic *as well as* The New York Times, *where this article was featured as the cover story of the February 27, 2000,* The New York Times Magazine. *It immediately struck a chord with Americans and was fervently discussed on* Talk of the Nation *and other call-in radio and television shows.*

To get to the house where Stephen and Megan Scheibner live with their seven children, you skirt past Allentown, Pa., and drive for another half-hour into the hills above the Lehigh Valley. The Scheibner place is on Blue Mountain Road, a few miles past a forlorn establishment called Binnie's Hot Dogs and Family Food. Standing behind their white clapboard farmhouse, where the backyard unfurls over three and a half acres and where, in summer, you can see a tangled strawberry patch and a tree fort, you could swear you were deep in the country and maybe deep in the past too. The front of the house is a different matter. It's practically on top of a busy road that leads to the local ski resorts; the view is of a housing development under construction.

Inside, there is no such ambivalence. Although the Scheibners are well off and their house is comfortably appointed—Steve is a pilot with American Airlines and a commander in the Naval Reserves—what might strike many visitors first is what's missing. In the Scheibner household, where the children are 12, 11, 9, 7, 6, 4 and 20 months, there is no Pokemon or "Star Wars" paraphernalia. There are no Britney Spears or Ricky Martin tapes. There are no posters of Leonardo DiCaprio or Michael Jordan taped to the walls, no pots of lip gloss or bottles of metallic nail polish scattered around. No Mortal Kombat, no "Goosebumps." No broadcast TV—though the family does watch carefully selected videos, which often means movies from the 1940's and 50's. (The older kids are big Cary Grant fans.) There is no giggling about the cute guys and girls at school, because the Scheibners are home-schooled and besides, their parents don't believe in dating. There is little sign of eye-rolling preteen rebellion, because Steve and his wife, Megan, don't believe in that either, and have set up their lives in such a way that it is unlikely to manifest itself. Katie, the oldest, reads Louisa May Alcott and reissued girls' classics like the Elsie Dinsmore books, and is partial to white patent-leather Mary Janes worn with ankle-length floral dresses. Peter, who comes next, likes Tolkien and the muscularly Christian boys' adventure stories written by the 19th-century author G. A. Henty, and favors chinos and logo-free button-down shirts. Peter wants to be a missionary in Russia, which he describes as a "forsaken" country; Katie wants to be a home-schooling mom. They are each other's best friends. And if they quarrel, it's not in a way that involves the dissing of one another in viciously up-to-the-minute slang.

There is no sports gear lying around the Scheibner household, because Megan feels that team sports breed competitive "behavior that we would not deem Christ-like"; more important, they interfere with the weekly rhythm of schooling, service and worship. Holidays don't disrupt much, either. The Scheibners don't celebrate Halloween—Satanic overtones—though one year the three oldest children dressed up as a couple of shepherds and a sheep and went door to door handing out evangelical tracts. At Christmas, they decorate the house and take baskets of food to their neighbors and to the poor, but they don't indulge in a buy-fest.

Megan, who is 37, guesses she has been to a mall "maybe three times" in the seven years the family has lived in Pennsylvania, and she can't remember the correct name of Toys "R" Us. For the children's clothes, she does a lot of her shopping at consignment stores because she objects to "the way most girls' stuff looks like it was designed for 20-year-olds and the boys' clothes all have some cartoon character on them." This Christmas, as they have for the past several years, the kids got a shared family gift—a "Sunday box" of special games and toys they can take out only on the Sabbath. It contained a Noah's Ark puzzle, several books, a tape of Christian children's songs with titles like "Keep Your Tongue From Evil," and a board game called Sticky Situations, a Christian version of Chutes and Ladders based on such moral dilemmas as what you should do if the most unpopular kid you know invites you over.

5   None of this is what Steve and Megan Scheibner would say first about themselves. What they would say first is that they are Christians—fundamentalist Baptists who were born again when, as teenagers, they found Jesus Christ and accepted the doctrine of salvation. And yet the way they practice their faith puts them so sharply and purposefully at odds with the larger culture that it is hard not to see the Scheibners, conservative and law-abiding though they are, as rebels.

We have arrived, it seems, at a moment in our history when the most vigorous and coherent counterculture around is the one constructed by conservative Christians. That sounds odd to many of us—especially, perhaps, to secular liberals, who cherish our own 60's-inflected notions of what an "alternative lifestyle" should look like. Ever since Theodore Roszak first coined it in 1968, the word "counterculture" has retained its whiff of patchouli, its association with free love, long hair and left-wing youth. "The counterculture," as Roszak defined it, "is the embryonic base of New Left politics, the effort to discover new types of community, new family patterns, new sexual mores . . . new personal identities on the far side of power politics."

Yet today it is conservative Christians like the Scheibners who, more self-consciously than any other large social group, buck mainstream notions of what constitutes a fulfilled life. Indeed, much of what Roszak said of the 60's counterculture could be said of them too. It's true that the "patterns" and "mores" they have discovered are not so much new ones as reinvigorated traditional ones. Parent-sanctioned courtship, the merging of school and home, the rejection of peer-group segregation, the moral value of thrift—all are ideas that, in the United States, last held real sway in the 19th century. But the impatience that people like the Scheibners display with acquisition, their unflagging commitment to putting the group—in their case, the family—above individual ambition, their rejection of pop culture, their characterization of themselves as, in Steve's words, "people who question absolutely everything," make them radical in ways that would be recognizable to some 60's counterculturists too.

There are about 20 million evangelical Christians in the U.S. today; together with fundamentalists, who tend to be more withdrawn from public life and more theologically conservative, they make up about 25 percent of the American population. Many of them lead lives that are far less sequestered and culturally abstemious than the Scheibners'. (Only 6 percent of conservative Christians educate their children at home, for instance, though the numbers are growing.) Some lead even more walled-off lives: at a conference for home-schooling families in Virginia last summer, I heard one speaker urge parents to reconsider sending their kids to college—even a Bible college—because dorm life encouraged "fornication" and "homosexual rape." But nearly all evangelicals struggle with the question of how staunchly they should separate their families from a majority culture they believe flouts their values.

A sense of this struggle came to the fore last spring, when Paul Weyrich published his "turn off, tune out, drop out" letter—the very phrase self-consciously echoing the hippie slogan. Weyrich, a founder of the Christian right, now urged "a strategy of separation," a "sort of quarantine" for Christians who he argued had been trying too hard, and at too much cost to their own morality, to insert themselves into the mainstream. "We need," he wrote "to drop out of this culture, and find places, even if it is where we physically are right now, where we can live godly, righteous and sober lives."

10   In their 1999 book, *Blinded by Might*, Cal Thomas, a conservative columnist, and Ed Dobson, a Baptist minister, offered a similar analysis, arguing that "religious conservatives have heard sermons that man's ways are not God's ways. . . . In politics they have fused the two, causing damage to both church and state." In a series of forceful columns, Thomas went on to argue that for Christians, worldly power was "not a calling, but a distraction" from the next world and

that the faithful often stumbled in the public square anyway. Consider Prohibition: "Good people diagnosed a social ill, but they used the wrong methods to correct it," he wrote. "The lesson: by and large, the Christian mission should be to change hearts, not laws."

Weyrich, Thomas and Dobson found few adherents among the leaders of the Christian right, but they touched off an emotional debate at the grass roots. Embittered by Clinton's survival of the impeachment scandal, some conservative Christians were despairing of politics altogether: how could Christians hope to influence a polity that supported a manifestly immoral leader? Even those who did not feel quite so deeply estranged from the American electorate still found something meaningful and provocative in the call to concentrate on discipleship, not politics. In an article in *Christianity Today,* the former Reagan aide Don Eberly wrote, "The greatest fallacy that has emerged in recent years is the expectation that national politicians and other civil authorities should take the lead in restoring biblical righteousness or, worse, using political power to create a 'Christian America.'"

It would be premature to declare the end of religious-right political activism. There are too many issues, from abortion to same-sex marriage, that continue to galvanize the faithful. But it cannot be denied that as a political force, the religious right is flagging. The Christian Coalition is deeply in the red. The two presidential candidates most identified with savvy Christian conservatism—Gary Bauer and Steve Forbes—have dropped out of the race, while the protest candidate Alan Keyes blusters on to tiny audiences. Yet even as Christian political movements flounder, the strategies that might be thought of as countercultural—home-schooling, building up a self-contained pop culture—are flourishing.

Not long after this debate was under way, I met the Scheibners. I had become interested in the idea of a Christian counterculture, and I wanted to write about a family who seemed to be living it out. I wasn't looking for people involved in a violent or illegal confrontation with the government—militia types, say—nor for people who belonged to a tradition with a long history of separateness, like the Amish. What I was looking for were people who were, as Steve Scheibner later described his family, "selective separatists": people who voted and paid taxes, worked in the mainstream world and even did community service, but who quite deliberately chose, as Megan put it, "not to participate in those parts of the culture that do not bring glory to God."

Partly I was interested because as a mother of young children, I had grappled with some of the same questions about what to keep at bay and for how long. TV or no TV? Did I want my 3-year-old to start playing on the computer now so he wouldn't be behind or hold off as long as possible, knowing his life will be colonized by dot-com this and digital that soon enough? Did toy guns lead inexorably to a taste for brutal video games? When you are awash in media and awash in stuff, what hope do you have of picking and choosing anyway? Could you do so only if armed with a totalizing worldview like the Scheibners'? How feasible—and how desirable—was it to "drop out" anyway?

15   When Megan Scheibner answered a message I posted on a Christian Internet discussion list last summer, her e-mail convinced me that I had found the right

family. "We don't isolate our family," she wrote, "but we do feel like we are called to shelter them from evil until they are spiritually ready to stand firm." Sheltering them, she explained, meant screening out almost all pop culture. "We have seen the fruit in kind, polite children," she went on to say. "Others have noticed, too, and this has given us many opportunities to share, i.e., one time at Pizza Hut, the man at the next table bought us lunch because the kids were so nice to each other. . . . Only God gets the glory for things like this. Neither my husband nor I were raised in Christian homes, but God has been faithful to show us his desire for our family, and then as we obey, He has blessed us abundantly."

On a rainy Sunday morning in August, I arrived, with my husband and son, for my first visit to the Scheibner house. The family was busy conducting its own Sunday school, and Megan sent Emma, then 8, out to greet us. Like all of the Scheibner children, Emma addressed me as Mrs. Talbot and my husband as Mr. Talbot. It seemed pointless to insist that they call me by my first name, and downright mean to introduce the idea that my husband and I have different last names, so there it stood. Of another 8-year-old, it might be fair to say that she bounded out of the house, but Emma walked delicately, on the balls of her feet, self-consciously ladylike. With a curtsy, she conducted us inside. All seven of the Scheibner children, and three of their friends, sat cross-legged on the tan carpet in the living room, reviewing their catechisms and listening to a sermon delivered by their father.

It may be because he is a pilot or because he has spent much of his adult life in the military or because he believes so firmly in parental authority, but Steve Scheibner seems at ease in the role of teacher and preacher to his own children in a way that few parents I know would be. Not that anything in his appearance or demeanor suggests an old-fashioned patriarch. He's a young-looking 39, slim, sharp-featured and dark-haired; he can be sarcastic; and he uses lots of guy lingo like "Bogus!" and "Where the rubber hits the road." But he's also got a storehouse of metaphors and concepts for child-rearing and for life that he dips into without hesitation or doubt. Steve explains to me later that he and Megan don't like the way many churches, including their own, shunt kids off to children's services where "they hear about Jonah and the whale for the umpteenth time." They think that children are capable of more or less following the main sermon by the age of 3; when they start their own church in Brunswick, Me., next summer (Steve is studying at a seminary now), there will be booster seats in the pews.

For now, though, he has taken to conducting his own Sunday school, with another couple and their children. Megan, in a smocked denim dress, a headband and no makeup, sits next to him. Though it's only 9 A.M., all the children look freshly scrubbed and shiny-haired, outfitted in their Sunday best. When little Baleigh cranes her neck to peer at us with a radiant, inquisitive smile, her mom gives her a whispered scolding, accompanied by the look a border collie might give a straying sheep. She turns around immediately.

At 10:30, Steve piles the kids into the van and drives to church, and Megan stays behind to talk to me. She'll miss church this morning, which she hardly ever does, but there's another service tonight, which the family always attends as well. In her high-ceilinged kitchen, where one wall is lined with homemade preserves, she tells me about their decision to teach their kids at home. "I worked in a day-care center for a while as a young Navy wife, and it really shocked me—the lack of discipline, the hitting, biting, screeching. We always thought we would home-school, but somehow we lost the nerve for a while and with Katie we sent her to kindergarten at a private Christian school for a year. But what we noticed was that she got more interested in what her peers were doing than in what her family was doing! We felt like our family-centered little girl was being pulled away from us."

20   Family identity is extremely important to the Scheibners—they have their own sayings, code words, even a family song. The turning outward that most parents expect of their children and accept, with varying degrees of wistfulness, was to them an intolerable betrayal. "We didn't want to lose our children to other people's ideas and ideologies," Megan will say, or, "We wanted our children's hearts, and we really feel we have them." Home-schooling afforded the prospect that the older kids would help with the younger ones and the younger ones would emulate the older ones instead of their peers.

While we talk, Megan is cooking gravy and pot roast and two kinds of pie, and when the rest of the family comes home it's time for Sunday lunch at the big butcher block table Steve made for them. Despite the presence of seven children, lunch is an orderly business. Interruptions are kept to a minimum—talking out of turn elicits the border-collie look. Still, Peter, who has been studying pirates, chats charmingly about Bluebeard, and Katie reminds me that there were female pirates who "fought like demons." There is a lot of anticipatory discussion of the pies. But lunch, like most meals in the Scheibner household, is also an occasion for moral pedagogy.

The thing about living in a culture from which you feel estranged, and which you therefore do not trust to reinforce your own values, is that you must be vigilant, you can't lose an opportunity to remind your children that they are different, and why. The Scheibners surround themselves as much as possible with a culture of their own making and friends of their own choosing who share their religion, but it's not as though they actually live in a 19th-century village. Just the other week, Katie innocently typed in "girls.com" on the computer—the Scheibner kids are allowed to do research on the Internet—and got hit with a dozen porn sites.

Just before pie is served, Steve asks Katie, as he has many times before, to explain what courtship is. Shyly, she looks down at her plate. "I don't know," she says. To which her mother replies, "You can do better than that, young lady." And she can. She has known the word, at least, since she was 9 and her father took her out for ice cream and a portentous chat. The Scheibners believe that dating, because it usually involves breaking up, is, as Steve puts it, "practice for divorce."

It goes without saying that they do not approve of premarital sex, but what is a little more surprising is that they do not approve of premarital emotional intimacy either. If a couple are courting, they are supposed to be seriously considering each other as husband and wife, and they are supposed to do so with some overt participation by parents or other elders. Ideally, they should not be alone together, or if they are it ought to be in a public place—a Friendly's, say—where liquor is not served and where they are unlikely to give in to temptation. As Steve later explained to me: "If a girl dates 100 guys before she gets married, she's given her heart away 100 times but every time she gets it back, it's a little more scarred. So, when I took Katie out, I had bought this cheap little wedding ring in my size, and I gave it to her and I said: 'This is yours and what it represents is your heart. Go ahead and try it on.' Well, of course it was about as big as three of her fingers. So I said, 'See, it doesn't fit you, but it does fit Daddy, so if you don't mind, I want you to give Daddy your heart and let him hold on to it until the appropriate time when I will give it back to you and you in turn will give it to the man you marry.'"

25   Katie looks up—she's a good girl who wants to please—and murmurs: "It's better than dating. It's waiting for the right man." Now Peter raises his hand. For him, this is all a little more abstract and a little less embarrassing, and he knows he has the answer. "It's keeping your heart pure!"

"Right!" says his father approvingly.

After lunch, Katie goes upstairs without prompting to put young Baleigh and Stephen down for their three-hour afternoon naps—nap time is inviolable at the Scheibner house—and Peter and Emma cheerily start in on the dishes. To a girl and boy, the Scheibner kids are a pleasure to talk to; they're polite and brimming with book-gotten information. They're also a little otherworldly, a bit unnervingly preprogrammed.

When the family came to Washington, where I live, to attend a rally for home-schoolers on the Capitol steps, I went along. It was a hot day and I was nine months pregnant, so I sat down, and while the rest of the children stood patiently with Megan and Steve, Molly, the 7-year-old, wandered over to me. Molly is the dreamy one, the dress-up artist—the one who likes to trail around the house in her mother's wedding gown and who says she wants to be a princess when she grows up. Her hair is honey-colored and waist length, and so, naturally, she maintains a lively interest in the general subject of hair. On the steps, she began doing what a lot of little girls with a lively interest in hair would do, which was to brush mine and, with my permission, to poke through my purse looking for hair ornaments. But though the motions seemed familiar, the dialogue was disconcertingly awry.

'Is President Clinton a Christian?" Molly asked in her singsong voice.

30   "I think he would say so, yes."

"No. He's not. He lies. Do you have a barrette?"

The sun was beating down. A boy skateboarded by in a black T-shirt reading, "Jesus: The Force Without a Dark Side."

"I know who is always against us," Molly continued.

"Who?"

35   "Satan." Brush. Brush.

"Really? What does he do?"

"Makes us lie." Brush. Brush. "Makes us sin." Brush. Brush. "Makes us turn our back on God. What's Play-Doh?"

For more moderate Americans, the persistence of the evangelical strain in our culture is a mystery that both requires and defies explanation. After the embarrassment of the Scopes trial, conservative Christians of all stripes were supposed to have sunk into the past like woolly mammoths in a tar pit. The re-emergence of a Christian right in the mid-80's took no one by greater surprise than the liberal academics and journalists who were frequently called upon to account for it, and to whom the equation of secularity and modernity was itself sacrosanct. As a result, much of the commentary on conservative Christians has tended to portray them, the historian Alan Brinkley points out, "as a group somehow left behind by the modern world—economically, culturally, psychologically." They were, in short, H. L. Mencken's "rustic gorillas" updated, but barely.

The trouble with this theory of "status discontent"—of conservative Christians as downwardly mobile rubes—was that most of them were neither. On "most measures of backwardness," as the sociologist Christian Smith puts it, evangelicals look no different—and frequently look more advanced—than their counterparts who identify themselves as mainline or liberal Protestants, as Catholics or as nonreligious. Of all these groups, evangelicals are the least likely to have had only a high school education or less. They are more likely than liberals or the nonreligious to belong to the $50,000-and-above income bracket. And they are no more likely to live in rural areas than anyone else; the new centers of conservative Christianity, it turns out, are the prosperous suburbs in Midwestern states like Kansas and Oklahoma.

40 Moreover, if you started with a theory of conservative Christians as orphans of history stranded in the modern world, you were more or less helpless to explain why the movement has been flourishing—both in new converts and in retention of members—since the 70's. Smith, a professor of sociology at the University of North Carolina, has one convincing answer. He argues that American evangelicalism is flourishing "because of and not in spite of its confrontation with modern pluralism." In other words, the fragmentation of American culture has encouraged the flowering of all kinds of minority groups, from gays to conservative Christians. More important, modern pluralism allows evangelicals to rub up against ideas and sensibilities that offend them, and this is itself a revitalizing force. "Contemporary pluralism," Smith has written, "creates a situation in which evangelicals can perpetually maintain but can never resolve their struggle with the nonevangelical world."

Over the past few years, engaging in this daily struggle to lead a "godly, righteous and sober life" has been made much easier by the exponential growth of Christian media. People like the Scheibners now have a storehouse of goods and services to which they can return, again and again, to refresh themselves and be entertained without guilt. The ability to encapsulate themselves in a culture of their own making removes some of the incentive to reform the culture at large, while at the same time offering a more fully realized reproof of it—a parallel world, imagined to the last, vivid detail.

Christian books and TV are just the beginning. The contemporary Christian music scene, with its groovily-named bands like Leaderdogs for the Blind and the Insyderz, is a $1-billion-a-year business. You can now buy, over the Internet, everything from Christian computer games to poseable biblical action figures. In the video market, "VeggieTales," a popular kids' series featuring animated vegetables enacting biblical parables, is just one among hundreds of titles—from the "Mother Goose Gospel" to "The Adventures of Prayer Bear."

Conservative Christianity has its own chaste heartthrobs, like Joshua Harris, the raffishly cute author of "I Kissed Dating Good-Bye," and the singer Rebecca St. James, the Alanis Morissette of the W. W. J. D. set. It even has its own indie film scene with movies like "End of the Harvest," in which "a college philosophy club meeting filled with atheists humiliates a new believer who tries to prove to them the existence of God." It has its own magazines for every demographic niche, including *Hopscotch* and *Boys' Quest* for kids 6 to 13, which promise "no teen themes, no boyfriends, girlfriends, makeup, fashion or violence and NO ADVERTISING!"

Combine all this with the fact that the number of home-schoolers has been increasing since 1985 at a rate of 15 to 20 percent a year—there are now about 1.2, million—while enrollment at evangelical colleges grew 24 percent between 1990 and 1996 (compared with an enrollment increase of 5 percent at other private colleges), and it seems fair to say that conservative Christians can live as much as they choose within a culture of their own construction. And that a lot of them are choosing to do so much of the time.

45   For some people, this separatist impulse has been strengthened by a newfound disillusionment with politics. It's not that conservative Christians are fleeing civic duty altogether: evangelicals still vote, for example, at a higher rate than do members of almost any other major religious group. It's more a matter of emphasis—of saying, maybe we were seduced by the promise of political power, and now we have to free ourselves from its thrall and concentrate anew on living faithfully and saving souls.

Steve Scheibner is certainly a patriotic guy: he has served in the Navy for 17 years, most recently flying drug-interdiction flights in the Caribbean. But whereas he once thought of running for political office, he now feels he "could have a greater and longer lasting impact on the lives of people as a pastor." He and Megan are Republicans, and they always vote, but they're not going to be active participants in Campaign 2000. Jerry Falwell, Ralph Reed and most other religious-right leaders don't impress Steve much—they "are mostly political creatures," he says. The one candidate he admires is the firebrand Alan Keyes, who doesn't stand a chance of getting the Republican nomination. The political issue the Scheibners say they care most about is being left alone to home-school, and they see the discipling of others—the training of hearts already opened up to Christ—as their best hope for making a difference in the world.

One icy evening in January, nine young couples crowd into the Scheibners' living room for a class Megan and Steve teach on parenting the Christian way. Angie Dalrymple and her husband, Bruce, have come because they are both new Christians—"my husband got saved in March and I got saved in April"—and she needs help picking her way through unfamiliar moral terrain. Just last week, the Dalrymples' 9-year-old son, Josh, who has also been born again, was facing all kinds of grief at his public school because he now insists on "dressing real nice." Given that he had already ostentatiously thrown his Pokemon cards away, explaining to his classmates that an obsession with the cards could lead to a lifetime fascination with the dark side, he was taking some risks as it was. But Josh is big, which helps, and Angie coaxed him to "get rid of the tie, but keep the button-down shirts." She's proud of him but sometime she feels he's getting ahead of her, spiritually speaking. When his 4-year-old brother, Cody, talked back to her the other day, Josh called his attention to the Ten Commandments on the wall. Now Josh is saying he wants to be home-schooled, and Angie admits to the group that her first thought was, "Whoa, there." She and her husband, a machinist, have already stopped drinking and cursing, cut up their credit cards and canceled their cable TV. How many more changes are there going to be? She's glad to have the group for support.

The agenda for the evening involves watching a video produced by the Christian child-rearing gurus Gary and Ann Marie Ezzo, whose advocacy of rigid schedules for feeding babies, among other things, has been widely criticized by mainstream pediatricians. Tonight's program, though, is a gentler offering, focused on the need to help your child grow morally by giving him "the moral reason why" when you reprimand him for, say, careening around the churchyard and knocking old ladies off-balance—the example given in the video. The evening's discussion also gives the Scheibners a chance to touch on one of their favorite metaphors: the funnel.

The Scheibners think that most parents today err by trying to be "buddies to their babies and little kids." As Megan puts it, they start out with "a big fat funnel, and then, when the kids get to be 13 or 14 and become rebellious, they try to tighten it, and by then it's too late." The Scheibners' idea, they explain, is that you start off with a tight funnel, then gradually open it so that by the time your kids get to be teenagers, you can trust them. They reject what is, in essence, the modern idea of adolescence—that a teenager's alienation from his parents is an inevitable, even necessary step on the way to individuation. For Megan and Steve, rebellion within the family is not an acceptable option; they need a united front at home to wage rebellion against the larger culture. And more important, they believe that obedience to parents trains a child for obedience to God. When the Lord calls him to do something, he has to be ready to say, "Yes, Lord, here I am." So kids need practice in the prompt and cheerful response to commands, learning to do as their parents ask in what the Scheibners refer to as the RAH spirit—for "the Right way, All the way, the Happy way."

50   In other classes, Steve will talk about the need to stand firm when your children push, how you must be the wall that doesn't give way. He'll defend spanking, a practice that the Scheibners have thought through in detail. (Never do it in anger; never do it when you've lost control; use a flexible instrument so you don't break down muscle.)

The atmosphere tonight is a little like a consciousness-raising session—there's an earnest aura of learning together and sustaining one another in a benighted world. During the short break, everybody stands around drinking Diet Cokes and eating the taco salad someone brought, but there's not a lot of small talk. Steve is indisputably the leader, but he's willing to make himself vulnerable with a well-placed confession or two. He mentions, for example, his own upbringing in a very 70's family that left him with nothing in what he likes to call his "moral warehouse." His parents divorced when he was 2; his dad was a pianist who played in clubs, drank a lot and dropped in and out; his two sisters were out of control. "We didn't eat meals together and we had free run. My mom would see me going out the door with a six-pack and say, 'Have fun.'"

Megan's not talking about it tonight, but her story is not all that different. She was the youngest and the only girl her family. In high school, she played tennis competitively and was a waitress after school to save money for a car and a trip to Europe as a pompom girl. Her parents doted on her and couldn't wait for her to start reeling in the boyfriends. "When I was 15, I started dating a college boy, and for my mom, that was just the apex," Megan told me. Tennis kept her straight for a while, but after she suffered a serious ankle injury in her senior year, her "safeguard" was gone and she started drinking as competitively as she had played tennis. She spent summers at Delaware beaches, where, as she says, "it's always happy hour somewhere," and it wasn't long before she had "quite a reputation as a party girl." "Makes me sick now to think of it," she says. Billy Joel and Jackson Browne provided the soundtrack for her life. She says now: "I still wake up some mornings with the lyrics of their songs running through my head. Unbelievable! Anyone who thinks music doesn't affect teens is woefully unaware."

Both she and Steve found Christ when they hooked up with a teen ministry called Young Life. Steve was impressed by the "air of confidence" and "inner peace" he detected in a Young Life staff member named Scott, who was then 24 but willing to hang out with teenagers. "There was something about him that was different, and it kept bugging me and I kept asking him and he kept saying Jesus Christ." Steve didn't want to hear that at first, but after a while he and Scott started talking about the Bible, and something fell into place.

As for Megan, she says she got sick of the beach scene and the sense of purposelessness that washed over her every morning. She found she needed to stop worrying about "having the right boyfriend" to "try and be quiet and learn who it was Christ called me to be." She had started calling herself a Christian in high school, but she hadn't really admitted her sinfulness, let alone renounced it. As a sophomore at West Chester College in Pennsylvania, she finally did, and her "measuring stick" became the Word of God. "He wasn't interested in what I looked like on the outside, but who I was on the inside. Galatians 5:22 says, 'The fruit of the Spirit is love, joy, peace, patience, kindness, goodness, faithfulness, gentleness, self-control.' Suddenly instead of looking in the mirror to see how I was doing, I had to check my heart." She found it an enormous relief "to have the focus off me, me, me."

55   Megan and Steve initially shocked their families with their conversions. One of Steve's sisters, now a Christian herself, was then a graduate student in philosophy at Penn and told him he was "committing intellectual suicide." Megan's mother, "an intelligent woman who considered herself a feminist," as Megan recalls, thought her only daughter was ruining her life. Considering this was at the end of the Me Decade, Steve and Megan were choosing a radical path indeed.

In the Young Life chapter they joined at West Chester, Steve and Megan were the two resident sticklers. They were the ones who, if somebody in Bible study suggested going out for beers afterward, would catch each other's eyes and say naaah. They were friends first, but their sense of needing to start life anew—their joint weariness with their past selves—brought them closer, and they married just after Steve joined the Navy. He was 23 and she was a year younger. Now the two of them have created a life that sometimes, as Steve jokes with the class that night, "can look a little like a bad 'Ozzie and Harriet' rerun."

"Hey," interrupts a young mother in the class. "There are worse things!"

It could be a rallying cry for the group.

10:30 A.M., a school day at the Scheibners'. It's a scene remarkable, as usual, for its orderliness. Everybody has been up since at least 7:30 (all the kids go to bed by 8:30, so rising early is no problem); they've completed their morning clean-up chores, which Megan reminds them of by affixing a yellow Post-it with a specific assignment directly onto each child's body. They have sung hymns, read some Scripture and gone over their catechisms for the day; they have said the Pledge of Allegiance together. The house is warm and tidy and smells pleasantly of the chili Megan is cooking for lunch.

60 Downstairs, in the sunny family room, Baleigh is quietly playing a computer game, while Stephen, the baby, bounces up and down in his playpen. In the "library," a room lined with floor-to-ceiling bookshelves made by Steve, Molly is practicing her handwriting, while Nate works on his reading and tries not to let his mind wander to the dinosaur picture he wants to draw when it's free time. Emma perches on a high stool at the kitchen counter, doing sums in her math book. Upstairs, at a pair of scuffed red old-fashioned school desks, Katie studies grammar while Peter reads about Jamestown in a textbook called "America's Providential History." ("Since God is the author of history and He is carrying out His plan on the earth through history, any view of the history of America, or any country, that ignores God is not true history.")

A week at the Scheibner household follows a neat and repetitive arc, constructed along what the Scheibners call the Loving Our Family Guidelines. Each day has a theme, and a biblical verse to go with it. Monday is Ministry Day ("For God is not unrighteous to forget your work and labor of love, which you have shown toward His name, in that you have ministered to the saints and do minister," Hebrews 6:10). On this day, the children might deliver meals to sick or housebound neighbors. Tuesday is Give Day ("For God so loved the world that He gave his only Son, that whosoever believes in Him should not perish but have eternal life," John 3:16), and so in addition to their regular schoolwork, the kids are supposed to think of something to give one another. Wednesday is Serve Day ("By love serve one another," Galatians 5:13), and the Scheibners do so by performing each other's chores. The family spends every Wednesday evening at Awana Bible Club, a Bible memorization program with about 80 kids in its local chapter. Thursday is Edify Day ("Love edifies," I Corinthians 8:1), which means the kids are supposed to make an effort to compliment each other—and not in a fakey way either. Friday is Prefer Day ("Be kindly affectioned one to another with brotherly love, in honor preferring one another," Romans 12:10), which means, for example, letting your sibling pick the hymn the family will sing in the morning. Friday evenings, Katie and Peter help set up the refreshments for the parenting class, then put the younger kids to bed. Saturday is mostly a preamble to Sunday, but sometimes Megan and the older kids will do some volunteer work at the local homeless shelter, and then follow it up with a special treat—a trip to Friendly's, a rented Shirley Temple video, a game of red rover in the backyard.

One consequence of teaching your children at home—and of carefully customizing their media intake—is that you almost never have the experience of hearing them say something you are surprised and sorry that they know. Maybe your 3-year-old comes home one day with a rather specific question about pro wrestling. Or maybe he has somehow sucked out of the cultural ether the message that you "gotta catch 'em all." Maybe your kid is older and it's something worse. Home-schooling appeals to the parental fantasy of unchallenged dominion over—or at the very least familiarity with—all the detritus that crowds the shelves of your child's "moral warehouse."

I think all parents must be subject to this desire now and again, though comparatively few are willing to remake their lives in the service of it. If your kid were with you all the time, you figure, she would not ask questions that reminded you of your lapses in judgment or vigilance; she would not be in possession of information that you regarded with embarrassment or regret. On the other hand, neither would she be likely to come home with a delightful bit of knowledge that you had nothing to do with putting in her head—a sweet and silly song, a smattering of Spanish, a moral lesson as imparted by someone else—because you might not have known it, perhaps, or thought to plant it there.

Once I asked Steve and Megan if any of their kids ever did come out and say something that shocked them or made them wonder where he or she could possibly have heard it. "That doesn't happen often," Steve replied. "Every now and then we get one of those, but we spend so much time together that it just doesn't happen."

65 Megan and Steve tend not to let their own guard down much around their kids either. Lately, in fact, they have even stopped watching movies with more adult themes by themselves. "We never did used to rent R- rated movies," Steve says, "but we would get a movie that would use some curse words or maybe had some brief nudity." They'd watch it after the kids were asleep and "justify it by saying, 'Oh, but it's a great story.' Well, now we've changed our view on that. I can't ask them to do something I'm not willing to do," Steve continues. "I don't want to be a hypocrite. And you know my relationship with God is just the same as theirs. My soul and my spirit is just as precious to God as their little souls and their little spirits, so how can I justify watching something that is vulgar and obscene for them? Isn't it vulgar and obscene for me too?"

To many of us, the specter of so much control suggests the possibility, even the inevitability, of rebellion. The Scheibners' oldest children are 12 and 11. What happens when they hit their teen years? Won't their hermetically sealed world spring a leak? Generational self-definition is a dearly held precept in our culture, which is why it seems to make sense to us that both Megan and Steve come from religiously indifferent families in which they defiantly distinguished themselves by their theological conservatism.

When you ask the Scheibners to imagine the future for their own kids, though, they can't picture them going astray. Peter has wanted to be a missionary for the longest time now, and since he and his parents regard this as something he has been called to do, they entertain few doubts about his doing it. Admittedly, it's hard to imagine Peter as a renegade. He is the kind of kid who, when asked in all innocence whether he ever listens furtively to his beloved "Lord of the Rings" tape in bed, looks shocked and says, "Oh, no, when it's time to go to bed, it's time to go to bed." He loves being home-schooled, and not long ago took it upon himself to write a letter to Senator Rick Santorum of Pennsylvania. It read, in part, "I have the joy of knowing I am going to heaven because when I was 4, I asked Jesus to come into my heart and save me from sin."

After spending some time with the Scheibner family, I was not particularly surprised to learn that evangelical Christians have one of the highest intergenerational retention rates of any major religion—meaning that, as Christian Smith puts it, "they have a great ability to raise children who do not become theologically liberal or nonreligious when they grow up." Certainly they work extremely hard to prevent what they see as the tragedy of apostasy. And the new availability of Christian media and of home-school curriculums helps enormously. A generation ago, evangelical families who wanted to shield their children from mainstream culture had little to replace it with, other than self-denial. Now they can offer goodies of their own. And new companies and institutions are springing up all the time to meet their needs. The Scheibners, for instance, are very excited about the founding of the first college primarily for Christian home-schoolers, Patrick Henry, in Purcelleville, Va., which will be accepting its inaugural class of students in the fall. Among other things, Patrick Henry will ask its students to sign a pledge in which they promise to court and not date.

And after college? Neither Megan nor Steve is outright opposed to their daughters' working, especially before they have children. Like many conservative Christians, they warm to the idea of a wife running her own little business from the home. "Proverbs 31 talks about the woman who made purple linens at home and sold them," Steve points out. But they warm even more to the idea of their daughters "having an eye to serve without compensation," as Megan says. They think too many working women have forgotten the virtues of volunteerism. And if one of their girls was to pursue a full-fledged career, Steve says, "we'd still love her and encourage her and, after all, at some point it's her life," but they would also find it hard to disguise their disappointment. "A career takes away from what I think their primary happiness will be, which is being a good mother," Steve says.

70 And then he gives a little speech that bears the distinctive hallmarks of the new Christian counterculture. "You know," he says, "you may have lots of pats on the back at work, you may have a successful career and a lot of money and great cars to drive, but in the end it always lets you down. Look at any number of gazillionaires out there—men, women, it doesn't make any difference—who have awful, tragic lives. Those things are not the things that satisfy. The things that satisfy are raising a good family, having love."

America has a long history of separatist movements, and within that history, there are, to put it bluntly, the bad separatists and the good ones. In the former category are the stockpilers of guns, the people who don't pay taxes or vaccinate their children—people who lack any sense of their duty as citizens. And in the latter category are people like the Scheibners. Indeed you could argue that their sort of separatism is good for the culture at large—or at least represents a reasonable compromise. If they are committed to teaching Creationism, for example, better that they teach it at home than insist that the public schools do. Besides, a culture that lacks a thriving and reproving counterculture is always in trouble. The very existence of alternative ways of life like the Scheibners' keeps alive a debate about the role of morality and religion in our culture and politics that probably ought never be declared over and done.

And yet you have to wonder about a way of life that requires such rigorous policing of its psychic boundaries. There is something poignant, for a parent like me anyway, about the idea of sons and daughters who love you as uncomplicatedly in their teenage years as they do when they were small—who are, indeed, your best friends—but there is something unreal about it too. There is something inspiring about the prospect of an American childhood in which advertising does not invade the imagination so relentlessly, but something claustrophobic about the notion that the only alternative is a sequestered family life. There is something fundamentally right and useful about the argument that American culture promotes independence at the expense, often, of the more nurturing virtues, but something sad and scared about the idea that the safest solution to this is early marriage. If the Scheibner philosophy allows girls to linger longer at the threshold of adolescence—not having to worry about being thin or sexy—it also pushes them much earlier into wifely domesticity.

By next summer, the Scheibners will be living in Maine, and they are looking forward to the move. Steve is eager to "plant" his new church. Megan thinks "the slower pace of life" there will make it that much easier to shelter the children from evil. The younger kids are excited about going crabbing and maybe seeing a moose or two on the rambling, wooded acreage where their new house will be. Katie, the oldest, is excited, too. She says she's hoping to find "a little place of my own, where I could read or think, and nobody would know about it."

▩ QUESTIONS FOR INQUIRY AND ACTION ▩

1. Talbot says the Scheibner family has isolated itself from the rest of society in order to "buck mainstream notions of what constitutes a fulfilled life." From details provided in the article, what is the Scheibners' view of a fulfilled life? What is your view? Where does your view of a good life come from—TV shows, your parents, a religious community?

2. Evangelical Christians such as the Scheibners, who have withdrawn from public life, believe their values are incompatible with the larger culture's. What are the Scheibners' values? How are those values ridiculed in the media and the culture at large? Are the Scheibners right to withdraw from our culture?

3. Do you think it is better for people professing a particular religious faith to become politically active or to withdraw from public life? Are there other forms of injustice in American society that might prompt citizens to withdraw and form

their own, alternative communities? Do you think active countercultural movements and separatist movements are good for the United States as a country? Are they good for our democratic system?

4. Because she believes the Scheibners' life is so different from our own, Talbot takes us through a detailed description of their daily routine. If you do not live like this, could you adopt their lifestyle? In what ways would you benefit from such an arrangement? In what ways might you suffer?

James McBride
Black Power

James McBride's "Black Power" is a chapter of his memoir The Color of Water: A Black Man's Tribute to His White Mother *(New York: Riverhead Books, 1996). It began life as an essay he wrote about his mother for the* Boston Globe's *Mother's Day 1981 edition; readers were so moved by the essay that they urged him to tell his mother's full story. McBride has worked as jazz saxophonist and composer as well as a journalist for the* Washington Times.

When I was a boy, I used to wonder where my mother came from, how she got on this earth. When I asked her where she was from, she would say, "God made me," and change the subject. When I asked her if she was white, she'd say, "No. I'm light-skinned," and change the subject again. Answering questions about her personal history did not jibe with Mommy's view of parenting twelve curious, wild, brown-skinned children. She issued orders and her rule was law. Since she refused to divulge details about herself or her past, and because my stepfather was largely unavailable to deal with questions about himself or Ma, what I learned of Mommy's past I learned from my siblings. We traded information on Mommy the way people trade baseball cards at trade shows, offering bits and pieces fraught with gossip, nonsense, wisdom, and sometimes just plain foolishness. "What does it matter to you?" my older brother Richie scoffed when I asked him if we had any grandparents. "You're adopted anyway."

My siblings and I spent hours playing tricks and teasing one another. It was our way of dealing with realities over which we had no control. I told Richie I didn't believe him.

"I don't care if you believe me or not," he sniffed. "Mommy's not your real mother. Your real mother's in jail."

"You're lying!"

5   "You'll see when Mommy takes you back to your real mother next week. Why do you think she's been so nice to you all week?"

Suddenly it occurred to me that Mommy *had* been nice to me all week. But wasn't she nice to me all the time? I couldn't remember, partly because within my confused eight-year-old reasoning was a growing fear that maybe Richie was right. Mommy, after all, did not really look like me. In fact, she didn't look like Richie, or David—or any of her children for that matter. We were all clearly black, of various shades of brown, some light brown, some medium brown, some very light-skinned, and all of us had curly hair. Mommy was, by her own definition, "light-skinned," a statement which I had initially accepted as fact but at some point later decided was not true. My best friend Billy Smith's mother was as light as Mommy was and had red hair to boot, but there was no question in my mind that Billy's mother was black and my mother was not. There was something inside me, an ache I had, like a constant itch that got bigger and bigger as I grew, that told me. It was in my blood, you might say, and however the notion got there, it bothered me greatly. Yet Mommy refused to acknowledge her whiteness. Why she did so was not clear, but even my teachers seemed to know she was white and I wasn't. On open school nights, the question most often asked by my schoolteachers was: "Is James adopted?" which always prompted an outraged response from Mommy.

I told Richie: "If I'm adopted, you're adopted too."

"Nope," Richie replied. "Just you, and you're going back to your real mother in jail."

"I'll run away first."

"You can't do that. Mommy will get in trouble if you do that. You don't want to see Ma get in trouble, do you? It's not her fault that you're adopted, is it?"

He had me then. Panic set in. "But I don't want to go to my real mother. I want to stay here with Ma. . . "

"You gotta go. I'm sorry, man."

This went on until I was in tears. I remember pacing about nervously all day while Richie, knowing he had ruined my life, cackled himself to sleep. That night I lay wide awake in bed waiting for Mommy to get home from work at two A.M., whereupon she laid the ruse out as I sat at the kitchen table in my tattered Fruit of the Loom underwear. "You're not adopted," she laughed.

"So you're my real mother?"

"Of course I am." Big kiss.

"Then who's my grandparents?"

"Your grandpa Nash died and so did your grandma Etta."

"Who were they?"

"They were your father's parents."

"Where were they from?"

"From down south. You remember them?"

I had a faint recollection of my grandmother Etta, an ancient black woman with a beautiful face who seemed very confused, walking around with a blue dress and a fishing pole, the bait, tackle, and line dragging down around her ankles. She didn't seem real to me.

"Did you know them, Ma?"

"I knew them very, very well."

"Did they love you?"

"Why do you ask so many questions?"

"I just want to know. Did they love you? Because your own parents didn't love you, did they?"

"My own parents loved me."

"Then where are they?"

30   A short silence. "My mother died many, many years ago," she said. "My father, he was a fox. No more questions tonight. You want some coffee cake?" Enough said. If getting Mommy's undivided attention for more than five minutes was a great feat in a family of twelve kids, then getting a midnight snack in my house was a greater thrill. I cut the questions and ate the cake, though it never stopped me from wondering, partly because of my own growing sense of self, and partly because of fear for her safety, because even as a child I had a clear sense that black and white folks did not get along, which put her, and us, in a pretty tight space.

In 1966, when I was nine, black power had permeated every element of my neighborhood in St. Albans, Queens. Malcolm X had been killed the year before and had grown larger in death than in life. Afros were in style. The Black Panthers were a force. Public buildings, statues, monuments, even trees, met the evening in their original bland colors and reemerged the next morning painted in the sparkling "liberation colors" of red, black, and green. Congas played at night on the streets while teenyboppers gathered to talk of revolution. My siblings marched around the house reciting poetry from the Last Poets, a sort of rap group who recited in-your-face poetry with conga and fascinating vocal lines serving as a musical backdrop, with songs titled "Niggers Are Scared of Revolution" and "On the Subway." Every Saturday morning my friends and I would pedal our bicycles to the corner of Dunkirk Street and Ilion Avenue to watch the local drag racers near the Sun Dew soft drink factory, trying to see who could drive the fastest over a dip in the road that sent even the slowest-moving car airborne. My stepfather hit that dip at fifteen miles an hour in his '64 Pontiac and I bounced high in my seat. These guys hit it at ninety and their cars flew like birds, barreling through the air and landing fifteen feet away, often skidding out of control, sometimes smacking against the wall of the Sun Dew factory before wobbling away in a pile of bent metal, grilles, and fenders. Their cars had names like "Smokin' Joe" and "Miko" and "Dream Machine" scrawled on the hoods, but our favorite was a gleaming black, souped-up GTO with the words "Black Power" written in smooth white script across the hood and top. It was the fastest and its driver was, of course, the coolest. He drove like a madman, and after leaving some poor Corvette in the dust, he'd power his mighty car in a circle, wheel it around, and do a victory lap for us, driving by at low speed, one muscled arm angling out the window, his car rumbling powerfully, while we whistled and cheered, raising our fists and yelling, "Black power!" He'd laugh and burn rubber for us, tires screeching, roaring away in a burst of gleaming metal and hot exhaust, his taillights flashing as he disappeared into the back alleyways before the cops had a chance to bust him. We thought he was God.

But there was a part of me that feared black power very deeply for the obvious reason. I thought black power would be the end of my mother. I had swallowed the white man's fear of the Negro, as we were called back then, whole. It began with a sober white newsman on our black-and-white television set introducing a news clip showing a Black Panther rally, led by Bobby Seale or Huey Newton or one of those young black militant leaders, screaming to hundreds and hundreds of angry African-American students, "Black power! Black power! Black power!" while the crowd roared. It frightened the shit out of me. I thought to myself, *These people will kill Mommy.* Mommy, on the other hand, seemed unconcerned. Her motto was, "If it doesn't involve your going to school or church, I could care less about it and my answer is no whatever it is."

She insisted on absolute privacy, excellent school grades, and trusted no outsiders of either race. We were instructed never to reveal details of our home life to any figures of authority: teachers, social workers, cops, storekeepers, or even friends. If anyone asked us about our home life, we were taught to respond with, "I don't know," and for years I did just that. Mommy's house was an entire world that she created. She appointed the eldest child at home to be "king" or "queen" to run the house in her absence and we took it from there, creating court jesters, slaves, musicians, poets, pets, and clowns. Playing in the street was discouraged and often forbidden and if you did manage to slip out, "Get your butt in this house before dark," she would warn, a rule she enforced to the bone. I often played that rule out to its very edge, stealing into the house at dusk, just as the last glimmer of sunlight was peeking over the western horizon, closing the door softly, hoping Mommy had gone to work, only to turn around and find her standing before me, hands on hips, whipping belt in hand, eyes flicking angrily back and forth to the window, then to me, lips pursed, trying to decide whether it was light or dark outside. "It's still light," I'd suggest, my voice wavering, as my siblings gathered behind her to watch the impending slaughter.

"That looks like light to you?" she'd snap, motioning to the window.

"Looks pretty dark," my siblings would chirp from behind her. "It's definitely dark, Ma!" they'd shout, stifling their giggles. If I was lucky a baby would wail in another room and she'd be off, hanging the belt on the doorknob as she went. "Don't do it again," she'd warn over her shoulder, and I was a free man.

But even if she had any interest in black power, she had no time to talk about it. She worked the swing shift at Chase Manhattan Bank as a typist, leaving home at three P.M. and returning around two A.M., so she had little time for games, and even less time for identity crises. She and my father brought a curious blend of Jewish-European and African-American distrust and paranoia into our house. On his end, my father, Andrew McBride, a Baptist minister, had his doubts about the world accepting his mixed family. He always made sure his kids never got into trouble, was concerned about money, and trusted the providence of the Holy Father to do the rest. After he died and Mommy remarried, my stepfather, Hunter Jordan, seemed to pick up where my father left off, insistent on education and church. On her end, Mommy had no model for raising us other than the experience of her own Orthodox Jewish family, which despite the seeming flaws—an unbending nature, a stridency, a focus on money, a deep distrust of all outsiders, not to mention her father's tyranny—represented the best and worst of the immigrant mentality: hard work, no nonsense, quest for excellence, distrust of authority figures, and a deep belief in God and education. My parents were nonmaterialistic. They believed that money without knowledge was worthless, that education tempered with religion was the way to climb out of poverty in America, and over the years they were proven right.

Yet conflict was a part of our lives, written into our very faces, hands, and arms, and to see how contradiction lived and survived in its essence, we had to look no farther than our own mother. Mommy's contradictions crashed and slammed against one another like bumper cars at Coney Island. White folks, she felt, were implicitly evil toward blacks, yet she forced us to go to white schools to get the best education. Blacks could be trusted more, but anything involving blacks was probably slightly substandard. She disliked people with money yet was in constant need of it. She couldn't stand racists of either color and had great distaste for bourgeois blacks who sought to emulate rich whites by putting on airs and "doing silly things like covering their couches with plastic and holding teacups with their pinkies out." "What fools!" she'd hiss. She wouldn't be bothered with parents who bragged about their children's accomplishments, yet she insisted we strive for the highest professional goals. She was against welfare and never applied for it despite our need, but championed those who availed themselves of it. She hated restaurants and would not enter one even if the meals served were free. She actually preferred to be among the poor, the working-class poor of the Red Hook Housing Projects in Brooklyn, the cement mixers, bakers, doughnut makers, grandmothers, and soul-food church partisans who were her lifelong friends. It was with them that she and my father started the New Brown Memorial Baptist Church, a small storefront church which still stands in Red Hook today. Mommy loves that church and to this day still loves Red Hook, one of the most dangerous and neglected housing projects in New York City. On any given day she'll get up in the morning, take the New Jersey Transit train from her home in Ewing, New Jersey, to Manhattan, then take the subway to Brooklyn, and wander around the projects like the Pope, the only white person in sight, waving to friends, stepping past the drug addicts, smiling at the young mothers pushing their children in baby carriages, slipping into the poorly lit hallway of 80 Dwight Street while the young dudes in hooded sweatshirts stare balefully at the strange, bowlegged old white lady in Nikes and red sweats who slowly hobbles up the three flights of dark, urine-smelling stairs on arthritic knees to visit her best friend, Mrs. Ingram in apartment 3G.

As a boy, I often found Mommy's ease among black people surprising. Most white folks I knew seemed to have a great fear of blacks. Even as a young child, I was aware of that. I'd read it in the paper, between the lines of my favorite sport columnists in the *New York Post* and the old *Long Island Press,* in their refusal to call Cassius Clay Muhammad Ali, in their portrayal of Floyd Patterson as a "good Negro Catholic," and in their burning criticism of black athletes like Bob Gibson of the St. Louis Cardinals, whom I idolized. In fact I didn't even have to open the paper to see it. I could see it in the faces of the white people who stared at me and Mommy and my siblings when we rode the subway, sometimes laughing at us, pointing, muttering things like, "Look at her with those little niggers." I remember when a white man shoved her angrily as she led a group of us onto an escalator, but Mommy simply ignored him. I remember two black women pointing at us, saying, "Look at that white bitch," and a white man screaming at Mommy somewhere in Manhattan, calling her a "nigger lover." Mommy ignored them all, unless the insults threatened her children, at which time she would turn and fight back like an alley cat, hissing, angry, and fearless. She had a casual way of ignoring affronts, slipping past insults to her whiteness like a seasoned boxer slips punches. When Malcolm X, the supposed demon of the white man, was killed, I asked her who he was and she said, "He was a man ahead of his time." She actually liked Malcolm X. She put him in nearly the same category as her other civil rights heroes, Paul Robeson, Jackie Robinson, Eleanor Roosevelt, A. Philip Randolph, Martin Luther King, Jr., and the Kennedys—any Kennedy. When Malcolm X talked about "the white devil" Mommy simply felt those references didn't apply to her. She viewed the civil rights achievements of black Americans with pride, as if they were her own. And she herself occasionally talked about "the white man" in the third person, as if she had nothing to do with him, and in fact she didn't, since most of her friends and social circle were black women from church. "What's the matter with these white folks?" she'd muse after reading some craziness in the *New York Daily News*. "They're fighting over this man's money now that he's dead. None of them wanted him when he was alive, and now look at them. Forget it, honey"—this is Mommy talking to the newspaper—"your husband's dead, okay? He's dead—pop! You had your chance. Is money gonna bring him back? No!" Then she'd turn to us and deliver the invariable lecture: "You don't need money. What's money if your mind is empty! Educate your mind! Is this world crazy or am I the crazy one? It's probably me."

Indeed it probably was—at least, I thought so. I knew of no other white woman who would board the subway in Manhattan at one o'clock every morning and fall asleep till she got to her stop in Queens forty-five minutes later. Often I could not sleep until I heard her key hit the door. Her lack of fear for her safety—particularly among blacks, where she often stuck out like a sore thumb and seemed an easy target for muggers—had me stumped. As a grown man, I understand now, understand how her Christian principles and trust in God kept her going through all her life's battles, but as a boy, my faith was not that strong. Mommy once took me to Harlem to visit my stepsister, Jacqueline, whom we called Jack and who was my father's daughter by a previous marriage and more like an aunt than a sister. The two of them sat in Jack's parlor and talked into the night while Jack cooked big plates of soul food, macaroni and cheese, sweet potato pies, and biscuits for us. "Take this home to the kids, Ruth," Jack told Ma. We put the food in shopping bags and took it on the subway without incident, but when we got off the bus in St. Albans near our house, two black men came up behind us and one of them grabbed Mommy's purse. The shopping bag full of macaroni and cheese and sweet potato pies burst open and food flew everywhere as Mommy held on to her purse, spinning around in a crazy circle with the mugger, neither saying a word as they both desperately wrestled for the purse, whirling from the sidewalk into the dark empty street like two ballerinas locked in a death dance. I stood frozen in shock, watching. Finally the mugger got the purse and ran off as his buddy laughed at him, and Mommy fell to the ground.

40 She got up, calmly took my hand, and began to walk home without a word.

"You okay?" she asked me after a few moments.

I nodded. I was so frightened I couldn't speak. All the food that Jack had cooked for us lay on the ground behind us, ruined. "Why didn't you scream?" I asked, when I finally got my tongue back.

"It's just a purse," she said. "Don't worry about it. Let's just get home."

The incident confirmed my fears that Mommy was always in danger. Every summer we joined the poor inner-city kids the Fresh Air Fund organization sent to host families or to summer camps for free. The luckier ones among my siblings got to stay with host families, but I had to go to camps where they housed ten of us in a cabin for two weeks at a time. Sometimes they seemed closer to prison or job corps than camp. Kids fought all the time. The food was horrible. I was constantly fighting. Kids called me Cochise because of my light skin and curly hair. Despite all that, I loved it. The first time I went, Mommy took me to the roundup point, a community center in Far Rockaway, once the home of middle-class whites and Jews like playwright Neil Simon, but long since turned black, and it seemed that the only white person for miles was my own mother. The camp organizers set up a table inside where they removed our shoes and shirts and inspected our toes for athlete's foot, checked us for measles and chicken pox, then sent us outside to board a yellow school bus for the long journey to upstate New York. As I sat on the bus peering out the window at Mommy, the only white face in a sea of black faces, a black man walked up with his son. He had a mustache and a goatee and wore black leather pants, a black leather jacket, a ton of jewelry, and a black beret. He seemed outstandingly cool. His kid was very handsome, well dressed, and quite refined. He placed his kid's bags in the back of the bus and when the kid went to step on the bus, instead of hugging the child, the father offered his hand, and father and son did a magnificent, convoluted black-power soul handshake called the "dap," the kind of handshake that lasts five minutes, fingers looping, thumbs up, thumbs down, index fingers collapsing, wrists snapping, bracelets tingling. It seemed incredibly hip. The whole bus watched. Finally the kid staggered breathlessly onto the bus and sat behind me, tapping at the window and waving at his father, who was now standing next to Mommy, waving at his kid.

45 "Where'd you learn that handshake?" someone asked the kid.

"My father taught me," he said proudly. "He's a Black Panther."

The bus roared to life as I panicked. A Black Panther? Next to Mommy? It was my worst nightmare come true. I had no idea who the Panthers truly were. I had swallowed the media image of them completely.

The bus clanked into gear as I got up to open my window. I wanted to warn Mommy. Suppose the Black Panther wanted to kill her? The window was stuck. I tried to move to another window. A counselor grabbed me and sat me down. I said, "I have to tell my mother something."

"Write her a letter," he said.

50 I jumped into the seat of the Black Panther's son behind me—his window was open. The counselor placed me back in my seat.

"Mommy, Mommy!" I yelled at the closed window. Mommy was waving. The bus pulled away.

I shouted, "Watch out for him!" but we were too far away and my window was shut. She couldn't hear me.

I saw the Black Panther waving at his son. Mommy waved at me. Neither seemed to notice the other.

When they were out of sight, I turned to the Black Panther's son sitting behind me and punched him square in the face with my fist. The kid held his jaw and stared at me in shock as his face melted into a knot of disbelief and tears.

▨ QUESTIONS FOR INQUIRY AND ACTION ▨

1. McBride writes that "conflict was a part of our lives, written into our very faces, hands, and arms"; what does he mean by this statement? Where does the conflict come from, and how does McBride's mother deal with it?

2. McBride argues that his mother's model for raising her children "represented the best and worst of the immigrant mentality: hard work, no nonsense, quest for excellence, distrust of authority figures, and a deep belief in God and education." Research your own family history. Is this an accurate description of your own family's experience in America? Why or why not?

3. Do you see McBride's mother as a model of interracial relations in America or an exception? How would your parents react if you dated someone of another race?

4. Reread the Black Panthers' *Ten Point Plan*. What does "Black Power" mean in the Panthers' program and in McBride's story? How are they similar, and how are they different? Why, in the story, does McBride punch the son of a Black Panther?

Fatima Mernissi
Moonlit Nights of Laughter

Fatima Mernissi was born in Fez, Morocco, and is a professor of sociology at the Universite Mohammed V, Agdal, Rabat, Morocco. She is the author of several critical books about Islam and Muslim society, including Islam and Democracy: Fear of the Modern World *(1992) and* Beyond the Veil: Male-Female Dynamics in a Modern Muslim Society *(1975). "Moonlit Nights of Laughter" is from her autobiographical* Dreams of Trespass: Tales of a Harem Girlhood *(New York: Addison-Wesley, 1994).*

On Yasmina's farm, we never knew when we would eat. Sometimes, Yasmina only remembered at the last minute that she had to feed me, and then she would convince me that a few olives and a piece of her good bread, which she had baked at dawn, would be enough. But dining in our harem in Fez was an entirely different story. We ate at strictly set hours and never between meals.

To eat in Fez, we had to sit at our prescribed places at one of the four communal tables. The first table was for the men, the second for the important women, and the third for the children and less important women, which made us happy, because that meant that Aunt Habiba could eat with us. The last table was reserved for the domestics and anyone who had come in late, regardless of age, rank, or sex. That table was often overcrowded, and was the last chance to get anything to eat at all for those who had made the mistake of not being on time.

Eating at fixed hours was what Mother hated most about communal life. She would nag Father constantly about the possibility of breaking loose and taking our immediate family to live apart. The nationalists advocated the end of seclusion and the veil, but they did not say a word about a couple's right to split off from their larger family. In fact, most of the leaders still lived with their parents. The male nationalist movement supported the liberation of women, but had not come to grips with the idea of the elderly living by themselves, nor with couples splitting off into separate households. Neither idea seemed right, or elegant.

Mother especially disliked the idea of a fixed lunch hour. She always was the last to wake up, and liked to have a late, lavish breakfast which she prepared herself with a lot of flamboyant defiance, beneath the disapproving stare of Grandmother Lalla Mani. She would make herself scrambled eggs and *baghrir*, or fine crêpes, topped with pure honey and fresh butter, and, of course, plenty of tea. She usually ate at exactly eleven, just as Lalla Mani was about to begin her purification ritual for the noon prayer. And after that, two hours later at the communal table, Mother was often absolutely unable to eat lunch. Sometimes, she would skip it altogether, especially when she wanted to annoy Father, because to skip a meal was considered terribly rude and too openly individualistic.

5   Mother dreamed of living alone with Father and us kids. "Whoever heard of ten birds living together squashed into a single nest?" she would say. "It is not natural to live in a large group, unless your objective is to make people feel miserable." Although Father said that he was not really sure how the birds lived, he still sympathized with Mother, and felt torn between his duty towards the traditional family and his desire to make her happy. He felt guilty about breaking up the family solidarity, knowing only too well that big families in general, and harem life in particular, were fast becoming relics of the past. He even prophesied that in the next few decades, we would become like the Christians, who hardly ever visited their old parents. In fact, most of my uncles who had already broken away from the big house barely found the time to visit their mother, Lalla Mani, on Fridays after prayer anymore. "Their kids do not kiss hands either," ran the constant refrain. To make matters worse, until very recently, all my uncles had lived in our house, and had only split away when their wives' opposition to communal life had become unbearable. That is what gave Mother hope.

The first to leave the big family was Uncle Karim, Cousin Malika's father. His wife loved music and liked to sing while being accompanied by Uncle Karim, who played the lute beautifully. But he would rarely give in to his wife's desire to spend an evening singing in their salon, because his older brother Uncle Ali thought it unbecoming for a man to sing or play a musical instrument. Finally, one day, Uncle Karim's wife just took her children and went back to her father's house, saying that she had no intention of living in the communal house ever again. Uncle Karim, a cheerful fellow who had himself often felt constrained by the discipline of harem life, saw an opportunity to leave and took it, excusing his actions by saying that he preferred to give in to his wife's wishes rather than forfeit his marriage. Not long after that, all my other uncles moved out, one after the other, until only Uncle Ali and Father were left. So Father's departure would have meant the death of our large family. "As long as [my] Mother lives," he often said, "I wouldn't betray the tradition."

Yet Father loved his wife so much that he felt miserable about not giving in to her wishes and never stopped proposing compromises. One was to stock an entire cupboardful of food for her, in case she wanted to discreetly eat sometimes, apart from the rest of the family. For one of the problems in the communal house was that you could not just open a refrigerator when you were hungry and grab something to eat. In the first place, there were no refrigerators back then. More importantly, the entire idea behind the harem was that you lived according to the group's rhythm. You could not just eat when you felt like it. Lalla Radia, my uncle's wife, had the key to the pantry, and although she always asked after dinner what people wanted to eat the next day, you still had to eat whatever the group—after lengthy discussion—decided upon. If the group settled on couscous with chick-peas and raisins, then that is what you got. If you happened to hate chick-peas and raisins, you had no choice but to shut up and settle for a frugal dinner composed of a few olives and a great deal of discretion.

"What a waste of time," Mother would say. "These endless discussions about meals! Arabs would be much better off if they let each individual decide what he or she wanted to swallow. Forcing everyone to share three meals a day just complicates things. And for what sacred purpose? None of course." From there, she would go on to say that her whole life was an absurdity, that nothing made sense, while Father would say that he could not just break away. If he did, tradition would vanish: "We live in difficult times, the country is occupied by foreign armies, our culture is threatened. All we have left is these traditions." This reasoning would drive Mother nuts: "Do you think that by sticking together in this big, absurd house, we will gain the strength we need to throw the foreign armies out? And what is more important anyway, tradition or people's happiness?" That would put an abrupt end to the conversation. Father would try to caress her hand but she would take it away. "This tradition is choking me," she would whisper, tears in her eyes.

So Father kept offering compromises. He not only arranged for Mother to have her own food stock, but also brought her things he knew she liked, such as dates, nuts, almonds, honey, flour, and fancy oils. She could make all the desserts and cookies she wanted, but she was not supposed to prepare a meat dish or a major meal. That would have meant the beginning of the end of the communal arrangement. Her flamboyantly prepared individual breakfasts were enough of a slap in the face to the rest of the family. Every once in a long while, Mother *did* get away with preparing a complete lunch or a dinner, but she had to not only be discreet about it but also give it some sort of exotic overtone. Her most common ploy was to camouflage the meal as a nighttime picnic on the terrace.

10 These occasional tête-à-tête dinners on the terrace during moonlit summer nights were another peace offering that Father made to help satisfy Mother's yearning for privacy. We would be transplanted to the terrace, like nomads, with mattresses, tables, trays, and my little brother's cradle, which would be set down right in the middle of everything. Mother would be absolutely out of her mind with joy. No one else from the courtyard dared to show up, because they understood all too well that Mother was fleeing from the crowd. What she most

enjoyed was trying to get Father to depart from his conventional self-controlled pose. Before long, she would start acting foolishly, like a young girl, and soon, Father would chase her all around the terrace, when she challenged him. "You can't run anymore, you have grown too old! All you're good for now is to sit and watch your son's cradle." Father, who had been smiling up to that point, would look at her at first as if what she had just said had not affected him at all. But then his smile would vanish, and he would start chasing her all over the terrace, jumping over tea-trays and sofas. Sometimes both of them made up games which included my sister and Samir (who was the only one of the rest of the family allowed to attend our moonlit gatherings) and myself. More often, they completely forgot about the rest of the world, and we children would be sneezing all the next day because they had forgotten to put blankets on us when we had gone to sleep that night.

After these blissful evenings, Mother would be in an unusually soft and quiet mood for a whole week. Then she would tell me that what ever else I did with my life, I had to take her revenge. "I want my daughters' lives to be exciting," she would say, "very exciting and filled with one hundred percent happiness, nothing more, nothing less." I would raise my head, look at her earnestly, and ask what one hundred percent happiness meant, because I wanted her to know that I intended to do my best to achieve it. Happiness, she would explain, was when a person felt good, light, creative, content, loving and loved, and free. An unhappy person felt as if there were barriers crushing her desires and the talents she had inside. A happy woman was one who could exercise all kinds of rights, from the right to move to the right to create, compete, and challenge, and at the same time could feel loved for doing so. Part of happiness was to be loved by a man who enjoyed your strength and was proud of your talents. Happiness was also about the right to privacy, the right to retreat from the company of others and plunge into contemplative solitude. Or to sit by yourself doing nothing for a whole day, and not give excuses or feel guilty about it either. Happiness was to be with loved ones, and yet still feel that you existed as a separate being, that you were not there just to make them happy. Happiness was when there was a balance between what you gave and what you took. I then asked her how much happiness she had in her life, just to get an idea, and she said that it varied according to the days. Some days she had only five percent; others, like the evenings we spent with Father on the terrace, she had full-blown one hundred percent happiness.

Aiming at one hundred percent happiness seemed a bit overwhelming to me, as a young girl, especially since I could see how much Mother labored to sculpt her moments of happiness. How much time and energy she put into creating those wonderful moonlit evenings sitting close to Father, talking softly in his ear, her head on his shoulder! It seemed quite an accomplishment to me because she had to start working on him days ahead of time, and then she had to take care of all the logistics, like the cooking and the moving of the furniture. To invest so much stubborn effort just to achieve a few hours of happiness was impressive, and at least I knew it could be done. But how, I wondered, was I going to create such a high level of excitement for an entire lifetime? Well, if Mother thought it was possible, I should certainly give it a try.

"Times are going to get better for women now, my daughter," she would say to me. "You and your sister will get a good education, and you'll walk freely in the streets and discover the world. I want you to become independent, independent and happy. I want you to shine like moons. I want your lives to be a cascade of serene delights. One hundred percent happiness. Nothing more, nothing less." But when I asked her for more details about how to create that happiness, Mother would grow very impatient. "You have to work at it. One develops the muscles for happiness, just like for walking and breathing."

So every morning, I would sit on our threshold, contemplating the deserted courtyard and dreaming about my beautiful future, a cascade of serene delights. Hanging on to the romantic moonlit terrace evenings, challenging your beloved man to forget about his social duties, relax and act foolish and gaze at the stars while holding your hand, I thought, could be one way to go about developing muscles for happiness. Sculpting soft nights, when the sound of laughter blends with the spring breezes, could be another.

15   But those magical evenings were rare, or so they seemed. During the days, life took a much more rigid and disciplined turn. Officially, there was no jumping around or foolishness allowed in the Mernissi household—all that was confined to clandestine times and spaces, such as late afternoons in the courtyard when the men were out, or evenings on the deserted terraces.

▩ QUESTIONS FOR INQUIRY AND ACTION ▩

1. Mernissi's mother taught her that "happiness was to be with loved ones, and yet still feel that you existed as a separate being, that you were not there just to make them happy." In what ways does Mernissi's mother act for her own happiness, and in what ways does she act for her family's happiness? Are there conflicts between the two?

2. Mernissi centers her story on the individual family's dinner. This is an aspect of American family life that many cultural commentators have observed is fading out: we no longer sit down and eat dinner together as a family. Is this true in your experience? Why is it important to eat dinner together as a family?

3. Write about one of your family's rituals or practices, especially one that varies from what appears to be mainstream practice. Do you prize that ritual and consider it important to your definition of family life? Is it a safe haven from the outside world's practices? Or are you embarrassed by it and ready to discontinue it when you create your own family?

4. Inquire into organizations that cater to various kinds of families, especially families with different cultural traditions from mainstream Americans. What specific needs do those families have?

CASE STUDY

A More Perfect Union: Defining Family Through the Marriage Protection Amendment

Marriage Protection Amendment

This is the text of H.J. Res. 106, called the Marriage Protection Amendment, introduced September 23, 2004, by Rep. Marilyn Musgrave, R-Colo.

JOINT RESOLUTION

Proposing an amendment to the Constitution of the United States relating to marriage.

Resolved by the Senate and House of Representatives of the United States of America in Congress assembled (two-thirds of each House concurring therein), That the following article is proposed as an amendment to the Constitution of the United States, which shall be valid to all intents and purposes as part of the Constitution when ratified by the legislatures of three-fourths of the several States:

Article—

SECTION 1. SHORT TITLE.

This Article may be cited as the "Marriage Protection Amendment".

SECTION 2. MARRIAGE AMENDMENT.

Marriage in the United States shall consist solely of the union of a man and a woman. Neither this Constitution, nor the constitution of any State, shall be construed to require that marriage or the legal incidents thereof be conferred upon any union other than the union of a man and a woman.

Rick Santorum
The Meaning of Family

Rick Santorum is a United States Senator from Pennsylvania. He was elected to the U.S. House of Representatives in 1990 and to the Senate in 1994. A Republican who has become well-known for his conservative stances against abortion and against the constitutional right to privacy that prevents the government from regulating consensual acts among adults, Santorum is also a leading opponent of same-sex marriage. "The Meaning of Family" is a chapter from his book It Takes a Family: Conservatism and the Common Good *(Wilmington, DE: Intercollegiate Studies Institute, 2005). The book's title is intended as a challenge to* It Takes a Village; and Other Lessons Children Teach Us, *by Hillary Rodham Clinton.*

I have been talking about the "traditional" family. By that, I mean a family constituted by a mother and a father who have committed themselves to each other in lifelong marriage, together with their children. This is "traditional," but the reason it is a traditional relationship is because it is fundamentally *natural.* But it is just there that the village elders dig in their heels and cry "Foul!" To the liberal mind, such a definition is "restrictive." It limits our "freedom" to choose who and how we will love. It "excludes" what liberals like to think of as simply "different kinds of families," no better and no worse than the natural family. Liberals get nervous at the very word *natural,* since nature is what we are as human beings, which we cannot change or choose otherwise.

In the tradition of my own faith community, the Catholic Church, we speak about the *natural law,* which we might think of as the operating instructions for human beings. The promise of the natural law is that we will be happiest, and freest, when we follow the law built into our nature as men and women. For liberals, however, *nature* is too confining, and thus is the enemy of *freedom.* Consequently, when liberals think about society, they see only "individuals"—*not* men and women and children. Men and women and children have natures, but liberal "individuals" are abstractions, free to choose anything at all and unconfined by purportedly illusory factors like gender. At first, the liberal vision may sound attractive—because freedom is attractive. The only problem is that it is a false vision, because nature is nature, and the freedom to choose against the natural law is not really freedom at all.

That all sounds pretty philosophical. But take cohabitation, or living together outside of marriage, as an example. Today's conventional wisdom holds that it is better than harmless, that it is a healthy way for a couple to "test drive" marriage. Some even say that cohabitation is better than marriage, since people should be together only when they are in love with one another, and we can never know how and whom we will love in the future: a vow of lifelong love, they say, is unrealistic. Today, the majority of men and women under the age of 30 believe that living together before marriage is a good way to avoid an eventual divorce. About half of all unmarried women between the ages of 25 and 39 have lived with a man whom they were not married to at some point in the past, and about one-quarter are currently living with a man without the benefit of marriage.

The problem is that the myth that living together leads to better marriages is wrong. The opposite is true. One study found that marriages preceded by cohabitation have nearly a 50 percent greater chance of ending in divorce than marriages that were not preceded by cohabitation. Furthermore, children born to parents who are just living together instead of married do not fare very well. Teenagers, for example, growing up with unmarried, cohabiting parents have more emotional and behavioral problems than do teenagers living with their married mother and father.

5   Despite all the evidence, as a society today we will go to almost any length to avoid telling ourselves, and others, the truth: marriage is better than living

together. Too few of us dare say living together without the benefit of marriage is *wrong*. We are afraid to make any such "value judgment." But that is exactly what we need to do. We parents owe it to our children to be honest, to give them a vision of the highest good. Failure to affirm a moral vision to our children is a form of *abandonment* by parents and by society. It leaves our children defenseless against the endless parade of influences the popular culture has in store for them.

And we need to be honest about the latest liberal assault on our marriage tradition as well. Even a year or two ago, few Americans imagined that we would be facing the issue of same-sex marriage today. Thanks to a few activist justices on the U.S. Supreme Court and to even more activist judges in Massachusetts, however, America is on the verge of undergoing a social revolution simply without any historical precedent. There are few places where the clash between what freedom means and its impact on families is clearer than when it comes to transforming the definition of marriage.

Liberals believe that the traditional family is neither natural nor vital, that it's an antiquated social convention which has not only outlived its usefulness, but is now inherently discriminatory and repressive toward legitimate alternative "families." As the Massachusetts high court said to the legislature of Massachusetts concerning the *Goodrich* case, "For no rational reason the marriage laws of the Commonwealth discriminate against a defined class (homosexuals); no amount of tinkering with language will eradicate that stain." So traditional marriage is a stain on the fabric of America that needs to be "Shouted out." How have we come to this?

It may come as a shock to some, but marriage is not, and never has been, just about the sex life of consenting adults. However, given the self-centeredness of our popular culture, it is not surprising that many adults today see marriage as about them being happy as individuals. This is one of the reasons our divorce rate is so high. Since marriage has become more and more about adult happiness, and less and less about children and their well-being, it is no wonder other groups in society want to use marriage for the same purpose. In fact, one of the criticisms I often hear when I speak with proponents of same-sex marriage is that heterosexuals have so deconstructed marriage through no-fault divorce that today marriage is only about adults, so why shouldn't it include them too? Touché! But do I need to say in response that two wrongs don't make a right?

Society's interest in protecting marriage goes beyond the public recognition of a romantic relationship and making people feel accepted. I've made the case that the reason our society has such a strong interest in strengthening the institution of marriage is because marriage as we traditionally understood it is far and away the best place for raising children—who happen to be the future of any society. All of the "legal incidents" of marriage built up over the years aim to secure a stable family in which to welcome children. Every known society has some form of marriage. And it's always about bringing together a male and female into the kind of sexual union where the interests of children under the care of their own mother and father are protected. Marriage is the word for the way in which we connect a man, a woman, and their children into one loving family. It represents our best attempt to see that every child receives his or her birthright: the right to know and be known by, to love and be loved by, his or her own mother and father.

10   When liberals, through unelected judges, order us to change this understanding of marriage into something radically different, the result is likely to be dangerous for children and for society. When the state declares two men marrying is just as valuable to society as the union of husband and wife, this is not neutrality, it is radical social engineering. It commits the government to the position that family structure does not matter; that children don't need fathers (or mothers for that matter), just abstract individual "caregivers." It shifts marriage further away from its core purpose of protecting the needs of (and the need for) children. It would transform our public understanding of marriage so that marriage would mean something like mere cohabitation, an adult relationship to be formed as adults please, rather than as children need.

Do we need to confuse future generations of Americans even more about the role and importance of an institution that is so critical to the common good? It is because children have a right to a faithfully married mother and father that we must oppose this radical redefinition—not because we are mean-spirited.

Moreover, once the government commits to same-sex marriage as a civil right, it will use the power of the state to enforce this new vision of marriage. Public schools will teach it, of course. But the logic of same-sex marriage will lead inevitably to even more government intrusion on the freedom of people and faith communities who continue to define marriage as the union of husbands and wives. What do I mean? When in *Loving v. Virginia* the Supreme Court ruled that state laws banning interracial marriage were unconstitutional, that ruling seemed at first to affect only private individuals. But sixteen years later, the IRS ruled that religious groups that opposed interracial marriage could be stripped of their tax-exempt status, because they were not operating for the public good. The Supreme Court ruled furthermore that the First Amendment's protection of the free exercise of religion provided no defense. Of course, I agree that laws against interracial marriage were unjust. My point is this: If we apply the logic of a civil right to same-sex marriage, people who believe children need mothers and fathers will be treated in the public square like racists, and churches that persist in teaching the traditional norm will risk the loss of their tax-exempt status. In other words, such churches will be treated as outlaws. How can we turn boys into good family men in a society that treats the idea that fathers matter as a form of bigotry?

Same-sex marriage is really "liberal marriage." That is, the "right" of homosexuals to "marry" one another is a logical result of what *must* happen to the definition of marriage if we view society as composed of nothing but abstract, autonomous *individuals*, rather than of men and women with their given natures. Abstract individuals, after all, are completely interchangeable and completely "free" to define who and what they are. To the liberal mind, therefore, there is no "rational basis" for limiting marriage only to people of opposite sexes; and that is what the four left-wing judges in Massachusetts held. Our village elders now declare that those holding to the traditional understanding of marriage are simply irrational.

But there is one more thing about these abstract, autonomous individuals that the left say are the real basis of society. Call it the liberal's marriage paradox. Individuals are free to do anything they want, including to redefine marriage, gender, and basic social institutions in pursuit of individual desire and preference. There is only one thing that individuals cannot do if they are to remain autonomous: they cannot commit themselves permanently to another human being. To do so would be a kind of slavery. As a result, the left's view of any marriage contract is that it is really only a kind of cohabitation, the choice of two people, each day, to continue together, but always with the perfect freedom to leave whenever either chooses. Of course, all too many marriages today end in divorce, and to most Americans that is a tragedy. But in "liberal marriage," there can never be any real expectation of permanence. In a society in which the liberal understanding of marriage becomes the law of the land, divorce would not only be the norm rather than the exception, but the institution of marriage would disappear altogether.

Just imagine two or three generations from now, if we legalize same-sex marriage today, what young adults will understand about marriage. Keep in mind that they will have been raised in a society that considers marriage nothing more than a romantic and sexual coupling between men and men, women and women, and men and women. The law will have declared it so, dissenters will be pressured into silence, and public schools will embrace and teach same-sex marriage as the law of the land. Laws have meaning, and therefore, laws *teach*. When something is legal it has the presumption that it is moral and right. If the sexual unions of men with men and women with women have equal dignity with the union of men and women, then marriage cannot be understood as having anything intrinsically to do with children. Society will teach the next generation that marriage is a self-centered endeavor primarily about adult satisfaction, not children's well-being.

15   What happens to a society that disconnects marriage from babies in this way? The connection has already been strained by the consequences of children being born out of wedlock and the damage wrought by our divorce culture. Same-sex marriage severs this connection completely. Once same-sex marriage becomes firmly entrenched as the law of the land, we can expect to get even more children being raised outside of marriage. And we will also have fewer children, period.

We don't need to hypothesize about what would happen if America definitively adopted the liberal conception of marriage: all we need to do is look to Europe today. European law has begun not only to acknowledge same-sex unions as marriages but also to treat cohabiting couples just the same as married couples. America, a mobile society, has always had somewhat higher divorce rates than Europe, but today European countries are catching up fast. And Europeans appear firmly committed to the most disastrous family trend of all: they are simply not having children.

The Council of Europe's Demographic Yearbook 2003 reports,

> In all European countries, except Turkey, the total fertility rate is currently below replacement level . . . . The main features of nuptiality are the declining number of marriages, the rise in the number of separations, and the appearance of other forms of union, particularly cohabitation. There has also been a widespread parallel increase in the number of births outside marriage. In certain countries, such as Iceland, Norway, Sweden, Estonia, and the former German Democratic Republic, such births represent more than 50 percent of the total.

The report goes on to state, "Generally speaking, natural growth (the excess of births over deaths) is declining in Europe, and in more and more cases is negative or only marginally positive. In 1990, three countries—Germany, Bulgaria and Hungary—had negative natural growth for the first time. By 2002, it was negative in fifteen countries . . . ."

20   Relatively few Americans are aware of this dramatic change. "Very low fertility" is a birthrate below 1.5 children. Europe's *total* fertility rate from 1995 to 2000 was 1.42 children per woman. In 2002, 28 nations experienced very low fertility, including Switzerland (1.4), Germany (1.3), Austria (1.3), Italy (1.3), Spain (1.2), Greece (1.3), Japan (1.3), Russia (1.3), the Czech Republic (1.1), and most other Eastern European nations.

What are the consequences of low fertility rates? At the April 2, 2004, meeting of the Population Association of America, United Nations demographer Joseph Chamie warned, "A growing number of countries view their low birth rates with the resulting population decline and aging to be a serious crisis, jeopardizing the basic foundations of the nation and threatening its survival. Economic growth and vitality, defense, and pensions and health care for the elderly, for example, are all areas of major concern."

Scholars do not agree on all the causes of low fertility, but the increasing disconnect between marriage and childbearing plays a clear role. At the Expert Group Meeting on Policy Responses to Population Aging and Population Decline in New York in October 2000, demographer Patrick Festy observed:

> Low fertility can also be linked to the movement away from marriage, which many western European countries have experienced for the recent decades. Of course, marriage is no longer a precondition for childbearing in most of these populations, but it remains true that married couples have a higher fertility than non-married people, even those who live in a "marriage-like" cohabitation.

What all of this means is that the nations of Europe are slowly dying off—sometimes not so slowly. Today, European governments are struggling with an increasingly aging population, large-scale immigration challenges, a rise in disturbing ultranationalism, and all of the individual and community issues that arise when children grow up without fathers. And not surprisingly, Europeans seem incapable of making the changes in their welfare and pension systems that are absolutely necessary to prevent a future fiscal crisis. Why not? Because without children, they have no future. They are failing in their responsibility to be stewards of their inheritance—because they do not see anyone after them who will inherit.

25   Irving Kristol once wrote that the most subversive question that can be posed to civilization is: Why not? Thanks to the decision of four activist liberal judges in Massachusetts, that is a question we now must face as Americans. In order to answer the question of "Why not?" with respect to same-sex marriage, we have to come to a fuller understanding of what marriage is. Is it simply about publicly honoring a romantic attachment? That's what the highest court in Ontario, Canada, believes. Just in time for the June wedding season of 2003 that court wrote, as it ruled in favor of same-sex marriages:

> Marriage is, without dispute, one of the most significant forms of personal relationship . . . . Through the institution of marriage, individuals can publicly express their love and commitment to each other. Through this institution, society publicly recognizes

expressions of love and commitment between individuals, granting them respect and legitimacy as a couple.

Marriage in this view means nothing more to society, to what we are as a people, and to our future, than making people feel accepted. The state's interest in promoting and stamping approval upon a marriage starts and stops with tolerance, and is therefore meaningless.

When we think about it for just a minute, Americans with loving hearts may be tempted to agree with Ontario's highest court. But if we think about it for ten minutes or longer, I think Americans will come to recognize that traditional marriage is what it is for good reasons. Who could have imagined that it would take courage to say: there is a rational basis for limiting marriage only to persons of the opposite sex? But we need that courage today. In a compassionate society, adult interests and agendas cannot be allowed to trump the basic needs and rights of children. A forward-thinking society reaches out to children in every family form, but it never deliberately endorses or encourages adults to deprive their children of a mother or a father. Men and women marry for many reasons. But the reason the law is involved in marriage is to protect society's future.

Unfortunately, as I will discuss in detail later, our courts are changing the landscape of the family by de facto amending our Constitution. Starting its campaign with the line of cases establishing the so-called right to privacy, the shock troops of the village elders are now battering at the gates of the fortress of marriage. The gates will not long hold. The fortress is but a few years away—at most!—of being laid to ruin, unless we, like the apparently doomed warriors at Helms Deep in the movie *The Two Towers,* make that last charge against the foe. Like them, it will take all of our effort, and the help of forces unseen, but it is a fight that must be waged.

30   That is why I support the Marriage Protection Amendment and commend President Bush for doing likewise. The amendment would spell out in our Constitution what our founding fathers could not have fathomed would someday need to be said: that marriage is the union of one man and one woman. I fully understand that amending the Constitution is the most solemn of legislative changes and therefore should only be used as a last resort. But I fear we have reached the moment of last resort. Unlike the courts, Congress does not have the power to change the Constitution through a simple majority of one body. Congress must amend the Constitution as our founders provided for in that Constitution. The amendment must pass the House and the Senate with a supermajority of two-thirds and then be ratified by a supermajority of three-fourths of the states. It is a long and difficult process.

In 2004, thanks to the tremendous work by citizen groups led by, among others, Dr. James Dobson and Maggie Gallagher, the fine scholarship of Stanley Kurtz, and the leadership in the Senate of Senator Bill Frist, the Marriage Protection Amendment was brought to the floor for a vote. The Senate Democrat leadership refused to allow the amendment to be debated, amended, and voted upon. Senator Frist was forced to file cloture to end the Democrats' filibuster. But the vote failed to get even a simple majority. This is going to be a tough fight. But I am heartened by the fact that in the eleven states that held referendums on marriage in 2004, the supporters of traditional marriage won every time, and almost always by a large margin.

Like so many important issues in our nation's history, it may take years for the Marriage Protection Amendment to pass. But like many other great struggles to ensure the common good, I am confident that it will one day become law.

Maggie Gallagher
What Marriage Is For

Maggie Gallagher is President of the Institute for Marriage and Public Policy, whose mission is "research and public education on ways that law and public policy can strengthen marriage as a social institution." She is also editor of the Web site MarriageDebate.com and the co-author, with Linda Waite, of The Case for Marriage: Why Married People Are Happier, Healthier, and Better-Off Financially. *"What Marriage Is For" was originally published in the* Weekly Standard *(August 4–11, 2003).*

Gay marriage is no longer a theoretical issue. Canada has it. Massachusetts is expected to get it any day. The Goodridge decision there could set off a legal, political, and cultural battle in the courts of 50 states and in the U.S. Congress. Every politician, every judge, every citizen has to decide: Does same-sex marriage matter? If so, how and why?

The timing could not be worse. Marriage is in crisis, as everyone knows: High rates of divorce and illegitimacy have eroded marriage norms and created millions of fatherless children, whole neighborhoods where lifelong marriage is no longer customary, driving up poverty, crime, teen pregnancy, welfare dependency, drug abuse, and mental and physical health problems. And yet, amid the broader negative trends, recent signs point to a modest but significant recovery.

Divorce rates appear to have declined a little from historic highs; illegitimacy rates, after doubling every decade from 1960 to 1990, appear to have leveled off, albeit at a high level (33 percent of American births are to unmarried women); teen pregnancy and sexual activity are down; the proportion of homemaking mothers is up; marital fertility appears to be on the rise.

Research suggests that married adults are more committed to marital permanence than they were twenty years ago. A new generation of children of divorce appears on the brink of making a commitment to lifelong marriage. In 1977, 55 percent of American teenagers thought a divorce should be harder to get; in 2001, 75 percent did.

5   A new marriage movement—a distinctively American phenomenon—has been born. The scholarly consensus on the importance of marriage has broadened and deepened; it is now the conventional wisdom among child welfare organizations. As a Child Trends research brief summed up: "Research clearly demonstrates that family structure matters for children, and the family structure that helps children the most is a family headed by two biological parents in a low-conflict marriage.

Children in single-parent families, children born to unmarried mothers, and children in stepfamilies or cohabiting relationships face higher risks of poor outcomes . . . . There is thus value for children in promoting strong, stable marriages between biological parents."

What will court-imposed gay marriage do to this incipient recovery of marriage? For, even as support for marriage in general has been rising, the gay marriage debate has proceeded on a separate track. Now the time has come to decide: Will unisex marriage help or hurt marriage as a social institution?

Why should it do either, some may ask? How can Bill and Bob's marriage hurt Mary and Joe? In an exchange with me in the just-released book "Marriage and Same Sex Unions: A Debate," Evan Wolfson, chief legal strategist for same-sex marriage in the Hawaii case, *Baer v. Lewin*, argues there is "enough marriage to share." What counts, he says, "is not family structure, but the quality of dedication, commitment, self-sacrifice, and love in the household."

Family structure does not count. Then what is marriage for? Why have laws about it? Why care whether people get married or stay married? Do children need mothers and fathers, or will any sort of family do? When the sexual desires of adults clash with the interests of children, which carries more weight, socially and legally?

These are the questions that same-sex marriage raises. Our answers will affect not only gay and lesbian families, but marriage as a whole.

10 In endorsing gay marriage on June 10, 2003, the highest court in Ontario, Canada, explicitly endorsed a brand new vision of marriage along the lines Wolfson suggests: "Marriage is, without dispute, one of the most significant forms of personal relationships . . . . Through the institution of marriage, individuals can publicly express their love and commitment to each other. Through this institution, society publicly recognizes expressions of love and commitment between individuals, granting them respect and legitimacy as a couple."

The Ontario court views marriage as a kind of Good Housekeeping Seal of Approval that government stamps on certain registered intimacies because, well, for no particular reason the court can articulate except that society likes to recognize expressions of love and commitment. In this view, endorsement of gay marriage is a no-brainer, for nothing really important rides on whether anyone gets married or stays married. Marriage is merely individual expressive conduct, and there is no obvious reason why some individuals' expression of gay love should hurt other individuals' expressions of non-gay love.

There is, however, a different view—indeed, a view that is radically opposed to this: Marriage is the fundamental, cross-cultural institution for bridging the male-female divide so that children have loving, committed mothers and fathers. Marriage is inherently normative: It is about holding out a certain kind of relationship as a social ideal, especially when there are children involved.

Marriage is not simply an artifact of law; neither is it a mere delivery mechanism for a set of legal benefits that might as well be shared more broadly. The laws of marriage do not create marriage, but in societies ruled by law they help trace the boundaries and sustain the public meanings of marriage.

In other words, while individuals freely choose to enter marriage, society upholds the marriage option, formalizes its definition, and surrounds it with norms and reinforcements, so we can raise boys and girls who aspire to become the kind of men and women who can make successful marriages. Without this shared, public aspect, perpetuated generation after generation, marriage becomes what its critics say it is: a mere contract, a vessel with no particular content, one of a menu of sexual lifestyles, of no fundamental importance to anyone outside a given relationship.

15　　The marriage idea is that children need mothers and fathers, that societies need babies, and that adults have an obligation to shape their sexual behavior so as to give their children stable families in which to grow up.

Which view of marriage is true? We have seen what has happened in our communities where marriage norms have failed. What has happened is not a flowering of libertarian freedom, but a breakdown of social and civic order that can reach frightening proportions. When law and culture retreat from sustaining the marriage idea, individuals cannot create marriage on their own.

In a complex society governed by positive law, social institutions require both social and legal support. To use an analogy, the government does not create private property. But to make a market system a reality requires the assistance of law as well as culture. People have to be raised to respect the property of others, and to value the traits of entrepreneurship, and to be law-abiding generally. The law cannot allow individuals to define for themselves what private property (or law-abiding conduct) means. The boundaries of certain institutions (such as the corporation) also need to be defined legally, and the definitions become socially shared knowledge. We need a shared system of meaning, publicly enforced, if market-based economies are to do their magic and individuals are to maximize their opportunities.

Successful social institutions generally function without people's having to think very much about how they work. But when a social institution is contested—as marriage is today—it becomes critically important to think and speak clearly about its public meanings.

Again, what is marriage for? Marriage is a virtually universal human institution. In all the wildly rich and various cultures flung throughout the ecosphere, in society after society, whether tribal or complex, and however bizarre, human beings have created systems of publicly approved sexual union between men and women that entail well-defined responsibilities of mothers and fathers. Not all these marriage systems look like our own, which is rooted in a fusion of Greek, Roman, Jewish, and Christian culture. Yet everywhere, in isolated mountain valleys, parched deserts, jungle thickets, and broad plains, people have come up with some version of this thing called marriage. Why?

20　　Because sex between men and women makes babies, that's why. Even today, in our technologically advanced contraceptive culture, half of all pregnancies are unintended: Sex between men and women *still* makes babies. Most men and women are powerfully drawn to perform a sexual act that can and does generate life. Marriage is our attempt to reconcile and harmonize the erotic, social, sexual, and financial needs of men and women with the needs of their partner and their children.

How to reconcile the needs of children with the sexual desires of adults? Every society has to face that question, and some resolve it in ways that inflict horrendous cruelty on children born outside marriage. Some cultures decide these children don't matter: Men can have all the sex they want, and any children they create outside of marriage will be throwaway kids; marriage is for citizens—slaves and peasants need not apply. You can see a version of this elitist vision of marriage emerging in America under cover of acceptance of family diversity. Marriage will continue to exist as the social advantage of elite communities. The poor and the working class? Who cares whether their kids have dads? We can always import people from abroad to fill our need for disciplined, educated workers.

Our better tradition, and the only one consistent with democratic principles, is to hold up a single ideal for all parents, which is ultimately based on our deep cultural commitment to the equal dignity and social worth of all children. All kids need and deserve a married mom and dad. All parents are supposed to at least try to behave in ways that will give their own children this important protection. Privately, religiously, emotionally, individually, marriage may have many meanings. But this is the core of its public, shared meaning: Marriage is the place where having children is not only tolerated but welcomed and encouraged, because it gives children mothers and fathers.

Of course, many couples fail to live up to this ideal. Many of the things men and women have to do to sustain their own marriages, and a culture of marriage, are *hard*. Few people will do them consistently if the larger culture does not affirm the critical importance of marriage as a social institution. Why stick out a frustrating relationship, turn down a tempting new love, abstain from sex outside marriage, or even take pains not to conceive children out of wedlock if family structure does not matter? If marriage is not a shared norm, and if successful marriage is not socially valued, do not expect it to survive as the generally accepted context for raising children. If marriage is just a way of publicly celebrating private love, then there is no need to encourage couples to stick it out for the sake of the children. If family structure does not matter, why have marriage laws at all? Do adults, or do they not, have a basic obligation to control their desires so that children can have mothers and fathers?

The problem with endorsing gay marriage is not that it would allow a handful of people to choose alternative family forms, but that it would require society at large to gut marriage of its central presumptions about family in order to accommodate a few adults' desires.

25   The debate over same-sex marriage, then, is not some sideline discussion. It *is* the marriage debate. Either we win—or we lose the central meaning of marriage. The great threat unisex marriage poses to marriage as a social institution is not some distant or nearby slippery slope, it is an abyss at our feet. If we cannot explain why unisex marriage is, in itself, a disaster, we have already lost the marriage ideal.

Same-sex marriage would enshrine in law a public judgment that the desire of adults for families of choice outweighs the need of children for mothers and fathers. It would give sanction and approval to the creation of a motherless or fatherless family as a deliberately chosen "good." It would mean the law was neutral as to whether children had mothers and fathers. Motherless and fatherless families would be deemed just fine.

Same-sex marriage advocates are startlingly clear on this point. Marriage law, they repeatedly claim, has nothing to do with babies or procreation or getting mothers and fathers for children. In forcing the state legislature to create civil unions for gay couples, the high court of Vermont explicitly ruled that marriage in the state of Vermont has nothing to do with procreation. Evan Wolfson made the same point in "Marriage and Same Sex Unions": "[I]sn't having the law pretend that there is only one family model that works (let alone exists) a lie?" He goes on to say that in law, "marriage is not just about procreation—indeed is not necessarily about procreation at all."

Wolfson is right that in the course of the sexual revolution the Supreme Court struck down many legal features designed to reinforce the connection of marriage to babies. The animus of elites (including legal elites) against the marriage idea is not brand new. It stretches back at least thirty years. That is part of the problem we face, part of the reason 40 percent of our children are growing up without their fathers.

It is also true, as gay-marriage advocates note, that we impose no fertility tests for marriage: Infertile and older couples marry, and not every fertile couple chooses procreation. But every marriage between a man and a woman is capable of giving any child they create or adopt a mother and a father. Every marriage between a man and a woman discourages either from creating fatherless children outside the marriage vow. In this sense, neither older married couples nor childless husbands and wives publicly challenge or dilute the core meaning of marriage. Even when a man marries an older woman and they do not adopt, his marriage helps protect children. How? His marriage means, if he keeps his vows, that he will not produce out-of-wedlock children.

30   Does marriage discriminate against gays and lesbians? Formally speaking, no. There are no sexual-orientation tests for marriage; many gays and lesbians do choose to marry members of the opposite sex, and some of these unions succeed. Our laws do not require a person to marry the individual to whom he or she is most erotically attracted, so long as he or she is willing to promise sexual fidelity, mutual caretaking, and shared parenting of any children of the marriage.

But marriage is unsuited to the wants and desires of many gays and lesbians, precisely because it is designed to bridge the male-female divide and sustain the idea that children need mothers and fathers. To make a marriage, what you need is a husband and a wife. Redefining marriage so that it suits gays and lesbians would require fundamentally changing our legal, public, and social conception of what marriage is in ways that threaten its core public purposes.

Some who criticize the refusal to embrace gay marriage liken it to the outlawing of interracial marriage, but the analogy is woefully false. The Supreme Court overturned anti-miscegenation laws because they frustrated the core purpose of marriage in order to sustain a racist legal order. Marriage laws, by contrast, were not invented to express animus toward homosexuals or anyone else. Their purpose is not negative, but positive: They uphold an institution that developed, over thousands of years, in thousands of cultures, to help direct the erotic desires of men and women into a relatively narrow but indispensably fruitful channel. We need men and women to marry and make babies for our society to survive. We have no similar public stake in any other family form—in the union of same-sex couples or the singleness of single moms.

Meanwhile, *cui bono?* To meet the desires of whom would we put our most basic social institution at risk? No good research on the marriage intentions of homosexual people exists. For what it's worth, the Census Bureau reports that 0.5 percent of households now consist of same-sex partners. To get a proxy for how many gay couples would avail themselves of the health insurance benefits marriage can provide, I asked the top 10 companies listed on the Human Rights Campaign's website as providing same-sex insurance benefits how many of their employees use this option. Only one company, General Motors, released its data. Out of 1.3 million employees, 166 claimed benefits for a same-sex partner, *one one-hundredth of one percent.*

People who argue for creating gay marriage do so in the name of high ideals: justice, compassion, fairness. Their sincerity is not in question. Nevertheless, to take the already troubled institution most responsible for the protection of children and throw out its most basic presumption in order to further adult interests in sexual freedom would not be high-minded. It would be morally callous and socially irresponsible.

35   If we cannot stand and defend this ground, then face it: The marriage debate is over. Dan Quayle was wrong. We lost.

WRITING STYLE

CREATING A PAMPHLET

The Slippery Slope of Same-Sex Marriage, published by the Family Research Council (FRC) in 2004, is an example of a pamphlet created as part of a public education and political lobbying campaign. One of the policy publications of the FRC, the pamphlet was developed in response to the debate over a constitutional amendment banning same-sex marriages. The author, Timothy J. Dailey, Ph.D., is a Senior Fellow of the Center for Marriage and Family Studies at the Family Research Council.

The pamphlet was published in both a paper form and as a downloadable document available from the Web site of the FRC http://www.frc.org/. We suggest you download a copy to refer to while reading this Writing Style box and creating your own pamphlets. You can find the pamphlet on the FRC's Center for Marriage and Family Studies page: http://www.frc.org/get.cfm?c=PROTECTMARRIAGE.

The 13-page pamphlet is a detailed, highly-polished piece of work financed by the Family Research Council in Washington, D.C. Your own pamphlets, especially while you are in school, may not be this involved. However, this kind of public writing can easily be done by students and can be tailored to events taking place on your campus and in your communities, and can be a fast and effective way of informing and mobilizing a group of people. Regardless of their size and the magnitude of the issue they address, pamphlets have as their goal to educate and persuade people who are not expected to know much about the issue at hand. Notice how this pamphlet provides:

- *A catchy introduction.* A photograph of part of a horse's eyes accompanies the opening section, "A Man and His Horse," which compares a Missouri man's desire to marry his horse to the logic employed by supporters of same-sex marriage. This story serves as a thesis for the pamphlet's "slippery slope" argument.

- *An overview of the issue and its importance.* To underscore the urgency of the issue and how it will affect readers and their communities, gay marriage is introduced as a threat to marriage, and the key arguments the pamphlet will address are introduced in a set of bullet points, for example, "Gay marriage threatens the institutions of marriage and the family," "Gay marriage is not a civil rights issue," and "Homosexuality is rightly viewed as unnatural."

- *Specific consequences of the issue.* Readers are urged to view this issue as public rather than private, with consequences that reach beyond individual family units. The pamphlet depicts marriage and family arrangements that jeopardize couples' intimacy and their attention to children: polyamorous "group marriages" and a "frat house concept" of family with "revolving bedroom doors." Homosexual marriage "cheapens and degrades" heterosexual marriage, it is argued, and causes "cumulative damage" to a society.

- *Encouragement for readers to take action on the issue.* The pamphlet concludes with a focus on the federal constitutional amendment, and addresses readers as citizens who have the "obligation to make our voices heard in the political process" and that "[t]hose who value the family have a God-given duty to become involved in what is shaping as the preeminent moral issue of our day: protecting the very institution of marriage."

- *Bibliography and sources for further research.* The pamphlet's endnotes provide resources for readers to examine the evidence used by the FRC for their argument.

- *Visual interest.* To break up the text into manageable chunks and provide interest to readers, the pamphlet includes boldfaced subheadings to direct readers from section to section, as well as different fonts, graphs, photographs, and other illustrations.

Discuss your response to this pamphlet. For instance, its goal is to educate the public. But it also has a specific argument to make and agenda to promote. Should the pamphlet attempt to be balanced in its coverage, to provide the FRC's point of view, and to leave it to readers to make their own decisions? Or is it more ethical to openly state the agenda of the authors?

Tom Tomorrow
A Brief History of Marriage in America

Tom Tomorrow is a political cartoonist whose weekly strip This Modern World *is published widely and is a regular feature at Salon.com and in the* Village Voice, *among other periodicals. In 1998, he won the first place Robert F. Kennedy Journalism Award for Cartooning, and in 2000, the Professional Freedom and Responsibility Award from the National Association for Education in Journalism and Mass Communication. This cartoon appeared on March 1, 2004.*

Jonathan Rauch
What Is Marriage For?

Journalist Jonathan Rauch is a Senior Writer and columnist (of the award-winning "Social Studies") for National Journal *magazine, a Washington-based weekly on government, politics, and public policy. He is also a correspondent for the* Atlantic Monthly *and a visiting scholar at the Brookings Institution. "What Is Marriage For?" is a chapter from his book* Gay Marriage: Why It Is Good for Gays, Good for Straights, and Good for America *(Henry Holt, 2004).*

When I was six years old, I went with my family from Phoenix, where I was born and raised, to visit New York. I remember only a little about that trip, apart from a visit to the Statue of Liberty, but seeing *Fiddler on the Roof* on Broadway remains vivid. It was my first play and a great play to boot, and Tevye's dream frightened me half to death, but another, more tender scene also stayed with me.

Tevye is a poor milkman in a Jewish shtetl (village) in czarist Russia. Life there is hardscrabble and traditional, and he is at first scandalized and then grudgingly helpful when his children break with custom by rejecting arranged marriages and insisting on marrying for love. Shaken, Tevye one day asks his wife, Golde: "Do you love me?"

The question strikes Golde as bizarre. "Do I *what?*" she sings. "Go inside, go lie down. Maybe it's indigestion." Tevye is undeterred and presses the question. "You're a fool!" his wife replies.

"But do you love me?"

5 "After twenty-five years," she grumbles, "why talk about love right now?" Still he insists: "Do you love me?"

"I'm your wife."

For Golde this is the answer. Or as much of an answer as she needs. She has done her job as a spouse; why would he want more? But Tevye sings on: "But do you love me?"

"Do I love him?"

And now, at last, she gives her answer:

10
> *For twenty-five years I've lived with him,*
> *Fought with him, starved with him,*
> *Twenty-five years my bed is his.*
> *If that's not love, what is?*

"Then you love me!" says Tevye.

15 "I suppose I do."

"And I suppose I love you, too."

The 1960s were the dawn of the era of love. Love was in the air, love was all around, all we needed was love, what the world needed now was love sweet love,

love would keep us together, we should make love not war, we emblazoned LOVE on postage stamps and honored it with statues in public squares. Probably not coincidentally, it was also the age when the American divorce rate soared, to levels never before seen. Love was up, marriage was down. If the light of love dimmed in your marriage, or if it shined in new directions, then follow your heart. You and your partner and your children and everyone would be happier.

That was the air I breathed as I grew up, and yet even a six-year-old was capable of recognizing, in *Do You Love Me?*, a different and in some respects wiser view of love. Later on in my life, some years after my parents divorced (when I was twelve), it occurred to me to wonder: Did Tevye and Golde know something that many of us might have forgotten?

What is marriage for? That ought to be the easiest question in the world to answer. So many people get married, so much cultural experience has accumulated, and so many novels and dramas and counselors and manuals and "Dear Abby" columns crowd the world. Yet, until recently, when the gay-marriage debate forced the issue, hardly anyone gave much thought to the question. Such answers as were given were shallow or incoherent, especially at first. Gay activists said: Marriage is for love and we love each other, therefore we should be able to marry. Traditionalists said: Marriage is for procreation, and homosexuals do not procreate, therefore you should not be able to marry. That pretty well covered the spectrum. Secular thinking on the matter has been shockingly sketchy.

20   In its religious dress, marriage has a straightforward justification. It is as it is because that is how God wants it. As the Vatican said in 2003, "Marriage is not just any relationship between human beings. It was established by the Creator with its own nature, essential properties and purpose." Depending on the religion, God has various things to say about the nature and purpose of marriage. Modern marriage is, of course, based on traditions which religion helped to codify and enforce. But religious doctrine has no special standing in the world of secular law and policy, although it certainly holds and deserves influence. Moreover, a lot of what various religions say about marriage is inconsistent with or downright opposed to the consensus view of marriage today. The biblical patriarchs were polygamous and effectively owned their wives; in any number of religious traditions today, equality within marriage remains anathema. The law allows routine divorce and remarriage, something Jesus unequivocally condemned. If we want to know what marriage is for in modern America, we need a sensible secular doctrine.

You could try the dictionary. If you did, you might find something like: "**marriage** (n). The formal union of a man and woman, typically recognized by law, by which they become husband and wife" (*Oxford American College Dictionary*). Not much help there. Or: "**marriage** (n). The state of being married; a legal contract, entered into by a man and a woman, to live together as husband and wife" (*Funk & Wagnalls Standard College Dictionary*). Maybe your dictionary does better.

You could turn to the statute books. Law is, after all, dense with legal prerogatives enjoyed by married couples and dense with cases (often divorces) allocating assets and resolving conflicts. But you will find surprisingly little about what marriage is for and what must or must not, or should or should not, go on within it. Instead, you will find definitions like the one a Washington State court provided in a 1974 case in which two men tried to get a marriage license. Marriage, said the court, is defined as "the legal union of one man and one woman." The case revealed marriage, writes the philosopher Richard Mohr, "at least as legally understood, to be nothing but an empty space, delimited only by what it excludes—gay couples."

One way to get a handle on what marriage is for would be to ask what married people must do. Or, at a bare minimum, what it is they must *not* do in order to remain married. Here, astonishingly, the answer turns out to be, more or less: nothing. Nearly all civic institutions require you to do or not do at least something. If you want to be a voter, you need to register, re-register when you move, go to the polls, prove your identity, and vote in a specified manner. In many places, if you are convicted of a felony, you lose your vote. If you want to own property, you have to buy it legally (often a complicated process) and pay applicable taxes, or it will cease to be yours. If you want to be a driver, you must prove you can drive safely and see adequately; if you disobey the rules or lose your sight, your license may be revoked. By contrast, few if any behaviors automatically end a marriage. If a man beats his wife—about the worst thing he can do to her—he may be convicted of assault, but the marriage is not automatically dissolved. Couples can be adulterous (or "open") yet still be married, as long as that is what they choose to be. They can be celibate, too; consummation is not required. They can live together or apart, in the same house or in different countries: there is no residency or cohabitation requirement. There is no upper age limit. Spouses need not know each other or even meet before receiving a marriage license. They need not regularly see each other; a prisoner of war or a sailor or an adventurer can be separated from his wife for years and be no less married. They can have children or not. Not only can felons marry, they can do so on their way to the electric chair.

Secular law nowadays makes all sorts of provisions for people who *are* married, but it sets only a few rules for people who want to *get* married. Marriage happens only with the consent of the parties. The parties are not children. The number of parties is two. The parties are not closely related. One is a man and the other is a woman.

25   Within those rules, a marriage is whatever the spouses agree it is. So the laws say almost nothing about what marriage is for: just who can be married. All in all, it is an impressive and also rather astonishing victory for modern individualism that so important an institution should be bereft of any formal social instruction as to what should go on inside it.

What is marriage for? If the dictionaries and the law are of little help, perhaps we can find clues by asking: What *was* marriage for? A backward glance, however, sheds less light than one might hope. Mostly what it establishes is that, in the past century and more, marriage has changed nearly beyond recognition.

Most cultures, throughout history, have been polygamous. One man marries several women, at least in society's upper echelons. (The converse, one woman marrying several men, is rare, almost unheard of.) Polygamy was largely about hierarchy: it helped men to dominate women, and it helped high-status men, with their multiplicity of highly desirable wives, dominate low-status men. The higher a man's status, the more wives he typically had. Among human societies, as among animals, it is monogamy that is the rarity. "A huge majority—980 of the 1,154 past or present societies for which anthropologists have data—have permitted a man to have more than one wife," says Robert Wright in *The Moral Animal: The New Science of Evolutionary Psychology* (1994). "And that number includes most of the world's hunter-gatherer societies, societies that are the closest thing we have to a living example of the context of human evolution."

The imposition of monogamy was an important step toward the development of modern liberalism . . . . The advent of monogamy did not, however, make for anything like modern marriage. For, in secular society, marriage was largely a matter of business: cementing family ties, forging social or economic alliances, providing social status for men and economic security for women, conferring dowries, and so on. Marriages were typically arranged, and "love" in the modern sense was certainly no prerequisite. Family, in the days before the modern corporation, was business, and marriages were mergers and acquisitions. It would have seemed silly, under the circumstances, to allow individuals to marry on the basis of anything as whimsical as infatuation, or at least to allow marriages that were not carefully vetted and specifically approved by family elders. Elopement, in the upper social strata, was not only a scandal but a blow to a family's stability and standing. E. J. Graff, in her book *What Is Marriage For?* (1999), quotes from an eighteenth-century advice manual: "Children are so much the goods, the possessions of their parents, that they cannot, without a kind of theft, give themselves away without the allowance of those that have the right in them." Anyone who has read Jane Austen knows that the economic and business aspects of marriage remained prominent well into the nineteenth century.

In the recent past, and in some predominantly religious quarters to this day, marriage was about gender specialization. Men rightly do certain things, and women rightly do others, and to form a complete social unit, the two sexes must form a complementary partnership. Marriage is that partnership. Here again, love may be desirable, but it is no prerequisite. A marriage is successful if the two partners are conscientiously fulfilling their roles: the man attending to work and the world of affairs, the woman to home and children. In Japan today, remnants of this system persist, and it works surprisingly well. Spouses view their marriage as a partnership: an investment in security and status for themselves and their children. Because Japanese couples don't expect as much emotional fulfillment as Americans do, they are less inclined to break up. They also take a somewhat more relaxed attitude toward adultery. As long as each partner is doing his or her job, what's a little extracurricular activity?

30   In contemporary America, women expect to have opportunities to work outside the home, and men are expected to change diapers and even, however ineptly, help with the dishes. Marriage-as-business and marriage-as-gender-specialization linger only as vestiges. In the West today, of course, love is a defining element. Love sus-

tains marriage, many people will tell you, and marriage sanctifies love—but it is the love, not the marriage, which makes the bond. That was the view I grew up with.

The notion of lifelong love is charming, if ambitious, and certainly love is a desirable and important element of marriage. In the modern world, a loveless wedding is not likely to produce a lasting marriage. Love is not, however, the defining element of marriage in society's eyes, and it never has been. You may or may not love your husband, but the two of you are just as married either way. You may love your mistress, but that does not make her your wife. To a large extent, marriage is defined not in tandem with love but in contradistinction to it: marriage is special precisely because it imposes obligations whether or not you and your spouse love each other. Love helps make sense of marriage from an emotional point of view, but it is not particularly important in making sense of marriage from the social-policy point of view.

With the rise of the gay-marriage debate, another view has come to the fore: marriage is about children . . . . At present, suffice to say that marriage is unquestionably good for children, but children are not and cannot be the only reason for marriage. No society denies marriage to the infertile; no society requires couples to promise they will have children; no society nullifies marriage if children don't turn up; for that matter, no modern society mandates marriage if they do. For the record, I would be the last to deny that children are a central reason for the privileged status of marriage. When men and women get together, children are a likely outcome; and, as we are learning in all sorts of unpleasant ways, when children appear without two parents, many kinds of trouble can follow. Without belaboring the point, I hope I won't be accused of saying that children are a trivial reason for marriage. They just cannot be the only reason.

What are the others? I can think of several possibilities, such as the provision of economic security for women (or men), or the orderly transfer of cultural and financial capital between families or generations. There is a lot of intellectual work to be done to sort the essential from the inessential purposes of marriage. It seems to me, however, that the two strongest candidates are these: settling the young, particularly young men; and providing reliable care-givers. Both purposes are critical to the functioning of a humane, stable society, and both are better served by marriage—that is, by one-to-one lifelong commitment—than by any other institution.

We all need a home; humans are nesting animals. Odysseus bore his trials by keeping the memory of home alive. Countless generations of soldiers and wanderers have done the same. Home may be a place or it may be a nomadic community; it can mean parents, friends, familiar customs, native language, citizenship, and the pub or pool hall down the block. For many people, however, it means one thing above all. It is the place where someone waits for you.

35   Leaving aside children, young adults are the people who need home the most and who have it the least. For many people, the period we call "leaving home"— leaving one's parents' home—is a time of great excitement but also great vulnerability. Most of us, at age eighteen or twenty-two, aren't yet very good at managing life. We lack status and feel less beholden to the society around us than we will

later on, when we have money or memberships or mortgages. We want a lot of sex but tend to have trouble handling it. And, often, we are lonely.

The result can be trouble: idleness, depression, debauchery, drugs, unwanted pregnancy, an unwanted child. The problems of young men are especially worrisome, for society as well as for the young men.

"Men are more aggressive than women," writes James Q. Wilson, the prominent political scientist, in his 1993 book *The Moral Sense*. "In every known society, men are more likely than women to play roughly, drive recklessly, fight physically, and assault ruthlessly, and these differences appear early in life." He goes on to speak of the male's need to hunt, defend, attack.

> Much of the history of civilization can be thought of as an effort to adapt these male dispositions to contemporary needs by restricting aggression or channeling it into appropriate channels. That adaptation has often required extraordinary measures, such as hunting rituals, rites of passage, athletic contests, military discipline, guild apprenticeships, or industrial authority.

Most of the men I know are gentle souls, hardly uncivilized. Remember, though, that men often change when they gather in groups—or packs, or gangs. Wherever unattached young men gather in packs, you see no end of mischief: wildings in Central Park, gangs in Los Angeles, football hooligans in Britain, skin-heads in Germany, hazings in college fraternities, gang bangs in prisons, grope lines in the military, and, in a different but ultimately no less tragic way, the bathhouses and wanton sex of gay San Francisco or New York in the 1970s. It is probably fair to say that civilizing young men is one of any society's two or three biggest problems.

40   "Of all the institutions through which men may pass—schools, factories, the military—marriage has the largest effect," writes Wilson. The stabilizing and settling effect of marriage is unmatched. "An unmarried man between twenty-four and thirty-five years of age is about three times as likely to murder another male as is a married man the same age," observes Wright. "He is also more likely to incur various risks—committing robbery, for example—to gain the resources that may attract women. He is more likely to rape."

Marriage confers status: to be married, in the eyes of society, is to be grown up. Marriage creates stakes: someone depends on you. Marriage creates a safe harbor for sex. Marriage puts two heads together, pooling experience and braking impulsiveness. Of all the things a young person can do to move beyond the vulnerabilities of early adulthood, marriage is far and away the most fruitful. We all need domesticating, not in the veterinary sense but in a more literal, human sense: we need a home. We are different people when we have a home: more stable, more productive, more mature, less self-obsessed, less impatient, less anxious. And marriage is the great domesticator.

Nowadays, of course, people marry later. A lot of people don't marry until their thirties. But civilization is not unraveling and packs of marauding youths have not taken over the streets. If marriage is so important to settling down, why do so many people manage to settle down *before* marrying?

The answer, I think, is this: marriage is a great domesticator, but so is the *prospect* of marriage. If you hope to get married, and if your friends and peers hope to get married, you will socialize and date more carefully. If you're a young woman, you will avoid getting pregnant unintentionally or gaining what used to be called a reputation. If you're a young man, you will reach for respectability. You will devote yourself to your work, try to build status, and earn money to make yourself marriageable (often true of women, too). People who expect to get married observe and emulate husbands and wives. For those on the path toward marriage, most of what they do is conditioned by the assumption that single life is a temporary phase. Because you aspire to marry, you prepare to marry. You make yourself what people used to call marriage material.

Nothing I've just said is intended to imply that people who don't want to get married or who don't manage to get married (a small minority, as it happens: about 90 percent of Americans get married) are uncivilized, dangerous, or pathetic. The point is that, whether you marry or not, it is the prospect and the possibility of marriage that makes us a society of homebodies, which is a wonderful thing to be.

45   Of course, women and older men do not generally travel in marauding or orgiastic packs. As the years go by, even the most impetuous tend to settle down. In that respect, age does some of the same work as marriage (and vice versa; ask any comedian). As life goes on, however, a second core rationale for marriage comes more strongly into play.

I have a good job. I have money. I have health insurance. I have friends. I have relatives. But my relatives live far away. My friends are busy. And no amount of money can allay what has to be one of the most elemental fears humans can know: the fear of enduring some catastrophe alone. Tomorrow, maybe, my little car gets hit by a big bus. Everything goes black. When I awake, I am surrounded by doctors and nurses, but without someone there especially for me, I am alone in the sense that matters most. I lose the power to work or walk or feed myself. A service comes by to check on me once a day. Meals on Wheels brings lunch. Nonetheless, I am alone. No one is there for *me*. God forbid it should ever happen. But we all know the fear.

Society worries, too. A second enormous problem for society is what to do when someone is beset by catastrophe. It could be cancer, a broken back, unemployment, depression; it could be exhaustion from work, stress under pressure, or an all-consuming rage. From society's point of view, an unattached person is an accident waiting to happen. The burdens of contingency are likely to fall, immediately and sometimes crushingly, on people—relatives, friends, neighbors—who have enough problems of their own, and then on charities and welfare agencies. We all suffer periods of illness, sadness, distress, fury. What happens to us, and what happens to the people around us, when we desperately need a hand but find none to hold?

If marriage has any meaning at all, it is that when you collapse from a stroke, there will be another person whose "job" is to drop everything and come to your aid. Or that when you come home after being fired, there will be someone to talk you out of committing a massacre or killing yourself. To be married is to know there is someone out there for whom you are always first in line.

No group could make such a commitment in quite the same way, because of a free-rider problem. If I were to marry three or four people, the pool of potential caregivers would be larger, but the situation would, perversely, make all of them less reliable: each could expect one of the others to take care of me (and each may be reluctant to do more than any of the others are willing to do—a common source of conflict among siblings who need to look after an aging parent). The pair bond, one to one, is the only kind which is inescapably reciprocal, perfectly mutual. Because neither of us has anyone else, we are there for each other.

50   All by itself, marriage is society's first and, often, second and third line of support for the troubled individual. A husband or wife is the social worker of first resort, the psychiatrist of first resort, the cop and counselor and insurer and nurse and 911 operator of first resort. Married people are happier, healthier, and live longer; married men have lower rates of homicide, suicide, accidents, and mental illness. In 1858, reports Graff, a British public-health statistician named William Farr noticed that, on average, married people outlive singles. "Marriage," said Farr, "is a healthy state. The single individual is much more likely to be wrecked on his voyage than the lives joined together in matrimony." Graff goes on to say:

> The data have been eerily consistent ever since: whether measuring by death rate, morbidity (health problems such as diabetes, kidney disease, or ischemic heart disease), subjective or stress-related complaints (dizziness, shortness of breath, achiness, days in bed during past year, asthma, headaches), or psychiatric problems (clinical depression or debilitating anxiety after a cancer diagnosis), married people do better than unmarried—single, widowed, divorced.

Might that just be because healthier people are more likely to marry? Maybe. But the conclusion remains the same even when studies compare matched populations, factor out confounding variables, or follow individuals over time. Moreover, married people do better than cohabiting couples, and their unions are more enduring—and, again, the generalization seems to hold even when researchers account for the fact that cohabitors and married people may be different. Marriage itself appears to be good for you. Why? I'm sure the answer is complicated. But in large part it must boil down to something pretty simple. Married people have someone to look after them, and they know it.

The gay-marriage debate is a storm that swirls around a single question. What makes marriage marriage? That is, what are marriage's essential attributes, and what are its incidental ones? As we will see, various people give various answers. They point to children, for instance. Or the ability to have children. Or heterosexual intercourse. Or monogamy. Clearly, marriage has many important attributes, and it would be unrealistic to expect agreement on what counts the most. But I think one attribute is more important than any of the others. If I had to pare marriage to its essential core, I would say that marriage is two people's lifelong commitment, recognized by law and by society, to care for each other. To get married is to put yourself in another person's hands, and to promise to take that person into your hands, and to do so within a community which expects both of you to keep your word.

Because, in theory, there is no reason why a male-male or female-female couple could not make and sustain the promise of lifelong caregiving, opponents of same-sex marriage are reluctant to put the caregiving commitment at the heart, rather than the periphery, of marriage. Against them, I adduce what I think are three strong kinds of evidence that caregiving is at the core of marriage: law, social opinion, and something else.

55   Law, as I said earlier, says almost nothing about what married people must do in order to be married; but it does weave a dense entanglement of prerogatives and special standings around any couple legally deemed to be wed. Spouses are generally exempted from having to testify against each other in court. They can make life-or-death decisions on each other's behalf in case of incapacity. They have hospital visitation rights. A doctor cannot refuse to tell them their spouse's condition. They have inheritance rights. They can file taxes as a single unit. On and on. The vast majority of the ways in which the law recognizes marriage—practically all of them, if you stop to think about it—aim at facilitating and bolstering the caregiving commitment. They are tools of trust and teamwork. A husband can speak to his wife candidly without fear that she will be served with a subpoena and rat him out. When one spouse is gravely ill, doctors and friends and other family members defer to the second spouse as caregiver in chief. Because spouses make a unique commitment to care for each other in life, their assets are presumed to merge when one of them dies—a recognition of what each has given up for the other. Most of what are usually thought of as the legal benefits of marriage are really gifts with strings attached. Or maybe strings with gifts attached. The law is saying: "You have a unique responsibility to care for each other. Here are the tools. Do your job."

Marriage creates kin. In olden times, marriage merged families to create alliances between clans. Today, marriage takes two people who are (except very rarely) not even remotely related and makes them each other's closest kin. Matrimony creates family out of thin air. Children cannot do this, nor can money, monogamy (that's just "going steady"), or lawyers. Only marriage does it.

Social opinion, I think, follows the same principle. Legally speaking, spouses are married until officially divorced. Socially speaking, however, under what circumstance would you regard someone as not just an imperfect spouse but as a nullifier of the marriage compact—a nonspouse? Adultery springs to mind. But the world is full of spouses who cheat or have cheated and who still manage to carry on in marriage. About 20 percent of American husbands admit to infidelity. Perhaps the betrayed spouse doesn't know, or knows but has forgiven, or has decided to live with the situation. I know more than one couple who have been through an adultery crisis and survived. An adulterous spouse is not a good spouse but, in the eyes of most people, would be a flawed spouse rather than a nonspouse.

What would lead me to think of someone as a nonspouse? Only, I think, abandonment. Mrs. Smith is diagnosed with a brain tumor. She will need treatment and care. Mr. Smith, an able-bodied adult with no history of mental illness, responds by leaving town. Now and then he calls her, chats for a few minutes as a friend might do, and then goes on about his business. He leaves Mrs. Smith in the hands of her sister, who has to fly in from Spokane. When the doctors call, he lets the answering machine take a message. "She can sign on our bank account," he says. "Let her hire help."

I have heard of people getting divorced in the face of a crisis. But I have never heard of anyone behaving like Mr. Smith while claiming to be married; and if Mr. Smith behaved that way, even his closest friends would think him beyond the pale. They would say he was having a breakdown—"not himself" (meaning, no longer the husband Mrs. Smith thought she had). Everyone else would just be shocked. Mrs. Smith, if she survived, would get a divorce.

Decent opinion has understood for centuries that, whatever else marriage may be, it is a commitment to be there. In 1547 (according to Graff), Archbishop Thomas Granmer wrote that marriage is for "mutual society, help, and comfort, that the one ought to have of the other, both in prosperity and in adversity." I mentioned a third strong kind of evidence for my view that the prime-caregiver status is the sine qua non of marriage. Here it is:

60   *To have and to hold from this day forward, for better for worse, for richer for poorer, in sickness and in health, to love, cherish, and to obey, till death us do part.*

I doubt there is a single grown-up person of sound mind in America who does not know what those words signify. They are from the Book of Common Prayer, dating from 1662. "Obey" is gone today, but otherwise not much has changed in four and a half centuries:

   Wilt thou love her, comfort her, honor and keep her in sickness and in health; and, forsaking all others, keep thee only unto her, so long as ye both shall live?

So go the ancient vows, the first for her, the second for him. The text speaks twice of care and comfort "in sickness and in health," twice of love, twice of a lifetime bond. Those three, it implies, are interwoven: the commitment to care for another for life is the love which exceeds all others, the love of another even above oneself. There is no promise of children here, either to have them or to raise them, no mention of sex, no mention of inheritance, not a word about personal fulfillment. Perhaps the writers of the vow meant to put in those things but forgot. Or perhaps they placed at the center of marriage what most married people today also place there: "in sickness and in health, to love and cherish, till death us do part."

I know a couple who have been married, now, for sixty years. I know them well, although it would not be proper to name them. But they are people I love.

65   Often it is hard to spend time with them, because they needle each other, raise their voices, speak harshly—not all the time, but often, and almost always unnecessarily. One says, "Where's your coat?" and the other says, "Whatsa matter, I always have to have a coat?" They do not show affection for each other. If this is love, it is not the kind of love I would prefer for myself. It's not the kind of marriage I would like, either.

The wife freely admits that the marriage has not been pleasant for many years. So I asked her: Why did you stick with it? Because, she said, for her generation divorce just wasn't something you thought about. Because, after a certain point, inertia took over. But then she said something else, something which, from the sudden firmness in her voice, I took to be her real answer. "Jon," she said, "he has been there for me. He has *always* been there. Whenever I needed him, he came through."

Tevye and Golde concluded that they must love each other, or else what could you call their twenty-five years of living and fighting and starving together? They were singing, of course, not about passionate love, or romantic love, or erotic love. They were singing of the unique kind of love which grows between two people who learn they can trust each other through anything. They were singing about marriage.

Barrie Jean Borich
When I Call Her My Husband

Barrie Jean Borich is a writer of creative nonfiction and poetry. She teaches in the Graduate Liberal Studies M.F.A. in Writing Program at Hamline University in St. Paul, Minnesota. "When I Call Her My Husband" is a chapter from My Lesbian Husband: Landscapes of a Marriage *(Greywolf Press, 2000). It won the 2000 American Library Association Gay/Lesbian/Bisexual/Transgender Nonfiction Book Award and was a finalist for the Minnesota Book Award and the Lambda Literary Award.*

Linnea and I have been lovers for all these years, and I wonder—are we married?

I ask her as we sit at our red kitchen table, in our South Minneapolis corner duplex with peeling walls and crumbling Victorian trim. Outside, the stoplight on Portland Avenue sends a shallow green, yellow, red wash in through the front windows as gearhead cars and accessorized Caddies with dark-tinted glass shriek through the intersection. As downtown commuters in tidy Hondas plod home south after work. As Harley guys rumble past with pipes clattering. As red Isuzu Troopers with big speakers in the back cruise by slow, bellowing with low bass, hip-hop, thump-da-thumps. As another family of kids we haven't seen before careens around the corner on bikes, the little ones on Big Wheels, pumping to keep up with tires growling and buckling over loose stones and broken glass.

Inside, our three cats lounge beneath the ceiling fan. Our dog digs through her basket of bones and toys. We are surrounded by the clutter of ourselves. Snapshots of friends and nieces. Funny postcards of women in vintage drag. Homemade valentines too sweet to throw away. Herb tinctures, and big bottles of vitamins. Big bottles of olive oil and every kind of tea. Glossy urbane magazines and mail-order catalogues for things we never order—books on tape, or down comforters, or loose-fitting casual clothing. Piles of clippings from the

Village Voice that we don't have time to read. City newspapers and poetry books or volumes of lesbian and gay theory or books about quantum physics or *Star Trek* or dogs. Our moderate collection of plastic dinosaurs, including the five-foot-long, blowup pteranodon hanging from the kitchen ceiling. Our large and varied collection of holy statues and candles, Catholic and Orthodox, mostly the Madonna, along with a few other saints and goddesses: Saint Lucy with her eyes on a plate, Kannon with her many arms, Marilyn in plunging black décolletage, shell ladies from ocean-beach resorts, and a piñata rendition of Madonna (the pop star) we made a few years back for a party. All this is seven years of us. So are we married?

I ask her in the summer as we ride in her Chevy Blazer truck on our way to a week in a one-room cabin on the shore of blue-gray and unblinking Lake Superior, the dog's head hanging between us from her spot in the back as the forests along the northern highway grow more blue-green and needled.

5   I ask her in the winter over big bowls of steaming seafood soup at our usual table, between bright white walls and abstract prints of fish, in the nonsmoking section of our favorite restaurant, run by a Chinese family emigrated here from Vietnam. Mostly daughters, black-haired and half our size, one-by-one they interrupt us to admire the silver jewelry Linnea buys me at gem shows, to ask us questions about our relationship, to describe how *their* lives are changing—a wedding engagement, a new baby, a college acceptance on the East Coast.

In all these spots, public and private, I ask Linnea, "Are we married?"

Her response is always to move closer, pull me closer if she can. Let's say we're at home, lying side-by-side in the king-sized bed that we bought with our only joint charge card (Slumberland). The bed is one of just three joint purchases we've made in our first seven years. The others were a TV and a queen-sized water bed that we sold later when we started waking up aching, my back, her knees. The water bed was our first joint purchase, and I cried when we bought it in our second year together because it was so complicated. There were enough boards and rubber and cords to fill up the back of a pickup truck. "I moved my whole life to Minnesota in a Pinto," I sobbed. "And now just the bed takes up a whole truck." Now we lie on our king-sized King Koil on a plain steel base, big enough for both of us, the dog, and a cat or two if there isn't any roughhousing. We're still waiting to be able to afford a frame for this extravagant mattress. We want something showy and romantic, like a Victorian sleigh bed, to match our feeling for each other. But our dreams surpass our credit limits. If the state of marriage is determined by property, we may not have enough to qualify.

So we're lying in this bed on a Sunday evening, the dog curled up just under my stocking feet, one of the cats annoying me by obsessively kneading at my chest, and I ask her, "Do you think we're married?"

Linnea rolls over, shooing away the cat, resting her belly alongside my hip as her chin nuzzles my shoulder. "I think you're my wife," she says.

10   I laugh and squeeze in closer, turn so I can kiss the soft exposed flesh below her ear. She is completely serious and not serious at all, in that queer way we

learn to roll with a language we are at once completely a part of and completely excluded from.

"Yes, honey," I say. "You are my wife, too." But this is not the right word for it. I can feel the vague tensing in her limbs as she holds me, the structure of her embrace still solid as something deeper steps away. What is it in her that is compromised, knocked off its feet, when I call her wife? A sort of manhood? But this is not the right word either. "I don't know the word," she would say. "But I'm not a man."

So I press myself even closer, sliding my thigh up to rest between her legs, sliding my hip up against her hip so I can feel our bones touch. The evening sun falling through the lace we have hung on our bedroom window scatters bright, sun-colored roses across her face and chest.

"Not your wife," she says.

"My handsome wife?" I try.

15   "I don't like wife."

It's true, it doesn't fit her. But who does the word wife fit? Fishwife. Housewife. I don't like it either. But when Linnea calls me her wife all that falls away. Then it is a word filled with all the attention she gives me, plump with kisses on the neck as my thighs part to her hands. We can only use this word if we steal it. Hidden in our laps it's better.

Better for me. When I say, wife, her jaw muscles stiffen. She becomes strange, unknowable to me while the sun outside falls behind clouds, while there is no light dappling our bare arms and faces, while the surface of our skin chills.

"OK," I say. "How about husband?"

With this word, husband, I feel her relax, the flow between us returning. Can I call her my husband without meaning a man? Without meaning a woman who wants to be a man? Without even meaning a woman who acts like a man? Even now, over thirteen years a lesbian, I still meet men I am attracted to, but just from the surface layers of my skin. No man can touch my face, my lips, and cause everything in me to drop, bones to water, as Linnea can, as women like her, butch lesbians, do. Who in the world can fly you to the moon, set you to swoon, send you down with that old black magic in a Tony Bennett ballad kind of love fever? For me it's a woman who would rather be a husband than a wife.

20   When I call Linnea my husband I mean that she's a woman who has to lead when we slow dance, who is compelled to try to dip and twirl me, no matter that I have rarely been able to relax on a dance floor since I stopped drinking. She leads me between the black walls of a gay bar, our faces streaked with neon and silver disco light, the air so dark Linnea's black leather belt and both pairs of our black boots seem to vanish, leaving parts of us afloat in the heavy smell of booze and cigarettes. She leads me slipping under streamers and lavender balloons, in the center of the light cast by several dozen candles, on some friend's polished oak dining-room floor cleared for party dancing. She leads me across a Sunday morning, sun streaming into our living room through southern exposed windows, so bright it sets the dust spinning. We dance clumsily on the purple oriental rug we

bought cheap at a garage sale, the worn wool covered with cat and dog hair, the dog barking and nipping at our heels, me in stocking feet, Linnea wearing athletic shoes because the arches of her feet went bad a few years back.

When I call her my husband I mean that she's a woman I saw dressed seriously in a skirt and heels just once, early on, when she still tried to cross over for job interviews. Her head, shoulders, hands looked too large, her gait too long, an inelegant drag queen. This is a woman who's happiest straddling a motorcycle, who wears a black leather jacket and square-toed biking boots even when she's not riding. For years I've been telling her that her thick, curly hair would look fantastic long, wild with its own life like the hair of Botticelli's Venus or Arlo Guthrie's hair in the *Alice's Restaurant* days, but she will always be a woman who wears her hair short, cut to look slicked back at the sides, a grease-free DA. She's a woman who does not look like a man, yet is often mistaken for one, a woman who meets a clamor of gasps when she enters into the pale green light of shopping-mall rest rooms. The other women are caught with their naked hands motionless over the bright white sinks. The boldest and least observant among them checks her own reflection in the mirror, straightens her back, breaks from the pack to protect the others, points to some unseeable place on the other side of the cloister wall—"*This* is the *women's* room."

I mean Linnea is a woman who once stood at the center of the Gay Nineties Saturday-night throb, her Levi's tight across the ass, her black leather boots and black leather jacket absorbing the speckled silver light refracting from the spangled curtains of the drag stage. She was caught in a fast second of instinct when she swung around and decked a drunk flat in the nose. He had reached between her legs from behind to grab what he thought was her dick. "He got two surprises that night," is what Linnea says about it.

I mean Linnea is a woman who is a woman because she was born with a woman's body. The large breasts and tender nipples. The monthly swelling, cramps, and blood. The opening up into her that she will do anything to protect, even break a man's nose in the glittering dark of a bar where drag queens sway on a sequined stage in sequined gowns and sequined eyelashes, *their* breasts made of foam rubber or silicone, *their* dicks taped up safe between their buttocks, as they smile like pop stars before paparazzi and mouth the words of Whitney Houston songs.

When I say husband I mean the woman lying beside me on a cool spring Sunday evening while the thinning light streaked over our bed from the west turns rose-colored. "You are my husband," I whisper to her, and we both laugh a little under our breaths, as we kiss, as she rocks me until I am nearly asleep, as the light flickers and sinks into night, as we listen to Luis outside in the yard behind ours crooning in Spanish to his four little dogs while his pet parrots shriek, as our dog pants alongside our bed, waiting for her supper, as the cat kneads my chest, using her claws, and I shoo her off to the floor. "But does that mean we're married?" I whisper to Linnea. But she is drifting off into a nap. We won't solve this today. The rose light flickers and I drift off with her.

George Lakoff
What's in a Word?

George Lakoff is Professor of Linguistics at the University of California at Berkeley and a Senior Fellow at the Rockridge Institute. He is the author of the influential book, Moral Politics: How Liberals and Conservatives Think *(Second Edition, 2002), and co-author, with Mark Johnson, of* Metaphors We Live By *(1980). His most recent book is* Don't Think of an Elephant: Know Your Values, Frame the Debate *(2004). "What's in a Word?" was posted on AlterNet, an independent Internet media site, on February 18, 2004.*

What's in a word? Plenty, if the word is "marriage."

Marriage is central to our culture. Marriage legally confers over 600 benefits, but that is only its material aspect. Marriage is an institution, the public expression of lifelong commitment based on love. It is the culmination of a period of seeking a mate, and, for many, the realization of a major goal, often with a buildup of dreams, dates, gossip, anxiety, engagement, shower, wedding plans, rituals, invitations, bridal gown, bridesmaids, families coming together, vows, and a honeymoon. Marriage is the beginning of family life, commonly with the expectation of children and grandchildren, family gatherings, in-laws, little league games, graduations, and all the rest.

Marriage is also understood in terms of dozens of deep and abiding metaphors: a journey through life together, a partnership, a union, a bond, a single object of complementary parts, a haven, a means for growth, a sacrament, a home. Marriage confers a social status—a married couple with new social roles. And for a great many people, marriage legitimizes sex. In short, marriage is a big deal.

Like most important concepts, marriage comes with a variety of prototypical cases: The ideal marriage is happy, lasting, prosperous, with children, a nice home, and friendships with other married couples. The typical marriage has its ups and downs, its joys and difficulties, typical problems with children and in-laws. The nightmare marriage ends in divorce, due perhaps to incompatibility, abuse, or betrayal. It is a rich concept with a cultural stereotype: it is between a man and a woman.

5   Because marriage is central to family life, it has a political dimension. As I discuss in my book *Moral Politics,* conservative and progressive politics are organized around two very different models of married life: a strict father family and a nurturing parent family.

The strict father is moral authority and master of the household, dominating both the mother and children and imposing needed discipline. Contemporary conservative politics turns these family values into political values: hierarchical authority, individual discipline, military might. Marriage in the strict father family *must* be heterosexual marriage: the father is manly, strong, decisive, dominating—a role model for sons and a model for daughters of a man to look up to.

The nurturing parent model has two equal parents, whose job is to nurture their children and teach their children to nurture others. Nurturance has two dimensions: empathy and responsibility, for oneself and others. Responsibility requires strength and competence. The strong nurturing parent is protective and caring, builds trust and connection, promotes family happiness and fulfillment, fairness, freedom, openness, cooperation, community development. These are the values of a strong progressive politics. Though the stereotype again is heterosexual, there is nothing in the nurturing family model to rule out same-sex marriage.

In a society divided down the middle by these two family models and their politics, we can see why the issue of same-sex marriage is so volatile. What is at stake is more than the material benefits of marriage and the use of the word. At stake is one's identity and most central values. This is not just about same-sex couples. It is about which values will dominate in our society.

When conservatives speak of the "defense of marriage," liberals are baffled. After all, no individual's marriage is being threatened. It's just that more marriages are being allowed. But conservatives see the strict father family, and with it, their political values as under attack. They are right. This is a serious matter for their politics and moral values as a whole. Even civil unions are threatening, since they create families that cannot be traditional strict father families.

10   Progressives are of two minds. Pragmatic liberals see the issue as one of benefits—inheritance, health care, adoption, etc. If that's all that is involved, civil unions should be sufficient—and they certainly are an advance. Civil unions would provide equal *material* protection under the law. Why not leave civil unions to the state and marriage to the churches, as in Vermont?

Idealistic progressives see beyond the material benefits, important as they are. Most gay activists want more than civil unions. They want full-blown marriage, with all its cultural meanings—a public commitment based on love, all the metaphors, all the rituals, joys, heartaches, family experiences—and a sense of normality, on a par with all other people. The issue is one of personal freedom: the state should not dictate who should marry whom. It is also a matter of fairness and human dignity. Equality under the law includes social and cultural, as well as material benefits. The slogan here is "freedom to marry."

Language is important. The radical right uses "gay marriage." Polls show most Americans overwhelmingly against anti-gay discrimination, but equally against "gay marriage." One reason, I believe, is that "marriage" evokes the idea of sex and most Americans do not favor gay sex. Another is that the stereotype of marriage is heterosexual. "Gay" for the right connotes a wild, deviant, sexually irresponsible lifestyle. That's why the right prefers "gay marriage" to "same-sex marriage."

But "gay marriage" is a double-edged sword. President Bush chose not to use the words "gay marriage" in his State of the Union Address. I suspect that the omission occurred for a good reason. His position is that "marriage" is defined as between a man and a woman, and so the term "gay marriage" should be an oxymoron, as meaningless as "gay apple" or "gay telephone." The more "gay marriage" is used, the more normal the idea of same-sex marriage becomes, and the clearer it becomes that "marriage" is not defined to exclude the very possibility. This is exactly why some gay activists want to use "same-sex marriage" or even "gay marriage."

The Democratic presidential nominees are trying to sidestep the issue. Kerry and Dean claim marriage is a matter for the church, while the proper role for the state is civil unions and a guarantee of material benefits. This argument makes little sense to me. The ability of ministers, priests, and rabbis to perform marriage ceremonies is granted by governments, not by religions. And civil marriage is normal and widespread. Besides, it will only satisfy the pragmatic liberals. Idealistic conservatives will see civil unions as tantamount to marriage, and idealistic progressives will see them as falling far short of equal protection. It may work in Vermont and perhaps in Massachusetts, but it remains to be seen whether such an attempt to get around the issue will play in most of the country.

15 And what of the constitutional amendment to define marriage legally as between a man and a woman? Conservatives will be for it, and many others with a heterosexual stereotype of marriage may support it. But it's unlikely to get enough progressive support to pass. The real question is, will the very proposal of such an amendment help George Bush keep the White House?

It's hard to tell right now.

But the progressives who are *not* running for office can do a lot. Progressives need to reclaim the moral high ground—of the grand American tradition of freedom, fairness, human dignity, and full equality under the law. If they are pragmatic liberals, they can talk this way about the civil unions and material benefits. If they are idealistic progressives, they can use the same language to talk about the social and cultural, as well as the material benefits of marriage. Either way, our job as ordinary citizens is to reframe the debate, in everything we say and write, in terms of our moral principles.

The rest of us have to put our ideas out there so that candidates can readily refer to them. For example, when there is a discussion in your office, church, or other group, there is a simple response to someone who says, "I don't think gays should be able to marry, do you?" The response is, "I believe in equal rights, period. I don't think the state should be in the business of telling people who they can or can't marry." The media does not have to accept the right wing's frames. What can a reporter ask besides "Do you support gay marriage?" Try this: "In San Francisco, there has been a lot discussion of the freedom to marry, as a matter of equal rights under the law. How do you feel about this?"

Reframing is everybody's job.

▩ QUESTIONS FOR INQUIRY AND ACTION ▩

1. List the values your family has taught you. Write an essay using several short narratives that shows readers how you were taught these values. Use your essay to answer the larger question: Does the type of family we live in influence the kind of values we are taught?

2. In the various arguments in support of and opposition to the federal Marriage Protection Amendment and gay marriage in general, much depends on people's definitions of the concept of "marriage." Point out the definitions you see in the various selections, implicit as well as explicit, and explain how beginning with different definitions—with different assumptions, in other words—affects the direction and conclusion of the arguments.

3. Interview several individuals from various family and marriage structures (for instance, single parents, gay or lesbian parents, unmarried cohabiting partners, or children from any of these families) on their views about marriage. Write an essay comparing and contrasting your views with theirs. Are their views better or worse for promoting good citizenship than your own?

4. Watch several different television shows depicting same-sex couples and/or families. Report to your class on these couples' and families' interactions with one another and with heterosexual couples and their families. Do you think these depictions undermine your society's views on marriage and the family, or do these shows reflect the kinds of marriageable relationships and families already in society?

▩ CONTINUING THE CASE STUDY ▩
Should Congress Define the American Family?

In the case study, all of the authors show concern for the future of families. Rick Santorum and Maggie Gallagher worry that legally expanding the definition of marriage to include same-sex couples would destabilize the core institution of our society. In contrast, Jonathan Rauch argues that allowing same-sex couples to marry will stabilize our society by encouraging more people to settle down and focus on families, an idea illustrated in Barrie Jean Borich's portrait of her partnership. Tom Tomorrow's cartoon reminds us that definitions of marriage have changed over the years, and George Lakoff calls our attention to the importance of the language we use to frame our debates over marriage and family.

Regardless of our personal beliefs and feelings, should we legislate, or make laws, that determine who can and cannot form a family? Assuming everyone wants strong families in our society—that is, people who provide us with affection, companionship, preparation for life, and financial, emotional, and spiritual support—what is the most effective means for securing these strong families? Should we encourage common values through social interaction and role modeling rather than through enacting laws? Or are laws the best means for urging the seriousness of this matter and for maintaining the definition and structure over generations?

For this exercise, divide into small groups of about four people each. Each of you will become a legislative subcommittee. Your subcommittee's task is to determine whether your state ought to adopt or revise an amendment to the state constitution defining what is and is not a family.

First, in your groups, answer the following questions:

Should we enact legislation to determine who can and cannot form a family?

(a) If you decide yes, first answer why we should do so. Then write your proposed legislation to define the family.

(b) If you decide no, first answer why we should not do so. Then decide what we should do instead to ensure strong families.

Write a group memo announcing your decision, explaining the rationale behind your decision, and proposing your solution. Then reconvene as a class. Have each group present its memos to the entire class and develop a debate among the groups. What common ground can you find? Can you reach a consensus? If not, what divides you?

CHAPTER 7

The Higher Education Community

The university is the only institution in Western society whose business
it is to search for and transmit truth regardless of all competing or
conflicting pressures and demands; pressures for immediate usefulness,
for social approval, pressures to serve the special interests of
government, a class, a professional group, a race, a faith, even a
nation.

—*Henry Steele Commager*

▓ GETTING STARTED ▓ Exploring Your Campus

To get the most out of your college experience, explore the social, professional,
and academic resources available to you as a student. To answer the following
questions, use a variety of research strategies including telephone interviews,
personal observation, and library research. Depending on the size of your college,
you may want to do this exercise individually or in groups.

- What official and unofficial student groups are available?
- What student political groups are active on campus?
- Where can you go to experience the arts?
- Where can you go to play a sport?
- Where can you go to conduct different types of research?
- What career planning resources are available?
- Where can you go to meet other students?
- Where can you go to worship or learn about different religions?
- What groups are available to get involved in social issues?
- What resources are available to get involved in the local
  community?

After you have compiled a list of available resources, meet as a class to
answer the following questions:

1. Which of these groups are most prominent on campus? What resources are
   most used? What does the prominence of these groups and resources say
   about your college?

2. Based on group participation and the use of school resources, do students at your college emphasize the school's social, professional, or academic qualities? Do students balance these qualities in healthy ways?

In the above quote, Henry Steele Commager represents colleges as ivy towers, resistant to the challenges of industry, public opinion, and government. A brief tour of any campus, however, would show that colleges and the communities in which they reside are intertwined. Changes in the larger society do affect what colleges do and how they operate. The growing numbers of nontraditional and international students, the emergence of private education providers, and increased public scrutiny of college programs are reshaping higher education communities.

The fact that these communities are not recreated every time the social or political landscape changes, however, testifies to the enduring appeal of their vision. In Thomas Jefferson's "Plan for Public Education in Virginia" (1817) and in the mission statements of colleges and universities across the country we find the same drive for knowledge, justice, beauty, and wisdom. We find these drives expressed not just in the classrooms, but in many aspects of a college's social life. Higher education communities offer students a wonderful and unique opportunity to pause and reflect on themselves and their world; they also offer students the resources and expertise to get involved in other communities.

The case study in this chapter demonstrates the possible tensions that arise from colleges and universities intersecting with larger communities. On January 26, 2005, Ohio Senate Bill 24 was introduced; it seeks to institutionalize within the state's colleges and universities the Academic Bill of Rights, a set of principles advocating for student access to a plurality of viewpoints. Here is one passage from that bill:

> Students . . . shall not be discriminated against on the basis of their political, ideological, or religious beliefs. Faculty and instructors shall not use their courses or their positions for the purpose of political, ideological, religious, or antireligious indoctrination.

Individual advocates such as David Horowitz and organizations such as NoIndoctrination.org and Students for Academic Freedom argue that members of our higher education communities are using their authority as educators to indoctrinate students into a particular set of liberal political, social, and religious views. Educators such as Stanley Fish, however, see the Academic Bill of Rights as a Trojan horse, a tool for pushing more conservative viewpoints and faculty members into higher education communities. The Academic Bill of Rights debates push us to consider why colleges exist, what students can expect in the college classroom, and what relationship those colleges should have to outside communities.

Arthur Levine and Jeanette S. Cureton
Collegiate Life: An Obituary

Arthur Levine is president and professor of education at Columbia University's Teachers College. Jeanette S. Cureton is an independent academic researcher, formerly at the Harvard Graduate School of Education. Together they have produced a number of works on education, including the book When Hope and Fear Collide: A Portrait of Today's College Student *(1998). "Collegiate Life: An Obituary" is an excerpt from that book; it originally appeared in the magazine* Change *(May–June 1998).*

In 1858, John Henry Cardinal Newman wrote *The Idea of a University*. His ideal was a residential community of students and teachers devoted to the intellect. To him, a college was "an alma mater, knowing her children one by one, not a foundry, or a mint, or a treadmill." Given a choice between an institution that dispensed with "residence and tutorial superintendence and gave its degrees to any person who passed an examination in a wide range of subjects" or "a university which. . . merely brought a number of young men together for three or four years," he chose the latter.

Newman's ideal was so appealing that it has been embraced regularly over the years by higher education luminaries from Robert Hutchins and Paul Goodman to Alexander Meiklejohn and Mortimer Adler. Belief in it remains a staple of nearly every college curriculum committee in the country.

But that ideal is moribund today. Except for a relatively small number of residential liberal arts colleges, institutions of higher education and their students are moving away from it at an accelerating pace. The notion of a living-learning community is dead or dying on most campuses today.

This is a principal finding of several studies we conducted between 1992 and 1997, which involved our surveying a representative sample of 9,100 undergraduate students and 270 chief student affairs officers, as well as holding focus groups on 28 campuses. The details of the studies can be found [at the end of this article], along with information about earlier surveys undertaken by Arthur Levine for the Carnegie Council on Policy Studies in Higher Education, which we use for the sake of comparison. Unless otherwise indicated, all findings we report in this article come from the surveys outlined. While much of this article focuses on students of traditional age, the current student generation is, in fact, multigenerational.

Demographics

5 A major reason for the changes we describe is simply demographic. In comparison with their counterparts of the 1960s and 1970s, undergraduates today are more racially diverse and, on average, considerably older. In fact, since 1980, the

lion's share of college enrollment growth has come from students who might be described as nontraditional. By 1993, 24 percent of all college students were working full-time, according to our Undergraduate Survey; at two-year colleges, this figure had reached 39 percent.

By 1995, 44 percent of all college students were over 25 years old; 54 percent were working; 56 percent were female; and 43 percent were attending part-time. Currently, fewer than one in six of all undergraduates fit the traditional stereotype of the American college student attending full-time, being 18 to 22 years of age, and living on campus (see U.S. Department of Education, in Resources).

What this means is that higher education is not as central to the lives of today's undergraduates as it was to previous generations. Increasingly, college is just one of a multiplicity of activities in which they are engaged every day. For many, it is not even the most important of these activities; work and family often overshadow it.

As a consequence, older, part-time, and working students—especially those with children—often told us in our surveys that they wanted a different type of relationship with their colleges from the one undergraduates historically have had. They preferred a relationship like those they already enjoyed with their bank, the telephone company, and the supermarket.

What Students Want

Think about what you want from your bank. We know what we want: an ATM on every corner. And when we get to the ATM, we want there to be no line. We also would like a parking spot right in front of the ATM, and to have our checks deposited the moment they arrive at the bank, or perhaps the day before! And we want no mistakes in processing—unless they are in our favor. We also know what we do not want from our banks. We do not want them to provide us with softball leagues, religious counseling, or health services. We can arrange all of these things for ourselves and don't wish to pay extra fees for the bank to offer them.

10   Students are asking roughly the same thing from their colleges. They want their colleges to be nearby and to operate at the hours most useful to them—preferably around the clock. They want convenience: easy, accessible parking (at the classroom door would not be bad); no lines; and a polite, helpful, efficient staff. They also want high-quality education but are eager for low costs. For the most part, they are willing to comparison shop, and they place a premium on time and money. They do not want to pay for activities and programs they do not use.

In short, students increasingly are bringing to higher education exactly the same consumer expectations they have for every other commercial establishment with which they deal. Their focus is on convenience, quality, service, and cost.

They believe that since they are paying for their education, faculty should give them the education they want; they make larger demands on faculty than past students ever have. They are also the target audience for alternatives to traditional higher education. They are likely to be drawn to distance education, which offers the convenience of instruction at home or the office. They are prime candidates for stripped-down versions of college, located in the suburbs and business districts of our cities, that offer low-cost instruction made possible by heavy faculty teaching loads, mostly part-time faculties, limited selections of majors, and few electives. Proprietary institutions of this type are springing up around the country.

On campus, students are behaving like consumers, too. More than nine out of 10 chief student affairs officers told us in last year's Student Affairs Survey that student power in college governance has increased during the 1990s (or at least has remained the same), but that undergraduates are less interested in being involved in campus governance than in the past.

A small minority of undergraduates continue to want voting power or control over admissions decisions, faculty appointments, bachelor's degree requirements, and the content of courses; however, a decreasing percentage desire similar roles in residential regulations and undergraduate discipline, areas in which students would seem most likely to want control. Overall, the proportion of students who want voting or controlling roles in institutional governance is at its lowest level in a quarter century, according to comparisons between our 1993 Undergraduate Survey and the 1969 and 1976 Carnegie Council surveys.

15   This is precisely the same attitude most of us hold with regard to the commercial enterprises we patronize. We don't want to be bothered with running the bank or the supermarket; we simply want them to do their jobs and do them well—to give us what we need without hassles or headaches. That is, help the consumers and don't get in their way. Students today are saying precisely the same things about their colleges.

Social Life

From a personal perspective, students are coming to college overwhelmed and more damaged than in the past. Chief student affairs officers in 1997 reported rises in eating disorders (on 58 percent of campuses), classroom disruption (on 44 percent), drug abuse (on 42 percent), alcohol abuse (on 35 percent), gambling (on 25 percent), and suicide attempts (on 23 percent).

As a consequence, academic institutions are being forced to expand their psychological counseling services. Three out of five colleges and universities reported last year that the use of counseling services had increased. Not only are counselors seeing students in record numbers, but the severity of the students' problems and the length of time needed to treat them are greater than in the past.

Students tell us they are frightened. They're afraid of deteriorating social and environmental conditions, international conflicts and terrorism, multiculturalism and their personal relationships, financing their education and getting jobs, and the future they will face. Nearly one-third of all college freshmen (30 percent) grew up with one or no parent (see Sax et al., in Resources). As one dean of students we talked with concluded, "Students expect the [college] community to respond to their needs—to make right their personal problems and those of society at large."

The effect of these accumulated fears and hurts is to divide students and isolate them from one another. Students also fear intimacy in relationships; withdrawal is easier and less dangerous than engagement.

20 Traditional dating is largely dead on college campuses. At institutions all over the country, students told us, in the words of a University of Colorado undergraduate, "There is no such thing as dating here." Two-person dating has been replaced by group dating, in which men and women travel in unpartnered packs. It's a practice that provides protection from deeper involvement and intimacy for a generation that regularly told us in focus group interviews that they had never witnessed a successful adult romantic relationship. Romantic relationships are seen as a burden, as a drag or potential anchor in a difficult world. Yet sexual relationships have not declined, even in the age of AIDS. Student descriptions of sexual activity are devoid of emotional content; they use words such as "scoping," "clocking," "hooking," "scamming," "scrumping," "mashing," and "shacking" to describe intimate relations.

In general, with increasing pressures on students, collegiate social life occupies a smaller part of their lives. In the words of an undergraduate at the University of the District of Columbia, "Life is just work, school, and home." In fact, one-fifth of those queried on our campus site visits (21 percent) defined their social lives in terms of studying; for another 11 percent, sleeping was all they cared about. When we asked students at the University of Colorado for the best adjective to describe this generation, the most common choice was "tired."

But not all of the retreat from social life is time-based. Chief student affairs officers describe students as loners more often now than in the past. Requests for single rooms in residence halls have skyrocketed. The thought of having a roommate is less appealing than it once was.

Similarly, group activities that once connected students on college campuses are losing their appeal and are becoming more individualized. For instance, the venue for television watching has moved from the lounge to the dorm room. Film viewing has shifted from the theater to the home VCR. With student rooms a virtual menagerie of electronic and food-preparation equipment, students are living their lives in ways that allow them to avoid venturing out if they so choose.

Student Organizational Mitosis

None of this is to say that collegiate social life is dead, but its profile and location have changed. On campus, there is probably a greater diversity of activities available than ever before, but each activity—in the words of the chief student affairs officer of the University of Southern Mississippi—"appeals to smaller pockets of students."

25 This is, in many respects, the consequence of student organizational mitosis and the proliferation of the divides between undergraduates. For instance, the business club on one college campus divided into more than a dozen groups—including women's; black; Hispanic; gay, lesbian, and bisexual; and Asian and Filipino business clubs.

Deans of students regularly told us last year that "there is less larger-group socializing" and that "more people are doing things individually and in separate groups than campus-wide." In contrast to the Carnegie Council's 1979 study, current students describe themselves in terms of their differences, not their commonalities. Increasingly, they say they associate with people who are like themselves rather than different.

In the main, when students do take time to have fun, they are leaving campus to do so. Our Campus Site Visits study indicated that drinking is the primary form of recreation for 63 percent of students, followed closely by going to clubs and bars (59 percent) and simply getting off campus (52 percent). By contrast, the latter two activities were not mentioned in the Carnegie Council's 1979 study.

Drinking was not a surprise. It was the first choice in our earlier study, but there is more binge drinking today. Drinking to get drunk has become the great escape for undergraduates.

Escaping from campus is a trend that goes hand in hand with the high numbers of students living in off-campus housing—more than triple the percentage in the late 1960s. Only 30 percent of students we surveyed reported living on campus. Add to this the fact that students are also spending less time on campus because of jobs and part-time attendance, and the result is that increasingly campuses are places in which instruction is the principal activity. Living and social life occur elsewhere.

Multiculturalism

30 Campuses are more deeply divided along lines of race, gender, ethnicity, sexuality, and other differences today than in the past. A majority of deans at four-year colleges told us last year that the climate on campus can be described as politically correct (60 percent), civility has declined (57 percent), students of different racial and ethnic groups often do not socialize together (56 percent), reports of sexual harassment have increased (55 percent), and students feel uncomfortable expressing unpopular or controversial opinions (54 percent).

Multiculturalism is a painful topic for many students. The dirty words on college campuses now are no longer four letters: they are-six-letter words like "racist" and "sexist"—and "homophobic," which is even longer. Students don't want to discuss the topic. In focus group interviews, students were more willing to tell us intimate details of their sex lives than to discuss diversity on campus.

Tension regarding diversity and difference runs high all across college life. Students talked about friction in the classroom; in the residence halls; in reactions to posters placed on campus or to visiting speakers; in campus activities and the social pursuits of the day; in hiring practices; in testing; in the dining room, library, bookstore, and sports facilities; in every aspect of their campus lives. In this sense, the campus in the 1990s is a less hospitable place for all undergraduates, regardless of background, than it once was.

Academics

Although instruction remains the principal on-campus activity that brings undergraduates together, the academic arena is experiencing its own form of student disengagement. Pursuit of academic goals is clearly utilitarian. It's as if students have struck a bargain with their colleges. They're going to class all right, but they're going by the book: they're doing what's necessary to fulfill degree requirements and gain skills for a job, but then they're out the door. They're focused and career-oriented, and see college as instrumental in leading to a lucrative career. "Task-oriented students who focus on jobs" is how a Georgia Tech student affairs official labeled them.

Although students do not believe that a college education provides a money-back guarantee of future success, they feel that without one, a good job—much less a lucrative or prestigious job—is impossible to obtain. At the very least, it's a kind of insurance policy to hedge bets against the future. As a student at Portland (Oregon) Community College put it, "College is the difference between white-collar and blue-collar work." Fifty-seven percent of undergraduates we surveyed in 1993 believed that the chief benefit of a college education is increasing one's earning power—an 11 percentage-point increase since 1976.

35   By contrast, the value placed on nonmaterial goals (that is, learning to get along with people and formulating the values and goals of one's life) has plummeted since the late 1960s, dropping from 71 and 76 percent respectively to 50 and 47 percent. Whereas in 1969 these personal and philosophic goals were cited by students as the primary reasons for attending college, in 1993, students placed them at the bottom of the list.

Although a great number of students are focused and intent on pursuing career goals, many also face a variety of academic hurdles. They are coming to college less well prepared academically. Nearly three-fourths (73 percent) of deans in 1997 reported an increase within the last decade in the proportion of students requiring remedial or developmental education at two-year (81 percent) and four-year (64 percent) colleges.

Nearly one-third (32 percent) of all undergraduates surveyed reported having taken a basic skills or remedial course in reading, writing, or math, up from 29 percent in 1976. Despite high aspirations, a rising percentage of students simply are not prepared for the rigors of academe. Another academic hurdle for students is a growing gap between how students learn best and how faculty teach. According to research by Charles Schroeder of the University of Missouri-Columbia, published in the September/October 1993 *Change*, more than half of today's students perform best in a learning situation characterized by "direct, concrete experience, moderate-to-high degrees of structure, and a linear approach to learning. They value the practical and the immediate, and the focus of their perception is primarily on the physical world." According to Schroeder, three-quarters of faculty, on the other hand, "prefer the global to the particular; are stimulated by the realm of concepts, ideas, and abstractions; and assume that students, like themselves, need a high degree of autonomy in their work."

Small wonder, then, that frustration results and that every year faculty believe students are less well prepared, while students increasingly think their classes are incomprehensible. On the faculty side, this is certainly the case. The 1997 Student Affairs Survey revealed that at 74 percent of campuses, faculty complaints about students are on the rise. One result is that students and faculty are spending less time on campus together. With work and part-time attendance, students increasingly are coming to campus just for their classes. This explains, in part, why students are taking longer to complete college. Fewer than two out of five are able to graduate in four years (see Astin et al., in Resources). Twenty-eight percent now require a fifth year to earn a baccalaureate, according to U.S. Department of Education statistics from 1996. In reality, obtaining the baccalaureate degree in four years is an anomaly today, particularly at public and less selective institutions.

The Future

The overwhelming majority of college students believe they will be successful. But their fears about relationships, romance, and their future happiness were continuing themes in every focus group. Their concerns about finances were overwhelming. There was not one focus group in which students did not ask whether they would be able to repay their student loans, afford to complete college, get a good job, or avoid moving home with Mom and Dad.

40   The college graduate driving a cab or working at the Gap was a universal anecdote. There was more mythology here than there were concrete examples, however. College graduates being forced to drive taxis is one of the great American legends, rivaled only by the tale of George Washington and the cherry tree.

Finances were a constant topic of discussion. Students told us of the need to drop out, stop out, and attend college part-time because of tuition costs. They told us of the lengths they had to go to pay tuition—even giving blood. More than one in five (21 percent) who participated in the Undergraduate Survey said that someone who helped pay their tuition had been out of work while they attended college.

At heart, undergraduates are worried about whether we can make it as a society, and whether they can actually make it personally. In our surveys, the majority did say they expected to do better than their parents. But in our focus groups, students regularly told us, "We're going to be the first generation that doesn't surpass our parents in making more money." "How will I buy a house?" "How will I send my kids to college?"

This is a generation of students desperately clinging to the American Dream. Nearly nine out of 10 (88 percent) students are optimistic about their personal futures, but their hope, though broadly professed, is fragile and gossamer-like. Their lives are being challenged at every turn: in their families, their communities, their nation, and their world. This is a generation where hope and fear collide.

Conclusion

In sum, these changes in America's undergraduates add up to a requiem for historic notions of collegiate life—the ivory tower, the living-learning community, the residential college, and all the rest. But the changes are not sudden; they began even before Cardinal Newman wrote his classic. Most are a natural consequence of the democratization of higher education. This is what happens when 65 percent of all high school graduates go on to college and higher education is open to the nation's population across the lifespan. Four years of living in residence becomes a luxury few can afford.

45   So how should higher education respond? Dismissing the present or recalling a golden era lost are not particularly helpful—for the most part the changes are permanent. But there are a few things colleges can do.

The first is to focus. Most colleges have less time with their students on campus than in the past. They need to be very clear about what they want to accomplish with students and dramatically reduce the laundry lists of values and goals that constitute the typical mission statement.

The second is to use all opportunities available to educate students. Required events, such as orientation, should be used to educate rather than to deal with logistics. The awards a college gives should represent the values it most wants to teach. The same is true for speakers. The in-house newsletter can be used to educate. And of course, maybe the best advice is that almost any event can be used for educational purposes if the food and music are good enough. Third, build on the strengths unique to every generation of students. For instance, current undergraduates, as part of their off-campus activities, are involved in public service— an astounding 64 percent of them, according to the Undergraduate Survey. Service learning, then, becomes an excellent vehicle to build into the curriculum and cocurriculum of most colleges.

Fourth, work to eliminate the forces that push students off campus unnecessarily. For example, most colleges talk a great deal about multiculturalism, but in general have not translated the rhetoric into a climate that will make the campus more hospitable to current students.

50   In like manner, using financial aid more to meet need than to reward merit would lessen the necessity for students to work while attending college. These are steps any college with the will and commitment can take. Both campus life and our students would benefit greatly.

Resources

* Astin, A.W., L. Tsui, and J. Avalos. *Degree Attainment Rates at American Colleges and Universities: Effects of Race, Gender, and Institutional Type,* Los Angeles: Higher Education Research Institute, UCLA, 1996.
* Sax, L.J., A.W. Astin, W.S. Korn, and K.M. Mahoney. *The American Freshman: National Norms for Fall 1997,* Los Angeles: Higher Education Research Institute, UCLA, 1997.
* U.S. Department of Education. National Center for Education Statistics. *Condition of Education, 1996* (NCES 96304), Washington, DC: U.S. Government Printing Office, 1996.
* ———. National Center for Education Statistics. *Digest of Education Statistics, 1997* (NCES 98-015), Washington, DC: U.S. Government Printing Office, 1997.

Studies Used in This Article

The studies of undergraduate student life that form the basis of this article and of the book *When Hope and Fear Collide: A Portrait of Today's College Student* were conducted by the authors between 1992 and 1997 at the Harvard Graduate

School of Education. The first—the Undergraduate Survey—included a 1993 questionnaire sent to a random sample of 9,100 students at institutions stratified by Carnegie type.

The second—the Student Affairs Survey—consisted of questionnaires sent in 1992 and again in 1997 to a random sample of 270 student affairs officers at institutions also stratified by Carnegie type. The third—Campus Site Visits—involved interviews conducted between 1993 and 1995 with nearly 50 student affairs officers and 300 students, both individually and in focus groups, at 28 diverse campuses across the country. The data from the completed questionnaires were weighted by Carnegie category to reflect the composition of American higher education.

In this article, the authors use for comparison with the above-listed surveys similar ones conducted in the 1960s and 1970s by Arthur Levine for the Carnegie Council on Policy Studies in Higher Education. All of these studies targeted students of both traditional and nontraditional age in two- and four-year institutions varying in control (public versus private), mission, size, selectivity, gender distribution, racial and ethnic mix, religious orientation, residential status, and regional location.

▨ QUESTIONS FOR INQUIRY AND ACTION ▨

1. Why do Levine and Cureton title their article "an obituary"? What elements of an obituary are present in the article?

2. Why do the authors compare colleges to banks? Does this analogy accurately describe your desired relationship with your school, too? If not, what analogy would you use?

3. How diverse is your campus? How do you define diversity? Is it simply a matter of race or ethnicity? Why or why not? Is diversity a difficult subject on your campus, so much so that, as Levine and Cureton discovered, students would be more willing to talk about their intimate lives than diversity at their schools?

4. Why are you in college? Survey others on your campus, using Levine and Cureton's questions and categories, to get a sense of the priorities, similarities, and differences at your institution.

Roger H. Garrison
Why Am I in College?

Roger H. Garrison was a professor of English at Briarcliff College. His work inspired the foundation of the National Great Teachers Seminar in 1969. He is also the author of a number of books on writing and teaching, including A Guide to Creative Writing, How a Writer Works, and Teaching in a Junior College: a

Brief Professional Orientation *(1968)*. The following selection is a chapter from *The Adventure of Learning in College (1959)*.

First among the signs of intellectual maturity we would wish for an ideal person is the achievement of an insight into his own make-up, a realistic understanding of his own assets and liabilities, an understanding of his own dominant trends and motivations. . .

Lawrence E. Cole

Before you skip over the above quotation, try an experiment with it. For each pronoun, substitute "I" or "my." For *ideal person* substitute "myself." How suddenly pertinent the generalized words become! Now the quotation says in effect: if I am to be a mature person, I will know what I am, where I'm strong and weak, and where I am aiming my life.

Where *are* you aiming your life? This may sound like too broad or moralistic a question. But what life *means* is and always has been the main concern of education. Education, fundamentally, is a *moral* enterprise. Harvard's President Nathan Pusey recently said: "The chief aim of undergraduate education is to discover what it means to be a man. This has always to be done in personal, individual terms." For you to discover the meaning of maturity and the direction of your life is therefore an inclusive aim of your studies.

Presumably you are in college because you want an education. You might well ask the next two logically inevitable questions: *What* is an education? *Why* do I want it?

The first question is, of course, difficult; it has almost as many answers as there are people who try to respond to it. And in the current literature on education, there are literally yards of library shelves taken up with books that discuss the matter. But there are some clear and useful general ideas on the meaning of an education that should help you think about it for yourself in practical and immediate terms.

5   Obviously, an education is something more than the acquiring of mere information. Pieces of knowledge, no matter how largely accumulated, are dead lumps unless you know what to do with them. As one philosopher put it bluntly, "A merely well-informed man is the most useless bore on God's earth." Yet the culture in which we live seems to put large and often spectacular premiums on the possession of factual knowledge. It would not be surprising, for example, if you have been impressed, and perhaps influenced, by the television and radio quiz programs of the past decade: winners in these fact-derbies have often walked away with fortunes in money and goods. Clearly, at least in this limited activity, the possession of great stores of random facts has a measurable pay-off. Yet actually there is little qualitative difference between the responses of quiz contestants in various categories of "knowledge," and the old-fashioned circus and vaudeville performances of trained animals who can "count," "talk," and perform other feats of "reasoning." Both quiz contestants and trained animals perform under special, limited conditions.

But life is never as tidy or controlled as a quiz program; in real living, the rewards usually go to the person who knows when and how to ask the right questions—not to the person who has sets of answers to predetermined questions. Life never has any predetermined questions either; it has only problems which must be coped with and dilemmas which rarely, if ever, come when they are supposed to, in the form they should.

To use the word "problems" is to presuppose questions. Most real learning starts with questions. One distinction between the educated person and the ignorant person is awareness of the importance of questions. The ignorant person is satisfied with answers; the educated person realizes that answers have limitations because they usually signal an end to investigation. There is nothing more empty or irrelevant than the answer to a question that nobody asks.

You can be given answers. You can be well trained without being well educated. For instance, if you want to be a trained engineer, you can find many institutions where superior engineering training is available; and if you work faithfully and intelligently at your courses, you will graduate as a trained engineer. If you want to be an *educated* engineer, you can manage that, too, and at those same institutions, but only after you develop some clear ideas about the differences between education and training, and after you understand what one is and the other is not.

Training is good, training is necessary, and training is a key part of education. To be trained means that one is fitted or qualified in the doing of something. In our complicated and competitive society, training in some skill is imperative. But to be educated is to know not only how to *do*, but to understand the meaning and significance of what one does. An educated person knows how and when to ask *why* of his own activity. Too often the trained man, like the expert, knows everything about his job except what it is for.

10   I agree wholly with A. N. Whitehead's comment: "There can be no adequate technical education which is not liberal, and no liberal education which is not technical: that is, no education which does not impart both technique and intellectual vision. . . Education should turn out the pupil with something he knows well and something he can do well[1]. . . .

There are endless illustrations in any business, and sometimes in the professions, of the differences between a merely trained man and an educated one. Recently, I took a group of students on a field trip to one of the country's largest manufacturers of rugs and carpets. We planned to make a two-hour tour of the factory, followed by a seminar with some of the management people on matters of the company's labor relations, rates of pay, employee status, and the like. Our guides for the tour were two friendly young men, both of whom had moved up from factory jobs and were now studying in the company's Management Education program as potential executives. As the tour began, we divided into two groups, with a guide for each. Throughout the tour, I alternated from group to group, listening as the guides explained production flow,

---

[1] *Alfred N. Whitehead,* The Aims of Education, *The Macmillan Company, 1929, chap. 4, p. 74.*

various types of looms, the designing of rugs and carpets and all the operations going on in front of us.

I soon noticed some pointed differences between our two guides. Though both were courteous and obviously knew their way around the complex factory processes, one of them seemed limited in his knowledge and understanding. When we stood by a loom or a sizing machine, he spoke surely and with authority, telling us in detail how the machine worked, what skills were needed to run it, and how it related to the sequence of operations in the factory. But when the students asked him questions about labor and manufacturing costs, sources of raw material, or any queries, in fact, which went beyond immediate functions, his replies were evasive and vague. He admitted freely that he didn't understand these matters well. "I thought I knew a lot about rugs," he said, "but all I really know is how to run some of these machines."

The other guide, however, enlarged his information with comments about the company's labor policy, the current state of the raw wool market, the economics of marketing and distribution, and the close relation between consumer research and the development of new designs and materials. These added facts were not merely sidelights or garnishing; they were expanded and intelligent attempts to increase the students' understanding of the total meaning of the work they were observing.

After the tour was over, I thanked our guides. As we talked I found that although both men had worked for several years in the plant and were trained in the use of the machines, the first guide—the one whose comments had been narrowly technical—had only that month begun his course in Management Education. The other guide had for eighteen months been taking university night courses in sociology, economics, and human relations, as well as following his regular studies in the Management program. The company's personnel director said to me later: "This fellow has all the makings of a fine executive some day. He knows the technical problems, but he can also think past them. In fact, he knows how to keep on learning about more than just the rug business. We need more men like that. We don't find enough of them."

15   The point is this: an educated person knows enough to ask the kinds of questions that open up, illuminate, and expand a subject, that set it in a new or fresh perspective, and that place it in significant relationships to other subjects. . . .

Let me say again that I have no intention of belittling trained skill, no matter how limited, nor of comparing it unfavorably with a "general education." All too often, to be "generally" educated means to be a dilettante, shallowly acquainted with much but usefully skilled in nothing—to be a person who, in Whitehead's phrases, has learned to execute "intellectual minuets" with "inert ideas." I remember, with sharp and still embarrassing clarity after more than two decades, a history professor who took me aside one morning, waved a sophomore paper I had written (with a C-minus grade) and said: "Young man, this is too slick, too superficial, too smooth on the surface, no texture underneath. You've got a good mind; why don't you dig a well for yourself instead of dilettanting around the edge?" I can still hear his voice. The honest outrage against superficiality of a cultivated, wise man taught me more than I learned in many another full-year course. . . .

Up to this point, I have been talking in general terms; obviously the question, "What *is* an education?" has not been answered except in the vaguest way. Just as you may take many months, or longer, in college to begin to discover for yourself what is meant by "an education," so it will take me the next dozen chapters even to suggest ways for you to begin to see the fullness of its meaning. In the last analysis, a liberal education is best described in the personal qualities of those who achieve it.

But the second question asked at the beginning of this chapter is almost indistinguishable from the first. You seek a college education. *Why?* What are you in college *for?*

Suppose you reply: "I want to be an industrial chemist, and good jobs in chemistry just aren't given to noncollege people." This is a reasonable and realistic answer. To be a good chemist (or a good *anything*) means much hard preparation first. But if you are asked, "*Why* do you want to be a chemist?" the answer is more difficult. You may say again, with perfect reasonableness, that industrial chemistry is a respectable, useful, and often creative business, that good chemists make a comfortable living, and that in a technological culture, chemists are needed and effective citizens. These are good answers—solid and rational and practical.

20   But why do you want to be a chemist? Only to make a good living? Only to be in a respectable and useful business or profession? Only to be a working element of society? Are these motives enough for *you?*

The full answer to this, if there is a full answer, implies far more than surface response about the necessary practical matters of making a living. The further answers you give have much to do with your *character.* They go deeply and personally to your motives and your hopes for yourself. They give your philosophy of life by answering, indirectly, the question, "What is the meaning of your life?" and fundamentally, the question, "What kind of a human being do you want to be?"

These are the hard, tangled, *basic* questions that education poses when you get to college. And this is why education is essentially a moral venture. It is relatively uncomplicated to get "know-how" training. Industries as well as schools and colleges do a superior job of teaching people how to perform detailed and complicated functions. We in America are an active people partly because we know how to teach one another to build, to make, to accomplish, and to invent. But education further says to you: learning to do something is fine and necessary, but what are you doing it *for?* Your trained skill, it says, is a function of your personality, to be sure, but are *you* merely a function or a skill? What more are you? What is the nature of your self? What is the meaning and direction of the group of selves we call society? What is your relation to your fellow men? What is your social function? Your *human* function?

Put it another way. Education's main concern is with the nature of decent, enlightened, effective human living—and this is a moral concern. The first goal of a liberal education is *your* personal growth as a generous-hearted, generous-minded human being. "Liberal" means generous and liberal means free. Surely, it is the least to expect of an educated person that he should have matured and become enriched *as a person,* one able to think freely, responsibly, and effectively. The world has plenty of experts, but does it have enough people who have both the imagination and the moral courage to make the best uses of the ideas and processes the experts create?

Before you shrug off this sort of talk, I urge you to follow the argument to its conclusion.

25   I have discovered that these apparently philosophical questions are crucial and real for intelligent college students. In some deep, inarticulate way, you recognize that an effective life is something more than a career, or raising a family, or being a good citizen. You urgently want to find for yourself what that "something more" is. Nor is this desire for inner certainty and purpose exclusive with college students. Many a person, in the midst of a successful career, wishes with inexpressible poignancy that he had begun in his teens to search how to make sense out of life, how to assert life, how to become a full, productive, serene human being. What kind of a human being do you want to be? What kind of human being *are* you now? These are not philosophers' or moralists' questions only. They are the most practical questions that can be asked.

Let's see why. You are, after all, given a legal twenty-one years to catch up with the major ideas and skills and insights of human experience. When you are technically adult, your society expects you to know how to work with other people and how to behave and express yourself without hurting others or yourself in the process. You are expected to know where you are going, and why. This is what being "grown up" implies. But the mental clinics and hospitals, jails, offices, and streets of our cities and towns are crowded with unhappy, tense, and nervous people who have not faced these fundamental questions about themselves. Moving restlessly from job to job, from pleasure to pleasure, from escape to escape, they try to find happiness by searching for conditions outside themselves that appear to lead to happiness. They do not seem to recognize that happiness comes from discovering what kind of person you want to be and can be, and then being it, serenely and confidently.

That is why I am suggesting that a *real* education (that is, an ultimately useful education) is not only the acquiring of knowledge and skill, but something more fundamental, more complex, and more significant.

Obviously, going to college will not guarantee happiness or tell you what kind of human being you ought to be. A lot of triumphs have been claimed for college education, but guaranteed maturity is not one of them. However, college is one of the few institutions in our society that is deliberately set up to help you explore the nature of human life and its meanings for you. Among all your motives for being in college—the practical ones of career, the general ones of culture, the unexpressed ones of great expectations—you might consider the aim of personal growth, or the opportunity for personal growth, as possibly the most important.

Indeed, this is the first and most inclusive stated purpose of most of the colleges and universities in the United States. At the beginning of nearly every general catalogue of course offerings, colleges state, with varying persuasiveness, the broad and humane aims I have suggested here. I recently examined several dozen of these, and I will quote briefly from two of the most typical. One, from a college division of a large university, reads: ". . . [This institution] provides the resources for the fullest personal, professional, and specialized development. . . . It provides each student with that liberal education best designed for. . . leadership. It gives him a background. . . that helps him to understand the human organism. . . ." Another, the catalogue of a small, coeducational college reads: ". . . The aim of ———— College is to give its students a sound education in preparation for the responsibilities of mature citizenship through the disciplines of a broad, rich, extensive curriculum. . . ."

30   You are in college because you are after adult learning. A college, if it lives up to its stated aims and pretensions, says: All right—most of your fact learning and drill and academic training up to now has been preparatory. You have had to learn multiplication tables, grammar, history, natural sciences, and the like, because you must have such facts as tools for any reasonable thinking. You will have to learn many more fact tools while you are at college. But now you are going to be asked in addition, and more pointedly: What *good* is all this information? On what bases is it good? These are questions of value and their implications go beyond mere fact knowledge. Questions of value have many levels, depending upon what "values" you are talking about.

A college, if it is doing the job it should, is not and cannot be concerned mainly with stuffing facts into you, or simply training you in a skill, or teaching you how to make a living. A college's real business is with the creative development of your best personal powers. Its business is to help you to a realistic awareness of yourself as an effective participant in your society. Its business is to lead you to a knowledge and appreciation of the extent and value of the culture that you have inherited. Its business is to stimulate you to develop a wide and open-minded sympathy for values and cultures not your own. Its business is to give you concrete and continuing experience with the meaning of the word "excellent" in both vocational and nonvocational studies. Its total concern is to discipline those capacities of mind and those qualities of personality which are best characterized by the adjective "mature." (You might look up the word "discipline" in an unabridged dictionary, investigating especially its root meanings from Latin.)

What you truly study when you go to college is not simply algebra, French, biology, English, physics, or sociology. What you study is *Man*—historically, presently, potentially; Man doing, Man thinking, Man puzzling, Man creating. No matter how genuine your desire or impatience to get at your specialty, whatever it is, you will merely develop a sterile *expertise* unless you recognize that the study of literature is as much a part of scientific training as advanced calculus, that the study of biology or physics is as much a part of the educating of a future English teacher as a course in Shakespeare, that semantics and sociology are intertwined. Knowledge is seamless; it is not compartmented.

Learning and growth are synonymous. How you learn in college is how you grow in college. You may test the validity of this assertion simply by recalling any recent situation or experience in your life in which you felt yourself *grow* in any way toward skill, mastery, or capacity to cope with a problem. How you felt during and after such an experience is how learning usually feels.

This can be said in another way by summarizing the function of a college or university: *the college exists to help you learn how to think for yourself and how to use the tools of thinking in a grown-up, morally responsible, and socially effective way.* This is a large order, a formidable one, both for you and for the college. Of course. Real learning is a formidable undertaking because it involves real thinking. All real thinking is hard; indeed I don't think there is such a thing as "easy" thinking. (William James once remarked on the "atrocious harmlessness" of most so-called thinking.) Knowledge or insights that are worth anything cannot be watered down or simplified. A real education does not come in prepackaged outlines and digests any more than you as an individual can be labeled, ticketed, and handily indexed under a single category. *The complexity of learning is precisely the complexity of the individual in relation to his experience.*

35   To be educated is to be *changed*, to be enlarged and reoriented as a person. To change is hard. Most of us resist changing or being changed. Yet if you graduate from college with your freshman habits, prejudices, and questions strengthened and more deep-seated, then no matter how much information you absorb, or how impressively you develop a skill or technique, you have not been educated but merely veneered, varnished with a cultural or technical gloss. (Varnish is a durable finish, but exposed to weather over any length of time it cracks, peels, and exposes the bare surface underneath.) Your education is going to be a personal business if it demands that you change yourself. It will demand your deep personal commitment, and may therefore be, on more than one occasion, a bewildering, frustrating, and even painful affair.

■ QUESTIONS FOR INQUIRY AND ACTION ■

1. Garrison wrote this piece in 1959. In what ways is his message relevant or irrelevant to students today?

2. Compare and contrast Garrison's piece with Peter Sacks's "The Sandbox Experiment." Are the authors arguing similar points? Who are their respective audiences, and what are the authors' respective purposes in writing? Which of these writers do you think is more persuasive? Why?

3. In your writer's notebook, answer Garrison's two main questions: What is education for you, and why do you want it? Compare your answers with your classmates'.

4. After answering question three above, review your college's mission statement and your courses' syllabi. Then, talk with your professors. Does your college have the same educational goals that you do? How do the college and its faculty help you reach your educational goals?

Mark Edmundson

On the Uses of a Liberal Education:
As Lite Entertainment for Bored
College Students

Mark Edmundson is the Daniels Family Distinguished Teaching Professor of Arts & Sciences at the University of Virginia. He has written several books including Why Read? *(2004),* Nightmare on Main Street: Angels, Sado-Masochism, and the Culture of Gothic *(1997),* Literature Against Philosophy, Plato to Derrida *(1995), and a memoir of one of his own teachers entitled* Teacher: The One Who Made the Difference *(2002). He has also written for the* Raritan, *the* New Republic, The New York Times Magazine, *and the* Nation. *Edmundson's essay was published in* Harper's *(September 1997).*

Today is evaluation day in my Freud class, and everything has changed. The class meets twice a week, late in the afternoon, and the clientele, about fifty undergraduates, tends to drag in and slump, looking disconsolate and a little lost, waiting for a jump start. To get the discussion moving, they usually require a joke, an anecdote, an off-the-wall question—When you were a kid, were your Halloween getups ego costumes, id costumes, or superego costumes? That sort of thing. But today, as soon as I flourish the forms, a buzz rises in the room. Today they write their assessments of the course, their assessments of me, and they are without a doubt wide-awake. "What is your evaluation of the instructor?" asks question number eight, entreating them to circle a number between five (excellent) and one (poor, poor). Whatever interpretive subtlety they've acquired during the term is now out the window. Edmundson: one to five, stand and shoot.

And they do. As I retreat through the door—I never stay around for this phase of the ritual—I look over my shoulder and see them toiling away like the devil's auditors. They're pitched into high writing gear, even the ones who struggle to squeeze out their journal entries word by word, stoked on a procedure they have by now supremely mastered. They're playing the informed consumer, letting the provider know where he's come through and where he's not quite up to snuff.

5   But why am I so distressed, bolting like a refugee out of my own classroom, where I usually hold easy sway? Chances are the evaluations will be much like what they've been in the past—they'll be just fine. It's likely that I'll be commended for being "interesting" (and I am commended, many times over), that I'll be cited for my relaxed and tolerant ways (that happens, too), that my sense of humor and capacity to connect the arcana of the subject matter with current culture will come in for some praise (yup). I've been hassled this term, finishing a manuscript, and so haven't given their journals the attention I should have, and for that I'm called—quite civilly, though—to account. Overall, I get off pretty well.

Yet I have to admit that I do not much like the image of myself that emerges from these forms, the image of knowledgeable, humorous detachment and bland tolerance. I do not like the forms themselves, with their number ratings, reminiscent of the sheets circulated after the TV pilot has just played to its sample audience in Burbank. Most of all I dislike the attitude of calm consumer expertise that pervades the responses. I'm disturbed by the serene belief that my function—and, more important, Freud's, or Shakespeare's, or Blake's—is to divert, entertain, and interest. Observes one respondent, not at all unrepresentative: "Edmundson has done a fantastic job of presenting this difficult, important & controversial material in an enjoyable and approachable way."

Thanks but no thanks. I don't teach to amuse, to divert, or even, for that matter, to be merely interesting. When someone says she "enjoyed" the course—and that word crops up again and again in my evaluations—somewhere at the edge of my immediate complacency I feel encroaching self-dislike. That is not at all what I had in mind. The off-the-wall questions and the sidebar jokes are meant as lead-ins to stronger stuff—in the case of the Freud course, to a complexly tragic view of life. But the affability and the one-liners often seem to be all that land with the students; their journals and evaluations leave me little doubt.

I want some of them to say that they've been changed by the course. I want them to measure themselves against what they've read. It's said that some time ago a Columbia University instructor used to issue a harsh two-part question. One: What book did you most dislike in the course? Two: What intellectual or characterological flaws in you does that dislike point to? The hand that framed that question was surely heavy. But at least it compels one to see intellectual work as a confrontation between two people, student and author, where the stakes matter. Those Columbia students were being asked to relate the quality of an encounter, not rate the action as though it had unfolded on the big screen.

Why are my students describing the Oedipus complex and the death drive as being interesting and enjoyable to contemplate? And why am I coming across as an urbane, mildly ironic, endlessly affable guide to this intellectual territory, operating without intensity, generous, funny, and loose?

10   Because that's what works. On evaluation day, I reap the rewards of my partial compliance with the culture of my students and, too, with the culture of the university as it now operates. It's a culture that's gotten little exploration. Current critics tend to think that liberal-arts education is in crisis because universities have been invaded by professors with peculiar ideas: deconstruction, Lacanianism, feminism, queer theory. They believe that genius and tradition are out and that P.C., multiculturalism, and identity politics are in because of an invasion by tribes of tenured radicals, the late millennial equivalents of the Visigoth hordes that cracked Rome's walls.

But mulling over my evaluations and then trying to take a hard, extended look at campus life both here at the University of Virginia and around the country eventually led me to some different conclusions. To me, liberal-arts education is as ineffective as it is now not chiefly because there are a lot of strange theories in the air. (Used well, those theories can be illuminating.) Rather, it's that university culture, like American culture writ large, is, to put it crudely, ever more devoted to consumption and entertainment, to the using and using up of goods and images. For someone growing up in America now, there are few available alternatives to the cool consumer worldview. My students didn't ask for that view, much less create it, but they bring a consumer weltanschauung to school, where it exerts a powerful, and largely unacknowledged, influence. If we want to understand current universities, with their multiple woes, we might try leaving the realms of expert debate and fine ideas and turning to the classrooms and campuses, where a new kind of weather is gathering.

From time to time I bump into a colleague in the corridor and we have what I've come to think of as a Joon Lee fest. Joon Lee is one of the best students I've taught. He's endlessly curious, has read a small library's worth, seen every movie, and knows all about showbiz and entertainment. For a class of mine he wrote an essay using Nietzsche's Apollo and Dionysus to analyze the pop group The Supremes. A trite, cultural-studies bonbon? Not at all. He said striking things about conceptions of race in America and about how they shape our ideas of beauty. When I talk with one of his other teachers, we run on about the general splendors of his work and presence. But what inevitably follows a JL fest is a mournful reprise about the divide that separates him and a few other remarkable students from their contemporaries. It's not that some aren't nearly as bright—in terms of intellectual ability, my students are all that I could ask for. Instead, it's that Joon Lee has decided to follow his interests and let them make him into a singular and rather eccentric man; in his charming way, he doesn't mind being at odds with most anyone.

It's his capacity for enthusiasm that sets Joon apart from what I've come to think of as the reigning generational style. Whether the students are sorority/fraternity types, grunge aficionados, piercer/tattooers, black or white, rich or middle class (alas, I teach almost no students from truly poor backgrounds), they are, nearly across the board, very, very self-contained. On good days they display a light, appealing glow; on bad days, shuffling disgruntlement. But there's little fire, little passion to be found.

This point came home to me a few weeks ago when I was wandering across the university grounds. There, beneath a classically cast portico, were two students, male and female, having a rip-roaring argument. They were incensed, bellowing at each other, headstrong, confident, and wild. It struck me how rarely I see this kind of full-out feeling in students anymore. Strong emotional display is forbidden. When conflicts arise, it's generally understood that one of the parties will say something sarcastically propitiating ("whatever" often does it) and slouch away.

15   How did my students reach this peculiar state in which all passion seems to be spent? I think that many of them have imbibed their sense of self from consumer culture in general and from the tube in particular. They're the progeny of 100 cable channels and omni-present Blockbuster outlets. TV, Marshall McLuhan famously said, is a cool medium. Those who play best on it are low-key and nonassertive; they blend in. Enthusiasm, à la Joon Lee, quickly looks absurd. The

form of character that's most appealing on TV is calmly self-interested though never greedy, attuned to the conventions, and ironic. Judicious timing is preferred to sudden self-assertion. The TV medium is inhospitable to inspiration, improvisation, failures, slipups. All must run perfectly.

Naturally, a cool youth culture is a marketing bonanza for producers of the right products, who do all they can to enlarge that culture and keep it grinding. The Internet, TV, and magazines now teem with what I call persona ads, ads for Nikes and Reeboks and Jeeps and Blazers that don't so much endorse the capacities of the product per se as show you what sort of person you will be once you've acquired it. The Jeep ad that features hip, outdoorsy kids whipping a Frisbee from mountaintop to mountaintop isn't so much about what Jeeps can do as it is about the kind of people who own them. Buy a Jeep and be one with them. The ad is of little consequence in itself, but expand its message exponentially and you have the central thrust of current consumer culture—buy in order to be.

Most of my students seem desperate to blend in, to look right, not to make a spectacle of themselves. (Do I have to tell you that those two students having the argument under the portico turned out to be acting in a role-playing game?) The specter of the uncool creates a subtle tyranny. It's apparently an easy standard to subscribe to, this Letterman-like, Tarantino-like cool, but once committed to it, you discover that matters are rather different. You're inhibited, except on ordained occasions, from showing emotion, stifled from trying to achieve anything original. You're made to feel that even the slightest departure from the reigning code will get you genially ostracized. This is a culture tensely committed to a laid-back norm.

Am I coming off like something of a crank here? Maybe. Oscar Wilde, who is almost never wrong, suggested that it is perilous to promiscuously contradict people who are much younger than yourself. Point taken. But one of the lessons that consumer hype tries to insinuate is that we must never rebel against the new, never even question it. If it's new—a new need, a new product, a new show, a new style, a new generation—it must be good. So maybe, even at the risk of winning the withered, brown laurels of crankdom, it pays to resist newness-worship and cast a colder eye.

Praise for my students? I have some of that too. What my students are, at their best, is decent. They are potent believers in equality. They help out at the soup kitchen and volunteer to tutor poor kids to get a stripe on their resumes, sure. But they also want other people to have a fair shot. And in their commitment to fairness they are discerning; there you see them at their intellectual best. If I were on trial and innocent, I'd want them on the jury.

20   What they will not generally do, though, is indict the current system. They won't talk about how the exigencies of capitalism lead to a reserve army of the unemployed and nearly inevitable misery. That would be getting too loud, too brash. For the pervading view is the cool consumer perspective, where passion and strong admiration are forbidden. "To stand in awe of nothing, Numicus, is perhaps the one and only thing that can make a man happy and keep him so," says Horace in the Epistles, and I fear that his lines ought to hang as a motto over the university in this era of high consumer capitalism.

It's easy to mount one's high horse and blame the students for this state of affairs. But they didn't create the present culture of consumption. (It was largely my own generation, that of the Sixties, that let the counterculture search for pleasure devolve into a quest for commodities.) And they weren't the ones responsible, when they were six and seven and eight years old, for unplugging the TV set from time to time or for hauling off and kicking a hole through it. It's my generation of parents who sheltered these students, kept them away from the hard knocks of everyday life, making them cautious and overfragile, who demanded that their teachers, from grade school on, flatter them endlessly so that the kids are shocked if their college profs don't reflexively suck up to them.

Of course, the current generational style isn't simply derived from culture and environment. It's also about dollars. Students worry that taking too many chances with their educations will sabotage their future prospects. They're aware of the fact that a drop that looks more and more like one wall of the Grand Canyon separates the top economic tenth from the rest of the population. There's a sentiment currently abroad that if you step aside for a moment, to write, to travel, to fall too hard in love, you might lose position permanently. We may be on a conveyor belt, but it's worse down there on the filth-strewn floor. So don't sound off, don't blow your chance.

But wait. I teach at the famously conservative University of Virginia. Can I extend my view from Charlottesville to encompass the whole country, a whole generation of college students? I can only say that I hear comparable stories about classroom life from colleagues everywhere in America. When I visit other schools to lecture, I see a similar scene unfolding. There are, of course, terrific students everywhere. And they're all the better for the way they've had to strive against the existing conformity. At some of the small liberal-arts colleges, the tradition of strong engagement persists. But overall, the students strike me as being sweet and sad, hovering in a nearly suspended animation.

Too often now the pedagogical challenge is to make a lot from a little. Teaching Wordsworth's "Tintern Abbey," you ask for comments. No one responds. So you call on Stephen. Stephen: "The sound, this poem really flows." You: "Stephen seems interested in the music of the poem. We might extend his comment to ask if the poem's music coheres with its argument. Are they consistent? Or is there an emotional pain submerged here that's contrary to the poem's appealing melody?" All right, it's not usually that bad. But close. One friend describes it as rebound teaching: they proffer a weightless comment, you hit it back for all you're worth, then it comes dribbling out again. Occasionally a professor will try to explain away this intellectual timidity by describing the students as perpetrators of postmodern irony, a highly sophisticated mode. Everything's a slick counterfeit, a simulacrum, so by no means should any phenomenon be taken seriously. But the students don't have the urbane, Oscar Wilde-type demeanor that should go with this view. Oscar was cheerful, funny, confident, strange. (Wilde, mortally ill, living in a Paris flophouse: "My wallpaper and I are fighting a duel to the death. One or the other of us has to go.") This generation's style is considerate, easy to please, and a touch depressed.

25   Granted, you might say, the kids come to school immersed in a consumer mentality—they're good Americans, after all—but then the university and the professors do everything in their power to fight that dreary mind-set in the interest of higher ideals, right? So it should be. But let us look at what is actually coming to pass.

Over the past few years, the physical layout of my university has been changing. To put it a little indecorously, the place is looking more and more like a retirement spread for the young. Our funds go to construction, into new dorms, into renovating the student union. We have a new aquatics center and ever-improving gyms, stocked with StairMasters and Nautilus machines. Engraved on the wall in the gleaming aquatics building is a line by our founder, Thomas Jefferson, declaring that everyone ought to get about two hours' exercise a day. Clearly even the author of the Declaration of Independence endorses the turning of his university into a sports-and-fitness emporium.

But such improvements shouldn't be surprising. Universities need to attract the best (that is, the smartest and the richest) students in order to survive in an ever more competitive market. Schools want kids whose parents can pay the full freight, not the ones who need scholarships or want to bargain down the tuition costs. If the marketing surveys say that the kids require sports centers, then, trustees willing, they shall have them. In fact, as I began looking around, I came to see that more and more of what's going on in the university is customer driven. The consumer pressures that beset me on evaluation day are only a part of an overall trend.

From the start, the contemporary university's relationship with students has a solicitous, nearly servile tone. As soon as someone enters his junior year in high school, and especially if he's living in a prosperous zip code, the informational material—the advertising—comes flooding in. Pictures, testimonials, videocassettes, and CD ROMs (some bidden, some not) arrive at the door from colleges across the country, all trying to capture the student and his tuition cash. The freshman-to-be sees photos of well-appointed dorm rooms; of elaborate phys-ed facilities; of fine dining rooms; of expertly kept sports fields; of orchestras and drama troupes; of students working alone (no overbearing grown-ups in range), peering with high seriousness into computers and microscopes; or of students arrayed outdoors in attractive conversational garlands.

Occasionally—but only occasionally, for we usually photograph rather badly; in appearance we tend at best to be styleless—there's a professor teaching a class. (The college catalogues I received, by my request only, in the late Sixties were austere affairs full of professors' credentials and course descriptions; it was clear on whose terms the enterprise was going to unfold.) A college financial officer recently put matters to me in concise, if slightly melodramatic, terms: "Colleges don't have admissions offices anymore, they have marketing departments." Is it surprising that someone who has been approached with photos and tapes, bells and whistles, might come in thinking that the Freud and Shakespeare she had signed up to study were also going to be agreeable treats?

30   How did we reach this point? In part the answer is a matter of demographics and (surprise) of money. Aided by the G.I. bill, the college-going population in America dramatically increased after the Second World War. Then came the baby

boomers, and to accommodate them, schools continued to grow. Universities expand easily enough, but with tenure locking faculty in for lifetime jobs, and with the general reluctance of administrators to eliminate their own slots, it's not easy for a university to contract. So after the baby boomers had passed through—like a fat meal digested by a boa constrictor—the colleges turned to energetic promotional strategies to fill the empty chairs. And suddenly college became a buyer's market. What students and their parents wanted had to be taken more and more into account. That usually meant creating more comfortable, less challenging environments, places where almost no one failed, everything was enjoyable, and everyone was nice.

Just as universities must compete with one another for students, so must the individual departments. At a time of rank economic anxiety, the English and history majors have to contend for students against the more success-insuring branches, such as the sciences and the commerce school. In 1968, more than 21 percent of all the bachelor's degrees conferred in America were in the humanities; by 1993, that number had fallen to about 13 percent. The humanities now must struggle to attract students, many of whose parents devoutly wish they would study something else.

One of the ways we've tried to stay attractive is by loosening up. We grade much more softly than our colleagues in science. In English, we don't give many Ds, or Cs for that matter. (The rigors of Chem 101 create almost as many English majors per year as do the splendors of Shakespeare.) A professor at Stanford recently explained grade inflation in the humanities by observing that the undergraduates were getting smarter every year; the higher grades simply recorded how much better they were than their predecessors. Sure.

Along with softening the grades, many humanities departments have relaxed major requirements. There are some good reasons for introducing more choice into curricula and requiring fewer standard courses. But the move, like many others in the university now, jibes with a tendency to serve—and not challenge—the students. Students can also float in and out of classes during the first two weeks of each term without making any commitment. The common name for this time span—shopping period—speaks volumes about the consumer mentality that's now in play. Usually, too, the kids can drop courses up until the last month with only an innocuous "W" on their transcripts. Does a course look too challenging? No problem. Take it pass-fail. A happy consumer is, by definition, one with multiple options, one who can always have what he wants. And since a course is something the students and their parents have bought and paid for, why can't they do with it pretty much as they please?

A sure result of the university's widening elective leeway is to give students more power over their teachers. Those who don't like you can simply avoid you. If the clientele dislikes you en masse, you can be left without students, period. My first term teaching I walked into my introduction to poetry course and found it inhabited by one student, the gloriously named Bambi Lynn Dean. Bambi and I chatted amiably awhile, but for all that she and the pleasure of her name could offer, I was fast on the way to meltdown. It was all a mistake, luckily, a problem with the scheduling book. Everyone was waiting for me next door. But in a dozen years of teaching I haven't forgotten that feeling of being ignominiously marooned. For it happens to others, and not always because of scheduling glitches. I've seen older colleagues go through hot embarrassment at not having enough students sign up for their courses: they graded too hard, demanded too much, had beliefs too far out of keeping with the existing disposition. It takes only a few such instances to draw other members of the professoriat further into line.

35   And if what's called tenure reform—which generally just means the abolition of tenure—is broadly enacted, professors will be yet more vulnerable to the whims of their customer-students. Teach what pulls the kids in, or walk. What about entire departments that don't deliver? If the kids say no to Latin and Greek, is it time to dissolve classics? Such questions are being entertained more and more seriously by university administrators.

How does one prosper with the present clientele? Many of the most successful professors now are the ones who have "decentered" their classrooms. There's a new emphasis on group projects and on computer-generated exchanges among the students. What they seem to want most is to talk to one another. A classroom now is frequently an "environment," a place highly conducive to the exchange of existing ideas, the students' ideas. Listening to one another, students sometimes change their opinions. But what they generally can't do is acquire a new vocabulary, a new perspective, that will cast issues in a fresh light.

The Socratic method—the animated, sometimes impolite give-and-take between student and teacher—seems too jagged for current sensibilities. Students frequently come to my office to tell me how intimidated they feel in class; the thought of being embarrassed in front of the group fills them with dread. I remember a student telling me how humiliating it was to be corrected by the teacher, by me. So I asked the logical question: "Should I let a major factual error go by so as to save discomfort?" The student— a good student, smart and earnest—said that was a tough question. He'd need to think about it.

Disturbing? Sure. But I wonder, are we really getting students ready for Socratic exchange with professors when we push them off into vast lecture rooms, two and three hundred to a class, sometimes face them with only grad students until their third year, and signal in our myriad professorial ways that we often have much better things to do than sit in our offices and talk with them? How bad will the student-faculty ratios have to become, how teeming the lecture courses, before we hear students righteously complaining, as they did thirty years ago, about the impersonality of their schools, about their decline into knowledge factories? "This is a firm," said Mario Savio at Berkeley during the Free Speech protests of the Sixties, "and if the Board of Regents are the board of directors, . . . then . . . the faculty are a bunch of employees and we're the raw material. But we're a bunch of raw material that don't mean . . . to be made into any product."

Teachers who really do confront students, who provide significant challenges to what they believe, can be very successful, granted. But sometimes such professors generate more than a little trouble for themselves. A controversial teacher can send students hurrying to the deans and the counselors, claiming to have been offended. ("Offensive" is the preferred term of repugnance today, just as "enjoyable" is the summit of praise.) Colleges have brought in hordes of counselors and deans to make sure that everything is smooth, serene, unflustered, that everyone has a good time. To the counselor, to the dean, and to the university legal squad, that which is normal, healthy, and prudent is best.

40   An air of caution and deference is everywhere. When my students come to talk with me in my office, they often exhibit a Franciscan humility. "Do you have a moment?" "I know you're busy. I won't take up much of your time." Their presences tend to be very light; they almost never change the temperature of the room. The dress is nondescript: clothes are in earth tones; shoes are practical—cross-trainers, hiking boots, work shoes, Dr. Martens, with now and then a stylish pair of raised-sole boots on one of the young women. Many, male and female both, peep from beneath the bills of monogrammed baseball caps. Quite a few wear sports, or even corporate, logos, sometimes on one piece of clothing but occasionally (and disconcertingly) on more. The walk is slow; speech is careful, sweet, a bit weary, and without strong inflection. (After the first lively week of the term, most seem far in debt to sleep.) They are almost unfailingly polite. They don't want to offend me; I could hurt them, savage their grades.

Naturally, there are exceptions, kids I chat animatedly with, who offer a joke, or go on about this or that new CD (almost never a book, no). But most of the traffic is genially sleepwalking. I have to admit that I'm a touch wary, too. I tend to hold back. An unguarded remark, a joke that's taken to be off-color, or simply an uncomprehended comment can lead to difficulties. I keep it literal. They scare me a little, these kind and melancholy students, who themselves seem rather frightened of their own lives.

Before they arrive, we ply the students with luscious ads, guaranteeing them a cross between summer camp and lotusland. When they get here, flattery and non-stop entertainment are available, if that's what they want. And when they leave? How do we send our students out into the world? More and more, our administrators call the booking agents and line up one or another celebrity to usher the graduates into the millennium. This past spring, Kermit the Frog won himself an honorary degree at Southampton College on Long Island; Bruce Willis and Yogi Berra took credentials away at Montclair State; Arnold Schwarzenegger scored at the University of Wisconsin-Superior. At Wellesley, Oprah Winfrey gave the commencement address. (Wellesley—one of the most rigorous academic colleges in the nation.) At the University of Vermont, Whoopi Goldberg laid down the word. But why should a worthy administrator contract the likes of Susan Sontag, Christopher Hitchens, or Robert Hughes—someone who might actually say something, something disturbing, something offensive—when he can get what the parents and kids apparently want and what the newspapers will softly commend—more lite entertainment, more TV?

Is it a surprise, then, that this generation of students—steeped in consumer culture before going off to school, treated as potential customers by the university well before their date of arrival, then pandered to from day one until the morning of the final kiss-off from Kermit or one of his kin—are inclined to see the books they read as a string of entertainments to be placidly enjoyed or languidly cast down? Given the way universities are now administered (which is more and more to say, given the way that they are currently marketed), is it a shock that the kids don't come to school hot to learn, unable to bear their own ignorance? For some measure of self-dislike, or self-discontent—which is much different than simple depression—seems to me to be a prerequisite for getting an education that matters. My students, alas, usually lack the confidence to acknowledge what would be their most precious asset for learning: their ignorance.

Not long ago, I asked my Freud class a question that, however hoary, never fails to solicit intriguing responses: Who are your heroes? Whom do you admire? After one remarkable answer, featuring T. S. Eliot as hero, a series of generic replies rolled in, one gray wave after the next: my father, my best friend, a doctor who lives in our town, my high school history teacher. Virtually all the heroes were people my students had known personally, people who had done something local, specific, and practical, and had done it for them. They were good people, unselfish people, these heroes, but most of all they were people who had delivered the goods.

45   My students' answers didn't exhibit any philosophical resistance to the idea of greatness. It's not that they had been primed by their professors with complex arguments to combat genius. For the truth is that these students don't need debunking theories. Long before college, skepticism became their habitual mode. They are the progeny of Bart Simpson and David Letterman, and the hyper-cool ethos of the box. It's inane to say that theorizing professors have created them, as many conservative critics like to do. Rather, they have substantially created a university environment in which facile skepticism can thrive without being substantially contested.

Skeptical approaches have potential value. If you have no all-encompassing religious faith, no faith in historical destiny, the future of the West, or anything comparably grand, you need to acquire your vision of the world somewhere. If it's from literature, then the various visions literature offers have to be inquired into skeptically. Surely it matters that women are denigrated in Milton and in Pope, that some novelistic voices assume an overbearing godlike authority, that the poor are, in this or that writer, inevitably cast as clowns. You can't buy all of literature wholesale if it's going to help draw your patterns of belief.

But demystifying theories are now overused, applied mechanically. It's all logocentrism, patriarchy, ideology. And in this the student environment—laid-back, skeptical, knowing—is, I believe, central. Full-out debunking is what plays with this clientele. Some have been doing it nearly as long as, if more crudely than, their deconstructionist teachers. In the context of the contemporary university, and cool consumer culture, a useful intellectual skepticism has become exaggerated into a fundamentalist caricature of itself. The teachers have buckled to their students' views.

At its best, multiculturalism can be attractive as well-deployed theory. What could be more valuable than encountering the best work of far-flung cultures and becoming a citizen of the world? But in the current consumer environment, where flattery plays so well, the urge to encounter the other can devolve into the urge to find others who embody and celebrate the right ethnic origins. So we put aside the African novelist Chinua Achebe's abrasive, troubling *Things Fall Apart* and gravitate toward hymns on Africa, cradle of all civilizations.

What about the phenomenon called political correctness? Raising the standard of civility and tolerance in the university has been—who can deny it?—a very good thing. Yet this admirable impulse has expanded to the point where one is enjoined to speak well—and only well—of women, blacks, gays, the disabled, in fact of virtually everyone. And we can owe this expansion in many ways to the student culture. Students now do not wish to be criticized, not in any form. (The culture of consumption never criticizes them, at least not overtly.) In the current university, the movement for urbane tolerance has devolved into an imperative against critical reaction, turning much of the intellectual life into a dreary Sargasso Sea. At a certain point, professors stopped being usefully sensitive and became more like careful retailers who have it as a cardinal point of doctrine never to piss the customers off.

50   To some professors, the solution lies in the movement called cultural studies. What students need, they believe, is to form a critical perspective on pop culture. It's a fine idea, no doubt. Students should be able to run a critical commentary against the stream of consumer stimulations in which they're immersed. But cultural studies programs rarely work, because no matter what you propose by way of analysis, things tend to bolt downhill toward an uncritical discussion of students' tastes, into what they like and don't like. If you want to do a Frankfurt School-style analysis of *Braveheart*, you can be pretty sure that by mid-class Adorno and Horkheimer will be consigned to the junk heap of history and you'll be collectively weighing the charms of Mel Gibson. One sometimes wonders if cultural studies hasn't prospered because, under the guise of serious intellectual analysis, it gives the customers what they most want—easy pleasure, more TV. Cultural studies becomes nothing better than what its detractors claim it is—Madonna studies—when students kick loose from the critical perspective and groove to the product, and that, in my experience teaching film and pop culture, happens plenty.

On the issue of genius, as on multiculturalism and political correctness, we professors of the humanities have, I think, also failed to press back against our students' consumer tastes. Here we tend to nurse a pair of—to put it charitably—disparate views. In one mode, we're inclined to a programmatic debunking criticism. We call the concept of genius into question. But in our professional lives per se, we aren't usually disposed against the idea of distinguished achievement. We argue animatedly about the caliber of potential colleagues. We support a star system, in which some professors are far better paid, teach less, and under better conditions than the rest. In our own profession, we are creating a system that is the mirror image of the one we're dismantling in the curriculum. Ask a professor what she thinks of the work of Stephen Greenblatt, a leading critic of Shakespeare, and you'll hear it for an hour. Ask her what her views are on Shakespeare's genius and she's likely to begin questioning the term along with the whole "discourse of evaluation." This dual sensibility may be intellectually incoherent. But in its awareness of what plays with students, it's conducive to good classroom evaluations and, in its awareness of where and how the professional bread is buttered, to self-advancement as well.

My overall point is this: It's not that a leftwing professorial coup has taken over the university. It's that at American universities, left-liberal politics have collided with the ethos of consumerism. The consumer ethos is winning.

Then how do those who at least occasionally promote genius and high literary ideals look to current students? How do we appear, those of us who take teaching to be something of a performance art and who imagine that if you give yourself over completely to your subject you'll be rewarded with insight beyond what you individually command?

I'm reminded of an old piece of newsreel footage I saw once. The speaker (perhaps it was Lenin, maybe Trotsky) was haranguing a large crowd. He was expostulating, arm waving, carrying on. Whether it was flawed technology or the man himself, I'm not sure, but the orator looked like an intricate mechanical device that had sprung into fast-forward. To my students, who mistrust enthusiasm in every form, that's me when I start riffing about Freud or Blake. But more and more, as my evaluations showed, I've been replacing enthusiasm and intellectual animation with standup routines, keeping it all at arm's length, praising under the cover of irony.

55   It's too bad that the idea of genius has been denigrated so far, because it actually offers a live alternative to the demoralizing culture of hip in which most of my students are mired. By embracing the works and lives of extraordinary people, you can adapt new ideals to revise those that came courtesy of your parents, your neighborhood, your clan—or the tube. The aim of a good liberal-arts education was once, to adapt an observation by the scholar Walter Jackson Bate, to see that "we need not be the passive victims of what we deterministically call 'circumstances' (social, cultural, or reductively psychological-personal), but that by linking ourselves through what Keats calls an 'immortal free masonry' with the great we can become freer—freer to be ourselves, to be what we most want and value."

But genius isn't just a personal standard; genius can also have political effect. To me, one of the best things about democratic thinking is the conviction that genius can spring up anywhere. Walt Whitman is born into the working class and thirty-six years later we have a poetic image of America that gives a passionate dimension to the legalistic brilliance of the Constitution. A democracy needs to constantly develop, and to do so it requires the most powerful visionary minds to interpret the present and to propose possible shapes for the future. By continuing to notice and praise genius, we create a culture in which the kind of poetic gamble that Whitman made—a gamble in which failure would have entailed rank humiliation, depression, maybe suicide—still takes place. By rebelling against established ways of seeing and saying things, genius helps us to apprehend how malleable the present is and how promising and fraught with danger is the future. If we teachers do not endorse genius and self-overcoming, can we be surprised when our students find their ideal images in TV's latest persona ads?

A world uninterested in genius is a despondent place, whose sad denizens drift from coffee bar to Prozac dispensary, unfired by ideals, by the glowing image of the self that one might become. As Northrop Frye says in a beautiful and now dramatically unfashionable sentence, "The artist who uses the same energy and genius that Homer and Isaiah had will find that he not only lives in the same palace of art as Homer and Isaiah, but lives in it at the same time." We ought not to deny the existence of such a place simply because we, or those we care for, find the demands it makes intimidating, the rent too high.

What happens if we keep trudging along this bleak course? What happens if our most intelligent students never learn to strive to overcome what they are? What if genius, and the imitation of genius, become silly, outmoded ideas? What you're likely to get are more and more one-dimensional men and women. These will be people who live for easy pleasures, for comfort and prosperity, who think of money first, then second, and third, who hug the status quo; people who believe in God as a sort of insurance policy (cover your bets); people who are never surprised. They will be people so pleased with themselves (when they're not in despair at the general pointlessness of their lives) that they cannot imagine humanity could do better. They'll think it their highest duty to clone themselves as frequently as possible. They'll claim to be happy, and they'll live a long time.

It is probably time now to offer a spate of inspiring solutions. Here ought to come a list of reforms, with due notations about a core curriculum and various requirements. What the traditionalists who offer such solutions miss is that no matter what our current students are given to read, many of them will simply translate it into melodrama, with flat characters and predictable morals. (The unabated capitalist culture that conservative critics so often endorse has put students in a position to do little else.) One can't simply wave a curricular wand and reverse acculturation.

60   Perhaps it would be a good idea to try firing the counselors and sending half the deans back into their classrooms, dismantling the football team and making the stadium into a playground for local kids, emptying the fraternities, and boarding up the student-activities office. Such measures would convey the message that American colleges are not northern outposts of Club Med. A willingness on the part of the faculty to defy student conviction and affront them occasionally—to be usefully offensive—also might not be a bad thing. We professors talk a lot about subversion, which generally means subverting the views of people who never hear us talk or read our work. But to subvert the views of our students, our customers, that would be something else again.

Ultimately, though, it is up to individuals—and individual students in particular—to make their own way against the current sludgy tide. There's still the library, still the museum, there's still the occasional teacher who lives to find things greater than herself to admire. There are still fellow students who have not been cowed. Universities are inefficient, cluttered, archaic places, with many unguarded corners where one can open a book or gaze out onto the larger world and construe it freely. Those who do as much, trusting themselves against the weight of current opinion, will have contributed something to bringing this sad dispensation to an end. As for myself, I'm canning my low-key one-liners; when the kids' TV-based tastes come to the fore, I'll aim and shoot. And when it's time to praise genius, I'll try to do it in the right style, full-out, with faith that finer artistic spirits (maybe not Homer and Isaiah quite, but close, close), still alive somewhere in the ether, will help me out when my invention flags, the students doze, or the dean mutters into the phone. I'm getting back to a more exuberant style; I'll be expostulating and arm waving straight into the millennium, yes I will.

▦ QUESTIONS FOR INQUIRY AND ACTION ▦

1. Edmundson says that students tend to evaluate professors using words like "interesting," "enjoyable," or "too hard" because they have been conditioned by society to see college classes as entertainment. What words do you tend to use in your evaluations of teachers? What qualities do you tend to comment on in those evaluations?

2. Edmundson makes several unflattering characterizations of the college experience (e.g., colleges have transformed their campuses into student versions of Club Med). Make a more complete list of Edmundson's characterizations and then observe your own campus and classrooms for one week. Are these generalizations supported by your observations? Why or why not?

3. How do Edmundson's ideas align with those of bell hooks on classroom teaching? Do they share the same views of and assumptions about students?

4. Near the end of the article, Edmundson suggests that one way to resist our culture of consumerism is to find heroes in those geniuses who show us a "glowing image of the self that one might become." Identify five heroes in your life. Do they tend to support or challenge the values associated with consumerism?

STOP AND THINK

THE CONSUMER MODEL FOR UNIVERSITIES

In the first essay, Arthur Levine and Jeanette Cureton record changes to higher education communities as a result of changes in the culture at large. Changing demographics (i.e., who is coming to college) and the changing values, experiences, and priorities of students are pushing changes in what courses are offered, where money is spent in an institution, and how education is experienced.

In particular, Levine and Cureton see growing pressure on colleges and universities to treat students as consumers. The narratives of bell hooks, Peter Sacks, and Mark Edmundson offer examples of how individual teachers are responding to these changes, and to the values associated with consumer culture.

You can contribute to this discussion by providing your own experience as a student. Write an essay or participate in a class discussion that answers the questions "Do you want the same things from your college as from other service

continued on next page

providers: convenience, ease, affordability, and pleasure? Why or why not?" Here are some additional questions to consider as you answer the larger question:

1. What does your college's mission statement say is the college's purpose? Is that purpose clear in the college's advertising materials?
2. What is your purpose in going to college? Have you been able to successfully accomplish your purpose so far?
3. What steps could the college take to better help you accomplish your purpose? Are these steps compatible with its mission?
4. Have your experiences with college professors and counselors been consistent with the college's mission? With your own purpose?
5. What might you change about yourself that would improve your experience in college? Would you change those views, values, or behaviors? Why or why not?

bell hooks
Engaged Pedagogy

bell hooks is the pen name of Gloria Watkins, a feminist theorist, a social critic, an educator, and a poet. She has taught at Yale University and Oberlin College and is currently Distinguished Professor of English at City University of New York. She has authored numerous essays and more than a dozen books, from Ain't I a Woman: Black Women and Feminism *(1981),* Black Looks: Race and Representation *(1992), and* Where We Stand: Class Matters *(2000) to* Remembered Rapture: The Writer at Work *(1999). "Engaged Pedagogy" is the first chapter of her book* Teaching to Transgress: Education as the Practice of Freedom *(New York: Routledge, 1994).*

To educate as the practice of freedom is a way of teaching that anyone can learn. That learning process comes easiest to those of us who teach who also believe that there is an aspect of our vocation that is sacred; who believe that our work is not merely to share information but to share in the intellectual and spiritual growth of our students. To teach in a manner that respects and cares for the souls of our students is essential if we are to provide the necessary conditions where learning can most deeply and intimately begin.

Throughout my years as student and professor, I have been most inspired by those teachers who have had the courage to transgress those boundaries that would confine each pupil to a rote, assembly-line approach to learning. Such teachers approach students with the will and desire to respond to our unique beings, even if the situation does not allow the full emergence of a relationship based on mutual recognition. Yet the possibility of such recognition is always present.

Paulo Freire and the Vietnamese Buddhist monk Thich Nhat Hanh are two of the "teachers" who have touched me deeply with their work. When I first began college, Freire's thought gave me the support I needed to challenge the "banking system" of education, that approach to learning that is rooted in the notion that all students need to do is consume information fed to them by a professor and be able to memorize and store it. Early on, it was Freire's insistence that education could be the practice of freedom that encouraged me to create strategies for what he called "conscientization" in the classroom. Translating that term to critical aware-ness and engagement, I entered the classrooms with the conviction that it was cru-cial for me and every other student to be an active participant, not a passive consumer. Education as the practice of freedom was continually undermined by professors who were actively hostile to the notion of student participation. Freire's work affirmed that education can only be liberatory when everyone claims knowl-edge as a field in which we all labor. That notion of mutual labor was affirmed by Thich Nhat Hanh's philosophy of engaged Buddhism, the focus on practice in con-junction with contemplation. His philosophy was similar to Freire's emphasis on "praxis"—action and reflection upon the world in order to change it.

In his work Thich Nhat Hanh always speaks of the teacher as a healer. Like Freire, his approach to knowledge called on students to be active participants, to link awareness with practice. Whereas Freire was primarily concerned with the mind, Thich Nhat Hanh offered a way of thinking about pedagogy which empha-sized wholeness, a union of mind, body, and spirit. His focus on a holistic approach to learning and spiritual practice enabled me to overcome years of social-ization that had taught me to believe a classroom was diminished if students and professors regarded one another as "whole" human beings, striving not just for knowledge in books, but knowledge about how to live in the world.

5   During my twenty years of teaching, I have witnessed a grave sense of dis-ease among professors (irrespective of their politics) when students want us to see them as whole human beings with complex lives and experiences rather than simply as seekers after compartmentalized bits of knowledge. When I was an undergraduate, Women's Studies was just finding a place in the academy. Those classrooms were the one space where teachers were willing to acknowledge a connection between ideas learned in university settings and those learned in life practices. And, despite those times when students abused that freedom in the classroom by only wanting to dwell on personal experience, feminist classrooms were, on the whole, one location where I witnessed professors striving to create participatory spaces for the sharing of knowl-edge. Nowadays, most women's studies professors are not as committed to explor-ing new pedagogical strategies. Despite this shift, many students still seek to enter feminist classrooms because they continue to believe that there, more than in any other place in the academy, they will have an opportunity to experience education as the practice of freedom.

Progressive, holistic education, "engaged pedagogy" is more demanding than conventional critical or feminist pedagogy. For, unlike these two teaching prac-tices, it emphasizes well-being. That means that teachers must be actively com-mitted to a process of self-actualization that promotes their own well-being if they are to teach in a manner that empowers students. Thich Nhat Hanh emphasized that "the practice of a healer, therapist, teacher or any helping pro-fessional should be directed toward his or herself first, because if the helper is unhappy, he or she cannot help many people." In the United States it is rare that anyone talks about teachers in university settings as healers. And it is even more rare to hear anyone suggest that teachers have any responsibility to be self-actualized individuals.

Learning about the work of intellectuals and academics primarily from nineteenth-century fiction and nonfiction during my pre-college years, I was certain that the task for those of us who chose this vocation was to be holistically questing for self-actualization. It was the actual experience of college that disrupted this image. It was there that I was made to feel as though I was terribly naive about "the profession." I learned that far from being self-actualized, the university was seen more as a haven for those who are smart in book knowledge but who might be otherwise unfit for social interaction. Luckily, during my undergraduate years I began to make a distinction between the practice of being an intellectual/teacher and one's role as a member of the academic profession.

It was difficult to maintain fidelity to the idea of the intellectual as someone who sought to be whole—well-grounded in a context where there was little emphasis on spiritual well-being, on care of the soul. Indeed, the objectification of the teacher within bourgeois educational structures seemed to denigrate notions of wholeness and uphold the idea of a mind/body split, one that promotes and supports compartmentalization.

This support reinforces the dualistic separation of public and private, encouraging teachers and students to see no connection between life practices, habits of being, and the roles of professors. The idea of the intellectual questing for a union of mind, body, and spirit had been replaced with notions that being smart meant that one was inherently emotionally unstable and that the best in oneself emerged in one's academic work. This meant that whether academics were drug addicts, alcoholics, batterers, or sexual abusers, the only important aspect of our identity was whether or not our minds functioned, whether we were able to do our jobs in the classroom. The self was presumably emptied out the moment the threshold was crossed, leaving in place only an objective mind—free of experiences and biases. There was fear that the conditions of that self would interfere with the teaching process. Part of the luxury and privilege of the role of teacher/professor today is the absence of any requirement that we be self-actualized. Not surprisingly, professors who are not concerned with inner well-being are the most threatened by the demand on the part of students for liberatory education, for pedagogical processes that will aid them in their own struggle for self-actualization.

10 Certainly it was naive for me to imagine during high school that I would find spiritual and intellectual guidance in university settings from writers, thinkers, scholars. To have found this would have been to stumble across a rare treasure. I learned, along with other students, to consider myself fortunate if I found an interesting professor who talked in a compelling way. Most of my professors were not the slightest bit interested in enlightenment. More than anything they seemed enthralled by the exercise of power and authority within their mini-kingdom, the classroom.

This is not to say that there were not compelling, benevolent dictators, but it is true to my memory that it was rare—absolutely, astonishingly rare—to encounter professors who were deeply committed to progressive pedagogical practices. I was dismayed by this; most of my professors were not individuals whose teaching styles I wanted to emulate.

My commitment to learning kept me attending classes. Yet, even so, because I did not conform—would not be an unquestioning, passive student—some professors treated me with contempt. I was slowly becoming estranged from education. Finding Freire in the midst of that estrangement was crucial to my survival as a student. His work offered both a way for me to understand the limitations of the type of education I was receiving and to discover alternative strategies for learning and teaching. It was particularly disappointing to encounter white male professors who claimed to follow Freire's model even as their pedagogical practices were mired in structures of domination, mirroring the styles of conservative professors even as they approached subjects from a more progressive standpoint.

When I first encountered Paulo Freire, I was eager to see if his style of teaching would embody the pedagogical practices he described so eloquently in his work. During the short time I studied with him, I was deeply moved by his presence, by the way in which his manner of teaching exemplified his pedagogical theory. (Not all students interested in Freire have had a similar experience.) My experience with him restored my faith in liberatory education. I had never wanted to surrender the conviction that one could teach without reinforcing existing systems of domination. I needed to know that professors did not have to be dictators in the classroom.

While I wanted teaching to be my career, I believed that personal success was intimately linked with self-actualization. My passion for this quest led me to interrogate constantly the mind/body split that was so often taken to be a given. Most professors were often deeply antagonistic toward, even scornful of, any approach to learning emerging from a philosophical standpoint emphasizing the union of mind, body, and spirit, rather than the separation of these elements. Like many of the students I now teach, I was often told by powerful academics that I was misguided to seek such a perspective in the academy. Throughout my student years I felt deep inner anguish. Memory of that pain returns as I listen to students express the concern that they will not succeed in academic professions if they want to be well, if they eschew dysfunctional behavior or participation in coercive hierarchies. These students are often fearful, as I was, that there are no spaces in the academy where the will to be self-actualized can be affirmed.

15   This fear is present because many professors have intensely hostile responses to the vision of liberatory education that connects the will to know with the will to become. Within professorial circles, individuals often complain bitterly that students want classes to be "encounter groups." While it is utterly unreasonable for students to expect classrooms to be therapy sessions, it is appropriate for them to hope that the knowledge received in these settings will enrich and enhance them.

Currently, the students I encounter seem far more uncertain about the project of self-actualization than my peers and I were twenty years ago. They feel that there are no clear ethical guidelines shaping actions. Yet, while they despair, they are also adamant that education should be liberatory. They want and demand more from professors than my generation did. There are times when I walk into classrooms overflowing with students who feel terribly wounded in their psyches (many of them see therapists), yet I do not think that they want therapy from me. They do want an education that is healing to the uninformed, unknowing spirit. They do want knowledge that is meaningful. They rightfully expect that my colleagues and I will not offer them information without addressing the connection between what they are learning and their overall life experiences.

This demand on the students' part does not mean that they will always accept our guidance. This is one of the joys of education as the practice of freedom, for it allows students to assume responsibility for their choices. Writing about our teacher/student relationship in a piece for the *Village Voice*, "How to Run the Yard: Off-Line and into the Margins at Yale," one of my students, Gary Dauphin, shares the joys of working with me as well as the tensions that surfaced between us as he began to devote his time to pledging a fraternity rather than cultivating his writing:

> People think academics like Gloria [my given name] are all about difference: but what I learned from her was mostly about sameness, about what I had in common as a black man to people of color; to women and gays and lesbians and the poor and anyone else who wanted in. I did some of this learning by reading but most of it came from hanging out on the fringes of her life. I lived like that for a while, shuttling between high points in my classes and low points outside. Gloria was a safe haven. . . Pledging a fraternity is about as far away as you can get from her classroom, from the yellow kitchen where she used to share her lunch with students in need of various forms of sustenance.

This is Gary writing about the joy. The tension arose as we discussed his reason for wanting to join a fraternity and my disdain for that decision. Gary comments, "They represented a vision of black manhood that she abhorred, one where violence and abuse were primary ciphers of bonding and identity." Describing his assertion of autonomy from my influence he writes, "But she must have also known the limits of even her influence on my life, the limits of books and teachers."

Ultimately, Gary felt that the decision he had made to join a fraternity was not constructive, that I "had taught him openness" where the fraternity had encouraged one-dimensional allegiance. Our interchange both during and after this experience was an example of engaged pedagogy.

20   Through critical thinking—a process he learned by reading theory and actively analyzing texts—Gary experienced education as the practice of freedom. His final comments about me: "Gloria had only mentioned the entire episode once after it was over, and this to tell me simply that there are many kinds of choices, many kinds of logic. I could make those events mean whatever I wanted as long as I was honest." I have quoted his writing at length because it is testimony affirming engaged pedagogy. It means that my voice is not the only account of what happens in the classroom.

Engaged pedagogy necessarily values student expression. In her essay, "Interrupting the Calls for Student Voice in Liberatory Education: A Feminist Poststructuralist Perspective," Mimi Orner employs a Foucauldian framework to suggest that

Regulatory and punitive means and uses of the confession bring to mind curricular and pedagogical practices which call for students to publicly reveal, even confess, information about their lives and cultures in the presence of authority figures such as teachers.

When education is the practice of freedom, students are not the only ones who are asked to share, to confess. Engaged pedagogy does not seek simply to empower students. Any classroom that employs a holistic model of learning will also be a place where teachers grow, and are empowered by the process. That empowerment cannot happen if we refuse to be vulnerable while encouraging students to take risks. Professors who expect students to share confessional narratives but who are themselves unwilling to share are exercising power in a manner that could be coercive. In my classrooms, I do not expect students to take any risks that I would not take, to share in any way that I would not share. When professors bring narratives of their experiences into classroom discussions it eliminates the possibility that we can function as all-knowing, silent interrogators. It is often productive if professors take the first risk, linking confessional narratives to academic discussions so as to show how experience can illuminate and enhance our understanding of academic material. But most professors must practice being vulnerable in the classroom, being wholly present in mind, body, and spirit.

Progressive professors working to transform the curriculum so that it does not reflect biases or reinforce systems of domination are most often the individuals willing to take the risks that engaged pedagogy requires and to make their teaching practices a site of resistance. In her essay, "On Race and Voice: Challenges for Liberation Education in the 1990s," Chandra Mohanty writes that

> resistance lies in self-conscious engagement with dominant, normative discourses and representations and in the active creation of oppositional analytic and cultural spaces. Resistance that is random and isolated is clearly not as effective as that which is mobilized through systemic politicized practices of teaching and learning. Uncovering and reclaiming subjugated knowledge is one way to lay claims to alternative histories. But these knowledges need to be understood and defined pedagogically, as questions of strategy and practice as well as of scholarship, in order to transform educational institutions radically.

Professors who embrace the challenge of self-actualization will be better able to create pedagogical practices that engage students, providing them with ways of knowing that enhance their capacity to live fully and deeply.

■ QUESTIONS FOR INQUIRY AND ACTION ■

1. What does the word pedagogy mean? What does hooks mean by an "engaged pedagogy"? How does she describe it in her essay?

2. Read hooks's essay with Peter Sacks's "The Sandbox Experiment." How does each of these professors describe the experience of teaching? What is each one's theory of pedagogy, or teaching? Which one would you rather have as a teacher, and why?

3. Research the concept of liberatory education. What are its tenets? How did it come about? Who practices it, and for what reasons?

4. Notice the teaching approaches used by your and your friends' professors. Do many professors at your institution teach like hooks does? Do you think they should? If so, how would you discuss the subject with them?

Peter Sacks
The Sandbox Experiment

Peter Sacks is the pseudonym for a former journalist who taught journalism at a large suburban community college. Earlier in his journalistic career he wrote for a number of newspapers and was nominated for a Pulitzer Prize. His latest work is Standardized Minds: The High Price of America's Testing Culture and What We Can Do to Change It *(Perseus Publishing, 2000). "The Sandbox Experiment" is a chapter from his book* Generation X Goes to College: An Eye-Opening Account of Teaching in Postmodern America *(Open Court, 1996).*

Having been given my ultimatum by those who held the key to The Castle as to how I might become a permanent fixture there myself (had I been so inclined), I had a good long talk with Sandy. We talked the evening after my tenure meeting with the Big Committee, after they told me my student evaluations must significantly improve, or else. My conversation with Sandy that night ultimately inspired me to keep going in my journey into teaching, rather than simply write off the whole experience. The actual possibility of Failure—yes, Failure with a capital F— was haunting me, and my self-confidence was waning. "People who can't do, teach, and I can't even succeed as a teacher." That was the demon in my head. And for a driven Boomer who had learned how to compete adequately in a world with millions of other Boomers, steering clear of Failure was probably what kept me going in my experiment at teaching. I still wanted to know exactly what one had to do to succeed—or survive, perhaps—teaching the MTV generation. In one of those classic moments in life, Sandy and I landed upon the perfect solution.

I was in my study when she got home. She plopped on the floor in my study. "So, what happened?" she asked, referring to my meeting that day with the Big Committee.

"Well, it's pretty simple. Either my student evaluations improve or I'm out."

"So that's what it takes to be a good teacher? Just make the students happy?"

5   "I suppose so. Otherwise, I'm gone. Oh, yeah, and they want me to take an *acting* course," I said, my voice dripping with sarcasm. "I'm not entertaining enough for the MTV crowd." . . .

I don't recall exactly how the idea came to me, but after I rejected Prozac as the means to become a successful teacher of Generation X, I got another idea. If one option was to chemically change my personality with a drug to be more outgoing, entertaining, and nurturing, then the opposite approach would be to consciously alter my behavior and actually *manipulate my environment.* There seemed little doubt that the system was actually pushing me in that direction. It suddenly became clear to me that being a good teacher didn't seem to really matter in the system of rewards and punishments teachers faced; excellence wasn't really the point. It was becoming increasingly clear that the real point was whether you kept students sufficiently amused and entertained.

Like the Prozac idea, the scheme I would simply call "the Sandbox Experiment" started out as something of a joke. As Sandy and I sat there on the carpet in my little study. I said, "What I should do is to become like a kindergarten teacher and do everything possible to make my classes like playtime. I'll call class the Sandbox. And we'll play all kinds of games and just have fun, and I'll give all my students good grades, and everyone will be happy. Students will get what they want—whether they learn anything or not doesn't matter. The College will get what it wants, which are lots of happy students. And I'll get good evaluations, because students are happy and contented."

From that seed, we then brainstormed what my new classes ought to be like, and sitting there on the carpet (in our sandbox positions) we came up with the essential outline of my new syllabus. To hell with the fundamentals; my little sandbox would emphasize amusement. We'd do restaurant and movie reviews, write about sports, have lots of guest speakers, write advertising copy (which I knew next to nothing about)—I would shamelessly plug into popular culture and the demands of this generation to be amused.

But that wasn't all. I'd have to alter my whole attitude toward people who hated me because they thought I was passing myself off as somehow superior to them. But that's an overstatement of the problem. Hints of one of the most important yet subtle characteristics of these students had been emerging in my evaluations for months, and it had something to do with their revolting against the traditional balance of power between the teacher and themselves. Sure, by most measures I was somewhat accomplished as a journalist who undoubtedly knew far more about the subject I was teaching than students did. But many students were still uncomfortable with the idea that my knowledge and skills were important or even relevant. They seemed far more comfortable with what some educators might call a "collaborative approach." That's a fancy sounding phrase, but it boiled down to mean that students felt what they knew about a subject was just as valuable as what I knew. And who was I, trying to shove my version of the world down their throats? I'll admit, I did come across as if I knew more—a lot more—about journalism than my students. And in doing so I violated this seemingly unwritten code: Don't *act* as if you know more than the students, even though you do.

10   And so I devised a few techniques to cope with this peculiar attitude. First, I would tell students on the first day of class to call me Peter; that would help break down barriers and assure them that I thought of myself as their equal. Second, I vowed not to tell them anything about my background in journalism. Doing so seemed only to intimidate them and draw attention to our inequality. Psychologists

probably have a term for it, but I could see how disoriented students would be if faced with the contradiction of thinking they are both my equal and my inferior in the classroom at the same time. Something would have to give, and it would probably take the form of irrational behavior, sullenness, or other behaviors that were unproductive for me and them. So, from then on, I would be a blank slate, and they'd call me by my first name, simply a "resource" for students to "facilitate" their learning. In the fashionable jargon of some educators, we would be "partners" in the "learning process."

Welcome to teaching in collaborative, multicultural, multivalued, postmodern America, I thought. Form, method, and style had triumphed over substance. For, in the end, it really didn't seem to matter what I knew about my field when it came to teaching. I remember talking to my brother, who was trained as an actor, about my teaching job. At thirty, he was at the older end of Generation X and had recently finished a graduate degree in drama. I said, "My students would probably consider you a better journalism teacher than me, because you know how to act, with just enough knowledge, you could simply play that role." He thought about what I said a minute, then slowly nodded his head and said, "Unfortunately, I think you're probably right." The irony, of course, was that The College hired me over people who had far more teaching experience than I had because of my journalism experience, and yet I had to play down my expertise in order to become a successful teacher. This truly was a strange world, I thought.

Finally, there was the question of grades. It is here that I made what is surely the most important decision about my little Sandbox Experiment, and the one loaded with ethical dilemmas. I decided that, just to see what would happen, I would consciously give what, in my own estimation, were outrageously good grades. I hypothesized that when students were receiving poor grades, they would blow out of proportion characteristics about a teacher that bothered them. But if students were content with their grades, they wouldn't make such a fuss out of other things about a class, such as the difficulty of the readings or my speaking style, which students said wasn't sufficiently entertaining.

And so, in my mind, I became a teaching teddy bear. In the metaphorical sandbox I created, students could do no wrong, and I did almost anything possible to keep all of them happy, all of the time, no matter how childish or rude their behavior, no matter how poorly they performed in the course, no matter how little effort they gave. If they wanted their hands held, I would hold them. If they wanted a stapler (or a Kleenex) and I didn't have one, I'd apologize. If they wanted to read the newspaper while I was addressing the class or if they wanted to get up and leave in the middle of a lecture, go for it. Call me spineless. I confess. But in the excessively accommodative culture that I found myself in, "our students" as many of my colleagues called them, had too much power for me to afford irritating them with demands and challenges I had previously thought were part and parcel of the collegiate experience. Metaphorically speaking, if they needed that ride to school I refused to give them in my dream in the mountains, now I'd give them a ride, and then I'd ask if there was anything else I could do to please. But to be sure, it wasn't always easy for me.

But you're probably thinking, "That's unethical. You're buying off students with high grades." You readers who are also parents of college-aged students might well be adding. "We're paying tuition for you to teach, regardless of how students behave."

15   I do understand the sentiment. But I believe that my Sandbox Experiment was defensible. First, grades are relative, and the grades I gave out during my experiment were in fact more equal to what was common at The College than the grades I'd been giving before the experiment. . . . I stumbled into the realization that the average grade at The College, as for most colleges and universities, was a solid B. That's compared to the C average I tried to maintain before the experiment, which I believe compelled many students to evaluate me so harshly. As a result, I brought down my standards to match those of the rest of The College, and it was professionally suicidal to try to do otherwise. As I shall describe below, in often subtle and occasionally quite overt ways, I was in fact strongly encouraged by college administrators and colleagues to do just that. In short, I had to get real. Second, . . . it became clear to me from my work on the Save Our Standards committee that one way or another most other instructors were watering down standards, essentially buying off students with lots of spoon-feeding and undeserved grades.

Is it a valid defense to say that "everybody was doing it?" Well, as far as I could tell, everybody *was* doing it, this pandering to students. And they weren't doing so for selfish gain—as opposed to Bill Clinton and Newt Gingrich trying to outdo each other on tax breaks for middle-class voters. The teachers at my college, rather, were going easy on students because they were afraid for their jobs. That's how grade inflation had become institutionalized, and virtually nobody was willing to acknowledge this. Given the incentives of benefits and punishments teachers faced, pandering became quite rational and justifiable, however unfortunate its collective results.

Still, I remained troubled in my choice to relax my personal standards in order to determine just what kinds of behavior the educational system rewarded. As a social experiment, I felt, my one true justification was that the end would justify the means. In an absolute sense, I might have been wrong to act in the way the system was compelling me to act; but now, I am confessing, and hoping that the virtue of my act lies in exposing the corruption that has enveloped much of higher education.

My Sandbox Experiment was to get its first key test in my journalism class. I was fortunate to get a pretty good group of students with which to deploy my new methods. There were Steve and Holly, both a bit older students with whom I could easily engage in small talk. There was just one hard-core grunger who had pieces of metal protruding from her nose and ears, but she was bright and a pretty fair writer and I got along well with her. There were several Asian students, including Japanese and Koreans who almost always made life easier for a teacher because they worked hard, listened well and didn't give you a lot of crap. But there was also Caitlin. Remember her? She was the one who didn't have any tastebuds because of a cold and wondered if she still had to complete her restaurant review.

Did I change? Let me show you the ways.

20   I became a master of hand-holding and spoon-feeding. Take Daniel, for instance, a student of mine who was an official of some sort in student government. He was outspoken, often absent—and potentially dangerous to a teacher who might demand too much of him. For one assignment, I showed a videotape of a speech so students could write a speech story. Daniel missed that day but didn't tell me he'd be absent. Nevertheless, I agreed to give him a written copy of the speech so he could do the assignment anyway. Before my Sandbox Experiment, I wouldn't have allowed him to make up the assignment. Still, I couldn't suppress saying when handing him the speech. "If this were a real job, you'd be fired by now." I sort of winced to myself as I said it, but I couldn't help it. Another time, Daniel hadn't attended class for a few days and he did the wrong assignment for a story. Instead of flunking the paper, as I would have done before, I let him do the correct assignment—and gave him extra credit for the wrong assignment.

When I used to take attendance, if somebody came in late I'd mark them absent anyway. Now I would go out of my way to erase the little 0 (absent) and write in an X (present) if a student walked in after I'd taken attendance. Whereas in the past I'd demand some sort of proof to document an absence, now I'd simply take a student's word. And nearly any excuse would do. If they cared enough to lie, then I didn't care.

Indeed, my self-inflicted lobotomy was very hard to live with at times, especially toward the end of the quarter when my nerves and patience wore thin. Sometimes when students were being real jerks, I'd say things I'd later regret and then try to figure out a way to make it up to the student I might have offended.

Caitlin, for instance, was the sort of student I might have flunked or given D's before, but now I indulged her incompetency, figuring that she was potentially one more happy student who would say good things about me come evaluation time. One day she came to me with another excuse (besides nonfunctioning tastebuds) about why she hadn't done an assignment. This was toward the end of the quarter, and I could only keep up this little act of mine for so long. I gave her the same line I laid on Daniel: "You know, if this were a job, you'd be fired by now." Whereas Daniel could handle my criticism, Caitlin couldn't. She started crying and then left the room to compose herself. I felt bad about coming down on her—and I envisioned Caitlin's retaliation on her evaluation of me: *"What a jerk! He treats us like he's the boss and this were a job or something! He has no compassion."* And I imagined how the Big Committee would respond to such words. So, when Caitlin returned to the classroom, at the end of the hour, I walked up to her desk and said, "Caitlin, are you okay? I'm sorry if I came down on you too hard. You're doing fine," I lied.

I also took to plain old bullshitting with students, going out of my way to be informal with them whenever I could, and it was working well in my new journalism class. I talked with Rick about skiing, Tanya about jogging. "How was your weekend?" I'd say. When Heather, the grunger, took time off from in the middle of the quarter to take a vacation in New Orleans, rather than get irritated that she had missed so much class, I asked her, "So how was your vacation? Did you enjoy Mardi Gras?"

25 Of course, my newfound happy-face approach to being a college instructor would have meant nothing if I didn't follow through on the grading end. It's one thing to try to be a nice guy; there's nothing wrong in trying to communicate better with your students. But when it came to my new grading system, I was a shameless lush, handing out mostly A's and B's, often for work that I would have given C's before. But while I felt shameless, I had to remind myself that nearly nine of ten students got A's and B's at The College—and the same went for top schools like Stanford.

I recall one news story a student wrote, containing so much muddled language that it was nearly impossible to follow. According to my theoretical grading system, the story should have gotten a D because it required so much work to whip it into shape. This is what the new me wrote on the student's paper: "Okay. Some unclear spots that don't make sense, mechanical problems, style errors (use your stylebook)."

And I gave the paper a warm and friendly B minus.

Over the entire quarter, that journalism class "earned" an average grade of 3.5, equivalent to an A minus. Compare that to the 2.3 average (a C) in the introductory journalism class that got on my case so hard during my first quarter at The College.

And so went the first phase of my grand experiment. . . .

30 The following quarter was the make or break time for me, the one that would resolve one way or another my fate as a college teacher. Since my Machiavellian formula seemed to be achieving the desired results, I tried hard not to change anything about my courses or my rather calculated behavior. The danger, however, was that I was becoming more confident, and students could interpret confidence as superciliousness, which I wanted to avoid. There was potentially great danger for an instructor trying to cope with students. Whenever they'd act childish, rude, or bored, a teacher might have to pinch himself real hard to keep from blowing up, walking out of the room, and telling them to all go back to high school or whatever Neverneverland they'd come out from.

My journalism class, as usually seemed to be the case, put me to the greatest test. It seemed that there was something about the journalism sequence at The College that attracted more than its share of difficult students. We had no professional school of journalism, and so most of the students had no interest at all in going into journalism or mass communications but were taking the course to satisfy a writing requirement.

This particular class was a special dog. Whereas my "turnaround" class the previous term had included some motivated students, by whom I was generally viewed favorably—this class had several quintessential members of Generation X who tested the limits of my patience.

As with all my writing classes, I had students first do drafts that they would then revise before turning in a final draft. I'd let them work on drafts during class time and allow them to get feedback from their peers. I'd also try to look at the drafts to give the students an idea whether they were on the right track. Doing the drafts was so important that I made them worth 15 percent of the final grade. As I've mentioned before, students at The College as a general rule would not do anything if it didn't directly affect their grade in a significant way. But in this class, I had a core of people who didn't do drafts, week after week after week, 15 percent of their grade be damned.

If my journalism class were a movie, it would have looked something like this:

Camera: Long shot from the back of a good-sized classroom, as college students file in to take their chairs. Sounds of tables and chairs being shuffled, voices in small talk. Zoom to teacher at the head of the class, smiling and casually talking to a student about skiing conditions over the weekend. After a few minutes at 11 A.M. sharp, he removes his rear end from the table (posing in a very casual, friendly way), stands up, and starts talking to the whole class.

Teacher: "Okay, folks, go ahead and pass me up a copy of your drafts due today. Then break up into your groups. Remember, today we're working on leads."

Camera: Scan back to students. Little movement detected. Two or three people take their assignments from folders and pass them to the student ahead. The rest of the class stares at the teacher, expressionless.

Teacher (*incredulous*): "Do I have everyone's draft? Is this it?"

Camera: Seeing no further movement from the inert students, the teacher moves back to his power position in the front of the podium, adjusts his body uncomfortably a second, then speaks.

Teacher: "Let me remind everyone that the drafts are worth 15 percent of your grade. If you don't come prepared, there's not any productive work we can do during class."

Camera: Scan back to class, still inert and silent, zoom in on two young men in the back sitting together at a table. Both have long hair. Not hippie long. More grunge or metal anti-hippie long, both in their early twenties. One sports a baseball hat and a goatee. The other has no baseball hat. He's a grunge-metal cross: long-sleeved checkered work shirt unbuttoned to his chest, showing a black T-shirt with the name of a metal band blasted across it. Slumped in their chairs, they stare alternatively at the teacher and down to their desk, obviously bored.

Narrator Voice-over (*teacher staring back at class*): "Look at these idiots. I've got three drafts. What the hell am I going to do today? I have a notion to just cancel class and send them home. How would Tom Hanks or Harrison Ford say it if this were a movie? 'You people make me sick. Get the hell out of here, come back when you've done the work. You're wasting my time.' . . . Yeah, right. In my dreams."

Teacher: "Okay, tell you what. Break up into your groups, give feedback to the ones who've done their drafts and the rest of you go over your outlines with each other and try to come up with an interesting angle for your leads."

35   And so I caved, and I caved over and over that quarter as I tried to please in the midst of mindlessness, to my students' deep sense of entitlement, and to the inordinate amount of power the system had given them. . . .

How well did the Sandbox Experiment work? In a word, it succeeded fabulously. That term's evaluations were the best I'd ever received at The College. In fact, they were sterling. The score in my writing class—when students were asked whether they would "recommend this class to other students"—18 Yes and 0 No; average grade I gave the class: 3.0. How about this comment: "I found (the instructor) was always willing to help me if I had any questions on my papers. I found his style of writing refreshing, and not like other stale writing classes I've had." And the final score in that problematic journalism class: 10 Yes and 1 No; average final grade I gave in the class: 3.0.

Still, I couldn't help but be amused at one of the comments a student wrote about the journalism class: "The teacher did not seem to have a good grasp of the material. I don't think he is qualified to teach this course." Apparently, at least for this particular student, I'd gone a bit overboard in striving for the humble approach and playing the role of teacher as facilitator. Either that, or he didn't have a clue about anything that went on in the class, and believe me, that's a distinct possibility. . . .

▓ QUESTIONS FOR INQUIRY AND ACTION ▓

1. Characterize Sacks's persona. How does he address and relate to us as readers? Who does he think will be reading the book? How can you tell?

2. Put Sacks into conversation with bell hooks in "Engaged Pedagogy." What does each have to say about the roles and relationships of college students and their professors?

3. Are students really as bad as Sacks describes them? Do students at your institution fit his descriptions? Through interviews, surveys, or library research, create a history of professors' opinions of students at your school. Have professors always thought that their students are lazy and uninterested, or is the situation really worse today?

4. Organize a reading and discussion group around this essay. Invite other students and faculty to express their views and enter into dialogue on classroom culture and the student-teacher relationship.

CASE STUDY

Free to Teach, Free to Learn: Academic Freedom and the Academic Bill of Rights

David Horowitz
Why an Academic Bill of Rights Is Necessary

David Horowitz is president of the Center for the Study of Popular Culture and editor-in-chief of the online journal FrontPage Magazine. *He is a frequent political commentator and an advocate for the academic bill of rights, a document aimed at combating political indoctrination on college and university campuses. He has coauthored several books with Peter Collier, including* Destructive Generation: Second Thoughts About the Sixties *(1989) and Horowitz's autobiography* Radical Son *(1997). They also wrote several histories including* The Kennedys: An American Drama *(1985),* The Fords: An American Epic *(1987), and* The Roosevelts: An American Saga *(1994). The following essay appeared at* FrontPageMagazine.com *(March 15, 2005).*

Ohio Senate Bill 24, which has been sponsored by Senator Mumper and is now before this Committee, and which is based on my Academic Bill of Rights, is not about Republicans and Democrats, liberals and conservatives, left and right. It is about what is appropriate to a higher education, and in particular what is an appropriate discourse in the classrooms of an institution of higher learning.

All higher education institutions in this country embrace principles of academic freedom that were first laid down in 1915 in the famous *General Report* of the American Association of University Professors, titled "The Principles of Tenure and Academic Freedom." The *Report* admonishes faculty to avoid "taking unfair advantage of the student's immaturity by indoctrinating him with the teacher's own opinions before the student has had an opportunity to fairly examine other opinions upon the matters in question, and before he has sufficient knowledge and ripeness of judgment to be entitled to form any definitive opinion of his own."

In other words, an education—as distinct from an indoctrination—makes students aware of a spectrum of scholarly views on matters of controversy and opinion, and does not make particular answers to such controversial matters the goal of the instruction. This is sound doctrine and common sense, and in one form or another it is recognized in the academic freedom guidelines of all accredited institutions of higher learning in the United States.

Unfortunately, it is a principle increasingly honored in the breach and not in the observance in American universities today. All too frequently, professors behave as political advocates in the classroom, express opinions in a partisan manner on controversial issues irrelevant to the academic subject, and even grade students in a manner designed to enforce their conformity to professorial prejudices. (Numerous instances of these abuses are available on the websites www.studentsforacademicfreedom.org and www.noindoctrination.org.)

5   Why this abuse of the academic classroom has occurred in the last academic generation is a matter for historians. Why it has not been remedied by existing institutional supports for academic freedom is the business of Senate Bill 24 and the Academic Bill of Rights.

To anticipate, it is the view of the authors of this legislation that the academic freedom protections to prevent indoctrination in the classroom are generally buried in "faculty handbooks," as faculty "responsibilities," never codified as a student right. Therefore when they are neglected there is no remedy for students who are victims of professorial abuse. Nor does there exist any grievance machinery that specifically recognizes this academic freedom right or that provides a policy for redress. The purpose of Senate Bill 24 and legislation in other states based on the Academic Bill of Rights is to rectify this omission.

It is not an education when a mid-term examination contains a required essay on the topic, "Explain Why President Bush Is A War Criminal," as did a criminology exam at the University of Northern Colorado in 2003. It is not an education when a professor of property law harangues his class on why all Republicans are racist as happened at the Colorado University Law School in 2004. It is not an education when a widely-used required "Peace Studies" textbook, described by the professor as a "masterpiece," explains that the Soviet Union was a force for peace in the Cold War and the United States was not, that "revolutionary violence" is the only justifiable violence, and that the United States is the greatest terrorist state—and does so without making students aware that there are other interpretations of this history and other views that should be considered on these matters. This extremist text, *Peace and Conflict Studies*, written by two university professors who explain in their preface that they are partisans of the political left is the required "academic" textbook for students in the Peace Studies course at Ohio State University (Marion).

At Foothills College in California, a pro-life professor compared women who have abortions to the deranged mother Andrea Yates who drowned her six children. The professor then gave D's and F's to students who expressed opinions in favor of abortion. Abortion is a matter that is both profoundly controversial and also emotional, and involves the deepest and most personal values. It is also a matter of opinion. It is not the task of a professor to provide his students with politically correct opinions.

It is the task of professors—whether they are politically left or politically conservative—to teach students *how* to think and not *what* to think about matters that are controversial. An education should make students aware of the range of scholarly views on a subject, teach students how to marshal evidence in behalf of a point of view, and instruct them how to make a logical case for their conclusions. An education is not about providing students with the correct conclusions on controversial matters.

10   We live in a democracy that is based on the proposition that there is no correct conclusion available to ordinary mortals, that no one—not even professors—are in possession of absolute truth. If there were only one correct conclusion to all controversial issues there would be no need for a multi-party democracy, since the only party necessary would be the one with the truth. No such party exists. No such professor exists. Therefore, Ohio Senate Bill 24 states that "*students [shall] have access to a broad range of serious scholarly opinion pertaining to the subjects they study*," and further that: "*Students shall be graded solely on the basis of their reasoned answers and appropriate knowledge of the subjects and disciplines they study and shall not be discriminated against on the basis of their political, ideological, or religious beliefs. Faculty and instructors shall not use their courses or their positions for the purpose of political, ideological, religious, or antireligious indoctrination.*"

    Three principal objections have been made to the Senate Bill 24, all of them groundless. The first is that the Bill would impose "political standards" on higher education. This is an invention of opponents of the Bill, whose text could not be clearer on this matter: "*students [shall] have access to a **broad range of serious scholarly opinion** pertaining to the subjects they study.*" In other words, the standards "imposed" by the Bill are scholarly not political.

    The second objection is that the Bill "limits free speech" and in particular would impose limits on the ability of professors to express themselves freely in the classroom. A typical "news" headline in the *Cleveland Plain Dealer,* reporting Senator Mumper's legislation, transforms a bill expressly designed to *promote* academic freedom into its opposite: "Legislator Wants Law To Restrict Professors."

    This false charge originates with the American Association of University Professors, which long ago abandoned its commitment to academic freedom where students are concerned. The AAUP was entirely absent from the battle against speech codes in the 1990s—the most dramatic infringement of free speech rights on college campuses since the McCarthy era. I am acutely conscious of this dereliction because my Individual Rights Foundations was actively engaged in those battles.

    The AAUP has particularly singled out the following clause in the Senate Bill for disapproval: "Faculty and instructors shall not infringe the academic freedom and quality of education of their students by persistently introducing controversial matter into the classroom or coursework that has no relation to their subject of study and that serves no legitimate pedagogical purpose." According to the AAUP and opponents of the Bill generally, this stipulation is an infringement of the free speech rights of professors.

15   Presumably it would be perfectly appropriate as far as the AAUP and these opponents of the Bill are concerned if a professor of property law were to devote an entire class to explaining why Americans deserved to die on 9/11, or a professor of Women's Studies devoted an entire class to discussing how the terrible results

of the 2004 presidential election could be countered or a Metallurgy professor confronted students in a class on "Organic Materials" with the question of whether it was right for the Governor of California to leave his state to campaign for George Bush in Ohio, or whether a Spanish language professor used her class time to tell her students "I wish George Bush were dead." All these incidents happened at quality American universities (Colorado, Stanford, and Ripon) within the last school year.

In fact, the issue here is not the free speech rights of professors as private citizens, but what is appropriate to a classroom, and in particular what form of discourse constitutes indoctrination as distinct from education. We don't go to our doctors' offices expecting to get a lecture on politics. That is because doctors are professionals whose responsibility is to minister to all their patients regardless of their patients' political beliefs. Introducing passionately divisive matters into a medical consultation can injure the trust between doctors and their patients, which is essential to the healing mission. Why is the profession of education any different? When students go to their professors' offices, for example, they go for advice and help. When professors plaster their office doors with partisan cartoons that mock the deeply held beliefs of students on matters like abortion and party affiliation—which they regularly do—this creates a wall between faculty and students, which is injurious to the counseling process. How can a professor teach a student whom he regards as a partisan adversary? The answer is he cannot.

Can professors, under this guideline, discuss controversial matters in class? Of course they can. But their purpose must be educational and not political. They can present students with the opposing views that define a controversy, show them how to marshal evidence for one view or the other and teach them how to construct a case in behalf of their own viewpoint. What they must not do is jump into the controversy on one side, wielding all the authority of their greater experience and superior knowledge, backed by their grading power. They are not in the classroom to recruit students to their political or religious agendas. They are there to teach them. It does not take a rocket scientist to understand the difference. A classroom is not—or should not be—a political soap box.

The truly insurmountable problem for opponents of this injunction is that the principle of restricting professorial speech in the classroom to what is professionally appropriate is not only a long-standing principle of academic freedom, it is a principle *already embraced* (if not practiced) by most universities. The Faculty Handbook of Ohio State University, for example, instructs professors as follows: "Academic freedom carries with it correlative academic responsibilities. The principal elements include the responsibility of teachers to " . . . (5) Refrain from persistently introducing matters that have no bearing on the subject matter of the course, . . . (7) Differentiate carefully between official activities as teachers and personal activities as citizens, and to act accordingly."

Is it feasible for professors to keep the political opinions and prejudices they hold as citizens out of the classroom? I attended school for 19 years from kindergarten to the graduate level, where I received my M.A. 43 years ago. In all that time I do not remember a single teacher or a single professor on a single occasion in any classroom reveal or express their political beliefs. If my teachers could be that professional, so can this generation of educators.

20   The principle of professional restraint in the classroom could not be stated more clearly than in the Ohio State University handbook and it is expressed in the very wording of Senate Bill 24 to which apparently the same administrators who are responsible for the Faculty Handbook and the same professors who are supposed to be guided by it now strenuously object. Apparently, the principle of academic freedom is acceptable when it is only a faculty responsibility that can be disregarded. When it is proposed as a student right that might be enforced, it becomes objectionable.

There is a reason that the Academic Bill of Rights and the Faculty Handbook have nearly identical wording. Both are derived from the long-standing Academic Freedom guidelines of the American Association of University Professors, which the present leaders of the AAUP have turned their backs on now seek to repudiate: Thus, the *1940 Statement of Principles on Academic Freedom and Tenure* of the AAUP states: "Teachers are entitled to freedom in the classroom in discussing their subject, but they should be careful not to introduce into their teaching controversial matter which has no relation to their subject."

The real problem has now been revealed, and the third of the three objections to the bill—the complaint that this would be a legislative interference in academic affairs—is answered: it wouldn't be an interference because the university itself has already adopted the principles of this Bill; the problem is that they will not enforce them.

The reasons for enacting Senate Bill 24 are that too many faculty members at our universities no longer observe their responsibility to teach and not to indoctrinate students; that university administrations no longer enforce their faculty guidelines on academic freedom; and that the existing guidelines are not codified as student rights; as result students currently have no way to redress their grievances. In this situation legislatures have a fiduciary responsibility—as the elected representatives of the taxpayers who fund these institutions—to step in and provide a remedy. If they do not, the future of our universities is bleak.

Informational Posters from Students for Academic Freedom and NoIndoctrination.org

Students for Academic Freedom is a coalition of students organized to promote intellectual diversity on campus. NoIndoctrination.org is a nonprofit, nonpartisan coalition of parents dedicated to educating students about their rights. The organizations are similar in their efforts to identify instances where professors, staff, or administrators use their positions of authority to indoctrinate students in a particular set of values and beliefs. The organizations encourage students to publicize their complaints on their Web sites (www.studentsforacademicfreedom. org and www.noindoctrination.org). The SAF also encourages students to organize local campus chapters. The two posters included in this case study can be found at their respective Web sites.

Is Your Professor Using The Classroom As A Political Soapbox?

Join Students for Academic Freedom

First Meeting: Monday, January 19
Time: 6pm
Location: College Hall, Room 101

Students for Academic Freedom is a nation-wide coalition of students who are committed to academic freedom and intellectual diversity. Many of us feel that our classes and professors are too one-sided in presenting the issues, and believe that professors are violating our academic freedom by singling out students for their religious or political beliefs. Educators have an obligation not to use the classroom as a political soapbox or to indoctrinate their students. Join us for our first meeting on Monday to learn how you can stand up for your right to a real education.

You can't get a good education if they're only telling you half the story

For more information, visit www.studentsforacademicfreedom.org or contact Sammy Student at name@school.edu.

Stanley Fish
"Intellectual Diversity": the Trojan Horse of a Dark Design

Stanley Fish taught English at the University of California at Berkeley, Johns Hopkins University, and Duke University, where he also taught law. From 1999 to 2004, he served as the Dean of Arts and Sciences at the University of Illinois at Chicago. In 2005, he became the Davidson-Kahn Distinguished University Professor of

Humanities and Law at Florida International University. Much of Fish's work has focused on the role of communities in providing assumptions, values and beliefs through which members make sense of what they read and experience. His works on American culture and political life include There's No Such Thing As Free Speech: And It is a Good Thing, Too *(1994) and* The Trouble with Principle *(1999). This article appeared in* The Chronicle of Higher Education *(February 13, 2004).*

Whenever I've been asked who won (or is winning) the culture wars in the academy, I say it depends on what you mean by winning.

If victory for the right meant turning back or retarding the growth of programs like women's studies, African-American studies, Chicano studies, Latino studies, cultural studies, gay and lesbian (and now transgender) studies, postmodern studies, and poststructuralist theory, then the left won big time, for these programs flourish (especially among the young) and are the source of much of the intellectual energy in the liberal arts.

But if the palm is to be awarded to the party that persuaded the American public to adopt its characterization of the academy, the right wins hands down, for it is now generally believed that our colleges and universities are hotbeds (what is a "hotbed" anyway?) of radicalism and pedagogical irresponsibility where dollars are wasted, nonsense is propagated, students are indoctrinated, religion is disrespected, and patriotism is scorned.

The left may have won the curricular battle, but the right won the public-relations war.

5   The right did this in the old-fashioned way, by mastering the ancient art of rhetoric and spinning a vocabulary that, once established in the public mind, performed the work of argument all by itself. The master stroke, of course, was the appropriation from the left (where it had been used with a certain self-directed irony) of the phrase "political correctness," which in fairly short order became capitalized and transformed from an accusation to the name of a program supposedly being carried out by the very persons who were the accusation's object. That is, those who cried "political correctness" hypostatized an entity about which they could then immediately complain. This was genius.

Now they're doing it again, this time by taking a phrase that seems positively benign and even progressive (in a fuzzy-left way) and employing it as the Trojan horse of a dark design. That phrase is "intellectual diversity," and the vehicle that is bringing it to the streets and coffee shops of your hometown is David Horowitz's Academic Bill of Rights, which has been the basis of legislation introduced in Congress, has stirred some interest in a number of states, and has been the subject of editorials (both pro and con) in leading newspapers.

Opponents of the Academic Bill of Rights contend that despite disclaimers of any political intention and an explicit rejection of quotas, the underlying agenda is the decidedly political one of forcing colleges and universities to hire conservative professors in order to assure ideological balance.

Horowitz replies (in print and conversation) that he has no desire to impose ideological criteria on the operations of the academy; he does not favor, he tells me, legislation that would have political bodies taking over the responsibility of making curricular and hiring decisions. His hope, he insists, is that colleges and universities will reform themselves, and he offers the Academic Bill of Rights (which is the product of consultation with academics of various persuasions) as a convenient base-line template to which they might refer for guidance.

For the record, and as one of those with whom he has consulted, I believe him, and I believe him, in part, because much of the Academic Bill of Rights is as apolitical and principled as he says it is. It begins by announcing that "the central purposes of a University are the pursuit of truth, the discovery of new knowledge through scholarship and research, the study and reasoned criticism of intellectual and cultural traditions . . . and the transmission of knowledge and learning to a society at large." (I shall return to the clause deleted by my ellipsis.)

10 The bill goes on to define academic freedom as the policy of "protecting the intellectual independence of professors, researchers and students in the pursuit of knowledge and the expression of ideas from interference by legislators or authorities within the institution itself."

In short, "no political, ideological or religious orthodoxy will be imposed on professors." Nor shall a legislature "impose any orthodoxy through its control of the university budget," and "no faculty shall be hired or fired or denied promotion or tenure on the basis of his or her political or religious beliefs." The document ends by declaring that academic institutions "should maintain a posture of organizational neutrality with respect to the substantive disagreements that divide researchers on questions within, or outside, their fields of inquiry."

It's hard to see how anyone who believes (as I do) that academic work is distinctive in its aims and goals and that its distinctiveness must be protected from political pressures (either external or internal) could find anything to disagree with here. Everything follows from the statement that the pursuit of truth is a—I would say *the*—central purpose of the university. For the serious embrace of that purpose precludes deciding what the truth is in advance, or ruling out certain accounts of the truth before they have been given a hearing, or making evaluations of those accounts turn on the known or suspected political affiliations of those who present them.

While it may be, as some have said, that the line between the political and the academic is at times difficult to discern—political issues are legitimately the subject of academic analysis; the trick is to keep analysis from sliding into advocacy— it is nevertheless a line that can and must be drawn, and I would go so far as to agree with Horowitz when he criticizes professors who put posters of partisan identification on their office doors and thus announce to the students who come for advice and consultation that they have entered a political space.

But it is precisely because the pursuit of truth is the cardinal value of the academy that the value (if it is one) of intellectual diversity should be rejected.

15 The notion first turns up, though not by name, in the clause I elided where Horowitz lists among the purposes of a university "the teaching and general development of students to help them become creative individuals and productive citizens of a pluralistic society."

Teaching, yes—it is my job to introduce students to new materials and equip them with new skills; but I haven't the slightest idea of how to help students become creative individuals. And it is decidedly not my job to produce citizens for a pluralistic society or for any other. Citizen building is a legitimate democratic activity, but it is not an academic activity. To be sure, some of what happens in the classroom may play a part in the fashioning of a citizen, but that is neither something you can count on—there is no accounting for what a student will make of something you say or assign—nor something you should aim for. As admirable a goal as it may be, fashioning citizens for a pluralistic society has nothing to do with the pursuit of truth.

For Horowitz, the link between the two is to be found in the idea of pluralism: Given the "unsettled character of all human knowledge" and the fact (which is a fact) "that there is no humanly accessible truth that is not in principle open to challenge," it follows, he thinks, that students being prepared to live in a pluralistic society should receive an education in pluralism; and it follows further, he says, that it is the obligation of teachers and administrators "to promote intellectual pluralism" and thereby "protect the principle of intellectual diversity."

But it is a mistake to go from the general assertion that no humanly accessible truth is invulnerable to challenge to the conclusion that therefore challenges must always be provided. That is to confuse a theory of truth with its pursuit and to exchange the goal of reaching it for a resolution to keep the question of it always open.

While questions of truth may be generally open, the truth of academic matters is not general but local; questions are posed and often they do have answers that can be established with certainty; and even if that certainty can theoretically be upset—one cannot rule out the future emergence of new evidence—that theoretical possibility carries with it no methodological obligation. That is, it does not mandate intellectual diversity, a condition that may attend some moments in the pursuit of truth when there is as yet no clear path, but not a condition one must actively seek or protect.

20   To put it simply, intellectual diversity is not a stand-alone academic value, no more than is free speech; either can be a help in the pursuit of truth, but neither should be identified with it; the (occasional) means should not be confused with the end.

Now if intellectual diversity is not an academic value, adherence to it as an end in itself will not further an academic goal; but it will further some goal, and that goal will be political. It will be part of an effort to alter the academy so that it becomes an extension of some partisan vision of the way the world should be.

Such an effort will not be a perversion of intellectual diversity; intellectual diversity as a prime academic goal is already a perversion and its transformation into a political agenda, despite Horowitz's protestations and wishes to the contrary, is inevitable and assured. It is just a matter of which party seizes it and makes it its own.

For a while (ever since the *Bakke* decision), it was the left that flew the diversity banner and put it to work in the service of affirmative action, speech codes, hostile-environment regulations, minority hiring, and more. Now it is the right's turn, and Horowitz himself has mapped out the strategy and laid bare the motives:

"I encourage [students] to use the language that the left has deployed so effectively on behalf of its own agendas. Radical professors have created a 'hostile learning' environment for conservative students. There is a lack of 'intellectual diversity' on college faculties and in academic classrooms. The conservative viewpoint is 'under-represented' in the curriculum and on its reading lists. The university should be an 'inclusive' and intellectually 'diverse' community" ("The Campus Blacklist," April 2003).

25   It is obvious that for Horowitz these are debating points designed to hoist the left by its own petard; but the trouble with debating points is that they can't be kept in bounds. Someone is going to take them seriously and advocate actions that Horowitz would probably not endorse.

Someone is going to say, let's monitor those lefty professors and keep tabs on what they're saying; and while we're at it, let's withhold federal funds from programs that do not display "ideological balance" ("balance" is also an unworthy academic goal); and let's demand that academic institutions demonstrate a commitment to hiring conservatives; and let's make sure that the material our students read is pro-American and free of the taint of relativism; and let's publish the names of those who do not comply.

This is not a hypothetical list; it is a list of actions already being taken. In fact, it is a list one could pretty much glean from the Web site of State Senator John K. Andrews Jr., president of the Colorado Senate (http://www.andrewsamerica.com/), a site on which the Academic Bill of Rights is invoked frequently.

Andrews, like everyone else doing the intellectual diversity dance, insists that he opposes "any sort of quotas, mandated hiring or litmus test"; but then he turns around and sends a letter to Colorado's universities asking them to explain how they promote "intellectual diversity."

Anne D. Neal, of the Lynne-Cheney-inspired American Council of Trustees and Alumni, plays the same double game in a piece entitled "Intellectual Diversity Endangered" (http://www.cfif.org/htdocs/freedomline/current/guest_commentary/student_right_to_learn.htm). First she stands up for the value of academic freedom ("no more important value to the life of the mind"), but then she urges university trustees to see to it "that all faculty . . . present points of view other than their own in a balanced way" (something you might want to do but shouldn't have to do) and to "insist that their institutions offer broad-based survey courses," and "to monitor tenure decisions" for instances of "political discrimination," and to "conduct intellectual diversity reviews and to make the results public."

30   These are only two examples of what the mantra of "intellectual diversity" gets you. And to make the point again, these are not examples of a good idea taken too far, but of a bad idea taken in the only direction—a political direction—it is capable of going. As a genuine academic value, intellectual diversity is a nonstarter. As an imposed imperative, it is a disaster.

▒ QUESTIONS FOR INQUIRY AND ACTION ▒

1. Stanley Fish argues that promoting intellectual diversity should not be confused with the pursuit of truth, a university's primary mission. He believes conservative citizens might use the Academic Bill of Rights to change teaching, course

offerings, and university policy to be more favorable to their own values and beliefs. Examine the two posters in this case study; do you see these posters as an effort to promote truth? Consult the organizations' respective Web sites for a fuller picture of their missions.

2. Politics is an ongoing debate about how our communities organize themselves, direct resources, and manage people's lives. Write an essay that answers the question "Can education be separated from politics?"

3. Horowitz argues that too many faculty take advantage of their positions to "express opinions in a partisan manner on controversial issues irrelevant to the academic subject, and even grade students in a manner designed to enforce their conformity to professorial prejudices." Interview five other students to see whether this is really the case. Ask them how often this occurs (i.e., how many of their teachers have shared ideological viewpoints, how often those with strong biases have expressed their views in class). Compare with the stories on the two Web sites *www.studentsforacademicfreedom.org* and *www.noindoctrination.org*. Is this the serious concern Horowitz suggests it is based on your limited study?

▨ CONTINUING THE CASE STUDY ▨
How Do Colleges Enforce a Civil Community?

Judicial boards are usually formal groups of students, faculty, and administrators that decide how a college should respond to violations of the college's student code of conduct. The intent of these boards is to enforce behavioral expectations in an academic community so members' rights and safety are protected.

This simulation encourages you to research judicial boards on your campus and to divide yourselves into smaller groups that parallel the composition of your school's board. You will then read the scenario below and research the definition of disorderly conduct (you might consult your student handbook, library materials, Web sites, or the dean of students). Then, discuss, as a group, whether the individual in the scenario has indeed violated the school's code of conduct and, if so, what the school should do about it. In the process of making your ruling, you will collaboratively reflect upon and argue about ethical issues central to your college community.

The Scenario: Disorderly Conduct Violation

Heather Klein is appealing the sanctions for disorderly conduct imposed upon her by the Dean of Students. Klein has been forbidden from attending her American History I course because of a series of incidents in which she challenged the instructor's authority. The worst occurred on November 4, 2005, when she called the instructor several profane names in front of the class and stormed out of the room.

According to Klein, instructor Bill Johnson has done a terrible job teaching them American history. He is seldom prepared, refuses to answer questions, and often wastes class time criticizing President George W. Bush and the war in Iraq. On several occasions, Klein had asked whether a particular subject would be on an exam. The instructor repeatedly told her to "Quit worrying about it." Without American History I, Klein, who is a post-secondary option student (that is, she is a high school student taking college classes), will not graduate high school on time. She would like to be permitted to finish the course or complete her assignments independently of lectures. To support her complaints, the dean acknowledged that several other students had registered complaints about the instructor's poor teaching and strong political views.

According to instructor Bill Johnson, Klein repeatedly challenged him when he did not know the answer to a question. He alleges that she would say things like "How did you ever get to become a college teacher?" He also alleges that she repeatedly objected to his efforts to bring alternative viewpoints into the classroom (e.g., the viewpoints of slaves, Chinese railroad workers, and Irish laborers) and to draw connections between past events and contemporary issues like the war in Iraq. He says he warned Klein both privately and during class that her continued disruptive behavior would result in expulsion from the class. After the November 4 incident, he refused to let her back in.

How should the college handle this? Should Ms. Klein be banned from the class regardless of the consequences to her?

Whether you write individual or group essays, or simply discuss the case, you might work through the following items essential to your board's recommendation:

- *Describe the case from your perspective.* How you frame the situation (e.g., is this a case of immaturity or deliberate malice) will show why your recommendation is appropriate. To support your interpretation of the event, you can draw on relevant details from the scenario and your own comparable experiences.

- *Identify your proposed judgment.* You can explain a) whether the accused violated the code of conduct and b) what sanction you would recommend if guilty.

- *Explain why your recommendation is better than others.* You can strengthen your case by anticipating and answering possible objections to your recommendation.

- *Outline step-by-step how the student should be sanctioned and/or what the school can do to avoid future incidents.* If you believe the accused is guilty of violating the code of conduct, outline how your recommended sanctions should be implemented.

Once your group has made a recommendation, you might reflect on the experience by answering the following questions:

1. What views of the college community emerged from your discussions? How do they relate to the views expressed by bell hooks, Roger H. Garrison, and the others?

2. Judicial boards usually have the authority to make rulings on student behavior, not faculty behavior. What procedures are in place at your college for addressing poor teaching, harassment, or verbal abuse? Are these procedures fair to all parties involved?

3. What other behaviors are you witnessing on your campus? Does the student code of conduct work on your campus? In other words, are students' rights and safety being protected so they can freely pursue their educations?

CHAPTER 8

Citizens of the World: Our Global Community

"Time" has ceased, "space" has vanished. We now live in a global village . . . a simultaneous happening.

—*Marshall McLuhan,* The Gutenberg Galaxy

▓ **GETTING STARTED** ▓   Becoming a Global Citizen

Study the satirical illustration, a map entitled "The World According to the United States of America," located on the following page.

1. What assumptions are made about the ways the United States views the rest of the world? Do you think these assumptions are warranted?

2. Is it important to think of ourselves as global citizens and not just as citizens of individual nations? What might change in terms of our perceptions and our actions if we imagine ourselves to be global citizens?

In how many different ways do we imagine being citizens of an international community? The writer Pico Iyer, of Indian descent, born in England, raised in California, now living in Japan, describes himself as a "global soul," one who is at home everywhere and, paradoxically, not at home anywhere. And familiar to us now is the term "global village," coined in 1967 by the cultural critic Marshall McLuhan, which describes how communications media allow us to connect with nearly anyone, nearly anywhere, in the world, at nearly any time.

What does it mean to *live* in a global village, though? What connotations does the word *village* have? Even though we may see ourselves as more connected in one global village, we still tend to divide and classify the world into West and East, Northern and Southern hemispheres, First World and Third World, developed and developing nations. In most formulations the language we use implies that the rest of the world

The World According to the United States of America

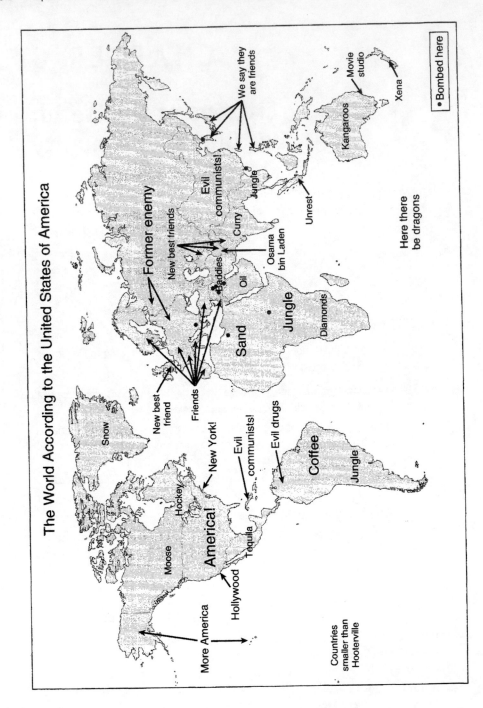

Bombed here

We say they are friends

Movie studio

Xena

Kangaroos

Evil communists!

Jungle

Unrest

Here there be dragons

Former enemy

New best friends

Curry

Osama bin Laden

Baddies

Oil

Sand

Jungle

Diamonds

New best friend

Friends

Snow

New York!

Evil communists!

Evil drugs

Hockey

Coffee

Jungle

Moose

America

Tequila

Hollywood

More America

Countries smaller than Hooterville

is moving toward being more like North America and Western Europe and that these societies are therefore superior. What holds us together as one global community? Capitalism? Mass media? Humanism?

Since the September 11, 2001 terrorist attacks on the World Trade Center in New York City, conflicts between religious and political cultures, between Western and Eastern lifestyles and liberties, and between Christianity and Islam have been the subject of numerous newspaper reports, editorials, television specials, and, increasingly, works of art and popular culture such as novels and films. Are our civilizations colliding? Are we becoming less of a global culture and more a split, opposed set of cultures? Or a number of local, segregated cultures?

The case study in this chapter examines the idea of a "clash of civilizations" in our contemporary global community. In the words of Harvard professor Samuel P. Huntington's influential 1993 *Foreign Affairs* article "The Clash of Civilizations?" "the fundamental source of conflict in this new world will not be primarily ideological or primarily economic. The great divisions among humankind and the dominating source of conflict will be *cultural.*" Benjamin Barber's article "Jihad vs. McWorld," written for the *Atlantic Monthly* magazine in March 1992, gave us vivid terms to imagine and describe the clash of cultures. Jihad, traditional tribal culture, comes into conflict with McWorld, secular culture based on an unregulated market.

Complicating the clash of civilizations theory is the argument that there is perhaps not just a clash of civilizations between the West and East, the Christian and Islamic worlds, but a clash *within* civilizations between a modern, secular democracy based on reason, and a traditional theocracy in which religious beliefs direct public policy. Understanding the global clashes between civilizations, then, may also (and first) mean understanding the local clashes.

Peter Mayer
Earth Town Square

Peter Mayer is a singer-songwriter based in Stillwater, Minnesota. According to his Web site, Peter Mayer "writes songs for a small planet—songs about interconnectedness and the human journey; songs about the beauty and the mystery of the world. Whimsical, humorous, and profound, his music takes you up mountains, across oceans, into space, and back home again. A native of Minnesota with a background in Theology, Peter is not big on love songs, but prefers delving into science, nature, and things spiritual." "Earth Town Square" is the title cut of his album Earth Town Square *(Blue Boat, 2002).*

Earth Town Square

Once, we were lonely islands
Divided by horizons
A hundred thousand tribes surviving, scattered far and wide
Hearing only stories
5   Of distant territories
Peering out across the miles between our shorelines

Then, we harnessed nature's forces
Straddled backs of horses
Waging wars and crossing borders as our numbers grew
10   We bought and sold and traded
Oceans were navigated
And fates entwined by rails and roads and telephones, and soon
We cracked the code of flight
Spoke via satellite at the speed of light, and

15   Now it's feeling like a small town
With six billion people downtown
At a little sidewalk fair
In Earth Town Square
There are Germans selling Audis
20   Filled with gasoline from Saudis
To Australians sipping Kenyan coffee in their Chinese shoes
Argentines are meeting Mongols
Over french fries from MacDonald's
And the place looks strangely tiny when you see it from the moon
25   And there's music in the park, kalimbas and guitars
Bagpipes and sitars

Now it's feeling like a small town
With six billion people downtown
Even Babel can't compare
30   To Earth Town Square

And as each hour goes by, ten thousand more arrive
And the din gets louder on Main Street
Where you can watch downtown boom
And wonder if we'll make room
35   For everybody there
In Earth Town Square

▓ QUESTIONS FOR INQUIRY AND ACTION ▓

1. What image does the idea of an "Earth town square" evoke? What connotations does it have for you? Where would the earth town square be located? What would it be like?

2. Read the lyrics to "Earth Town Square" in conversation with Pico Iyer's "The Global Village Finally Arrives." What do they have in common? How do they describe the world?

3. Peter Mayer has released six CDs. Listen to songs off of the various albums and describe Mayer's worldview as expressed in the songs. What other musicians would you compare him with?

4. Write a song that expresses your sense of being a citizen of the world. What would you emphasize? What would be the tone or mood of your song?

Pico Iyer
The Global Village Finally Arrives

Pico Iyer is a popular and respected travel writer and essayist. His many books include Video Night in Katmandu *(1989),* The Global Soul: Jet Lag, Shopping Malls, and the Search for Home *(2001), and the novel* Abandon *(2003), which is framed by the conflict between Islamic and secular Western values. "The Global Village Finally Arrives" appeared in a special issue of* Time *magazine called "The New Face of America" (Fall 1993).*

This is the typical day of a relatively typical soul in today's diversified world. I wake up to the sound of my Japanese clock radio, put on a T shirt sent me by an uncle in Nigeria and walk out into the street, past German cars, to my office.

Around me are English-language students from Korea, Switzerland and Argentina—all on this Spanish-named road in this Mediterranean-style town. On TV, I find, the news is in Mandarin; today's baseball game is being broadcast in Korean. For lunch I can walk to a sushi bar, a tandoori palace, a Thai cafe or the newest burrito joint (run by an old Japanese lady). Who am I, I sometimes wonder, the son of Indian parents and a British citizen who spends much of his time in Japan (and is therefore—what else?—an American permanent resident)? And where am I?

I am, as it happens, in Southern California, in a quiet, relatively uninternational town, but I could as easily be in Vancouver or Sydney or London or Hong Kong. All the world's a rainbow coalition, more and more; the whole planet, you might say, is going global. When I fly to Toronto, or Paris, or Singapore, I disembark in a world as hyphenated as the one I left. More and more of the globe looks like America, but an America that is itself looking more and more like the rest of the globe. Los Angeles famously teaches 82 different languages in its schools. In this respect, the city seems only to bear out the old adage that what is in California today is in America tomorrow, and next week around the globe.

In ways that were hardly conceivable even a generation ago, the new world order is a version of the New World writ large: a wide-open frontier of polyglot terms and postnational trends. A common multiculturalism links us all—call it Planet Hollywood, Planet Reebok or the United Colors of Benetton. Taxi and hotel and disco are universal terms now, but so too are karaoke and yoga and pizza. For the gourmet alone, there is tiramisu at the Burger King in Kyoto, echt angel-hair pasta in Saigon and enchiladas on every menu in Nepal.

But deeper than mere goods, it is souls that are mingling. In Brussels, a center of the new "unified Europe," 1 new baby in every 4 is Arab. Whole parts of the Paraguayan capital of Asuncion are largely Korean. And when the prostitutes of Melbourne distributed some pro-condom pamphlets, one of the languages they used was Macedonian. Even Japan, which prides itself on its centuries-old socially engineered uniculture, swarms with Iranian illegals, Western executives, Pakistani laborers and Filipina hostesses.

5   The global village is defined, as we know, by an international youth culture that takes its cues from American pop culture. Kids in Perth and Prague and New Delhi are all tuning in to *Santa Barbara* on TV, and wriggling into 501 jeans, while singing along to Madonna's latest in English. CNN (which has grown 70-fold in 13 years) now reaches more than 140 countries; an American football championship pits London against Barcelona. As fast as the world comes to America, America goes round the world—but it is an America that is itself multi-tongued and many hued, an America of Amy Tan and Janet Jackson and movies with dialogue in Lakota.

For far more than goods and artifacts, the one great influence being broadcast around the world in greater numbers and at greater speed than ever before is people. What were once clear divisions are now tangles of crossed lines: there are 40,000 "Canadians" resident in Hong Kong, many of whose first language is Cantonese. And with people come customs: while new immigrants from Taiwan and Vietnam and India—some of the so-called Asian Calvinists—import all-American values of hard work and family closeness and entrepreneurial energy to America, America is sending its values of upward mobility and individualism and melting-pot hopefulness to Taipei and Saigon and Bombay.

Values, in fact, travel at the speed of fax; by now, almost half the world's Mormons live outside the U.S. A diversity of one culture quickly becomes a diversity of many: the "typical American" who goes to Japan today may be a third-generation Japanese American, or the son of a Japanese woman married to a California serviceman, or the offspring of a Salvadoran father and an Italian mother from San Francisco. When he goes out with a Japanese woman, more than two cultures are brought into play.

None of this, of course, is new: Chinese silks were all the rage in Rome centuries ago, and Alexandria before the time of Christ was a paradigm of the modern universal city. Not even American eclecticism is new: many a small town has long known Chinese restaurants, Indian doctors and Lebanese grocers. But now all these cultures are crossing at the speed of light. And the rising diversity of the planet is something more than mere cosmopolitanism: it is a fundamental recoloring of the very complexion of societies. Cities like Paris, or Hong Kong, have always had a soigne, international air and served as magnets for exiles and emigres, but now smaller places are multinational too. Marseilles speaks French with a distinctly North African twang. Islamic fundamentalism has one of its strongholds in Bradford, England. It is the sleepy coastal towns of Queensland, Australia, that print their menus in Japanese.

The dangers this internationalism presents are evident: not for nothing did the Tower of Babel collapse. As national borders fall, tribal alliances, and new man-made divisions, rise up, and the world learns every day terrible new meanings of the word Balkanization. And while some places are wired for international transmission, others (think of Iran or North Korea or Burma) remain as isolated as ever, widening the gap between the haves and the have-nots, or what Alvin Toffler has called the "fast" and the "slow" worlds. Tokyo has more telephones than the whole continent of Africa.

10   Nonetheless, whether we like it or not, the "transnational" future is upon us: as Kenichi Ohmae, the international economist, suggests with his talk of a "borderless economy," capitalism's allegiances are to products, not places. "Capital is now global," Robert Reich, the Secretary of Labor, has said, pointing out that when an Iowan buys a Pontiac from General Motors, 60% of his money goes to South Korea, Japan, West Germany, Taiwan, Singapore, Britain and Barbados. Culturally we are being re-formed daily by the cadences of world music and world fiction: where the great Canadian writers of an older generation had names like Frye and Davies and Laurence, now they are called Ondaatje and Mistry and Skvorecky.

As space shrinks, moreover, time accelerates. This hip-hop mishmash is spreading overnight. When my parents were in college, there were all of seven foreigners living in Tibet, a country the size of Western Europe, and in its entire history the country had seen fewer than 2,000 Westerners. Now a Danish student in Lhasa is scarcely more surprising than a Tibetan in Copenhagen. Already a city like Miami is beyond the wildest dreams of 1968; how much more so will its face in 2018 defy our predictions of today?

It would be easy, seeing all this, to say that the world is moving toward the Raza Cosmica (Cosmic Race), predicted by the Mexican thinker Jose Vasconcelos in the '20s—a glorious blend of mongrels and mestizos. It may be more relevant to suppose that more and more of the world may come to resemble Hong Kong, a stateless special economic zone full of expats and exiles linked by the lingua franca of English and the global marketplace. Some urbanists already see the world as a grid of 30 or so highly advanced city-regions, or technopoles, all plugged into the same international circuit.

The world will not become America. Anyone who has been to a baseball game in Osaka, or a Pizza Hut in Moscow, knows instantly that she is not in Kansas. But America may still, if only symbolically, be a model for the world. E Pluribus Unum, after all, is on the dollar bill. As Federico Mayor Zaragoza, the director-general of UNESCO, has said, "America's main role in the new world order is not as a military superpower, but as a multicultural superpower."

The traditional metaphor for this is that of a mosaic. But Richard Rodriguez, the Mexican-American essayist who is a psalmist for our new hybrid forms, points out that the interaction is more fluid than that, more human, subject to daily revision. "I am Chinese," he says, "because I live in San Francisco, a Chinese city. I became Irish in America. I became Portuguese in America." And even as he announces this new truth, Portuguese women are becoming American, and Irishmen are becoming Portuguese, and Sydney (or is it Toronto?) is thinking to compare itself with the "Chinese city" we know as San Francisco.

▒ QUESTIONS FOR INQUIRY AND ACTION ▒

1. When Iyer notes that "deeper than mere goods, it is souls that are mingling," what does he mean?

2. "The world will not become America," Iyer claims in the penultimate paragraph. Compare his argument with James L. Watson's "China's Big Mac Attack." Do you think they are in disagreement?

3. Research globalization trends: are we moving more toward a statelessness governed chiefly by an open marketplace, or will we experience a resurgence of nationalism and concern for national borders and identities? What are the alternatives?

4. Rewrite Iyer's opening paragraph, inserting your own data. Are your possessions and activities also indicative of a global culture?

James L. Watson
China's Big Mac Attack

James L. Watson is Fairbank Professor of Chinese Society and Professor of Anthropology at Harvard University. A distinguished scholar of China, he has written many articles and books and edited Golden Arches East: McDonald's in East Asia, *an anthropological study of McDonald's in five cities in East Asia (Hong Kong, Beijing, Taipei, Seoul, and Tokyo). "China's Big Mac Attack" was published in* Foreign Affairs *(May–June 2000).*

Ronald McDonald Goes to China

Looming over Beijing's choking, bumper-to-bumper traffic, every tenth building seems to sport a giant neon sign advertising American wares: Xerox, Mobil, Kinko's, Northwest Airlines, IBM, Jeep, Gerber, even the Jolly Green Giant. American food chains and beverages are everywhere in central Beijing: Coca-Cola, Starbucks, Kentucky Fried Chicken, Häagen-Daas, Dunkin' Donuts, Baskin-Robbins, Pepsi, TCBY, Pizza Hut, and of course McDonald's. As of June 1999, McDonald's had opened 235 restaurants in China. Hong Kong alone now boasts 158 McDonald's franchises, one for every 42,000 residents (compared to one for every 30,000 Americans).

Fast food can even trump hard politics. After NATO accidentally bombed the Chinese embassy in Belgrade during the war in Kosovo, Beijing students tried to organize a boycott of American companies in protest. Coca-Cola and McDonald's were at the top of their hit list, but the message seemed not to have reached Beijing's busy consumers: the three McDonald's I visited last July were packed with Chinese tourists, local yuppies, and grandparents treating their "little emperors and empresses" to Happy Meals. The only departure from the familiar American setting was the menu board (which was in Chinese, with English in smaller print) and the jarring sound of Mandarin shouted over cellular phones. People were downing burgers, fries, and Cokes. It was, as Yogi Berra said, deja vu all over again; I had seen this scene a hundred times before in a dozen countries. Is globalism—and its cultural variant, McDonaldization—the face of the future?

Imperialism and a Side of Fries

American academe is teeming with theorists who argue that transnational corporations like McDonald's provide the shock troops for a new form of imperialism that is far more successful, and therefore more insidious, than its militarist antecedents. Young people everywhere, the argument goes, are avid consumers of soap operas, music videos, cartoons, electronic games, martial-arts books, celebrity posters, trendy clothing, and faddish hairstyles. To cater to them, shopping malls, supermarkets, amusement parks, and fast-food restaurants are popping up everywhere. Younger consumers are forging transnational bonds of empathy and shared interests that will, it is claimed, transform political alignments in ways that most world leaders—old men who do not read *Wired*—cannot begin to comprehend, let alone control. Government efforts to stop the march of American (and Japanese) pop culture are futile; censorship and trade barriers succeed only in making forbidden films, music, and Web sites irresistible to local youth.

One of the clearest expressions of the "cultural imperialism" hypothesis appeared in a 1996 *New York Times* op-ed by Ronald Steel: "It was never the Soviet Union, but the United States itself that is the true revolutionary power. . . . We purvey a culture based on mass entertainment and mass gratification. . . . The cultural message we transmit through Hollywood and McDonald's goes out across the world to capture, and also to undermine, other societies. . . . Unlike traditional conquerors, we are not content merely to subdue others: We insist that they be like us." In his recent book, *The Lexus and the Olive Tree*, Thomas Friedman presents a more benign view of the global influence of McDonald's. Friedman has long argued in his *New York Times* column that McDonald's and other manifestations of global culture serve the interests of middle classes that are emerging in autocratic, undemocratic societies. Furthermore, he notes, countries that have a McDonald's within their borders have never gone to war against each other. (The NATO war against Serbia would seem to shatter Friedman's Big Mac Law, but he does not give up easily. In his July 2, 1999 column, he argued that the shutdown and rapid reopening of Belgrade's six McDonald's actually prove his point.)

5   If Steel and his ideological allies are correct, McDonald's should be the poster child of cultural imperialism. McDonald's today has more than 25,000 outlets in 119 countries. Most of the corporation's revenues now come from operations outside the United States, and a new restaurant opens somewhere in the world every 17 hours.

McDonald's makes heroic efforts to ensure that its food looks, feels, and tastes the same everywhere. A Big Mac in Beijing tastes virtually identical to a Big Mac in Boston. Menus vary only when the local market is deemed mature enough to expand beyond burgers and fries. Consumers can enjoy Spicy Wings (red-pepper-laced chicken) in Beijing, kosher Big Macs (minus the cheese) in Jerusalem, vegetable McNuggets in New Delhi, or a McHuevo (a burger with fried egg) in Montevideo. Nonetheless, wherever McDonald's takes root, the core product—at least during the initial phase of operation—is not really the food but the experience of eating in a cheerful, air-conditioned, child-friendly restaurant that offers the revolutionary innovation of clean toilets.

Critics claim that the rapid spread of McDonald's and its fast-food rivals undermines indigenous cuisines and helps create a homogeneous, global culture. Beijing and Hong Kong thus make excellent test cases since they are the dual epicenters of China's haute cuisine (with apologies to Hunan, Sichuan, and Shanghai loyalists). If McDonald's can make inroads in these two markets, it must surely be an unstoppable force that levels cultures. But the truth of this parable of globalization is subtler than that.

The Secret of My Success

How did McDonald's do it? How did a hamburger chain become so prominent in a cultural zone dominated by rice, noodles, fish, and pork? In China, adult consumers often report that they find the taste of fried beef patties strange and unappealing. Why, then, do they come back to McDonald's? And more to the point, why do they encourage their children to eat there?

The history of McDonald's in Hong Kong offers good clues about the mystery of the company's worldwide appeal. When Daniel Ng, an American-trained engineer, opened Hong Kong's first McDonald's in 1975, his local food-industry competitors dismissed the venture as a nonstarter: "Selling hamburgers to Cantonese? You must be joking!" Ng credits his boldness to the fact that he did not have an M.B.A. and had never taken a course in business theory.

10   During the early years of his franchise, Ng promoted McDonald's as an outpost of American culture, offering authentic hamburgers to "with-it" young people eager to forget that they lived in a tiny colony on the rim of Maoist China. Those who experienced what passed for hamburgers in British Hong Kong during the 1960s and 1970s will appreciate the innovation. Ng made the fateful decision not to compete with Chinese-style fast-food chains that had started a few years earlier (the largest of which, Cafe de Coral, was established in 1969). The signs outside his first restaurants were in English; the Chinese characters for McDonald's (Cantonese Mak-dong-lou, Mandarin Mai-dang-lao) did not appear until the business was safely established. Over a period of 20 years, McDonald's gradually became a mainstay of Hong Kong's middle-class culture. Today the restaurants are packed wall-to-wall with busy commuters, students, and retirees who treat them as homes away from home. A 1997 survey I conducted among Hong Kong university students revealed that few were even aware of the company's American origins. For Hong Kong youth, McDonald's is a familiar institution that offers comfort foods that they have eaten since early childhood.

Yunxiang Yan, a UCLA anthropologist, hints that a similar localization process may be underway in Beijing. McDonald's there is still a pricey venue that most Chinese treat as a tourist stop: you haven't really "done" Beijing unless you have visited the Forbidden City, walked around Tiananmen Square, and eaten at the "Golden Arches." Many visitors from the countryside take Big Mac boxes, Coke cups, and napkins home with them as proof that they did it right. Yan also discovered that working-class Beijing residents save up to take their kids to McDonald's and hover over them as they munch. (Later the adults eat in a cheaper, Chinese-style restaurant.) Parents told Yan that they wanted their children to "connect" with the world outside China. To them, McDonald's was an important stop on the way to Harvard Business School or the MIT labs. Yan has since discovered that local yuppies are beginning to eat Big Macs regularly. In 20 years, he predicts, young people in Beijing (like their counterparts in Hong Kong today) will not even care about the foreign origin of McDonald's, which will be serving ordinary food to people more interested in getting a quick meal than in having a cultural experience. The key to this process of localization is China's changing family system and the emergence of a "singleton" (only-child) subculture.

The Little Emperors

In China, as in other parts of East Asia, the startup date for McDonald's corresponds to the emergence of a new class of consumers with money to spend on family entertainment. Rising incomes are dramatically changing lifestyles, especially among younger couples in China's major cities. Decisions about jobs and purchases no longer require consultations with an extended network of parents, grandparents, adult siblings, and other kin. More married women in Hong Kong, Beijing, and Shanghai work outside the home, which in turn affects child-rearing practices, residence patterns, and gender relations. At least in the larger cities, men no longer rule the roost. One of China's most popular television shows features a search for the "ideal husband," a man who does the shopping, washes the dishes, and changes the baby's diapers—behavior inconceivable in Mao's heyday.

Most Chinese newlyweds are choosing to create their own homes, thereby separating themselves from parents and in-laws. The traditional system of living with the groom's parents is dying out fast, even in the Chinese countryside. Recent research in Shanghai and Dalian (and Taipei) shows that professional couples prefer to live near the wife's mother, often in the same apartment complex. The crucial consideration is household labor—child care, cooking, shopping, washing, and cleaning. With both husband and wife working full time, someone has to do it, and the wife's mother is considered more reliable (and less trouble) than the husband's mother, who would expect her daughter-in-law to be subservient.

In response to these social and economic changes, a new Chinese family system is emerging that focuses on the needs and aspirations of the married couple—the conjugal unit. Conjugality brings with it a package of attitudes and practices that undermine traditional Chinese views regarding filial piety and Confucianism. Should younger couples strive, irrespective of personal cost, to promote the welfare of the larger kin group and support their aging parents? Or should they concentrate on building a comfortable life for themselves and their offspring? Increasingly, the balance is shifting toward conjugality and away from the Confucian norms that guided earlier generations.

15   The shift also coincides with a dramatic decline in China's birth rate and a rise in the amount of money and attention lavished on children. The Communist Party's single-child family policy has helped produce a generation of "little emperors and empresses," each commanding the undivided affection and economic support of two parents and (if lucky) four grandparents. The Chinese press is awash with articles bemoaning the rise of singletons who are selfish, maladjusted, and spoiled beyond repair—although psychologists working on China's singletons find them little different from their American or European counterparts.

McDonald's opened in Beijing in 1992, a time when changes in family values were matched by a sustained economic boom. The startup date also coincided with a public "fever" for all things American—sports, clothing, films, food, and so on. American-style birthday parties became key to the company's expansion strategy. Prior to the arrival of McDonald's, festivities marking youngsters' specific birth dates were unknown in most of East Asia. In Hong Kong, for instance, lunar-calendar dates of birth were recorded for use in later life—to help match prospective marriage partners' horoscopes or choose an auspicious burial date. Until the late 1970s and early 1980s, most people paid little attention to their calendar birth date if they remembered it at all. McDonald's and its rivals now promote the birthday party—complete with cake, candles, and silly hats—in television advertising aimed directly at kids.

McDonald's also introduced other localized innovations that appeal to younger customers. In Beijing, Ronald McDonald (a.k.a. Uncle McDonald) is paired with an Aunt McDonald whose job is to entertain children and help flustered parents. All over East Asia, McDonald's offers a party package that includes food, cake, gifts, toys, and the exclusive use of a children's enclosure sometimes known as the Ronald Room. Birthday parties are all the rage for upwardly mobile youngsters in Hong Kong, Beijing, and Shanghai. Given that most people in these cities live in tiny, overcrowded flats, the local Kentucky Fried Chicken or McDonald's is a convenient and welcoming place for family celebrations.

For the first time in Chinese history, children matter not simply as future providers but as full-scale consumers who command respect in today's economy. Until the 1980s, kids rarely ate outside the home. When they did, they were expected to eat what was put in front of them. The idea that children might actually order their own food would have shocked most adults; only foreign youngsters were permitted to make their opinions known in public, which scandalized everyone within earshot. Today children have money in their pockets, most of which they spend on snacks. New industries and a specialized service sector have emerged to feed this category of consumers, as the anthropologist Jun Jing has noted in his new book *Feeding China's Little Emperors*. In effect, the fast-food industry helped start a consumer revolution by encouraging children as young as three or four to march up to the counter, slap down their money, and choose their own food.

In Hong Kong, McDonald's has become so popular that parents use visits to their neighborhood outlet as a reward for good behavior or academic achievement. An old friend told me that withholding McDonald's visits was the only threat that registered with his wayward son. "It is my nuclear deterrent," he said.

20   McDonald's could not have succeeded in East Asia without appealing to new generations of consumers—children from 3 to 13 and their harried, stressed-out parents. No amount of stealth advertising or brilliant promotions could have done the trick alone. The fast-food industry did not create a market where none existed; it responded to an opportunity presented by the collapse of an outdated Confucian family system. In effect, McDonald's tailgated the family revolution as it swept through East Asia, first in Japan and Hong Kong (1970s), then in Taiwan and South Korea (1980s), and finally in China (1990s). There is no great mystery here, unless one is predisposed to seeing imperialist plots behind every successful business.

Grimace

In 1994 students protesting against California's Proposition 187, which restricted state services to immigrants, ransacked a McDonald's in Mexico City, scrawling "Yankee go home" on the windows. In August 1999 French farmers dumped tons of manure and rotting apricots in front of their local McDonald's to protest U.S.

sanctions on European food imports. During the past five years, McDonald's restaurants have been the targets of violent protests—including bombings—in over 50 countries, in cities including Rome, Macao, Rio de Janeiro, Prague, London, and Jakarta.

Why McDonald's? Other transnationals—notably Coca-Cola, Disney, and Pepsi—also draw the ire of anti-American demonstrators, but no other company can compete with the "Golden Arches." McDonald's is often the preferred site for anti-American demonstrations even in places where the local embassies are easy to get at. McDonald's is more than a purveyor of food; it is a saturated symbol for everything that environmentalists, protectionists, and anticapitalist activists find objectionable about American culture. McDonald's even stands out in the physical landscape, marked by its distinctive double-arched logo and characteristic design. Like the Stars and Stripes, the Big Mac stands for America.

Despite the symbolic load it carries, McDonald's can hardly be held responsible for the wholesale subversion of local cuisines, as its many critics claim. In China's larger cities, traditional specialties are supported by middle-class connoisseurs who treat eating out as a hobby and a diversion. Beijing's food scene today is a gourmet's paradise compared to the grim days of Maoist egalitarianism, when China's public canteens gave real meaning to the term "industrialized food." Party leaders may have enjoyed haute cuisine on the sly, but for most people, eating extravagantly was a counterrevolutionary crime. During the 1960s, refugee chefs kept microregional specialties alive in the back streets of Hong Kong and Taipei, where Panyu-style seafood, Shandong noodles, and Shunde vegetarian delights could be had at less than a dollar a head. Today, many Cantonese and Taiwanese lament the old refugees' retirement and complain that no one has carried on their culinary traditions: the chefs' own children, of course, have become brokers, lawyers, and professors.

Meanwhile, there has been an explosion of exotic new cuisines in China's cities: Thai, Malaysian, Indonesian, French, Spanish, Nepali, Mexican, and Hong Kong's latest hit, Louisiana creole. Chinese-style restaurants must now compete with these "ethnic" newcomers in a vast smorgasbord. The arrival of fast food is only one dimension of a much larger Chinese trend toward the culinary adventurism associated with rising affluence.

25   McDonald's has not been entirely passive, as demonstrated by its successful promotion of American-style birthday parties. Some try to tag McDonald's as a polluter and exploiter, but most Chinese consumers see the company as a force for the improvement of urban life. Clean toilets were a welcome development in cities where, until recently, a visit to a public restroom could be harrowing. The chain's preoccupation with cleanliness has raised consumer expectations and forced competitors to provide equally clean facilities. Ray Kroc, the legendary founder of McDonald's, was once asked if he had actually scrubbed out toilets during the early years of his franchise: "You're damn right I did," he shot back, "and I'd clean one today if it needed it." In a 1993 interview, Daniel Ng described his early efforts to import the Kroc ethos to his Hong Kong franchise. After an ineffectual first try, one new employee was ordered to clean the restrooms again. The startled

worker replied that the toilets were already cleaner than the collective facilities he used at home. Ng told him that standards at McDonald's were higher and ordered him to do it again.

Another innovation is the line, a social institution that is seldom appreciated until it collapses. When McDonald's opened in Hong Kong, customers clumped around the cash registers, pushing their money over the heads of the people ahead of them—standard procedure in local train stations, banks, and cinemas. McDonald's management appointed an employee (usually a young woman) to act as queue monitor, and within a few months, regular consumers began to enforce the system themselves by glaring at newcomers who had the effrontery to jump ahead. Today the line is an accepted feature of Hong Kong's middle-class culture, and it is making headway in Beijing and Shanghai. Whether or not McDonald's deserves the credit for this particular innovation, many East Asian consumers associate the "Golden Arches" with public civility.

Have It Your Way

At first glance McDonald's appears to be the quintessential transnational, with its own corporate culture nurtured at Hamburger University in Oak Brook, Illinois. But James Cautalupo, the president of McDonald's Corporation, maintains that his strategy is to become as much a part of local culture as possible and protests when people call McDonald's a multinational or a transnational. "I like to call us multilocal," he told *The Christian Science Monitor* in 1991. McDonald's goes out of its way to find local suppliers whenever it enters a new market. In China, for instance, the company nurtures its own network of russet-potato growers to provide french fries of the requisite length. McDonald's has also learned to rely on self-starters like Daniel Ng to run its foreign franchises—with minimal interference from Oak Brook. Another winning strategy, evident everywhere in East Asia, is promoting promising young "crew" (behind-the-counter) workers into management's ranks. Surprisingly few managers are dispatched from the Illinois headquarters. Yan found only one American, a Chinese-speaker, on McDonald's Beijing management team.

Crities of the fast-food industry assume that corporations always call the shots and that consumers have little choice but to accept what is presented to them. In fact, the process of localization is a two-way street, involving changes in the local culture as well as modifications of the company's standard mode of operation.

The hallmark of the American fast-food business is the displacement of labor costs from the corporation to consumers. For the system to work, consumers must be educated—or "disciplined"—so that they voluntarily fulfill their side of an implicit bargain: we (the corporation) will provide cheap, fast service if you (the customer) carry your own tray, seat yourself, eat quickly, help clean up afterward, and depart promptly to make room for others. Try breaking this contract in Boston or Pittsburgh by spreading out your newspaper and starting to work on a crossword puzzle in McDonald's. You will soon be ousted—politely in Pittsburgh, less so in Boston.

30　　　Key elements of McDonald's pan-national system—notably lining up and self-seating—have been readily accepted by consumers throughout East Asia. Other aspects of the Oak Brook model have been rejected, especially those relating to time and space. In Hong Kong, Taipei, and Beijing, consumers have turned their neighborhood restaurants into leisure centers for seniors and after-school clubs for students. Here, "fast" refers to the delivery of food, not its consumption.

Between 3:00 and 5:30 P.M. on Hong Kong weekdays, McDonald's restaurants are invaded by armies of young people in school uniforms. They buy a few fries, pour them out on a tray for communal snacking, and sit for at least an hour—gossiping, studying, and flirting. During the midmorning hours, the restaurants are packed with white-haired retirees who stay even longer, drinking tea or coffee (free refills for senior citizens) and lingering over pancake breakfasts. Many sit alone, reading newspapers provided by the management. Both retirees and students are attracted by the roomy tables, good light, and air-conditioning—a combination not easily found in Hong Kong, Beijing, or Shanghai. In effect, local citizens have appropriated private property and converted it into public space.

The process of localization correlates closely to the maturation of a generation of local people who grew up eating fast food. By the time the children of these pioneer consumers entered the scene, McDonald's was an unremarkable feature of the local landscape. Parents see the restaurants as havens for their school-age children: smoking is banned and (in China and Hong Kong) no alcohol is served, effectively eliminating drugs and gangs. McDonald's has become so local that Hong Kong's youth cannot imagine life without it.

Everyone has heard the story: Japanese little leaguers tour California and spot a McDonald's, whereupon they marvel that America also has Japanese food. Such anecdotes are not apocryphal. The children of visiting colleagues from Taiwan and South Korea were overjoyed when they saw a McDonald's near their temporary homes in the Boston suburbs: "Look! They have our kind of food here," one eight-year-old Korean exclaimed. The stories also work within East Asia: last year, Joe Bosco, an anthropologist at the Chinese University of Hong Kong, took several of his students to Taipei for a study tour. After a week of eating Taiwanese restaurant food, Bosco's charges began to complain that they missed home-style cooking. "Okay," Bosco said, "where do you want to eat tonight?" The students all said, "McDonald's!"

Next to Godliness

In China's increasingly affluent cities, parents now worry more about what their children eat outside the home. Rumors frequently sweep through Beijing and Shanghai with the same story line: migrants from the countryside set up a roadside stall selling youtiar, deep-fried dough sticks eaten with rice gruel for breakfast. To expand the batter, they add industrial detergent to the mix, creating a powerful poison that kills everyone who eats it. Families of the deceased rush back to the scene to discover that the stall has disappeared; the local police are more interested in silencing the survivors than pursuing the culprits. Such stories are, of course, unverifiable, but they carry a "truth" that resists official denials, much like urban legends in the United States. Last summer's food scare in Belgium over dioxin-laced eggs and the recent British mad-cow fiasco were well covered in the Chinese media, feeding the anxieties of urbanites with no reliable system of consumer protection.

35   McDonald's appeals to China's new elites because its food is safe, clean, and reliable. Western intellectuals may scoff at McDonald's for its unrelenting monotony, but in many parts of the world (including China) this is precisely what consumers find so attractive. Why else would competitors go to such extremes to imitate McDonald's? In Beijing one can find fast-food restaurants with names such as McDucks, Mcdonald's, and Mordornal. In Shanghai a local chain called Nancy's Express used a sign with one leg of the double arches missing, forming an "N." Another popular chain of noodle shops, called Honggaoliang (Red sorghum), advertises itself with a large "H" that bears an uncanny resemblance to the "Golden Arches." All over China, competitors dress their staff in McDonald's-style uniforms and decorate their restaurants in yellow. Corporate mascots inspired by Ronald McDonald—clowns, ducks, cowboys, cats, hamburger figures, mythic heroes, and chickens—parade along the sidewalks of Chinese cities. Local fast-food chains frequently engage in public exhibitions of cleanliness: one worker mops the floors and polishes the windows, all day long, every day. The cleaners usually restrict their efforts to the entryway, where the performance can best be seen by passersby.

So Lonely

During McDonald's first three years in China, Communist Party officials could barely restrain their enthusiasm over this new model of modernization, hygiene, and responsible management. By 1996, however, media enthusiasm cooled as state authorities began to promote an indigenous fast-food industry based on noodles, barbecued meats, soups, and rice pots. Now that McDonald's, Kentucky Fried Chicken, and Pizza Hut had shown the way, party officials reasoned, local chains should take over the mass market. (No such chain has seriously challenged McDonald's, but a Shanghai-based restaurateur has fought a much-reported "battle of the chickens" with KFC.)

Meanwhile, China faces yet another family revolution, this one caused by the graying of the population. In 1998, 10 percent of China's people were over 60; by 2020, the figure is expected to rise to approximately 16 percent. In 2025, there will be 274 million people over 60 in China—more than the entire 1998 U.S. population. Since Beijing has made few provisions for a modern social-security system, the implications are profound. The locus of consumer power will soon shift generations as the parents of today's little emperors retire. Unlike the current generation of retirees—the survivors of Maoism—China's boomers will not be content with 1950s-level pensions, and they cannot expect their children to support them. Like their counterparts in the American Association of Retired Persons, future retirees in China are likely to be a vociferous, aggressive lot who will demand more state resources.

So what will happen to child-centered industries? If its experience in Hong Kong is any guide, McDonald's will survive quite handily as a welcoming retreat from the isolation and loneliness of urban life. The full ramifications of China's single-child policy will not be felt for another 20 years. Having one grandchild for every four grandparents is a recipe for social anomie on a truly massive scale. The consequences of China's demographic time bomb can already be seen on the streets of Hong Kong, where the family began to shrink decades ago. Tens of thousands of retirees roam Hong Kong's air-conditioned shopping malls, congregate in the handful of overcrowded parks, and turn their local McDonald's during the midmorning hours into a substitute for the public gardens, opera theaters, and ancestral halls that sheltered their parents. What stands out at McDonald's is the isolation among Hong Kong elders as they try to entertain themselves. Americans may be bowling alone and worrying about the decline of family life, but in early 21st-century Hong Kong, no one even seems concerned about the emergence of a civil society that ignores the elderly.

Whose Culture Is It Anyway?

Is McDonald's leading a crusade to create a homogenous, global culture that suits the needs of an advanced capitalist world order? Not really. Today's economic and social realities demand an entirely new approach to global issues that takes consumers' perspectives into account. The explanatory device of "cultural imperialism" is little more than a warmed-over version of the neo-Marxist dependency theories that were popular in the 1960s and 1970s—approaches that do not begin to capture the complexity of today's emerging transnational systems.

40 The deeper one digs into the personal lives of consumers anywhere, the more complex matters become. People are not the automatons many theorists make them out to be. Hong Kong's discerning consumers have most assuredly not been stripped of their cultural heritage, nor have they become the uncomprehending dupes of transnational corporations.

In places like Hong Kong, it is increasingly difficult to see where the transnational ends and the local begins. Fast food is an excellent case in point: for the children who flock to weekend birthday parties, McDonald's is self-evidently local. Similarly, the Hong Kong elders who use McDonald's as a retreat from the loneliness of urban life could care less about the company's foreign origin. Hong Kong's consumers have made the "Golden Arches" their own.

One might also turn the lens around and take a close look at American society as it enters a new millennium. Chinese food is everywhere, giving McDonald's and KFC a run for their money in such unlikely settings as Moline and Memphis. Mandarin is fast becoming a dominant language in American research laboratories, and Chinese films draw ever more enthusiastic audiences. Last Halloween, every other kid in my Cambridge neighborhood appeared in (Japanese-inspired) Power Ranger costumes, striking poses that owe more to Bruce Lee than to Batman. Whose culture is it, anyway? If you have to ask, you have already missed the boat.

▓ QUESTIONS FOR INQUIRY AND ACTION ▓

1. What strategies does Watson use to make this explanation of a complex subject — one that is not a simple pro or con situation—engaging for his readers?

2. Read the family section of this essay along with the readings in the Family as Community chapter. How does Watson make nuanced connections between global-

ization, capitalism, and changes in family structures? Have "family values" changed?

3. Watson comments that in Hong Kong and places like it "it is increasingly difficult to see where the transnational ends and the local begins." Write about ways you have been influenced by other cultures, ways that transnational culture has blended into your local culture.

4. Can we be global citizens without forcing American culture on the rest of the world? Is being a global village just about being able to buy a McDonald's hamburger and a Coke anywhere in the world?

STOPANDTHINK

THE OLYMPIC GAMES

The Olympics have a long history. The first contest, in 776 B.C.E. in Greece, was merely a foot race. By the fifth century B.C.E., they were in full swing, with city-states such as Athens, Corinth, and Sparta vying for glory. Athleticism became a core value of Greek culture as each city-state strove to have the most athletic citizens, for all Greek citizens could participate in the games. (This did not count women and slaves, but it did mean that the participating men were not solely athletes.) Not only an athletic contest, the Olympic Games were also a religious festival, and originally included competitions in artistic and poetic composition. They were also an important time for political negotiation, because the rule was that all hostilities—all wars—would be suspended during the games. Traditional enemies would compete as athletes instead of warriors, and citizens could talk informally about political struggles rather than killing one another over them. In the Roman period, the Olympics degenerated into a spectator sport. Instead of being made up of all citizens, the athletes were mostly slaves or gladiators, performing for an audience. In the nineteenth century, when Greece won its independence from the Ottoman Empire, the Olympic Games were revived, though only on a national level, in 1859, 1870, 1875, and 1889. The first modern international Olympics were reinstated in Athens in 1896, through the work of Baron Pierre de Coubertin, who emphasized the original spirit of love of sport and international cooperation.

Athens hosted the 2004 Summer Olympic Games. In an article for *Kathimerini*, the daily newspaper in Athens, writer John Ross refers to the Olympics as "an exercise in globalism par excellence, with a much longer duration than other institutions like the World Trade Organization, the United Nations, or the Internet." Athletes will often speak of feeling a sense of "world citizenship" when they participate in the Olympic rituals and celebrations.

At the same time, and paradoxically, the Olympics are an exercise in nationalism, as each athlete competes fiercely to capture the most glory for his or her country. Athletes who compete year-round on teams outside their own nations return to their homelands to compete on the national team at Olympics time.

continued on next page

Some nations stake their reputations on the success of their athletes, with the result that we've seen an increase in cheating through the use of performance-enhancing drugs.

Are you a fan of the Olympics? When the next games appear on television (Beijing in 2008, Vancouver 2010), watch them and take notes on the international and nationalistic aspects of the competition. Compare the global aspects of the Olympics with the globalism described in the other readings in this chapter. For example, notice the displays of the various nations' athletes, the speeches made by athletes, the press coverage of the host city and nation, even the advertisements of the corporate sponsors.

One aspect of the Olympics that has not been widely discussed is the impact they make on the cities that host them. Research the beneficial and detrimental effects—economically, politically, and socially—on the host communities.

Ngugi wa Thiong'o
Decolonising the Mind

Ngugi wa Thiong'o is a Kenyan dramatist, novelist, and essayist, and is generally considered East Africa's leading writer. His early novels Weep Not, Child *and* A Grain of Wheat *concern the Mau Mau uprising against British colonial rule, and his play* The Trial of Dedan Kimathi *(with Micere Githae Mugo) celebrates the leader of the Mau Mau revolution. Ngugi's openly critical attitude toward both British and Kenyan rulers resulted in his year-long imprisonment, the banishment of his theater group, and his later self-exile to London. "Decolonising the Mind" is an excerpt from his book* Decolonising the Mind: The Politics of Language in African Literature *(New York: Heinemann, 1986).*

I was born into a large peasant family: father, four wives and about twenty-eight children. I also belonged, as we all did in those days, to a wider extended family and to the community as a whole.

We spoke Gĩkũyũ as we worked in the fields. We spoke Gĩkũyũ in and outside the home. I can vividly recall those evenings of story-telling around the fireside. It was mostly the grown-ups telling the children but everybody was interested and involved. We children would re-tell the stories the following day to other children who worked in the fields picking the pyrethrum flowers, tea-leaves or coffee beans of our European and African landlords.

The stories, with mostly animals as the main characters, were all told in Gĩkũyũ. Hare, being small, weak but full of innovative wit and cunning, was our hero. We identified with him as he struggled against the brutes of prey like lion, leopard, hyena. His victories were our victories and we learnt that the apparently weak can outwit the strong. We followed the animals in their struggle against hostile nature—drought, rain, sun, wind—a confrontation often forcing them to search for forms of co-operation. But we were also interested in their struggles amongst themselves, and particularly between the beasts and the victims of prey. These twin struggles, against nature and other animals, reflected real-life struggles in the human world.

Not that we neglected stories with human beings as the main characters. There were two types of characters in such human-centred narratives: the species of truly human beings with qualities of courage, kindness, mercy, hatred of evil, concern for others; and a man-eat-man two-mouthed species with qualities of greed, selfishness, individualism and hatred of what was good for the larger co-operative community. Cooperation as the ultimate good in a community was a constant theme. It could unite human beings with animals against ogres and beasts of prey, as in the story of how dove, after being fed with castor-oil seeds, was sent to fetch a smith working far away from home and whose pregnant wife was being threatened by these man-eating two-mouthed ogres.

5   There were good and bad story-tellers. A good one could tell the same story over and over again, and it would always be fresh to us, the listeners. He or she could tell a story told by someone else and make it more alive and dramatic. The differences really were in the use of words and images and the inflexion of voices to effect different tones.

We therefore learnt to value words for their meaning and nuances. Language was not a mere string of words. It had a suggestive power well beyond the immediate and lexical meaning. Our appreciation of the suggestive magical power of language was reinforced by the games we played with words through riddles, proverbs, transpositions of syllables, or through nonsensical but musically arranged words. [1] So we learnt the music of our language on top of the content. The language, through images and symbols, gave us a view of the world, but it had a beauty of its own. The home and the field were then our pre-primary school but what is important, for this discussion, is that the language of our evening teach-ins, and the language of our immediate and wider community, and the language of our work in the fields were one.

And then I went to school, a colonial school, and this harmony was broken. The language of my education was no longer the language of my culture. I first went to Kamaandura, missionary run, and then to another called Maanguuũ run by nationalists grouped around the Gĩkũyũ Independent and Karinga Schools Association. Our language of education was still Gĩkũyũ. The very first time I was ever given an ovation for my writing was over a composition in Gĩkũyũ. So for my first four years there was still harmony between the language of my formal education and that of the Limuru peasant community.

---

[1] *Example from a tongue twister: "Kaana ka Nikoora koona koora: na ko koora koona kaana ka Nikoora koora koora." I'm indebted to Wangui wa Coro for this example. 'Nichola's child saw a baby frog and ran away: and when the baby frog saw Nichola's child it also ran away.' A Gĩkũyũ speaking child has to get the correct tone and length of vowel and pauses to get it right. Otherwise it becomes a jumble of k's and r's and na's* [Author's note].

It was after the declaration of a state of emergency over Kenya in 1952 that all the schools run by patriotic nationalists were taken over by the colonial regime and were placed under District Education Boards chaired by Englishmen. English became the language of my formal education. In Kenya, English became more than a language: it was *the* language, and all the others had to bow before it in deference.

Thus one of the most humiliating experiences was to be caught speaking Gĩkũyũ in the vicinity of the school. The culprit was given corporal punishment— three to five strokes of the cane on bare buttocks—or was made to carry a metal plate around the neck with inscriptions such as I AM STUPID or I AM A DONKEY. Sometimes the culprits were fined money they could hardly afford. And how did the teachers catch the culprits? A button was initially given to one pupil who was supposed to hand it over to whoever was caught speaking his mother tongue. Whoever had the button at the end of the day would sing who had given it to him and the ensuing process would bring out all the culprits of the day. Thus children were turned into witch-hunters and in the process were being taught the lucrative value of being a traitor to one's immediate community.

10   The attitude to English was the exact opposite: any achievement in spoken or written English was highly rewarded; prizes, prestige, applause; the ticket to higher realms. English became the measure of intelligence and ability in the arts, the sciences, and all the other branches of learning. English became *the* main determinant of a child's progress up the ladder of formal education.

As you may know, the colonial system of education in addition to its apartheid racial demarcation had the structure of a pyramid: a broad primary base, a narrowing secondary middle, and an even narrower university apex. Selections from primary into secondary were through an examination, in my time called Kenya African Preliminary Examination, in which one had to pass six subjects ranging from Maths to Nature Study and Kiswahili. All the papers were written in English. Nobody could pass the exam who failed the English language paper no matter how brilliantly he had done in the other subjects. I remember one boy in my class of 1954 who had distinctions in all subjects except English, which he had failed. He was made to fail the entire exam. He went on to become a turn boy in a bus company. I who had only passes but a credit in English got a place at the Alliance High School, one of the most elitist institutions for Africans in colonial Kenya. The requirements for a place at the University, Makerere University College, were broadly the same: nobody could go on to wear the undergraduate red gown, no matter how brilliantly they had performed in all the other subjects unless they had a credit—not even a simple pass!—in English. Thus the most coveted place in the pyramid and in the system was only available to the holder of an English language credit card. English was the official vehicle and the magic formula to colonial elitedom.

Literary education was now determined by the dominant language while also reinforcing that dominance. Orature (oral literature) in Kenyan languages stopped. In primary school I now read simplified Dickens and Stevenson alongside Rider Haggard. Jim Hawkins, Oliver Twist, Tom Brown—not Hare, Leopard, and Lion—were now my daily companions in the world of imagination. In secondary school, Scott and G. B. Shaw vied with more Rider Haggard, John Buchan, Alan Paton, Captain W. E. Johns. At Makerere I read English: from Chaucer to T. S. Eliot with a touch of Graham Greene.

Thus language and literature were taking us further and further from ourselves to other selves, from our world to other worlds.

What was the colonial system doing to us Kenyan children? What were the consequences of, on the one hand, this systematic suppression of our languages and the literature they carried, and on the other the elevation of English and the literature it carried? To answer those questions, let me first examine the relationship of language to human experience, human culture, and the human perception of reality.

15   Language, any language, has a dual character: it is both a means of communication and a carrier of culture. Take English. It is spoken in Britain and in Sweden and Denmark. But for Swedish and Danish people English is only a means of communication with non-Scandinavians. It is not a carrier of their culture. For the British, and particularly the English, it is additionally, and inseparably from its use as a tool of communication, a carrier of their culture and history. Or take Swahili in East and Central Africa. It is widely used as a means of communication across many nationalities. But it is not the carrier of a culture and history of many of those nationalities. However in parts of Kenya and Tanzania, and particularly in Zanzibar, Swahili is inseparably both a means of communication and a carrier of the culture of those people to whom it is a mother-tongue.

Culture transmits or imparts those images of the world and reality through the spoken and the written language, that is through a specific language. In other words, the capacity to speak, the capacity to order sounds in a manner that makes for mutual comprehension between human beings is universal. This is the universality of language, a quality specific to human beings. It corresponds to the universality of the struggle against nature and that between human beings. But the particularity of the sounds, the words, the word order into phrases and sentences, and the specific manner, or laws, of their ordering is what distinguishes one language from another. Thus a specific culture is not transmitted through language in its universality but in its particularity as the language of a specific community with a specific history. Written literature and orature are the main means by which a particular language transmits the images of the world contained in the culture it carries.

Language as communication and as culture are then products of each other. Communication creates culture: culture is a means of communication. Language carries culture, and culture carries, particularly through orature and literature, the entire body of values by which we come to perceive ourselves and our place in the world. How people perceive themselves affects how they look at their culture, at their politics and at the social production of wealth, at their entire relationship to nature and to other beings. Language is thus inseparable from ourselves as a community of human beings with a specific form and character, a specific history, a specific relationship to the world.

So what was the colonialist imposition of a foreign language doing to us children?

The real aim of colonialism was to control the people's wealth: what they produced, how they produced it, and how it was distributed; to control, in other words, the entire realm of the language of real life. Colonialism imposed its control of the social production of wealth through military conquest and subsequent political dictatorship. But its most important area of domination was the mental universe of the colonised, the control, through culture, of how people perceived themselves and their relationship to the world. Economic and political control can never be complete or effective without mental control. To control a people's culture is to control their tools of self-definition in relationship to others.

20   For colonialism this involved two aspects of the same process: the destruction or the deliberate undervaluing of a people's culture, their art, dances, religions, history, geography, education, orature and literature, and the conscious elevation of the language of the coloniser. The domination of a people's language by the languages of the colonising nations was crucial to the domination of the mental universe of the colonised.

Take language as communication. Imposing a foreign language, and suppressing the native languages as spoken and written, were already breaking the harmony previously existing between the African child and the three aspects of language. Since the new language as a means of communication was a product of and was reflecting the 'real language of life' elsewhere, it could never as spoken or written properly reflect or imitate the real life of that community. This may in part explain why technology always appears to us as slightly external, *their* product and not *ours*. The word "missile" used to hold an alien faraway sound until I recently learnt its equivalent in Gĩkũyũ, *ngurukuhĩ*, and it made me apprehend it differently. Learning, for a colonial child, became a cerebral activity and not an emotionally felt experience.

But since the new, imposed languages could never completely break the native languages as spoken, their most effective area of domination was the third aspect of language as communication, the written. The language of an African child's formal education was foreign. The language of the books he read was foreign. The language of his conceptualisation was foreign. Thought, in him, took the visible form of a foreign language. So the written language of a child's upbringing in the school (even his spoken language within the school compound) became divorced from his spoken language at home. There was often not the slightest relationship between the child's written world, which was also the language of his schooling, and the world of his immediate environment in the family and the community. For a colonial child, the harmony existing between the three aspects of language as communication was irrevocably broken. This resulted in the disassociation of the sensibility of that child from his natural and social environment, what we might call colonial alienation. The alienation became reinforced in the teaching of history, geography, music, where bourgeois Europe was always the centre of the universe.

This disassociation, divorce, or alienation from the immediate environment becomes clearer when you look at colonial language as a carrier of culture.

Since culture is a product of the history of a people which it in turn reflects, the child was now being exposed exclusively to a culture that was a product of a world external to himself. He was being made to stand outside himself to look at himself. *Catching Them Young* is the title of a book on racism, class, sex, and politics in children's literature by Bob Dixon. "Catching them young" as an aim was even more true of a colonial child. The images of this world and his place in it implanted in a child take years to eradicate, if they ever can be.

25 Since culture does not just reflect the world in images but actually, through those very images, conditions a child to see that world in a certain way, the colonial child was made to see the world and where he stands in it as seen and defined by or reflected in the culture of the language of imposition.

And since those images are mostly passed on through orature and literature it meant the child would now only see the world as seen in the literature of his language of adoption. From the point of view of alienation, that is of seeing oneself from outside oneself as if one was another self, it does not matter that the imported literature carried the great humanist tradition of the best in Shakespeare, Goethe, Balzac, Tolstoy, Gorky, Brecht, Sholokhov, Dickens. The location of this great mirror of imagination was necessarily Europe and its history and culture and the rest of the universe was seen from the centre.

But obviously it was worse when the colonial child was exposed to images of his world as mirrored in the written languages of his coloniser. Where his own native languages were associated in his impressionable mind with low status, humiliation, corporal punishment, slow-footed intelligence and ability or downright stupidity, non-intelligibility and barbarism, this was reinforced by the world he met in the works of such geniuses of racism as a Rider Haggard or a Nicholas Monsarrat; not to mention the pronouncement of some of the giants of western intellectual and political establishment, such as Hume (". . .the negro is naturally inferior to the whites. . ."),[2] Thomas Jefferson (". . .the blacks. . . are inferior to the whites on the endowments of both body and mind. . ."),[3] or Hegel with his Africa comparable to a land of childhood still enveloped in the dark mantle of the night as far as the development of self-conscious history was concerned. Hegel's statement that there was nothing harmonious with humanity to be found in the African character is representative of the racist images of Africans and Africa such a colonial child was bound to encounter in the literature of the colonial languages.[4] The results could be disastrous.

In her paper read to the conference on the teaching of African literature in schools held in Nairobi in 1973,[5] entitled "Written Literature and Black

---

[2] *Quoted in Eric Williams,* A History of the People of Trinidad and Tobago, *London 1964, p. 32 [Author's note].*
[3] *Ibid, p. 31 [Author's note].*
[4] *In references to Africa in the introduction to his lectures in* The Philosophy of History *Hegel gives historical, philosophical, rational expression and legitimacy to every conceivable European racist myth about Africa. Africa is even denied her own geography where it does not correspond to myth. Thus Egypt is not part of Africa; and North Africa is part of Europe. Africa proper is the especial home of ravenous beasts, snakes of all kinds. The African is not part of humanity. Only slavery to Europe can raise him, possibly, to the lower ranks of humanity. Slavery is good for the African, "Slavery is in and for itself injustice, for the essence of humanity is freedom; but for this man must be matured. The gradual abolition of slavery is therefore wiser and more equitable than its sudden removal." (Hegel,* The Philosophy of History, *Dover edition, New York: 1956, pp. 91–9.) Hegel clearly reveals himself as the nineteenth-century Hitler of the intellect [Author's note].*
[5] *The paper is now in Akivaga and Gachukiah's* The Teaching of African Literature in Schools, *published by Kenya Literature Bureau.*

Images," the Kenyan writer and scholar Professor Mĩcere Mũgo related how a reading of the description of Gagool as an old African woman in Rider Haggard's *King Solomon's Mines* had for a long time made her feel mortal terror whenever she encountered old African women. In his autobiography *This Life*, Sidney Poitier describes how, as a result of the literature he had read, he had come to associate Africa with snakes. So on arrival in Africa and being put up in a modern hotel in a modern city, he could not sleep because he kept on looking for snakes everywhere, even under the bed. These two have been able to pinpoint the origins of their fears. But for most others the negative image becomes internalised and it affects their cultural and even political choices in ordinary living.

▓ QUESTIONS FOR INQUIRY AND ACTION ▓

1. Ngugi wa Thiong'o opens his essay by describing the stories he was told as a child. How does this effectively prepare the readers for his analysis of language and culture?

2. "Language and literature were taking us further and further from ourselves to other selves, from our world to other worlds." Compare this with your experiences with reading and studying literature. Was the literature you were taught from your own language and culture? Could you see yourself in it? Was that important to you?

3. Have you studied a second or third language? If so, write about the experience of thinking in another language. How have you experienced language as a carrier of culture? How does learning a language help you understand and empathize with people who speak that language?

4. Research the history of colonialism in Kenya. How did this affect their educational system? How does it still affect their public education system, even though it has been years since Kenya was officially a colony?

Roz Chast
One Morning, While Getting Dressed

Roz Chast is a cartoonist whose work appears often in The New Yorker, *the* Sciences, *and the* Harvard Business Review. *She has also published collections of cartoons, including* Childproof: Cartoons about Parents and Children, *and has illustrated four children's books, including* Meet My Staff. *"One Morning, While Getting Dressed" appeared in the November 29, 1999, edition of* The New Yorker.

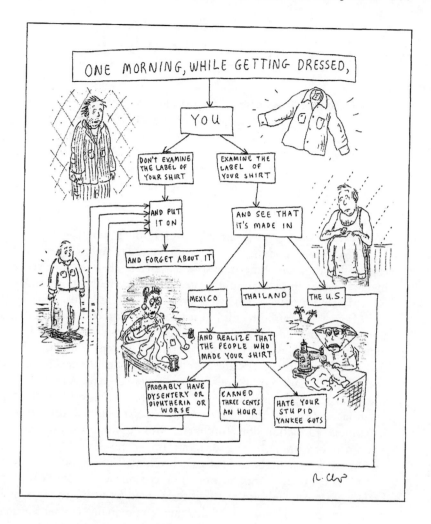

▦ QUESTIONS FOR INQUIRY AND ACTION ▦

1. What is the "thesis" or argument of this cartoon? How do cartoons make their statements differently from written texts?

2. Compare this cartoon with Marisa Acocella's cartoon in Chapter 1. Both appeared in *The New Yorker*. What do they assume about the audience for that magazine?

3. Research the work of Roz Chast. How can you discern the tone and point of view of her cartoon? Is this a typical cartoon for her? How would you describe her cartooning style?

4. Draw your own cartoon to make an argument. You might illustrate an essay you've written and compare the two forms of expression. For instance, what does the cartoon permit you to express that the essay does not, and vice versa?

Slavenka Drakulić
On Bad Teeth

Slavenka Drakulić is a Croatian journalist and essayist who writes about politics and culture for the Nation *and other periodicals. She is the author of a number of books, several of which have been translated into English, including* How We Survived Communism and Even Laughed *(1991) and* S: A Novel about the Balkans *(2000). "On Bad Teeth" is from her collection of essays entitled* Café Europa: Life After Communism *(New York: Norton, 1997).*

In a way, I was initiated into capitalism through toothpaste.

When I first visited the States in 1983, I loved to watch TV commercials. This is when I noticed that Americans were obsessed by their teeth. Every second commercial seemed to be for a toothpaste. Where I come from, toothpaste is toothpaste. I couldn't believe there were so many different kinds. What were they all *for?* After all, the purpose of it is just to clean your teeth. In my childhood there were two kinds, mint flavour and strawberry flavour, and both of them had the same brand name, Kalodont. For a long time I was convinced that Kalodont was the word for toothpaste, because nobody at home used the generic word. We never said, "Do you have toothpaste?", we said, "Do you have Kalodont?" It is hardly surprising, then, that such a person would react with nothing short of disbelief when faced with the American cosmetic (or is it pharmaceutical?) industry and its endless production line. Toothpaste with or without sugar, with or without flour, with or without baking soda, calcium, vitamins. . .

Over the years, on subsequent visits I continued to be fascinated by this American obsession with toothpaste, from the common varieties all the way up to Rembrandt, the most snobbish brand, if there could be such a thing as snobbishness about toothpaste. I soon learned that there could: in one women's magazine I saw it recommended as a Christmas present! Needless to say, in every commercial for toothpaste at least one bright, impressively beautiful set of teeth flashes across the screen, but this image is not confined to selling toothpaste. As we all know, beautiful teeth are used to advertise beer, hair shampoo, cars, anything. Indeed, they are an indispensable feature of any American advertisement. The foreigner soon learns that they stand not only as a symbol for both good looks and good health, but for something else as well.

If you think that such advertising might be part of the Americans' national obsession with health in general, you are not far from the truth. Americans seem to be passionate about their health and their looks, which appear to be interchangeable qualities. Health and good looks are essential badges of status among the middle classes. Nothing but narcissism, you could retort, but it is more than that. This connection between teeth and social status is not so evident to an Eastern European. I personally had some doubts about those TV teeth, I thought that they must be artificial, some kind of prosthesis made out of plastic or porcelain. They were just too good to be true. How could people have such fine teeth? Intrigued, I decided to take a good look around me.

5 I noticed that the people I met, that is mostly middle-class urban professionals, generally do have a set of bright, white teeth of their own, not unlike the TV teeth. It was even more surprising to me that I could detect no cavities, no missing teeth, no imperfections. I was astonished. The secret was revealed to me when a friend took her son to the dentist. When they returned, the little boy's upper teeth were fixed with a dreadful-looking kind of iron muzzle: a brace, I learned. It was obviously painful for him. "Poor little thing!" I exclaimed, but his mother showed no mercy. Moreover, she was proud that she could afford this torture device. I was puzzled. When she explained to me that the brace cost between $2,000 and $3,000, her attitude seemed even more sinister. I eventually realised that the mystery of beautiful teeth is not only about hygiene, but about money. She had money enough to get her son's teeth fixed, and the little boy was brave enough to stand the pain, because somehow he understood that this was a requirement of his social status. All the other boys from his private school had braces, too. He was going to grow up being well aware of the fact that his healthy, beautiful teeth were expensive and, therefore, an indication of prestige. Moreover, his mother could count on him to brush them three times a day, with an electric toothbrush and the latest toothpaste promising even healthier and more beautiful teeth, as if that were possible. In the long run, all the discomfort would be worth it.

Seeing the boy's brace, the connection between health and wealth in America became a bit clearer to me. Clean, healthy teeth feature so much in advertising because Americans have no free dental care, and neither is it covered by any medical insurance. Therefore, if you invest money and educate your child early enough (a bit of suffering is needed, too), you will save a lot later. But how much money did this take? I got my answer when I had to visit a dentist myself. On one of my last visits my filling fell out, and just to have it refilled with some temporary white stuff, whatever it was, I had to pay $100. This would be a minor financial catastrophe for any Eastern European citizen used to free dental care in his own country; it was expensive even by American standards. Only then did I become fully aware of what it means not to have free dental care.

Predictably enough, I was outraged. How was it possible for dental work to be so expensive in this country? For $100 back home I could have coated my tooth in pure gold! And why was it that such an affluent country did not provide its citizens with basic services like free dental work? This was one of the very few areas in which we from former communist countries had some advantage over Americans—and we would like to keep it.

On my way home, I thought what a blessing it was that we did not have to worry about our teeth, or about whether we could afford to look after them—or at least, we did not have to worry yet, in my country, anyway. However, immediately upon my arrival in Zagreb, I realised that I could allow myself such rose-tinted thoughts only as long as I was on the other side of the Atlantic, from where everything at home looked a bit blurred, especially the general state of people's teeth. Back at home, I was forced to adjust my view. It was as if I had been myopic before and now I had got the right pair of glasses and could finally see properly. And what I saw did not please me at all.

On the bus from the airport I met one of my acquaintances, a young television reporter. For the first time I noticed that half of his teeth were missing and that those which remained looked like the ruins of a decayed medieval town. I had known this guy for years, but I had never thought about the state of the inside of his mouth before, or if I had, I'd considered it totally unimportant. Now I also noticed that, in order to hide his bad teeth, he had grown a moustache and developed a way of laughing which didn't involve him opening his mouth too wide. Even so, his bad teeth were still obvious.

10   This encounter did not cheer me up. Sitting next to the young reporter, I wondered how he managed to speak in front of a TV camera without making a mistake that would reveal his terrible secret. Without smiling, perhaps? This would be perfectly acceptable, because he reports on the war, but wasn't he tired of this uncomfortable game of hide-and-seek? Wouldn't it be much more professional and make life easier if he visited a good dentist and got it all over with? But this is not something we are supposed to talk about. How do you say such a thing to a person if he is not your intimate friend? You can't just say, "Listen, why don't you do something about your teeth?" Perhaps I should have pulled out my toothpaste and handed it to him, or casually dropped the name of my dentist, something like what my friend did last summer. A woman standing next to her in a streetcar emanated an extremely unpleasant odour from her hairy armpits. My friend could not stand it. She pulled her own deodorant stick out of her handbag and gave it to the woman. The funny thing is that the woman accepted it without taking offence. I, on the other hand, could not risk offending my acquaintance.

I continued my investigations at home. Yes, I admit that I looked into the mouths of friends, relatives, acquaintances, neighbours—I could not help it. I discovered that the whole nation had bad teeth, it was just that I had not been able to see it before. I concluded that the guy on the bus was only a part of the general landscape, that he was no exception, and that therefore his failure to attend to his teeth was perfectly normal. I tried to explain this attitude to myself: perhaps people were afraid of drilling? Of course. Who isn't? But if nothing else, there must be an aesthetic drive in every human being, or one would at least think so. Yet, for some reason, aesthetics and communism don't go well together and though we might call our current state post-communism, we still have a communist attitude in such matters.

You could also argue that dentists, being employed by the state, are not well paid. Consequently, they don't put much effort into their job. You can claim as well that the materials they use are not of good quality. That is all probably true. But, I still believe that having your teeth repaired to a mediocre standard is preferable to treasuring the medieval ruins in your mouth or being toothless altogether.

There is no excuse that sounds reasonable enough for such negligence. The problem is that the condition of your teeth in Eastern Europe is regarded as a highly personal matter, not a sign of your standard of living or a question for public discussion. Having good teeth is simply a matter of being civilised and well mannered. Strangely enough, however, dirty shoes, dirty fingernails or dandruff are no longer tolerated: these are considered impolite, even offensive. Yet like such matters of personal hygiene, good teeth are not only a question of money. Dental work has been free for the last forty years. At present there co-exists a mixture of both state-run general medical care, which includes dental care, and private dentists. If you want, you can have excellent dental work done. I know people who travel from Vienna to Bratislava, Budapest, Ljubljana or Zagreb to have their teeth repaired more cheaply. But if you asked people in Eastern Europe who can afford it why they don't go to a private dentist for a better service, they would probably tell you that this is not their priority at the moment. Instead they want to fix their car, or buy a new carpet.

It is clear that leaders and intellectuals here certainly don't care about such a minor aspect of their image. They are preoccupied with the destiny of their respective nations, they do not have time for such trivial matters. The American idea that it is not very polite for a public figure to appear with bad teeth, just as it would be inappropriate to make a speech in your pyjamas, is not understood here. You can meet exquisitely dressed politicians or businessmen, but wait until they open their mouths! If these public figures are not worried about this aspect of their looks, why should ordinary people be concerned about theirs? They too have more important things to do, for example surviving. There is also that new breed, the *nouveau riche* of post-communism. Previously everything was valued by one's participation in politics, now it is slowly replaced by money. The arrogance of these people originates there. Unfortunately, money does not guarantee good manners, or a regular visit to the dentist for that matter.

15   I can only try to imagine the horrors when free dental work is replaced by private dentists whose prices nobody can afford. How many decades will we have to wait until our teeth look like American ones? It is a question of perception. In order to improve your looks, you have to be convinced that it is worth the trouble. In other words, we are dealing with a problem of self-esteem, with a way of thinking, rather than a superficial question. Bad teeth are the result of bad dentists and bad food, but also of a specific culture of thinking, of not seeing yourself as an individual. What we need here is a revolution of self-perception. Not only will that not come automatically with the new political changes, but I am afraid that it will also take longer than any political or economic developments. We need to accept our responsibilities towards both others and ourselves. This is not only a wise sort of investment in the future, as we can see in the case of Americans, it also gives you the feeling that you have done what you can to improve yourself, be it your teeth, your health, your career, education, environment or society in general.

Individual responsibility, including the responsibility for oneself, is an entirely new concept here, as I have stated many times elsewhere. This is why the revolution of self-perception has a long way to go. As absurd as it may sound, in the old days one could blame the Communist Party even for one's bad teeth. Now there is no one to blame, but it takes time to understand that. If you have never had it, self-respect has to be learned. Maybe our own teeth would be a good place to start.

But I can see signs of coming changes. Recently a good friend borrowed some money from me in order to repair her apartment. When the time came to give it back, she told me that I would have to wait, because she needed the money for something very urgent. She had finally decided to have her teeth fixed by a private dentist. No wonder she was left without a penny. But what could I have said to that? I said the only thing I could say: "I understand you, this must come first."

Finally, I guess it is only fair that I should declare the state of my own teeth. I am one of those who much too often used the free dental work so generously provided by the communist state for the benefit of its people. I was afraid of the dentist, all right, but also brave enough to stand the pain because I had overcome the psychological barrier at an early age.

When I was in the third grade a teacher showed us a cartoon depicting a fortress— a tooth—attacked by bad guys—bacteria. They looked terribly dangerous, digging tunnels and ditches with their small axes until the fortress almost fell into their hands. Then the army of good guys, the white blood cells, arrived and saved it at the last moment. The teacher explained to us how we could fight the bad guys by brushing our teeth regularly with Kalodont and by visiting a dentist every time we spotted a little hole or felt pain. I took her advice literally—I was obviously very impressed by the cartoon, just as I was impressed by the American TV commercials thirty years later. The result is that today I can say that I have good teeth, although six of them are missing. How did that happen? Well, when I spotted a little cavity, I would immediately go to the dentist all by myself. This was mistake number one. You could not choose your own dentist at that time, and my family had to go to a military hospital. A dentist there would usually fill the cavity, but for some reason the filling would soon fall out. Then he would make an even bigger hole and fill it again, until eventually there was not much tooth left.

20   Those "dentists" were in fact young students of dentistry drafted into the army. For them, this was probably an excellent chance to improve their knowledge by practising on patients. When they'd finished practising on me a more experienced dentist would suggest I had the tooth out. What could I, a child, do but agree? This was mistake number two, of course. I had to learn to live with one gap in my jaw, then another, and another. Much later I had two bridges made by a private dentist. He didn't even ask me why I was missing six of my teeth; he knew how things had worked in those days. My only consolation was that I did not have to pay much for my bridgework.

Like everyone else in the post-communist world, I had to learn the meaning of the American proverb "There is no such thing as a free lunch." The Americans are right. You don't get anything properly done if you don't pay for it sooner or later.

▨ QUESTIONS FOR INQUIRY AND ACTION ▨

1. Drakulić's description of braces is funny because she defamiliarizes something that is commonplace to us. What is the effect of that passage on you? In what ways is having braces, and, consequently, straight teeth, a sign of social status?

2. Observe the details Drakulić gives us about Eastern Europe. Which details seem to typify what we think of as "Eastern European." How has Eastern Europe been distinguished from Western Europe and the United States?

3. Beautiful teeth are "an indispensable feature of any American advertisement," Drakulić declares. Is this true? Go through magazine ads and catalogues, observe billboards and TV commercials. How many people have beautiful teeth? How many of the models show their teeth prominently? Look at ads from 10, 20, 30, 40 years ago. Do we show our teeth more now than we used to?

4. Do you have dental insurance? Research dental insurance. How common is it on employers' health plans? Is it included in your own or your parents' employers' health plan? What percentage of Americans have it? What are the connections between what is considered necessary or cosmetic, and what people have to pay for themselves?

CASE STUDY

Jihad vs. McWorld: Seeking a Way of Talking about Civilizations in Conflict

Benjamin R. Barber
Jihad vs. McWorld

Benjamin R. Barber is the Gershon and Carol Kekst Professor of Civil Society and Distinguished University Professor at the University of Maryland and a principal of the Democracy Collaborative. He is the author of a number of plays and novels as well as many academic books on political science and democracy including Strong Democracy: Participatory Politics for a New Age *(1984) and* A Passion for Democracy: American Essays *(1998). "Jihad vs. McWorld" first appeared as the March 1992 cover story for the* Atlantic *magazine; Barber later developed it into the book* Jihad vs. McWorld *(Times Books, 1995), which became an international bestseller and has been translated into twenty languages.*

Just beyond the horizon of current events lie two possible political futures—both bleak, neither democractic. The first is a retribalization of large swaths of humankind by war and bloodshed: a threatened Lebanonization of national states in which culture is pitted against culture, people against people, tribe against tribe—a Jihad in the name of a hundred narrowly conceived faiths against every kind of interdependence, every kind of artificial social cooperation and civic mutuality. The second is being borne in on us by the onrush of economic and ecological forces that demand integration and uniformity and that mesmerize the world with fast music, fast computers, and fast food—with MTV, Macintosh, and McDonald's pressing nations into one commercially homogenous global network: one McWorld tied together by technology, ecology, communications, and commerce. The planet is falling precipitantly apart and coming reluctantly together at the very same moment.

These two tendencies are sometimes visible in the same countries at the same instant: thus Yugoslavia, clamoring just recently to join the New Europe, is exploding into fragments; India is trying to live up to its reputation as the world's largest integral democracy while powerful new fundamentalist parties like the Hindu nationalist Bharatiya Janata Party, along with nationalist assassins, are imperiling its hard-won unity. States are breaking up or joining up: the Soviet Union has disappeared almost overnight, its parts forming new unions with one another or with likeminded nationalities in neighboring states. The old interwar national state based on territory and political sovereignty looks to be a mere transitional development.

The tendencies of what I am here calling the forces of Jihad and the forces of McWorld operate with equal strength in opposite directions, the one driven by parochial hatreds, the other by universalizing markets, the one re-creating ancient subnational and ethnic borders from within, the other making national borders porous from without. They have one thing in common: neither offers much hope to citizens looking for practical ways to govern themselves democratically. If the global future is to pit Jihad's centrifugal whirlwind against McWorld's centripetal black hole, the outcome is unlikely to be democratic—or so I will argue.

McWorld, or the Globalization of Politics

Four imperatives make up the dynamic of McWorld: a market imperative, a resource imperative, an information-technology imperative, and an ecological imperative. By shrinking the world and diminishing the salience of national borders, these imperatives have in combination achieved a considerable victory over factiousness and particularism, and not least of all over their most virulent traditional form—nationalism. It is the realists who are now Europeans, the utopians who dream nostalgically of a resurgent England or Germany, perhaps even a resurgent Wales or Saxony. Yesterday's wishful cry for one world has yielded to the reality of McWorld.

5   *The market imperative.* Marxist and Leninist theories of imperialism assumed that the quest for ever-expanding markets would in time compel nation-based capitalist economies to push against national boundaries in search of an international economic imperium. Whatever else has happened to the scientistic predictions of Marxism, in this domain they have proved farsighted. All national economies are now vulnerable to the inroads of larger, transnational markets within which trade is free, currencies are convertible, access to banking is open, and contracts are enforceable under law. In Europe, Asia, Africa, the South Pacific, and the Americas such markets are eroding national sovereignty and giving rise to entities—international banks, trade associations, transnational lobbies like OPEC and Greenpeace, world news services like CNN and the BBC, and multinational corporations that increasingly lack a meaningful national identity—that neither reflect nor respect nationhood as an organizing or regulative principle.

The market imperative has also reinforced the quest for international peace and stability, requisite of an efficient international economy. Markets are enemies of parochialism, isolation, fractiousness, war. Market psychology attenuates the psychology of ideological and religious cleavages and assumes a concord among producers and consumers—categories that ill fit narrowly conceived national or religious cultures. Shopping has little tolerance for blue laws, whether dictated by pub-closing British paternalism, Sabbath-observing Jewish Orthodox fundamentalism, or no-Sunday-liquor-sales Massachusetts puritanism. In the context of common markets, international law ceases to be a vision of justice and becomes a workaday framework for getting things done—enforcing contracts, ensuring that governments abide by deals, regulating trade and currency relations, and so forth.

Common markets demand a common language, as well as a common currency, and they produce common behaviors of the kind bred by cosmopolitan city life everywhere. Commercial pilots, computer programmers, international bankers, media specialists, oil riggers, entertainment celebrities, ecology experts, demographers, accountants, professors, athletes—these compose a new breed of men and women for whom religion, culture, and nationality can seem only marginal elements in a working identity. Although sociologists of everyday life will no doubt continue to distinguish a Japanese from an American mode, shopping has a common signature throughout the world. Cynics might even say that some of the recent revolutions in Eastern Europe have had as their true goal not liberty and the right to vote but well-paying jobs and the right to shop (although the vote is proving easier to acquire than consumer goods). The market imperative is, then, plenty powerful; but, notwithstanding some of the claims made for "democratic capitalism," it is not identical with the democratic imperative.

The resource imperative. Democrats once dreamed of societies whose political autonomy rested firmly on economic independence. The Athenians idealized what they called *autarky*, and tried for a while to create a way of life simple and austere enough to make the polis genuinely self-sufficient. To be free meant to be independent of any other community or polis. Not even the Athenians were able to achieve autarky, however: human nature, it turns out, is dependency. By the time of Pericles, Athenian politics was inextricably bound up with a flowing empire held together by naval power and commerce—an empire that, even as it appeared to enhance Athenian might, ate away at Athenian independence and autarky. Master and slave, it turned out, were bound together by mutual insufficiency.

The dream of autarky briefly engrossed nineteenth-century America as well, for the underpopulated, endlessly bountiful land, the cornucopia of natural resources, and the natural barriers of a continent walled in by two great seas led many to believe that America could be a world unto itself. Given this past, it has been harder for Americans than for most to accept the inevitability of interdependence. But the rapid depletion of resources even in a country like ours, where they once seemed inexhaustible, and the maldistribution of arable soil and mineral resources on the planet, leave even the wealthiest societies ever more resource-dependent and many other nations in permanently desperate straits.

10   Every nation, it turns out, needs something another nation has; some nations have almost nothing they need.

The information-technology imperative. Enlightenment science and the technologies derived from it are inherently universalizing. They entail a quest for descriptive principles of general application, a search for universal solutions to particular problems, and an unswerving embrace of objectivity and impartiality.

Scientific progress embodies and depends on open communication, a common discourse rooted in rationality, collaboration, and an easy and regular flow and exchange of information. Such ideals can be hypocritical covers for power-mongering by elites, and they may be shown to be wanting in many other ways, but they are entailed by the very idea of science and they make science and globalization practical allies.

Business, banking, and commerce all depend on information flow and are facilitated by new communication technologies. The hardware of these technologies tends to be systemic and integrated—computer, television, cable, satellite, laser, fiber-optic, and microchip technologies combining to create a vast interactive communications and information network that can potentially give every person on earth access to every other person, and make every datum, every byte, available to every set of eyes. If the automobile was, as George Ball once said (when he gave his blessing to a Fiat factory in the Soviet Union during the Cold War), "an ideology on four wheels," then electronic telecommunication and information systems are an ideology at 186,000 miles per second—which makes for a very small planet in a very big hurry. Individual cultures speak particular languages; commerce and science increasingly speak English; the whole world speaks logarithms and binary mathematics.

Moreover, the pursuit of science and technology asks for, even compels, open societies. Satellite footprints do not respect national borders; telephone wires penetrate the most closed societies. With photocopying and then fax machines having infiltrated Soviet universities and samizdat literary circles in the eighties, and computer modems having multiplied like rabbits in communism's bureaucratic warrens thereafter, glasnost could not be far behind. In their social requisites, secrecy and science are enemies.

15   The new technology's software is perhaps even more globalizing than its hardware. The information arm of international commerce's sprawling body reaches out and touches distinct nations and parochial cultures, and gives them a common face chiseled in Hollywood, on Madison Avenue, and in Silicon Valley. Throughout the 1980s one of the most-watched television programs in South Africa was *The Cosby Show*. The demise of apartheid was already in production. Exhibitors at the 1991 Cannes film festival expressed growing anxiety over the "homogenization" and "Americanization" of the global film industry when, for the third year running, American films dominated the awards ceremonies. America has dominated the world's popular culture for much longer, and much more decisively. In November of 1991 Switzerland's once insular culture boasted best-seller lists featuring *Terminator 2* as the No. 1 movie, *Scarlett* as the No. 1 book, and Prince's *Diamonds and Pearls* as the No. 1 record album. No wonder the Japanese are buying Hollywood film studios even faster than Americans are buying Japanese television sets. This kind of software supremacy may in the long term be far more important than hardware superiority, because culture has become more potent than armaments. What is the power of the Pentagon compared with Disneyland? Can the Sixth Fleet keep up with CNN? McDonald's in Moscow and Coke in China will do more to create a global culture than military colonization ever could. It is less the goods than the brand names that do the work, for they convey life-style images that alter perception and challenge behavior. They make up the seductive software of McWorld's common (at times much too common) soul.

Yet in all this high-tech commercial world there is nothing that looks particularly democratic. It lends itself to surveillance as well as liberty, to new forms of manipulation and covert control as well as new kinds of participation, to skewed, unjust market outcomes as well as greater productivity. The consumer society and the open society are not quite synonymous. Capitalism and democracy have a relationship, but it is something less than a marriage. An efficient free market after all requires that consumers be free to vote their dollars on competing goods, not that citizens be free to vote their values and beliefs on competing political candidates and programs. The free market flourished in junta-run Chile, in military-governed Taiwan and Korea, and, earlier, in a variety of autocratic European empires as well as their colonial possessions.

The ecological imperative. The impact of globalization on ecology is a cliché even to world leaders who ignore it. We know well enough that the German forests can be destroyed by Swiss and Italians driving gas-guzzlers fueled by leaded gas. We also know that the planet can be asphyxiated by greenhouse gases because Brazilian farmers want to be part of the twentieth century and are burning down tropical rain forests to clear a little land to plough, and because Indonesians make a living out of converting their lush jungle into toothpicks for fastidious Japanese diners, upsetting the delicate oxygen balance and in effect puncturing our global lungs. Yet this ecological consciousness has meant not only greater awareness but also greater inequality, as modernized nations try to slam the door behind them, saying to developing nations, "The world cannot afford your modernization; ours has wrung it dry!"

Each of the four imperatives just cited is transnational, transideological, and transcultural. Each applies impartially to Catholics, Jews, Muslims, Hindus, and Buddhists; to democrats and totalitarians; to capitalists and socialists. The Enlightenment dream of a universal rational society has to a remarkable degree been realized—but in a form that is commercialized, homogenized, depoliticized, bureaucratized, and, of course, radically incomplete, for the movement toward McWorld is in competition with forces of global breakdown, national dissolution, and centrifugal corruption. These forces, working in the opposite direction, are the essence of what I call Jihad.

Jihad, or the Lebanonization of the World

OPEC, The World Bank, the United Nations, the International Red Cross, the multinational corporation . . . there are scores of institutions that reflect globalization. But they often appear as ineffective reactors to the world's real actors: national states and, to an ever greater degree, subnational factions in permanent rebellion against uniformity and integration—even the kind represented by universal law and justice. The headlines feature these players regularly: they are cultures, not countries; parts, not wholes; sects, not religions; rebellious factions and dissenting minorities at war not just with globalism but with the traditional nation-state. Kurds, Basques, Puerto Ricans, Ossetians, East Timoreans, Quebecois, the Catholics of Northern Ireland, Abkhasians, Kurile Islander Japanese, the Zulus of Inkatha, Catalonians, Tamils, and, of course, Palestinians—people without countries, inhabiting nations not their own, seeking smaller worlds within borders that will seal them off from modernity.

20   A powerful irony is at work here. Nationalism was once a force of integration and unification, a movement aimed at bringing together disparate clans, tribes, and

cultural fragments under new, assimilationist flags. But as Ortega y Gasset noted more than sixty years ago, having won its victories, nationalism changed its strategy. In the 1920s, and again today, it is more often a reactionary and divisive force, pulverizing the very nations it once helped cement together. The force that creates nations is "inclusive," Ortega wrote in *The Revolt of the Masses.* "In periods of consolidation, nationalism has a positive value, and is a lofty standard. But in Europe everything is more than consolidated, and nationalism is nothing but a mania. . . ."

This mania has left the post-Cold War world smoldering with hot wars; the international scene is little more unified than it was at the end of the Great War, in Ortega's own time. There were more than thirty wars in progress last year, most of them ethnic, racial, tribal, or religious in character, and the list of unsafe regions doesn't seem to be getting any shorter. Some new world order!

The aim of many of these small-scale wars is to redraw boundaries, to implode states and resecure parochial identities: to escape McWorld's dully insistent imperatives. The mood is that of Jihad: war not as an instrument of policy but as an emblem of identity, an expression of community, an end in itself. Even where there is no shooting war, there is fractiousness, secession, and the quest for ever smaller communities. Add to the list of dangerous countries those at risk: In Switzerland and Spain, Jurassian and Basque separatists still argue the virtues of ancient identities, sometimes in the language of bombs. Hyperdisintegration in the former Soviet Union may well continue unabated—not just a Ukraine independent from the Soviet Union but a Bessarabian Ukraine independent from the Ukrainian republic; not just Russia severed from the defunct union but Tatarstan severed from Russia. Yugoslavia makes even the disunited, ex-Soviet, nonsocialist republics that were once the Soviet Union look integrated, its sectarian fatherlands springing up within factional motherlands like weeds within weeds within weeds. Kurdish independence would threaten the territorial integrity of four Middle Eastern nations. Well before the current cataclysm Soviet Georgia made a claim for autonomy from the Soviet Union, only to be faced with its Ossetians (164,000 in a republic of 5.5 million) demanding their own self-determination within Georgia. The Abkhasian minority in Georgia has followed suit. Even the good will established by Canada's once promising Meech Lake protocols is in danger, with Francophone Quebec again threatening the dissolution of the federation. In South Africa the emergence from apartheid was hardly achieved when friction between Inkatha's Zulus and the African National Congress's tribally identified members threatened to replace Europeans' racism with an indigenous tribal war. After thirty years of attempted integration using the colonial language (English) as a unifier, Nigeria is now playing with the idea of linguistic multiculturalism—which could mean the cultural breakup of the nation into hundreds of tribal fragments. Even Saddam Hussein has benefited from the threat of internal Jihad, having used renewed tribal and religious warfare to turn last season's mortal enemies into reluctant allies of an Iraqi nationhood that he nearly destroyed.

The passing of communism has torn away the thin veneer of internationalism (workers of the world unite!) to reveal ethnic prejudices that are not only ugly and deep-seated but increasingly murderous. Europe's old scourge, anti-Semitism, is back with a vengeance, but it is only one of many antagonisms. It appears all too easy to throw the historical gears into reverse and pass from a Communist dictatorship back into a tribal state.

Among the tribes, religion is also a battlefield. ("Jihad" is a rich word which generic meaning is "struggle"—usually the struggle of the soul to avert evil. Strictly applied to religious war, it is used only in reference to battles where the faith is under assault, or battles against a government that denies the practice of Islam. My use here is rhetorical, but does follow both journalistic practice and history.) Remember the Thirty Years War? Whatever forms of Enlightenment universalism might once have come to grace such historically related forms of monotheism as Judaism, Christianity, and Islam, in many of their modern incarnations they are parochial rather than cosmopolitan, angry rather than loving, proselytizing rather than ecumenical, zealous rather than rationalist, sectarian rather than deistic, ethnocentric rather than universalizing. As a result, like the new forms of hypernationalism, the new expressions of religious fundamentalism are fractious and pulverizing, never integrating. This is religion as the Crusaders knew it: a battle to the death for souls that if not saved will be forever lost.

25   The atmospherics of Jihad have resulted in a breakdown of civility in the name of identity, of comity in the name of community. International relations have sometimes taken on the aspect of gang war—cultural turf battles featuring battle factions that were supposed to be sublimated as integral parts of large national, economic, postcolonial, and constitutional entities.

The Darkening Feature of Democracy

These rather melodramatic tableaux vivants do not tell the whole story, however. For all their defects, Jihad and McWorld have their attractions. Yet, to appear and insist, the attractions are unrelated to democracy. Neither McWorld nor Jihad is remotely democratic in impulse. Neither needs democracy; neither promotes democracy.

McWorld does manage to look pretty seductive in a world obsessed with Jihad. It delivers peace, prosperity, and relative unity—if at the cost of independence, community, and identity (which is generally based on difference). The primary political values required by the global market are order and tranquility, and freedom—as in the phrases "free trade," "free press," and "free love." Human rights are needed to a degree, but not citizenship or participation—and no more social justice and equality than are necessary to promote efficient economic production and consumption. Multinational corporations sometimes seem to prefer doing business with local oligarchs, inasmuch as they can take confidence from dealing with the boss on all crucial matters. Despots who slaughter their own populations are no problem, so long as they leave markets in place and refrain from making war on their neighbors (Saddam Hussein's fatal mistake). In trading partners, predictability is of more value than justice.

The Eastern European revolutions that seemed to arise out of concern for global democratic values quickly deteriorated into a stampede in the general direction of free markets and their ubiquitous, television-promoted shopping malls.

East Germany's Neues Forum, that courageous gathering of intellectuals, students, and workers which overturned the Stalinist regime in Berlin in 1989, lasted only six months in Germany's mini-version of McWorld. Then it gave way to money and markets and monopolies from the West. By the time of the first all-German elections, it could scarcely manage to secure three percent of the vote. Elsewhere there is growing evidence that glasnost will go and perestroika—defined as privatization and an opening of markets of Western bidders—will stay. So understandably anxious are the new rulers of Eastern Europe and whatever entities are forged from the residues of the Soviet Union to gain access to credit and markets and technology—McWorld's flourishing new currencies—that they have shown themselves willing to trade away democratic prospects in pursuit of them: not just old totalitarian ideologies and command-economy production models but some possible indigenous experiments with a third way between capitalism and socialism, such as economic cooperatives and employee stock-ownership plans, both of which have their ardent supporters in the East.

Jihad delivers a different set of virtues: a vibrant local identity, a sense of community, solidarity among kinsmen, neighbors, and countrymen, narrowly conceived. But it also guarantees parochialism and is grounded in exclusion. Solidarity is secured through a war against outsiders. And solidarity often means obedience to a hierarchy in governance, fanaticism in beliefs, and the obliteration of individual selves in the name of the group. Deference to leaders and intolerance toward outsiders (and toward "enemies within") are hallmarks of tribalism—hardly the attitudes required for the cultivation of new democratic women and men capable of governing themselves. Where new democratic experiments have been conducted in retribalizing societies, in both Europe and the Third World, the result has often been anarchy, repression, persecution, and the coming of new, noncommunist forms of very old kinds of despotism. During the past year, Havel's velvet revolution in Czechoslovakia was imperiled by partisans of "Czechland" and of Slovakia as independent entities. India seemed little less rent by Sikh, Hindu, Muslim, and Tamil infighting than it was immediately after the British pulled out, more than forty years ago.

30   To the extent that either McWorld or Jihad has a natural politics, it has turned out to be more of an antipolitics. For McWorld, it is the antipolitics of globalism: bureaucratic, technocratic, and meritocratic, focused (as Marx predicted it would be) on the administration of things—with people, however, among the chief things to be administered. In its politico-economic imperatives McWorld has been guided by laissez-faire market principles that privilege efficiency, productivity, and beneficence at the expense of civic liberty and self-government.

For Jihad, the antipolitics of tribalization has been explicitly antidemocratic: one-party dictatorship, government by military junta, theocratic fundamentalism—often associated with a version of the *Fuhrerprinzip* that empowers an individual to rule on behalf of a people. Even the government of India, struggling for decades to model democracy for a people who will soon number a billion, longs for great leaders; and for every Mahatma Gandhi, Indira Gandhi, or Rajiv Gandhi taken from them by zealous assassins, the Indians appear to seek a replacement who will deliver them from the lengthy travail of their freedom.

The Confederal Option

How can democracy be secured and spread in a world whose primary tendencies are at best indifferent to it (McWorld) and at worst deeply antithetical to it (Jihad)? My guess is that globalization will eventually vanquish retribalization. The ethos of material "civilization" has not yet encountered an obstacle it has been unable to thrust aside. Ortega may have grasped in the 1920s a clue to our own future in the coming millennium.

Everyone sees the need of a new principle of life. But as always happens in similar crises—some people attempt to save the situation by an artificial intensification of the very principle which has led to decay. This is the meaning of the "nationalist" outburst of recent years. . . things have always gone that way. The last flare, the longest; the last sigh, the deepest. On the very eve of their disappearance there is an intensification of frontiers—military and economic.

Jihad may be a last deep sigh before the eternal yawn of McWorld. On the other hand, Ortega was not exactly prescient; his prophecy of peace and internationalism came just before blitzkrieg, world war, and the Holocaust tore the old order to bits. Yet democracy is how we remonstrate with reality, the rebuke our aspirations offer to history. And if retribalization is inhospitable to democracy, there is nonetheless a form of democratic government that can accommodate parochialism and communitarianism, one that can even save them from their defects and make them more tolerant and participatory: decentralized participatory democracy. And if McWorld is indifferent to democracy, there is nonetheless a form of democratic government that suits global markets passably well—representative government in its federal or, better still, confederal variation.

35   With its concern for accountability, the protection of minorities, and the universal rule of law, a confederalized representative system would serve the political needs of McWorld as well as oligarchic bureaucratism or meritocratic elitism is currently doing. As we are already beginning to see, many nations may survive in the long term only as confederations that afford local regions smaller than "nations" extensive jurisdiction. Recommended reading for democrats of the twenty-first century is not the U.S. Constitution or the French Declaration of Rights of Man and Citizen but the Articles of Confederation, that suddenly pertinent document that stitched together the thirteen American colonies into what then seemed a too loose confederation of independent states but now appears a new form of political realism, as veterans of Yeltsin's new Russia and the new Europe created at Maastricht will attest.

By the same token, the participatory and direct form of democracy that engages citizens in civic activity and civic judgment and goes well beyond just voting and accountability—the system I have called "strong democracy"—suits the political needs of decentralized communities as well as theocratic and nationalist party dictatorships have done. Local neighborhoods need not be democratic, but they can be. Real democracy has flourished in diminutive settings: the spirit of liberty, Tocqueville said, is local. Participatory democracy, if not naturally apposite to tribalism, has an undeniable attractiveness under conditions of parochialism.

Democracy in any of these variations will, however, continue to be obstructed by the undemocratic and antidemocratic trends toward uniformitarian globalism and intolerant retribalization which I have portrayed here. For democracy to persist in our brave new McWorld, we will have to commit acts of conscious political will—a possibility, but hardly a probability, under these conditions. Political will requires much more than the quick fix of the transfer of institutions. Like technology transfer, institution transfer rests on foolish assumptions about a uniform world of the kind that once fired the imagination of colonial administrators. Spread English justice to the colonies by exporting wigs. Let an East Indian trading company act as the vanguard to Britain's free parliamentary institutions. Today's well-intentioned quick-fixers in the National Endowment for Democracy and the Kennedy School of Government, in the unions and foundations and universities zealously nurturing contacts in Eastern Europe and the Third World, are hoping to democratize by long distance. Post Bulgaria a parliament by first-class mail. FedEx the Bill of Rights to Sri Lanka. Cable Cambodia some common law.

Yet Eastern Europe has already demonstrated that importing free political parties, parliaments, and presses cannot establish a democratic civil society; imposing a free market may even have the opposite effect. Democracy grows from the bottom up and cannot be imposed from the top down. Civil society has to be built from the inside out. The institutional superstructure comes last. Poland may become democratic, but then again it may heed the Pope, and prefer to found its politics on its Catholicism, with uncertain consequences for democracy. Bulgaria may become democratic, but it may prefer tribal war. The former Soviet Union may become a democratic confederation, or it may just grow into an anarchic and weak conglomeration of markets for other nations' goods and services.

Democrats need to seek out indigenous democratic impulses. There is always a desire for self-government, always some expression of participation, accountability, consent, and representation, even in traditional hierarchical societies. These need to be identified, tapped, modified, and incorporated into new democratic practices with an indigenous flavor. The tortoises among the democratizers may ultimately outlive or outpace the hares, for they will have the time and patience to explore conditions along the way, and to adapt their gait to changing circumstances. Tragically, democracy in a hurry often looks something like France in 1794 or China in 1989.

40   It certainly seems possible that the most attractive democratic ideal in the face of the brutal realities of Jihad and the dull realities of McWorld will be a confederal union of semi-autonomous communities smaller than nation-states, tied together into regional economic associations and markets larger than nation-states—participatory and self-determining in local matters at the bottom, representative and accountable at the top. The nation-state would play a diminished role, and sovereignty would lose some of its political potency. The Green movement adage "Think globally, act locally" would actually come to describe the conduct of politics.

This vision reflects only an ideal, however—one that is not terribly likely to be realized. Freedom, Jean-Jacques Rousseau once wrote, is a food easy to eat but hard to digest. Still, democracy has always placed itself out against the odds. And democracy remans both a form of coherence as binding as McWorld and a secular faith potentially as inspiriting as Jihad.

Letters to the Editor

The following letters were published in the June 1992 edition of the Atlantic *magazine in response to Benjamin Barber's "Jihad vs. McWorld," which appeared in the March 1992 edition.*

Benjamin Barber makes a number of good points in his essay. But there are several aspects of the McGlobalization phenomenon that are hardly democracy-neutral. From my years of experience as a business manager in one of America's largest corporations, I can say without equivocation that the *only* goal of these organizations is profit. In my company *nothing,* including giving to charitable groups, is done unless it can somehow be connected to protecting or increasing profits. This singular sense of purpose is understood and communicated throughout the organization, and only those people who demonstrate complete fidelity to this principle are guaranteed success and continued employment.

Peter Townsend said years ago that the only way to beat the system is to join it. He was wrong. McWorld has very effective immune systems with which to weed out undesirables from within. Our corporations are not at fault for this situation; business only optimizes the job that society has entrusted to it. Our democratic government can and must protect itself by protecting the civil rights of employees. Or has democracy already been swallowed up by the system? I, for one, think it has.

Robert Fireovid
Pittsfield, Mass.

Benjamin Barber puts forth the old, tired liberal argument that free-market enterprise is the antithesis of democratic government. That his preferences are socialistic is apparent when he drones incessantly about the supposed "impersonalization" of the global-market influence and when he comments that McWorld is "bureaucratic, technocratic, and meritocratic, focused (as Marx predicted it would be) on the administration of things." He ignores the very fact that these market forces are developed and nurtured at their best only in democracies (the United States, Great Britain, Japan, and Germany) and that they were the very forces that brought down totalitarian communism (Eastern Europe) and exposed the insipidness of socialism (Sweden, France).

Walter L. Wojak
Terre Haute, Ind.

I agree with the conclusion but not the negative tone of Benjamin Barber's article. Barber emphasizes the threats to democracy in recent international trends. However, the simultaneous development of ethnic separatisms (what he calls Jihad) and transnational entities like the European Community (what he calls McWorld) presents an unprecedented opportunity to escape two major dead ends of the twentieth century.

After the First World War, Woodrow Wilson attempted to carve up Europe into separate nation-states, a manifest impossibility given the great number and overlapping territories of European ethnic groups. Shortly thereafter, Lenin and Stalin tried to destroy the separate nationalities of the Soviet Union by amalgamating them into a centralized state dominated by the Communist Party. The bankruptcy of this policy has only recently been made manifest.

Both the Americans and the Soviets spurned the example of the Austro-Hungarian Empire, which covered most of Central Europe before the First World War. Yet that loosely federated, multinational state provided a better combination of central authority and decentralized autonomy than the successor states that replaced it.

At present the European Community has an enormous opportunity to recreate the Austro-Hungarian Empire on a more legitimate, and democratic, basis, by recognizing the symbolic and cultural importance of separate ethnic groups yet drawing them into a more universal economic and political federation. Professor Barber should draw attention to this window of opportunity and not muddle the argument with loaded terms such as Jihad and McWorld.

Edward R. Kantowicz
Chicago, Ill.

WRITING STYLE

WRITING LETTERS TO THE EDITOR

Letters to the editor are one of the most accessible ways for beginning writers to communicate their views to the public. However, because they are so short and direct, writers often believe, incorrectly, that they are easy to write well. Examine the letters to the editor written in response to Benjamin Barber's article "Jihad vs. McWorld." What qualities do you like or dislike in the letters? What qualities make a letter more or less effective? Write down some of the qualities of those letters you think are successful and compare them to the following list of suggestions for how to write a letter to the editor.

- *Always review the newspaper's or magazine's policies for printing letters.* Some editors will only accept letters under a certain length or submitted in particular ways (e.g., with full name and address included; or, in some cases, hand-delivered with a picture ID). Knowing the policies ahead of time can save you time and frustration.

continued on next page

- *Submit your letter as soon as possible.* If you are responding to a previous article or editorial, you should submit your letter within two or three days for a newspaper story, or within the next couple of weeks for a monthly periodical. After that time, the editor and readers will have moved on to other issues. If your letter raises a new issue then you should submit your letter when it might have the strongest impact on the public (e.g., you might raise concerns about a candidate's environmental policies a few days before an election so your ideas are still fresh in readers' minds as they go to the polls).

- *Keep the letter short.* Letters longer than 150 words may get published but they will often be cut down by the editor. Editors want to print as many different letters as possible within a small space, so writing a short, concise letter will increase your chances for getting it published.

- *Identify the issue or argument you are responding to up front.* Readers want to be able to locate your views in a particular conversation quickly so identify the issue or argument in the first sentence and state your purpose in writing (e.g., to agree, disagree, qualify, and so on). However, do not waste too much space reminding readers of the issue or what another arguer said; those who take the time to read your letter will probably know the issue or other arguer's ideas already.

- *Make sure the letter is focused, well-organized, and specific.* Because letters are short, you should decide what aspect of the issue or argument you want to focus on. Then, you can include facts, expert testimony, examples, and specific discussion—those elements that will most convince your readers. Following a clear structure will make it easier for people to read (e.g., identify the issue or argument you are responding to, state your view, and then support your view with evidence). A focused, well-organized, and specific letter will also help your writing persona, projecting competence and expertise to readers.

- *Avoid an abusive or condescending tone.* Saying that another arguer is an idiot or a creeping worm will usually reflect badly on your own writing persona, undermining your professionalism and sincerity. In addition, such a tone may prevent the editor from printing your letter. Instead, treat disagreements as opportunities to inquire about the issue.

- *Include your name, address, phone number, and signature.* Editors usually will not publish letters unless they can verify who wrote it.

- *Don't get discouraged.* Editors receive dozens of letters every day; consequently they cannot publish every letter they receive, no matter how good they are. If they do not print your letter, try again the next time you are moved to write, and keep trying.

Samuel P. Huntington
from The Clash of Civilizations?

Samuel P. Huntington is the Albert J. Weatherhead III University Professor in the Department of Government at Harvard University and Chairman of the Harvard Academy of International and Area Studies. He is the author of many books including American Politics: The Promise of Disharmony *(1981) and* Who Are We? The Challenges to America's National Identity *(2004). "The Clash of Civilizations?" was first published in the journal* Foreign Affairs *(Summer 1993) and was later developed into the book* The Clash of Civilizations and the Remaking of World Order *(1996).*

The Next Pattern of Conflict

World politics is entering a new phase, and intellectuals have not hesitated to proliferate visions of what it will be—the end of history, the return of traditional rivalries between nation states, and the decline of the nation state from the conflicting pulls of tribalism and globalism, among others. Each of these visions catches aspects of the emerging reality. Yet they all miss a crucial, indeed a central, aspect of what global politics is likely to be in the coming years.

It is my hypothesis that the fundamental source of conflict in this new world will not be primarily ideological or primarily economic. The great divisions among humankind and the dominating source of conflict will be cultural. Nation states will remain the most powerful actors in world affairs, but the principal conflicts of global politics will occur between nations and groups of different civilizations. The clash of civilizations will dominate global politics. The fault lines between civilizations will be the battle lines of the future.

Conflict between civilizations will be the latest phase in the evolution of conflict in the modern world. For a century and a half after the emergence of the modern international system with the Peace of Westphalia, the conflicts of the Western world were largely among princes—emperors, absolute monarchs and constitutional monarchs attempting to expand their bureaucracies, their armies, their mercantilist economic strength and, most important, the territory they ruled. In the process they created nation states, and beginning with the French Revolution the principal lines of conflict were between nations rather than princes. In 1793, as R. R. Palmer put it, "The wars of kings were over; the wars of peoples had begun." This nineteenth-century pattern lasted until the end of World War I. Then, as a result of the Russian Revolution and the reaction against it, the conflict of nations yielded to the conflict of ideologies, first among communism, fascism-Nazism and liberal democracy, and then between communism and liberal democracy. During the Cold War, this latter conflict became embodied in the struggle between the two superpowers, neither of which was a nation state in the classical European sense and each of which defined its identity in terms of its ideology.

5   These conflicts between princes, nation states and ideologies were primarily conflicts within Western civilization, "Western civil wars," as William Lind has labeled them. This was as true of the Cold War as it was of the world wars and the earlier wars of the seventeenth, eighteenth and nineteenth centuries. With the end of the Cold War, international politics moves out of its Western phase, and its centerpiece becomes the interaction between the West and non-Western civilizations and among non-Western civilizations. In the politics of civilizations, the peoples and governments of non-Western civilizations no longer remain the objects of history as targets of Western colonialism but join the West as movers and shapers of history.

The Nature of Civilizations

During the Cold War the world was divided into the First, Second and Third Worlds. Those divisions are no longer relevant. It is far more meaningful now to group countries not in terms of their political or economic systems or in terms of their level of economic development but rather in terms of their culture and civilization.

What do we mean when we talk of a civilization? A civilization is a cultural entity. Villages, regions, ethnic groups, nationalities, religious groups, all have distinct cultures at different levels of cultural heterogeneity. The culture of a village in southern Italy may be different from that of a village in northern Italy, but both will share in a common Italian culture that distinguishes them from German villages. European communities, in turn, will share cultural features that distinguish them from Arab or Chinese communities. Arabs, Chinese and Westerners, however, are not part of any broader cultural entity. They constitute civilizations. A civilization is thus the highest cultural grouping of people and the broadest level of cultural identity people have short of that which distinguishes humans from other species. It is defined both by common objective elements, such as language, history, religion, customs, institutions, and by the subjective self-identification of people. People have levels of identity: a resident of Rome may define himself with varying degrees of intensity as a Roman, an Italian, a Catholic, a Christian, a European, a Westerner. The civilization to which he belongs is the broadest level of identification with which he intensely identifies. People can and do redefine their identities and, as a result, the composition and boundaries of civilizations change.

Civilizations may involve a large number of people, as with China ("a civilization pretending to be a state," as Lucian Pye put it), or a very small number of people, such as the Anglophone Caribbean. A civilization may include several nation states, as is the case with Western, Latin American and Arab civilizations, or only one, as is the case with Japanese civilization. Civilizations obviously blend and overlap, and may include subcivilizations. Western civilization has two major variants, European and North American, and Islam has its Arab, Turkic and Malay subdivisions. Civilizations are nonetheless meaningful entities, and while the lines between them are seldom sharp, they are real. Civilizations are dynamic; they rise and fall; they divide and merge. And, as any student of history knows, civilizations disappear and are buried in the sands of time.

Westerners tend to think of nation states as the principal actors in global affairs. They have been that, however, for only a few centuries. The broader reaches of human history have been the history of civilizations. In *A Study of History*, Arnold Toynbee identified 21 major civilizations; only six of them exist in the contemporary world.

Why Civilizations Will Clash

10 Civilization identity will be increasingly important in the future, and the world will be shaped in large measure by the interactions among seven or eight major civilizations. These include Western, Confucian, Japanese, Islamic, Hindu, Slavic-Orthodox, Latin American and possibly African civilization. The most important conflicts of the future will occur along the cultural fault lines separating these civilizations from one another.

Why Will This Be the Case?

First, differences among civilizations are not only real; they are basic. Civilizations are differentiated from each other by history, language, culture, tradition and, most important, religion. The people of different civilizations have different views on the relations between God and man, the individual and the group, the citizen and the state, parents and children, husband and wife, as well as differing views of the relative importance of rights and responsibilities, liberty and authority, equality and hierarchy. These differences are the product of centuries. They will not soon disappear. They are far more fundamental than differences among political ideologies and political regimes. Differences do not necessarily mean conflict, and conflict does not necessarily mean violence. Over the centuries, however, differences among civilizations have generated the most prolonged and the most violent conflicts.

Second, the world is becoming a smaller place. The interactions between peoples of different civilizations are increasing; these increasing interactions intensify civilization consciousness and awareness of differences between civilizations and commonalities within civilizations. North African immigration to France generates hostility among Frenchmen and at the same time increased receptivity to immigration by "good" European Catholic Poles. Americans react far more negatively to Japanese investment than to larger investments from Canada and European countries. Similarly, as Donald Horowitz has pointed out, "An Ibo may be . . . an Owerri Ibo or an Onitsha Ibo in what was the Eastern region of Nigeria. In Lagos, he is simply an Ibo. In London, he is a Nigerian. In New York, he is an African." The interactions among peoples of different civilizations enhance the civilization-consciousness of people that, in turn, invigorates differences and animosities stretching or thought to stretch back deep into history.

Third, the processes of economic modernization and social change throughout the world are separating people from longstanding local identities. They also weaken the nation state as a source of identity. In much of the world religion has moved in to fill this gap, often in the form of movements that are labeled "fundamentalist." Such movements are found in Western Christianity, Judaism, Buddhism and Hinduism, as well as in Islam. In most countries and most religions the people active in fundamentalist movements are young, college-educated, middle-class technicians, professionals and business persons. The "unsecularization of the world," George Weigel has remarked, "is one of the dominant social facts of life in the late twentieth century." The revival of religion, "la revanche de Dieu," as Gilles Kepel labeled it, provides a basis for identity and commitment that transcends national boundaries and unites civilizations.

Fourth, the growth of civilization-consciousness is enhanced by the dual role of the West. On the one hand, the West is at a peak of power. At the same time, however, and perhaps as a result, a return to the roots phenomenon is occurring among non-Western civilizations. Increasingly one hears references to trends toward a turning inward and "Asianization" in Japan, the end of the Nehru legacy and the "Hinduization" of India, the failure of Western ideas of socialism and nationalism and hence "re-Islamization" of the Middle East, and now a debate over Westernization versus Russianization in Boris Yeltsin's country. A West at the peak of its power confronts non-Wests that increasingly have the desire, the will and the resources to shape the world in non-Western ways.

15   In the past, the elites of non-Western societies were usually the people who were most involved with the West, had been educated at Oxford, the Sorbonne or Sandhurst, and had absorbed Western attitudes and values. At the same time, the populace in non-Western countries often remained deeply imbued with the indigenous culture. Now, however, these relationships are being reversed. A de-Westernization and indigenization of elites is occurring in many non-Western countries at the same time that Western, usually American, cultures, styles and habits become more popular among the mass of the people.

Fifth, cultural characteristics and differences are less mutable and hence less easily compromised and resolved than political and economic ones. In the former Soviet Union, communists can become democrats, the rich can become poor and the poor rich, but Russians cannot become Estonians and Azeris cannot become Armenians. In class and ideological conflicts, the key question was "Which side are you on?" and people could and did choose sides and change sides. In conflicts between civilizations, the question is "What are you?" That is a given that cannot be changed. And as we know, from Bosnia to the Caucasus to the Sudan, the wrong answer to that question can mean a bullet in the head. Even more than ethnicity, religion discriminates sharply and exclusively among people. A person can be half-French and half-Arab and simultaneously even a citizen of two countries. It is more difficult to be half-Catholic and half-Muslim.

Finally, economic regionalism is increasing. The proportions of total trade that were intraregional rose between 1980 and 1989 from 51 percent to 59 percent in Europe, 33 percent to 37 percent in East Asia, and 32 percent to 36 percent in North America. The importance of regional economic blocs is likely to continue to increase in the future. On the one hand, successful economic regionalism will reinforce civilization-consciousness. On the other hand, economic regionalism may succeed only when it is rooted in a common civilization. The European Community rests on the shared foundation of European culture and Western Christianity. The success of the North American Free Trade Area depends on the convergence now underway of Mexican, Canadian and American cultures. Japan, in contrast, faces difficulties in creating a comparable economic entity in East Asia because Japan is a society and civilization unique to itself. However strong the trade and investment links Japan may develop with other East Asian countries, its cultural differences with those countries inhibit and perhaps preclude its promoting regional economic integration like that in Europe and North America.

Common culture, in contrast, is clearly facilitating the rapid expansion of the economic relations between the People's Republic of China and Hong Kong, Taiwan, Singapore and the overseas Chinese communities in other Asian countries. With the Cold War over, cultural commonalities increasingly overcome ideological differences, and mainland China and Taiwan move closer together. If cultural commonality is a prerequisite for economic integration, the principal East Asian economic bloc of the future is likely to be centered on China. This bloc is, in fact, already coming into existence. As Murray Weidenbaum has observed,

> Despite the current Japanese dominance of the region, the Chinese-based economy of Asia is rapidly emerging as a new epicenter for industry, commerce and finance. This strategic area contains substantial amounts of technology and manufacturing capability (Taiwan), outstanding entrepreneurial, marketing and services acumen (Hong Kong), a fine communications network (Singapore), a tremendous pool of financial capital (all three), and very large endowments of land, resources and labor (mainland China) . . . . From Guangzhou to Singapore, from Kuala Lumpur to Manila, this influential network—often based on extensions of the traditional clans—has been described as the backbone of the East Asian economy.[1]

20   Culture and religion also form the basis of the Economic Cooperation Organization, which brings together ten non-Arab Muslim countries: Iran, Pakistan, Turkey, Azerbaijan, Kazakhstan, Kyrgyzstan, Turkmenistan, Tadjikistan, Uzbekistan and Afghanistan. One impetus to the revival and expansion of this organization, founded originally in the 1960s by Turkey, Pakistan and Iran, is the realization by the leaders of several of these countries that they had no chance of admission to the European Community. Similarly, Caricom, the Central American Common Market and Mercosur rest on common cultural foundations. Efforts to build a broader Caribbean-American economic entity bridging the Anglo-Latin divide, however, have to date failed.

As people define their identity in ethnic and religious terms, they are likely to see an "us" versus "them" relation existing between themselves and people of different

---

[1]*Murray Weidenbaum, "Greater China: The Next Economic Superpower?," St. Louis: Washington University Center for the Study of American Business,* Contemporary Issues, *Series 57, February 1993, pp. 2–3.*

ethnicity or religion. The end of ideologically defined states in Eastern Europe and the former Soviet Union permits traditional ethnic identities and animosities to come to the fore. Differences in culture and religion create differences over policy issues, ranging from human rights to immigration to trade and commerce to the environment. Geographical propinquity gives rise to conflicting territorial claims from Bosnia to Mindanao. Most important, the efforts of the West to promote its values of democracy and liberalism as universal values, to maintain its military predominance and to advance its economic interests engender countering responses from other civilizations. Decreasingly able to mobilize support and form coalitions on the basis of ideology, governments and groups will increasingly attempt to mobilize support by appealing to common religion and civilization identity.

The clash of civilizations thus occurs at two levels. At the micro-level, adjacent groups along the fault lines between civilizations struggle, often violently, over the control of territory and each other. At the macro-level, states from different civilizations compete for relative military and economic power, struggle over the control of international institutions and third parties, and competitively promote their particular political and religious values.

The Fault Lines Between Civilizations

The fault lines between civilizations are replacing the political and ideological boundaries of the Cold War as the flash points for crisis and bloodshed. The Cold War began when the Iron Curtain divided Europe politically and ideologically. The Cold War ended with the end of the Iron Curtain. As the ideological division of Europe has disappeared, the cultural division of Europe between Western Christianity, on the one hand, and Orthodox Christianity and Islam, on the other, has reemerged. The most significant dividing line in Europe, as William Wallace has suggested, may well be the eastern boundary of Western Christianity in the year 1500. This line runs along what are now the boundaries between Finland and Russia and between the Baltic states and Russia, cuts through Belarus and Ukraine separating the more Catholic western Ukraine from Orthodox eastern Ukraine, swings westward separating Transylvania from the rest of Romania, and then goes through Yugoslavia almost exactly along the line now separating Croatia and Slovenia from the rest of Yugoslavia. In the Balkans this line, of course, coincides with the historic boundary between the Hapsburg and Ottoman empires. The peoples to the north and west of this line are Protestant or Catholic; they shared the common experiences of European history—feudalism, the Renaissance, the Reformation, the Enlightenment, the French Revolution, the Industrial Revolution; they are generally economically better off than the peoples to the east; and they may now look forward to increasing involvement in a common European economy and to the consolidation of democratic political systems. The peoples to the east and south of this line are Orthodox or Muslim; they historically belonged to the Ottoman or Tsarist empires and were only lightly touched by the shaping events in the rest of Europe; they are generally less advanced economically; they seem much less likely to develop stable democratic political systems. The Velvet Curtain of culture has replaced the Iron Curtain of ideology as the most significant dividing line in Europe. As the events in Yugoslavia show, it is not only a line of difference; it is also at times a line of bloody conflict.

Conflict along the fault line between Western and Islamic civilizations has been going on for 1,300 years. After the founding of Islam, the Arab and Moorish surge west and north only ended at Tours in 732. From the eleventh to the thirteenth century the Crusaders attempted with temporary success to bring Christianity and Christian rule to the Holy Land. From the fourteenth to the seventeenth century, the Ottoman Turks reversed the balance, extended their sway over the Middle East and the Balkans, captured Constantinople, and twice laid siege to Vienna. In the nineteenth and early twentieth centuries as Ottoman power declined Britain, France, and Italy established Western control over most of North Africa and the Middle East.

25   After World War II, the West, in turn, began to retreat; the colonial empires disappeared; first Arab nationalism and then Islamic fundamentalism manifested themselves; the West became heavily dependent on the Persian Gulf countries for its energy; the oil-rich Muslim countries became money-rich and, when they wished to, weapons-rich. Several wars occurred between Arabs and Israel (created by the West). France fought a bloody and ruthless war in Algeria for most of the 1950s; British and French forces invaded Egypt in 1956; American forces went into Lebanon in 1958; subsequently American forces returned to Lebanon, attacked Libya, and engaged in various military encounters with Iran; Arab and Islamic terrorists, supported by at least three Middle Eastern governments, employed the weapon of the weak and bombed Western planes and installations and seized Western hostages. This warfare between Arabs and the West culminated in 1990, when the United States sent a massive army to the Persian Gulf to defend some Arab countries against aggression by another. In its aftermath NATO planning is increasingly directed to potential threats and instability along its "southern tier."

This centuries-old military interaction between the West and Islam is unlikely to decline. It could become more virulent. The Gulf War left some Arabs feeling proud that Saddam Hussein had attacked Israel and stood up to the West. It also left many feeling humiliated and resentful of the West's military presence in the Persian Gulf, the West's overwhelming military dominance, and their apparent inability to shape their own destiny. Many Arab countries, in addition to the oil exporters, are reaching levels of economic and social development where autocratic forms of government become inappropriate and efforts to introduce democracy become stronger. Some openings in Arab political systems have already occurred. The principal beneficiaries of these openings have been Islamist movements. In the Arab world, in short, Western democracy strengthens anti-Western political forces. This may be a passing phenomenon, but it surely complicates relations between Islamic countries and the West.

Those relations are also complicated by demography. The spectacular population growth in Arab countries, particularly in North Africa, has led to increased migration to Western Europe. The movement within Western Europe toward minimizing internal boundaries has sharpened political sensitivities with respect to this development. In Italy, France and Germany, racism is increasingly open, and political reactions and violence against Arab and Turkish migrants have become more intense and more widespread since 1990. On both sides the inter-action between Islam and the West is seen as a clash of civilizations. The West's "next confrontation," observes M. J. Akbar, an Indian Muslim author, "is defi-nitely going to come from the Muslim world. It is in the sweep of the Islamic nations from the Maghreb to Pakistan that the struggle for a new world order will begin." Bernard Lewis comes to a similar conclusion:

> We are facing a mood and a movement far transcending the level of issues and policies and the governments that pursue them. This is no less than a clash of civilizations—the perhaps irrational but surely historic reaction of an ancient rival against our Judeo-Chris-tian heritage, our secular present, and the worldwide expansion of both.[2]

Historically, the other great antagonistic interaction of Arab Islamic civiliza-tion has been with the pagan, animist, and now increasingly Christian black peo-ples to the south. In the past, this antagonism was epitomized in the image of Arab slave dealers and black slaves. It has been reflected in the on-going civil war in the Sudan between Arabs and blacks, the fighting in Chad between Libyan-supported insurgents and the government, the tensions between Orthodox Christians and Muslims in the Horn of Africa, and the political conflicts, recurring riots and com-munal violence between Muslims and Christians in Nigeria. The modernization of Africa and the spread of Christianity are likely to enhance the probability of violence along this fault line. Symptomatic of the intensification of this conflict was the Pope John Paul II's speech in Khartoum in February 1993 attacking the actions of the Sudan's Islamist government against the Christian minority there.

30   On the northern border of Islam, conflict has increasingly erupted between Orthodox and Muslim peoples, including the carnage of Bosnia and Sarajevo, the simmering violence between Serb and Albanian, the tenuous relations between Bulgarians and their Turkish minority, the violence between Ossetians and Ingush, the unremitting slaughter of each other by Armenians and Azeris, the tense relations between Russians and Muslims in Central Asia, and the deployment of Russian troops to protect Russian interests in the Caucasus and Central Asia. Religion reinforces the revival of ethnic identities and restimulates Russian fears about the security of their southern borders. This concern is well captured by Archie Roosevelt:

> Much of Russian history concerns the struggle between the Slavs and the Turkic peoples on their borders, which dates back to the foundation of the Russian state more than a thousand years ago. In the Slavs' millennium-long confrontation with their eastern neigh-bors lies the key to an understanding not only of Russian history, but Russian character. To understand Russian realities today one has to have a concept of the great Turkic eth-nic group that has preoccupied Russians through the centuries.[3]

The conflict of civilizations is deeply rooted elsewhere in Asia. The historic clash between Muslim and Hindu in the subcontinent manifests itself now not

---

[2] Bernard Lewis, "The Roots of Muslim Rage," The Atlantic Monthly, vol. 266, September 1990, p. 60; Time, June 15, 1992, pp. 24–28.
[3] Archie Roosevelt, For Lust of Knowing, Boston: Little, Brown, 1988, pp. 332–333.

only in the rivalry between Pakistan and India but also in intensifying religious strife within India between increasingly militant Hindu groups and India's substantial Muslim minority. The destruction of the Ayodhya mosque in December 1992 brought to the fore the issue of whether India will remain a secular democratic state or become a Hindu one. In East Asia, China has outstanding territorial disputes with most of its neighbors. It has pursued a ruthless policy toward the Buddhist people of Tibet, and it is pursuing an increasingly ruthless policy toward its Turkic-Muslim minority. With the Cold War over, the underlying differences between China and the United States have reasserted themselves in areas such as human rights, trade and weapons proliferation. These differences are unlikely to moderate. A "new cold war," Deng Xiaoping reportedly asserted in 1991, is under way between China and America.

The same phrase has been applied to the increasingly difficult relations between Japan and the United States. Here cultural difference exacerbates economic conflict. People on each side allege racism on the other, but at least on the American side the antipathies are not racial but cultural. The basic values, attitudes, behavioral patterns of the two societies could hardly be more different. The economic issues between the United States and Europe are no less serious than those between the United States and Japan, but they do not have the same political salience and emotional intensity because the differences between American culture and European culture are so much less than those between American civilization and Japanese civilization.

The interactions between civilizations vary greatly in the extent to which they are likely to be characterized by violence. Economic competition clearly predominates between the American and European subcivilizations of the West and between both of them and Japan. On the Eurasian continent, however, the proliferation of ethnic conflict, epitomized at the extreme in "ethnic cleansing," has not been totally random. It has been most frequent and most violent between groups belonging to different civilizations. In Eurasia the great historic fault lines between civilizations are once more aflame. This is particularly true along the boundaries of the crescent-shaped Islamic bloc of nations from the bulge of Africa to central Asia. Violence also occurs between Muslims, on the one hand, and Orthodox Serbs in the Balkans, Jews in Israel, Hindus in India, Buddhists in Burma and Catholics in the Philippines. Islam has bloody borders . . . .

The West Versus the Rest

35 The West is now at an extraordinary peak of power in relation to other civilizations. Its superpower opponent has disappeared from the map. Military conflict among Western states is unthinkable, and Western military power is unrivaled. Apart from Japan, the West faces no economic challenge. It dominates international political and security institutions and with Japan international economic institutions. Global political and security issues are effectively settled by a directorate of the United States, Britain and France, world economic issues by a directorate of the United States, Germany and Japan, all of which maintain

extraordinarily close relations with each other to the exclusion of lesser and largely non-Western countries. Decisions made at the U.N. Security Council or in the International Monetary Fund that reflect the interests of the West are presented to the world as reflecting the desires of the world community. The very phrase "the world community" has become the euphemistic collective noun (replacing "the Free World") to give global legitimacy to actions reflecting the interests of the United States and other Western powers.[4] Through the IMF and other international economic institutions, the West promotes its economic interests and imposes on other nations the economic policies it thinks appropriate. In any poll of non-Western peoples, the IMF undoubtedly would win the support of finance ministers and a few others, but get an overwhelmingly unfavorable rating from just about everyone else, who would agree with Georgy Arbatov's characterization of IMF officials as "neo-Bolsheviks who love expropriating other people's money, imposing undemocratic and alien rules of economic and political conduct and stifling economic freedom."

Western domination of the U.N. Security Council and its decisions, tempered only by occasional abstention by China, produced U.N. legitimation of the West's use of force to drive Iraq out of Kuwait and its elimination of Iraq's sophisticated weapons and capacity to produce such weapons. It also produced the quite unprecedented action by the United States, Britain and France in getting the Security Council to demand that Libya hand over the Pan Am 103 bombing suspects and then to impose sanctions when Libya refused. After defeating the largest Arab army, the West did not hesitate to throw its weight around in the Arab world. The West in effect is using international institutions, military power and economic resources to run the world in ways that will maintain Western predominance, protect Western interests and promote Western political and economic values.

That at least is the way in which non-Westerners see the new world, and there is a significant element of truth in their view. Differences in power and struggles for military, economic and institutional power are thus one source of conflict between the West and other civilizations. Differences in culture, that is basic values and beliefs, are a second source of conflict. V. S. Naipaul has argued that Western civilization is the "universal civilization" that "fits all men." At a superficial level much of Western culture has indeed permeated the rest of the world. At a more basic level, however, Western concepts differ fundamentally from those prevalent in other civilizations. Western ideas of individualism, liberalism, constitutionalism, human rights, equality, liberty, the rule of law, democracy, free markets, the separation of church and state, often have little resonance in Islamic, Confucian, Japanese, Hindu, Buddhist or Orthodox cultures. Western efforts to

---

[4]*Almost invariably Western leaders claim they are acting on behalf of "the world community." One minor lapse occurred during the run-up to the Gulf War. In an interview on "Good Morning America," Dec. 21, 1990, British Prime Minister John Major referred to the actions "the West" was taking against Saddam Hussein. He quickly corrected himself and subsequently referred to "the world community." He was, however, right when he erred.*

propagate such ideas produce instead a reaction against "human rights imperialism" and a reaffirmation of indigenous values, as can be seen in the support for religious fundamentalism by the younger generation in non-Western cultures. The very notion that there could be a "universal civilization" is a Western idea, directly at odds with the particularism of most Asian societies and their emphasis on what distinguishes one people from another. Indeed, the author of a review of 100 comparative studies of values in different societies concluded that "the values that are most important in the West are least important worldwide."[5] In the political realm, of course, these differences are most manifest in the efforts of the United States and other Western powers to induce other peoples to adopt Western ideas concerning democracy and human rights. Modern democratic government originated in the West. When it has developed in non-Western societies it has usually been the product of Western colonialism or imposition.

The central axis of world politics in the future is likely to be, in Kishore Mahbubani's phrase, the conflict between "the West and the Rest" and the responses of non-Western civilizations to Western power and values.[6] Those responses generally take one or a combination of three forms. At one extreme, non-Western states can, like Burma and North Korea, attempt to pursue a course of isolation, to insulate their societies from penetration or "corruption" by the West, and, in effect, to opt out of participation in the Western-dominated global community. The costs of this course, however, are high, and few states have pursued it exclusively. A second alternative, the equivalent of "band-wagoning" in international relations theory, is to attempt to join the West and accept its values and institutions. The third alternative is to attempt to "balance" the West by developing economic and military power and cooperating with other non-Western societies against the West, while preserving indigenous values and institutions; in short, to modernize but not to Westernize . . . .

Implications for the West

This article does not argue that civilization identities will replace all other identities, that nation states will disappear, that each civilization will become a single coherent political entity, that groups within a civilization will not conflict with and even fight each other. This paper does set forth the hypotheses that differences between civilizations are real and important; civilization-consciousness is increasing; conflict between civilizations will supplant ideological and other forms of conflict as the dominant global form of conflict; international relations, historically a game played out within Western civilization, will increasingly be de-Westernized and become a game in which non-Western civilizations are actors and not simply objects; successful political, security and economic international institutions are more likely to develop within civilizations than across civilizations;

---

[5]Harry C. Triandis, the New York Times, Dec. 25, 1990, p. 41, and "Cross-Cultural Studies of Individualism and Collectivism," Nebraska Symposium on Motivation, vol. 37, 1989, pp. 41–133.
[6]Kishore Mahbubani, "The West and the Rest," The National Interest, Summer 1992, pp. 3–13.

conflicts between groups in different civilizations will be more frequent, more sustained and more violent than conflicts between groups in the same civilization; violent conflicts between groups in different civilizations are the most likely and most dangerous source of escalation that could lead to global wars; the paramount axis of world politics will be the relations between "the West and the Rest"; the elites in some torn non-Western countries will try to make their countries part of the West, but in most cases face major obstacles to accomplishing this; a central focus of conflict for the immediate future will be between the West and several Islamic-Confucian states.

40   This is not to advocate the desirability of conflicts between civilizations. It is to set forth descriptive hypotheses as to what the future may be like. If these are plausible hypotheses, however, it is necessary to consider their implications for Western policy. These implications should be divided between short-term advantage and long-term accommodation. In the short term it is clearly in the interest of the West to promote greater cooperation and unity within its own civilization, particularly between its European and North American components; to incorporate into the West societies in Eastern Europe and Latin America whose cultures are close to those of the West; to promote and maintain cooperative relations with Russia and Japan; to prevent escalation of local inter-civilization conflicts into major inter-civilization wars; to limit the expansion of the military strength of Confucian and Islamic states; to moderate the reduction of Western military capabilities and maintain military superiority in East and Southwest Asia; to exploit differences and conflicts among Confucian and Islamic states; to support in other civilizations groups sympathetic to Western values and interests; to strengthen international institutions that reflect and legitimate Western interests and values and to promote the involvement of non-Western states in those institutions.

In the longer term other measures would be called for. Western civilization is both Western and modern. Non-Western civilizations have attempted to become modern without becoming Western. To date only Japan has fully succeeded in this quest. Non-Western civilizations will continue to attempt to acquire the wealth, technology, skills, machines and weapons that are part of being modern. They will also attempt to reconcile this modernity with their traditional culture and values. Their economic and military strength relative to the West will increase. Hence the West will increasingly have to accommodate these non-Western modern civilizations whose power approaches that of the West but whose values and interests differ significantly from those of the West. This will require the West to maintain the economic and military power necessary to protect its interests in relation to these civilizations. It will also, however, require the West to develop a more profound understanding of the basic religious and philosophical assumptions underlying other civilizations and the ways in which people in those civilizations see their interests. It will require an effort to identify elements of commonality between Western and other civilizations. For the relevant future, there will be no universal civilization, but instead a world of different civilizations, each of which will have to learn to coexist with the others.

David Brooks
All Cultures Are Not Equal

David Brooks is an Op-Ed columnist for the New York Times. *He has also been a senior editor at* The Weekly Standard *and a contributing editor at* Newsweek *and the* Atlantic Monthly, *and he is currently a commentator on* The Newshour with Jim Lehrer. *Brooks is the author of* Bobos In Paradise: The New Upper Class and How They Got There *(2001) and* On Paradise Drive: How We Live Now (And Always Have) in the Future Tense *(2004). "All Cultures Are Not Equal" was Brooks's column in the* New York Times *on August 10, 2005.*

Let's say you are an 18-year-old kid with a really big brain. You're trying to figure out which field of study you should devote your life to, so you can understand the forces that will be shaping history for decades to come.

Go into the field that barely exists: cultural geography. Study why and how people cluster, why certain national traits endure over centuries, why certain cultures embrace technology and economic growth and others resist them.

This is the line of inquiry that is now impolite to pursue. The gospel of multiculturalism preaches that all groups and cultures are equally wonderful. There are a certain number of close-minded thugs, especially on university campuses, who accuse anybody who asks intelligent questions about groups and enduring traits of being racist or sexist. The economists and scientists tend to assume that material factors drive history—resources and brain chemistry—because that's what they can measure and count.

But none of this helps explain a crucial feature of our time: while global economies are converging, cultures are diverging, and the widening cultural differences are leading us into a period of conflict, inequality and segmentation.

5   Not long ago, people said that globalization and the revolution in communications technology would bring us all together. But the opposite is true. People are taking advantage of freedom and technology to create new groups and cultural zones. Old national identities and behavior patterns are proving surprisingly durable. People are moving into self-segregating communities with people like themselves, and building invisible and sometimes visible barriers to keep strangers out.

If you look just around the United States you find amazing cultural segmentation. We in America have been "globalized" (meaning economically integrated) for centuries, and yet far from converging into some homogeneous culture, we are actually diverging into lifestyle segments. The music, news, magazine and television markets have all segmented, so there are fewer cultural unifiers like *Life* magazine or Walter Cronkite.

Forty-million Americans move every year, and they generally move in with people like themselves, so as the late James Chapin used to say, every place becomes more like itself. Crunchy places like Boulder attract crunchy types and become crunchier. Conservative places like suburban Georgia attract conservatives and become more so.

Not long ago, many people worked on farms or in factories, so they had similar lifestyles. But now the economy rewards specialization, so workplaces and lifestyles diverge. The military and civilian cultures diverge. In the political world, Democrats and Republicans seem to live on different planets.

Meanwhile, if you look around the world you see how often events are driven by groups that reject the globalized culture. Islamic extremists reject the modern cultures of Europe, and have created a hyperaggressive fantasy version of traditional Islamic purity. In a much different and less violent way, some American Jews have moved to Hebron and become hyper-Zionists.

10 From Africa to Seattle, religiously orthodox students reject what they see as the amoral mainstream culture, and carve out defiant revival movements. From Rome to Oregon, antiglobalization types create their own subcultures.

The members of these and many other groups didn't inherit their identities. They took advantage of modernity, affluence and freedom to become practitioners of a do-it-yourself tribalism. They are part of a great reshuffling of identities, and the creation of new, often more rigid groupings. They have the zeal of converts.

Meanwhile, transnational dreams like European unification and Arab unity falter, and behavior patterns across nations diverge. For example, fertility rates between countries like the U.S. and Canada are diverging. Work habits between the U.S. and Europe are diverging. Global inequality widens as some nations with certain cultural traits prosper and others with other traits don't.

People like Max Weber, Edward Banfield, Samuel Huntington, Lawrence Harrison and Thomas Sowell have given us an inkling of how to think about this stuff, but for the most part, this is open ground.

If you are 18 and you've got that big brain, the whole field of cultural geography is waiting for you.

WRITING STYLE

WRITING EDITORIALS AND OPINION PIECES

The purposes of editorials and opinion pieces often vary; a writer may wish to call attention to a public concern, express a political viewpoint, call readers to support or reject a cause, or even entertain with light-hearted commentary on people, events, or issues. Yet most editorials have one point in common: They try to start or stimulate public discussion. Examine David Brooks's editorial written for the *New York Times*. As you read it, write down those qualities you think make it successful. Then, compare your list with the following suggestions for writing your own editorials and opinion pieces:

- *Stay close to the latest news or events.* Editorials usually follow public conversation closely. Writers can usually get their views published so long as the public is still discussing the issue, but writers may want to time their advice to best achieve their purposes. For example, someone wanting to write an editorial discouraging legislation that restricts the ownership of handguns would want to publish his or her editorial shortly before legislators are scheduled to meet to discuss it.

- *Maintain a clear focus, good organization and specific details.* Editorials and opinion pieces are usually several paragraphs; consequently, you may want to focus on one or two points so you can support those points with good evidence. An easy-to-follow structure with plenty of transitions also helps readers navigate your arguments easily.

- *Include background information if the issue is new or unknown.* Like a news article, an editorial and opinion piece may need to inform readers what the issue is, who is involved, and why they should care. However, because these works are short, you should stick to the minimum details needed to communicate your views.

- *Hook the readers in and keep their interest.* Because editorials and opinion pieces must compete with many other works for the readers' attention, they usually lure the reader in with a strong, even controversial tone or with a clever organizational strategy (e.g., the writer turns a seemingly impersonal issue like geography into something personal by organizing the piece around an imagined person—"an 18-year-old-kid with a really big brain"—who will be affected by globalization and can in turn affect changes in the world). You can keep readers' interest by including anecdotes or dramatic quotations in those places where your readers' attention may waver.

- *Engage readers' emotions when appropriate.* Appeal to readers' emotions for those issues that invite emotional responses. You might shock them with graphic details or statistics; you might inspire them with the stories of individuals. Make sure the emotional appeals are appropriate and natural; in other words, don't use them to discourage readers' critical thinking.

Barbara Ehrenreich
Christian Wahhabists

Barbara Ehrenreich, a social critic and essayist, is a frequent contributor to Harper's and Time magazines. Her book on the working poor, Nickel and Dimed: On (Not) Getting By in America (2002), was a best-seller and was followed by her expose of white collar struggles, Bait and Switch: The (Futile) Pursuit of the American Dream (2005). She is a columnist with the Progressive magazine, where "Christian Wahhabists" first appeared in January 2002.

There has been a lot of loose talk, since September 11, about a "clash of civilizations" between musty, backward-looking, repressive old Islam and the innovative and freedom-loving West. "It is a clash between positivism and a reactionary, negative world view," columnist H.D.S. Greenway writes in *The Boston Globe.*

Or, as we learn in *The Washington Post:* While the West used the last two centuries to advance the cause of human freedom, "The Islamic world, by contrast, was content to remain in its torpor, locked in rigid orthodoxy, fearful of freedom."

So it is a surprise to find, on turning to the original text—Samuel P. Huntington's 1996 *The Clash of Civilizations and the Remaking of World Order* (Simon & Schuster)—a paragraph-long analogy between the Islamic fundamentalist movement and the Protestant Reformation: "Both are reactions to the stagnation and corruption of existing institutions; advocate a return to a purer and more demanding form of their religion; preach work, order, and discipline."

Whoa, there! Weren't the Protestants supposed to be the up-and-coming, progressive, force vis-a-vis the musty old Catholics? And if we were supposed to root for the Protestants in our high school history texts, shouldn't we be applauding the Islamic "extremists" now?

5   Huntington doesn't entertain the analogy between Islamic fundamentalism and reforming Protestantism for very long. But let's extend the analogy, if only because it implicitly challenges the notion that we are dealing with two radically different, mutually opposed, "civilizations."

Like the Protestants of the sixteenth century, the Islamic fundamentalists are a relatively new and innovative force on the scene. Wahhabism—the dour and repressive creed espoused by Saudi Arabia, Osama bin Laden, and other Islamic fundamentalists throughout the world—dates from only the mid-eighteenth century. Deobandism, the strain of Islam that informed the Taliban (and which has, in recent decades, become almost indistinguishable from Wahhabism), arose in India just a little over a century ago. So when we talk about Islamic fundamentalism, we are not talking about some ancient and venerable "essence of Islam"; we are talking about something new and even "modern." As Huntington observes, the appeal of fundamentalism is to "mobile and modern-oriented younger people."

Islamic fundamentalism is a response—not to the West or to the "modern"—but to earlier strands of Islam, just as Protestantism was a response to Catholicism. Wahhabism arose in opposition to both the (thoroughly Muslim) Ottoman Empire and to the indigenous Sufism of eighteenth-century Arabia.

Sufism is part of Islam, too—much admired in the West for its relative tolerance, its mysticism and poetry, its danced, ecstatic rituals. But it is also, especially in its rural forms, a religion that bears more than a casual resemblance to late medieval Catholicism: Sufism encourages the veneration of saint-like figures at special shrines and their celebration of festivities—sometimes rather raucous ones, like the carnivals and saints' days of medieval Catholicism—throughout the year.

Just as the Protestants smashed icons, prohibited carnivals, and defaced cathedrals, the Wahhabists insisted on a "reformed" style of Islam, purged of all the saints, festivities, and music. Theirs is what has been described as a "stripped-down" version of Islam, centered on short prayers recited in undecorated mosques to the one god and only to him.

10   The Taliban imposed Wahhabism in Afghanistan as soon as they came to power in 1996 and took on, as their first task, the stamping out of Sufism.

The closest Reformation counterpart to today's Islamic fundamentalists were the Calvinists, whose movement arose a few decades after Lutheranism. Pundits often exclaim over the Islamic fundamentalists' refusal to recognize a church-state division—as if that were a uniquely odious feature of "Islamic civilization"—but John Calvin was a militant theocrat himself, and his followers carved out Calvinist mini-states wherever they could.

In sixteenth-century Swiss cantons and seventeenth-century Massachusetts, Calvinists and Calvinist-leaning Protestants banned dancing, gambling, drinking, colorful clothing, and sports of all kinds. They outlawed idleness and vigorously suppressed sexual activity in all but its married, reproductively oriented, form.

Should he have been transported back into a Calvinist-run Zurich or Salem, a member of the Taliban or a Wahhabist might have found only one thing that was objectionable: the presence of unveiled women. But he would have been reassured on this point by the Calvinists' insistence on women's subjugation. As a man is to Jesus, asserted the new Christian doctrine, so is his wife to him.

Calvinism—or "Puritanism" as it is known in America—was of course immensely successful. Max Weber credited it with laying the psychological groundwork for capitalism: work hard, defer gratification, etc. Within the West, the Calvinist legacy carries on most robustly in America, with its demented war on drugs, its tortured ambivalence about pornography and sex, its refusal to accord homosexuals equal protection under the law. It even persists in organized form as the Christian right, which continues to nurture the dream of a theocratic state. Recall the statement by one of our leading warriors against Islamic fundamentalist terrorism—John Ashcroft—that "we have no king but Jesus."

15　　In a world that contains Christian Wahhabists like Ashcroft and Islamic Calvinists like bin Laden, what sense does it make to talk about culturally monolithic "civilizations" like "Islam" and "the West"? Any civilization worthy of the title is, at almost any moment of its history, fraught with antagonistic world views and balanced on the finely poised dialectics of class, race, gender, and ideology. We talk of "Roman civilization," for example, forgetting that the Roman elite spent the last decades before Jesus's birth bloodily suppressing its own ecstatic, unruly, Dionysian religious sects.

There is no "clash of civilizations" because there are no clear-cut, and certainly no temperamentally homogeneous, civilizations to do the clashing. What there is, and has been again and again throughout history, is a clash of alternative cultures. One, represented by the Islamic and Christian fundamentalists—as well as by fascists and Soviet-style communists—is crabbed and punitive in outlook, committed to collectivist discipline, and dogmatically opposed to spontaneity and pleasure. Another, represented both in folk traditions and by elite "enlightenment" thought, is more open, liberatory, and trusting of human impulses.

Civilizations can tilt in either direction. And individuals—whether they are Christian, Muslim, or neither have a choice to make between freedom, on the one hand, and religious totalitarianism on the other.

Seyla Benhabib
Unholy Wars

Seyla Benhabib, born in Istanbul, Turkey, is Eugene Meyer Professor of Political Science and Philosophy at Yale University. She is the author of many books, including Democracy and Difference: Changing Boundaries of the Political *(1996) and, most recently,* The Claims of Culture: Equality and Diversity in the Global Era *(2002). From 1994–1997, Benhabib was Editor-in-Chief (with Andrew Arato) of* Constellations: An International Journal of Critical and Democratic

Theory. *"Unholy Wars"* was published in Constellations *in 2002; it was later reprinted in* Nothing Sacred: Women Respond to Religious Fundamentalism and Terror, *edited by Betsy Reed (Thunder's Mouth Press/Nation Books, 2002).*

It has become clear since September 11 that we are faced with a new form of struggle that threatens to dissolve the boundaries of the political in liberal democracies. The terror network of Osama bin Laden, and its various branches in Egypt, Pakistan, Malaysia, Indonesia, the Philippines, Algeria, and among Islamist groups in western Europe, is wider, more entrenched, and more sophisticated than it was believed to be. The attacks unleashed by these groups (and their potential sympathizers in the U.S. and Europe among the neo-Nazis and white supremacists), especially the use of the biological weapon anthrax to contaminate the civilian population via the mail, indicate a new political and military phenomenon which challenges the framework of state-centric politics.

Historians always warn us that the unprecedented will turn out to have some forerunners somewhere and that what seems new today will appear old when considered against the background of some longer time span. Nevertheless to "think the new" in politics is the vocation of the intellectual. This is a task at which Susan Sontag, Fred Jameson, and Slavoj Zizek have failed us by interpreting these events along the tired paradigm of an antiimperalist struggle by the "wretched of the earth."[1] Neglecting the internal dynamics and struggles within the Islamic world and the history of regional conflicts in Afghanistan, Pakistan, India, and Kashmir, these analyses assure us that we can continue to grasp the world through our usual categories, and that by blaming the policies and actions of western governments one can purge oneself of the enmity and hatred which is directed toward one as a member of such western societies. These analyses help us neither to grasp the unprecedented nature of the events unfolding since September 11, 2001, nor to appreciate the internal dynamics within the Arab-Muslim world which have given rise to them.

The line between *military and civilian targets,* between military and civilian populations, had already been erased during the aerial bombings of World War II. This is not what is new since September 11. Faced with the total mobilization of society, initiated by fascism and National Socialism, it was the democracies of the world, and not some marginal terrorist group hiding in the mountains of Afghanistan, that first crossed that line and initiated "total war." The civilian population at large became the hostage of the enemy, as during the bombing of London by the Nazis and then of Dresden, Hiroshima, and Nagasaki by the Allies.

In the 1950s, the Algerian War marked a new variation in this process of the erasure of the line between the front and the home, the soldier and the civilian. The Algerian Resistance against the French aimed at destroying the *normalcy of everyday life* for the civilians of the occupying population. By blowing up the French residents of Algeria in cafes, markets, and stations, the Resistance not only

---

[1] *See Susan Sontag,* New Yorker, *September 24, 2001; Fred Jameson,* London Review of Books *23, no. 19 (October 4, 2001); and Slavoj Zizek, "The Desert of the Real: Is this the End of Fantasy?" In These Times, October 29, 2001.*

reminded them that they were the enemy but that there could be no "normal life" under conditions of colonial occupation. Since that time, this kind of terror—which fights against the superior military and technical weapons of a mightier enemy by tearing apart the fabric of everyday life through interrupting normal routines, and by rendering every bus or railroad station, each street corner or gathering place, a potential target—has become one of the favorite "weapons of the weak." The strategy of this kind of struggle is to make life so unlivable for the enemy civilians that they concede defeat even if they enjoy superior military power. The Palestinian Intifada at least in part follows the Algerian model: by creating conditions of continuous fear, insecurity, and violence in the land of Palestine, it aims at destroying the resolve of the Israeli civilian population to continue a normal life.[2] In recent years, however, infiltrators from Islamist groups like the Hamas and the Hizbollah into the ranks of the Palestinians, and the widespread practice of "suicide bombings," are changing the nature of the Intifada as well.

5   The bombing of the World Trade Center and the Pentagon is unlike both the total war waged in the struggle against fascism and the terrorism against the occupier initiated by the Algerians. These new attacks, perpetrated against a civilian population in its own land and against a country in no state of declared hostility with the attackers, not only defy all categories of international law but reduce politics to apocalyptic symbols. Until Osama bin Laden released his terse video celebrating September 11, his deed had *no* political name: In whose name or for whom was his group acting? What political demands was it voicing? The brief references to the stationing of U.S. troops in Saudi Arabia, to U.S. sanctions against Iraq, and to U.S. support of Israel were shrouded in the language of *jihad* (holy war) and obfuscated by allusions to the lost glory of Islam in the thirteenth century through the loss of "al Andalus" (Spain) to the Christians. While it is conceivable that Palestinian terror could end one day if Israel withdrew from the occupied West Bank, released Palestinian prisoners of war, found a settlement for the refugees, and somehow resolved the question of Jerusalem, it is unclear, what, if anything, could end the *jihad* of the Osama bin Laden network against the U.S. and its allies. Theirs is a war of "holy" vengeance, a war designed to humiliate the mighty "Satan" in New York and Washington by turning the weapons of the most developed technology against the society which created them.

The result is a sublime combination of high tech wizardry and moral and political atavism, which some have named "jihad online." But this unholy politics threatens to undo the moral and political distinctions that ought to govern our lives, distinctions between enemy, friend, and bystander; guilt, complicity, and responsibility; conflict, combat, and war. We have to live by them even if others do not.

---

[2] *The analogy is not quite accurate, for the French colonizers eventually left Algeria. Despite all theories to the contrary, the Jewish population of Palestine are not colonizers in the traditional sense of the term. They are not there to exploit the indigenous population or their resources, but to establish a "Jewish homeland"—however problematic and tragic this vision may be. The refusal of much of the Arab world to understand the uniqueness of the dream that motivated the Zionist enterprise makes it easy for them to assimilate Israel to the model of the western oppressor while presenting themselves as the colonized and the oppressed. Israel was not established to be a colonizing force; it has become so increasingly since the occupation of the West Bank, and since its growing dependence on Palestinian labor to run its expanding economy.*

One of the most commonly heard contentions in the aftermath of September 11 was that even if the terrorist attacks upon the World Trade Center and Washington equaled war in the civilian and property damage they inflicted, the deliberateness and precision with which they were executed, and the brazenness with which they violated customary moral, legal, and international norms, the U.S. Congress could not actually declare "war," not because the enemy was as yet unknown, but because a state can declare war only against another state. The idea that a democratic nation-state would declare war upon a global network of loosely organized sympathizers of a religious-cum-civilizational cause strained all categories of international law with which the world has lived since 1945 and in which nation-states are the principal recognized actors. For this reason, the current military action in Afghanistan has not been preceded by a declaration of war; rather the Congress has authorized the president to do whatever is necessary to fight the global terror network and to bring the perpetrators to justice, but declared war neither on the Taliban (whom most nations do not recognize as a legitimate regime) nor on the Afghani people. It is as if the territory, the terrain of Afghanistan, is our enemy, in that this terrain offers a sanctuary and an operational base for one of the great fugitives of our time—Osama bin Laden. Ironically, the people of Afghanistan have themselves fallen "captive" or "prisoner" to one who operates on their territory, and to whom the Taliban had granted refuge. Afghanistan is a decaying or failed nation-state, and this very condition of decay permits us to understand all the more vividly the principles of national sovereignty which have governed international relations since the Second World War.

Recall here Max Weber's classically modernist definition of the state as "the legitimate monopoly over the use of violence within a recognized and bounded territory.[3] Modern statehood is based upon the coupling together of the principles of *territoriality, administrative and military monopoly,* including the use of violence, and the *legitimacy* to do so. When states decay, dissolve, or secede, these three principles fall asunder. Their territory can become a staging ground for operations not only of guerilla warfare, but of drug smuggling, weapons production, contraband, and other illegal activities; administrative and military competence is overtaken by units at the substate level such as warlords, commandos, traditional chieftains, or religious leaders; and legitimacy loses its representational quality in that there is no longer a unified people to whose will it either refers or defers—legitimacy either flows from the barrel of a gun or from other sources of supra- and subnational ideological worldviews, be these race-, religion-, or civilization-based.

The decaying and weak nation-states of the contemporary world bear similarities as well as differences with the totalitarian regimes of the mid-twentieth century. The breakdown of the rule of law, the destruction of representative and democratic institutions, the pervasiveness of violence, and the universalization of fear are features of both state-forms. Although at times they mobilized "the movement" against

---

[3] *"However, the monopolization of legitimate violence by the political-territorial association and its rational consociations into an institutional order is nothing primordial, but a product of evolution." Max Weber,* Economy and Society, *vol. 2, ed. Guenther Roth and Claus Wittich (Berkeley: University of California Press, 1978), 904–905.*

the state bureaucracy, the totalitarian regimes of the mid-twentieth century by and large strengthened and rebuilt the state by rendering it subservient to their ideologies. But the postmodern/quasifeudal states of the present, like Afghanistan, Chechnya, Bosnia, and Rwanda, emerge as a result not of the strengthening but of the destruction of the territorial and administrative unity of the state in the name of subunities, which are then globally networked. As Hannah Arendt has shown us, totalitarian movements also had globalizing ambitions in that they touted supranational ideologies like pan-Germanism and pan-Slavism.[4] Yet the global ideologies of today's terror movements are both larger and smaller in range: instead of the ideology of linguistic or cultural unity among the Slavic or Germanic nations, for example, today we are dealing with ideologies aimed at tribes, ethnicities, or a vision of a community of believers that transcends them all—namely the Islamic *umma* of the faithful. The new unit of totalitarianism is the terrorist cell, not the party or the movement; the goal of this new form of war is not just the destruction of the enemy but the extinction of a way of life. *The emergence of nonstate agents capable of waging destruction at a level hitherto thought to be only the province of states and the emergence of a supranational ideological vision with an undefinable moral and political content, which can hardly be satisfied by ordinary political tactics and negotiations, are the unprecedented aspects of our current condition.*

10   This remark should not be taken to suggest that I attribute an overarching rationality or normativity to the state use of violence. State terrorism can also be brutal, unjust, and merciless—recall the war of the Yugoslav state against the Bosnians and the Kosovar Albanians! The point I am emphasizing, however, is that in liberal democracies the monopoly which the state claims over the use of the means of violence is always in principle, if not in fact, subject to the rule of law and to democratic legitimation by the citizenry. These internal constraints upon the legitimate use of violence are then carried into the international arena, where sovereign states bind themselves to limit their use of violence through entering into pacts and associations, signing treaties, etc.

The end of the bipolar world of the cold war brought with it not just multi-plurality but a global society in which nonstate actors have emerged as players possessing the means of violence but who are not subject to usual constraints of international law and treaties. All treaties which have hitherto governed the nonuse and proliferation of biological, chemical, and nuclear weapons have been rendered irrelevant: those who will deploy them have never been their signatories. Furthermore, not being recognized as legitimate political entities, these groups have no responsibility and accountability toward the populations in whose midst they act and which harbor them. Suppose Osama bin Laden and his group possess Scud missiles with nuclear war-heads, which they may have obtained either from Iraq or from the Russian Mafia or other weapons smugglers. What would prevent them from firing these missiles against population centers in Afghanistan, Pakistan, India, or Israel if this would serve some purpose? Since they are accountable to no one, the collateral damage which they may cause even to their own allies and sym-

---

[4]*Hannah Arendt*, The Origins of Totalitarianism *(New York: Harcourt, Brace, Jovanovich, 1979 (1951)), pt. 3.*

pathizers is of no concern to them. Whereas terrorist groups like the Basque ETA and the IRA still have to be governed by some sense of proportion in the damage they inflict and the violence they engage in, in order not to lose all sympathy for their cause in world public opinion, these new terror networks are not motivated by fore-seeable political goals analogous to the independence of the Basque land from Spain and France, the removal of the Irish Loyalist population and unity with Catholic Ire-land, and the like. Nor are these groups fighting for hearts and minds in the West by seeking the conversion of the population to Islam and to Islamic ways of life. When it was practiced by Islamic armies in the centuries after the death of Muhammad (632 A.D.), *jihad*—which can also mean the struggle of the soul with itself to lead the virtuous life as dictated by the Qur'an[5]—aimed at the conquest of the land of the "infidels" in order to force their conversion to Islam. People of all races, colors, ethnicities, and tongues could convert to Islam and become "good Muslims." It is this option of conversion which has made Islam into the biggest Abrahamic reli-gion of the world; ironically, it is the very absence of this conversion mission that is striking in the new jihad.

The new jihad is not only apocalyptic; it is nihilistic. A Taliban spokesman's statement that his people love death as much as the Americans love life is an expression of superb nihilism. The eroticization of death, as evidenced on the one hand by the frequently heard vulgarisms about *huris*, the dark-eyed virgins who are to meet the warriors in the afterlife, but on the other hand and more importantly by the destruction of one's own body in an act of supreme violence which dismembers and pulverizes it, is remarkable. Human beings have died throughout the centuries for causes they believed in, to save their loved ones, to protect their country or their principles, to save the faith, to exercise solidarity, and the like. But the emergence of "suicide bombings" among Islamist groups on a mass scale is astonishing. As many Qur'anic scholars have pointed out, there is no theological justification for this: it is one thing to die in war and yet another to make the destruction of one's body along with those of others the supreme weapon. In order to quell such waves of suicide bombings, the Israeli authorities resorted to an atavistic practice: they made it publicly known that they would bury the remains of suicide bombers in shrouds of pigs' skin (an animal that is considered "*haram*"—taboo—by Jews and Muslims alike) in order to prevent their ascent into heaven in accordance with Islamic faith. It is of course hard to know whether men of the sophistication and worldliness of Muhammad Atta and others, who have lived in the capitals of Europe and the West and who have attended universities as well as bars, movie houses as well as brothels, believe in the afterlife. I personally doubt it. Not only is it clear that the very strict version of Islam—Wahhabism—which Osama bin Laden follows is not shared by all even within his own group, but the Egyptian Brotherhood which was the original orga-nization for many Islamist philosophies in the 1950s had its own version of things, as do members of the Algerian terror network. These networks of young militants

---

[5] Roxanne Euben, *"Killing (for) Politics: Jihad, Martyrdom, and Political Action,"* lecture given in the Political Theory Colloquium, Yale University, October 16, 2001. Forthcoming, Political Theory *(February 2002).*

who trot the globe from Bosnia to Afghanistan, from Paris to Indonesia, and back to Baghdad, Hamburg, or New York, are like Islamic soldiers of fortune, in search not of riches but an elusive and decisive encounter with death. In this regard they bear more resemblance to chiliastic sects among all world religions than to the Muslim armies of the Umayyad, the Abassids, or the Ottomans. While using friendly Muslim governments and their hospitality for their own purposes, these groups pose a clear threat to any established form of authority—which may have been one reason why the Saudis renounced Osama bin Laden's citizenship and rendered him an international fugitive.

As in the past century, faced with a novel form of totalitarianism, democracies confront unique challenges. The presence of an enemy who is neither a military adversary nor a representative agent of a known state creates confusion as to whether police and other law enforcement agencies or the military should take the lead in the investigation and the struggle; the lines between acts of crime and acts of war get blurred. The concept of an "internal enemy," which is now being promoted against "suspect groups" through surveillance, wiretapping, and stricter immigration controls, is not one that democracies can live with. The category of the terrorist as an "internal enemy," as one who is among us, even if not one of us, strains the democratic community by revealing that the rule of law is not all-inclusive and that violence lurks at the edges of everyday normalcy. Our thinking about foreigners, refugees, and asylees becomes colored by the image of others as potential enemies; the "other" becomes the criminal. We may be at a point in history when the state-centric system is indeed waning: global terrorism and the formation of a global economy and civil society are part of the same maelstrom. Yet our laws as well as institutions, practices as well as alliances, are governed by state-centric terms which presuppose the unity of territoriality, the monopoly over the use of the means of violence, and the attainment of legitimacy through representative institutions. It is of course supremely ironic that President Bush, who advocated a new version of American unilateralism and isolationism and who denounced "nation building," now finds himself supporting multilateral actions with allies like Pakistan, Saudi Arabia, and Syria, whose democratic legitimacy is highly questionable, but also reconstructing a post-Taliban government in Afghanistan. Can we find responses to this new challenge that will break the vicious cycles of violence, incomprehension, and repression at home and war abroad?

Although the attacks have so far been directed against the U.S., and although the U.S. is justified under international law in invoking the right of self-defense to justify the current war,[6] the U.S. and its NATO allies have resorted to the clause of collective security and Article 5 of NATO, which guarantees the security of each member of the alliance. I support this course of action, and I would further endorse the call by UN President Kofi Annan to declare terrorism a "crime against humanity," and to try the terrorists, if and when they are captured, before an international tribunal. Furthermore, the UN General Assembly should condemn the Taliban regime for

---

[6]For a lucid elucidation of the current situation from the standpoint of international law, see Richard Falk, "A Just Response," Nation, October 8, 2001.

committing crimes against humanity not only for harboring Osama bin Laden and his men, but for the way the Taliban have trampled upon the human rights of their own women. There is no reason why the human rights of women to work, to be educated, to walk on the street, to dress as they wish, etc. should be considered any less sacred and any less in need of defense than the rights of ethnic minorities. In response to the events of September 11 and to future threats, multilateral responses that enjoy cross-cultural legitimacy and reflect some of the new norms of international law—like crimes against humanity or genocide, as defined under the Statute of Rome of the International Criminal Court—should be invoked. Unfortunately, the current actions of the Bush administration tend exactly in the opposite direction: the captured Taliban and al Qaeda soldiers have been declared "non-military combatants" and will be tried by military tribunals, held in the extra-territorial space of Guantà-namo Bay, which is not subject to U.S. constitutional protections. As with the abdication of the Kyoto and Salt II agreements, around this issue too the Bush administration preaches internationalism but practices unilateralism.

15   Of course—and this cannot be said clearly enough by the citizens of western democracies—a radical revision of U.S. and NATO policy vis-à-vis the Arab world and south-central Asia is needed. The U.S. and its allies have to stop propping up military dictatorships and religious conservatives in these areas in order simply to secure oil supplies. Democratic movements within the burgeoning civil societies of countries like Egypt, Turkey, Jordan, and the new Iran must be supported. A general UN conference must be convened to deal with the rights of nations, ethnicities, and other minorities without states in this region, like the Kurds in Turkey, Iraq, and Iran; the Shi'ites in Iraq; and the Baha'is as well as the Azeris in Iran. Efforts analogous to the Marshall Plan in postwar Europe or the Soros Foundation in Eastern Europe must be developed and furthered for entire regions. But even if all these things are assumed, I believe that a more daunting cultural struggle and civilizational malaise is unfolding before our eyes.

II

As many have noted (including former Prime Minister of Pakistan Benazir Bhutto), the events of September 11 at first seemed to offer a belated confirmation of Samuel Huntington's famous thesis of the clash of civilizations. Huntington wrote:

> It is my hypothesis that the fundamental source of conflict in this new world will not be primarily ideological or primarily economic. The great divisions among humankind and the dominating source of conflict will be cultural. Nation states will remain the most powerful actors in world affairs, but the principal conflicts of global politics will occur between nations and groups of different civilizations. The fault lines between civilizations will be the battle lines of the future.[7]

Proceeding from a holistic understanding of cultures and civilizations—terms which he at times conflated and others distinguished—Huntington was unable

---

[7]*Samuel Huntington*, The Clash of Civilizations and the Remaking of World Order *(New York: Simon and Schuster, 1996), 2.*

to differentiate one "civilization" from another, with the consequence that, apart from "the West and the rest," he could not specify how many civilizations there were and how they were to be differentiated.[8] Edward Said pointed out that Huntington made civilizations and identities into:

> shut-down, sealed-off entities that have been purged of the myriad currents and counter-currents that animate human history, and over centuries have made it possible for that history not only to contain wars of religion and imperial conquest but also to be one of exchange, cross-fertilization, and sharing.[9]

20   It is precisely this history of crossfertilization—exchange as well as confrontation—between Islamic cultures and the West that we must pay increasing attention to. One of the principal thinkers of the Islamist[10] movement, Sayyid Qutb, an Egyptian who studied philosophy in France and briefly visited the United States, developed a civilizational critique of the West for its corruption, coldness, heartlessness, and individualism. His critique resonates with themes from the works of Nietzsche as well as Heidegger, from Adorno and Horkheimer as well as contemporary communitarians.[11] Describing the current condition of the West as one of "*jahiliyyah*," a lack of knowledge and a condition of ignorance, the Islamists advocate a return to Qur'anic law—the *shariah*—and Muslim precepts to combat the corruption of the western way of life. To combat the condition of *jahiliyyah*, it is necessary to rebel and establish a countercommunity (*jama'a*) and spread it through *jihad*.[12] Very often, the Islamists' struggle against *jahiliyyah* takes the form of a struggle against established authorities in their own countries and their "corrupt," westernizing policies.

This clash within Islamic countries between Islamist religious forces and modernizers like Kemal Ataturk in Turkey, Habib Burgiba in Tunisia, Gemal Abdel Nasser, Anwar Sadat and Hosni Mubarek in Egypt, the deposed Reza Shah Pahlavi in Iran, and even Saddam Hussein in Iraq, is long, deep, and powerful. The modernizers in these countries have usually come from military rather than civilian backgrounds, and by transforming one of the few intact institutions of the old regime—namely the military bureaucracy—into an instrument of political power and hegemony, they have consolidated their authority, often with limited popular support and democratic institutions. All over the Islamic Arab world this *military modernization* paradigm, in which Syria and Iraq had participated through the Ba'ath regimes in the 1970s, has lost ground. The defeat of the Egyptian armies in the hands of Israel during the Six Day War and the Israeli occupation of the West Bank are reminders to the military elite of these countries, less of the plight of the Palestinians, whom they have massacred and oppressed when it suited their interests (remember Black September

---

[8]*See my forthcoming* The Claims of Culture: Equality and Diversity *(Princeton: Princeton University Press, 2002). I discuss the conceptual and explanatory difficulties of Huntington's theses in the Introduction.*
[9]*Edward Said on Samuel Huntington, in* al-Ahram Weekly On-Line,
http://www.ahram.org.eg/weekly/standard/aaw.gif no. 555, October 11–17, 2001.
[10]*Roxanne Euben observes that "'Islamism' is another, slightly less controversial way of referring to Islamic fundamentalism." ("Killing (for) Politics")*
[11]*See Roxanne Euben's excellent book,* Enemy in the Mirror: Islamist Fundamentalism and the Limits of Modern Rationalism *(Princeton: Princeton University Press, 1999).*
[12]*Euben, "Killing (for) Politics," 8.*

in Jordan in 1970, in which Palestinians were killed by the thousands, or the persecution of the Palestinians by the Saudis because of their support for Saddam Hussein during the Gulf War) than of the failure of their own truncated projects of modernization. Israel is a thorn in the side of these regimes, whose very presence is a reminder of their own failure to modernize in military, technological, and economic terms.

The revival of Islamist movements is best understood in the light of the failure of most of these societies to succeed in combining a prosperous economy *with* political democracy and a Muslim identity.[13] Islamism emerges as a plausible civilizational project not just against the West, but against the failure of westernizing elites who have managed to import only a truncated modernity into their own societies. Some of these modernizing elites had considered themselves "socialists" of sorts. The Ba'ath regimes in Syria and Iraq, and even the kind of pan-Arabism envisaged by Nasser in the early 1960s, advocated strong redistributionist economic measures, built up huge public sectors (in state-owned utilities, for example), and practiced what could be called "statist modernization" from above. The demise of the Soviet Union has left these states with no patrons. Need we remind ourselves that the mobilization of the Islamist *mujahedeen* in Afghanistan began against the Soviet invasion of the country in 1979—an invasion the Soviets engaged in to support their own backers, the leftist *fedayyeen*?

The collapse of really existing socialisms and the failure of state-guided modernization from above have created an enormous vacuum in the ideological life of these societies. And into this vacuum have rushed Islamist fundamentalists. Osama bin Laden is the most spectacular member of a long chain of critics in the Islamic world, who, more often than not, have directed their local struggles against their own corrupt and authoritarian regimes (Nasser banned the Islamist Muslim Brotherhood and hanged some of its leaders) toward the outside, toward the external enemy.

III

I want to end with Max Weber's question: Which directions do religious rejections of the world take and why?[14] There is a fundamental conflict between secular, capitalist modernity, driven by profit, self-interest, and individualism, and the ethical worldviews of the world's religions. The religious worldviews preach various forms of abstinence, renunciation of riches, the pursuit of virtue in the path of God, the exercise of solidarity among members of the faith, and the disciplining of everyday life to do the work of the Lord. What is it, Weber asked, that enables some religious interpretations of the world to make their peace with the new world of modernity? For Weber the Protestant ethic exhibited its "elective affinity" to capitalism by transforming the abstinent and methodical pursuit of one's vocation in the service of God into the methodical, predictable, disciplined pursuit of work and profit in this world. This process took several centuries and not all early modern Christians accepted its logic: Millennarian movements which

---

[13] See Sayres S. Rudy for an in-depth social theoretical analysis of some of these issues, "Subjectivity, Political Evaluation, and Islamist Trajectories," in Birgit Schaebler and Leif Stenberg, eds., Globalization and the Muslim World (Albany: SUNY Press, 2002).

[14] Max Weber, "Religious Rejections of the World and their Directions," Economy and Society, vol. 1.

rejected the capitalist control of everyday life for the sake of disciplined labor and profit accompanied the rise of western modernity.

25   The Protestant—and more narrowly Calvinist—transformation of religious salvation into an earthly vocation of hard work in the service of an unpredictable God is one among the many paths that the religious accommodation with the world can take. It is also possible to split the religious and mundane spheres in such a way that one altogether withdraws from engagement with the world; the religious abnegation of the world remains an option. A third option—besides engagement or withdrawal—is to *compartmentalize* by separating the spheres of life which come under the ethical dictates of religion from those like the public spheres of the economy in which more flexibility and compromise are possible. Throughout the Islamic world, such a strict separation of religious observance (in the domain of family life and everyday practices of prayer, cleanliness, food, and sexuality) from the sphere of the economy in the "bazaar" (the marketplace) was practiced. This separation of the home from the market was made possible by the practice of Islamic tolerance toward the other Abrahamanic religions, like Judaism and Christianity. The Ottomans adopted this "separate spheres" model, and permitted the wide array of ethnic groups and peoples whom they dominated to govern themselves in their own communal affairs according to their own religious and customary traditions (the so-called *millet* system). Global modernization is destroying the fragile balance between these separate spheres; this may explain in turn the obsessive preoccupation with controlling female sexuality which all Islamist groups exhibit.

Technical modernization, which brings along with it the gadgets of modernity like computers, videos, DVDs, cell phones, and satellite dishes, is no threat to the Islamists.[15] In fact, there is a ruthless exploitation of these new media to convey one's message to believers. Neither is finance capitalism as such problematic from an Islamic perspective. Attempts exist all over the Muslim world to reconcile the *shariah* with modern financial institutions. Whether it is the *hawale* method of money transfers, which bypass modern banks and rely on personalized contacts among money lenders, or the obligation of the rich to share 5 percent of their wealth with the poor, as dictated in the *Qur'an* (a practice that is partially behind the founding of the *madrassas*—institutions of religious learning—for war orphans in Afghanistan by wealthy individuals all over the Islamic world), institutional innovations to make Islam compatible with global capitalism are taking place. The threat to the separate spheres model is primarily a threat to family and personal life.

Global capitalism is bringing images of sexual freedom and decadence, female emancipation and equality among the sexes, into the homes of patriarchal and authoritarian Muslim communities. It is Hollywood which is identified as America, and not the Constitution, the Supreme Court, or the legacy of Puritanism

---

[15]*At the end of the 1980s, when I first visited Germany as a Humboldt fellow in Munich, I was taken aback by the sale of cassettes and videotaped versions of chants from the Qur'an in big shopping centers. Recorded by well-known* Muezzins *(cantors), these tapes permitted the faithful to utilize the technology of the society around them while remaining true to themselves. The irony is that the chanting of the Qur'an, like the reading of the Old Testament, and unlike the reading of the Bible, is supposed to be a communal and collective act of chanting, telling, and recalling. The medium of Western technology threatens this communal fabric. The result may be "religion à la carte," as this phenomenon has been called, for many Muslims as well.*

and town meetings. These fast circulating images of sexual liberty and decadence, physical destruction and violence, sell very well globally because their message is blunt and can be extricated from local cultural nuance.

In a global world, it is not only images that travel; individuals all over the Islamic world are part of a large diaspora to the West. Sizeable Muslim communities exist in every large European and North American capital. These migrant communities attempt to practice the separate life-spheres model in their new homes. But the children of Muslim migrants are caught between worlds; be it through educational institutions or the influence of mass culture, they are torn between the authoritarian and patriarchal family structures from which they emerge and the new world of freedom into which they enter. There is a continuous renegotiation of clashing moral codes and value orientations in the minds of this younger generation, particularly regarding women. If we want to understand why so many educated, relatively well-off Muslim males who had lived in Hamburg and Paris would participate in the actions of September 11, we have to understand the psychology of Muslim immigrants in their encounters with secular liberal democracies of the West. Given the failure of their own home-grown versions of modernity like Nasserism and the Ba'ath movement, given the global entertainment industry's profound assault on their identity as Muslims, and given the profound discrimination and contempt which they experience in their host societies as new immigrants who are perceived to have "backward" morals and ways of life, many young Muslims today turn to Islamism and fundamentalism. Commenting on *l'affaire foulard* (the headscarf affair) in France, in which some female students took to wearing traditional headscarfs less as a sign of submission to religious patriarchy than as an emblem of difference and defiance against homogenizing French republican traditions, the French sociologists Gaspard and Khosrokhavar capture these set of complex symbolic negotiations as follows:

> [The headscarf] mirrors in the eyes of the parents and the grandparents the illusions of continuity whereas it is a factor of discontinuity; it makes possible the transition to otherness (modernity), under the pretext of identity (tradition); it creates the sentiment of identity with the society of origin whereas its meaning is inscribed within the dynamic of relations with the receiving society . . . . [I]t is the vehicle of the passage to modernity within a promiscuity which confounds traditional distinctions, of an access to the public sphere which was forbidden to traditional women as a space of action and the constitution of individual autonomy . . . .[16]

30   We can intervene in this process of complex cultural negotiations as dialogue partners in a global civilization only insofar as we make an effort to understand the struggles of others whose idioms and terms may be unfamiliar to us, but which, by the same token, are also not so different from similar struggles at other times in our own cultures; through acts of strong hermeneutical generosity, we can still extend our moral imagination to view the world through the others' eyes.[17] While I believe that at this stage of the conflict the use of force against the Osama bin Laden network is inevitable and justified, the real political task ahead

---

[16] *Francoise Gaspard and Farhad Khosrokhar,* Le Foulard et la République *(Paris: Découverte, 1995), 44–45. My translation.*

[17] *I deal with the ethics of communication and multiculturalism in* The Claims of Culture, *ch. 5.*

is to engage in a dialogue with millions of Muslims around this globe—beyond vengeance and without apocalyptic expectations. Democracies cannot fight holy wars. Reason, compassion, respect for the dignity of human life, the search for justice, and the desire for reconciliation are the democratic virtues which are now pitted against acts of apocalyptic hatred and vengeance.

▨ QUESTIONS FOR INQUIRY AND ACTION ▨

1. Describe the definitions of citizenship and community found in Jihad and in McWorld. How are they strikingly different? Can you find any common ground?

2. In the last section of "Jihad vs. McWorld," Barber recommends reading the Articles of Confederation. You can find them at a number of sites online. Read and discuss them with your class. What would a democracy based on the Articles of Confederation look like? How would our lives change as a result?

3. How are Ehrenreich's and Benhabib's analyses of the situation different from Huntington's, Barber's, and Brooks's? How does taking a feminist perspective change the questions we ask about a situation? How might a feminist perspective also change the solutions we develop to solve the problems caused by these clashes?

4. As you saw in Ursula Le Guin's "The Ones Who Walk Away from Omelas" in Chapter 3, fiction is often used as a means of working through social problems. Write a short story that addresses the clash of civilizations as you see it. What do you think is at the root of the clash? How would you dramatize that in your story?

▨ CONTINUING THE CASE STUDY ▨

Why Are Women at the Center of the Clash of Civilizations?

The status of women may seem peripheral or just coincidental to the cultural, religious, and political tensions that Samuel P. Huntington popularized as a "clash of civilizations." Yet, as writers like Barbara Ehrenreich remind us, the role of women is critical to both progressive and to fundamentalist or traditional cultures—indeed, it *defines* them in large part. In the one, the emphasis is on progressive freedoms and rights that bring women to the same plane as men. This may include access to higher education and career paths, voting privileges, choice of a marriage partner and equality in the partnership, use of contraception, and so on. In the latter, the stress is on reinstating traditional relationships and roles, in which women are the deferential helpmates, mothers, and nurturers, playing a complementary and stabilizing role for the culture. This may include more social control of how women act and dress, participate in public life, and experience their civil rights.

To test the idea that women's status is a key area wherein tensions between and within cultures are expressed, try the following activity. Divide your class into several small groups. Each group will be a *think tank,* a group organized to study and develop solutions for social problems. Each think tank is charged to analyze the notion that women are at the center of the clash of civilizations, to theorize why that might be, and to propose solutions to alleviate the cultural clashes and violence against women.

1. Begin by making a chart of clashes between progressive and traditional cultures just within the United States. For instance, how do the Promise Keepers and the National Organization of Women, or Focus on the Family and the National Council of Churches, define marriage and family, the role of religious belief in education and in government policy? (You can also use the readings in Chapter 6 on The Family as Community with the readings in this chapter and case study to provide some specific examples and voices.)

2. In your chart, make a note of whenever women, their bodies, and their roles in the family and in public society are mentioned as a concern. (For example, look at restrictions on clothing, sexuality, contraception, marriage relations, mothering, careers, etc.)

3. With your think tank group, theorize why women would be considered a group that needs to be controlled. Why would men (and other women) think it necessary to control the actions of women? What is potentially powerful or threatening about women?

   Next discuss this argument by Rosemary Radford Ruether, a professor of theology:

   > Women seem to have become the scapegoats for male fears of loss of control in society. In a world where anonymous global forces control and decide the economies of nations, control over women seems to become the place where men can imagine that they are reclaiming order against chaos, their dignity, honor, and security in a world where there is little available on the macro level. With life out of control for many men, rigid control of the women in their homes becomes the place where they can imagine that they are still in charge. (From "The War on Women," *Conscience*, Winter 2001/2002.)

   Do you agree with Ruether? Does this description seem to fit Islamic fundamentalists? What about American Christian fundamentalists?

4. Outline steps you would take to begin to address and alleviate the clashes between progressive and traditional civilizations. Where would you start? At the personal, local, state, or national level? How would your proposals help to alleviate the violence to women that is often a part of these cultural clashes? Each think tank should write a report that assesses the current situation within the United States (and/or between the United States and other countries), and proposes both short-term and long-term solutions.

CHAPTER 9

Citizens of the Earth: The Planetary Community

An ethic, ecologically, is a limitation on freedom of action in the struggle for existence. An ethic, philosophically, is a differentiation of social from anti-social conduct. These are two definitions of one thing. The thing has its origin in the tendency of interdependent individuals or groups to evolve modes of cooperation. The ecologist calls these symbioses. Politics and economics are advanced symbioses in which the original free-for-all competition has been replaced, in part, by cooperative mechanisms with an ethical content.

We abuse land because we regard it as a commodity belonging to us. When we see land as a community to which we belong, we may begin to use it with love and respect.

—*Aldo Leopold, from* A Sand County Almanac

■ GETTING STARTED ■ Taking Your Ecological Footprint

The creators of the Redefining Progress Web site ask, "Ever wondered how much 'nature' your lifestyle requires?" Take the Ecological Footprint Quiz to find out. You can find it at the site: http://www.earthday.net/footprint/index.asp.

1. Have each person in your class take the Ecological Footprint Quiz, which poses 15 multiple-choice questions about your eating habits, modes of transportation, and living conditions.

2. You will each end with a score that tells you how many "biologically productive acres" you use by your lifestyle. There are 4.5 biologically productive acres per person in the world; most residents of the United States use 24 each. The results also tell you that if everyone lived like you, we would need X-number of additional planet Earths to sustain your lifestyle.

3. Compare your results with your class members'. Whose results are best, and why? What are the deciding factors? You can try taking the quiz again, changing your eating habits or usual modes of transportation to see whether it improves your score.

In Chapter 1, we discussed citizenship as the quality of our membership in a community. What is the quality of our membership in the Earth community, home to billions of species? What would it mean to think of ourselves as "citizens" of the Earth?

When we imagine ourselves as citizens of the Earth, environmental concerns are probably our primary civic responsibility. We may see ourselves as stewards of the planet and feel a sense of personal responsibility for securing and maintaining its health. As Leopold's statement above argues, though, we need to see land, our planet, as a community to which we belong, rather than a commodity that belongs to us. Ethically we need to cooperate with the planet and view ourselves as interdependent members of its community rather than autonomous rulers of it. We also need to cooperate with one another and put ethical limits on our freedom to consume and waste resources. Environmental concerns transcend national boundaries, so we need to work in cooperation with other countries and individuals toward the health of the planet. So-called developing countries are often polluting their environment and rapidly draining resources in an attempt to attain the affluent lifestyle enjoyed by many people in the United States and Western Europe, while the people of the United States still use far more than our share of the world's natural resources.

The case study for this chapter asks you to imagine what kind of relationship you have with the planet. People have long debated about who cares most for the planet, with disagreements flaring between, for instance, hunters and vegetarians over humans' relationships to animals. Members of the Sierra Club and of the National Rifle Association generally view the other as an enemy and find little to agree on, but will find common ground in their concern to preserve the natural environment. While they agree on conservationist ends, however, they often remain in disagreement over *why* they believe in conservation, and over *how* they characterize their relationship with the planet. Whatever the case, when we imagine our interactions with nature as being in a relationship with it—whether we take the role of ruler, steward, student, devotee, partner, child, or some other position—we may notice more clearly the ways our personal choices affect the overall health, well-being, and longevity of the planet.

Regina Austin and Michael Schill
Activists of Color

Regina Austin is William A. Schnader Professor at the University of Pennsylvania Law School. Michael Schill is Dean and Professor of Law at UCLA. Both previously worked as attorneys and write about issues of law and justice in minority communities. This excerpt is taken from the chapter "Black, Brown, Red, and Poisoned" that Austin and Schill contributed to the book Unequal Protection: Environmental Justice and Communities of Color, *edited by Robert D. Bullard (Sierra Club Books, 1994).*

People of color throughout the United States are receiving more than their fair share of the poisonous fruits of industrial production. They live cheek by jowl with waste dumps, incinerators, landfills, smelters, factories, chemical plants, and oil refineries whose operations make them sick and kill them young. They are poisoned by the air they breathe, the water they drink, the fish they catch, the vegetables they grow, and, in the case of children, the very ground they play on. Even the residents of some of the most remote rural hamlets of the South and Southwest suffer from the ill effects of toxins. . . .[1]

The Path of Least Resistance

The disproportionate location of sources of toxic pollution in communities of color is the result of various development patterns. In some cases, the residential communities where people of color now live were originally the homes of whites who worked in the facilities that generate toxic emissions. The housing and the industry sprang up roughly simultaneously.[2] Whites vacated the housing (but not necessarily the jobs) for better shelter as their socioeconomic status improved, and poorer black and brown folks who enjoy much less residential mobility took their place. In other cases, housing for African Americans and Latino Americans was built in the vicinity of existing industrial operations because the land was cheap and the people were poor. For example, Richmond, California, was developed

---

[1]*Activist Pat Bryant uses the term "poisoning" in lieu of "pollution" to convey the idea that harm is being caused deliberately with the knowledge and aid of government officials. See Pat Bryant, "Toxics and Racial Justice,"* Social Policy 20 (Summer 1989): 48–52; Pat Bryant, "A Lily-White Achilles Heel," *Environmental Action 21 (January–February 1990): 28–29.*

[2]*See Community Environmental Health Center at Hunter College,* Hazardous Neighbors? Living Next Door ro Industry in Greenpoint-Williamsburg *(New York: Hunter College, Community Environmental Health Center, 1989). This study details the nature of the toxic risks posed by industrial concerns in a community composed primarily of Hasidic Jews and Puerto Ricans.*

downwind from a Chevron oil refinery when African Americans migrated to the area to work in shipyards during World War II.[3]

In yet a third pattern, sources of toxic pollution were placed in existing minority communities. The explanations for such sitings are numerous; some reflect the impact of racial and ethnic discrimination. The impact, of course, may be attenuated and less than obvious. The most neutral basis for a siting choice is probably the natural characteristics of the land, such as mineral content of the soil.[4] Low population density would appear to be a similar criterion. It has been argued, however, that in the South, a sparse concentration of inhabitants is correlated with poverty, which is in turn correlated with race. "It follows that criteria for siting hazardous waste facilities which include density of population will have the effect of targeting rural black communities that have high rates of poverty."[5]Likewise, the compatibility of pollution with preexisting uses might conceivably make some sites more suitable than others for polluting operations. Pollution tends to attract other sources of pollutants, particularly those associated with toxic disposal. For example, Chemical Waste Management, Incorporated (Chem Waste) has proposed the construction of a toxic waste incinerator outside of Kettleman City, California, a community composed largely of Latino farm workers.[6] Chem Waste also has proposed to build a hazardous waste incinerator in Emelle, a predominantly African American community located in the heart of Alabama's "black belt." The company already has hazardous waste landfills in Emelle and Kettleman City.

According to the company's spokeswoman, Chem Waste placed the landfill in Kettleman City "because of the area's geological features. Because the landfill handles toxic waste, . . . it is an ideal spot for the incinerator"; the tons of toxic ash that the incinerator will generate can be "contained and disposed of at the installation's landfill."[7] Residents of Kettleman City face a "triple whammy" of threats from pesticides in the fields, the nearby hazardous waste landfill, and a proposed hazardous waste incinerator. This case is not unique.

After reviewing the literature on hazardous waste incineration, one commentator has concluded that "[m]inority communities represent a 'least cost' option for waste incineration. . . because much of the waste to be incinerated is already in these communities."[8] Despite its apparent neutrality, then, siting based on

---

[3]*Citizens for a Better Environment*, Richmond at Risk: Community Development and Toxic Hazards from Industrial Polluters *(San Francisco: Citizens for a Better Environment, 1989), pp. 21–22.*

[4]*Conner Bailey and Charles Faupel, "Environmentalism and Civil Rights in Sumter County, Alabama," pp. 159, 170–171* in Proceedings of the Michigan Conference on Race and the Incidence of Environmental Hazards, *ed. Bunyan Bryant and Paul Mohai (Ann Arbor: University of Michigan, School of Natural Resources, 1990).*

[5]*Ibid., p. 171.*

[6]*Miles Corwin, "Unusual Allies Fight Waste Incinerator."* Los Angeles Times, *February 24, 1991, p. A3.*

[7]*Ibid., p. A36.*

[8]*Harvey White, "Hazardous Waste Incineration and Minority Communities: The Case of Alsen, Louisiana,"* in *Bryant and Mohai,* Race and the Incidence of Environment Hazards *pp. 142, 148–149.*

compatibility may be related to racial and ethnic discrimination, particularly if such discrimination influenced the siting of preexisting sources of pollution.

Polluters know that communities of low-income and working-class people with no more than a high school education are not as effective at marshalling opposition as communities of middle- or upper-income people. People of color in the United States have traditionally had less clout with which to check legislative and executive abuse or to challenge regulatory laxity. Private corporations, moreover, can have a powerful effect on the behavior of public officials. Poor minority people wind up the losers to them both.[9] People of color are more likely than whites to be economically impoverished, and economic vulnerability makes impoverished communities of color prime targets for "risky" technologies. Historically, these communities are more likely than others to tolerate pollution-generating commercial development in the hope that economic benefits will inure to the community in the form of jobs, increased taxes, and civic improvements.[10] Once the benefits start to flow, the community may be reluctant to forgo them even when they are accompanied by poisonous spills or emissions. This was said to be the case in Emelle, in Sumter County, Alabama, site of the nation's largest hazardous waste landfill.[11] Sumter County's population is roughly 70 percent African American, and 30 percent of its inhabitants fall below the poverty line. Although the landfill was apparently leaking, it was difficult to rally support against the plant among African American politicians because its operations contributed an estimated $15.9 million to the local economy in the form of wages, local purchases of goods and services, and per-ton landfill user fees.[12] Of course, benefits do not always materialize after the polluter begins operations. . . . In other cases, there is no net profit to distribute among the people. New jobs created by the poisonous enterprises are "filled by highly skilled labor from outside the community," while the increased tax revenues go not to "social services or other community development projects, but . . . toward expanding the infrastructure to better serve the industry."[13]

Once a polluter has begun operations, the victims' options are limited. Mobilizing a community against an existing polluter is more difficult than organizing opposition to a proposed toxic waste–producing activity. Resignation sets in, and the resources for attacking ongoing pollution are not as numerous, and the tactics not as potent, as those available during the proposal stage. Furthermore,

---

[9]See Conger Beasley, "Of Pollution and Poverty: Keeping Watch in 'Cancer Alley,'" Buzzworm (July–August 1990); 38, 41–42 (describing the Louisiana politics that produced the string of petrochemical plants lining what is known as Cancer Alley).

[10]Robert D. Bullard, "Environmental Blackmail in Minority Communities," in Bryant and Mohai, Race and the Incidence of Environmental Hazards, pp. 60, 64–65.

[11]See Robert D. Bullard, Dumping in Dixie: Race, Class, and Environmental Quality (Boulder, CO: Westview Press, 1990), pp. 69–73; Bailey and Faupel, "Environmentalism and Civil Rights in Sumter County," pp. 169–170, 172–173.

[12]Bailey and Faupe, "Environmentalism and Civil Rights in Sumter County," p. 163.

[13]Dana Alston, Taking Back Our Lives: A Report to the Panos Institute on Environment, Community Development, and Race in the United States (Washington, D.C.: The Panos Institute, 1990). p. 11.

though some individuals are able to escape toxic poisoning by moving out of the area, the flight of others will be blocked by limited incomes, housing discrimination, and restrictive land use regulations.[14]

Threat to Barrios, Ghettos, and Reservations

Pollution is no longer accepted as an unalterable consequence of living in the "bottom" (the least pleasant, poorest area minorities can occupy) by those on the bottom of the status hierarchy. Like anybody else, people of color are distressed by accidental toxic spills, explosions, and inexplicable patterns of miscarriages and cancers, and they are beginning to fight back, from Maine to Alaska.[15]

To be sure, people of color face some fairly high barriers to effective mobilization against toxic threats, such as limited time and money; lack of access to technical, medical, and legal expertise; relatively weak influence in political and media circles; and ideological conflicts that pit jobs against the environment.[16] Limited fluency in English and fear of immigration authorities will keep some of those affected, especially Latinos, quiescent. Yet despite the odds, poor minority people are responding to their poisoning with a grass-roots movement of their own.

Activist groups of color are waging grass-roots environmental campaigns all over the country. Although they are only informally connected, these campaigns reflect certain shared characteristics and goals. The activity of activists of color is indicative of a grass-roots movement that occupies a distinctive position relative to both the mainstream movement and the white grass-roots environmental movement. The environmental justice movement is antielitist and antiracist. It capitalizes on the social and cultural differences of people of color as it cautiously builds alliances with whites and persons of the middle class. It is both fiercely environmental *and* conscious of the need for economic development in economically disenfranchised communities. Most distinctive of all, this movement has been extremely outspoken in challenging the integrity and bona fides of mainstream establishment environmental organizations.

15   People of color have not been mobilized to join grass-roots environmental campaigns because of their general concern for the environment. Characterizing a problem as being "environmental" may carry weight in some circles, but it has much less impact among poor minority people. It is not that people of color are uninterested in the environment—a suggestion the grass-roots activists find insulting. In fact, they are more likely to be concerned about pollution than are people who are wealthier and white.[17] Rather, in the view of many people of color, environmentalism is

---

[14]*Robert D. Bullard and Beverly H. Wright, "Blacks and the Environment,"* Humboldt Journal of Social Relations 14 *(Summer 1987): 165, 180.*

[15]*Robert D. Bullard,* People of Color Environmental Groups Directory 1992 *(Riverside, CA: University of California, 1992). pp. i–iv.*

[16]*See generally Dorceta Taylor, "Blacks and the Environment: Toward an Explanation of the Concern and Action Gap between Blacks and Whites,"* Environment and Behavior 22 *(March 1989): 175.*

[17]*Susan Cutter, "Community Concern for Pollution: Social and Environmental Influences,"* Environment and Behavior 13 *(1981): 105–124.*

associated with the preservation of wildlife and wilderness, which simply is not more important than the survival of people and the communities in which they live; thus, the mainstream movement has its priorities skewed.

The mainstream movement, so the critique goes, embodies white, bourgeois values, values that are foreign to African Americans, Latino Americans, Asian Americans, and Native Americans. Environmental sociologist Dorceta Taylor has characterized the motivations of those who make donations to mainstream organizations as follows:

> [In part, the] motivation to contribute is derived from traditional Romantic and Transcendental ideals—the idea of helping to conserve or preserve land and nature for one's own present and future use, or for future generations. Such use involves the ability to get away from it all; to transcend earthly worries, to escape, to commune with nature. The possibility of having a transcendental experience is strongly linked to the desire to save the places where such experiences are likely to occur.[18]

Even the more engaged environmentalists, those whose involvement includes participation in demonstrations and boycotts, are thought to be imbued with romantic and transcendental notions that favor nature over society and the individual's experience of the natural realm over the collective experience.

There are a number of reasons why people of color might not share such feelings. Their prospects for transcendental communion with nature are restricted. Parks and recreational areas have been closed to them because of discrimination, inaccessibility, cost, their lack of specialized skills or equipment, and residence requirements for admission.[19] They must find their recreation close to home. Harm to the environment caused by industrial development is not really their responsibility because they have relatively little economic power or control over the exploitation of natural resources. Since rich white people messed it up, rich white people ought to clean it up. In any event, emphasis on the environment in the abstract diverts attention and resources from the pressing, concrete problems that people of color, especially those with little or no income, confront every day.

Nonetheless, communities of color have addressed environmental problems that directly threaten them on their own terms. The narrowness of the mainstream movement, which appears to be more interested in endangered nonhuman species and pristine, undeveloped land than at-risk humans, makes poor minority people *think* that their concerns are not "environmental." Cognizant of this misconception and eschewing terminology that artificially compartmentalizes people's troubles minority grass-roots environmental activists take a multidimensional approach to pollution problems. Thus, the sickening, poisonous odor emitted by landfills and sewage plants are considered matters of public health or government accountability, while workplace contamination is a labor issue, and lead-based paint in public housing projects is a landlord-tenant problem.[20] The very names of some of the organiza-

---

[18]Dorceta Taylor, *"Can the Environmental Movement Attract and Maintain the Support of Minorities?"* in Bryant and Mohai, Race and the Incidence of Environmental Hazards, *p. 35.*

[19]Taylor, *"Blacks and the Environment,"* pp. 187–190.

[20]Arnoldo Garcia, *"Environmental Inequities,"* Crossroads *(June 1990), p. 16 (interview with activist Richard Moore).*

tions and the goals they espouse belie the primacy of environmental concerns. The Southwest Organizing Project of Albuquerque (SWOP) has been very successful in mobilizing people around issues of water pollution and workplace contamination. For example, SWOP fought for the rollback of charges levied against a group of home owners who were forced to hook up with a municipal water system because nitroglycerine had contaminated private wells. SWOP then campaigned to make the federal government assume responsibility for the pollution, which was attributed to operations at a nearby military installation. Yet in a briefing paper titled "Major National Environmental Organizations and the Problem of the 'Environmental Movement,'" SWOP describes itself as follows:

> SWOP does not consider itself an "environmental" organization but rather a community-based organization which addresses toxics issues as part of a broader agenda of action to realize social, racial, and economic justice. We do not single out the environment as necessarily having a special place above all other issues; rather, we recognize that issues of toxic contamination fit within an agenda which can (and in our practical day-to-day work, does) include employment, education, housing, health care, and other issues of social, racial, and economic justice. . . .[21]

20   In the estimation of the grass-roots folks, . . . race and ethnicity surpass class as explanations for the undue toxic burden heaped on people of color. Activists see these environmental inequities as unfair and unjust—practices that many feel should be illegal. Of course, it is hard to prove that racial discrimination is responsible for siting choices and government inaction in the environmental area, particularly in a court of law. One need only point to the examples of *Bean v. Southwestern Waste Management* (Houston, Texas), *Bordeaux Action Committee v. Metropolitan Nashville* (Nashville, Tennessee), and *R.I.S.E. v. Kay* (King and Queen County, Virginia) to see the limited utility of current antidiscrimination doctrine in redressing the plight of poisoned communities of color.

Environmental activists of color draw a good deal of their inspiration from the modern civil rights movement of the 1960s. That movement was advanced by hard-won Supreme Court decisions. These organizers hope that a civil rights victory in the environmental area will validate their charges of environmental racism, help to flesh out the concept of environmental equity, serve as a catalyst for further activism, and, just possibly, force polluters to reconsider siting in poor minority communities.

Capitalizing on the Resources of Common Culture

For people of color, social and cultural differences such as language are not handicaps but the communal resources that facilitate mobilization around issues like toxic poisoning. As members of the same race, ethnicity, gender, and even age cadre, would-be participants share cultural traditions, modes, and mores that encourage cooperation and unity. People of color may be more responsive to organizing efforts than whites because they already have experience with collective action through community groups and institutions such

---

[21] Southwest Organizing Project, "Major National Environmental Organizations and the Problem of the 'Environmental Movement,'" (February 1990) (unpublished briefing paper).

as churches, parent-teacher associations, and town watches or informal social networks.[22] Shared criticisms of racism, a distrust of corporate power, and little expectation that government will be responsive to their complaints are common sentiments in communities of color and support the call to action around environmental concerns.

Grass-roots environmentalism is also fostered by notions that might be considered feminist or womanist. Acting on a realization that toxic poisoning is a threat to home and family, poor minority women have moved into the public realm to confront corporate and government officials whose modes of analysis reflect patriarchy, white supremacy, and class and scientific elitism. There are numerous examples of women of color whose strengths and talents have made them leaders of grass-roots environmental efforts.[23] The organization Mothers of East Los Angeles (MELA) illustrates the link between group culture and mobilization in the people of color grass-roots environmental movement.[24] Persistent efforts by MELA-defeated proposals for constructing a state prison and a toxic-waste incinerator in the group's mostly Latino American neighborhood in East Los Angeles.

25   Similarly, the Lumbee Indians of Robeson County, North Carolina, who attach spiritual significance to a river that would have been polluted by a hazardous waste facility proposed by the GSX Corporation, waged a campaign against the facility on the ground of cultural genocide. Throughout the campaign, "Native American dance, music, and regalia were used at every major public hearing. Local Lumbee churches provided convenient meeting locations for GSX planning sessions. Leaflet distribution at these churches reached significant minority populations in every pocket of the county's nearly 1,000 square miles."[25] Concerned Citizens of Choctaw defeated a plan to locate a hazardous waste facility on their lands in Philadelphia, Mississippi. The Good Road Coalition, a grass-roots Native American group based on the Rosebud Reservation in South Dakota, defeated plans by a Connecticut-based company to build a 6,000-acre garbage landfill on the Rosebud. Local residents initiated a recall election, defeating several tribal council leaders and the landfill proposal. The project, dubbed "dances with garbage," typifies the lengths that the Lakota people and other Native Americans will go to preserve their land—which is an essential part of their religion and culture.

---

[22]Bullard, Dumping in Dixie, pp. 95–98.

[23]See Jim McNeil, "Hazel Johnson: Talkin' Toxics," In These Times (May 23–June 5, 1990), p. 4 (interview with the founder of Chicago's Southeast Side's People for Community Recovery); Claude Engle, "Profiles: Environmental Action in Minority Communities," Environmental Action (January–February 1990), p. 22 (profiling Jessie Deerln Water, founder of Native Americans for a Clean Environment; Cora Tucker, founder of Citizens for a Better America; and Francesca Cavazos, director of the Maricopa County Organizing Project); Cynthia Hamikon, "Women, Home, and Community: The Struggle in an Urban Environment," Race, Poverty, and the Environment Newsletter (April 1990), p. 3.

[24]See Mary Pardo, "Mexican American Women Grassroots Community Activists: 'Mothers of East Los Angeles,'" Frontiers: A Journal of Women's Studies 11 (1990): 1; Dick Russell, "Environmental Racism," Amicus Journal 11 (Spring 1989): 22–23, 29–31.

[25]Richard Regan and M. Legerton, "Economic Slavery or Hazardous Wastes? Robeson County's Economic Menu," in Communities in Economic Crisis: Appalachia and the South, John Gaventa and Alex Willingham, eds. (Philadelphia: Temple University Press, 1990), pp. 146, 153–154.

Consider, finally, the Toxic Avengers of El Puente, a group of environmental organizers based in the Williamsburg section of Brooklyn, New York.[26] The name is taken from the title of a horror movie. The group attacks not only environmental racism but also adultism and adult superiority and privilege. The members, whose ages range from nine to twenty-eight, combine their activism with programs to educate themselves and others about the science of toxic hazards.

The importance of culture in the environmental justice movement seems not to have produced the kind of distrust and misgivings that might impede interaction with white working-class and middle-class groups engaged in grass-roots environmental activism. There are numerous examples of ethnic-based associations working in coalitions with one another, with majority group associations, and with organizations from the mainstream.[27] There are also localities in which the antagonism and suspicion that are the legacy of white racism have kept whites and African Americans from uniting against a common toxic enemy. The link between the minority groups and the majority groups seems grounded in material exchange, not ideological fellowship. The white groups attacking toxins at the grass-roots level have been useful sources of financial assistance and information about tactics and goals. . . .

People of color have provided the crucial leadership for the growing environmental justice movement in the United States. This movement, in all aspects of its operations, is antielitist, antiracist, class conscious, populist, and participatory. It attacks environmental problems as being intertwined with other pressing economic, social, and political ills. It capitalizes on the social and cultural strengths of people of color and demands in turn that their lifestyles, traditions, and values be respected by polluters and mainstream environmental organizations alike.

30   The environmental justice movement is still in its embryonic stages. Its ideology has yet to be fully developed, let alone tested. Moreover, it is too easy for outsiders to criticize the trade-offs and compromises poor people and people of color bearing toxic burdens have made. It is important to understand the movement on its own terms if one hopes to make policy proposals that will be of use to those struggling to save themselves. Grass-roots people have proven that they are capable of *leading, speaking,* and *doing* for themselves.

▓ QUESTIONS FOR INQUIRY AND ACTION ▓

1. Why is using the term "poisoning" rather than "polluting" powerful? Is it accurate? How conscious is our poisoning/polluting?

2. Austin and Schill observe, "In the view of many people of color, environmentalism is associated with the preservation of wildlife and wilderness, which simply is not more important than the survival of people and the communities in which they

---

[26]Marguerite Holloway. "*The Toxic Avengers Take Brooklyn,*" City Limits *(December 1989), p. 8*
[27]M. Oliviero, Minorities and the Environment: An Inquiry for Foundations *(report to the Nathan Cummings Foundation) (New York: Nathan Cummings Foundation, 1991). pp. 17–18, 21–24.*

live; thus, the mainstream movement has its priorities skewed." Based on the other readings in this chapter and your own experiences with environmentalism, would you agree? How could the different perspectives and priorities be brought into effective dialogue?

3. Explore Austin and Schill's argument that people of color "may be more responsive to organizing efforts than whites because they already have experience with collective action through community groups and institutions such as churches, parent-teacher associations, and town watches or informal social networks," and that they are in allegiance with feminist or womanist ideals. Write about your own experience with collective action, whether formal or informal. Was your experience similar to that described by Austin and Schill?

4. Where are the toxic waste dumps, the incinerators, the landfills, and the like, in your community? Go on a field trip to visit these sites, and observe the neighborhoods around them. Who lives there? What kinds of housing do they have? Where do the children play?

David W. Orr
Saving Future Generations
from Global Warming

David W. Orr is Professor and Chair of the Environmental Studies program at Oberlin College. He lectures frequently around the country on environmental issues and is the author of Earth in Mind: Essays on Education, Environment, and the Human Prospect *(1994) and* Ecological Literacy: Education and the Transition to a Postmodern World *(1992). "Saving Future Generations from Global Warming" was published in the* Chronicle of Higher Education *(April 21, 2000).*

We all live by robbing Asiatic coolies, and those of us who are "enlightened"
all maintain that those coolies ought to be set free; but our standard of living,
and hence our "enlightenment," demands that the robbery shall continue.
                                                                George Orwell

How many of us think about George Orwell when we hear about global warming? We've all seen the facts before. Nineteen ninety-eight was by far the warmest year ever recorded. Nineteen ninety-seven was the second-warmest. Mounting scientific evidence indicates that the combustion of fossil fuels, deforestation, and poor land-use practices will cause a major, and perhaps self-reinforcing, shift in global climate, given present trends. With climatic change will come severe weather extremes, super storms, droughts, famine, killer heat waves, rising sea levels, spreading disease, and accelerating rates of species loss—as well as bitter conflicts over declining supplies of fossil fuels, water, and food.

It is not far-fetched to think that human institutions, including democratic governments, will break down under such conditions. As the scientist Roger Revelle once noted, we are conducting a one-time experiment on the earth that cannot be reversed—and that never should have been run.

To see the situation more clearly, we need a perspective that transcends the minutiae of science, economics, and current politics. Future generations will bear the brunt of the effects of global warming. What will they think about the policy decisions we're making today? Will they applaud the precision of cost-benefit calculations that discount their prospects? Will they think us prudent for delaying action until even the most minute scientific doubts have been erased? Will they admire our stubborn devotion to inefficient vehicles, urban sprawl, and fossil-fuel consumption?

Hardly.

5   Think about an analogy. In the years leading up to the Civil War, defenders of slavery argued that: The advance of human culture and freedom depended on slavery; slaves were better off living in servitude than they otherwise would have been; freeing slaves would cause widespread economic and financial ruin; the issue of slavery was a matter of states' rights. Beneath all such arguments, of course, lay bedrock contempt for human equality, dignity, and freedom—as well as the perverse self-interest George Orwell so clearly described.

The parallels with arguments justifying our extravagant use of fossil fuels, if not exact, are nonetheless instructive. Our tacit position is: Civilization depends on the consumption of fossil fuels; a warmer world will be, on balance, a good thing; conserving energy and using solar energy are too expensive; the issue is a matter of the rights of individuals to drive the kinds of cars they want, live how they want, and the Devil take the hindmost.

Both the use of human beings as slaves and the use of fossil fuels inflate the wealth of some by robbing others. Both systems work only so long as someone or something is undervalued. Both require that some costs be ignored. Both warp the politics and culture of society. In the case of slavery, the effects were egregious, brutal, and immediate. But massive use of fossil fuels simply defers the costs, different but no less burdensome, onto our descendants. Moreover, slavery could be dismantled; future generations can have no reprieve from the consequences of our dereliction.

Of course, we do not intend to enslave subsequent generations, but the fact is that we are placing them in bondage to degraded climatic and ecological conditions. They will know that we failed to act on their behalf with alacrity, even after it became clear that our inaction would severely damage their prospects—and for reasons that will be regarded as no more substantial than those once used to support slavery.

At the same time, there is substantial evidence that taking steps to vastly improve energy efficiency and to make an expeditious transition to a solar-powered society would accrue to our advantage, saving upwards of $200-billion per year. It would also be the moral thing to do. History rarely offers such a clear convergence of ethics and self-interest.

10   In a letter to James Madison, written in 1789, Thomas Jefferson argued that no generation had the right to impose debt on its descendants, lest the dead rule the future. A similar principle applies to our use of fossil fuels. Drawn from Jefferson, Aldo Leopold, and others, such a principle might be stated thus:

No person, institution, or nation has the right to participate in activities that contribute to large-scale, irreversible changes of the earth's biogeochemical cycles or that undermine the integrity, stability, and beauty of its biotic systems; the consequences of such activities would fall on succeeding generations as an irreversible form of remote tyranny.

That principle is likely to fall on deaf ears in Congress and most corporate boardrooms, where short-term thinking predominates. To whom should we address it, then?

At the top of my list are those who educate the young. Education is most powerful when done by example. Accordingly, I propose that every school, college, and university stand up and be counted on the issue of climatic change, by beginning—now—to develop plans that would reduce the emission of heat-trapping gases, eliminating or finding ways to offset emissions by the year 2020. The alternative is to violate Jefferson's principle, and to enslave the future.

Opposition to such a proposal will, predictably, follow three lines. Some people will argue that we do not know enough yet to act. Presumably, those same people would not wait until they smelled smoke in the house at 2 A.M. to purchase fire insurance. A second group will object that educational institutions cannot afford to act. To be sure, change would require initial expenses—but it would also provide quick savings from reducing energy use. The real problem has less to do with costs than with the failure of imagination in places where imagination is reportedly much valued.

15   A third objection will come from those who agree with the overall goal of stabilizing climate, but who argue that our business is education, not social change. That argument is based on the belief that what occurs in educational institutions must be uncontaminated by contact with the affairs of the world. It further assumes that education occurs only in classrooms. Such views, however, make us accessories to an unfolding tragedy.

The steps necessary to abolish fossil fuels are straightforward, requiring campuses to:

- audit their current energy use;
- prepare detailed engineering plans to upgrade energy efficiency and eliminate waste;
- develop plans to harness renewable energy sources sufficient to meet campus energy needs by 2020; and
- carry out those plans over the next 20 years, through the combined efforts of students, faculty and staff members, administrators, energy engineers, and technical experts.

Through such campus and community involvement, we can educate a broad constituency about the consequences of our present course and the possibilities and opportunities for change. We can, in effect, begin to build a grassroots movement for the long-delayed transition to energy efficiency and solar power.

One day, we will come to understand that true prosperity neither permits nor requires bondage of any human being, in any form, for any reason, now or ever.

▣ QUESTIONS FOR INQUIRY AND ACTION ▣

1. Analyze and discuss Orr's use of the analogy of slavery and our use of fossil fuels. How does he set the analogy up? What makes it effective?

2. Alan Thein Durning, an environmentalist writer, explains the concept of a worldview: "Everyone operates from a worldview. It is a set of simplifying assumptions, an informal theory, a picture of how the world works. Worldviews are rarely brought out into the light of day. So people are not usually aware of them. They sit down deep in human consciousness somewhere, quietly shaping reactions to new ideas and information, guiding decisions, and ordering expectations for the future." What do you think Orr might say in response to Durning? Set up a discussion or debate in your classroom to explore your own worldviews and the analogies and metaphors you use to imagine and support those worldviews.

3. Winona La Duke, an activist and Ralph Nader's running mate on the Green Party ticket for the 1996 and 2000 presidential elections, advocates a "Seventh Generation Amendment" to the United States Constitution, which would require that government decisions take into consideration their effect seven generations into the future. Research and discuss the implications of this amendment.

4. Inquire into the ways your own educational institution can improve its energy efficiency. Join with other students to become educated on the subject and lobby your administrators for action on your campus.

WRITING STYLE

THE PROBLEM/SOLUTION ESSAY

David W. Orr's essay "Saving Future Generations From Global Warming" fits the classic model for what has often been called in composition courses the "problem/solution essay." You may have written such an essay previously and will almost certainly write one in some form while you're in college. In life outside of college, while you may not write many formal problem/solution essays, you will probably quite frequently work through the same problem-solving process outlined here.

- *Introduce the problem.* In Orr's case he needs first to establish that there is indeed a problem that needs to be solved, because the existence and urgency of global warming has been contested and not everyone is convinced that we need to be taking action. Orr persuades his audience by using an analogy to slavery, which we are now embarrassed about but once accepted in our society.

continued on next page

- *Present the consequences of not solving the problem.* Continuing the slavery analogy, Orr argues that we will enslave our children and subsequent generations, "placing them in bondage to degraded climatic and ecological conditions."

- *Introduce the solution.* Immediately after stating the consequences of not taking action, Orr introduces his solution in one brief, specific paragraph that begins, "At the same time, there is substantial evidence that taking steps to vastly improve energy efficiency . . . "

- *Aim your solution at your audience.* For your proposal to be effective, you need to communicate directly with the people who can implement your solution. For Orr this means educators, so he published his work in the *Chronicle of Higher Education,* and appealed to educators' pride in knowledge and wisdom (later generations "will know that we failed to act on their behalf with alacrity") and in ethics ("It would also be the moral thing to do").

- *Acknowledge counterarguments.* There will always be objections to or hesitations about a particular solution. To show that you are an aware and considerate arguer, you need to acknowledge the counterarguments, accommodate them when you can, and carefully refute them when you need to assert your own solution as the right one. Orr acknowledges three lines of opposition and contests them.

- *Present a clear plan of action to implement your solution.* So that your readers do not simply nod their heads in agreement but then put your solution away, you will need to provide specific steps they can follow to begin to implement your solution. Orr offers four, and presents them in a bullet-point list for clarity.

- *Engage with your audience in the conclusion.* Finally, as you conclude your essay, connect with your readers to reinforce the common ground you share on the issue. Orr appeals to educators' commitment to enlightenment and reminds them of their mutual abhorrence of slavery.

John Haines
Snow

John Haines is a poet and nature writer. He lived in Alaska for years, hunting, fishing, trapping, gardening, writing, and finally homesteading. His many collections of poems and essays include News from the Glacier: Selected Poems, 1960–1980 *(1982),* You and I and the World *(1988), and* Fables and Distances: New and Selected Essays *(1996). "Snow" was originally published in* The Stars, the Snow, the Fire: Twenty-five Years in the Alaska Wilderness *(1989). It has been anthologized in* In Short: A Collection of Brief Creative Nonfiction, *edited by Judith Kitchen and Mary Paumier Jones (New York: W. W. Norton & Company, 1996).*

To one who lives in the snow and watches it day by day, it is a book to be read. The pages turn as the wind blows; the characters shift and the images formed by their combinations change in meaning, but the language remains the same. It is a shadow language, spoken by things that have gone by and will come again. The same text has been written there for thousands of years, though I was not here, and will not be here in winters to come, to read it. These seemingly random ways, these paths, these beds, these footprints, these hard, round pellets in the snow; they all have meaning. Dark things may be written there, news of other lives, their stories and excursions, their terrors and deaths. The tiny feet of a shrew or a vole make a brief, erratic pattern across the snow, and here is a hole down which the animal goes. And now the track of an ermine comes this way, swift and searching, and he too goes down that white-shadow of a hole.

A wolverine, and the loping, toed-in track I followed uphill for two miles one spring morning, until it finally dropped away into another watershed and I gave up following it. I wanted to see where he would go and what he would do. But he just went on, certain of where he was going, and nothing came of it for me to see but that sure and steady track in the snowcrust, and the sunlight strong in my eyes.

Snow blows across the highway before me as I walk—little, wavering trails of it swept along like a people dispersed. The snow people—where are they going? Some great danger must pursue them. They hurry and fall, the wind gives them a push, they get up and go on again.

I was walking home from Redmond Creek one morning late in January. On a divide between two watersheds I came upon the scene of a battle between a moose and three wolves. The story was written plainly in the snow at my feet. The wolves had come in from the west, following an old trail from the Salcha River, and had found the moose feeding in an open stretch of the overgrown road I was walking.

The sign was fresh, it must have happened the night before. The snow was torn up, with chunks of frozen moss and broken sticks scattered about; here and there, swatches of moose hair. A confusion of tracks in the trampled snow—the splayed, stabbing feet of the moose, the big, furred pads and spread toenails of the wolves.

I walked on, watching the snow. The moose was large and alone, almost certainly a bull. In one place he backed himself into a low, brush-hung bank to protect his rear. The wolves moved away from him—those moose feet are dangerous. The moose turned, ran on for fifty yards, and the fight began again. It became a running, broken flight that went on for nearly half a mile in the changing, rutted terrain, the red morning light coming across the hills from the sun low in the south. A pattern shifting and uncertain; the wolves relenting, running out into the brush in a wide circle, and closing again; another patch of moose hair in the trodden snow.

I felt that I knew those wolves. I had seen their tracks several times before during that winter, and once they had taken a marten from one of my traps. I believed them to be a female and two nearly grown pups. If I was right, she may have been teaching them how to hunt, and all that turmoil in the snow may have been the serious play of things that must kill to live. But I saw no blood sign that morning, and the moose seemed to have gotten the better of the fight. At the end of it he plunged away into thick alder brush. I saw his tracks, moving more slowly now, as he climbed through a low saddle, going north in the shallow, unbroken snow. The three wolves trotted east toward Banner Creek.

What might have been silence, an unwritten page, an absence, spoke to me as clearly as if I had been there to see it. I have imagined a man who might live as the coldest scholar on earth, who followed each clue in the snow, writing a book as he went. It would be the history of snow, the book of winter. A thousand-year text to be ready by a people hunting these hills in a distant time. Who was here, and who has gone? What were their names? What did they kill and eat? Whom did they leave behind?

▓ QUESTIONS FOR INQUIRY AND ACTION ▓

1. Why does Haines call snow "a book to be read"? What does this particular metaphor reveal about his relationship to the snow and the wilderness?

2. Compare Haines's description of natural life with the other readings in this chapter. How do you think Haines would define being part of a planetary community?

3. Take a walk in nature, observe the life around you, and tell the story of something you see there. What kinds of traits do you find yourself reading into the animal or plant or natural phenomena that you observe?

4. Take your narrative from question #3, and add a reflective component to it. Reflect on the appropriateness of applying a human mental construct—that is, of creating a narrative—to nonhuman processes.

Bruce Stockler
Saved by Sequoias

Bruce Stockler is a media relations consultant and humorist who has worked as a joke writer for Jay Leno and writes a column, "Crazy Talk," for Esquire *magazine. He is the author of* I Sleep at Red Lights: A True Story of Life After Triplets *(2003). "Saved by Sequoias" appeared in* Hemispheres *magazine, the magazine of United Airlines, June 2005.*

Golden hills undulate to the horizon. Five hard hours out of Los Angeles, we edge north on California Highway 99 toward Sequoia National Park and the Giant Forest. My buddy Greg and I are fleeing the daily grind of our jobs as magazine editors—the whole airbrushed media world. We want to stand amid the sequoias, the tallest living things on earth, and rebalance our lives. We want to hike up above the tree line, look back down at the world, and feel we have learned a lesson. We need these trees. We are counting on these trees to save us. "Look at the landscape," Greg says. "Yes," I say. "The rolling, restaurantless hills." Despite the verdant panorama of California's Central Valley, I can think only about one thing: lunch. The Meal Not Yet Eaten. I am not a veteran camper. I am anxious about being so far away from food. Greg can't be bothered. He is blissfully driving his beloved, cherry-red Alfa Romeo Spider, Dustin Hoffman's car in *The Graduate* and a fitting symbol of our ill-preparedness to tackle the possibility of mountain lions and rockslides and hypothermia. Also, my new boots are too tight. I am most comfortable in my socks, climbing up and down from the couch.

I try to psyche myself up for the austere and spiritual experience ahead. I will hike 20 miles. I will gain 2,000 feet of elevation. I will commune with nature. Truths will be revealed. Bears will grok my aura.

After spending years in Los Angeles, I am shocked to discover that the state of California is largely uninhabited. Even before we reached Bakersfield, the landscape has become uncluttered by billboards, automobiles, and other examples of human vulgarity. It's unnerving when you first notice there are no more telephone poles and power lines—that you are truly off the grid. We rattle along for 30 minutes without seeing another car.

"You could jam another 50 million people in this state," I say.

5   "We're not even halfway through it," Greg adds.

We float through the gentle, alluvial plain of the San Joaquin Valley, headed for Sequoia and then Yosemite, the glittering jewels of the Sierra Nevadas.

By nightfall, we reach the southeast edge of Sequoia National Park and turn in to the town of Three Rivers to set up camp. Greg pampers the Alfa, and I wander into a general store, my fat cells gasping for some attention.

In my trance of pseudo-starvation, I buy two pounds of ground beef, loaves of Italian bread, diet soda, chips, pretzels, and nuts. Still shaking from the terror of being separated from food, I scarf down pretzels and breadsticks while I shop. The store clerk watches me with disgust.

We quickly put up the borrowed, idiot-proof tent without injury. It is nylon, with two telescoping plastic poles that cross in the middle. The only possible way the tent could be simpler to open would be if it came equipped with a tiny park ranger who popped out of the handle like Jiminy Cricket. During the ride, I imagined bad feelings and harsh words, even a possible fistfight, arising from our failure to erect the tent, so a delayed surge of machismo now courses through me. We did it! We are men, facing nature, testing ourselves. We are the heirs of Magellan and Cortés. We have teriyaki sauce for marinating.

We camp along the shore of the splendid Kaweah River, which gurgles and bubbles pleasingly as I grill our burgers over the campfire.

10   "Geez," Greg says, looking down at his paper plate.

I have cooked up monstrous, heaping, 1-pound burgers. The slices of Italian bread peel off both sides of the heaving meat zeppelins and fall impotently to the ground.

"I can't eat this," Greg says. "This isn't even food."

I eat ravenously, meat juice running down to my elbows. I eat as though I have hiked the 500 miles from Los Angeles, instead of sitting in a car, worrying about french fries.

It is 2 or 3 a.m. Greg and I toss and turn, basting in our polystyrene bags, bellies bloated from cow flesh, salted snack foods, and super-premium ice cream bars. We are camped on a hilly spot, and the air mattresses keep sliding downhill.

I jolt awake to hear rustling outside the tent. With adrenaline weed-whacking my nerves, I look through the tent gathers.

15 "What?" Greg says, groggy and disoriented.

"Shhh!" I hiss. "I hear someone!"

Greg lights the gas lamp, and we tiptoe outside, shocked by the cold and dark. The half-moon provides a slim sanction of light in the unfamiliar, primeval darkness.

The Sequoia and King's Canyon parks comprise 863,700 acres. This isn't like looking into the woods behind your house. This is like looking into your DNA to see why you evolved the ability to invent jet engines and liquid cheese product.

We stare into nature's black mouth, listening.

20 Nothing. Before us lie galaxies of impenetrable unknown. The stars are aloof and godless. And then, in the shallow foreground, an amorphous shape moves in and out of the shadows, as though the darkness itself is being rearranged.

"Nyuugh!" I shout.

Greg swings the lamp around, creating crazy, bewildering shapes. Finally the lantern light falls upon our stalker. It is a small animal, perched on a rock.

"I think it's an otter," Greg says.

The creature lifts its nose into the air, flaps an appendage in our general direction.

25 "A river otter?" I say. "I don't think so."

"Freshwater otter, sure," Greg says.

"It's a seal," I say.

The animal splashes back into the river with a backflip.

"No, no. Seals are much bigger," Greg says, his confidence growing.

30 "Well, otters look like . . . badgers," I bluff.

We launch into an absurd, sleep-addled argument over marine life, citing vaguely remembered episodes of *Flipper, Sea Hunt*, even the cheaply animated *Marine Boy.*

Our biological ignorance is matched only by our lack of outdoor survival skills. It is 33 degrees Fahrenheit in the Sierra night, and we are outside in T-shirts and cotton workout shorts. The thermals are in the trunk of the car.

The otter frolics around the campsite in the early morning, hunting for leftovers—a garbage otter. Greg and I feel years younger and deliriously energized as we pack up our gear and drive to the Lodgepole Visitor Center. We bask, finally, under the protective shade of the sequoias.

We have two day-hikes planned on the Giant Forest trails, escalating in difficulty until we do a two-night back-pack in the backcountry. As we check the trail maps, I see a warning posted about giardia lamblia, a pathogen that afflicts drinking water across the Sierras. Once ingested, giardia causes vomiting, fever, severe cramps, and diarrhea.

35   If I harbor any anxiety greater than being far away from food, it is suffering from stomach problems and unsanitary or makeshift bathroom utilities.

     The giardia parasite multiplies my anxiety into a gastrointestinal doomsday scenario. Worse, thoughts of the parasite kill my long-held fantasy about swimming in virgin mountain streams, in water hard and clear as ice-cold diamonds, water dripped from God's hand onto the cooling Genesis rock, water from which I would emerge, somehow, reborn.

     "Let's go," Greg snaps. "It's too cold to swim, anyway. Nobody swims in the High Sierras."

     Everywhere we look in the Giant Forest, we are stunned. The sequoias are sentinels, ancient witnesses, 15 to 20 stories tall, whose roots displace acres of earth. To stand beside them is humbling. I feel like I should bury my credit cards.

     Greg and I follow a trail to General Sherman, the largest sequoia in the world. We stare up at this supernatural behemoth, consuming the tree's unnerving reality in short gulps.

40   The National Park Service brochure cheerfully describes the tree's curriculum vitae. We can see it with our eyes, but, being cogs in the information-age machine, we need to review the paperwork. The General Sherman tree is 274.9 feet tall. It measures 102.6 feet in circumference at its base, around which a fence has been built to protect its roots. Containing 52,500 cubic feet of wood, the General Sherman tree has notably been dubbed the "World's Largest Living Thing."

     Giddy from lack of sleep, we begin to joke around.

     "She's not so big," I say.

     "I know," answers Greg. "I saw a bigger tree in New Jersey."

     "Hey," I say. "If this is the Giant Forest, how come I don't see any giants?"

45   We insult General Sherman for a few brainless minutes. But we have failed to notice, on the other side of the tree, a man, his wife, and three kids, a nice, all-American family.

     The man begins to mutter and complain. I zoom in on my brochure, nervously, my lizard brain sensing our mistake. The man stares at us, his agitation growing with the continued sacrilege of our presence.

     I am unsure what to do. To return to the visitor center would require us to walk around the tree past the family. The alternative would be to run away into the forest.

     Suddenly, the wind changes, and the man's voice rings out.

     "It says so right here!" the man is saying.

50   "Calm down," the man's wife says.

     "The biggest tree in the whole world!" reads the man.

     "Will you please," his wife says.

     "$%#"

     "Dad, let's go!" whines the middle child, a boy.

55 The man's neck and forehead veins are bulging. He is tall and thin, not obviously dangerous, but rangy, a dictionary illustration of potential energy.

"It's really a very nice tree," I say loudly, to Greg.

"The problem with General Sherman is, he's not specific enough," Greg says, elbowing me and laughing. I nod anxiously in the angry man's direction. Greg turns, slowly, and quickly grasps the situation.

"Wonderful tree!" Greg says.

We skulk. It seems smarter to retreat into the woods and hope for the best.

The angry man is walking toward us. I do not feel that roller-coaster sense of panic until I see the wife. The anxious look on her face—her fear, for us—terrifies me.

60 We begin to jog, pretending this is just a crazy joke, but knowing we could be crushed, beaten, gutted. He could take our shoes and car keys and make us walk home to Los Angeles.

"You!" the man says. "Hey, you!"

I am running now. I am running as I have not run since I was 10 years old. Greg is at my side, panting. We pound through the cool dark groves.

The sequoias project a powerful aura of sadness. They are strange, these trees, antiquated, lost in time. They are 3,000 years old, a fact I can barely comprehend.

Perhaps the sequoias have lived too long. Now, in their old age, they suffer the plagues of logging, suburbia, and the dim-witted gawking of overweight tourists like me.

65 Months will pass before I realize that here is where I finally found my sanctuary. For a few screaming heartbeats we ran like animals, living in the blinding, purifying glare of the moment. We threw ourselves into the maternal embrace of the sequoias, and the sequoias saved us, after all.

Fifteen minutes later, barking for air, we stopped and sucked long draughts of sweet, gummy oxygen. We listened for the angry man, but he had gone.

We rambled through the Giant Forest, lost, but greedily awake, pardoned from our scorching incompetence. And yet we smiled nervously as we imagined the poor family's exhausting trip back to Akron, or Kalamazoo, or Erie, or wherever it is that decent human beings do not wake at 5 in the morning, drive furiously for eight hours, and camp overnight, just to inexplicably poke fun at nature's wild and incomprehensible charity.

▨ QUESTIONS FOR INQUIRY AND ACTION ▨

1. What is the significance of Stockler's story about the family he and Greg encounter next to General Sherman, the giant sequoia tree?

2. Compare Stockler's description of Sequoia National Park with John Haines's description of snow in this chapter. How would you describe each writer's relationship with the natural world he's describing?

3. Travel essayists seek to convey a sense of *place* in their writing. Unlike academic anthropological or naturalist writing, though, travel writing does not usually aim to be scientific or dispassionate. Instead, readers expect that the essay will largely

be about the author's own personal experience of the place, culminating in a moment of revelation when he discovers he learned something from the place he visited. How does Stockler's essay fit these conventions? Perform an analysis of this essay as a piece of travel literature.

4. Write a travel essay of your own to share your own experience of leaving home for a new place. Select the most vivid images and anecdotes for your readers.

William Wordsworth
The World Is Too Much With Us

William Wordsworth (1770–1850) was an English poet of what is called the Romantic movement, as was John Clare, whose poem "The Badger" we include here. Wordsworth spent much of his childhood and young adulthood in nature, and as an adult settled in the Lake District of northern England. Although he is famous for celebrating the power of nature, his poetry reveals feelings of loss in the face of industrialization and materialistic society. The sonnet "The World Is Too Much With Us" was composed between 1802 and 1804 and first published in 1807.

The world is too much with us; late and soon,
Getting and spending, we lay waste our powers;
Little we see in Nature that is ours;
We have given our hearts away, a sordid boon!
5 This Sea that bares her bosom to the moon;
The winds that will be howling at all hours,
And are up-gathered now like sleeping flowers,
For this, for everything, we are out of tune;
It moves us not.—Great God! I'd rather be
10 A pagan suckled in a creed outworn;
So might I, standing on this pleasant lea,
Have glimpses that would make me less forlorn;
Have sight of Proteus rising from the sea;
Or hear old Triton blow his wreathèd horn.

▦ QUESTIONS FOR INQUIRY AND ACTION ▦

1. This poem is a sonnet. Read it with attention to the conventions of the sonnet, especially the "turn" in the sestet or final six lines. How is the sestet a response to the first eight lines, or two quatrains?

2. Look up pagan, Proteus, and Triton in a dictionary. What is Wordsworth suggesting by using these classical allusions in his poem about modern life?

3. Compare this poem with the selections in the case study for this chapter. How does "The World Is Too Much With Us" convey a sense of relationship with the planet?

4. Compose your own poem to respond to the current state of the world. How does the form of the poem discipline your writing and make your descriptions more focused and precise than they might be in an essay?

Muriel Rukeyser
St. Roach

Muriel Rukeyser (1913–1980) was a political activist and poet who often wrote about the ethical issues of inequalities in gender, class, and race. Her first book of poems, Theory of Flight, *was published in the prestigious Yale Younger Poets Series in 1935 and launched her career. She has had a deep influence on a generation of American poets that includes Adrienne Rich and Anne Sexton. "St. Roach" can be found in her collection* The Gates *(New York: McGraw-Hill, 1976).*

For that I never knew you, I only learned to dread you,
for that I never touched you, they told me you are filth,
they showed me by every action to despise your kind;
for that I saw my people making war on you,
5   I could not tell you apart, one from another,
for that in childhood I lived in places clear of you,
for that all the people I met you by
crushing you, stamping you to death, they poured boiling
    water on you, they flushed you down,
10   for that I could not tell one from another
only that you were dark, fast on your feet, and slender.
    Not like me.
For that I did not know your poems
And that I did not know any of your sayings
15   And that I cannot speak or read your language
And that I do not sing your songs
And that I do not teach our children
        to eat your food
        or know your poems
20   or sing your songs
But that we say you are filthing our food
But that we know you not at all.
Yesterday I looked at one of you for the first time.
You were lighter than the others in color, that was
25   neither good nor bad.

I was really looking for the first time.
You seemed troubled and witty.

Today I touched one of you for the first time.
You were startled, you ran, you fled away
30   Fast as a dancer, light, strange and lovely to the touch.
I reach, I touch, I begin to know you.

▧ QUESTIONS FOR INQUIRY AND ACTION ▧

1. Why do you think Rukeyser titles this poem "St. Roach"? What is the effect of anthropomorphizing, or giving human qualities to, the roach?

2. The context in which we read something affects the way we interpret it. How does finding this poem at the end of a chapter on the "planetary community" affect the way you read and understood it? What if you found this poem in an anthology of gay and lesbian writers?

3. Poetry allows us to re-see our world. Compose a poem in which you carefully observe and minutely describe a familiar creature or object, re-seeing and understanding it anew.

4. If you live in a region where cockroaches are common, take a moment to look at one more closely. In other areas, choose an insect or creature that is similarly considered ugly and disgusting or scary and observe it closely. What do you notice differently as a result of having read Rukeyser's poem?

John Clare
The Badger

▧ ▧

John Clare (1793–1864) was an English poet of the Romantic movement, born into a poor farming family in Northamptonshire. He is primarily regarded as a nature poet although he wrote on a number of different subjects including politics, poverty, and love. In his age he was called a "ploughman poet," because he wrote about agriculture, and his first collection of poetry, Poems Descriptive of Rural Life and Scenery, *was printed in 1820 by Taylor and Hessey, who also published the poetry of John Keats. This poem, "The Badger," describes the practice of badger baiting, which was a public spectacle and form of amusement in the early nineteenth century.*

When midnight comes a host of dogs and men
Go out and track the badger to his den,
And put a sack within the hole and lie
Till the old grunting badger passes by.
5   He comes and hears—they let the strongest loose.

The old fox hears the noise and drops the goose.
The poacher shoots and hurries from the cry,
And the old hare half wounded buzzes by.
They get a forkéd stick to bear him down
10   And clap the dogs and take him to the town,
And bait him all the day with many dogs,
And laugh and shout and fright the scampering hogs.
He runs along and bites at all he meets:
They shout and hollo down the noisy streets.

15   He turns about to face the loud uproar
And drives the rebels to their very door.
The frequent stone is hurled where'er they go;
When badgers fight, then everyone's a foe.
The dogs are clapped and urged to join the fray;
20   The badger turns and drives them all away.
Though scarcely half as big, demure and small,
He fights with dogs for hours and beats them all.
The heavy mastiff, savage in the fray,
Lies down and licks his feet and turns away.
25   The bulldog knows his match and waxes cold
The badger grins and never leaves his hold.
He drives the crowd and follows at their heels
And bites them through—the drunkard swears and reels.

The frighted women take the boys away,
30   The blackguard laughs and hurries on the fray.
He tries to reach the woods, an awkward race,
But sticks and cudgels quickly stop the chase.
He turns again and drives the noisy crowd
And beats the many dogs in noises loud.
35   He drives away and beats them every one,
And then they loose them all and set them on.
He falls as dead and kicked by boys and men,
Then starts and grins and drives the crowd again;
Till kicked and torn and beaten out he lies
40   And leaves his hold and cackles, groans and dies.

▓ QUESTIONS FOR INQUIRY AND ACTION ▓

1. Follow the narrative thread of the poem and carefully describe the step by step action of the badger baiting.

2. Read this poem with "St. Roach." What common views do you find between the authors?

3. Research the life and works of John Clare. What was his upbringing like? How did his life affect his writing? How is he represented by scholars of Romantic poetry?

4. A Web site devoted to badgers includes this poem. You can access it at http://www.badgers.org.uk/badgerpages/eurasian-badger-14.html. How does Clare's poem speak to the concerns of those who care about badgers today? Is poetry an effective form of argument?

STOP AND THINK

THE VALUE OF POETRY TO CIVIC DIALOGUES

French philosopher Victor Cousin said in 1818, "We must have religion for religion's sake, morality for morality's sake, as with art for art's sake . . . the beautiful cannot be the way to what is useful, or to what is good, or to what is holy; it leads only to itself." Cousin's point is that we should not look to the poems of Wordsworth, Rukeyser, or Clare for suggestions on how to improve our communities. Poetry, and artistic works generally, concern themselves with beauty, the art of crafting language for pleasurable and powerful effects. The poet's duty is not to write poetry for the moral improvement of readers.

A close reading of the poems in this chapter, however, suggests the poets were interested in the same questions that challenge politicians, theologians, and other civic leaders: who are we, how should we live, and how should we organize ourselves? Poems can promote inquiry and action in a variety of ways. Poems can

- *Frame issues.* In "The World Is Too Much With Us," Wordsworth argues that our consumer culture encourages us to waste our life energies pursuing material gains, which makes us see the world only as raw materials. He frames the issue as an expressed wish to return to ancient worldviews in which the natural and supernatural were intertwined.

- *Reorient our values and ideas.* In "St. Roach," Rukeyser records her changing attitude towards cockroaches. She takes the time to really look at the roach and goes from despising them to almost admiring their strangeness.

- *Help us discover ideas for ourselves.* Rukeyser's story gives us a model for how we might rethink our attitudes toward any number of subjects. By actually taking time to observe and experience those subjects, we might change the ideas we have inherited about them.

- *Engage our emotions.* In "The Badger," Clare never tells us how we ought to feel about badger baiting, but by encouraging us to imagine what the badger experiences, he makes us feel anger and shame. We can direct these feelings to any number of contemporary examples where we cause animals to suffer for our entertainment.

We encourage you to bring in other poems to see whether they can contribute to the civic dialogues occurring in your classroom. Sometimes poems can contribute even when they are most concerned with truth and beauty; they push us to reexamine our values and priorities. They encourage us to think less on what we should do about any particular issue and more on how we might experience just being alive. What does "being alive" mean to your life as a citizen?

CASE STUDY

Caretakers of the Earth
Comparing Visions of Ecological Responsibility

Rachel Carson
from *Silent Spring*

Rachel Carson (1907–1964) was a biologist and ecologist known today for being a founder of the modern environmental movement. She wrote pamphlets on conservation and natural resources as well as several books including a prize-winning biography of the ocean, The Sea Around Us *(1952). After she witnessed the heavy use of synthetic chemical pesticides in World War II, she wrote* Silent Spring *to warn the public about the dangers of these pesticides to human health and the environment. She also testified before Congress on these concerns. The excerpt below comes from chapters one and two, "A Fable for Tomorrow" and "The Obligation to Endure," from* Silent Spring *(Houghton Mifflin, 1962).*

A Fable for Tomorrow

There was once a town in the heart of America where all life seemed to live in harmony with its surroundings. The town lay in the midst of a checkerboard of prosperous farms, with fields of grain and hillsides of orchards where, in spring, white clouds of bloom drifted above the green fields. In autumn, oak and maple and birch set up a blaze of color that flamed and flickered across a backdrop of pines. Then foxes barked in the hills and deer silently crossed the fields, half hidden in the mists of the fall mornings.

Along the roads, laurel, viburnum and alder, great ferns and wildflowers delighted the traveler's eye through much of the year. Even in winter the roadsides were places of beauty, where countless birds came to feed on the berries and on the seed heads of the dried weeds rising above the snow. The countryside was, in fact, famous for the abundance and variety of its bird life, and when the flood of migrants was pouring through in spring and fall people traveled from great distances to observe them. Others came to fish the streams, which flowed clear and cold out of the hills and contained shady pools where trout lay. So it had been from the days many years ago when the first settlers raised their houses, sank their wells, and built their barns.

Then a strange blight crept over the area and everything began to change. Some evil spell had settled on the community: mysterious maladies swept the flocks of chickens; the cattle and sheep sickened and died. Everywhere was a shadow of death.

The farmers spoke of much illness among their families. In the town the doctors had become more and more puzzled by new kinds of sickness appearing among their patients. There had been several sudden and unexplained deaths, not only among adults but even among children, who would be stricken suddenly while at play and die within a few hours.

There was a strange stillness. The birds, for example—where had they gone? Many people spoke of them, puzzled and disturbed. The feeding stations in the backyards were deserted. The few birds seen anywhere were moribund; they trembled violently and could not fly. It was a spring without voices. On the mornings that had once throbbed with the dawn chorus of robins, catbirds, doves, jays, wrens, and scores of other bird voices there was now no sound; only silence lay over the fields and woods and marsh.

5   On the farms the hens brooded, but no chicks hatched. The farmers complained that they were unable to raise any pigs—the litters were small and the young survived only a few days. The apple trees were coming into bloom but no bees droned among the blossoms, so there was no pollination and there would be no fruit.

The roadsides, once so attractive, were now lined with browned and withered vegetation as though swept by fire. These, too, were silent, deserted by all living things. Even the streams were now lifeless. Anglers no longer visited them, for all the fish had died.

In the gutters under the eaves and between the shingles of the roofs, a white granular powder still showed a few patches; some weeks before it had fallen like snow upon the roofs and the lawns, the fields and streams.

No witchcraft, no enemy action had silenced the rebirth of new life in this stricken world. The people had done it themselves.

This town does not actually exist, but it might easily have a thousand counterparts in America or elsewhere in the world. I know of no community that has experienced all the misfortunes I describe. Yet every one of these disasters has actually happened somewhere, and many real communities have already suffered a substantial number of them. A grim specter has crept upon us almost unnoticed, and this imagined tragedy may easily become a stark reality we all shall know.

10   What has already silenced the voices of spring in countless towns in America? This book is an attempt to explain.

The Obligation to Endure

The history of life on earth has been a history of interaction between living things and their surroundings. To a large extent, the physical form and the habits of the earth's vegetation and its animal life have been molded by the environment. Considering the whole span of earthly time, the opposite effect, in which life actually modifies its surroundings, has been relatively slight. Only within the moment of time represented by the present century has one species—man—acquired significant power to alter the nature of his world.

During the past quarter century this power has not only increased to one of disturbing magnitude but it has changed in character. The most alarming of all man's assaults upon the environment is the contamination of air, earth, rivers, and sea with dangerous and even lethal materials. This pollution is for the most part irrecoverable;

the chain of evil it initiates not only in the world that must support life but in living tissues is for the most part irreversible. In this now universal contamination of the environment, chemicals are the sinister and little-recognized partners of radiation in changing the very nature of the world—the very nature of its life. Strontium 90, released through nuclear explosions into the air, comes to earth in rain or drifts down as fallout, lodges in soil, enters into the grass or corn or wheat grown there, and in time takes up its abode in the bones of a human being, there to remain until his death. Similarly, chemicals sprayed on croplands or forests or gardens lie long in soil, entering into living organisms, passing from one to another in a chain of poisoning and death. Or they pass mysteriously by underground streams until they emerge and, through the alchemy of air and sunlight, combine into new forms that kill vegetation, sicken cattle, and work unknown harm on those who drink from once pure wells. As Albert Schweitzer has said, "Man can hardly even recognize the devils of his own creation."

It took hundreds of millions of years to produce the life that now inhabits the earth—eons of time in which that developing and evolving and diversifying life reached a state of adjustment and balance with its surroundings. The environment, rigorously shaping and directing the life it supported, contained elements that were hostile as well as supporting. Certain rocks gave out dangerous radiation; even within the light of the sun, from which all life draws its energy, there were short-wave radiations with power to injure. Given time—time not in years but in millennia—life adjusts, and a balance has been reached. For time is the essential ingredient; but in the modern world there is not time.

The rapidity of change and the speed with which new situations are created follow the impetuous and heedless pace of man rather than the deliberate pace of nature. Radiation is no longer merely the background radiation of rocks, the bombardment of cosmic rays, the ultraviolet of the sun that have existed before there was any life on earth; radiation is now the unnatural creation of man's tampering with the atom. The chemicals to which life is asked to make its adjustment are no longer merely the calcium and silica and copper and all the rest of the minerals washed out of the rocks and carried in rivers to the sea; they are the synthetic creations of man's inventive mind, brewed in his laboratories, and having no counterparts in nature.

15   To adjust to these chemical would require time on the scale that is nature's; it would require not merely the years of a man's life but the life of generations. And even this, were it by some miracle possible, would be futile, for the new chemicals come from our laboratories in an endless stream; almost five hundred annually find their way into actual use in the United States alone. The figure is staggering and its implications are not easily grasped—500 new chemicals to which the bodies of men and animals are required somehow to adapt each year, chemicals totally outside the limits of biologic experience.

Among them are many that are used in man's war against nature. Since the mid-1940's over 200 basic chemicals have been created for use in killing insects, weeds, rodents, and other organisms described in the modern vernacular as "pests"; and they are sold under several thousand different brand names.

These sprays, dusts, and aerosols are now applied almost universally to farms, gardens, forests, and homes—nonselective chemicals that have the power to kill every insect, the "good" and the "bad," to still the song of birds and the leaping of fish in the streams, to coat the leaves with a deadly film, and to linger on in soil—all this though the intended target may be only a few weeds or insects. Can anyone believe it is possible to lay down such a barrage of poisons on the surface of the earth without making it unfit for all life? They should not be called "insecticides," but "biocides."

The whole process of spraying seems caught up in an endless spiral. Since DDT was released for civilian use, a process of escalation has been going on in which ever more toxic materials must be found. This has happened because insects, in a triumphant vindication of Darwin's principle of the survival of the fittest, have evolved super races immune to the particular insecticide used, hence a deadlier one has always to be developed—and then a deadlier one than that. It has happened also because, for reasons to be described later, destructive insects often undergo a "flareback," or resurgence, after spraying, in numbers greater than before. Thus the chemical war is never won, and all life is caught in its violent crossfire.

Along with the possibility of the extinction of mankind by nuclear war, the central problem of our age has therefore become the contamination of man's total environment with such substances of incredible potential for harm—substances that accumulate in the tissues of plants and animals and even penetrate the germ cells to shatter or alter the very material of heredity upon which the shape of the future depends.

20   Some would-be architects of our future look toward a time when it will be possible to alter the human germ plasm by design. But we may easily be doing so now by inadvertence, for many chemicals, like radiation, bring about gene mutations. It is ironic to think that man might determine his own future by something so seemingly trivial as the choice of an insect spray.

All this has been risked—for what? Future historians may well be amazed by our distorted sense of proportion. How could intelligent beings seek to control a few unwanted species by a method that contaminated the entire environment and brought the threat of disease and death even to their own kind? Yet this is precisely what we have done. We have done it, moreover, for reasons that collapse the moment we examine them. We are told that the enormous and expanding use of pesticides is necessary to maintain farm production. Yet is our real problem not one of *overproduction?* Our farms, despite measures to remove acreages from production and to pay farmers *not* to produce, have yielded such a staggering excess of crops that the American taxpayer in 1962 is paying out more than one billion dollars a year as the total carrying cost of the surplus-food storage program. And is the situation helped when one branch of the Agriculture Department tries to reduce production while another states, as it did in 1958, "It is believed generally that reduction of crop acreages under provisions of the Soil Bank will stimulate interest in use of chemicals to obtain maximum production on the land retained in crops."

All this is not to say there is no insect problem and no need of control. I am saying, rather, that control must be geared to realities, not to mythical situations and that the methods employed must be such that they do not destroy us along with the insects.

The problem whose attempted solution has brought such a train of disaster in its wake is an accompaniment of our modern way of life. Long before the age of man, insects inhabited the earth—a group of extraordinarily varied and adaptable beings. Over the course of time since man's advent, a small percentage of the more than half a million species of insects have come into conflict with human welfare in two principal ways: as competitors for the food supply and as carriers of human disease.

Disease-carrying insects become important where human beings are crowded together, especially under conditions where sanitation is poor, as in time of natural disaster or war or in situations of extreme poverty and deprivation. Then control of some sort becomes necessary. It is a sobering fact, however, as we shall presently see, that the method of massive chemical control has had only limited success, and also threatens to worsen the very conditions it is intended to curb.

25   Under primitive agricultural conditions the farmer had few insect problems. These arose with the intensification of agriculture—the devotion of immense acreages to a single crop. Such a system set the stage for explosive increases in specific insect populations. Single-crop farming does not take advantage of the principles by which nature works; it is agriculture as an engineer might conceive it to be. Nature has introduced great variety into the landscape, but man has displayed a passion for simplifying it. Thus he undoes the built-in checks and balances by which nature holds the species within bounds. One important natural check is a limit on the amount of suitable habitat for each species. Obviously then, an insect that lives on wheat can build up its population to much higher levels on a farm devoted to wheat than on one in which wheat is intermingled with other crops to which the insect is not adapted.

The same thing happens in other situations. A generation or more ago, the towns of large areas of the United States lined their streets with the noble elm tree. Now the beauty they hopefully created is threatened with complete destruction as disease sweeps through the elms, carried by a beetle that would have only limited chance to build up large populations and to spread from tree to tree if the elms were only occasional trees in a richly diversified planting.

Another factor in the modern insect problem is one that must be viewed against a background of geologic and human history: the spreading of thousands of different kinds of organisms from their native homes to invade new territories. This worldwide migration has been studied and graphically described by the British ecologist Charles Elton in his recent book *The Ecology of Invasions*. During the Cretaceous Period, some hundred million years ago, flooding seas cut many land bridges between continents and living things found themselves confined in what Elton calls "colossal separate nature reserves." There, isolated from others of their kind, they developed many new species. When some of the land masses were joined again, about 15 million years ago, these species began to move out into new territories—a movement that is not only still in progress but is now receiving considerable assistance from man.

The importation of plants is the primary agent in the modern spread of species, for animals have almost invariably gone along with the plants, quarantine being a comparatively recent and not completely effective innovation. The United States Office of Plant Introduction alone has introduced almost 200,000 species and varieties of plants from all over the world. Nearly half of the 180 or so major insect enemies of plants in the United States are accidental imports from abroad, and most of them have come as hitchhikers on plants.

In new territory, out of reach of the restraining hand of the natural enemies that kept down its numbers in its native land, an invading plant or animal is able to become enormously abundant. Thus it is no accident that our most troublesome insects are introduced species.

30   These invasions, both the naturally occurring and those dependent on human assistance, are likely to continue indefinitely. Quarantine and massive chemical campaigns are only extremely expensive ways of buying time. We are faced, according to Dr. Elton, "with a life-and-death need not just to find new technological means of suppressing this plant or that animal"; instead we need the basic knowledge of animal populations and their relations to their surroundings that will "promote an even balance and damp down the explosive power of outbreaks and new invasions."

Much of the necessary knowledge is now available but we do not use it. We train ecologists in our universities and even employ them in our governmental agencies but we seldom take their advice. We allow the chemical death rain to fall as though there were no alternative, whereas in fact there are many, and our ingenuity could soon discover many more if given opportunity.

Have we fallen into a mesmerized state that makes us accept as inevitable that which is inferior or detrimental, as though having lost the will or the vision to demand that which is good? Such thinking, in the words of the ecologist Paul Shepard, "idealizes life with only its head out of water, inches above the limits of toleration of the corruption of its own environment . . . Why should we tolerate a diet of weak poisons, a home in insipid surroundings, a circle of acquaintances who are not quite our enemies, the noise of motors with just enough relief to prevent insanity? Who would want to live in a world which is just not quite fatal?"

Yet such a world is pressed upon us. The crusade to create a chemically sterile, insect-free world seems to have engendered a fanatic zeal on the part of many specialists and most of the so-called control agencies. On every hand there is evidence that those engaged in spraying operations exercise a ruthless power. "The regulatory entomologists . . . function as prosecutor, judge and jury, tax assessor and collector and sheriff to enforce their own orders," said Connecticut entomologist Neely Turner. The most flagrant abuses go unchecked in both state and federal agencies.

It is not my contention that chemical insecticides must never be used. I do contend that we have put poisonous and biologically potent chemicals indiscriminately into the hands of persons largely or wholly ignorant of their potentials for harm. We have subjected enormous numbers of people to contact with these poisons, without their consent and often without their knowledge. If the Bill of Rights contains no guarantee that a citizen shall be secure against lethal poisons distributed either by private individuals or by public officials, it is surely only because our forefathers, despite their considerable wisdom and foresight, could conceive of no such problem.

35   I contend, furthermore, that we have allowed these chemicals to be used with little or no advance investigation of their effect on soil, water, wildlife, and man himself. Future generations are unlikely to condone our lack of prudent concern for the integrity of the natural world that supports all life.

There is still very limited awareness of the nature of the threat. This is an era of specialists, each of whom sees his own problem and is unaware of or intolerant of the larger frame into which it fits. It is also an era dominated by industry, in which the right to make a dollar at whatever cost is seldom challenged. When the public protests, confronted with some obvious evidence of damaging results of pesticide applications, it is fed little tranquilizing pills of half truth. We urgently need an end to these false assurances, to the sugar coating of unpalatable facts. It is the public that is being asked to assume the risks that the insect controllers calculate. The public must decide whether it wishes to continue on the present road, and it can do so only when in full possession of the facts. In the words of Jean Rostand, "The obligation to endure gives us the right to know."

STOPANDTHINK

HOW DO YOU SEE NATURE?

We always see nature in relation to ourselves. In other words, the way we view nature always implies a relationship to it. At various times we may see it as a powerful, even divine force to which we must submit; as a commodity available to us to use for our own purposes; or as a vulnerable resource that needs our stewardship and protection.

Philip James de Loutherbourg's sublime painting *An Avalanche in the Alps* (1803) conveys the feeling of being overwhelmed by and tiny in the face of the magnificence and power of nature. The natural world is imbued with supernatural elements and the humans are insignificant in the grand scheme.

Used with permission from The Biltmore Company, Asheville, North Carolina.

We also tame nature into pleasing sights—picturesque scenes—for ourselves in the form of gardens and parks. The formal Italian Garden at Biltmore Estate, designed by the landscape architect Frederick Law Olmsted (who also designed Central Park in New York City), is carefully cultivated and composed; it is enclosed by a stone wall and hemlock hedge and was intended to look like an "outdoor room."

This photograph depicts nature as a personal playground. The snowboarder conveys the ecstasy and feeling of freedom that being in nature provides while he defies the natural laws of gravity and flies above the treetops.

This photo of the Earth was taken July 17, 1969, by the crew of Apollo 11. Seeing the Earth from the Moon—where it appeared vulnerable, a lonely planet floating in the darkness of space—changed many people's perceptions of and relationship to the planet, and helped foster the founding of Earth Day in 1970. Almost three decades later, with similar goals in mind, Al Gore proposed to put a static satellite in space to send us constantly updated pictures of the planet to remind us how fragile we are and to help us transcend cultural and national differences.

Richard Louv
Don't Know Much about Natural History: Education as a Barrier to Nature

Richard Louv is a visiting scholar at the Heller School for Social Policy and Management at Brandeis University. He has been a columnist and member of the advisory board for Parents *magazine, and is the author of several books, including* 101 Things You Can Do for Our Children's Future *(1993) and* The Web of Life: Weaving the Values that Sustain Us *(1996). "Don't Know Much about Natural History: Education as a Barrier to Nature" is a chapter from his latest book,* Last Child in the Woods: Saving Our Children from Nature-Deficit Disorder *(Algonquin Books, 2005).*

To a person uninstructed in natural history, his country or sea-side stroll is a walk through a gallery filled with wonderful works of art, nine-tenths of which have their faces turned to the wall.

—Thomas Huxley

David Sobel tells this story: A century ago, a boy ran along a beach with his gun, handmade from a piece of lead pipe. From time to time, he would stop, aim, and shoot at a gull. Today, such activity would be cause for time spent in juvenile hall, but for young John Muir, it was just another way to connect with nature. (Muir, it should be noted, was a bad shot, and apparently never killed a seagull.) Muir went on to become one of the initiators of modern environmentalism.

"Whenever I read Muir's description of shooting at seagulls to my students, they're shocked. They can't believe it," says Sobel, co-director of the Center for Place-based Education at Antioch New England Graduate School. He uses this example to illustrate just how much the interaction between children and nature has changed. Practitioners in the new fields of conservation psychology (focused on how people become environmentalists) and ecopsychology (the study of how ecology interacts with the human psyche) note that, as Americans become increasingly urbanized, their attitudes toward animals change in paradoxical ways.

To urbanized people, the source of food and the reality of nature are becoming more abstract. At the same time, urban folks are more likely to feel protective toward animals—or to fear them. The good news is that children today are less likely to kill animals for fun; the bad news is that children are so disconnected from nature that they either idealize it or associate it with fear—two sides of the same coin, since we tend to fear or romanticize what we don't know. Sobel, one of the most important thinkers in the realm of education and nature, views "ecophobia" as one of the sources of the problem.

Explaining Ecophobia

Ecophobia is fear of ecological deterioration, by Sobel's definition. In its older, more poetic meaning, the word ecophobia is the fear of home. Both definitions are accurate.

5   "Just as ethnobotanists are descending on tropical forests in search of new plants for medical uses, environmental educators, parents, and teachers are descending on second- and third-graders to teach them about the rainforests," Sobel writes in his volume, *Beyond Ecophobia: Reclaiming the Heart in Nature Education*. "From Brattleboro, Vermont, to Berkeley, California, schoolchildren . . . watch videos about the plight of indigenous forest people displaced by logging and exploration for oil. They learn that between the end of morning recess and the beginning of lunch, more than ten thousand acres of rainforest will be cut down, making way for fast-food, 'hamburgerable' cattle."

In theory, these children "will learn that by recycling their *Weekly Readers* and milk cartons, they can help save the planet," and they'll grow up to be responsible stewards of the earth, "voting for environmental candidates, and buying energy-efficient cars." Or maybe not. The opposite may be occurring, says Sobel. "If we fill our classrooms with examples of environmental abuse, we may be engendering a subtle form of dissociation. In our zest for making them aware of and responsible for the world's problems, we cut our children off from their roots." Lacking direct experience with nature, children begin to associate it with fear and apocalypse, not joy and wonder. He offers this analogy of disassociation: In response to physical and sexual abuse, children learn to cut themselves off from pain. Emotionally, they turn off. "My fear is that our environmentally correct curriculum similarly ends up distancing children from, rather than connecting them with, the natural world. The natural world is being abused and they just don't want to have to deal with it."

To some environmentalists and educators, this is contrarian thinking—even blasphemy. To others, the ecophobia thesis rings true. Children learn about the rain forest, but usually not about their own region's forests, or, as Sobel puts it, "even just the meadow outside the classroom door." He points out that "It is hard enough for children to understand the life cycles of chipmunks and milkweed, organisms they can study close at hand. This is the foundation upon which an eventual understanding of ocelots and orchids can be built."

By one measure, rain-forest curriculum is developmentally appropriate in middle or high school, but not in the primary grades. Some educators won't go that far, but they do agree with Sobel's basic premise that environmental education is out of balance. This issue is at the crux of the curriculum wars, particularly in the area of science. One teacher told me, "The science frameworks bandied about by state and local education boards have swung back and forth between the hands-on experiential approach and factoid learning from textbooks."

If educators are to help heal the broken bond between the young and the natural world, they and the rest of us must confront the unintended educational consequences of an overly abstract science education: ecophobia and the death of natural history studies. Equally important, the wave of test-based education reform that became dominant in the late 1990s leaves little room for hands-on experience in nature. Although some pioneering educators are sailing against the wind, participating in an international effort to stimulate the growth of nature education in and outside classrooms (which will be described in later chapters), many educational institutions and current educational trends are, in fact, part of the problem.

Silicon Faith

10 John Rick, who was quoted earlier in these pages about his community's restrictions on natural play, is a dedicated educator who left engineering to teach eighth-grade math. Rick is dismayed that nature has disappeared from the classroom, except for discussions of environmental catastrophe.

I asked Rick to describe an imaginary classroom saturated with the natural sciences and hands-on nature learning. "I keep coming back to a class devoid of nature," he answered. "Unfortunately, a class devoid of nature looks just like any classroom you would walk into today. We have industrialized the classroom to the extent that there is no room for nature in the curriculum." Curriculum standards adopted in the name of school reform restrict many districts to the basics of reading, writing, and mathematics. These are vital subjects, of course, but in Rick's opinion—and I share it—education reform has moved too far from what used to be called a well-rounded education. Rick elaborated:

> The society we are molding these kids toward is one that values consumer viability. The works of John Muir, Rachel Carson, or Aldo Leopold are seldom if ever taught to children in the public schools. Even in the sciences, where nature could play such an important role, the students study nature in a dry, mechanized way. How does the bat sonar work, how does a tree grow, how do soil amenities help crops grow? Kids see nature as a lab experiment.
>
> The alternative? I imagine a classroom that turns outward, both figuratively and literally. The grounds would become a classroom, buildings would look outward, and gardens would cover the campus. The works of naturalists would be the vehicle by which we would teach reading and writing. Math and science would be taught as a way to understand the intricacies of nature, the potential to meet human needs, and how all things are interlaced. A well-rounded education would mean learning the basics, to become part of a society that cherished nature while at the same time contributing to the well-being of mankind. Progress does not have to be patented to be worthwhile. Progress can also be measured by our interactions with nature and its preservation. Can we teach children to look at a flower and see all the things it represents: beauty, the health of an ecosystem, and the potential for healing?

Public education is enamored, even mesmerized, by what might be called silicon faith: a myopic focus on high technology as salvation. In 2001, the Alliance for Childhood, a nonprofit organization in College Park, Maryland, released "Fool's Gold: A Critical Look at Computers in Childhood," a report supported by more than eighty-five experts in neurology, psychiatry, and education, including Diane Ravitch, former U.S. assistant secretary of education; Marilyn Benoit, president-elect of the American Academy of Child and Adolescent Psychiatry; and primate researcher Jane Goodall. "Fool's Gold" charged that thirty years of research on educational technology had produced just one clear link between computers and children's learning. (On some standardized tests, "drill-and-practice programs appear to improve scores modestly—though not as much or as cheaply as one-on-one tutoring.") The co-signers of the "Fool's Gold" report went so far as to call for a moratorium on computer use in early childhood education, until the U.S. surgeon general can ascertain whether computers are hazardous to the health of young children. The public response was surprising. After "Fool's Gold" was released, MSNBC conducted an online poll of subscribers, asking if they supported such a moratorium. Of three thousand people who answered, 51 percent agreed. And these were Internet users.

15   The problem with computers isn't computers—they're just tools; the problem is that overdependence on them displaces other sources of education, from the arts to nature. As we pour money and attention into educational electronics, we allow less fashionable but more effective tools to atrophy. Here's one example: We know for a fact that the arts stimulate learning. A 1995 analysis by the College Board showed that students who studied the arts for more than four years scored forty-four points higher on the math portion and fifty-nine points higher on the verbal section of the SAT. Nonetheless, over the past decade, one-third of the nation's public-school music programs were dropped. During the same period, annual spending on school technology tripled, to $6.2 billion. Between early 1999 and September 2001, educational technology attracted nearly $1 billion in venture capital, according to Merrill Lynch and Company. One software company now targets babies as young as one day old. Meanwhile, many public school districts continue to shortchange the arts, and even more districts fail to offer anything approaching true hands-on experience with nature outside the classroom.

In some school districts, the arts are making a tentative comeback. The same cannot be said of hands-on nature education—yet. In recent years, farsighted educators and environmental organizations have made important inroads into the classroom and the public consciousness of the young, especially at the primary and secondary levels. Experiential, environment-based, or place-based education offers a promising alternative. Proponents of the arts revival in schools have successfully argued that the arts stimulate learning in math and science. Based on early research, a similar argument could now be made that nature education stimulates cognitive learning and reduces attention deficits.

Nonetheless, the school district in my own county—the sixth-largest district in America—illustrates the lack of synchronicity. San Diego County, larger in size and population than some states, is an ecological and sociological microcosm of America. It is, in fact, a place with more endangered and threatened species than any other county in the continental United States. The United Nations declared it one of the Earth's twenty-five "hot spots" of biodiversity. Yet, as of this writing, not one of the forty-three school districts within this county offers a single elective course in local flora and fauna. A few volunteers, including docents from the local Natural History Museum, do what they can. Across the nation, such neglect is the norm.

The Death of Natural History

Though current waves of school reform are less than nature-friendly, individual teachers—with help from parents, natural history museum docents, and other volunteers—can do much to improve the situation without organized, official sanction. To be truly effective, however, we must go beyond the dedication of individual teachers and volunteers, to question the assumptions and context of the nature-student gap. We should do everything we can to encourage the incipient movement of what is sometimes called "experiential education." We should also challenge some of the driving forces behind our current approach to nature, including a loss of respect for nature and the death of natural history in higher education.

A few years ago, I sat in the cluttered office of Robert Stebbins, professor emeritus at the Museum of Vertebrate Zoology at the University of California, Berkeley. He grew up ranging through California's Santa Monica Mountains, where he learned to cup his hands around his mouth and "call in the owls." For him, nature was still magical. For more than twenty years, Stebbins's reference work, *A Field Guide to Western Reptiles and Amphibians,* which he wrote and illustrated, has remained the undisputed bible of herpetology, and inspired countless youngsters to chase snakes. To Stebbins, our relationship with nature has been undermined by a shift in values.

20   For a decade, he and his students drove to the California desert to record animal tracks in areas frequented by all-terrain vehicles, or ATVs; Stebbins discovered that 90 percent of invertebrate animal life—insects, spiders, and other arthropods—had been destroyed in the ATV-scarred desert areas. While I spoke with him, he dropped scores of slides into an old viewer. "Look," he said. "Ten years of before-and-after photos." Grooves and slashes, tracks that will remain for centuries. Desert crust ripped up by rubber treads, great clouds of dirt rising high into the atmosphere; a gunshot desert tortoise, with a single tire track cracking its back; aerial photographs taken near Blythe, California, of ancient and mysterious Indian intaglios, carved images so large that they can only be perceived from the air. Across the flanks and back and head of a deer-like intaglio were claw marks left by ATVs. "If only these people knew what they were doing," said Stebbins.

What upset him most was not the destruction that had already occurred, but the devastation yet to come and the waning sense of awe—or simple respect—toward nature that he sensed in each successive generation. "One time, I was out watching the ATVs. I saw these two little boys trudging up a dune. I went running after them. I wanted to ask them why they weren't riding machines—maybe they were looking for something else out there. They said their trail bikes were broken. I asked them if they knew what was out there in the desert, if they'd seen any lizards. 'Yeah,' one of them said, 'But lizards just run away.' These kids were bored, uninterested. If only they knew."

Even among children who participate in nature activities, a conservation ethic is not assured. In a classroom in Alpine, California, I visited elementary-school pupils who reported spending far more time outside than I had heard reported in most settings across the country. Some of the students in this science class had watched bobcats play on the ridges; one boy had watched a mountain lion thread its way across his parents' acreage. Many of these young people were growing up in this far exurb in the mountains because their parents wanted them to be exposed to more nature. One boy said, "My mom didn't like the city because there was hardly any nature, so mom and dad decided to move here to Alpine. We live in an apartment. My grandma lives even farther out and she has huge property—most of it is grass, but part of it is just trees. I like to go there, because she has a baby mountain lion that comes down into her yard. When I was there on Sunday, we were going out to feed the goats and we saw a bobcat trying to catch birds. It's really cool."

I was glad to find a group of kids who seemed to enjoy nature as much as I had, but as they spoke, it became clear that, for nearly half of them, their favorite interaction with nature was vehicular, on small four-wheel ATVs, or "quads." "My dad and me ride in the desert and most of the time we don't follow the tracks. My dad races off-road cars. He says it's cool to go out there even if you're on a track because you can still see animals—and also it's fun to race." Another boy: "Every August we go to Utah, and my mom's friend up there has three quads; we ride for the fun of it but mostly to see animals like deer and skunk at night, and if you leave fish guts and go out at night you'll see, like, five black bears come out. It's cool." A third boy: "We go to the desert every weekend and they have races, there's one hill that nobody rides on because it's rocky, so we changed it so you go up, then jump off these cliffs; and up there we'll see snake holes and snakes. On hot days we go out and hunt for lizards." And a girl, displaying no sense of irony, added: "My dad had a four-wheel-drive truck and we go out in the desert, not out in nature or anything."

After the bell rang and the students left, Jane Smith, a teacher at the school for five years, and a social worker before that, raised her hands in exasperation. "It always amazes me. Most of these students don't make the connection that there's a conflict between ATVs and the land. Even after this project we did a week on energy conservation, and they didn't get it. Just didn't see it—and they still don't. Every weekend, Alpine empties out. Families head for the desert and the dunes. And that's the way it is."

25   Some of these young people, and their parents, are more likely to know the brand names of ATVs than the lizards, snakes, hawks, and cacti of the desert. As my friend, biologist Elaine Brooks, has said, "humans seldom value what they cannot name." Or experience. What if, instead of sailing to the Galápagos Islands and getting his hands dirty and his feet wet, Charles Darwin had spent his days cooped up in some office cubicle staring at a computer screen? What if a tree fell in the forest and no one knew its biological name? Did it exist?

"Reality is the final authority; reality is what's going on out there, not what's in your mind or on your computer screen," says Paul Dayton, who has been seething for years about the largely undocumented sea change in how science—specifically higher education—perceives and depicts nature. That change will shape—or distort—the perception of nature, and reality, for generations to come. Dayton is a professor of oceanography at Scripps Institution of Oceanography in La Jolla. He enjoys a worldwide reputation as a marine ecologist and is known for his seminal ecological studies, which he began in the 1960s, of the benthic (sea bottom) communities in the Antarctic. Two years ago, the Ecological Society of America honored Dayton and colleagues with the prestigious Cooper Ecology Award—marking a first for research of an oceanic system—for addressing "fundamental questions about sustainability of communities in the face of disturbance along environmental gradients." In 2004, the American Society of Naturalists presented him with the E. O. Wilson Naturalist Award.

Now, he sits in his office on a rainy spring day staring at the Pacific Ocean, dark and cold beyond the Scripps Pier. He has a terrarium in the room, where he keeps a giant centipede named Carlos, to whom Dayton feeds mice. Dayton approaches nature with a sense of awe and respect, but he doesn't romanticize it. When he was growing up in snow-clogged logging camps, the family didn't eat if his father didn't hunt. A compact, athletic man with graying hair, an infectious smile, and skin burnished by cold wind and hot sun, Dayton must sometimes feel as if he has slept through a long, hard Arctic night, and awakened in a foreign future in which nothing is named and nature is sold in stores or deconstructed into pure math. He tells me that most of his elite graduate students in marine ecology exhibit "no evidence of training in any type of natural history." Few upper-division ecology majors or undergraduates in marine ecology "know even major phyla such as arthropods or annelids."

Sitting a few feet away from him (and farther from Carlos), Bonnie Becker, a National Park Service marine biologist at Cabrillo National Monument, says Dayton's view is accurate. Recently, she realized that—despite her prior training—she could identify few of the more than one thousand marine invertebrate species that live off Point Loma. So she set up an informal tutoring group, mostly students teaching other students. "Word has gotten out," she says. "You know, have a beer and teach me everything you know about limpets." The people who name the animals, or even know the names, are fast becoming extinct. In San Diego and Orange counties, no more than a half-dozen people can come close to naming a significant number of marine invertebrates, and these are mainly museum workers and docents, and a few local government workers who monitor wastewater treatment and sewage out-falls. These people have few opportunities to pass on their knowledge to a new generation. "In a few years there will be nobody left to identify several major groups of marine organisms," Dayton says. "I wish I were exaggerating."

What we can't name can hurt us. "A guy in Catalina sent me photos of a snail he found," Dayton says. "The snail is moving north. It's not supposed to be where the guy found it. Something is going on with this snail or with its environment." Global warming? Maybe. "But if you don't know it's an invasive species, then you detect no change." It's easy enough to blame the public schools for a pervading ignorance, but Dayton places much of the responsibility on the dominance of molecular biology in higher education. Not that he has anything against molecular biology, and not that he doesn't encounter professors who buck the trend. But, he says, the explicit goal of the new philosophy of modern university science education is to get the "ologies"—invertebrate zoology, ichthyology, mammalogy, ornithology, and herpetology—"back in the nineteenth century where they belong." Shortly after I spoke with Paul Dayton at his Scripps office, he presented a paper, now in high demand as a reprint, at the American Society of Naturalists Symposium. In it he underscores the greater threat:

30   The last century has seen enormous environmental degradation: many populations are in drastic decline, and their ecosystems have been vastly altered . . . . These environmental crises coincide with the virtual banishment of natural sciences in academe, which eliminate the opportunity for both young scientists and the general public to learn the fundamentals that help us predict population levels and the responses by complex systems to environmental variation . . . . The groups working on molecular biology and theoretical ecology have been highly successful within their own circles and have branched into many specialties. These specialists have produced many breakthroughs important to those respective fields. However . . . this reductionist approach has contributed rather little toward actual solutions for the increasingly severe global realities of declining populations, extinctions, or habitat loss . . . . We must reinstate natural science courses in all our academic institutions to insure that students experience nature first-hand and are instructed in the fundamentals of the natural sciences.

What specifically, I asked Dayton, can be done to improve the situation? His answer was not hopeful. "Not only is there a huge elitist prejudice against natural history and for microbiology, [but] simple economics almost rule out a change, because good natural history classes must be small." Nonetheless, he hopes that greater public knowledge about the generational nature deficit will encourage politicians to "start demanding that universities teach the fundamentals of biology and explicitly define these fundamentals to include real natural history."

Unfortunately, finding anybody with enough natural history knowledge to teach such classes will be difficult. Dayton suggests that higher education "offer the courses and hire young professors eager to do the right thing" and organize the older naturalists, fading in number, to mentor the young students "never offered the opportunity to learn any natural history." At least one organization, the Western Society of Naturalists, has stepped to the plate with support for the training of young naturalists. If education and other forces, intentionally or unintentionally, continue to push the young away from direct experience in nature, the cost to science itself will be high. Most scientists today began their careers as children, chasing bugs and snakes, collecting spiders, and feeling awe in the presence of nature. Since such untidy activities are fast disappearing, how, then, will our future scientists learn about nature?

"I fear that they will not," says Dayton, staring out at that lost horizon. "Nobody even knows that this wisdom about our world has been driven from our students."

Rasheed Salahuddin, a high school principal who heads my local school district's one-week outdoor-education program, sees the corrosive effect of nature-fear. "Too many kids are associating nature with fear and catastrophe, and not having direct contact with the outdoors," he says. Salahuddin brings sixth-graders to the mountains and shows them the wonder. "Some of these kids are from Eastern

Europe, Africa, and the Middle East. They view the outdoors, the woods, as a dangerous place. They associate it with war, with hiding—or they view it in a solely utilitarian way, as a place to gather firewood."

35   Inner-city kids of all ethnic backgrounds show similar responses, he says. Some have never been to the mountains or the beach—or the zoo, even though it's within sight of their homes. Some of them spend their entire childhood inside an apartment, living in fear. They associate nature with the neighborhood park, which is controlled by gangs. "What does this say about our future?" asks Salahuddin. "Nature has been taken over by thugs who care absolutely nothing about it. We need to take nature back."

Steve Chapple
Eco-Rednecks

Steve Chapple is a contributing editor to Sports Afield *and the* San Francisco Examiner Sunday Magazine, *and a frequent essayist on politics, travel, and the environment for the* New York Times *and* Travel + Leisure, *among other periodicals. His books include* Kayaking the Full Moon: A Journey Down the Yellowstone River to the Soul of Montana *(1993), and, with David Brower,* Let the Mountains Talk, Let the Rivers Run: A Call to Those Who Would Save the Earth *(2000). "Eco-Rednecks" is a chapter from his book of essays entitled* Confessions of an Eco-Redneck: Or How I Learned to Gut-Shoot Trout & Save the Wilderness at the Same Time *(Plenum Press, 1997).*

It was the best fishing I've had in Montana. Every cast, whether perfect lay or clumsy drag upon the water, anything we threw—popper, hopper, or coachman—garnered a strike, until we were laughing in victory and sweating with the effort. Turned out, the reason it was so good was that it was the Saturday before fishing season opened. The fish had no idea we were breaking the law.

In my defense, I was only 10. My friend's mother had driven us up the Stillwater for a day's easy baby-sitting, and she was not, looking back on it, such a punctilious sportswoman.

Neither was her husband. He took us trolling on Yellowstone Lake in the park a little later in the summer. Soon enough, using red and white daredevils, we were more than a little over the limit and—exciting moment!—a patrol boat set out from the marina to check up on us.

"Empty the freezer!" shouted my friend's father. We kids tossed 30 or 40 dead cutthroats over the transom.

5   Then the great helmsman crisscrossed the Evinrude over the floating trout until they were, at best, chum. When the patrol boat drew alongside, he voluntarily threw open the cooler. He was a cocky bastard.

"You're one over," said the ranger, after counting.

"They were really biting!" explained my friend's father.

The ranger let us off.

The souls of those salmonids still weigh on my conscience, I guess. Today, we'd call my friend's father a game hog, maybe even a redneck, though in Montana, the sun never gets hot enough to pink a neck properly. As I recall, my friend's father had to open his mouth to spit, so he could not have been an authentic redneck, anyway.

10   At bottom, he was a meat hunter, devil take the hindquarters, catch and fillet. Nothing wrong with that, either—once you factor out excessive zeal—because food does not walk onto the plate, in my experience. It has to be killed first.

Even if you yourself don't kill what you eat, somebody else must. Your sister-in-law doesn't find shooting game birds to be a pleasant pastime? Well, has she ever watched cows being sledgehammered at the slaughterhouse? This is what lies behind the waitress's smile.

"I'm a vegetarian!" screams your sister-in-law.

And I can respect that. Vegetarianism will make emotional logic, to vegetarians, until the scientists of the next century play back the tapes of wheat tops screaming under the blades of the thresher.

Even then, there can be no difference, in the eyes of the Lord, between mycorrhiza soil bacteria and an elk steak. You walk, you step on beetles. It's kill or be killed, and let God sort out the giblets.

15   But how did we get to this pass? How have the small number of anti-hunters and those who eschew steak tartar come to be identified as environmentalists, and those of us who trout-box for breakfast and prefer antelope medallion to acorn souffle (which is not bad, actually) come to be imagined as unconcerned for the land?

It defies common sense. Who loves the mountains more than those who hunt them? Who has done more for wetlands than duck hunters? More to stop nickel-and-dime trailer courts, subdivisions, and septic tanks at streamside than trout and bass organizations? More to convince farmers not to rain-forest-torch the cover that runs alongside country roads than pheasant beaters? Those who enjoy tying into the bull trout, that tiger shark of the northern Rockies, are learning that acid mine waste must be stopped in the headwaters, because the bulls are like prize-fighters with bad lungs. They can't stand even minimal pollution.

These days, sportsman and environmentalist are apt to be the same person. There is a strange new animal stalking the woods of North America: the eco-redneck.

Of course, there is nothing new about eco-rednecks, really, except for the name. John James Audubon often shot and ate the birds he drew, as I've said. ("So we took our guns and went after Black-breasted Lark Buntings." *The Missouri River Journals,* 1843.) The two main founders of the modern conservation movement were forester Aldo Leopold, an avid hunter of deer along New Mexico's Gila, and, of course, Teddy "Hunting Trips of a Ranchman" Roosevelt: "The whitetail . . . keeps its place in the land in spite of the swinish game-butchers, who hunt for hides and not for sport or actual food, and who murder the gravid doe and the spotted fawn with as little hesitation as they would kill a buck of ten points. No one who is not himself a sportsman and lover of nature can realize the intense indignation—"

Whoa, Theodore!

20   I think what happened is some thoroughbred rednecks got control of the White House after the first Roosevelt and sullied the waters, which confused our minds. Consider this quote from a recent official of the Department of Interior: "If you can't shoot it, hook it, or screw it, it's not worth conserving." What's wrong with this is not elegance of prose. I like a direct speaker, always an endangered species inside the Beltway. The problem is snail-darters make good bait, spotted owls are a sign of a healthy forest, and if we don't let small-scale controlled burns put back forbs and grass at the edge of conifer forests, we won't have elk to shoot come fall. You see, in Washington, they're always willing to cut the forests to save the tees.

That, bottom line, may be why sportsmen and environmentalists are too often kept on opposite sides of the barbed wire: so they won't see how close they really are to each other.

Right now there is even a scheme afoot to chain-saw the cottonwoods along western rivers and mill them into coffins. A writer couldn't ask for a more perfect metaphor. In turn for caulking the juices of dead folks, countless bobcats, raccoons, whitetails, bald eagles, and rabbits will have to look elsewhere for homes, which they will not find, and the denuded banks of the streams and rivers themselves will erode faster than a hemophiliac's scab.

An eco-redneck is not ashamed to hug a tree. But he may be just primitive enough to punch out your lights if you try to embarrass him.

What does the proper eco-redneck dress like? Over his folding knife and his bag of urine gel powder (which masks his scent) he probably wears one of those new fleece pullovers made from recycled soft-drink containers. He prefers his petrol-garb in camo green, but he won't be truly happy until the Polar-Tek people come up with a way to spin fleece directly from crushed beer cans.

25   Like life itself, it all comes back to food and drink—or to the eco-redneck, to quail breast in a butter cognac sauce with a cold Bud beside the plate.

Frances Moore Lappé
from *Diet for a Small Planet*

Frances Moore Lappé is a bestselling author on issues of environmental sustainability. Along with Joseph Collins, she started the Institute for Food and Development Policy and wrote Food First: Beyond the Myth of Scarcity *(1977), an analysis of causes of world hunger and approaches to alleviating it. Her many books also include* The Quickening of America *(1994) and* Democracy's Edge *(2005). With her daughter, Anna Lappé, she runs the Small Planet Institute; you can read their blog at http://www.smallplanetinstitute.org/thoughts/index.php.*

Diet for a Small Planet was a groundbreaking book when it was first published in 1971; this excerpt is the introduction to the twentieth-anniversary edition (Ballantine Books, 1991).

No one has been more astonished than I at the impact of *Diet for a Small Planet*. It was born as a one-page handout in the late 1960s, and became a book in 1971. Since then it has sold close to two million copies in a half dozen languages. What I've discovered is that many more people than I could ever have imagined are looking for the same thing I was—a first step.

Mammoth social problems, especially global ones like world hunger and ecological destruction, paralyze us. Their roots seem so deep, their ramifications endless. So we feel powerless. How can *we* do anything? Don't we just have to leave these problems to the "experts"? We try to block out the bad news and hope against hope that somewhere someone who knows more than we do has some answers.

The tragedy is that this totally understandable feeling—that we must leave the big problems to the "experts"—lies at the very root of our predicament, because the experts are those with the greatest stake in the status quo. Schooled in the institutions of power, they take as given many patterns that must change if we are to find answers. Thus, the solutions can come only from people who are less "locked-in"—ordinary people like you and me. Only when we discover that we have both the capacity and the right to participate in making society's important decisions will solutions emerge. Of this I am certain.

But how do we make this discovery?

5 The world's problems appear so closely interwoven that there is no point of entry. Where do we begin when everything seems to touch everything else? Food, I discovered, was just the tool I needed to crack the seemingly impenetrable facade. With food as my grounding point I could begin to see meaning in what before was a jumble of frightening facts—and over the last ten years I've learned that my experience has been shared by thousands of others. Learning about the politics of food "not only changed my view of the world, but spurred me on to act upon my new vision," Sally Bachman wrote me from New York.

To ask the biggest questions, we can start with the most personal—what do we eat? What we eat is within our control, yet the act ties us to the economic, political, and ecological order of our whole planet. Even an apparently small change—consciously choosing a diet that is good both for our bodies and for the earth—can lead to a series of choices that transform our whole lives. "Food had been a major teacher in my life," Tina Kimmel of Alamosa, California, wrote me.

The process of change is more profound, I'm convinced, than just letting one thing lead to the next. . . .

> Previously when I went to a supermarket, I felt at the mercy of our advertising culture. My tastes were manipulated. And food, instead of being my most direct link with the nurturing earth, had become mere merchandise by which I fulfilled my role as a "good" consumer.

Feeling victimized, I felt powerless. But gradually I learned that every choice I made that aligned my daily life with an understanding of how I wanted things to be made me feel more powerful. As I became more convincing to myself, I was more convincing to other people. I *was* more powerful.

10 So while many books about food and hunger appeal to guilt and fear, this book does not. Instead, I want to offer you power. Power, you know, is not a dirty word!

Here's how it began for me . . .

In 1969 I discovered that half of our harvested acreage went to feed livestock. At the same time, I learned that for every 7 pounds of grain and soybeans fed to livestock we get on the average only 1 pound back in meat on our plates. Of all the animals we eat, cattle are the poorest converters of grain to meat: it takes 16 pounds of grain and soybeans to produce just 1 pound of beef in the United States today.

The final blow was discovering that much of what I had grown up believing about a healthy diet was false. Lots of protein is essential to a good diet, I thought, and the only way to get enough is to eat meat at virtually every meal. But I learned that, on the average, Americans eat twice the protein their bodies can even use. Since our bodies don't store protein, what's not used is wasted. Moreover, I learned that the "quality" of meat protein, better termed its "usability," could be matched simply by combining certain plant foods. Thus, the final myth was exploded for me.

I was shocked. While the world's experts talked only of scarcity, I had just discovered the incredible waste built into the American meat-centered diet. And nutritionally it was all unnecessary! My world view flipped upside down. Along with many others in the late 1960s, I had started out asking: "How close are we to the limit of the earth's capacity to provide food for everyone?" Then it began to dawn on me that I was part of a system actively *reducing* that capacity.

Hidden Resources Plowed into Our Steaks

15 What I failed to appreciate fully ten years ago was that the production system that generates our grain-fed-meat diet not only wastes our resources but helps destroy them, too. Most people think of our food-producing resources, soil and water, as renewable, so how can they be destroyed? The answer is that because our production system encourages farmers to continually increase their output, the natural cycle of renewal is undermined. The evidence for this is presented in Part II, but here are a few facts to give you some sense of the threats to our long-term food security:

- *Water costs.* Producing just one pound of steak uses 2,500 gallons of water— as much water as my family uses in a month! Livestock production, including water for U.S. crops fed to livestock abroad, accounts for about half of all water consumed in the United States, and increasingly that water is drawn from underground lakes, some of which are not significantly renewed by rainfall. Already irrigation sources in north Texas are running dry, and within decades the underground sources will be drawn down so far that scientists estimate a third of our current irrigation will be economically unfeasible.

- *Soil erosion.* Corn and soybeans, the country's major animal feed crops, are linked to greater topsoil erosion than any other crops. In some areas topsoil losses are greater now than during the Dust Bowl era. At current rates, the loss of topsoil threatens the productivity of vital farmland within our lifetime.
- *Energy costs.* To produce a pound of steak, which provides us with 500 calories of food energy, takes 20,000 calories of fossil fuel, expended mainly in producing the crops fed to livestock.
- *Import dependency.* Corn alone uses about 40 percent of our major fertilizers. U.S. agriculture has become increasingly dependent on imported fertilizer, which now accounts for 20 percent of our ammonia fertilizer and 65 percent of our potash fertilizer. And even though the United States is the world's leading producer of phosphates for fertilizer, at current rates of use we will be importing phosphates, too, in just 20 years.

A Symbol and a Symptom

20　　The more I learned, the more I realized that a grain-fed-meat diet is not the cause of this resource waste, destruction, and dependency. The "Great American Steak Religion" is both a symbol and a symptom of the underlying logic of our production system—a logic that makes it self-destructive.

Our farm economy is fueled by a blind production imperative. Because farmers are squeezed between rising production costs and falling prices for their crops, their profits per acre fall steadily—by 1979 hitting one-half of what they had been in 1945 (figures adjusted for inflation). So *just to maintain the same income* farmers must constantly increase production—planting more acres and reaping higher yields, regardless of the ecological consequences. And they must constantly seek new markets to absorb their increasing production. But since hungry people in both the United States and the third world have no money to buy this grain, what can be done with it?

One answer has been to feed about 200 million tons of grain, soybean products, and other feeds to domestic livestock every year. Another, especially in the last ten years, has been to sell it abroad. While most Americans believe our grain exports "feed a hungry world," *two-thirds* of our agricultural exports actually go to livestock—and the hungry abroad cannot afford meat. The trouble is that, given the system we take for granted, this all appears logical. So perhaps to begin we must stop taking so much for granted and ask, who really benefits from our production system? Who is hurt, now and in the future?. . .

The Traditional Diet

Over the years many people have been surprised when meeting the author of *Diet for a Small Planet.* I am not the gray-haired matron they expect. Nor am I a back-to-nature purist. (Sometimes I even wear lipstick!) But mouths really drop open when I explain that I am not a vegetarian. Over the last ten years I've hardly ever served or eaten meat, but I try hard to distinguish what I advocate from what people think of as "vegetarianism."

Most people think of vegetarianism as an ethical stance against the killing of animals, unconventional, and certainly untraditional. But what I advocate is the return to the traditional diet on which our bodies evolved. Traditionally the human diet has centered on plant foods, with animal foods playing a supplementary role. Our digestive and metabolic system evolved over millions of years on such a diet. Only very recently have Americans, and people in some other industrial countries, begun to center their diets on meat. So it is the meat-centered diet—and certainly the grain-fed-meat-centered diet—that is the fad.

25   I hope that my book will be of value to the growing numbers of people who refuse to eat meat in order to discourage the needless suffering of animals. But I believe that its themes can make sense to just about anyone, whether or not they are prepared to take an ethical stance against the killing of animals for human food.

Many counter the vegetarian's position against killing animals for human food by pointing out that in many parts of the world livestock play a critical role in sustaining human life: only livestock can convert grasses and waste products into meat. Where good cropland is scarce, this unique ability of grazing animals may be crucial to human survival. Intellectually, I agree. But I say "intellectually" because, although using livestock to convert inedible substances to protein for human beings makes sense to me, I found that once I stopped cooking meat, it no longer appealed to me. If all our lives we handle flesh and blood, maybe we become inured to it. Once I stopped, I never wanted to start again. But this view is a strictly personal one, and it is not the subject of this book.

An Escape or a Challenge?

For many who have come to appreciate the profound political and economic roots of our problems, a change in diet seems like a pretty absurd way to start to change things. Such personal decisions are seen simply as a handy way to diminish guilt feelings, while leaving untouched the structural roots of our problems. Yes, I agree—such steps *could* be exactly this and nothing more.

But taking ever greater responsibility for our individual life choices could be one way to change us—heightening our power and deepening our insight, which is exactly what we need most if we are ever to get to the roots of our society's problems. Changing the way we eat will not change the world, but it may begin to change us, and then we can be part of changing the world.

Examining any of our consumption habits has value only to the degree that the effort is both liberating and motivating. Learning why our grain-fed-meat diet developed and learning what does constitute a healthy and satisfying diet have been both for me. In one area of my life I began to feel that I could make real choices—choices based on knowledge of their consequences. Second, the more I learned about why the American diet developed to include not only more grain-fed meat but more processed food, the more I began to grasp the basic flaws in the economic ground rules on which our entire production system is based. I learned, for example, that the prices guiding our resource use are make-believe—they in no way tell us the real resource costs of production. Moreover, I came to see how our production system inevitably treats even an essential ingredient of life itself—food—as just another commodity, totally divorcing it from human need. Slowly it became clear that until the production of our basic survival goods is consciously tied to the fulfillment of human need there can be no solution to the tragedy of needless hunger that characterizes our time—even here in the United States.

We Are the Realists

30   Some call such views unrealistic, visionary, or idealistic. I respond that it is we who are awakening to the crisis of our planet—and to our own power to make critical changes—who are the realists. Those who believe that our system of waste and destruction should continue are the dreamers. Yes, *we* are the realists. We want to face up to the terrible problems confronting the human race and learn what each of us can do right now. At the same time, we are also visionaries, because we have a vision of the direction in which we want our society to move. . . .

▦ QUESTIONS FOR INQUIRY AND ACTION ▦

1. Make a chart of these four authors' representations of humans in the natural world. How would each describe the relationship between humans and the natural world? Create a Venn diagram to show the overlapping area or common ground among the four authors. On which aspects are they in most agreement? Are there points on which you find significant disagreement? If so, what are they?

2. Research arguments about vegetarianism. How much of an impact does an individual's vegetarian eating habits have on local, national, and international economies and natural resources?

3. How much has your education so far—elementary and secondary as well as higher education—encouraged you to spend time in nature observing and interacting with other species and life forms in order to learn about and from them? Have these been rewarding learning experiences?

4. Design a curriculum for one of your courses (particularly one that is *not* a "nature" or "environmentalism" course) that would tie the subject matter of the course to spending time in nature. How would it change the course? What would you learn about the course content that you would not learn in a traditional classroom?

▦ CONTINUING THE CASE STUDY ▦
How Lightly Do You Walk the Earth?

The readings in the case study address, in various ways, our personal impact on life on the Earth. Rachel Carson calls for humans to see ourselves as just one species interacting with the rest of the natural world in an interdependent and cooperative relationship. Richard Louv worries that we are developing a more and more abstract relationship with nature because we lack a direct experience with it, and Steve Chapple reasons that sportsmen make the most concerned environmentalists because of their extensive direct experiences with nature. Frances Moore Lappé examines the relationship between our individual eating habits and the "economic, political, and ecological order of the entire planet."

To continue this case study we ask you to continue the Getting Started exercise for this chapter in which you took the Ecological Footprint Quiz. Here are a few suggestions of things you might do to measure your impact upon the Earth in your daily life. You should feel free to adapt this to your own needs, and to add other experiments.

1. Conduct your research. Construct a chart to keep track of your responses to these and any other questions and experiments you create.

   - Measure your daily water usage.

     How much water do you use for brushing your teeth, showering, washing dishes, doing laundry, washing your car? How much does water cost you? Do you know where your water comes from? Where is the watershed for your region?

   - Record what you eat for a week.

     Record *everything* you eat—at home and in restaurants. When you eat, how often are you actually hungry? How often do you eat animal products (meat, eggs, dairy)? Do you know where your food comes from? Where do you shop for your food? Where do they get the food that you buy? How much of it is processed? How much of it is imported? How much comes from factories or factory-farms, and how much from smaller farms and industries? How much of it is organic? How much of it is genetically modified?

   - Record how much garbage you throw out in a week.

     Instead of throwing your garbage out as your can fills, keep all of the garbage inside for a week. How much do you accumulate? How many trash bags or pounds? What does your garbage consist of? Food? Packaging? How much of what you throw in the trash can be recycled or composted?

   - Keep track of your mode(s) of transportation for a week.

     How often do you drive a personal car? How often do you take the bus or other form of public transportation? How often do you ride your bike? How often do you walk, rollerblade, or skateboard?

   - Research the history of your neighborhood.

     How long have you lived in your house, apartment building, or residence hall? Did anyone live in that building before you? If so, do you know who the person was (or people were)? How long has the building itself been standing? What used to be on the land before the building was constructed? Has your neighborhood experienced gentrification—a process of renewal in which wealthier people move into and rebuild deteriorating areas, displacing poorer residents in the meantime?

2. Then, do some research to put your findings into a meaningful context. Treat this study just like the other case studies in this book. Some questions to consider:

- What was your most surprising discovery? Why did it surprise you?

- How did you discover that your daily living affects others' daily living, even if you have no physical contact with them or do not generally consider yourself to be in community with them?

- Where do people's interests or concerns compete or conflict? Where do people's interests conflict with the interests of animals or plants? Whose interests or concerns should get priority?

- What conclusions can you draw from your experiments?

- What are the ethical or political questions that this case study raises? Write a series of Questions for Inquiry and Action that stem from your experiments and results.

- What can you do to make a more positive impact on the Earth? What can you do immediately? What can you do over the long term?

CHAPTER 10

Communities of Faith

In one sense, an individual's homely, imperfect search for meaning says more about the origins of faith than the polished beauty of a great religious tradition can. An established religion may be a finished work of art, but the personal quest is a creative act, and thus just as authentic in what it says about innate human yearnings and desires . . . . It's one of the benefits of a tolerant age—that we, too, if we choose, can strip away the rich vestments of religious tradition and discover that naked faith is something separate and, ultimately, even more mysterious.

—*Jeremiah Creedon, "God with a Million Faces"*

▓ GETTING STARTED ▓ Observing Worship Practices in Faith Communities

Visit the worship services of three faith communities as a participant observer. Try to visit representatives of three different religions or spiritual schools of thought, although visiting three different denominations of the same religion can also be instructive. While you are there, participate as fully as you can while observing closely; afterward, record the details in your writer's notebook. Here are some questions to guide your observations and discussion with your class:

1. What were the primary similarities and differences between the faith communities and their services?

2. Which felt most like a community to you? Why? What aspects of a worship service—including the moments before and after the official service time—contribute to the feeling of community?

3. Can you feel a part of the community if you don't share the beliefs, or, perhaps more important, if you do not share the same rituals of expression (e.g., the same songs, prayers, images, practices)? How did you respond to unfamiliar or uncomfortable aspects of the services? Did you ask questions if you did not understand something? Did you refrain from reciting prayers or singing songs that you did not understand or that offended you? Did you go along politely because you did not want to offend the others' beliefs?

4. Did you ever find yourself hanging back from full participation? If so, why? Did you fear being "taken in"? Did you dread being asked why you were there and whether you would be back the next week? Did you feel like a phony?

Textbooks such as this one often include selections on political disputes between church and state, or they include discussions of religious freedom of expression, or sometimes historical or cultural essays about different religions. Rarely do you find substantive discussions of the *communities* of faith. Yet these communities are among the most important for people in their everyday lives, and it is often the dimension of communion with others, rather than specific doctrine, that binds the members of the communities together. The readings in this chapter illustrate how faith communities are often the most significant communities in people's lives.

One of the great attractions of a spiritual community is the sense of sanctuary it provides—not just the physical sanctuary of the house of worship, but the feeling of refuge and protection that being a part of the community confers. Spiritual expression is deeply personal, and when people live most of their days in a society that often finds open expression of faith disconcerting, congregants find it especially vital to have the outlet of the faith community. As a result, however, worship communities can be made up of a homogeneous group of people—people who feel safe in their similarities to one another and apprehensive of or even hostile to those they perceive as different.

While American culture prides itself on being tolerant of religious difference—of being a nation characterized by religious freedom—it is also often nervous about the public display of faith. While we tend to like our leaders to be people of faith, we do not actually want them to act upon their religious beliefs in making public policy. We fear they will impose their beliefs on others who do not share those beliefs. In short, our country is deeply conflicted over the role faith plays in civic life.

The case study for this chapter examines the role faith communities, particularly African-American churches, played in the early civil rights movement. As with many social justice movements—the abolitionist and temperance movements in the United States, the anti-apartheid movement in South Africa—faith communities, with their religious convictions and biblical rhetoric, led the way. Civil rights workers did not see themselves as pursuing a personal political agenda; their expressed goal was pursuing the "beloved community," as Martin Luther King put it, and "redeeming the soul of America," and they saw themselves as fulfilling God's plan. At the same time, those who opposed the civil rights movement often also based their action on faith and believed that segregation was God's plan.

Today, too, faith communities with their differing religious convictions clash over public policy decisions, as is seen perhaps most prominently in debates concerning abortion. These debates often place the pro-life movement, which is associated with conservative Christians, on one end, and the pro-choice movement, which is generally liberal (e.g., the Religious Coalition for Reproductive Choice) on the other. Yet, each side sees itself as acting in good faith and in line with God's will. Is faith really a private matter? What role do you think it should play in public, civic life?

Anne Lamott
Why I Make Sam Go to Church

Anne Lamott is a writer based in Marin County, California. She is the author of several novels and the very popular nonfiction works Operating Instructions: A Journal of My Son's First Year *(1993) and* Bird by Bird: Some Instructions on Writing and Life *(1994). "Why I Make Sam Go to Church" is from her book* Traveling Mercies: Some Thoughts on Faith *(New York: Pantheon Books, 1999).*

Sam is the only kid he knows who goes to church—who is made to go to church two or three times a month. He rarely wants to. This is not exactly true: the truth is he *never* wants to go. What young boy would rather be in church on the weekends than hanging out with a friend? It does not help him to be reminded that once he's there he enjoys himself, that he gets to spend the time drawing in the little room outside the sanctuary, that he only actually has to sit still and listen during the short children's sermon. It does not help that I always pack some snacks, some Legos, his art supplies, and bring along any friend of his whom we can lure into our churchy web. It does not help that he genuinely cares for the people there. All that matters to him is that he alone among his colleagues is forced to spend Sunday morning in church.

You might think, noting the bitterness, the resignation, that he was being made to sit through a six-hour Latin mass. Or you might wonder why I make this strapping, exuberant boy come with me most weeks, and if you were to ask, this is what I would say.

I make him because I can. I outweigh him by nearly seventy-five pounds.

But that is only part of it. The main reason is that I want to give him what I found in the world, which is to say a path and a little light to see by. Most of the people I know who have what I want—which is to say, purpose, heart, balance, gratitude, joy—are people with a deep sense of spirituality. They are people in community, who pray, or practice their faith; they are Buddhists, Jews, Christians—people banding together to work on themselves and for human rights.

They follow a brighter light than the glimmer of their own candle; they are part of something beautiful. I saw something once from the Jewish Theological Seminary that said, "A human life is like a single letter of the alphabet. It can be meaningless. Or it can be a part of a great meaning." Our funky little church is filled with people who are working for peace and freedom, who are out there on the streets and inside praying, and they are home writing letters, and they are at the shelters with giant platters of food.

5   When I was at the end of my rope, the people at St. Andrew tied a knot in it for me and helped me hold on. The church became my home in the old meaning of *home*—that it's where, when you show up, they have to let you in. They let me in. They even said, "You come back now."

My relatives all live in the Bay Area and I adore them, but they are all as skittishly self-obsessed as I am, which I certainly mean in the nicest possible way. Let's just say that I do not leave family gatherings with the feeling that I have just received some kind of spiritual chemotherapy. But I do when I leave St. Andrew.

"Let's go, baby," I say cheerfully to Sam when it is time to leave for church, and he looks up at me like a puppy eyeing the vet who is standing there with the needle.

Sam was welcomed and prayed for at St. Andrew seven months before he was born. When I announced during worship that I was pregnant, people cheered. All these old people, raised in Bible-thumping homes in the Deep South, clapped. Even the women whose grown-up boys had been or were doing time in jails or prisons rejoiced for me. And then almost immediately they set about providing for us. They brought clothes, they brought me casseroles to keep in the freezer, they brought me assurance that this baby was going to be a part of the family. And they began slipping me money.

Now, a number of the older black women live pretty close to the bone financially on small Social Security checks. But routinely they sidled up to me and stuffed bills in my pocket—tens and twenties. It was always done so stealthily that you might have thought they were slipping me bundles of cocaine. One of the most consistent donors was a very old woman named Mary Williams, who is in her mid-eighties now, so beautiful with her crushed hats and hallelujahs; she always brought me plastic Baggies full of dimes, noosed with little wire twists.

10   I was usually filled with a sense of something like shame until I'd remember that wonderful line of Blake's—that we are here to learn to endure the beams of love—and I would take a long deep breath and force these words out of my strangulated throat: "Thank you."

I first brought Sam to church when he was five days old. The women there very politely pretended to care how I was doing but were mostly killing time until it was their turn to hold Sam again. They called him "our baby" or sometimes "my baby." "Bring me my baby!" they'd insist. "Bring me that baby now!" "Hey, you're hogging that baby."

I believe that they came to see me as Sam's driver, hired to bring him and his gear back to them every Sunday.

Mary Williams always sits in the very back by the door. She is one of those unusually beautiful women—beautiful like a river. She has dark skin, a long broad nose, sweet full lips, and what the theologian Howard Thurman calls "quiet eyes." She raised five children as a single mother, but one of her boys drowned when he was young, and she has the softness and generosity and toughness of someone who has endured great loss. During the service she praises God in a nonstop burble, a glistening dark brook. She says, "Oh, yes.... Uh-huh.... My sweet Lord. Thank you, thank you."

Sam loves her, and she loves him, and she still brings us Baggies full of dimes even though I'm doing so much better now. Every Sunday I nudge Sam in her direction, and he walks to where she is sitting and hugs her. She smells him behind his ears, where he most smells like sweet unwashed new potatoes. This is in fact what I think God may smell like, a young child's slightly dirty neck. Then Sam leaves the sanctuary and returns to his drawings, his monsters, dinosaurs, birds. I watch Mary Williams pray sometimes. She clutches her hands together tightly and closes her eyes most of the way so that she looks blind; because she is so unself-conscious, you get to see someone in a deeply interior pose. You get to see all that intimate resting. She looks as if she's holding the whole earth together, or making the biggest wish in the world. Oh, yes, Lord. Uh-huh.

15   It's funny: I always imagined when I was a kid that adults had some kind of inner toolbox, full of shiny tools: the saw of discernment, the hammer of wisdom, the sandpaper of patience. But then when I grew up I found that life handed you these rusty bent old tools—friendships, prayer, conscience, honesty—and said, Do the best you can with these, they will have to do. And mostly, against all odds, they're enough.

Not long ago I was driving Sam and his friend Josh over to Josh's house where the boys were going to spend the night. But out of the blue, Josh changed his mind about wanting Sam to stay over. "I'm tired," he said suddenly, "and I want to have a quiet night with my mom." Sam's face went white and blank; he has so little armor. He started crying. I tried to manipulate Josh into changing his mind, and I even sort of vaguely threatened him, hinting that Sam or I might cancel a date with *him* sometime, but he stayed firm. After a while Sam said he wished we'd all get hit by a car, and Josh stared out the window nonchalantly. I thought he might be about to start humming. It was one of those times when you wish you were armed so you could attack the kid who has hurt your own child's feelings.

"Sam?" I asked. "Can I help in any way? Shall we pray?"

"I just wish I'd never been born."

But after a moment, he said yes, I should pray. To myself.

20   So I prayed that God would help me figure out how to stop living in the problem and to move into the solution. That was all. We drove along for a while. I waited for a sign of improvement. Sam said, "I guess Josh wishes I had never been born."

Josh stared out the window: dum de dum.

I kept asking God for help, and after a while I realized something—that Josh was not enjoying this either. He was just trying to take care of himself, and I made the radical decision to let him off the hook. I imagined gently lifting him off the hook of my judgment and setting him back on the ground.

And a moment later, he changed his mind. Now, maybe this was the result of prayer, or forgiveness; maybe it was a coincidence. I will never know. But even before Josh changed his mind, I did know one thing for sure, and this was that Sam and I would be going to church the next morning. Mary Williams would be sitting in the back near the door, in a crumpled hat. Sam would hug her; she would close her eyes and smell the soft skin of his neck, just below his ears.

What I didn't know was that Josh would want to come with us too. I didn't know that when I stopped by his house to pick up Sam the next morning, he would eagerly run out ahead of Sam to ask if he could come. And another thing I didn't know was that Mary Williams was going to bring us another bag of dimes. It had been a little while since her last dime drop, but just when I think we've all grown out of the ritual, she brings us another stash. Mostly I give them to street people. Some sit like tchotchkes on bookshelves around the house. Mary doesn't know that professionally I'm doing much better now; she doesn't know that I no longer really need people to slip me money. But what's so dazzling to me, what's so painful and poignant, is that she doesn't bother with what I think she knows or doesn't know about my financial life. She just knows we need another bag of dimes, and that is why I make Sam go to church.

▨ QUESTIONS FOR INQUIRY AND ACTION ▨

1. How does Lamott manage to evoke emotion without being sappy? Notice how she weaves tender, sentimental observations with sharp, witty comments.

2. Read through the essay with a highlighter and highlight each of Lamott's descriptions of a person or thing. Which ones are particularly vivid or real for you, and why? How do these vivid descriptions help her purpose in writing?

3. Lamott writes that "most of the people I know who have what I want—which is to say, purpose, heart, balance, gratitude, joy—are people with a deep sense of spirituality." Do you think this is generally true? Inquire into the happiness and purpose in lives of people who are not part of a "churchy web," as Lamott puts it.

4. To what extent is Lamott describing your own church experience? How could you find a faith community like hers if you haven't already? Is this the kind of community you would want? Why or why not?

STOP**AND**THINK

HOUSE CHURCHES:
DESIGNING YOUR OWN WORSHIP

A phenomenon has been growing across the United States and in other countries of the world affected by Christian missionaries: house churches. As their name indicates, house churches are worship services that take place in individuals' homes rather than in official institutions. Popular among evangelical Christians primarily, but also among liberal freethinkers and others, house churches allow participants a deeply intimate and personal fellowship that is not available in most church settings.

continued on next page

What is more, house churches also allow everyone present to participate fully in all of the elements of worship, from selecting, reading, and studying scriptures; to choosing hymns and making the music; to composing prayers; to sharing aloud experiences of faith; and even to preaching, although that aspect of worship generally has a diminished role in these settings. It is, in fact, what caused many people to leave institutionalized churches and set up their own worship services at home. The participants interact with one another more, too, rather than sit passively in the pews as fellow audience members.

What do you think is gained and what is lost in this kind of worship service? As individuals and small groups make meaning for themselves, are they more likely to become deeply informed and wise, or more likely not to tolerate any differences of opinion, scriptural interpretation, worship style, or lifestyle, and to ostracize anyone who is different?

On the other hand, what does the popularity of house churches say about our human need to make meaning by creating and participating in ritual for ourselves? Where in our lives do we have opportunities to create rituals and share them with others?

Stephen J. Dubner
Choosing My Religion

Stephen J. Dubner is an editor at the New York Times *and a feature writer for* The New York Times Magazine. *"Choosing My Religion" was the cover story of* The New York Times Magazine *on March 31, 1996. Dubner later expanded it into a memoir,* Turbulent Souls: A Catholic Son's Return to His Jewish Family *(1998).*

Not long ago, I was having Shabbos dinner with three friends. I am still new to all this. As the candles were lighted and a song was sung, I stumbled along. We washed our hands, then said the blessing as we dried them. I did know that you weren't supposed to speak until the bread had been blessed, so I went back to the table.

As I sat there, another silent ritual came to mind. I was raised in upstate New York and was the last of eight children. When it was your birthday, you had to eat your entire piece of cake without saying a word. If you broke your silence, a penalty awaited: molasses would be poured over your bare feet, then chicken feed sprinkled on, and you'd have to walk through the chicken coop and let the hens peck away.

Although the penalty was carried out a few times (never on me), what I remember best is the struggle to keep the silence, no matter how much everyone baited you. The whole thing was nonsense, and I had never thought about where it came from — until that Shabbos dinner a few weeks ago, when I suddenly wondered if one silence weren't somehow related to the other.

I did not grow up Jewish, but my parents did. Florence Greenglass and Solomon Dubner, both born in Brooklyn, were the children of Russian and Polish immigrants. On Christmas Eve of 1942, when Florence was a 21-year-old ballet dancer, she was baptized as a Roman Catholic. Two years later, she met Sol, a 28-year-old soldier home on furlough. The son of Orthodox Jews, he, too, was about to become a Catholic.

5   Unlike St. Augustine or Thomas Merton, my parents did not embrace Catholicism to atone for a wanton past. Unlike Saul of Tarsus, who became St. Paul, they saw no visions, heard no voices. Theirs were sober conversions of faith, brought about by no force or crises, or at least none visible from the surface.

The fallout was dramatic: no one in their families went to their wedding, and Sol's father never spoke to him again. They built new lives from top to bottom. They even changed their names. My mother chose Veronica as her baptismal name and has used it ever since; Sol, not surprisingly, became Paul.

They began having children, moved to a rural sprawl outside Albany and continued having children. After Joseph, the first son, and Mary, the first daughter, the rest of us had to settle for Joseph or Mary as our middle names. My namesake was St. Stephen, the first Christian martyr, who, I remember learning early on, was stoned to death by Jews.

We took our Catholicism very seriously. We never missed Mass; our father was a lector, and both our parents taught catechism. At 3 in the afternoon on Good Friday, we gathered in the living room for 10 minutes of silence in front of a painting of the Crucifixion. On top of a battered bookcase, our mother kept a simple shrine: a large wooden crucifix, a statue of a beatific Virgin Mary and several devotional candles, all nestled on a thick piece of red felt. Once a year, when our grandmother was due to visit, the shrine was packed away in a cardboard box. This wasn't a sin, our mother assured us, and was absolutely necessary, to keep our grandmother "from getting hysterical."

It did seem strange that our Jewish aunts and uncles and cousins almost never visited — not that I had the slightest idea of what a Jew or Judaism was. Our neighbors were farmers and auto mechanics named O'Donnell and Vandemeer. Only when our father died, when he was 57 and I was 10, did a handful of Jewish relatives make the trip upstate. Because our grandmother was dead by then, the shrine stayed put.

10   The matter of our having been Jewish was half footnote, half secret. A jar of gefilte fish sometimes found its way into the refrigerator, and our parents occasionally resorted to Yiddish for private conversation. But their ardent Catholicism allowed for scant inquiry into a different religious past. My brother Dave remembers asking our mother, when he was 7, why they had become Catholic. "Because we were young and we were searching for the truth, and we found it," she told him.

If I had known then what I know now, I might have recognized the remnants of my parents' past — for a religious conversion, I have come to learn, is imperfect. At best, the convert is a palimpsest. The old writing will always bleed through.

The gefilte fish, the birthday cake routine, the way our father would burst into "My Yiddishe Mama" — it all reminds me of the Marranos, the Jews who were forced during the Spanish Inquisition to convert to Catholicism and wound up practicing their Judaism in secret. Hundreds of years later, some fully assimilated Marrano families still clung to old Jewish rituals with no idea where they had come from.

But for my parents — and now, for me, as I am becoming a Jew — there is a pointed difference. We have chosen our religion, rejecting what we inherited for what we felt we needed. This is a particularly American opportunity and one that is being exploited in ever-increasing numbers. To be convinced, you only need to stick your head into an overflowing Catholic conversion workshop, a mosque filled with American-born blacks, a 5,000-member "megachurch" that caters to forward-looking Protestants or a tiny Pentecostal church packed with Hispanic immigrants who came here as Catholics. "Religious switching is more common now than it has ever been in American history," says Dean Hoge, a sociology professor at Catholic University in Washington, D.C., who has conducted many religious surveys.

Statistics on religious affiliation are notoriously slippery: the Government isn't allowed to gather such data, and the membership claims of religious organizations aren't entirely reliable. But, according to "One Nation Under God" (1993), by Barry A. Kosmin and Seymour P. Lachman, perhaps the most ambitious study to date of Americans and their religions, about 30 percent of Americans now switch denominations in their lifetimes. Kosmin and Lachman, who used a survey of 113,000 people, conclude that the most common reason for a switch is, predictably, intermarriage, followed by a shift in religious conviction and a geographical change.

To be sure, the majority of shifts are not particularly dramatic, tending to be from one Protestant denomination to another. (In a study of 500 people from 33 to 42 years old who had been confirmed as Presbyterians, Hoge found that 33 percent had already made a move, usually to another mainline Protestant denomination.) Still, Kosmin says, "There are more spiritual searches now than ever before, mainly because people are freer than ever before to search."

15   There is also the common phenomenon of intensely renewing your religion of birth as an adult — an especially strong movement among American Jews and middle-class blacks. Such journeys often fall under what is known as Hansen's Law, or the third-generation syndrome, noted by the sociologist Marcus Lee Hansen in the 1930's. According to Hansen's Law, a person looks beyond his parents' religion, which was watered down by assimilation, to the religion of his grandparents, splicing traditional rituals and beliefs into his modern life.

Americans born after World War II, simultaneously facing their parents' deaths and watching their children grow up with a flimsy religious identity, are particularly susceptible to Hansen's Law. The recent surge in American spirituality has sent even the most secular adults into what has become a religion bazaar, where the boundaries are far more fluid and the rules less rigid than when they were children. As late as 1960, even a Protestant-Catholic marriage might have kept at least one set of in-laws out of the church; since then, the charge toward ecumenism has been relentless.

Jack Miles, a former Jesuit and the author of the recent "God: A Biography," told me why he thought this is so: because America has long been that rare country where a religious identity, as opposed to a political identity, is optional. As citizens of a country that has absorbed, with a fair amount of grace, so many different religious traditions, we are bound to be more tolerant and experimental. Miles himself is proof: after leaving the seminary in 1970, he considered converting to Judaism, then flirted with Buddhism and is now a practicing Episcopalian.

By now, choosing a religion is no longer a novel idea. And sometimes all the switching can seem comically casual. At the first meeting of a Judaism class I've been taking, we all announced why we had come. "I grew up Catholic in New Zealand — Catholic school, the whole bit," said one earnest young man, who was there with his Jewish girlfriend. "I had more than my share of whacks on the behind. And, well, as I learned more about Judaism, I thought it was a cracking good religion, so I'm here to see more about it."

The movement toward choosing religion, rampant as it is, shouldn't be surprising. Ours is an era marked by the desire to define — or redefine — ourselves. We have been steadily remaking ourselves along ethnic, political, sexual, linguistic and cultural lines, carefully sewing new stripes into our personal flags and waving them with vigor. Now, more than ever, we are working on the religious stripe.

20   That, of course, is a tricky proposition, since religion comprises practically every strand of identity we possess, and since so many religious rituals are also our most important family rituals. Disengaging yourself from your family's religion often means disengaging yourself, to some extent, from your family.

Lately, I have fallen in with and sought out a variety of converts — or seekers or returnees or born-agains, as they variously call themselves. Judith Anderson, 34, is a practicing Buddhist who was raised, she said, in a "devoutly atheistic" Jewish family in Teaneck, N.J. Like many Jews who practice Buddhism, she hasn't renounced her Jewishness; still, her parents are distressed with the spiritual layer she has added to her life, and she is torn between satisfying herself and appeasing them.

"My heart really hurts right now," she told me. "If they knew half of what goes on in the Buddhist center I belong to, or half of what I say in the morning when I do chants, it would absolutely freak them out. So I will probably always edit what I say and what I expose them to." She keeps a small Buddhist shrine in her Manhattan apartment; when her parents visit, she takes most of it down.

Three of my four sisters are still practicing Catholics; none of my brothers are. Most of them are curious about my Godwrestling, as we sometimes call it, but they don't seem to want or need it for themselves. My mother, meanwhile, remains the most devoted Catholic I have ever known. Two summers ago, I was sitting with her on a screened-in porch in the Adirondacks. Everyone else was off swimming or fishing. To that point, I hadn't asked her how she felt about my push toward Judaism, since I was pretty sure I knew. Now, though, I decided to go ahead with the question.

She tilted her face toward me and almost smiled. "How can I tell you what to believe?" she said. "You have to be true to your own conscience, and you have to do what you think is right." Her answer surprised me and pleased me.

25   "But," she went on, "I see this as the loss of a great opportunity for you." She respected Judaism, she explained, but only as the foundation for Catholicism.

Her tone of voice encouraged no argument. A door slammed, and my niece ran in, dripping wet, wanting to tell Grandma about her swim. I was relieved to be interrupted. For the first time, I had felt the sting of rebuke that, a half-century ago, my parents must have felt tenfold.

It may be that the transcendent mystery of a religious conversion, like the transcendence of sex, is incommunicable. A conversion is a tangle of loneliness, ambition, fear and, of course, hope. It is never tidy. The memoirs written by converts are generally one of two kinds: the breathless account of an irreversible epiphany (I tend to be skeptical of these) and the story wherein a convert pokes around his soul and his mind, yet arrives at no more concrete an explanation than a pressing desire to change the course of his life.

The current boom in choosing religion exists precisely because such inquiry is allowed today — as opposed to when my parents converted. There has never been a more liberal time and place than pre-millennial America to explore a given religion, both intellectually and spiritually. Fifty years ago, challenging a religious text or arguing with doctrine bordered on the heretical; now it is fashionable. Most denominations have become adept at packaging themselves, at disseminating their doctrines and rewards. "It's supply-side religion," Barry Kosmin says. "It's a free-market situation, and anything you can do to survive in that market, you'll do."

What the trends don't reveal, of course, is the fiercely personal nature of any religious search. Daniel Dunn, 26, a database programmer in Boca Raton, Fla., who grew up in the United Church of Christ, became a Catholic after a serious water-skiing accident left him wondering why he hadn't died. "I would go every Sunday and sit in the back pew, just watching and listening to the weekly Scriptures," Dunn says. "I was able to relate to each one in some way, which I hadn't been able to do as a young person."

30   Everyone who chooses a religion is running toward — and away from — his own mountain of questions. As adults, at least people know how to ask those questions and, just as important, how to argue — with their religions, their consciences, their families. They experience the intoxicating jolt of learning a religion with the intellect of an adult rather than the rote acceptance of a child.

I recently met a 22-year-old woman named Fatima Shama, whose mother is a devout Catholic from Brazil and whose father, a Palestinian Muslim, isn't very religious, Shama said. Shama grew up Catholic in the Bronx; she saw Islam, as practiced by her aunts, as exceedingly anti-female. At college, though, she discovered literary interpretations of the Koran, many written by women.

"I realized that everything I'd been taught as a child was wrong," she told me. "I began to separate out the Islamic religion from the Arabic culture, to learn what was really what." She now practices Islam, albeit a more liberal form than her aunts do, and insists that she will marry an Arab-American Muslim. "All my brothers and sisters, they think I'm whacked," Shama said. "They always say to me, 'Where did you come from?' "

I have been asked the same question, now that I am becoming a Jew — or, as some would argue, as I am learning to be the Jew that I have always been. I was, after all, born of a Jewish mother; curious as my religious provenance may be, my bloodline would provide entry into either the state of Israel or a concentration camp.

Four years ago, I first sat down with my mother and a tape recorder. I had to know at least a little bit about my Jewish family, and how Florence Greenglass became Veronica Dubner. And I had to understand what made me so badly want to be Jewish when both my mother and father wanted so badly not to be.

35   What could be called the first existential thought of Florence Greenglass's life occurred in 1931, when she was 10. In bed with a cold, she heard her friends playing stickball outside and realized that, with or without her, life would go rambling on. From that day, she pondered the ephemerality of her existence, and her fate.

Her father, Harry, was an agnostic, a quietly affable man who ran a candy store on Lincoln Place in Brooklyn. Florence had an older sister and a mother, Esther, who disapproved of most things that Florence was interested in. Harry and Esther, born poor in Russia, were now inching toward the middle class. They were the only Jews in their neighborhood, which was mostly Catholic. Florence's grandmother was Orthodox and devout, but the rest of the family observed only Passover and a few other holidays.

Florence considered her Jewishness largely inconsequential. "Except I do remember one time, this girl standing up in class, in sixth grade," she told me. "This very, very blond girl, her name was Ann Ross. And she said, 'My father thinks that Hitler has the right idea about the Jews.' That was kind of a blow, to hear somebody come out and say that."

When Florence was 13, she began studying ballet in Manhattan. Her teacher, Asta Souvorina, was about 60, a former Russian ballerina and actress who had fled Moscow in 1917. Madame Souvorina, as her students always called her, had converted to Catholicism from Russian Orthodoxy. She was domineering, charming, melodramatic; an intellectual, a storyteller — a mentor in every sense. Florence became her star dancer, performing in her small company and later in nightclub acts.

Florence and some of the other girls virtually lived at the studio, where Mme. Souvorina held forth on many subjects. When she mentioned the Epistles of St. Paul, Florence was curious: she had no idea that a living, breathing person, a Jew no less, had left behind such a dramatic record of his newfound faith, and such a compelling explanation of everlasting life. She read Paul's letters and felt they had the ring of truth.

"Well, if you really believe, you ought to do something about it," Mme. Souvorina told her. "You ought to get baptized, because that's what Jesus said you should do."

40   But Florence had much to reconcile — the Virgin Birth, for instance, seemed highly implausible. Her search was long and gradual. She devoured literature and asked endless questions of priests and her Catholic friends. One day, she went to Mass at the Church of the Blessed Sacrament, on West 71st Street in Manhattan, just down Broadway from Mme. Souvorina's studio. She was 21.

Even now, after more than 50 years, my mother's eyes brighten at the memory, and her voice shoots up an octave: "The priest was saying, 'God said, "This is my beloved son in whom I am well pleased. Hear Him." ' Those words were the key to my conversion, actually — 'hear Him,' listen to Jesus and do what He said. And all of a sudden, everything made sense."

About two years ago, I asked my mother how she ultimately came to accept the Virgin Birth and the Resurrection on a literal level. "First of all, it's told in Scripture," she said. But how had she come to believe Scripture? "Because you feel that Scripture was divinely inspired, for one thing — it's not a fairy tale that's made up." But how was she convinced that the Gospels canonized in the New Testament were divinely inspired, as opposed to all the conflicting gospels that didn't make it in?

A long, jagged pause. "It's the gift of faith," she said, "and faith is a gift."

45   It's the gift of faith, and faith is a gift. Where could I go with that? I recalled how our parents used to parry any questions about Catholicism: faith, they told us, is a treasure that can neither be questioned nor fully explained.

Florence was baptized at Blessed Sacrament, and her new faith immediately became the most valuable thing in her life. Esther, her mother, was heartsick and furious — what kind of daughter would betray the family, betray the Jews? Esther tried to plead, bully, threaten her daughter out of it. Veronica, as she now called herself, put up a font of holy water in her bedroom; when she came home, it was missing. "My mother told me I was to blame for her arthritis," she remembers. "And when my father died, she said he died because of me."

She had anticipated her mother's anger. "But you see, this was calculated — you know what you're going to have to give up," she says. "And to me, it was worth it. It's like the story in the Scripture, where you sell everything you have to buy this pearl of great value. That's what you do when you find that pearl — you pay the price. And I could not have lived with myself if I hadn't done it."

A confession: much of the time my mother is telling me about her conversion, I am thinking about my father. When she mentions a book that influenced her, I ask if he read it, too. I prod her to remember more of his life, to think of more people I can interview about what he was like as a Jew and why he converted.

Instead, she sends me a letter from a nun named Sister June. "Dear Mrs. Dubner," it says. "I was with Paul when he died — it was very peaceful. I was praying with him — he opened his eyes halfway and seemed to look at me. I kept saying the name of Jesus in his ear. I rejoice that he sees the Lord face to face."

50   I have the urge to round up 10 Jews and drive upstate to the Catholic cemetery where he is buried, to recite the Mourner's Kaddish.

The evidence of my father's Catholicism is overwhelming. Yet in recreating his life, I found myself thinking of him as a Jew. I would cling to the un-Catholic stories I heard, no matter how wispy, like the time he came back to New York and immediately picked up a copy of *The Jewish Daily Forward*. He was proud he could still read Yiddish.

I never got to ask him what led to his conversion, but it probably wouldn't have mattered. He seems to have told no one. Even my mother's recollections are painfully featureless. His only significant written traces are 18 wartime letters he sent to my mother, all from after his baptism. I studied them endlessly — even the envelopes held potential clues — and scurried off to read the books he mentioned in them. I tracked down relatives who knew of my existence only as a shadowy member of "the Catholic part of the family" (or, occasionally, worse). Some of the reunions were cathartic: "What's this I hear about you becoming Jewish again?" one aunt asked me. "Oh, that's good, that's good."

In late 1944, Sol Dubner was home in New York on furlough. As a teen-ager, he had been sharp and full of ambition, but the war had worn him down, made him lonely, set him searching. He had spent two years with a medical unit at Army hospitals, most recently on Christmas Island. He had written home that he was the only Jew there. What he didn't write home was that after encountering a group of Christian missionaries, he had undergone a nondenominational baptism. And he was pretty sure he wanted to become a Catholic.

Back in Manhattan, he saw a posting for a dance sponsored by the Church of the Blessed Sacrament, and he went around to talk to the priest. "Tell me, Father," he said, "did you ever hear of another creature like me, a Jew who wants to become a Catholic?"

55 Actually, there were a few such creatures, the priest told him, whom Sol could find at a meeting of young Catholics the following night.

Although my mother insists that in the beginning it was only a friendship, other evidence suggests that she and Sol fell in love at the meeting that night. He asked question after question, especially about the Virgin Mary and why she was so key to Catholicism. Veronica, because she had asked the same questions herself two years earlier, could answer them. They spent much of Sol's furlough together, going to Mass regularly.

Sol returned to duty in January, at an Army hospital in Hawaii. "There's a good chance of my being baptized at this post as the chaplain here is pretty interested in my case," he wrote to Veronica.

The chaplain was a German-born Catholic priest named Ulrich J. Proeller. He is now 92 and lives in San Antonio. I called him to see what he could tell me of my father's conversion.

He said he couldn't recall a thing. A wartime conversion, he explained, was often no more than "a momentary transaction." Then he suddenly said: "I remember he was a very alert young fellow, very interested. It was a joy to instruct him.

60 "There were not many Jewish converts," he went on. "He took confidence in me somehow. And I was grateful — I wanted to create better feelings between the Christians and the Jews, since I had the experience of the Jews in Germany."

Father Proeller paused for a minute. "Wartime is good for converts," he finally said. "The Jews felt kind of lonely, you know, because they were so few, so they picked out what they thought was the best, as far as services were concerned, and they stuck with that."

He made it sound so casual! Like a recipe from an Army cookbook: Take one New York City Jew; place him in the middle of nowhere (preferably during a war that's killing Jews by the millions); add a flock of missionaries; top with a gung-ho priest (German if possible). Yield: one Catholic.

Sol, ecstatic after his baptism, wrote to Veronica steadily. March 29, 1945: "I know it would knock you for a loop to know that I am toying with the notion of becoming a priest after the war." Aug. 16, 1945: "At long last we have peace again! . . . If God wills it, I may be back home in four or five months!" Sept. 14, 1945: "It's going to be hard to make my family understand why I am a Catholic . . . . Perhaps I will find some room and board in New York till I decide what my future plans will be."

Sol's father, Shepsel, was one of the most rigorously observant Orthodox men in the neighborhood. He and his wife, Gussie, had come from a small Polish town called Pultusk, north of Warsaw. They settled in the Brownsville section of Brooklyn, where they ran a tiny kosher restaurant.

65 Sol, the fifth of six children, had wanted to be a writer, to play the saxophone, to study in France after high school. "Whatever he thought about doing, Shepsel would slap down," my Aunt Dottie told me. Sol never got along with his father, and often stayed with an older brother. "Shepsel was very, very strict, to a fault really," Dottie says. "It was because of the religion."

Gussie, meanwhile, was as gentle and encouraging as Shepsel was harsh, and Sol was extremely close to her. One day, he was walking home from high school, whistling. A neighbor shouted out the window: "Hey, Sol, what are you whistling for? Don't you know your mother's dead?" Gussie, 51, had had high blood pressure and died suddenly. On the day of her funeral, the street was packed with mourners.

Last year, before Rosh ha-Shanah, I went to a Judaica shop on West 30th Street to buy a tallis — a prayer shawl — and a yarmulke. A man with short red hair and eyeglasses, about 35, grabbed my arm as I walked in. "Come on, we need you," he said. It was time for afternoon prayers, and they were one man shy of the necessary 10.

"I can't — I have to get back to my office," I lied.

"Come on," he said. "A couple of minutes."

70 I sputtered again: can't . . . can't . . . can't. Finally: "I don't know how."

From behind the counter, a woman's voice: "Leave him alone already. You'll get someone else."

A minute later, a 10th man came in and I slunk off to buy my things. At home that night, I stood in front of a mirror, put on the yarmulke and started to wrap myself in the prayer shawl. I was feeling the deep tug of ritual. I got the shawl around my shoulders, though not without a struggle, but then the yarmulke fell off my head. I put it back on, then got my forearms tangled in the shawl, like a mummy. The yarmulke fell off again. As I grabbed for it, I heard the shawl rip.

For about two seconds, I laughed. Then I got sad, and angry — that I don't even know how to put on a prayer shawl. That, at 32, I have to sound out my Hebrew like a first grader. That, even if I had wanted to, I couldn't have been the 10th man.

My father was never overwhelmingly religious; none of Shepsel's children turned out to be. But he certainly knew his way around Judaism and what it would mean to abandon it. I tried to imagine his mind-set on Christmas Island. I knew that the war had depressed him, and that it was hardly an easy time to be even an American Jew. Ever since his mother died, his home situation had been rocky, and he wasn't exactly flush with career opportunities after the war.

75   Reading the New Testament with my father in mind, I came across any number of passages that might have seized him. In Matthew 19:29, for instance: "And everyone who has left houses, brothers, sisters, father, mother, children or land for the sake of my name will be repaid a hundred times over, and also inherit eternal life." But I couldn't imagine the son of an Old World Jew, even one who was willing to shed his Judaism, being satisfied by the Gospels alone, no matter how deft their politics and psychology.

One day, my mother mentioned a book that my father said had greatly influenced him: "Rebuilding a Lost Faith," by John L. Stoddard. Dots began to connect. In one wartime letter, Sol mentioned giving the same book to a friend, and his first job after the war was at P. J. Kenedy & Sons, the Catholic publisher that had put out the Stoddard book — surely not a coincidence.

I was nervous about reading the book. I wanted it to reveal the mystery of his conversion, and I dreaded that it wouldn't. It turned out to be a fairly dry piece of hard-sell apologetics; the last chapter is called "Some Catholic Privileges and Compensations." The moment I read Stoddard's passage about the special appeal of the Virgin Mary, I felt that I owned my father's secret:

"All hearts are not alike. Some unimpassioned souls prefer to pray to God alone . . . . Others are moved to hold communion with their Saviour only . . . . And there are others still, lone, orphaned hearts, who crave a mother's love and care, and find the greatest surcease of their pain by coming to the Mother of their crucified Redeemer . . . . There are in every life some moments when a mother's tenderness outweighs the world, and prayer to Mary often meets this want, especially when one's earthly mother is forever gone."

I wish I had my father's copy. Would those sentences be underlined? Tearstained? From the day he became a Catholic, my father was deeply devoted to Mary. He started a local chapter of the Blue Army, a group dedicated to Mary and the rosary, and constantly wore a scapular around his neck that contained her likeness. He took public-speaking courses, my mother told me, "because he wanted to go to church societies and speak about the Blessed Mother Mary."

80   After the war, Sol did move back in with his family, keeping his conversion secret. His father had grown even more religious in his old age. One day, while Sol was out of the house, Shepsel went to fold a pair of pants that Sol had draped over a chair. A rosary dropped out of the pocket. "If a knife had been plunged into him, I don't think he would have bled," my Aunt Irene told me. "I thought he was going to take his own life."

Instead, Shepsel went into a quiet rage. He declared his son dead and sat shiva, the seven-day mourning period. He announced that Sol was not to enter the house, nor was his name to be spoken. Sol was crushed. He tried to visit his father with Veronica, whom he was now planning to marry.

My mother, whose memory is amazingly Catholic-centric, cannot recall this meeting (which exasperates me to no end); I can only imagine the young couple, remotely hopeful and deathly nervous, standing before the seething old man.

They were married on March 2, 1946, at St. Brigid's Catholic Church in Brooklyn. Only a small group of friends, nearly all Catholics, attended. Shepsel kept his word about Sol, never even inquiring about his grandchildren.

Within a few years, Shepsel was dying of cancer in Kings County Hospital. Very near the end, he cried out: "Solly! Solly! Solly!" Maybe he regretted cutting off his son. Or maybe he was still angry. At the funeral, Sol wasn't allowed inside the chapel, or to stand near the grave. When I learned about this in interviews with relatives, I couldn't believe that my mother had never told me. As it turns out, she didn't know — my father never told her. Nor had anyone ever told Sol that his father had been calling his name in the hospital.

85   I wonder how his life might have been different had he known. Perhaps he — and my mother — wouldn't have been so determined to live as though their families and their Jewishness had never existed. As it was, they would build a future from the ground up, a foundation of secrets and hurt feelings plastered over by a seemingly endless supply of faith.

Like the graduates of some notorious boot camp, my brothers and sisters and I look back with a sort of perverse glee at the rigors of our Catholicism. My oldest sister, Mary, was so convinced of the church's omnipotence that when she walked into a Protestant church with some high-school friends, she was sure its walls would crash down on her head. We were expected to say our prayers with feeling, to go to Mass with joy and to confession with contrition. The boys were to become altar boys, and the girls were to emulate the Virgin Mary, in every way. Dating, if absolutely necessary, was to involve only other Catholics.

Our rebellions were many, but seldom vehement. When she went to college, Mary changed her name to Mona, for whom no saint is named. "Mary was just so religious," she says now. "I never told Mom and Dad why I changed, though, because I didn't want to hurt them. I resented them for requiring us to be so Catholic, but even then, I think, I knew that we had very decent parents."

They were, indeed, unerringly decent — and inexorably Catholic. Soon after they were married, they visited a Pennsylvania farm retreat run by the Catholic Worker organization. Between the sessions on social activism and prayer, they learned about baking bread and growing vegetables, and saw the appeal of living off the land. It made sense: they could embrace the proud poverty of Catholicism and still produce a large and healthy family. In 1959, they bought an old farmhouse on 36 acres upstate near a town called Duanesburg.

Our father had been scraping by on two and three blue-collar jobs. Now, he became a journalist, which he had wanted to be all along. He worked as a copy editor at *The Schenectady Gazette* and then as the religion page editor at *The Troy*

Record, for about $150 a week. Our mother ran the home operation: we milked our cow, slaughtered our chickens, baked our bread, tapped our maple trees and canned, pickled or froze anything that was remotely edible. We were eight Catholic Workers, obedient if reluctant. (We scraped the wheat germ off our oatmeal when Mom wasn't looking and fed our vitamins to the dogs.)

90   At school, we were the kids who could never pull off a trade from our bag lunches. But we were also a sort of minor dynasty, one Dubner rolling through after the next. We played music and sports, occasionally made class president or valedictorian. We were a dependable brand name — a serendipitously un-Jewish-sounding brand name. All told, we passed beautifully as a Catholic family. Our father started the parish library, and our mother was the prime link on the local prayer chain, phoning other parishioners when someone took ill. When abortion was legalized, she helped start the local Right-to-Life chapter; as a 10-year-old, I was enlisted to help make up "Abortion Is Murder" posters with Magic Markers and yellow cardboard.

    Along the way, our parents had discovered the charismatic renewal movement. I remember those prayer meetings more vividly than anything else from that time. About a dozen adults would gather in a ring of folding metal chairs; I was the only child there. They'd close their eyes and start to pray, quietly, addressing Jesus and God in what seemed to me startlingly intimate voices. They would open their pale blue booklets to sing, the melodies and words far more ethereal than our regular hymns. More silence, then they would start to mumble, their faces twisted in what looked like pain, and their voices would leap up and over one another's, jagged bursts of unknown syllables.

    I peeked through half-shut eyelids. Why were they making up this absurd language? Was I supposed to know it, too? It was several months before I heard someone refer to this drama as speaking in tongues; still, I didn't understand. The prayer meetings scared me, and I dreaded going, but in our family it was impractical to refuse a religious duty.

    Our father was now in his mid-50's. He had had a number of health problems, but since finding the charismatic movement, he was on an upswing. It lasted about two years. At a large meeting of charismatics in Albany in late 1973, he gave a short inspirational talk, then sat down and slumped forward in his seat. My mother thought he had fallen asleep. He spent a month in the hospital, and died just before Christmas.

    At his funeral Mass, I served as an altar boy while the rest of my family sat in the front pew. Afterward, in the sacristy, I remember coolly stripping off my cassock and hanging it neatly, the job done. I didn't cry, then or later: my mother, the priest, my parents' friends all told me how happy my father was in heaven, and how proud I should be that God wanted him.

95   I knew they really believed this, but I could neither believe nor disbelieve. To me, God was some sort of complicated magic trick, a foreign tongue I couldn't speak. Every Sunday, I let the communion wafer dissolve on my tongue undisturbed, as the nuns had taught; I waited for the transubstantiation, to feel God filling up my body, a feeling I dearly wanted. Week after week, it didn't happen.

After my father died, my mother began going to church even more often, every morning during the summer, and I usually went with her. I now believe that she may have mistaken my obedience for devotion, and that I encouraged her to do so. I had neither the courage nor the language to challenge her faith, much less reject it. I thought about God less and less, primarily as a punisher whose wrath I could escape by cleverness. Going off to college, I had a sharply defined religious identity that I was eager to shed.

For Rosh ha-Shanah last year, I decided to go with a friend, Ivan Kronenfeld, to an old Orthodox synagogue on the Lower East Side. Even though the service would last into the night and would be totally in Hebrew, I felt armed to the teeth. I had bought a prayer book with English transliterations; I had been taking my classes; I was wearing my brand-new tallis. No doubt about it, I thought: Today, I am a Jew.

I sat in the second row with Ivan, who is in his late 40's. In front of us were a tall, straight-backed man and his 15-year-old son. The boy wore eyeglasses and a suit like his father's, and the two of them moved like a dancer and his shadow: standing-bowing-sitting-standing-singing, all with effortless passion. The boy was called up to sing from the Torah, and his voice was sweet and clear.

For the first hour or so, I hung in. But I kept losing my way in the prayer book. The tallis felt scratchy on my neck. The Hebrew was flying by too fast to sing along. Watching the boy and his father, I hated them. I had come here to pray, to account for my jealousy and selfishness of the past year; now I was jealous of the boy and selfish enough to pretend that I wasn't. At the first break, I told Ivan I'd had enough, folded up my tallis and went home.

100   I had fallen in with Ivan a few years earlier, when I was studying and teaching writing in graduate school. A wise but decidedly unorthodox Jew, he was a brilliant, controlling mentor — an actor, a deal-maker, a raconteur, a scholar of boxing and psychology, of Marx and Maimonides. Once he heard my family's story, he became my Virgil, shuttling me from a claustrophobic little Hasidic shul in Brooklyn to the sagging Judaica shops and bookstores on the Lower East Side. He lectured me on Akiba, Spinoza, Disraeli, Salk, Arthur Miller, Hank Greenberg, and most of it stuck. I felt as though I were growing into my skin, as though I were coming home to a place that I hadn't known to exist. My mother, meanwhile, was sending me stacks of Catholic literature; for Easter, she gave me the New Testament on cassette.

Ivan introduced me to several rabbis, most of whom unhesitatingly pronounced me a Jew. I was proud, and confused. At shul, Ivan showed me how to touch the fringes of my tallis to the Torah, then to my lips, but I felt painfully awkward — half intruder, half impostor. As enthusiastic as I was about this new identity, I was growing leery of having it decreed by someone else. And Ivan, for all his sincerity, was, like Mme. Souvorina, not inclined to subtle encouragements.

I stopped trying to go to synagogue. Besides, I was busy exploring the secular precincts of an unspent Jewish youth: klezmer music, Ratner's deli, Jewish girlfriends, Sholem Aleichem and *The Forward,* now published in English. One friend bought a mezuza for my door; he didn't spend much, he joked, because he figured I'd be moving to Israel soon. I became what I wanted to become, a cultural and intellectual Jew — which left me wanting, as it had my parents.

But it left us wanting different things. My mother, recognizing life's temporality, was determined to insure a life everlasting. For reasons I can't explain, I was less consumed with beating back the darkness of death than with finding a schematic for the here and now.

About 18 months ago, I called my mother to tell her that I had taken on a book project, helping to put together the teachings of Menachem Mendel Schneerson, the late Lubavitcher Rebbe. Her first reaction was that it might be dangerous, because the Hasids were such obvious targets for anti-Semites. Then she said that it might be good for me, since understanding Judaism would deepen my understanding of Catholicism.

105   Working on the book meant thinking and reading about God a great deal, from the simplest Hasidic parables to the Talmud, the writings of Martin Buber and the medieval French scholar Rashi. It didn't take long to realize what a painfully narrow view of God I had grown up with. Now, my mind purged of fairy-tale images, unencumbered by fear, able to see that religion itself is man-made, I began to wrestle with a new idea of God. And I came to understand that the very act of wrestling is paramount. Quite organically, I had begun to think Jewishly about God.

For several months, I was content simply to relish this understanding. But I was bombarded by small, sacred moments. Now that my head was engaged, my soul demanded the same attention. I started going to synagogue again (and learning my way around the service), reading the Torah, having Shabbos dinner and studying the Talmud with friends. I started spending more time with Ivan.

As a Jew, I am still astoundingly ignorant, and sometimes compensate with enthusiasm, like trying to tackle the Orthodox Rosh ha-Shanah service last fall. I recognized my parents in this enthusiasm; it is common to the convert — a giddy rush to gather up the promises of a new and better life and hold them so tightly to your breast that they might pass through to your heart.

Sometimes they do. Eight days after the Rosh ha-Shanah service, I went back to Ivan's shul for Yom Kippur: I had decided that I didn't need to be perfect to be a good Jew. The straight-backed man and his son were in the front pew again, singing beautifully. The rabbi, a soft-voiced, sad-eyed old man, turned out to be the boy's grandfather. He stepped forward to give a sermon. During these days of reflection, he said, he had been asking himself what makes us keep on being Jews when it's such a struggle. "And I found the answer in six words," he said. "Six words in the Talmud, written by Rashi: 'He will not let us go.' "

It isn't a matter of our choosing whether to quit God, the old rabbi explained; it is God who chooses not to quit us.

110   Of course! I immediately understood that, as much as I had chosen my religion, I chose the one that had chosen me. I had come to Judaism for many, many reasons, but the journey soon developed its own relentless, inexplicable

momentum — the same sort of momentum, obviously, that had moved my parents in the opposite direction.

But was it even the opposite direction? True, the relative merits of Catholicism and Judaism could be argued endlessly, as my mother and I have tried; but hadn't my parents and I ultimately trodden the same path? Like Abraham, we left our native land and our father's house for a land we did not know. As much as ours were spiritual acts, they were cultural, familial and psychological acts as well. Choosing a religion means far more than choosing a new perspective on God — it informs how we talk, eat and vote, how we think about justice and history, money and sex. We choose a new religion to choose a new self, to set ourselves apart from where we have come. My parents, as it turns out, were practicing identity politics long before it had a name.

The day after Yom Kippur, I left on a trip to Poland. When I got to Pultusk, where my father's parents came from, I wanted to see where their parents were buried. As in most of Europe, the Nazis had made the Jews of Pultusk tear down their families' gravestones for building material. My hotel, a sprawling hilltop castle, was a former bishop's residence; during the war, it had been commandeered by the Nazis. The Jewish gravestones, I was told, had been used to pave the courtyard where I was just strolling.

My first taste of Jewish rage was deep; it was a shock to realize what I had become a part of. That night, lying in bed, I recognized how thoroughly my siblings and I had been spared that rage. I also recognized, for the first time, that had my parents not become such fervent Catholics, I probably wouldn't have been born — how many Jewish families of the 1950's and 60's, after all, had eight children?

My mother is a gentle woman, but her Catholicism runs so deep that I was sure she couldn't accept her youngest son as a Jew. Long after my intentions were known, she gave me for my birthday a coffee-table book called "The Living Gospels of Jesus Christ."

115   The first sign of detente was a newspaper clipping she sent last year, just after the Easter and Passover holidays. It was about a group of Jews in Sarajevo who had celebrated Passover with a famous 14th-century Haggadah that had miraculously survived the Bosnian war.

When the Rabbi Schneerson book came out, she sent me a note: "Great work! And I can see why you're attracted to Judaism. For me, Catholicism is the blossoming or fruition or completion of Judaism. Lots of love, Mom."

When we had first sat down to talk about her conversion, she was cooperative but unenthusiastic. Now she was calling to reminisce about her family seders. She would even call to talk about the family story that pained her the most: David Greenglass and Ethel Greenglass, who married Julius Rosenberg, were my mother's first cousins; she had known them fairly well as a girl. No one in my family was aware of this until a few years ago, and when I first asked my mother about it, she reached out and turned off the tape recorder.

Ours is still a fragile understanding, built as it is over such powerful waters. I believe it is an understanding, though, not a capitulation. I think she realizes that I did indeed inherit her faith, and the faith of my father, but that it has taken a different shape.

Just before Christmas, I drove upstate to my father's cemetery. I was ready to carry out my act of spiritual subterfuge: I had a yarmulke and the Mourner's Kaddish in my pocket. It took me a while to find his marker. I scraped off the snow, saw the cross and then his name. I never reached for the yarmulke. Would I want some son of mine saying the rosary when I'm lying in a Jewish cemetery? Painful as it has been to accept my father's choice, it was his choice, just as I've been free to make mine. I ended up having a conversation with him; it cleared up a lot of things. I did leave a little stone at the corner of his plot.

120   When I got home, there was a Christmas card from my mother, offering me a novena. And, in a separate envelope, a Hanukkah card. "I don't remember my letters enough to translate this," she wrote beneath the Hebrew lettering, "but I'm sure it's a good wish."

On the phone a few days later, she told me about spending Christmas Eve alone. With eight children, Christmas had always been a rambunctious affair, and in the past she had missed it. This year, she just quietly reflected on her faith: Dec. 24 was the anniversary of her baptism, 53 years ago. She thought about all her blessings, she said, and about my father, "happy as he can be, because he's got it all, face to face with God."

In the past, I would have shut out a comment like that — it's too far removed from what I believe. Now I just listened to the serenity in her voice. There was a long silence on the line. It was the sound of forgiveness, I'm sure, and it was traveling in two directions.

▪ QUESTIONS FOR INQUIRY AND ACTION ▪

1. "A religious conversion," Dubner writes, "is imperfect. At best, the convert is a palimpsest. The old writing will always bleed through." What is a palimpsest, and why is this metaphor appropriate and evocative?

2. "Everyone who chooses religion is running toward—and away from—his own mountain of questions." In your notebook, brainstorm what you think some of those questions are. Are they questions you, too, are asking?

3. Do your own research into "religious switching" by reading and talking with others. How common is it in your own communities? In your faith community, how many of the people were raised in that tradition?

4. Record an oral history of one of your grandparents or an older relative or friend. Ask him or her to talk with you about growing up within a particular religious tradition and how he or she has seen the experience of religion change over the years.

Michael Wolfe
Islam: the Next American Religion?

Michael Wolfe is a columnist for Beliefnet, *a multi-faith e-community (http://www.beliefnet.com/). He is the author of a number of books on Islam, including* The Hajj *(1993), a memoir of his pilgrimage to Mecca. He also worked on the PBS documentary,* Muhammad: Legacy of a Prophet, *which won a 2004 Cine Award Special Jury Prize for best documentary and aired around the world in a dozen languages on the National Geographic Channel. In response to the 9/11 crisis Wolfe edited* Taking Back Islam, *a collection of articles by 40 Muslims; it won a 2003 Wilbur Award for best book of the year on a religious theme. "Islam: the Next American Religion?" was first published as one of Wolfe's columns for* Beliefnet *February 4, 2004.*

The U.S. began as a haven for Christian outcasts. But what religion fits our current zeitgeist? The answer may be Islam.

Americans tend to think of their country as, at the very least, a nominally Christian nation.

Didn't the Pilgrims come here for freedom to practice their Christian religion? Don't Christian values of righteousness under God, and freedom, reinforce America's democratic, capitalist ideals?

True enough. But there's a new religion on the block now, one that fits the current zeitgeist nicely. It's Islam.

5   Islam is the third-largest and fastest growing religious community in the United States. This is not just because of immigration. More than 50% of America's six million Muslims were born here. Statistics like these imply some basic agreement between core American values and the beliefs that Muslims hold. Americans who make the effort to look beyond popular stereotypes to learn the truth of Islam are surprised to find themselves on familiar ground.

Is America a Muslim nation? Here are seven reasons the answer may be yes.

Islam is monotheistic. Muslims worship the same God as Jews and Christians. They also revere the same prophets as Judaism and Christianity, from Abraham, the first monotheist, to Moses, the law giver and messenger of God, to Jesus—not leaving out Noah, Job, or Isaiah along the way. The concept of a Judeo-Christian tradition only came to the fore in the 1940s in America. Now, as a nation, we may be transcending it, turning to a more inclusive "Abrahamic" view.

In January, President Bush grouped mosques with churches and synagogues in his inaugural address. A few days later, when he posed for photographers at a meeting of several dozen religious figures, the Shi'ite imam Muhammad Qazwini, of Orange County, Calif., stood directly behind Bush's chair like a presiding angel, dressed in the robes and turban of his south Iraqi youth.

Islam is democratic in spirit. Islam advocates the right to vote and educate yourself and pursue a profession. The Qur'an, on which Islamic law is based, enjoins Muslims to govern themselves by discussion and consensus. In mosques, there is no particular priestly hierarchy. With Islam, each individual is responsible for the condition of her or his own soul. Everyone stands equal before God.

10   Americans, who mostly associate Islamic government with a handful of tyrants, may find this independent spirit surprising, supposing that Muslims are somehow predisposed to passive submission. Nothing could be further from the truth. The dictators reigning today in the Middle East are not the result of Islamic principles. They are more a result of global economics and the aftermath of European colonialism. Meanwhile, like everyone else, average Muslims the world over want a larger say in what goes on in the countries where they live. Those in America may actually succeed in it. In this way, America is closer in spirit to Islam than many Arab countries.

Islam contains an attractive mystical tradition. Mysticism is grounded in the individual search for God. Where better to do that than in America, land of individualists and spiritual seekers? And who might better benefit than Americans from the centuries-long tradition of teachers and students that characterize Islam. Surprising as it may seem, America's best-selling poet du jour is a Muslim mystic named Rumi, the 800-year-old Persian bard and founder of the Mevlevi Path, known in the West as the Whirling Dervishes. Even book packagers are now rushing him into print to meet and profit from mainstream demand for this visionary. Translators as various as Robert Bly, Coleman Barks, and Kabir and Camille Helminski have produced dozens of books of Rumi's verse and have only begun to bring his enormous output before the English-speaking world. This is a concrete poetry of ecstasy, where physical reality and the longing for God are joined by flashes of metaphor and insight that continue to speak across the centuries.

Islam is egalitarian. From New York to California, the only houses of worship that are routinely integrated today are the approximately 4,000 Muslim mosques. That is because Islam is predicated on a level playing field, especially when it comes to standing before God. The Pledge of Allegiance (one nation, "under God") and Lincoln's Gettysburg Address (all people are "created equal") express themes that are also basic to Islam.

Islam is often viewed as an aggressive faith because of the concept of jihad, but this is actually a misunderstood term. Because Muslims believe that God wants a just world, they tend to be activists, and they emphasize that people are equal before God. These are two reasons why African Americans have been drawn in such large numbers to Islam. They now comprise about one-third of all Muslims in America.

Meanwhile, this egalitarian streak also plays itself out in relations between the sexes. Muhammad, Islam's prophet, actually was a reformer in his day. Following the Qur'an, he limited the number of wives a man could have and strongly recommended against polygamy. The Qur'an laid out a set of marriage laws that guarantees married women their family names, their own possessions and capital, the right to agree upon whom they will marry, and the right to initiate divorce. In Islam's early period, women were professionals and property owners, as increasingly they are today. None of this may seem obvious to most Americans because of cultural overlays that at times make Islam appear to be a repressive faith toward women—but if you look more closely, you can see the egalitarian streak preserved in the Qur'an finding expression in contemporary terms. In today's Iran, for example, more women than men attend university, and in recent local elections there, 5,000 women ran for public office.

15   **Islam shares America's new interest in food purity and diet.** Muslims conduct a monthlong fast during the holy month of Ramadan, a practice that many Americans admire and even seek to emulate. I happened to spend quite a bit of time with a non-Muslim friend during Ramadan this year. After a month of being exposed to a practice that brings some annual control to human consumption, my friend let me know, in January, that he was "doing a little Ramadan" of his own. I asked what he meant. "Well, I'm not drinking anything or smoking anything for at least a month, and I'm going off coffee." Given this friend's normal intake of coffee, I could not believe my ears.

Muslims also observe dietary laws that restrict the kind of meat they can eat. These laws require that the permitted, or halal, meat is prepared in a manner that emphasizes cleanliness and a humane treatment of animals. These laws ride on the same trends that have made organic foods so popular.

Islam is tolerant of other faiths. Like America, Islam has a history of respecting other religions. In Muhammad's day, Christians, Sabeans, and Jews in Muslim lands retained their own courts and enjoyed considerable autonomy. As Islam spread east toward India and China, it came to view Zoroastrianism, Hinduism, and Buddhism as valid paths to salvation. As Islam spread north and west, Judaism especially benefited. The return of the Jews to Jerusalem, after centuries as outcasts, only came about after Muslims took the city in 638. The first thing the Muslims did there was to rescue the Temple Mount, which by then had been turned into a garbage heap.

Today, of course, the long discord between Israel and Palestine has acquired harsh religious overtones. Yet the fact remains that this is a battle for real estate, not a war between two faiths. Islam and Judaism revere the same prophetic lineage, back to Abraham, and no amount of bullets or barbed wire can change that. As the *New York Times* recently reported, while Muslim/Jewish tensions sometimes flare on university campuses, lately these same students have found ways to forge common links. For one thing, the two religions share similar dietary laws, including ritual slaughter and a prohibition on pork. Joining forces at Dartmouth this fall, the first kosher/halal dining hall is scheduled to open its doors this autumn. That isn't all: They're already planning a joint Thanksgiving dinner, with birds dressed at a nearby farm by a rabbi and an imam. If the American Pilgrims were watching now, they'd be rubbing their eyes with amazement. And, because they came here fleeing religious persecution, they might also understand.

Islam encourages the pursuit of religious freedom. The Pilgrims landing at Plymouth Rock is not the world's first story of religious emigration. Muhammad and his little band of 100 followers fled religious persecution, too, from Mecca in the year 622. They only survived by going to Madinah, an oasis a few hundred miles north, where they established a new community based on a religion they could only practice secretly back home. No wonder then that, in our own day, many Muslims have come here as pilgrims from oppression, leaving places like Kashmir, Bosnia, and Kosovo, where being a Muslim may radically shorten your life span. When the 20th century's list of emigrant exiles is added up, it will prove to be heavy with Muslims, that's for sure.

20   All in all, there seems to be a deep resonance between Islam and the United States. Although one is a world religion and the other is a sovereign nation, both are traditionally very strong on individual responsibility. Like New Hampshire's motto, "Live Free or Die," America is wedded to individual liberty and an ethic based on right action. For a Muslim, spiritual salvation depends on these. This is best expressed in a popular saying: Even when you think God isn't watching you, act as if he is.

Who knows? Perhaps it won't be long now before words like *salat* (Muslim prayer) and *Ramadan* join *karma* and *Nirvana* in Webster's Dictionary, and Muslims take their place in America's mainstream.

▦ QUESTIONS FOR INQUIRY AND ACTION ▦

1. Analyze the rhetorical situation of Wolfe's essay. Who is the implied audience, and what seems to be his purpose for writing? Do you find his argument persuasive?

2. Put Wolfe's essay into conversation with Stephen Dubner's on Judaism and Anne Lamott's on Christianity. Each author came to his or her chosen religion later in life, and each cares deeply about it. How does each author describe his or her religion?

3. How popular is Islam in your local or state community? Are many of the Muslims in your community American converts, like Michael Wolfe, or are most of them Muslims who have immigrated to the United States from another country?

4. Attend a Muslim worship service either on your campus or elsewhere in your local community. Write a description of your experience.

STOPANDTHINK

WHAT'S YOUR SPIRITUAL COMMUNITY?

The Web site Beliefnet.com, which considers itself a "multi-faith e-community," includes, among its many articles and blogs, a number of quizzes to help readers think about their own spiritual and religious leanings. Their popular "Belief-O-Matic" quiz asks you questions about your conception of God, the afterlife, and human nature in order to help you place yourself among the various world religions. For instance, one of the questions is:

continued on next page

3. What are the origins of the physical universe and life on earth? Choose one.

☐ As in the book of Genesis, God created a mature universe and mature life forms from nothing in less than 7 days, less than 10,000 years ago.

☐ As in the book of Genesis, but "day" is not 24 hours, possibly refers to thousands (or even millions) of years, or to creation phases.

☐ God is creating and controlling the phenomena uncovered by scientists. Or there are other spiritual explanations, but not in conflict with scientific discovery.

☐ All matter and life forms are manifestations (or illusions) of the eternal Absolute (Ultimate Truth, Universal Soul or Mind, etc.).

☐ Only natural forces (like evolution) and no Creator or spiritual forces. Or not sure. Or not important.

☐ None of the above.

Another of their quizzes recognizes that many people find it difficult to answer a question phrased, "What is your religion?" because many people define themselves outside a traditionally religious framework. Instead, the quiz asks, "What is your spiritual type?" and includes questions such as the following.

Q2. When I think about issues of faith or spirituality, my foremost concern is:

☐ 1. A sense of connection to something larger than myself

☐ 2. A rational understanding of whether religious claims are valid

☐ 3. A personal relationship with God

☐ 4. A framework of morality and hope

Q20. In regards to religion and morality:

☐ 1. I think it's impossible to be moral without being religious

☐ 2. It's possible but difficult to be moral without reminders from religion

☐ 3. It's entirely possible to develop and live by a good moral code without religion

☐ 4. Religion makes it harder to be a moral person

When your responses are tallied, you are given a description of yourself from "Hardcore Skeptic" to "Questioning Believer" to "Candidate for Clergy." The point of the quiz is less to label you, though, than to spark reflection and discussion. *Beliefnet* includes links to join in conversation with others who share your spiritual leanings.

What is the appeal of quizzes to determine our spiritual beliefs? Does a quiz trivialize the importance of spiritual or religious belief?

Wendy Kaminer
The Last Taboo: Why America
Needs Atheism

Wendy Kaminer is a writer, lawyer, and public policy fellow at Radcliffe Public Policy Institute, Radcliffe College. She has authored a number of books of social critique including A Fearful Freedom: Women's Flight from Equality *(1990),* I'm Dysfunctional, You're Dysfunctional: The Recovery Movement and Other Self-Help Fashions *(1992), and* Sleeping with Extra-Terrestrials: The Rise of Irrationalism and Perils of Piety *(1999). "The Last Taboo: Why America Needs Atheism" was the cover story of the* New Republic *on October 14, 1996.*

It was King Kong who put the fear of God in me, when I was 8 or 9 years old. Blessed with irreligious parents and excused from attending Sunday school or weekly services, I had relatively little contact with imaginary, omnipotent authority figures until the Million Dollar Movie brought King Kong to our living room TV Tyrannical and invincible (I never found his capture and enslavement believable), he awakened my superstitions. Watching Kong terrorize the locals, I imagined being prey to an irrational, supernatural brute whom I could never outrun or outsmart. I couldn't argue with him, so my only hope was to grovel and propitiate him with sacrifices. Looking nothing like Fay Wray, I doubted I could charm him; besides, his love was as arbitrary and unpredictable as his wrath.

For the next several years, like the natives in the movie, I clung to rituals aimed at keeping him at bay. (I can only analyze my rituals with hindsight; at the time, I was immersed in them unthinkingly.) Instead of human sacrifices, I offered him neatness, a perfectly ordered room. Every night before going to bed, I straightened all the stuff on my desk and bureau, arranged my stuffed animals in rectangular tableaus and made sure all doors and drawers were tightly shut. I started at one end of the room and worked my way around, counterclockwise; when I finished, I started all over again, checking and rechecking my work three, four or five times.

Going to bed became an ordeal. I hated my rituals; they were tedious and time-consuming and very embarrassing. I knew they were stupid and always kept them secret until, eventually, I grew out of them. I still harbor superstitions, of course, but with less shame and more humor; I find them considerably less compelling.

If I were to mock religious belief as childish, if I were to suggest that worshiping a supernatural deity, convinced that it cares about your welfare, is like worrying about monsters in the closet who find you tasty enough to eat, if I were to describe God as our creation, likening him to a mechanical gorilla, I'd violate the norms of civility and religious correctness. I'd be excoriated as an example of the cynical, liberal elite responsible for America's moral decline. I'd be pitied for my spiritual blindness; some people would try to enlighten and convert me. I'd receive hate mail. Atheists generate about as much sympathy as pedophiles. But, while pedophilia may at least be characterized as a disease, atheism is a choice, a willful rejection of beliefs to which vast majorities of people cling.

5   Yet conventional wisdom holds that we suffer from an excess of secularism. Virtuecrats from Hillary Clinton to William Bennett to Patrick Buchanan blame America's moral decay on our lack of religious belief. "The great malady of the 20th century" is "'loss of soul,'" bestselling author Thomas Moore declares, complaining that "we don't believe in the soul." Of course, if that were true, there'd be no buyers for his books. In fact, almost all Americans (95 percent) profess belief in God or some universal spirit, according to a 1994 survey by *U.S. News and World Report*. Seventy-six percent imagine God as a heavenly father who actually pays attention to their prayers. Gallup reports that 44 percent believe in the biblical account of creation and that 36 percent of all Americans describe themselves as "born-again."

Adherence to mainstream religions is supplemented by experimentation with an eclectic collection of New Age beliefs and practices. Roughly half of all Catholics and Protestants surveyed by Gallup in 1991 believed in ESP; nearly as many believed in psychic healing. Fifty-three percent of Catholics and 40 percent of Protestants professed belief in UFOs, and about one-quarter put their faith in astrology. Nearly one-third of all American teenagers believe in reincarnation. Once I heard Shirley MacLaine explain the principles of reincarnation on the *Donahue* show. "Can you come back as a bird?" one woman asked. "No," MacLaine replied, secure in her convictions. "You only come back as a higher life form." No one asked her how she knew.

In this climate—with belief in guardian angels and creationism becoming commonplace—making fun of religion is as risky as burning a flag in an American Legion hall. But, by admitting that they're fighting a winning battle, advocates of renewed religiosity would lose the benefits of appearing besieged. Like liberal rights organizations that attract more money when conservative authoritarians are in power, religious groups inspire more believers when secularism is said to hold sway. So editors at the *Wall Street Journal* protest an "ardent hostility toward religion" in this country, claiming that religious people are "suspect." When forced by facts to acknowledge that God enjoys unshakable, non-partisan, majoritarian support, religion's proselytizers charge that our country is nonetheless controlled by liberal intellectual elites who disdain religious belief and have denied it a respected public role.

Educated professionals tend to be embarrassed by belief, Yale Law Professor Stephen Carter opined in *The Culture of Disbelief,* a best-selling complaint about the fabled denigration of religion in public life. Carter acknowledges that belief is widespread but argues that it has been trivialized by the rationalist biases of elites and their insistence on keeping religion out of the public sphere. Carter's thesis is echoed regularly by conservative commentators. Another recent *Wall Street Journal* editorial asserted that religious indoctrination is one of the most effective forms of drug treatment and wondered at the "prejudice against religion by much of our judicial and media elites." Newt Gingrich has attacked the "secular, anti-religious view of the left."

No evidence is adduced to substantiate these charges of liberal irreligiosity run rampant. No faithless liberals are named, no influential periodicals or articles cited—perhaps because they're chimeras. Review the list of prominent left-of-center opinion makers and public intellectuals. Who among them mocks religion? Several have gained or increased their prominence partly through their embrace of belief. Harvard Professor Cornel West is a part-time preacher; Michael Lerner came into public view as Hillary Clinton's guru; Gloria Steinem greatly expanded her mainstream appeal by writing about spirituality. Bill Moyers, who introduced New Age holy men Joseph Campbell and Robert Bly to the American public, regularly pays homage to faith in traditional and alternative forms in television specials. Popular spirituality authors, like Thomas Moore, are regarded as public intellectuals in spite or because of their pontifications about faith. Even secular political theorists, preoccupied with civic virtue, are overly solicitous of religion and religious communities.

10   The supposedly liberal, mainstream press offers unprecedented coverage of religion, taking pains not to offend the faithful. An op-ed piece on popular spirituality that I wrote for the *New York Times* this past summer was carefully cleansed by my editors of any irreverence toward established religion (although I was invited to mock New Age). I was not allowed to observe that, while Hillary Clinton was criticized for conversing with Eleanor Roosevelt, millions of Americans regularly talk to Jesus, long deceased, and that many people believe that God talks to them, unbidden. Nor was I permitted to point out that, to an atheist, the sacraments are as silly as a seance. These remarks and others were excised because they were deemed "offensive."

Indeed, what's striking about American intellectuals today, liberal and conservative alike, is not their Voltairean skepticism but their deference to belief and their utter failure to criticize, much less satirize, America's romance with God. They've abandoned the tradition of caustic secularism that once provided refuge for the faithless: people "are all insane," Mark Twain remarked in *Letters from the Earth.* "Man is a marvelous curiosity. . . he thinks he is the Creator's pet. . . he even believes the Creator loves him; has a passion for him; sits up nights to admire him; yes and watch over him and keep him out of trouble. He prays to him and thinks He listens. Isn't it a quaint idea." No prominent liberal thinker writes like that anymore.

Religion is "so absurd that it comes close to imbecility," H.L. Mencken declared in *Treatise on the Gods.* "The priest, realistically considered, is the most immoral of men, for he is always willing to sacrifice every other sort of good to the one good of his arcanum—the vague body of mysteries that he calls the truth."

Mencken was equally scornful of the organized church: "Since the early days, [it] has thrown itself violently against every effort to liberate the body and mind of man. It has been, at all times and everywhere, the habitual and incorrigible defender of bad governments, bad laws, bad social theories, bad institutions. It was, for centuries, an apologist for slavery, as it was an apologist for the divine right of kings." Mencken was not entirely unsympathetic to the wishful thinking behind virtually all religion—the belief that we needn't die, that the universe isn't arbitrary and indifferent to our plight, that we are governed by a supernatural being whom we might induce to favor us. Still, while a staunch defender of the right to say or think virtually anything, he singled out as "the most curious social convention of the great age in which we live" the notion that religious opinions themselves (not just the right to harbor them) "should be respected." Name one widely published intellectual today who would dare to write that.

Mencken would have been deeply dismayed by contemporary public policy discussions: left and right, they are suffused with piety. The rise of virtue talk—which generally takes the form of communitarianism on the left and nostalgia for Victorianism on the right—has resulted in a striking re-moralization of public policy debates. Today, it's rare to hear a non-normative analysis of social problems, one that doesn't focus on failings of individual character or collective virtue: discussions of structural unemployment have given way to jeremiads about the work ethic; approaches to juvenile crime focus on the amorality of America's youth, not the harsh deprivations that shape them. Among academic and media elites, as well as politicians, there is considerable agreement that social pathologies such as crime, drug abuse, teenage pregnancy and chronic welfare dependency are, at least in part, symptomatic of spiritual malaise—loss of faith in God or a more generalized anomie. (Some blame TV.) Try to imagine an avowed atheist running successfully for public office; it's hard enough for politicians to oppose prayer in school.

15   Today, proposals for silent school prayer promise to bring spirituality into the classroom, avoiding religious sectarianism. "Spirituality," a term frequently used to describe the vaguest intimations of supernatural realities, is popularly considered a mark of virtue and is as hostile to atheism as religious belief. Spirituality, after all, is simply religion deinstitutionalized and shorn of any exclusionary doctrines. In a pluralistic marketplace, it has considerable appeal. Spirituality embraces traditional religious and New Age practices, as well as forays into pop psychology and a devotion to capitalism. Exercises in self-esteem and recovery from various addictions are presented as spiritual endeavors by codependency experts ranging from John Bradshaw to Gloria Steinem. The generation of wealth is spiritualized by best-selling personal development gurus such as Deepak Chopra, author of *The Seven Spiritual Laws of Success,* which offers "the ability to create unlimited wealth with effortless ease." (Some sixty years ago, Napoleon Hill's best-selling *Think and Grow Rich* made readers a similar promise.)

Spirituality discourages you from passing judgment on any of these endeavors: it's egalitarian, ranking no one religion over another, and doesn't require people to choose between faiths. You can claim to be a spiritual person without professing loyalty to a particular dogma or even understanding it. Spirituality makes no intellectual demands on you; all it requires is a general belief in immaterialism (which can be used to increase your material possessions).

In our supposedly secular culture, atheists, like Madelyn Murray O'Hare, are demonized more than renegade believers, like Jimmy Swaggart. Indeed, popular Christian theology suggests that repentant sinners on their way to Heaven will look down upon ethical atheists bound for Hell. Popular spirituality authors, who tend to deny the existence of Hell, and evil, suggest that atheists and other skeptics are doomed to spiritual stasis (the worst fate they can imagine). You might pity such faithless souls, but you wouldn't trust them.

You might not even extend equal rights to them. America's pluralistic ideal does not protect atheism; public support for different belief systems is matched by intolerance of disbelief. According to surveys published in the early 1980s, before today's pre-millennial religious revivalism, nearly 70 percent of all Americans agreed that the freedom to worship "applies to all religious groups, regardless of how extreme their beliefs are"; but only 26 percent agreed that the freedom of atheists to make fun of God and religion "should be legally protected no matter who might be offended." Seventy-one percent held that atheists "who preach against God and religion" should not be permitted to use civic auditoriums. Intolerance for atheism was stronger even than intolerance of homosexuality.

Like heterosexuality, faith in immaterial realities is popularly considered essential to individual morality. When politicians proclaim their belief in God, regardless of their religion, they are signaling their trustworthiness and adherence to traditional moral codes of behavior, as well as their humility. Belief in God levels human hierarchies while offering infallible systems of right and wrong. By declaring your belief, you imply that an omnipotent, omniscient (and benign) force is the source of your values and ideas. You appropriate the rightness of divinity.

20   It's not surprising that belief makes so many people sanctimonious. Whether or not it makes them good is impossible to know. Considering its history, you can safely call organized religion a mixed blessing. Apart from its obvious atrocities—the Crusades or the Salem witch trials—religion is a fount of quotidian oppressions, as anyone who's ever lost a job because of sexual orientation might attest. Of course, religion has been a force of liberation, as well. The civil rights movement demonstrated Christianity's power to inspire and maintain a struggle against injustice. Today, churches provide moral leadership in the fight to maintain social welfare programs, and in recent history, whether opposing Star Wars or providing sanctuary to Salvadoran refugees, church leaders have lent their moral authority to war resistance. Over time, the clergy may have opposed as many wars as they started.

It is as difficult to try to quantify the effect of organized religion on human welfare as it is to generalize about the character, behavior and beliefs of all religious people. Religion is probably less a source for good or evil in people than a vehicle for them. "Religion is only good for good people," Mary McCarthy wrote, in the days when liberal intellectuals may have deserved a reputation for skepticism. It's equally difficult to generalize about the character of non-believers. Indeed, the disdain for self-righteousness that atheism and agnosticism tend to encourage make them particularly difficult to defend. How do you make the case for not believing in God without falling into the pit of moral certainty squirming with believers? You can't accurately claim that atheists are particularly virtuous or intelligent or even courageous: some are just resigned to their existential terrors.

Of course, whether or not atheists are in general better or worse citizens than believers, neither the formation of individual character nor religious belief is the business of government. Government is neither competent nor empowered to ease our existential anxieties; its jurisdiction is the material world of hardship and injustice. It can and should make life a little more fair, and, in order to do so, it necessarily enforces some majoritarian notions of moral behavior—outlawing discrimination, for example, or a range of violent assaults. But, in a state that respects individual privacy, law can only address bad behavior, not bad thoughts, and cannot require adherence to what are considered good thoughts—like love of God. Government can help make people comfortable, ensuring access to health care, housing, education and the workplace. But government cannot make people good.

Champions of more religion in public life are hard put to reconcile the prevailing mistrust of government's ability to manage mundane human affairs—like material poverty—with the demand that it address metaphysical problems, like poverty of spirit. It is becoming increasingly popular to argue, for example, that welfare recipients should be deprived of government largess for their own good, to defeat the "culture of dependency," while middle-class believers receive government subsidies (vouchers) to finance the private, religious education of their kids.

Even those "judicial elites" scorned by *Wall Street Journal* editorial writers for their hostility to religion are increasingly apt to favor state support for private religious activities. In a remarkable recent decision, *Rosenberger v. University of Virginia,* the Supreme Court held that private religious groups are entitled to direct public funding. Rosenberger involved a Christian student newspaper at the University of Virginia that was denied funding provided to other student groups because of its religiosity. A state-run institution, the university is subject to the First Amendment strictures imposed on any governmental entity. Reflecting obvious concern about state entanglement in the exercise of religion, the school's funding guidelines prohibited the distribution of student activities funds to religious groups. The guidelines did not discriminate against any particular religion or viewpoint; funds were withheld from any group that "primarily promotes or manifests a particular belief in or about a deity or an ultimate reality." The student paper at issue in the case was actively engaged in proselytizing.

25   Arguing that the University of Virginia had an obligation to pay for the publication of this paper, as it paid for other student activities, editors of the newspaper, *Wide Awake,* sued the school and ultimately prevailed in the Supreme Court, which, like other "elitist" institutions, has become more protective of religion than concerned about its establishment by the state. In a five to four decision, authored by Justice Anthony Kennedy, the Court held that the denial of funding to *Wide Awake* constituted "viewpoint discrimination." Religion was not "excluded as a subject matter" from fundable student discussions, the Court observed; instead funding guidelines excluded discussions of secular issues shaped by "student journalistic efforts with religious editorial viewpoints."

It is one of the ironies of the church/state debate that the equation of Christianity (and other sects) with worldly ideologies, such as Marxism, supply-side economics, theories of white supremacy, agnosticism or feminism, has been championed by the religious right. Those inclined to worship, who believe that their sect offers access to Heaven, are the last people you'd expect to argue that religion is just another product vying for shelf space in the marketplace, entitled to the same treatment as its competitors. You wouldn't expect critics of secularism to suggest that devout Christians are merely additional claimants of individual rights: religion is more often extolled by virtuecrats as an antidote to untrammeled individualism. But new Christian advocacy groups, modeled after advocacy groups on the left, are increasingly portraying practicing Christians as citizens oppressed by secularism and are seeking judicial protection. The American Center for Law and Justice (ACLG), founded by Pat Robertson, is one of the leaders in this movement, borrowing not just most of the acronym but the tactics of the American Civil Liberties Union in a fight for religious "rights."

It's worth noting that, in this battle over rights, science—religion's frequent nemesis—is often reduced to a mere viewpoint as well. Evolution is just a "theory," or point of view, fundamentalist champions of creationism assert; they demand equal time for the teaching of "creation science," which is described as an alternative theory, or viewpoint, about the origin of the universe. "If evolution is true, then it has nothing to fear from some other theory being taught," one Tennessee state senator declared, using liberal faith in the open marketplace of ideas to rationalize the teaching of creationism.

So far, the Supreme Court has rejected this view of creationism as an alternative scientific theory, and intellectual elites who are hostile to secularism but who champion religion's role in public life generally oppose the teaching of "creation science"; they are likely to ground their opposition in creationism's dubious scientific credibility, not its religiosity. Stephen Carter argues that the religious motivations of creationists are irrelevant; the religious underpinnings of laws prohibiting murder do not invalidate them, he observes.

Carter is right to suggest that legislation is often based in religion (which makes you wonder why he complains about secularism). You'd be hard-pressed to find a period in American history when majoritarian religious beliefs did not influence law and custom. From the nineteenth century through the twentieth, anti-vice campaigns—against alcohol, pornography and extramarital or premarital sex— have been overtly religious, fueled by sectarian notions of sin. Domestic relations laws long reflected particular religious ideas about gender roles (which some believe are divinely ordained). But religion's impact on law is usually recognized and deemed problematic only in cases involving minority religious views: Christian ideas about marriage are incorporated into law while the Mormon practice of polygamy is prohibited.

30   I'm not suggesting that religious people should confine their beliefs to the home or that religion, like sex, does not belong in the street. The First Amendment does not give you a right to fornicate in public, but it does protect your right to preach. Secularists are often wrongly accused of trying to purge religious ideals from public discourse. We simply want to deny them public sponsorship. Religious beliefs are essentially private prerogatives, which means that individuals are free to invoke them in conducting their public lives—and that public officials are not empowered to endorse or adopt them. How could our opinions about political issues not be influenced by our personal ideals?

Obviously, people carry their faith in God, Satan, crystals or UFOs into town meetings, community organizations and voting booths. Obviously, a core belief in the supernatural is not severable from beliefs about the natural world and the social order. It is the inevitable effect of religion on public policy that makes it a matter of public concern. Advocates of religiosity extol the virtues or moral habits that religion is supposed to instill in us. But we should be equally concerned with the intellectual habits it discourages.

Religions, of course, have their own demanding intellectual traditions, as Jesuits and Talmudic scholars might attest. Smart people do believe in Gods and devote themselves to uncovering Their truths. But, in its less rigorous, popular forms, religion is about as intellectually challenging as the average self-help book. (Like personal development literature, mass market books about spirituality and religion celebrate emotionalism and denigrate reason. They elevate the "truths" of myths and parables over empiricism.) In its more authoritarian forms, religion punishes questioning and rewards gullibility. Faith is not a function of stupidity but a frequent cause of it.

The magical thinking encouraged by any belief in the supernatural, combined with the vilification of rationality and skepticism, is more conducive to conspiracy theories than it is to productive political debate. Conspiratorial thinking abounds during this period of spiritual and religious revivalism. And, if only small minorities of Americans ascribe to the most outrageous theories in circulation these days—that a cabal of Jewish bankers run the world, that AIDS was invented in a laboratory by a mad white scientist intent on racial genocide—consider the number who take at face value claims that Satanists are conspiring to abuse America's children. According to a 1994 survey by *Redbook*, 70 percent of Americans believed in the existence of Satanic cults engaged in ritual abuse; nearly one-third believed that the FBI and local police were purposefully ignoring their crimes. (They would probably not be convinced by a recent FBI report finding no evidence to substantiate widespread rumors of Satanic abuse.)

As Debbie Nathan and Michael Snedeker report in *Satan's Silence*, these beliefs infect public life in the form of baseless prosecutions and convictions. If religion engenders civic virtue, by imparting "good" values, it also encourages public hysteria by sanctifying bad thinking.

Skepticism about claims of abuse involving Satanism or recovered memories would serve the public interest, not to mention the interests of those wrongly accused, much more than eagerness to believe and avenge all self-proclaimed victims. Skepticism is essential to criminal justice: guilt is supposed to be proven, not assumed. Skepticism, even cynicism, should play an equally important role in political campaigns, particularly today, when it is in such disrepute. Politicians have learned to accuse anyone who questions or opposes them of "cynicism," a popular term of opprobrium associated with spiritual stasis or soullessness. If "cynic" is a synonym for "critic," it's a label any thoughtful person might embrace, even at the risk of damnation.

This is not an apology for generalized mistrust of government. Blind mistrust merely mirrors blind faith and makes people equally gullible. Would a resurgence of skepticism and rationality make us smarter? Not exactly, but it would balance supernaturalism and the habit of belief with respect for empirical realities, which should influence the formulation of public policy more than faith. Rationalism would be an antidote to prejudice, which is, after all, a form of faith. Think, to cite one example, of people whose unreasoned faith in the moral degeneracy of homosexuals leads them to accept unquestioningly the claim that gay teachers are likely to molest their students. Faith denies facts, and that is not always a virtue.

■ QUESTIONS FOR INQUIRY AND ACTION ■

1. What is the effect of Kaminer's opening paragraph? What impression does it make on you? Describe her persona and imagined relationship with her readers.

2. How would you fit this reading with the others in this chapter on faith *communities* and citizenship? What does Kaminer add to the conversation?

3. Research atheism. What does it really mean? Who were some famous atheists and how did they write about their convictions? Do you see commonalities and patterns?

4. Kaminer argues that "the rise of virtue-talk—which generally takes the form of communitarianism on the left and nostalgia for Victorianism on the right—has resulted in a striking re-moralization of public policy debates." Is this true? Conduct a study of television and print news analysis and see how much and what kinds of "virtue-talk" you discover.

Bill McKibben

The Christian Paradox: How a Faithful Nation Gets Jesus Wrong

Bill McKibben is a scholar-in-residence at Middlebury College and the author of many books, including The End of Nature *(1989), a classic work on the environmental crisis;* Enough: Staying Human in an Engineered Age *(2004); and* Wandering Home: A Long Walk Across America's Most Hopeful Landscape *(2005). "The Christian Paradox: How a Faithful Nation Gets Jesus Wrong" appeared in* Harper's *magazine in August 2005.*

Only 40 percent of Americans can name more than four of the Ten Commandments, and a scant half can cite any of the four authors of the Gospels. Twelve percent believe Joan of Arc was Noah's wife. This failure to recall the specifics of our Christian heritage may be further evidence of our nation's educational decline, but it probably doesn't matter all that much in spiritual or political terms. Here is a statistic that does matter: Three quarters of Americans believe the Bible teaches that "God helps those who help themselves." That is, three out of four Americans believe that this uber-American idea, a notion at the core of our current individualist politics and culture, which was in fact uttered by Ben Franklin, actually appears in Holy Scripture. The thing is, not only is Franklin's wisdom not biblical; it's counter-biblical. Few ideas could be further from the gospel message, with its radical summons to love of neighbor. On this essential matter, most Americans—most American *Christians*—are simply wrong, as if 75 percent of American scientists believed that Newton proved gravity causes apples to fly up.

Asking Christians what Christ taught isn't a trick. When we say we are a Christian nation—and, overwhelmingly, we do—it means something. People who go to church absorb lessons there and make real decisions based on those lessons; increasingly, these lessons inform their politics. (One poll found that 11 percent of U.S. churchgoers were urged by their clergy to vote in a particular way in the 2004 election, up from 6 percent in 2000.) When George Bush says that Jesus Christ is his favorite philosopher, he may or may not be sincere, but he is reflecting the sincere beliefs of the vast majority of Americans.

And therein is the paradox. America is simultaneously the most professedly Christian of the developed nations and the least Christian in its behavior. That paradox—more important, perhaps, than the much touted ability of French women to stay thin on a diet of chocolate and cheese—illuminates the hollow at the core of our boastful, careening culture.

Ours is among the most spiritually homogenous rich nations on earth. Depending on which poll you look at and how the question is asked, somewhere around 85 percent of us call ourselves Christian. Israel, by way of comparison, is 77 percent Jewish. It is true that a smaller number of Americans—about 75 percent—claim they actually pray to God on a daily basis, and only 33 percent say they manage to get to church every week. Still, even if that 85 percent overstates actual practice, it clearly represents aspiration. In fact, there is nothing else that unites more than four fifths of America. Every other statistic one can cite about American behavior is essentially also a measure of the behavior of professed Christians. That's what America is: a place saturated in Christian identity.

5   But is it *Christian?* This is not a matter of angels dancing on the heads of pins. Christ was pretty specific about what he had in mind for his followers. What if we chose some simple criterion—say, giving aid to the poorest people—as a reasonable proxy for Christian behavior? After all, in the days before his crucifixion, when Jesus summed up his message for his disciples, he said the way you could tell the righteous from the damned was by whether they'd fed the hungry, slaked the thirsty, clothed the naked, welcomed the stranger, and visited the prisoner. What would we find then?

In 2004, as a share of our economy, we ranked second to last, after Italy, among developed countries in government foreign aid. Per capita we each provide fifteen cents a day in official development assistance to poor countries. And it's not because we were giving to private charities for relief work instead. Such funding increases our average daily donation by just six pennies, to twenty-one cents. It's also not because Americans were too busy taking care of their own; nearly 18 percent of American children lived in poverty (compared with, say, 8 percent in Sweden). In fact, by pretty much any measure of caring for the least among us you want to propose—childhood nutrition, infant mortality, access to preschool—we come in nearly last among the rich nations, and often by a wide margin. The point is not just that (as everyone already knows) the American nation trails badly in all these categories; it's that the overwhelmingly *Christian* American nation trails badly in all these categories, categories to which Jesus paid particular attention. And it's not as if the numbers are getting better: the U.S. Department of Agriculture reported last year that the number of households that were "food insecure with hunger" had climbed more than 26 percent between 1999 and 2003.

This Christian nation also tends to make personal, as opposed to political, choices that the Bible would seem to frown upon. Despite the Sixth Commandment, we are, of course, the most violent rich nation on earth, with a murder rate four or five times that of our European peers. We have prison populations greater by a factor of six or seven than other rich nations (which at least should give us plenty of opportunity for visiting the prisoners). Having been told to turn the other cheek, we're the only Western democracy left that executes its citizens, mostly in those states where Christianity is theoretically strongest. Despite Jesus' strong declarations against divorce, our marriages break up at a rate—just over half—that compares poorly with the European Union's average of about four in ten. That average may be held down by the fact that Europeans marry less frequently, and by countries, like Italy, where divorce is difficult; still, compare our success with, say, that of the godless Dutch, whose divorce rate is just over 37 percent. Teenage pregnancy? We're at the top of the charts. Personal self-discipline—like, say, keeping your weight under control? Buying on credit? Running government deficits? Do you need to ask?

Are Americans hypocrites? Of course they are. But most people (me, for instance) are hypocrites. The more troubling explanation for this disconnect between belief and action, I think, is that most Americans—which means most believers—have replaced the Christianity of the Bible, with its call for deep sharing and personal sacrifice, with a competing creed.

In fact, there may be several competing creeds. For many Christians, deciphering a few passages of the Bible to figure out the schedule for the End Times has become a central task. You can log on to *RaptureReady.com* for a taste of how some of these believers view the world—at this writing the Rapture Index had declined three points to 152 because, despite an increase in the number of U.S. pagans, "Wal-Mart is falling behind in its plan to bar code all products with radio tags." Other End-Timers are more interested in forcing the issue—they're convinced that the way to coax the Lord back to earth is to "Christianize" our nation and then the world. Consider House Majority Leader Tom DeLay. At church one day he listened as the pastor, urging his flock to support the administration, declared that "the war between America and Iraq is the gateway to the Apocalypse." DeLay rose to speak, not only to the congregation but to 225 Christian TV and radio stations. "Ladies and gentlemen," he said, "what has been spoken here tonight is the truth of God."

10   The apocalyptics may not be wrong. One could make a perfectly serious argument that the policies of Tom DeLay are in fact hastening the End Times. But

there's nothing particularly Christian about this hastening. The creed of Tom DeLay—of Tim LaHaye and his *Left Behind* books, of Pat Robertson's "The Antichrist is probably a Jew alive in Israel today"—ripened out of the impossibly poetic imagery of the Book of Revelation. Imagine trying to build a theory of the Constitution by obsessively reading and rereading the Twenty-fifth Amendment, and you'll get an idea of what an odd approach this is. You might be able to spin elaborate fantasies about presidential succession, but you'd have a hard time working backwards to "We the People." This is the contemporary version of Archbishop Ussher's seventeenth-century calculation that the world had been created on October 23, 4004 B.C., and that the ark touched down on Mount Ararat on May 5, 2348 B.C., a Wednesday. Interesting, but a distant distraction from the gospel message.

The apocalyptics, however, are the lesser problem. It is another competing (though sometimes overlapping) creed, this one straight from the sprawling megachurches of the new exurbs, that frightens me most. Its deviation is less obvious precisely because it looks so much like the rest of the culture. In fact, most of what gets preached in these palaces isn't loony at all. It is disturbingly conventional. The pastors focus relentlessly on *you* and your individual needs. Their goal is to service consumers—not communities but individuals: "seekers" is the term of art, people who feel the need for some spirituality in their (or their children's) lives but who aren't tightly bound to any particular denomination or school of thought. The result is often a kind of soft-focus, comfortable, suburban faith.

A *New York Times* reporter visiting one booming megachurch outside Phoenix recently found the typical scene: a drive-through latte stand, Krispy Kreme doughnuts at every service, and sermons about "how to discipline your children, how to reach your professional goals, how to invest your money, how to reduce your debt." On Sundays children played with church-distributed Xboxes, and many congregants had signed up for a twice-weekly aerobics class called Firm Believers. A list of bestsellers compiled monthly by the Christian Booksellers Association illuminates the creed. It includes texts like *Your Best Life Now* by Joel Osteen—pastor of a church so mega it recently leased a 16,000-seat sports arena in Houston for its services—which even the normally tolerant *Publishers Weekly* dismissed as "a treatise on how to get God to serve the demands of self-centered individuals." Nearly as high is Beth Moore, with her *Believing God*—"Beth asks the tough questions concerning the fruit of our Christian lives," such as "are we living as fully as we can?" Other titles include *Humor for a Woman's Heart*, a collection of "humorous writings" designed to "live a life above the stresses and strains of the day"; *The Five Love Languages*, in which Dr. Gary Chapman helps you figure out if you're speaking in the same emotional dialect as your significant other; and Karol Ladd's *The Power of a Positive Woman*. Ladd is the co-founder of USA Sonshine Girls—the "Son" in Sonshine, of course, is the son of God—and she is unremittingly upbeat in presenting her five-part plan for creating a life with "more calm, less stress."

Not that any of this is so bad in itself. We *do* have stressful lives, humor *does* help, and you *should* pay attention to your own needs. Comfortable suburbanites watch their parents die, their kids implode. Clearly I need help with being positive. And I have no doubt that such texts have turned people into better parents, better spouses, better bosses. It's just that these authors, in presenting their perfectly sensible advice, somehow manage to ignore Jesus' radical and demanding focus on *others*. It may, in fact, be true that "God helps those who help themselves," both financially and emotionally. (Certainly fortune does.) But if so it's still a subsidiary, secondary truth, more Franklinity than Christianity. You could eliminate the scriptural references in most of these bestsellers and they would still make or not make the same amount of sense. *Chicken Soup for the Zoroastrian Soul.* It is a perfect mirror of the secular bestseller lists, indeed of the secular culture, with its American fixation on self-improvement, on self-esteem. On self. These similarities make it difficult (although not impossible) for the televangelists to posit themselves as embattled figures in a "culture war"—they offer too uncanny a reflection of the dominant culture, a culture of unrelenting self-obsession.

Who am I to criticize someone else's religion? After all, if there is anything Americans agree on, it's that we should tolerate everyone else's religious expression. As a *Newsweek* writer put it some years ago at the end of his cover story on apocalyptic visions and the Book of Revelation, "Who's to say that John's mythic battle between Christ and Antichrist is not a valid insight into what the history of humankind is all about?" (Not *Newsweek*, that's for sure; their religious covers are guaranteed big sellers.) To that I can only answer that I'm a . . . Christian.

15   Not a professional one; I'm an environmental writer mostly. I've never progressed further in the church hierarchy than Sunday school teacher at my backwoods Methodist church. But I've spent most of my Sunday mornings in a pew. I grew up in church youth groups and stayed active most of my adult life—started homeless shelters in church basements, served soup at the church food pantry, climbed to the top of the rickety ladder to put the star on the church Christmas tree. My work has been, at times, influenced by all that—I've written extensively about the Book of Job, which is to me the first great piece of nature writing in the Western tradition, and about the overlaps between Christianity and environmentalism. In fact, I imagine I'm one of a fairly small number of writers who have had cover stories in both the *Christian Century,* the magazine of liberal mainline Protestantism, and *Christianity Today,* which Billy Graham founded, not to mention articles in *Sojourners,* the magazine of the progressive evangelical community co-founded by Jim Wallis.

Indeed, it was my work with religious environmentalists that first got me thinking along the lines of this essay. We were trying to get politicians to understand why the Bible actually mandated protecting the world around us (Noah: the first Green), work that I think is true and vital. But one day it occurred to me that the parts of the world where people actually had cut dramatically back on their carbon emissions, actually did live voluntarily in smaller homes and take public transit, were the same countries where people were giving aid to the poor and making sure everyone had health care—countries like Norway and Sweden, where religion was relatively unimportant. How could that be? For Christians there should be something at least a little scary in the notion that, absent the magical answers of religion, people might just get around to solving their problems and strengthening their communities in more straightforward ways.

But for me, in any event, the European success is less interesting than the American failure. Because we're not going to be like them. Maybe we'd be better off if we abandoned religion for secular rationality, but we're not going to; for the foreseeable future this will be a "Christian" nation. The question is, what kind of Christian nation?

The tendencies I've been describing—toward an apocalyptic End Times faith, toward a comfort-the-comfortable, personal-empowerment faith—veil the actual, and remarkable, message of the Gospels. When one of the Pharisees asked Jesus what the core of the law was, Jesus replied:

> You shall love the Lord your God with all your heart, and with all your soul, and with all your mind. This is the greatest and first commandment. And a second is like it, You shall love your neighbor as yourself. On these two commandments hang all the law and the prophets.

20　Love your neighbor as yourself: although its rhetorical power has been dimmed by repetition, that is a radical notion, perhaps the most radical notion possible. Especially since Jesus, in all his teachings, made it very clear who the neighbor you were supposed to love was: the poor person, the sick person, the naked person, the hungry person. The last shall be made first; turn the other cheek; a rich person aiming for heaven is like a camel trying to walk through the eye of a needle. On and on and on—a call for nothing less than a radical, voluntary, and effective reordering of power relationships, based on the principle of love.

I confess, even as I write these words, to a feeling close to embarrassment. Because in public we tend not to talk about such things—my theory of what Jesus mostly meant seems like it should be left in church, or confined to some religious publication. But remember the overwhelming connection between America and Christianity; what Jesus meant is the most deeply potent political, cultural, social question. To ignore it, or leave it to the bullies and the salesmen of the televangelist sects, means to walk away from a central battle over American identity. At the moment, the idea of Jesus has been hijacked by people with a series of causes that do not reflect his teachings. The Bible is a long book, and even the Gospels have plenty in them, some of it seemingly contradictory and hard to puzzle out. But love your neighbor as yourself—not do unto others as you would have them do unto you, but *love your neighbor as yourself*—will suffice as a gloss. There is no disputing the centrality of this message, not is there any disputing how easy it is to ignore that message. Because it is so counterintuitive, Christians have had to keep repeating it to themselves right from the start. Consider Paul, for instance, instructing the church at Galatea: "For the whole law is summed up in a single commandment," he wrote. "'You shall love your neighbor as yourself.'"

American churches, by and large, have done a pretty good job of loving the neighbor in the next pew. A pastor can spend all Sunday talking about the Rapture Index, but if his congregation is thriving you can be assured he's spending the other six days visiting people in the hospital, counseling couples, and sitting up with grieving widows. All this human connection is important. But if the theology makes it harder to love the neighbor a little farther away—particularly the poor and the weak—then it's a problem. And the dominant theologies of the moment do just that. They undercut Jesus, muffle his hard words, deaden his call, and in the end silence him. In fact, the soft-focus consumer gospel of the suburban megachurches is a perfect match for emergent conservative economic notions about personal responsibility instead of collective action. Privatize Social Security? Keep health care for people who can afford it? File those under "God helps those who help themselves."

Take Alabama as an example. In 2002, Bob Riley was elected governor of the state, where 90 percent of residents identify themselves as Christians. Riley could safely be called a conservative—right-wing majordomo Grover Norquist gave him a Friend of the Taxpayer Award every year he was in Congress, where he'd never voted for a tax increase. But when he took over Alabama, he found himself administering a tax code that dated to 1901. The richest Alabamians paid 3 percent of their income in taxes, and the poorest paid up to 12 percent; income taxes kicked in if a family of four made $4,600 (even in Mississippi the threshold was $19,000), while out-of-state timber companies paid $1.25 an acre in property taxes. Alabama was forty-eighth in total state and local taxes, and the largest proportion of that income came from sales tax—a super-regressive tax that in some counties reached into double digits. So Riley proposed a tax hike, partly to dig the state out of a fiscal crisis and partly to put more money into the state's school system, routinely ranked near the worst in the nation. He argued that it was Christian duty to look after the poor more carefully.

Had the new law passed, the owner of a $250,000 home in Montgomery would have paid $1,432 in property taxes—we're not talking Sweden here. But it didn't pass. It was crushed by a factor of two to one. Sixty-eight percent of the state voted against it—meaning, of course, something like 68 percent of the Christians who voted. The opposition was led, in fact, not just by the state's wealthiest interests but also by the Christian Coalition of Alabama. "You'll find most Alabamians have got a charitable heart," said John Giles, the group's president. "They just don't want it coming out of their pockets." On its website, the group argued that taxing the rich at a higher rate than the poor "results in punishing success" and that "when an individual works for their income, that money belongs to the individual." You might as well just cite chapter and verse from *Poor Richard's Almanack*. And whatever the ideology, the results are clear. "I'm tired of Alabama being first in things that are bad," said Governor Riley, "and last in things that are good."

25   A rich man came to Jesus one day and asked what he should do to get into heaven. Jesus did not say he should invest, spend, and let the benefits trickle down; he said sell what you have, give the money to the poor, and follow me. Few plainer words have been spoken. And yet, for some reason, the Christian Coalition of America—founded in 1989 in order to "preserve, protect and defend the Judeo-Christian values that made this the greatest country in history"—proclaimed last

year that its top legislative priority would be "making permanent President Bush's 2001 federal tax cuts."

Similarly, a furor erupted last spring when it emerged that a Colorado jury had consulted the Bible before sentencing a killer to death. Experts debated whether the (Christian) jurors should have used an outside authority in their deliberations, and of course the Christian right saw it as one more sign of a secular society devaluing religion. But a more interesting question would have been why the jurors fixated on Leviticus 24, with its call for an eye for an eye and a tooth for a tooth. They had somehow missed Jesus' explicit refutation in the New Testament: "You have heard that it was said, 'an eye for an eye and a tooth for a tooth.' But I say to you, Do not resist an evildoer. But if anyone strikes you on the right cheek, turn the other also."

And on and on. The power of the Christian right rests largely in the fact that they boldly claim religious authority, and by their very boldness convince the rest of us that they must know what they're talking about. They're like the guy who gives you directions with such loud confidence that you drive on even though the road appears to be turning into a faint, rutted track. But their theology is appealing for another reason too: it coincides with what we want to believe. How nice it would be if Jesus had declared that our income was ours to keep, instead of insisting that we had to share. How satisfying it would be if we were supposed to hate our enemies. Religious conservatives will always have a comparatively easy sell.

But straight is the path and narrow is the way. The gospel is too radical for any culture larger than the Amish to ever come close to realizing; in demanding a departure from selfishness it conflicts with all our current desires. Even the first time around, judging by the reaction, the Gospels were pretty unwelcome news to an awful lot of people. There is not going to be a modern-day return to the church of the early believers, holding all things in common—that's not what I'm talking about. Taking seriously the actual message of Jesus, though, should serve at least to moderate the greed and violence that mark this culture. It's hard to imagine a con much more audacious than making Christ the front man for a program of tax cuts for the rich or war in Iraq. If some modest part of the 85 percent of us who are Christians woke up to that fact, then the world might change.

It is possible, I think. Yes, the mainline Protestant churches that supported civil rights and opposed the war in Vietnam are mostly locked in a dreary decline as their congregations dwindle and their elders argue endlessly about gay clergy and same-sex unions. And the Catholic Church, for most of its American history a sturdy exponent of a "love your neighbor" theology, has been weakened, too, its hierarchy increasingly motivated by a single-issue focus on abortion. Plenty of vital congregations are doing great good works—they're the ones that have nurtured me—but they aren't where the challenge will arise; they've grown shy about talking about Jesus, more comfortable with the language of sociology and politics. More and more it's Bible-quoting Christians, like Wallis's *Sojourners* movement and that Baptist seminary graduate Bill Moyers, who are carrying the fight.

30   The best-selling of all Christian books in recent years, Rick Warren's *The Purpose-Driven Life*, illustrates the possibilities. It has all the hallmarks of self-absorption (in

one five-page chapter, I counted sixty-five uses of the word "you"), but it also makes a powerful case that we're made for mission. What that mission is never becomes clear, but the thirst for it is real. And there's no great need for Warren to state that purpose anyhow. For Christians, the plainspoken message of the Gospels is clear enough. If you have any doubts, read the Sermon on the Mount.

Admittedly, this is hope against hope; more likely the money changers and power brokers will remain ascendant in our "spiritual" life. Since the days of Constantine, emperors and rich men have sought to co-opt the teachings of Jesus. As in so many areas of our increasingly market-tested lives, the co-opters—the TV men, the politicians, the Christian "interest groups"—have found a way to make each of us complicit in that travesty, too. They have invited us to subvert the church of Jesus even as we celebrate it. With their help we have made golden calves of ourselves—become a nation of terrified, self-obsessed idols. It works, and it may well keep working for a long time to come. When Americans hunger for selfless love and are fed only love of self, they will remain hungry, and too often hungry people just come back for more of the same.

▓ QUESTIONS FOR INQUIRY AND ACTION ▓

1. Read McKibben's introductory paragraph. What strategies does he use to engage his readers and lead them into the thesis of the article?

2. What does McKibben mean when he says that the paradox that "America is simultaneously the most professedly Christian of the developed nations and the least Christian in its behavior . . . illuminates the hollow at the core of our boastful, careening culture"?

3. Read this article in relation to others in this book with a Christian perspective or Christian themes, e.g., Margaret Talbot's "A Mighty Fortress" in Chapter 6, Jeff Dietrich's "Refusing to Hope in a God of Technology" in Chapter 11, and Anne Lamott's "Why I Make Sam Go to Church" in this chapter. Based on what McKibben has said, are the people in these essays typical or atypical Christians?

4. What place would McKibben's argument have among the writers included in the case study on faith in the civil rights movement? Write a dialogue that you imagine taking place between Bill McKibben and Martin Luther King.

CASE STUDY

Living Out the Dream:
The Black Church and the Civil Rights Movement

Robert M. Franklin
Another Day's Journey: Faith Communities Renewing American Democracy

Robert M. Franklin is president of the Interdenominational Theological Center in Atlanta, and he has worked at Harvard Divinity School, Colgate-Rochester Divinity School, Candler School of Theology, and the Ford Foundation. He is also the author of Another Day's Journey: Black Churches Confronting the American Crisis *(1997) and* Liberating Visions: Human Fulfillment and Social Justice in African-American Thought *(1990). "Another Day's Journey: Faith Communities Renewing American Democracy" is included in* Religion, Race, and Justice in a Changing America *(New York: The Century Foundation Press, 1999).*

As a concession to a culture profoundly shaped by televised images, I invite you to consider my nomination for the nation's most significant icon depicting religion as a positive force in securing civil and human rights. It is the familiar portrait of Dr. Martin Luther King, Jr., delivering his "I Have a Dream" oration from the steps of the Lincoln Memorial. The image is so familiar that we may fail to grasp its extraordinary, multidimensional character. The black Baptist preacher standing at the foot of the monument to the emancipator is a stunning, riveting symbol suggestive of many values and issues that interest those of us who think about religion and civil rights.

For instance, in the portrait one encounters religion restraining its sectarian energies and harnessing them in the service of public order. Also, one sees a representative of a particular, Christian view of human nature and destiny standing in solidarity with other faith traditions. And one perceives in the King/Lincoln juxtaposition the graceful and mysterious power of religious faith to transform imperfect human beings into courageous exemplars of moral citizenship.

In that 1963 portrait, Lincoln is but a figure carved in marble, his complexity and contradictions concealed in cold stone. Before the stone stood a vibrant incarnation of the indomitable African-American spirit of authentic freedom. Recall the manner in which King began the famous speech: "Fivescore years ago, a great American, in whose symbolic shadow we stand today, signed the Emancipation Proclamation. This momentous decree came as a great beacon light of hope to millions of Negro slaves who had been seared in the flames of withering injustice. It came as a joyous daybreak to end the long night of their captivity. But one hundred years later, the Negro still is not free. . . ."[1] With those words, King paid respect to one of the nation's sacred ancestors, underscored the rude fact that Lincoln's agenda was unfinished, and positioned himself as a moral successor to the slain president.

Also in that extraordinary speech, King drew upon the two major philosophical traditions that have shaped the American culture and character: the covenant tradition based upon biblical notions of American exceptionalism; and the Enlightenment tradition of Immanuel Kant, John Locke, Thomas Jefferson, and others who asserted the inviolable rights of the individual. No one was more skilled than King at interweaving the great and noble ideas from varying intellectual traditions.

5   Recall his words that day as he placed his dream in the context of the hard work that lay before his listeners. "Even though we must face the difficulties of today and tomorrow, I still have a dream. It is a dream deeply rooted in the American dream that one day this nation will rise up and live out the true meaning of its creed—we hold these truths to be self-evident, that all men are created equal."[2] King believed that a dream inspired by references to particular biblical sources could live in dialectical and fruitful tension with ideals embraced by nontheistic rationalists. "I have a dream that one day every valley shall be exalted, every hill and mountain shall be made low, the rough places shall be made plain, and the crooked places shall be made straight and the glory of the Lord will be revealed and all flesh shall see it together."[3]

King did not merely search for common ground, he sought to create it out of the stuff of living traditions. In so doing, he was able to use theology and ethics as resources for renewing American public life. He used theology to prompt people to vote, to run for office, and to be concerned about the moral state of the society. A person who seeks to create common ground, build traditions, craft narratives, and negotiate coalitions exemplifies a quality of character that moral education should seek to inculcate.

We should also acknowledge that using theology and ethics as resources for renewing public life can have unforeseen negative consequences. For instance, many religious people who regard the concept of grace as central and significant to their faith may construe it to mean that they are acceptable to God despite their admitted racist behavior and attitudes, or their indifference to racial justice. Some people suggest that America in the post-civil rights movement era has come a long way through hard work and heroic effort, and that to push further

---

[1] See James M. Washington, ed., I Have a Dream: Writings and Speeches that Changed the World (San Francisco: Harper San Francisco, 1992), p. 102.
[2] Ibid., p. 104.
[3] Ibid., p. 105.

might be counterproductive. We should now focus on celebrating our progress rather than rousing bitter feelings by advocating additional progress. Grace, thereby, becomes a psychological mechanism that absolves responsibility for the contemporary condition of race relations and civil rights. This is the double edge of grace. Ironically, the theological shift from "salvation by works" to "salvation by grace" encourages complacency with the racial status quo. King understood, clearly, that the Bible and theological concepts could be misappropriated to justify social evil and felt that an important check upon this tendency would involve keeping the Bible and human reason in mutually critical dialogue.

In the pages that follow, I will provide: (1) a brief sketch of the character of black church culture that illustrates how a marginalized and particular religious tradition helped to renew democracy during the modern civil rights movement; (2) an analysis of King's concept of the "beloved community" as an ethical norm that should be used to critique, guide, and inspire public policy and individual behavior; and (3) a brief overview of the heroic role that faith communities are now playing to promote a more just society.

The Revolution Led by Preachers, Church Women, and Sunday School Children

In order to understand Dr. King's journey from Atlanta to the steps of the Lincoln Memorial in 1963, we need to understand something about the culture that produced him, and, thereby, revisit the ways in which culture is a vehicle of moral education. Paul Tillich said that culture is the form of religion, and religion is the substance of culture. If these claims are true, what system of values is available to children being reared in neighborhoods that are scarred by violent crime, adult joblessness, multigenerational dependence, aimlessness, disease, hopelessness, and wretched schools?

10   King's biographers all note that the black church and family were the context in which the boy King learned something about racism, poverty, and religion as a resource for mobilizing social change. James Cone has gone further, noting that the culture of the black church included theological concepts that played a critical role in shaping King's worldview and moral compass. These included notions of human freedom, social justice, black self-love, and collective power.

Historians such as Albert Raboeau (Princeton), the late James Melvin Washington (Union), and Evelyn Brooks Higginbotham (Harvard) have noted that black church culture is an amalgam of numerous symbolic and ritual traditions, including African traditional religions (ATR), Catholic popular piety, Protestant evangelicalism, and Islam. This collection of religious traditions infused the core practices of progressive African-American Christianity that produced King.

These core practices include the following:

1. A multisensory worship experience in which all of a human being's capacity to respond to God is engaged. Worship is conceived to be a sacred drama, a dance with the gods. Hence, drums are present to orchestrate the antiphonal call and response between the people and the deity. Colorful

choir robes and clergy vestments provide visual stimulation. Brass horns, electric guitars, tambourines, and clapping hands electrify the air with sound. Usually, the church kitchen is in operation, sending aromas of soul food wafting throughout the neighborhood. And, this sacred space is animated by lots of touching, hugging, holy kissing, and high-five greetings that bridge the social distance that is common in secular gatherings.

2. Intimate communal prayer, when led by a skilled leader, succeeds in weaving lonely personal concerns into a community of pain, struggle, reconciliation, and hope. Worshippers who approach the altar as separate individuals experience a transformation that sends them away as members of the body of Christ.

3. Choirs give triumphant voice to the church's confidence that it will not be vanquished by evil in the world. Triumphal songs are situationally rational and appropriate if those who sing them regard themselves as warriors in the midst of a great and bloody conflict between good and evil.

4. Prophetic preaching in the black church tradition is the focal point of worship. It is the high, holy moment in the liturgical drama. The brilliant historian of religion, Mircea Eliade, has observed that "for people in traditional societies, religion is a means of extending the world spatially upward so that communication with the other world becomes ritually possible, and extending it temporally backward so that the paradigmatic acts of the gods and mythical ancestors can be continually reenacted and indefinitely recoverable."[4] Eliade helps to illumine the genius of black preaching as he reminds us that words can be deployed to mediate an encounter with the holy. Words can usher the imagination into a transcendent realm where one may be empowered to give one's life on behalf of a noble cause. The black preacher, through the virtuosity of imaginative, narrative, lyrical, and poetic language and the co-creativity of a responsive congregation, unites the sacred and the human realms. Stated briefly, the entire liturgical culture of progressive black churches nurtures political sensibilities. These are the congregations that shape moral character and teach people to care about the moral condition of the society.

The biblical scholar Walter Bruggemann offers a cogent observation about such transformative liturgy: "Every act of a minister who could be prophetic is part of a way of evoking, forming, and reforming an alternative community. This applies to every facet and every practice of ministry. It is a measure of our enculturation that the various acts of ministry (for example, counseling, administration, even liturgy) have taken on lives and functions of their own rather than being seen as elements of the one prophetic ministry of formation and reformation of alternative community."[5]

Bruggemann's comment about "alternative community" reminds us again of King's dream narrative, and the fact that it was crafted in the genre of a sermon rather than as an essay, philosophical argument, or lecture. King and his counterparts were

---

[4] *Paraphrased in Lawrence W. Levine,* Black Culture and Black Consciousness: Afro-American Folk Thought from Slavery to Freedom *(New York: Oxford University Press, 1977), pp. 31–32.*
[5] *Walter Bruggemann,* The Prophetic Imagination *(Minneapolis: Fortress Press, 1978), p. 14.*

products of a liturgical culture that cultivated the capacity to engage in utopian discourse and to act boldly to achieve moral causes.

15   I shall have more to say about utopian discourse, black Christian preaching, and political theology when we consider King's notion of the beloved community.

Congregational Culture Authorizes a Variety of Political Responses

We should note briefly that blacks reared in the congregational context that I have described here, and on which I elaborate in my book, *Another Day's Journey: Black Churches Confronting the American Crisis* (Fortress Press, 1997), opted for a variety of political responses rather than simply the one embraced by King. I have characterized five major responses. They include the pragmatic accommodationists who cooperate with the political and economic status quo in the interest of maintaining social order. In that context, they believe that they can maximize their acquisition of goods. This was the political agenda of Booker T. Washington and the National Baptist Convention leader, Dr. Joseph H. Jackson. Accommodationists tend to embrace a theology of creation that emphasizes abundance in the natural order. A second response is that of the prophetic radicals who challenge the system to improve the life prospects of marginalized people. This was the orientation of W. E. B. Du Bois and Dr. King. Radicals tend to develop a theology of liberation and a view of God as an ally of oppressed people.

A third response could be characterized as redemptive nationalism, aimed at avoiding the conventional power structure in order to create a separate, ethnically pure order. This was the social vision of Marcus Garvey and of the young Malcolm X and Nation of Islam. Nationalists work from a theology of redemption in which God seeks to restore and redeem the halcyon days of the past, when ethnic kingdoms were distinct and uncontaminated by diversity. The fourth response is characterized as grassroots revivalism, which condemns and avoids the political systems of this world and focuses instead upon individual salvation and moral reform. This agenda was advanced by William J. Seymour, the father of black Pentecostalism. In this theological arena, God is working to save individuals by transforming them one by one. Faith does not have social consequences. Finally, the fifth response is positive thought materialism, which is indifferent to social justice and concerned primarily with opportunities to maximize individual health, wealth, and success. This is spirituality for the upwardly mobile classes who lack a social conscience. This is the outlook of Reverend "Ike," the New York religious showman, an outlook that may lack a full-blown example earlier in black history. Materialists work from a theology of prosperity in which God is a provider of material bounty.

This typology of political theologies should serve to remind us that black church culture is not a monolith, that it fosters and celebrates diversity. I am simply making the point that a variety of political responses emerged from the ecology of black worship culture. Those responses produced a variety of theological reflections upon the nature of the state, political objectives such as voting, citizenship, and running for office, and the relationship between religious and civil obligations.

The Underside of American Christianity

It is perplexing to consider that Christianity has had two thousand years to eradicate the multiple and overlapping forms of oppression based upon ethnicity, race, creed, culture, region, class, and gender, but has failed to do so. Why is this the case? And, more to the point of our discussion, why haven't Protestantism and Catholicism succeeded in canceling the power and grip of racism on the minds and behavior of the masses of their adherents? Is this a theological crisis? Does the tradition possess the resources to address racism in a compelling manner? Is it a human and cultural crisis that represents, yet again, the depths and variety of sinful human nature? King framed it poignantly when he noted the following in his "Letter from a Birmingham Jail":

> I have traveled the length and breadth of Alabama, Mississippi, and all the other southern states. On sweltering summer days and crisp autumn mornings I have looked at her beautiful churches with their lofty spires pointing heavenward. I have beheld the impressive outlay of her massive religious education buildings. Over and over again I have found myself asking: "What kind of people worship here? Who is their God? Where were their voices when the lips of Governor Barnett dripped with words of interposition and nullification? Where were they when Governor Wallace gave the clarion call for defiance and hatred? Where were their voices of support when tired, bruised, and weary Negro men and women decided to rise from the dark dungeons of complacency to the bright hills of creative protest?"[6]

20   Although prophetic religion should hold the state accountable for the moral exercise of power, when religion goes astray who can call it back to its foundation? This is where King's methodological and symbolic eclecticism in drawing up various traditions proved valuable. The biblical and the Enlightenment traditions could critique and correct each other.

Returning to my earlier comments about King's preaching as an instance of utopian discourse, I would like to briefly discuss the central thrust of King's political theology.

The Beloved Community as a Political and Ethical Norm

Moral philosopher and former Clinton domestic policy adviser William Galston has noted that "utopian thought is the political branch of moral philosophy" and that "among its many functions it guides our deliberation in devising courses of action, justifies our actions so that the grounds of action are reasons that others ought to accept, and serves as the basis for the evaluation of existing institutions and practices."[7] Utopian discourse becomes moral discourse as it seeks to guide action. It enables us to "imaginatively reconcile and transmute" the "contradictions of experience."

In his final book, *Where Do We Go From Here: Chaos or Community?*, King noted that the "good and just society is neither the thesis of capitalism nor the antithesis of Communism, but a socially conscious democracy which reconciles

---

[6]*Washington*, I Have a Dream, *p. 97.*

[7]*William Galston*, Justice and the Human Good *(Chicago: University of Chicago Press, 1980).*

the truths of individualism and collectivism."[8] He characterized his political philosophy with the term "democratic socialism." In his November 1966 Gandhi Memorial Lecture at Howard University, he said, "Public accommodations did not cost the nation anything; the right to vote did not cost the nation anything. Now we are grappling with basic class issues between the privileged and underprivileged. In order to solve this problem, not only will it mean the restructuring of American society but it will cost the nation something. . . ."[9]

King had always been attentive to the economic dimensions of authentic liberation. At the end of his life, his public ministry focused upon the nation's moral obligation to improve the economic plight of the least advantaged members of the community. When he was killed in Memphis, King was working on behalf of sanitation workers, and he was headed back to Washington, D.C., to lead a national "Poor People's Campaign." Had he lived, there would have been another great speech and another iconic photograph to juxtapose with the 1963 image.

Faith Communities in Pursuit of the Beloved Community

25   Today, many of the nation's 320,000 communities of faith are stepping up to tackle Dr. King's unfinished agenda. This includes the more than 70,000 African-American congregations that were part of the coalition of conscience that sustained the Civil Rights Movement and expanded democracy. In many distressed neighborhoods, churches are the only indigenous institutions that have significant assets: talented leaders, credibility, track records of service, armies of potential volunteers, physical space, financial resources, and the spiritual resources necessary to sustain courage and hope amidst adversity. Long after other secular nonprofit service agencies disappear for lack of funding, or employers disappear because of the cost of doing business, or government agencies disappear due to devolution, churches are there to pick up the pieces of people's lives, affirming their dignity and feeding bodies and souls.

Congregations provide basic charity, sustained nurture, social services, political advocacy, and comprehensive community development, on behalf of the poor. Congregations and clergy are helping to sustain civil society and resisting the nihilism of which Cornel West speaks.

Faith communities are working to renew American democracy and, as such, have earned a seat at the table of future public/private ventures. The most creative leaders of the black church tradition understand that the future of the beloved community will depend upon expanding our notion of civil rights to include basic economic rights and the fruits of our labor. Churches and clergy are working overtime to become leaders and partners in the community development enterprise.

To ensure that there will be thoughtful religious leaders capable of moving the nation forward, a number of institutions are engaged in exciting and noteworthy projects. Harvard Divinity School's Summer Leadership Institute trains clergy and lay leaders in the art of innovative community economic development. Through a

---

[8]*Martin Luther King, Jr.,* Where Do We Go From Here: Chaos or Community? *(Boston: Beacon Press, 1967), p. 187.*
[9]*King Center Archives.*

new initiative called "ITC FaithFactor," the Interdenominational Theological Center provides training, technical support, and vision to the vast army of religiously motivated volunteers who reside, work, and worship in and around this nation's most distressed neighborhoods. The "Sojourners" organization has helped to nurture a broad coalition of religious leaders (Call to Renewal) concerned with the moral decay as reflected in the resurgence of racism and other social evils.

Despite these resources and many others, the larger question remains: Can religion provide something unique and significant to the pursuit of a just society? Many of the revolutionaries of the 1960s, tutored by the writings of Karl Marx, answered negatively. Religion was (is) an opiate that enables people to tolerate injustice in pious quietude. Ironically, many black revolutionaries of the period had to admit that it was the black church and prophetic Christianity that were mobilizing people to risk their lives in the pursuit of freedom. Although many found escape and refuge in the church, others felt that authentic biblical religion is inescapably wedded to God's concern for a just social order. In fact, it is impossible to read the Hebrew prophets of the Hebrew Bible (Old Testament) without recognizing that God seems to have a lot to say about how people who enjoy privilege and power should relate to less advantaged people. God does not ignore politics, and politics involves a proactive concern for people with limited options and few material goods.

30 As religious leaders today have sought to apply this biblical agenda, or what the late theologian John Howard Yoder called "the politics of Jesus," they have felt the frustration of talking about justice, equality, and love in purely theological terms. Our largely secular society has found it possible to ignore such theological appeals, preferring instead the rhetoric of politics and law. Politicians and lawyers often ignore the contentious and fragmented presence of sectarian religious people. And many religious leaders have reconciled themselves to a marginal role in public life and public policy.

However, some ministers and lay people have resisted marginalization. Although some ministers have elected to run for public office—William Gray, Father Robert J. Drinan, Jesse Jackson, among others—and bring religious rhetoric into the public square, the majority have sought to find ways to talk about the biblical political agenda in their local parishes. It is at that level that tough decisions have to be made about what one will and can say in public about the "hard questions" affecting national life.

Frustration with being regarded as "a marginal voice" often encourages clergy to embrace the language of the modern state. Preachers begin to talk like politicians, and while gaining some credibility as political power brokers, in the process they tend to lose the prophetic edge that they can and should bring to the political debate and the process of creating a better society. This is a temptation to which Dr. King never yielded. He consistently employed theological concepts and language to challenge the modern state to be more just and inclusive. He gave opinions on practical and concrete political matters, but only insofar as they were outgrowths of the theological and ethical principles he espoused.

It is humbling, hopeful, and empowering to consider that preachers, church women, and Sunday school children led a revolution in our lifetime. They marched, prayed, voted, and challenged the nation to, in the words of Arthur Schlesinger, Jr., "conform America's political reality to her political rhetoric." They have now passed the baton to us.

In the words of a great rabbi, "the world is equally balanced between good and evil, our next act will tip the scale."

Martin Luther King, Jr.
Speech at Holt Street Baptist Church

Martin Luther King, Jr. (1929–1968), was one of the most famous and respected orators and civil rights leaders in American history. An ordained Baptist minister, he served with his father as co-pastor of Ebenezer Baptist Church in Atlanta from 1960 to 1968, and founded the Southern Christian Leadership Conference in Atlanta in 1957 and served as its president from 1957 to 1968. He was named Time's *Man of the Year in 1963 and won the Nobel Prize for Peace in 1964. His sermon "I Have a Dream" (1963) was an instant classic, and he was the author of several books, including* Where Do We Go from Here: Chaos or Community? *(1967). This speech is a portion of one delivered at Holt Street Baptist Church in Montgomery, Alabama on December 5, 1955, shortly after Rosa Parks's participation in the Montgomery Bus Boycott. The speech was included in the fourteen-part PBS television series* Eyes on the Prize: America's Civil Rights Years *and is reprinted in the* Eyes on the Prize Civil Rights Reader *(New York: Penguin, 1991).*

We are here this evening for serious business. We are here in a general sense because first and foremost we are American citizens, and we are determined to apply our citizenship to the fullness of its means. We are here because of our love for democracy, because of our deep-seated belief that democracy transformed from thin paper to thick action is the greatest form of government on earth. But we are here in a specific sense, because of the bus situation in Montgomery. We are here because we are determined to get the situation corrected.

This situation is not at all new. The problem has existed over endless years. For many years now Negroes in Montgomery and so many other areas have been inflicted with the paralysis of crippling fear on buses in our community. On so many occasions, Negroes have been intimidated and humiliated and oppressed because of the sheer fact that they were Negroes. I don't have time this evening to go into the history of these numerous cases. . . . But at least one stands before us now with glaring dimensions. Just the other day, just last Thursday to be exact, one of the finest citizens in Montgomery—not one of the finest Negro citizens but one of the finest citizens in Montgomery—was taken from a bus and carried to jail and arrested because she refused to get up to give her seat to a white person. . . . Mrs. Rosa Parks is a fine person. And since it had to happen I'm happy it happened to a person like Mrs. Parks, for nobody can doubt the boundless outreach of her integrity. Nobody can doubt the height of her character, nobody can doubt the depth of her Christian commitment and devotion to the teachings of Jesus. . . .

And just because she refused to get up, she was arrested. . . . You know my friends there comes a time when people get tired of being trampled over by the iron feet of oppression. There comes a time my friends when people get tired of being flung across the abyss of humiliation where they experience the bleakness of nagging despair. There comes a time when people get tired of being pushed out of the glittering sunlight of life's July and left standing amidst the piercing chill of an Alpine November.

We are here, we are here this evening because we're tired now. Now let us say that we are not here advocating violence. We have overcome that. I want it to be known throughout Montgomery and throughout this nation that we are Christian people. We believe in the Christian religion. We believe in the teachings of Jesus. The only weapon that we have in our hands this evening is the weapon of protest. And secondly, this is the glory of America, with all of its faults. This is the glory of our democracy. If we were incarcerated behind the iron curtains of a Communistic nation we couldn't do this. If we were trapped in the dungeon of a totalitarian regime we couldn't do this. But the great glory of American democracy is the right to protest for right.

5   My friends, don't let anybody make us feel that we ought to be compared in our actions with the Ku Klux Klan or with the White Citizens' Councils. There will be no crosses burned at any bus stops in Montgomery. There will be no white persons pulled out of their homes and taken out to some distant road and murdered. There will be nobody among us who will stand up and defy the Constitution of this nation. We only assemble here because of our desire to see right exist.

My friends, I want it to be known that we're going to work with grim and firm determination to gain justice on the buses in this city. And we are not wrong, we are not wrong in what we are doing. If we are wrong, then the Supreme Court of this Nation is wrong. If we are wrong, the Constitution of the United States is wrong. If we are wrong, God Almighty is wrong. If we are wrong, Jesus of Nazareth was merely a utopian dreamer and never came down to earth. If we are wrong, justice is a lie. And we are determined here in Montgomery to work and fight until justice runs down like water and righteousness like a mighty stream.

I want to say that with all of our actions we must stick together. Unity is the great need of the hour. And if we are united, we can get many of the things that we not only desire but which we justly deserve. And don't let anybody frighten you. We are not afraid of what we are doing, because we are doing it within the law. There is never a time in our American democracy that we must ever think we're wrong when we protest. We reserve that right. . . .

We, the disinherited of this land, we who have been oppressed so long are tired of going through the long night of captivity. And we are reaching out for the daybreak of freedom and justice and equality. . . . In all of our doings, in all of our deliberations. . . whatever we do, we must keep God in the forefront. Let us be Christian in all of our action. And I want to tell you this evening that it is not enough for us to talk about love. Love is one of the pinnacle parts of the Christian faith. There is another side called justice. And justice is really love in [application]. Justice is love correcting that which would work against love. . . . Standing beside love is always justice. And we are only using the tools of justice. Not only are we using the tools of persuasion but we've got to use the tools of coercion. Not only is this thing a process of education but it is also a process of legislation.

And as we stand and sit here this evening, and as we prepare ourselves for what lies ahead, let us go out with a grim and bold determination that we are going to stick together. We are going to work together. Right here in Montgomery when the history books are written in the future, somebody will have to say "There lived a race of people, black people, fleecy locks and black complexion, of people who had the moral courage to stand up for their rights." And thereby they injected a new meaning into the veins of history and of civilization. And we're gonna do that. God grant that we will do it before it's too late.

Bernice Johnson Reagon
Interview

Bernice Johnson Reagon, then Bernice Johnson, is a scholar, a composer, a singer, and an activist. She is Distinguished Professor of History at American University, curator emerita at the Smithsonian National Museum of American History, and artistic director of Sweet Honey In The Rock, the renowned African-American women's a cappella ensemble she founded in 1973. She is the author of, among other works, We'll Understand It Better By and By: Pioneering African-American Gospel Composers *(1992) and* We Who Believe in Freedom: Sweet Honey In The Rock: Still On the Journey *(1993). During the civil rights movement she was a student at all-black Albany State College and secretary of the local chapter of the NAACP. This interview is an excerpt from one taken in 1986; it is included in the fourteen-part PBS television series* Eyes on the Prize: America's Civil Rights Years *and is reprinted in the* Eyes on the Prize Civil Rights Reader *(New York: Penguin, 1991).*

Growing up in Albany, I learned that if you bring black people together, you bring them together with a song. To this day, I don't understand how people think they can bring anybody together without a song.

Now, the singing tradition in Albany was congregational. There were not soloists, there were song leaders.

When you ask somebody to lead a song, you're asking them to plant a seed. The minute you start the song, then the song is created by everybody there. It's almost like a musical explosion that takes place. But the singing in the movement was different from the singing in church. The singing is the kind of singing where you disappear.

The song-singing I heard in Albany I'd never heard before in my life, in spite of the fact that I was from that congregational singing culture. The only difference was that in Albany, Georgia, black people were doing some stuff around being black people. I know a lot of people talk about it being a movement and when they do a movement they're talking about buses and jobs and the ICC ruling, and the Trailways bus station. Those things were just incidents that gave us an excuse to be something of ourselves. It's almost like where we had been working before we had a chance to do that stuff was in a certain kind of space, and when we did those marches and went to jail, we expanded the space we could operate in, and that was echoed in the singing. It was a bigger, more powerful singing. . . .

5   After this first march, we're at Union Baptist Church, Charlie Jones [of SNCC] looks at me and said, "Bernice, sing a song." And I started "Over My Head I See Trouble in the Air." By the time I got to where "trouble" was supposed to be, I didn't see any trouble, so I put "freedom" in there. And I guess that was the first time I really understood using what I'd been given in terms of songs. I'd always been a singer but I had always, more or less, been singing what other people taught me to sing. That was the first time I had the awareness that these songs were mine and I could use them for what I needed them to. This sort of thing was important because I ended up being arrested in the second wave of arrests in Albany, Georgia. And I was in jail. And when we got to jail, Slater King was already in jail, and he said, "Bernice, is that you?" And I said, "Yeah." And he said, "Sing a song."

The voice I have now, I got the first time I sang in a movement meeting, after I got out of jail. Now I'm past that first meeting in Union Baptist, I've done "Lift Every Voice and Sing." I am a song leader, I lead every song in jail, but I did not lead the songs in jail in the voice I have now. The voice I have now I got that night and I'd never heard it before in my life. At that meeting, they did what they usually do. They said, "Bernice, would you lead us in a song?" And I did the same first song, "Over My Head I See Freedom in the Air," but I'd never heard that voice before. I had never been that me before. And once I became that me, I have never let that me go.

I like people to know when they deal with the movement that there are these specific things, but there is a transformation that took place inside of the people that needs to also be quantified in the picture. And the singing is just the echo of that. If you have a people who are transformed and they create the sound that lets you know they are new people, then certainly you've never heard it before. They have also never heard it before, because they've never been that before.

When I was in the mass meetings, I would be part of a group up at the front leading the songs. There would be Rutha Harris, Andrew Reed, Charlie Jones, Cordell Reagon, Charles Sherrod. We were all young people. The meetings always started with these freedom songs and the freedom songs were in-between all of the activities of the mass meetings. Most of the mass meeting was singing—there was more singing than there was talking. Most of the work that was done in terms of taking care of movement business had to do with nurturing the people who had come, and there would be two or three people who would talk but basically songs were the bed of everything. I'd had songs in college and high school and church, but in the movement all the words sounded differently. "This Little Light of Mine, I'm Going to Let It Shine," which I'd sung all my life, said something very different: "All in the street, I'm going to let it shine." I'd never even heard that before, 'cause, I mean, who would go into the street? That was not where you were supposed to be if you were an upstanding Christian person. "All in the jailhouse, I'm going to let it shine"— all of these new concepts of where, if you said it, this is where you could be.

What I can remember is being very alive and very clear, the clearest I've ever been in my life. I knew that every minute, I was doing what I was supposed to do. That was the way it was in jail, too, and on the marches. In "We Shall Overcome" there's a verse that says "God is on our side," and there was a theological discussion that said maybe we should say, "We are on God's side." God was lucky to have us in Albany doing what we were doing. I mean, what better case would he have? So it was really like God would be very, very happy to be on my side. There's a bit of arrogance about that, but that was the way it felt.

10 I think Albany settled the issue of jail and I think songs helped to do that because in the songs you could just name the people who were trying to use this against you—Asa Kelley, who was the mayor, Chief Pritchett, who was the police. This behavior is new behavior for black people in the United States of America. You would every once in a while have a crazy black person going up against some white person and they would hang him. But this time, with a song, there was nothing they could do to block what we were saying. Not only did you call their names and say what you wanted to say, but they could not stop your sound. Singing is different than talking because no matter what they do, they would have to kill me to stop me from singing, if they were arresting me. Sometimes they would plead and say, "Please stop singing." And you would just know that your word is being heard. There was a real sense of platformness and clearly empowerment, and it was like just saying, "Put me in jail, that's not an issue of power. My freedom has nothing to do with putting me in jail." And so there was this joy.

James Lawson
Student Nonviolent Coordinating Committee Statement of Purpose

The Student Nonviolent Coordinating Committee was formed during a meeting on April 15, 1960, of student leaders of the Southern sit-in movement. One hundred-twenty-six student delegates from fifty-six colleges in twelve Southern states, and students from nineteen northern schools as well as thirteen organi-

zations and fifty-seven observers were represented at the meeting at Shaw University in Raleigh, North Carolina. Reverend James Lawson, who was expelled from Vanderbilt University Divinity School because he refused to withdraw from the protest movement, drafted this Statement of Purpose, dated May 14, 1960, for the Temporary Student Nonviolent Coordinating Committee. It is reprinted in the Eyes on the Prize Civil Rights Reader (New York: Penguin, 1991).

Carrying out the mandate of the Raleigh Conference to write a statement of purpose for the movement, the Temporary Student Nonviolent Coordinating Committee submits for careful consideration the following draft. We urge all local, state or regional groups to examine it closely. Each member of our movement must work diligently to understand the depths of nonviolence.

We affirm the philosophical or religious ideal of nonviolence as the foundation of our purpose, the pre-supposition of our faith, and the manner of our action. Nonviolence as it grows from Judaic-Christian traditions seeks a social order of justice permeated by love. Integration of human endeavor represents the crucial first step towards such a society.

Through nonviolence, courage displaces fear; love transforms hate. Acceptance dissipates prejudice; hope ends despair. Peace dominates war; faith reconciles doubt. Mutual regard cancels enmity. Justice for all overthrows injustice. The redemptive community supersedes systems of gross social immorality.

Love is the central motif of nonviolence. Love is the force by which God binds man to himself and man to man. Such love goes to the extreme; it remains loving and forgiving even in the midst of hostility. It matches the capacity of evil to inflict suffering with an even more enduring capacity to absorb evil, all the while persisting in love.

5 By appealing to conscience and standing on the moral nature of human existence, nonviolence nurtures the atmosphere in which reconciliation and justice become actual possibilities.

▓ QUESTIONS FOR INQUIRY AND ACTION ▓

1. What are the unique qualities of the black churches in the United States? How have they contributed to the civil rights movement and ongoing social justice movements? How can white churches learn from them, from their theology to their liturgy and rituals of worship?

2. Bernice Johnson Reagon speaks to a *transformation* that needs to take place in order for a movement truly to effect change. The movement for social justice is beyond mere politics and economics; it needs to transform people in order to work. What do you think and feel about this?

3. Some theologians interpret the commandment "Thou Shalt Not Take the Lord's Name in Vain" not primarily to mean that we should not swear, but that we should

not act as if we know what God wants; in other words, that we should not act in God's name. Reflect on this. How do you respond to it? How would that affect the actions of faith communities around the world?

4. Wendy Kaminer states in "The Last Taboo" that "government can't make you good." Its purpose is not moral. What is its purpose? How can faith communities and government work together? *Should* they work together?

WRITING STYLE

PUBLIC LETTERS

Martin Luther King, Jr.'s "Letter from Birmingham Jail" is one of the most famous examples in American history of a *public letter*, or an *open letter*, that is, a letter addressed to a specific person or persons, but aimed generally at a large public reading audience. He wrote the letter in response to a statement published in the *Birmingham News*. Written by eight clergymen, the statement urged King and the activists in the Southern Christian Leadership Conference not to demonstrate for civil rights in Birmingham. You can read this statement along with the text of King's letter, and even listen to King himself reading the letter, at *The Martin Luther King, Jr. Papers Project* Web site at Stanford University: http://www.stanford.edu/group/King/popular_requests/

Public letters are generally longer and more substantive than letters to the editor, which are also a form of public letter. Public letters are often published on the editorial pages of newspapers. However, writers can also buy advertising space and print their letters as full-page advertisements in newspapers or magazines. More recently, the Internet has become a common forum for public letters, as it is relatively easy to publish material and to respond to others' arguments on it. King could have responded to the eight clergymen privately, in one collective letter copied to each of them, or in individual letters. Instead, he chose to respond openly and to publish his response in the newspaper, as they had done. By choosing this route, the clergymen sought public support for their views. Likewise, King ensured that this matter—which was a public matter—would not be relegated to private discussion. The citizens of Birmingham, the state of Alabama, and the United States as a whole deserved to be informed about various perspectives on racial integration and civil rights. If you are going to publish a letter openly addressing a particular figure or group of people, you will want to keep in the mind the following:

- *Write for a dual audience.* You choose to write a public letter so that you can seek public support for your views, rather than simply try to persuade a certain individual or organization. Therefore, you will be writing for two audiences simultaneously—the person or persons whose actions you want to comment on, and the larger public who will read the source in which you publish your thoughts. All of your choices as a writer will be made with this fact in mind. For example, notice how King uses the second person. He crafts the letter as if it were private, addressing it "My dear fellow clergymen" and referring to the audience as "you" throughout the letter. Yet that "you" simultaneously addresses the wider reading public. The use of "you" gives the letter a feeling of intimacy and inclusiveness. An alternative would be to write an open letter to the people of Alabama referring to the eight clergy-men as "they" and "them." What do you think the difference would be in the effect on both audiences?

- *Embrace your public audience.* Furthermore, if you want the reading public to take action on your letter, embrace them, even if indirectly. Observe how King often refers to "we" and "us," especially in such pronouncements as "We are caught in an inescapable network of mutuality, tied in a single garment of destiny. Whatever affects one directly, affects all indirectly." While the "we" and "us" refer to himself and the eight clergymen, they also refer to all the citizens reading his words. Similarly, when King expresses his disappoint-ment in "the white moderate," he can disarm the specific clergymen by tak-ing some of the blame off their own shoulders, while he suggests they share that blame with the white moderate reading public, who are in a position to make change through their sheer numbers.

- *Garner public support by showing you understand the opposer's point of view.* King could easily attack or dismiss the views of the clergymen. Instead, he chooses to show his understanding of their worldview before he presents his own alternative. His letter opens with his statement that he decided to respond to the clergymen's letter because "I feel that you are men of genuine good will and that your criticisms are sincerely set forth." Throughout he refers to the men as brothers, and concedes points where it is appropriate; for instance, he tells them "You are quite right in calling for negotiation." He extends credit to them, insisting "I am sure that none of you would want to rest content with the superficial kind of social analysis that deals merely with effects and does not grapple with underlying causes."

- *Anticipate counterarguments.* The need for public letters and open debate rarely arises from problems for which there is only one right solution, or one way to achieve the solution. Therefore, you need to anticipate the arguments that will oppose and critique your own. King works the clergymen's concerns into his own document—often by directly quoting them—from their notion that King is an "outsider coming in" to their community, to their fear that the demonstrators will demand immediate change. He mirrors their concerns and anticipates their responses to his concerns. By repeating their concerns in his letter, he shows that he read and understood their argument. At the same time, by anticipating their responses, he shows that he is a step ahead in his thinking.

- *Find common ground.* You will gather more support from the public as well as the individual whose work you are responding to if you find common grounds

continued on next page

for concern and a common language and culture to draw upon. King refers
frequently to figures, events, and ideals his audiences also hold dear: Jesus,
St. Paul, Martin Luther, Thomas Jefferson, the Boston Tea Party, and the
American Dream. He calls upon the assumption of their shared concern for
God and the growth of "the church" (meaning all of the clergymen's congregations and denominations) by proclaiming that "the judgment of God is
upon the church as never before" and that every day he meets young people
"whose disappointment with the church has turned into outright disgust."
All of these clergymen, and the adults in the community who are reading
the newspaper, have a vested interest in keeping young people engaged
with the church.

- *Recommend specific action for your audience to take.* Finally, while you've
got the attention of the public, instead of simply airing your grievances,
make specific recommendations for taking the action that will begin to
implement your solution. King announces almost immediately that "in any
nonviolent campaign there are four basic steps: collection of the facts to
determine whether injustices exist; negotiation; self-purification; and direct
action." Outline the ways in which he goes on to explain each of these in his
letter, ending with a call for direct action.

▨ CONTINUING THE CASE STUDY ▨
Where Do We Go from Here: How Do Social Change Movements Work?

The successes of the civil rights movement were the result of many years of education,
preparation, persistence, and, as the voices in this case study affirm, faith. Robert M.
Franklin, reflecting on the civil rights movement decades later, writes of the "graceful and
mysterious power of religious faith to transform imperfect human beings into courageous
exemplars of moral citizenship." Martin Luther King's speech at Holt Street Baptist Church,
delivered at an early stage in the movement, shortly after the Montgomery Bus Boycott, is
focused on strategizing for the long and hard work to come. Singer Bernice Johnson Reagon
emphasizes the power of music, especially singing, to bring people together, and James
Lawson's statement of purpose shows the importance of putting one's vision and goals into
writing (as well as the importance of students to the movement).

Martin Luther King's famous "Letter from Birmingham Jail," one of the most important
texts of the civil rights movement, outlines his steps for a nonviolent campaign. Direct
action is his *last* step; before that come stages of collecting facts, negotiating, and purifying oneself. Direct action is not intended as an end in itself, but as a means to get the people involved on either side to return to negotiating and resolving their differences. When we
are observing or even participating in social change movements, we often do not realize
that after the dramatic marches and protests, further work is necessary to change the laws
or the city ordinances and to transform institutional structures in order to reinforce the
objectives of the direct action.

When working with a case study on a historical event, we have the benefit of hindsight. We can analyze the process of change by breaking it down into its parts and observing what was most effective at each stage. In this exercise you will be using the tool of the Social Change Wheel to analyze an event in the civil rights movement and trace the methods used to effect change. The Social Change Wheel originated with Mark Langseth and Marie Troppe at Minnesota Campus Compact and has since been adapted by many others. The various sections of the wheel show the individual (and multiple) methodologies at work in any social change process—although the categories tend to overlap in actual application. Education is in the center. It is where we start, no matter which method we may turn to afterward.

Divide your class into groups of researchers. Each group should select one event of the civil rights movement (e.g., the Montgomery Bus Boycott, the integration of Little Rock's Central High School or the *Brown v. Board of Education* Supreme Court case, the various sit-ins at lunch counters, the organization of the Student Nonviolent Coordinating Committee, the Freedom Rides). The civil rights movement involves far more events than those referred to in this case study. You could begin your research with the *Eyes on the Prize Civil Rights Reader,* which includes documents, speeches, and other firsthand accounts from the various stages of the movement.

Each group will apply the Social Change Wheel to its event to analyze the effectiveness of that event. Observe the methods of the wheel that were used in the event in order to understand reasons for using the individual methods, for the sequence and coordination of various methods, and for the effectiveness of each method alone and in combination with other methods.

1. Write a description of *each* component of the Social Change Wheel with analysis of its individual effect on the event. (Some will be more important than others, depending on which event you choose.)

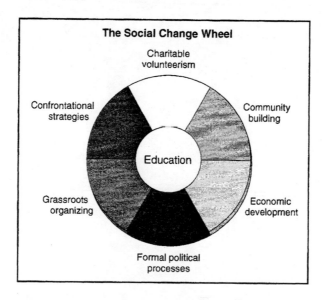

The Social Change Wheel

Charitable volunteerism

Confrontational strategies

Community building

Education

Grassroots organizing

Economic development

Formal political processes

2. Then based on your analysis, speculate on how including or excluding certain methods, sequencing methods in a certain way, and allocating resources to particular methods might have affected the outcome of the event. Write a one-page conclusion that analyzes the cumulative effect of the methods that were used and predicts how alternative methods might have changed the outcome.

3. Present your analyses and conclusions to the class. How has analyzing one event of the decades-long civil rights movement helped you to understand the movement more fully, as well as to understand the work that goes into creating social change?

4. Discuss ways you could use the Social Change Wheel to educate yourselves for effecting change in your own communities today. What issues concern you most? What resources do you have as students to help you take steps toward changing the situation?

CHAPTER 11

Virtual Communities

Technology is neither good nor bad, nor even neutral. Technology is
one part of the complex of relationships that people form with each
other and the world around them; it simply cannot be understood
outside of that concept.

—*Samuel Collins*

▓ GETTING STARTED ▓   H. G. Wells and the World Brain

The illustration below is of the Round Reading Room of the British Museum library.
H. G. Wells's *Work, Wealth, and the Happiness of Mankind* (1931) refers to such
libraries as "cells" of the "world's brain." Wells's hope for a "systematic ordering and
drawing together of human thought and knowledge" reached its clearest expression
in his book *World Brain* (1938). Since that time, scholars have used Wells's world

brain as a focal point for conversations about technology and community. You can begin to join that conversation by answering the questions below.

1. Do you see the Internet and other modern technologies as fulfilling H. G. Wells's dream of a world brain? In what ways do these technologies improve upon the model Wells imagined?

2. Brains not only store information, they organize, evaluate, and utilize it to solve problems. Brains also direct the body to act. In what ways do contemporary technologies also perform or fail to perform these actions? Can these technologies organize our communities to act in ways similar to a single body?

3. Like Wells, many contemporary scholars and computer experts envision a global information network. Seek out two other efforts to conceptualize this network. Compare and contrast them with Wells's world brain to explore their relative strengths and weaknesses as metaphors that explain this phenomenon.

In this final chapter, we explore communities defined primarily by the influence of digital technology, more specifically television and the Internet. Digital technology provides us with *subjects* of mutual interest (MP3s, television shows, virtual worlds, video games, and so on), *tools* for helping us meet and communicate with one another (cell phones, e-mail, Web logs, and so on), and *structures* for how we can think, organize, and act in the world. As Samuel Collins reminds us, our concerns with virtual communities are the same concerns we have with all of our other communities. We want to know how we can best live with one another.

New digital technologies like the Internet promise to improve the health and richness of our communal life and to create new opportunities for inquiry and action. Wells imagined his world brain to serve as more than an encyclopedia of human knowledge; he believed it could serve as the nerve center of a new social order, a planetary community. The implications of such a community urge us to reflect on these promises critically.

The chapter's case study provides an overview of one facet of our growing virtual community: Web logs. Enthusiasts for Web logs, or blogs, claim the Internet will enable us to build new communities, open our lives to more people, improve our ability to scrutinize politicians and businesses, and share information and resources more effectively. Critics complain that blogs have the potential to gum up our world brain, burdening us with too much trivial information and unsubstantiated opinions.

Esther Dyson
Communities

Esther Dyson is a well-known expert on the relationship between digital technology and society. She serves as the editor at large at CNET Networks, which publishes Release 1.0, *a newsletter for the technology industry. She also writes "Release 3.0," a column for the* New York Times, *and* Release 4.0, *her personal Weblog (http://weblog.edventure.com). "Communities" comes from her 1998 book* Release 2.1: A Design for Living in the Digital Age.

By 1997, "community" had become one of the trendiest words around, both on and off the Internet. In the context of this book and of the online world in general, a community is the unit in which people live, work, and play. Most individuals live in several communities online, just as they do in the physical world—family, church or temple, soccer club, professional society, workplace. Some communities are formal, with rules and duties, entrance requirements, and perhaps membership fees; others are less formal groupings with loose boundaries and revolving membership. As the world seems to get more complex and more overwhelming, and public life ever more scary, people look to communities for fellowship and security.

Used right, the Internet can be a powerful enabling technology fostering the development of communities because it supports the very thing that creates a community—human interaction. One benefit of the Internet is that it allows the formation of communities independent of geography. People need only share interests or goals and find one another. Conversely, people are not stuck in the communities they are born in—not entirely, at least. The programmer in India can argue with his peers in Silicon Valley or Budapest about the finer points of the Java programming language. Also, the Internet overcomes some of the barriers of time: both between time zones, and in the sense that it's quicker to send an e-mail than to drive to a community center—let alone cross the world. It's even quicker than finding an envelope and a stamp, and you can do it at your convenience, while the other person does it at *his* convenience.

There will be—there already is—a profusion of online communities. They are easy to find, and relatively easy to form. But what holds them together? Can a single person in fact be a member of twenty different communities, with each getting his attention fifteen minutes a day (for a total of five hours online)? Online communities may engage in conversations and other interaction through the medium of a particular Web site or through mailing lists or newsgroups—people linked together by text messages and increasingly through multimedia virtual places that they enter from time to time. A newsgroup is a virtual bulletin board, which members post to or read on their own schedule. A mailing list (or listserv) is like an active newsgroup; it sends regular messages out to its members, but it also generally maintains archives for people to search.

Online virtual places can be anything from a virtual room where people describe in text what is happening—"Alice looks at her shoes and bites her lip"[1]— to full-scale multimedia locations where people are represented by "avatars"—cartoon figures, images of themselves, or any other symbol they choose. Some of these places support voice or even video. Then there are "buddy lists," which enable you to see which of your friends or colleagues are currently online, and virtually tap them on the shoulder as if to say, "May I talk to you now?" (People can put up "do not disturb" signs, or say something like "Working on Berkman project; don't bother me otherwise.")

5   Online as offline, what you bring to a community determines what you get out of it. This ranges from a community of two, of which the canonical form is marriage, to a community of two thousand. People's online communities will reflect their daily lives as more and more people go online: their extended families; their colleagues at work, including customers and suppliers and possibly competitors; their school friends; and so on. As people move around physically, from school to camp and college and from job to job, from chance meetings on holidays to various kinds of interest groups, they will join new communities and probably drop out of others.

The Great Net Hope

For me, the great hope of the Net is that more and more people will be led to get involved with it, and that using it will change their overall experience of life. *Power in one sphere changes one's perception of one's capabilities in general.* Right now, politically, the United States is in a sorry state. Only 49 percent of the potential voters bothered to vote in the most recent presidential elections. (Compare that to Russia, where more people voted, but there's even less feeling of involvement.) People are rational, and they know that one person's vote won't change the outcome. Others feel a certain social responsibility, and so they vote anyway. But voting alone does not make a real democracy, any more than taxes are an expression of philanthropy.

From Cyberspace to Real Space

I feel this intensely because it so happens that I have never voted, although I have certainly paid a lot of taxes.[2] For many years, I just ignored the government and it ignored me. Then I started spending a lot of time in Washington because of the Electronic Frontier Foundation and the National Information Infrastructure Advisory Council, and my attitudes changed. To be sure, even with the advent

---

[1] *This compelling snip of text is courtesy of Amy Bruckman, a grad student at MIT who runs the MediaMOO online community.*

[2] *The one time I tried to register to vote I was told I had to go to some office with my birth certificate because I was born in Switzerland, even though I've been a U.S. citizen since childhood. I didn't have my birth certificate and it just seemed so complicated that I gave up. I feel a little embarrassed about it; my only lame excuse is that I have other priorities. I now have sent in a form to register, but I haven't voted yet.*

of the Net not everyone gets invited to Washington, but suddenly everyone is invited to contribute if he or she cares enough to go to any relevant Web site or discussion group. Although I haven't yet voted formally, I feel that I have a meaningful voice and a meaningful stake in what our government does. I'm a far more active citizen than before I raised my voice, and I care about the consequences. This doesn't mean that the folks in Washington are rushing to follow my advice. But if my ideas are valid, other people will amplify them and they will be heard.

The Net will involve a growing portion of the population in this kind of governance, and their feeling of empowerment will spread to other parts of their lives. The secret is that the Internet doesn't actually *do* much; it's a powerful tool for people to use. It's not something worth having, but it's a powerful lever for people to use to accomplish their own goals in collaboration with other people. It's more than a source of information; *it's a way for people to organize themselves. It gives them power for themselves, rather than over others.*

Net Participation

How many times have you wanted to complain about something, but you gave up because it was just too difficult? I recently flew Delta to Moscow and back from Warsaw, and neither time did they have power outlets for my computer, as they had more or less promised in their ads. I complained to the flight attendant. The next morning I went to register my complaint on the Delta Web site. An hour later, I got an automatic notification that my message had been received. And less than three weeks later, I actually got a nice e-mail from one D. E. Coherly that didn't look like a form letter; it specifically talked about the schedule for upgrading the aircraft with power outlets.

10   Sometimes, I'm in a better mood. I might even like to compliment a company on something in hopes that they'll keep doing it—Marriott's excellent in-room facilities for computers, for example—although in this case I'd rather do it in public so that other hotels will follow suit. (There—consider it done!)

Sometimes I want to write a letter to the editor, but it's just too inconvenient; by the time I get to a computer, type a letter, print it out, and fax it (let alone mail it), I've lost the urge.

People are not naturally lazy, but they avoid useless effort and are overwhelmed by competing demands. Though we're not quite there yet, in the future the Net *will* make it easier for people to participate in a variety of communities—and do so more effectively. Smart businesses will encourage consumer feedback; smart politicians will solicit and even listen to comments from constituents; smart newspapers will welcome letters by e-mail and foster online discussions.

And individuals will rise to the occasion. The Net will foster activity instead of passivity.

Basic Principles

Here are a few basic principles for communities, based on my own experience both on- and offline:

15
- Each participant should be clear about what he is *giving and what he hopes to get*. Overall, those desires should mesh, although they may well be different for each individual.
- There should be a way of determining who is in the community and who is outside it. Otherwise the community is meaningless.
- Community members should feel that they have invested in the community, and that therefore it is tough for them to leave. The ultimate punishment in a strong community is punishment, expulsion, excommunication, exile . . . . All those words signify the terror of being cast out of a community.
- The community's rules should be clear, and there should be recourse if they are broken.

Communities fail when these principles are not observed: for example, the marriage in which one person loves a partner who is deceiving him, as opposed to one where one partner provides sex in exchange for a life of ease. Some people might see the latter as a moral failure, but it is a valid community. The dance club where people are screened in or out by a bouncer may or may not be a valid community, depending no how well the bouncer knows the crowd and whether they know one another. On the other hand, a good bartender can create a wonderful community, as illustrated in countless plays and television shows, or by Rick in the movie *Casablanca*.

Vested Interest

20
What kinds of investment can one make in a community? There are two things people can give easily, especially over the Net: time and money. Paying $19.95 a month for America Online doesn't really make you part of the community, nor does it make it hard for you to leave (it may actually encourage you to do so to save money), but it does signify a certain commitment. Time is often more valuable. Emotionally, you will want to justify that spending of time or money because you value what you have paid for.

In the real world, community members often contribute (or own) real estate, which is why in the past voting rights were often restricted to landowners; they were considered the only ones with a true stake in the community (and they paid taxes for that privilege). Now, in many countries, language as well as birth is a gauge of membership. In the Baltics, for example, the old ethnic identities are reasserting themselves through language; Russian residents who went to Soviet/Russian schools and never learned the local language are now being disenfranchised in their local geographic communities. In the United States, use of Spanish is a political issue in border states such as California, Texas, and Florida.

Sharing food is another mark of community, reflected in everything from statements about breaking bread together to customs such as potluck dinners. In many communities, people share their labor, building houses for one family after another. On the Net, they share their time, ideas, and experiences—food for thought or discussion, so to speak . . . .

From here on, it's just excerpts, to save you the e-mail "overhead." . . .

The Role of Government vs. Self-help

Government can play a divisive role vis-à-vis communities. Often, the more government provides, the less community members themselves contribute.[3] For example, parents tend to identify less with a government-provided school than with a private school they raise money for and oversee themselves. Yet parents can "invest" in public schools too, by taking an active role in school administration, coaching soccer teams, running school events, and participating in parent-teacher meetings. Often, families join neighborhood communities through their children; single people tend to identify with their jobs or their after-work activities. All these facets of human nature translate easily to the online world. It's harder to build houses, but people can get together to build virtual environments, discussion groups, even markets.

25 It is often just as deadly for the government to take over communities as for commercial interests to do so. And in cyberspace the results are the same: The members fight and then flee. There's a community spirit that has more to do with influence than with voting, more to do with being heard than with ownership.

For-profit Communities

So, communities can be commercial, or they can be not-for-profit. The notion of commercial communities often offends people, although most people spend time in commercial environments every day. There are commercial communities at work; there are athletic clubs and hairdressers, bars and bookstores. Someone has to pay the rent—although the rent is usually a lot lower in cyberspace than in the physical world.

Often it works the other way: The "owner"—a company or an individual leader—thinks it owns the community. But then that owner finds out that even though it may own the facilities, collect the membership fees, and provide the towels, golf clubs, alcohol or online entertainment, hairdressing, or editorial services, the community owns whatever it is that keeps people from leaving. The "owner" may make and enforce the rules, but if he tries to change them without general consent, the community may well take over. Worse, it may just up and leave. Something like that faced San Francisco's WELL, where a tight-knit membership rejected new, financially oriented management.

There's no necessary conflict in an owner's making a profit. Conflict occurs when the members aren't happy. Running online communities will become a big market in the long run. Many will be local, closer to an extension of the local shopper paper than, say, *Time* magazine. Some will be sponsored by advertisers or supported by transaction fees. Others will change membership fees.[4]

---

[3] *Even in the physical world, the government doesn't entirely control the community. A city may think it "owns" the city streets, but at some point, if the government doesn't do its job, the citizens may take those streets back, with their own neighborhood associations or their own vigilante groups. But that process is much slower and more dangerous than what happens in cyberspace.*

[4] *What's the difference between a tax and a user/membership fee? Basically, one is required and the other is optional. Is the fee we pay to Microsoft for Windows really closer to a tax we pay for the sheer benefit of membership in a Microsoft-dominated world?*

Like terrestrial communities, good online communities require care and tending. Members need someone to resolve disputes, set the tone, find the sponsors, or collect the fees. Someone needs to maintain the database or whatever software manages the conversations, deal with the vendors who are supporting the community or communicating with it, and define the rules or modify them in accordance with community interests.

30 Online communities will vary broadly, and some community operators will do a good job while others won't. The criterion of a "good job" is set by the members—both the critical mass who stay, and those who leave. In the end, if the community does not operate in the interests of its members, whoever they are, it will not survive. But the damage is not as great as in physical communities, where buildings deteriorate, criminals take over, and the most defenseless people have nowhere else to go.

Not-for-profit Communities

One real benefit of the digital medium is its low cost, at least by developed-world standards. Just as the Net will foster a profusion of entrepreneurs who can now set up in business for themselves with little capital, so will it encourage philanthropic entrepreneurs. The Net lowers barriers to entry in all kinds of activities. Already there are a number of online museums, many online interest groups, and Web sites and mailing lists supporting interests ranging from Native-American culture to the worldwide fight against child labor. Such groups will proliferate.

It used to take market forces or huge amounts of charity to foster long-distance communications and the communities they support, now it's cheap. One of the organizations I'm involved in, the Eurasia Foundation, makes a tight budget go a long way in helping nonprofit organizations in the former Soviet Union keep their community together.

They can bolster their resolve in difficult circumstances and band together to lobby for new laws or spread information about existing laws that are being ignored by local authorities. The Net provides a continuing lifeline as graduates of Foundation-sponsored economics courses, journalism training, and other programs apply their new skills at home in local communities that often find their ideas strange and their enthusiasm suspect.

Online Support for Community

But there's more to the Net than just "virtual" communities. There are lots of "real" communities that also exist online. To listen to many people talk, you'd think we're all going to slip off into cyberspace and leave our daily lives behind. People who read about communities in cyberspace often get online, and then wonder what all the fuss is about. Yes, there are those chat rooms, but many of those are for people who want titillation more than community. You can't necessarily find community on the Net any more reliably than in real life.

35 Usually, you get into a community through an introduction, online or offline. Or you have to take a little time to establish your presence for others. Even online,

community still consists of the people behind the computers and the intangible—neither physical nor electronic—ties that bind them.

So it makes sense to think of the Net as community *support,* not a community (or communities) in itself. The Net can support all kinds of communities. As I've shown, my own communities tend to operate through e-mail. We use the Net for our communications, for sending and sharing information, for setting up meetings, for catching up on news. Other communities operate through the Web, with people posting and reacting to one another's comments, or even representing themselves as avatars. People can put up their own home pages describing themselves, but what makes a community is the interaction among people, not their mere presence.

Beyond that, I can imagine a lot of physical communities using the Net in more mundane ways: bulletin boards for teenagers offering babysitting services, listings of school events, sites for restaurants with constantly changing daily specials, news of local sports teams. People in companies can use online support to share information about sales prospects or competitors' activities; they can also organize company outings, complain about the state of the bathrooms, or recommend local coffee shops.

In the future, we'll take online community support for granted. Some communities will be mostly offline, some mostly online, and people's physical locations won't matter as much. But that won't be the key thing about any particular community. In any kind of community, the key thing will be its members. A technical system can support a community, but it needs active members to lead it and to make it worth joining.

Community Questions

Many facets of online communities aren't yet clear. What is the right size for a community? The answer certainly will vary according to a number of factors, but over time we should have a better understanding, much as we do of cities and villages today. How do communities split up into smaller communities when they get too large, or when a group simply decides to go off on its own for other reasons? One intriguing point, from anthropologist George Gumerman at the Santa Fe Institute in New Mexico, is that homogeneous communities can be relatively indifferent to size, whereas communities with complex social roles need to have the right number of people to fill those roles: one medicine man, one trainer of youth, one village chief, one spiritual leader, and so forth. If the community grows, too many people may be vying for one role; if it shrinks, certain roles may go unfilled. Such communities tend to have strong rules about family size, and about members joining or leaving the community. It will be interesting to see how that translates into online communities: one social director, one head of member programs, one advertising manager . . . .

What Doesn't Work

40 Clearly, some things do *not* foster community. You do not need a real identity, but you need *some* identity . . . . You need to have a voice, a reputation, a presence to be part of a community, because it is (at least) a two-way proposition.

Thus, "lurkers," people who only read or listen, are not really part of the community. They may fancy themselves to be, but no one would miss them if they left. They are fans, not friends. Lurkers may latch on to a culture, but they do not contribute to it. (That's why fandom is so eerie: There's usually no real communication between the fans and the stars, just lurkers and fantasies on one side and a PR machine on the other.)

Thus, a particular community may contain pseudonymous members who are valued on the basis of what they contribute to it. If someone's contribution is based on falsehood, then that individual may have a problem. But pseudonymity can also be a mask that allows a person to reveal a true identity rather than to hide one, or to allow a true expression of one facet of that individual's character.

Thus, a self-help group of anonymous people is hard to define as a community unless the members at least have persistent (though pseudonymous) identities. A monologue explaining who you are does not bring you into a community, however good it feels and however cathartic or liberating it may be.

There are good experiences without community . . . and there are bad communities. Imagine, for example, a community built around shared hatred of Jews or Serbians or the U.S. government, working on ways to "cleanse" the neighborhood or destroy supposed enemies. It may be a good example of a community, with shared contributions and common interests—but a horrible example of humanity.

That illustrates the biggest danger in the ease of forming and enclosing communities—their ability to insulate themselves from the rest of society. People in most physical communities encounter reality from time to time, be it on the streets of a neighborhood, a network television broadcast, or the front page of a newspaper. Online communities can exist sealed away from reality. Members can trade lies or illusions among themselves without fear of contradiction. (As I have said, the Net is a great medium for conspiracy, while television is best for propaganda.)

Tricky Questions: Freedom of Speech

45   Many social norms differ from community to community. They include censorship/freedom of speech, religion, the inclusion of children, and the like. On many of these issues, communities will simply agree to disagree, and observe and enforce the rules they think appropriate internally.

Freedom of speech is one of those near-absolute freedoms that Americans cherish and many other countries think we honor too much. In other societies, where convention governs more than law anyway, the sorts of things we may legally say in the United States are considered appalling and uncultured, to say nothing of offensive or dangerous. Americans (including me) answer back that this is the price we pay for freedom of speech—and our related freedoms to think for ourselves, to criticize our government, to believe as we want.

Communities will set their own standards for what is appropriate.

People who select or receive content from the Net can use filtering tools to determine what they see as individuals . . . , but here I'm talking about content within a community—what people say to one another, what they post in public "online spaces," and so forth. What will your company allow you to say about the chairman on the corporate intranet, or even outside on the Internet at large? How rude can you be when you disagree with someone? How much informality or bad spelling is tolerated at work? What about in a community of poets? How commercial can you be in a sports discussion group? Is Juan allowed to promote his sporting goods store when Alice asks a question about fishing tackle? How loudly can either of them criticize the person who sold her the fishing rod she uses now?

The answers to these questions are norms, not laws. Usually a community can handle them for itself. People chide one another, others complain; leaders calm things down. Over time, people in a group learn how to live together or they go off in search of more compatible (for them) communities.

50   Many terrestrial governments that fear freedom of speech will probably try to prohibit their citizens from visiting (let alone speaking in) Net communities outside their own countries. In the long run, that makes no sense. Apart from protecting children, the best response to "offensive" speech, however defined, is not to bury it, but to answer it. (The best response to obscenity is to ignore it. And the best response to child pornography, which involves actual children, is to track down and prosecute the people involved.)

More troubling than "indecency" is what to do with genuinely dangerous information such as bomb-making instructions, maps of sensitive security installations, and the like. There is no perfect answer. The kind of bomb-making information available in chemistry textbooks is best left free precisely so that it doesn't acquire the lure of the forbidden. And I do know that most laws against content can't ultimately be effective; they will simply drive information underground, where only the worst people can get at it. Nonetheless, some stuff shouldn't be published by the people who have it. Such information is often classified and can be kept off the Net by law and secrecy agreements at the source, and by the local decisions of communities that don't want the responsibility on their own heads.[5] Freedom of speech does not mean "obligation to publish."

Government censorship is unlikely to be effective in the long run, even though governments will keep trying. France outlawed the printing of polling information in the prelude to its recent national elections; those who cared simply got the information from the Net, published by French-language news sources in nearby Switzerland. Germany embroiled CompuServe in a lawsuit over porn and Nazi material, now on appeal.

Nonetheless, we live in a world where governments—even democratic governments—still do things Americans and others find unconscionable. As long as governments control people physically, they can instill fear and keep all but the most determined dissidents under intellectual control, too—not just by cutting wires or employing technical filtering tools and tapping lines (with encryption outlawed), but by getting neighbor to spy on neighbor. They will be able to control

---

[5]But in fact, way too much information is classified, most of it probably "dangerous" only to the officials involved.

the overall level of discourse in their countries if they are willing to lose many of the Net's benefits. But they will fail to keep their most dedicated dissident citizens from connecting with the rest of the world.

Changing Culture

Clearly, Net culture is changing. It is no longer dominated by upper-middle-class males who speak (only) English. The commercial community has found the Net, and it is increasingly a business medium. But grandparents and social workers have found it, too, Nonprofit organizations are big users, especially in far-flung locations where other means of communication are prohibitively expensive. In the United States and in wired regions such as Scandinavia, the Net is becoming a consumer medium. In most other countries, it's still too expensive and exotic for all but the most sophisticated home users . . . for now.

55   Eventually, there will be a global society of the connected, laid over more traditional local communities that are usually less well off—in terms of material things, education, connectivity, and even the sophistication to judge the merits of what's online. This global culture (it would be a stretch to call it a community) will probably offend the sensibilities of many "antiglobal" people, but it will grow as a proportion of the world's population.

Some parts of local culture can easily transfer to the Net; others are fundamentally hostile to it. I'm not comfortable saying that everyone in the world should be on the Net. But in the end, everyone will be, except for a few holdouts. The challenge is to make sure that those holdouts are offline by choice, not for lack of it.

▩ QUESTIONS FOR INQUIRY AND ACTION ▩

1. The Internet, Dyson argues, offers citizens the chance to empower themselves by organizing with other people. To organize effectively, Dyson provides several basic principles for community. Examine those principles. Based on your own experiences with the Net, are these principles sufficient? What principles would you change or add?

2. Dyson imagines a global culture of Internet users in the future. As this digital society grows, some aspects of local culture will join them while others will resist. As a class, list all the local communities to which you belong; then, discuss how these communities would or would not benefit from digital technology. Finally, discuss how digital technology could change those communities, whether they go online or not.

3. "Sharing food is another mark of community," writes Dyson, "reflected in everything from statements about breaking bread together to customs such as potluck dinners." Dyson's reference to food is metaphorical; people on the Net share "time, ideas, and experiences—food for thought or discussion." In the next essay, Jeff Dietrich also uses food as a metaphor for discussing technology; how would he respond to Dyson's points? Does he believe the Net might renew our communities?

4. Dyson describes the Internet as a "powerful enabling technology" that can promote human interaction. How have e-mail, chat rooms, blogs, or other forms of digital technology affected your human interactions? Have they broadened or improved your interactions as Dyson suggests they can? Ask the same questions of five other people representing different age groups, genders, ethnicities, or social classes. Compare and contrast what you learn.

Jeff Dietrich
Refusing to Hope in a God of Technology

Jeff Dietrich is a writer, an activist, and a member of the Los Angeles Catholic Worker. He writes regularly about religious issues for The Catholic Agitator. *"Refusing to Hope in a God of Technology" was published in* National Catholic Reporter *(March 14, 1997).*

"Hey, don't give me nonna that hard crust stuff, man. I ain't no Frenchy." For the majority of folks who eat at our soup kitchen, bread is not hard and crusty, does not have poppy seeds or sesame seeds, is not black or brown. It does not have the flavor of rye or yeast. In fact it has no flavor or character, mass or density, or substance. It is soft, white, bland and as flavorless as a cotton ball. It is bread in name only, made by machines for a people who have lost their memory of bread.

This is not a judgment on the people who eat at the Catholic Worker soup kitchen. It is just a minor example of the subtle but pervasive manner in which technology "transubstantiates" life into a mere simulation of itself, erasing all memories of what has gone before.

In recent months we have read articles of artists and monastics, Catholic Workers and peace activists embracing the Internet. It is not the technology itself that concerns us so much as the fact that these particular people who are apparently embracing this new technology with such enthusiasm should, by virtue of their "alternative" vocations, be more skeptical than they apparently are.

They should not so glibly repeat the hype and promise of technical progress. They should know that everything that is being said today about the positive benefits of the Internet was first said about the automobile and then about radio and television. It will bring us closer together, give us more and better leisure time, improve our intellect, save lives, promote community, give us more freedom, greater autonomy and personal power. How many times do we have to hear the same sales pitch before we realize that we are being sold a bill of goods? Soon they will forget the taste and substance of face-to-face community. Soon the only real community will be the "net," just as the only "real" bread is Wonder Bread.

5   Those who criticize new technology are often characterized as naive or romantic. But in truth it is the ones who uncritically embrace new technical innovations

that are being naive and idealistic. They put their hope in the power of technology to solve the very problems it has caused: alienation, pollution, unemployment and an epidemic of cancer-related diseases.

But as sociologist Jacques Ellul points out, "Technique is monistic." That is, "It is all one piece. All techniques are inseparably united and cannot be detached from the others. Nor can the technical phenomenon be broken down in such a way as to retain the good and reject the bad. Every technical advance is matched by a negative reverse side. History has proven that every technical application from its beginnings presents certain unforeseeable secondary effects which are much more disastrous than the lack of the technique would have been."

Though we cannot know all of the unforeseeable consequences of the information superhighway, we can certainly recognize the secondary effects of our current highway system: air pollution and traffic fatalities that every five years exceed the number of Americans killed in World War II; war, intrigue and death to secure oil in the Middle East; and endless suburban sprawl and more acres of asphalt than farm land.

Here in Los Angeles anyone without an automobile is a de facto second-class citizen without access to the better-paying jobs and decent housing that have migrated down the freeways to the suburbs. The same will also be true of everyone who finds himself stuck at the on-ramp of the information superhighway. It's a dead-end street for the poor.

In his recent book, *The Revolt of the Elites*, the late Christopher Lasch points out that the "new meritocratic elites" are already cruising down the information superhighway, losing all sense of connectedness with community, place and the common good. Their loyalties are international rather than regional, national or local. "They have more in common with their counterparts in Brussels and Hong Kong than with the masses of Americans not yet plugged into the network of global communications."

10   Our blindness to the disastrous secondary effects of technology is a result of our theological attachment to the technical phenomenon. We tend to think of technology as a neutral instrument. But in fact it is the physical embodiment of our cultural values of rationality and efficiency, and our collective desire to overcome the forces of nature: toil, suffering and death. As such it is a response to the Fall. It is a manifestation of our attempts to attain salvation without repentance or discomfort.

Thus we must recognize that our struggle is not against technology in itself but rather against the "spirituality of technology," against technology as a principality and power. Ellul says that technology, or "technique" as he calls it, is the "sacred organizing principle of our culture," somewhat like the force that Christianity exerted on the culture of medieval Europe.

In the past, technological growth was restrained by the culture. All traditional cultures are essentially religious and conservative, skeptical of anything new and innovative and focused primarily upon preserving the patterns and practices of the past. As a consequence, technology developed at a very slow pace and never disrupted cultural structures.

It is axiomatic that human institutions develop at a far slower pace than technical innovations. Just ask any businessman and he will tell you that in our world today change is the only constant. The survivors are the ones who have positioned themselves to "ride the cresting wave of the future." On the other hand, the vast majority of the world's population will drown, because they need the buoyancy provided by stable institutions.

It is often assumed that the prosperous working class of the industrial nations was created by the progressive development of technology. But the truth is that this prosperity was created not by machines but by the struggle and sacrifice of dedicated workers and the advent of the labor union. But labor unions took over 100 years to evolve, while the benefits they created have been destroyed in less than a generation by the onslaught of new information technologies. The constant cycle of technological change is disastrous for the poor. Long before any human institution can evolve to address this current technology, there will be a new destabilizing technical development.

15   Jacques Ellul is not a satisfying writer because he refuses to give us any solution to the problems of "technological society." He simply reminds us that as Christians we are called to be in the world but not of it. Ellul is painfully aware that we cannot simply reject technology and that it is impossible to give a pure witness to the simple non-technical life. But we can refuse to sing the songs of technology, we can refuse to repeat the mythology of technical progress, we can refuse to put our hope in the god of technology. And when we use technology, we can use it "confessionally," acknowledging our complicity in the degradation of the planet and the oppression of the poor.

Though I am a big fan of *Star Trek* and *The X-Files*, I do believe that Carl Jung was correct when he said that the current interest in space travel and flying saucers is a projection of desperate people seeking salvation no longer in God or repentance, but in a fantasy of space-traveling extraterrestrials. But Wendell Berry said: "We cannot look for happiness to any technological paradise or to any New Earth of outer space, but only to the world as it is, and as we have made it. The only life we may hope to live is here. . . . We can only wait here, where we are, in the world, obedient to its processes, patient in its taking away, and all that we deserve of earthly Paradise will come to us."

Our salvation lies in eating the true bread of life, not bread baked by machines and filled with chemicals—the bread of remembering, not the bread of forgetfulness.

▦ QUESTIONS FOR INQUIRY AND ACTION ▦

1. Examine Dietrich's use of the metaphor of bread. Why does he choose that metaphor? What does it allow him to argue?

2. Dietrich, writing for a Catholic magazine, uses language that he knows his audience will respond to, and he assumes shared values. He argues that "when we use technology, we can use it 'confessionally,' acknowledging our complicity in the

degradation of the planet and the oppression of the poor." What does he mean by this? In what ways would you agree or disagree?

3. Conduct an inquiry into the history of any one piece of technology, for instance, the telephone, automobile, or washing machine. What were the promises made about the advantages of that technology? In what ways did those promises come true or not?

4. Explore the effects of technology on a social movement that interests you or that you are involved in, perhaps through your service learning work. In what ways do the new technologies aid the activists and communities, and in what ways do the technologies impede progress and/or community building?

STOP AND THINK

78 QUESTIONS: A GUIDE TO LIVING WITH TECHNOLOGY

Participants in the 1993 and 1994 Megatechnology conferences created the following questions to promote critical thinking in our use of technology. As you read the questions, apply them in your mind to the technologies you use every day.

As articulated, debated, and refined by the participants in the 1993 and 1994 Megotechnology conferences, 78 tools to be used in dismantling the megamachine and restoring organic reality. Designed to be comfortable to everyone's grasp and to provide a lifetime of service if honed with hope and polished by imagination.

Ecological

What are its effects on the health of the planet and of the person?
Does it preserve or destroy biodiversity?
Does it preserve or reduce ecosystem integrity?
What are its effects on the land?
What are its effects on wildlife?
How much and what kind of waste does it generate?
Does it incorporate the principles of ecological design?
Does it break the bond of renewal between humans and nature?
Does it preserve or reduce cultural diversity?
What is the totality of its effects, its "ecology"?

Social

Does it serve community?
Does it empower community members?
How does it affect our perception of our needs?
Is it consistent with the creation of a communal, human economy?
What are its effects on relationships?
Does it undermine conviviality?
Does it undermine traditional forms of community?

How does it affect our way of seeing and experiencing the world?
Does it foster a diversity of forms of knowledge?
Does it build on, or contribute to, the renewal of traditional forms of knowledge?
Does it serve to commodify knowledge or relationships?
To what extent does it redefine reality?
Does it erase a sense of time and history?
What is its potential to become addictive?

Practical

What does it make?
Whom does it benefit?
What is its purpose?
Where was it produced?
Where is it used?
Where must it go when it's broken or obsolete?
How expensive is it?
Can it be repaired? By an ordinary person?
What is the entirety of its cost, the full cost accounting?

Moral

What values does its use foster?
What is gained by its use?
What are its effects beyond its utility to the individual?
What is lost in using it?
What are its effects on the least person in the society?

Ethical

How complicated is it?
What does it allow us to ignore?
To what extent does it distance agent from effect?
Can we assume personal, or communal, responsibility for its effects?
Can its effects be directly apprehended?
What ancillary technologies does it require?
What behavior might it make possible in the future?
What other technologies might it make possible?
Does it alter our sense of time and relationships in ways conducive to nihilism?

Vocational

What is its impact on craft?
Does it reduce, deaden, or enhance human creativity?
Is it the least imposing technology available for the task?
Does it replace, or does it aid, human hands and human beings?
Can it be responsive to organic circumstance?
Does it depress or enhance the quality of goods?
Does it depress or enhance the meaning of work?

continued on next page

Metaphysical

What aspect of the inner self does it reflect?
Does it express love?
Does it express rage?
What aspect of our past does it reflect?
Does it reflect cyclical or linear thinking?

Political

What is its mystique?
Does it concentrate or equalize power?
Does it require, or institute, a knowledge elite?
Is it totalitarian?
Does it require a bureaucracy for its perpetuation?
What legal empowerments does it require?
Does it undermine traditional moral authority?
Does it require military defense?
Does it enhance, or serve, military purposes?
How does it affect warfare?
Does it foster mass thinking or behavior?
Is it consistent with the creation of a global economy?
Does it empower transnational corporations?
What kind of capital does it require?

Aesthetic

Is it ugly?
Does it cause ugliness?
What noise does it make?
What pace does it set?
How does it affect quality of life (as distinct from standard of living)?

Jake Mulholland and Adrienne Martin
Tune Out

Jake Mulholland is a student at the University of Minnesota. Adrienne Martin is a student at Normandale Community College. They collaboratively designed, researched, and wrote "Tune Out" for their composition course when both were freshmen at Normandale Community College.

Our lives are hard-wired with technology. We are surrounded by computers and the Internet at work and at home. We drive complex cars with ABS brakes and GPS tracking down eight-lane super highways. We talk on cell phones with

SMS, schedule appointments on Palm Pilots, and cruise the Internet at 1.5 megabytes a second on DSL networks. Yet none of these technological wonders comes close to playing as big a role in our lives as do television and movies.

According to the *Kill Your TV* Website, by the time the average child reaches 18 years of age he or she has spent more time watching TV than attending school. The movie industry grossed 732 billion dollars last year. The average movie ticket costs $5.50. This means that 133.1 billion movies were viewed last year—and this excludes the multibillion dollar movie rental industry. TV is everywhere. Our daily rituals revolve around our favorite sitcoms and made-for-TV-movies. We wake to Al Roker telling us the forecast. We employ the television as a nanny. We eat dinner with Seinfeld, and Jay Leno lulls us to sleep at night.

With all the time spent in front of the TV and watching movies it would be hard to disagree that they play a major role in how we socialize, or how we interact with others. In the United States, 98% of households have at least one television and by the time today's children reach age 70, they will have spent approximately seven years watching TV. These statistics were nationwide and for all ages.

This made us wonder: How are *we* affected by TV? Would the denial of television and movies affect us? Would we toss and turn at night and be groggier in the mornings? Would we converse more with our friends and family? Would we find ourselves lost without the companionship of Frazier, Montel, and Chandler Bing or would we go on with life as though nothing had changed?

To discover how much TV has shaped our socializing, we decided to set up an experiment. First, we needed to assess how TV affects our lives. We did this by journaling our daily lives for one week, recording how TV and movies influenced them. We found that TV was habitual. It was not a scheduled daily event, but it was consistently watched at the same time every day. We watched TV regularly during the same times, like before bed and during dinner. For example, when Jake gets home from school, he automatically turns on his TV. He instinctively turns it on no matter what time it is or what's on. It has become a habit. Instead of calling a friend or playing catch with his brother he opts to watch the TV in place of real human contact. This has a direct effect on Jake's social life because he excludes himself from the activities going on around him. To simplify, we'll call this type of TV watching *habitual viewing*.

We also found that television was used for entertainment. In contrast to the habitual viewing, this refers to scheduled events for socializing. For instance, Jake planned an outing with friends to watch a movie. The movie wasn't the focus of the evening but provided a vehicle for communication and motivated their meeting. It has been our experience that people are uncomfortable getting together with no agenda in mind. In Jake's case, the movie created a comfortable atmosphere where everyone was able to openly discuss recent events and "hang out" without feeling like they weren't doing anything. The movie created the agenda and made it acceptable for them to meet. Other examples of this are Super Bowl parties and dinner-and-a-movie dates. We'll call this *scheduled viewing*. Because of the examples mentioned above, we hypothesized that TV and movies do play a role in our social lives and when TV and movies are absent we will interact more with others.

Next, we needed to show how TV and movies affect our social lives. Beginning April 4, we stopped watching TV and movies for one month and recorded the results in journals. We made it a point to write whenever we felt an impact of the absence of television or movies on our lives. This process would allow us to see how prevalent TV is in our lives and how we are affected when we try to avoid it. This was the most important part of our research because we experienced what life is like without TV in a TV-watching society. We had many fascinating results. Throughout our experiment we often felt separated from our families and friends because of their habitual television viewing. One instance in particular is that when Adrienne comes home from work at night she and her dad usually watch TV for about an hour before bed. This is the time they talk about their days and anything else going on. During the TV prohibition, Adrienne didn't sit with her dad because he continued the nightly ritual without her. They rarely talked and became distant from each other.

Jake had a similar experience. While visiting his girlfriend he found himself doing many activities alone while she was away at rehearsal. Although aware of Jake's project, her family would sit around watching TV while Jake had to find non-TV alternatives such as working out, playing guitar, and staring at the wall.

Watching TV has become such a habit for most people that they watch it even when there are better things to do. In the case with Adrienne's dad, you would think that he would stop watching TV, if only for a short time, to talk with Adrienne before bed. In Jake's case, it would seem obvious that someone at his girlfriend's house would make an effort to stop watching TV and spend some time with Jake. Instead, these people continued to habitually watch their programs. This shows that habitual viewing affects the way everyone socializes. The people in our examples are affected because they aren't socializing with us or with each other. We are affected because the presence of television limits who we are able to socialize with.

We also found that we had trouble sleeping at night because we had become so accustomed to watching TV before bed. Adrienne had it especially hard for the first week because her nightly ritual was to fall asleep with the TV on. Without it, she tossed until three or four in the morning. She became irritable with others, which directly affected how she socialized. The irritability made it hard for her to deal with those around her including her research partner, Jake, who thought she was a "real bitch" during that week.

The results were not all bad. We found that we spent our time more constructively. Instead of zoning out to pointless shows, we read more, completed various art projects and conversed more with those around us. Adrienne spent more time studying and on other school projects. She got an A on her second psychology test during the anti-TV campaign in contrast to her first test score of a C. Jake used his new-found free time lifting weights and went up fifty pounds on his bench press.

Although we did spend our time more constructively it took Jake longer than Adrienne to figure out alternative activities. Adrienne finished the many projects she had begun and, because of TV, never had time to finish. It had appeared to her that she had no time, but in actuality the few hours she spent watching TV every day is what kept her from getting these things done. While Adrienne had a waiting list full of projects Jake had no unfinished work to complete so he had to create new projects. This proved difficult for him during the first week and caused him some frustration. He spent his time literally staring at walls and listening to the buzzing in his ears but eventually found an escape through playing the guitar and reading. As time passed, Adrienne finished her projects and found it hard to remain busy. She experienced similar feelings as Jake did in the beginning. Jake found it easier to not watch TV as time went on because he was creating things to do.

Watching less TV increased our quality of life and in turn improved how we socialize. We learned new things, used our creativity, expanded our minds, and Adrienne's house has never been cleaner. Our social lives improved because we created more ways of engaging others in our activities. Adrienne and her dad began painting their walls, a project that had been on hold for months. It was a way for them to socialize without having to constantly be in conversation. Painting took the place of TV.

Another positive result is that we talked to those around us more than we did when we watched TV. Jake and his buddy Mark usually meet at Mark's house and talk over the television. During the month-long restriction, Jake and Mark had conversations free from TV interruptions. Jake and Mark were more focused on the conversation and had better social interaction.

Now that we had our results, we needed to find out if they were consistent with others' experiences. We did this by surveying 100 college-age students at Normandale Community College and comparing their viewing habits with the nation's scale. According to the *Kill Your TV* Web site, the nation watches 4.5 hours of TV a day. We found that Normandale students watched an average of 3.21 hours a day, which is significantly less time than the national survey showed. This difference can be explained by the sample used. Because Normandale is a community college, the students spend a lot of time commuting to school, then to work, which leaves little time for them to be at home watching TV or movies. If we broadened our sample to include similar-aged people who attend universities or don't go to school at all we would most likely find that the average number of hours viewed would increase because they have more spare time.

We completed our project by gathering a group of ten people together to abstain from TV and movies for one week and record their reactions in a questionnaire. This was essential to increase the credibility of our month-long research project. We needed a wider range of people who had similar experiences, such as feeling excluded from their social group, to strengthen our point. When we found those people in the sample had similar feelings we could extend our hypothesis to a wider range of people.

The most difficult part of this operation was finding volunteers to abstain from watching TV. We assumed that finding people to participate would be very simple because our surveys showed that the average Normandale student only watches about 3.21 hours of TV per day. In reality, it proved very difficult. When given the challenge, people would tell us how easy it would be to abstain from TV and movies, because they watched so little anyway, but when asked to participate they would decline. This shows that even though Normandale students watch little

TV, compared to the national average, the TV and movies they do watch they hold so dear that they won't give them up.

Because of the difficulty in finding Normandale students to do this project, we had to use outside sources, like family members and friends. These outside sources were supposed to help us increase the credibility of our one-month research but caused some experimental error because the test subjects for the survey and the one-week trial were not consistent. In addition, the questionnaires weren't as helpful as we had hoped they would be. Eight out of ten participants failed to complete the entire week without watching TV. Two failed after the first day. The two who made it through the week didn't have TVs. From these results we can assume that eight out of ten people can't go even a week without watching TV. This statement would be stronger if we had a larger sample and the project had been conducted for a longer period of time.

However, from our research we can establish that television and movies contribute greatly to how we socialize. The effects of this vary depending on what one wants to do with their time. TV can provide a relaxing getaway but usually inhibits us from socializing in other ways. We have concluded that TV has a negative effect on how we socialize. It prevents us from having quality conversations, prevents interaction with those around us, and causes us to waste our time.

Works Cited

Hardbeck, Daniel. *Kill Your TV*. 17 May 2001. *www.killyourtv.com.*

QUESTIONS FOR INQUIRY AND ACTION

1. Analyze Mulholland and Martin's paper as an example of a student research project. What kinds of projects could you develop for your own course? Are you allowed to do collaborative work in your courses? What would be appealing or discouraging about researching and writing collaboratively?

2. How would Mulholland and Martin converse with the television-watching narrator in Tony Earley's "Somehow Form a Family" in Chapter 6? In what ways do you think Mulholland and Martin would say that television affected that narrator's life?

3. Mulholland and Martin chose not to focus on the content of television shows but on the viewing time itself. Thus they are not making an argument about the beneficial or harmful elements of the popular culture of television. You might extend their work by exploring the social effects of watching different types of shows. Are some shows better than others in promoting social interaction or other desirable behaviors?

4. In this essay, Mulholland and Martin refer to the Kill Your TV Web site. The site encourages visitors to give up television for 30 days to see how much their lives will improve without it. Try the Kill Your TV challenge for yourself. Monitor your results by writing in your notebook whenever you miss watching TV. How does your life change when you are not watching TV?

Technorealism: An Overview

This overview and statement of principles was conceived by David Shenk, Steven Johnson, and Andrew Shapiro, and then developed through a collaboration of twelve technology writers. On March 12, 1998, the document was posted to the Technorealism Web site at www.technorealism.org. The site is maintained by the Historical Site Preservation Group.

In this heady age of rapid technological change, we all struggle to maintain our bearings. The developments that unfold each day in communications and computing can be thrilling and disorienting. One understandable reaction is to wonder: Are these changes good or bad? Should we welcome or fear them?

The answer is both. Technology is making life more convenient and enjoyable, and many of us healthier, wealthier, and wiser. But it is also affecting work, family, and the economy in unpredictable ways, introducing new forms of tension and distraction, and posing new threats to the cohesion of our physical communities.

Despite the complicated and often contradictory implications of technology, the conventional wisdom is woefully simplistic. Pundits, politicians, and self-appointed visionaries do us a disservice when they try to reduce these complexities to breathless tales of either high-tech doom or cyber-elation. Such polarized thinking leads to dashed hopes and unnecessary anxiety, and prevents us from understanding our own culture.

Over the past few years, even as the debate over technology has been dominated by the louder voices at the extremes, a new, more balanced consensus has quietly taken shape. This document seeks to articulate some of the shared beliefs behind that consensus, which we have come to call technorealism.

5   Technorealism demands that we think critically about the role that tools and interfaces play in human evolution and everyday life. Integral to this perspective is our understanding that the current tide of technological transformation, while important and powerful, is actually a continuation of waves of change that have taken place throughout history. Looking, for example, at the history of the automobile, television, or the telephone — not just the devices but the institutions they became — we see profound benefits as well as substantial costs. Similarly, we anticipate mixed blessings from today's emerging technologies, and expect to forever be on guard for unexpected consequences — which must be addressed by thoughtful design and appropriate use.

As technorealists, we seek to expand the fertile middle ground between techno-utopianism and neo-Luddism. We are technology "critics" in the same way, and for the same reasons, that others are food critics, art critics, or literary critics. We can be passionately optimistic about some technologies, skeptical and disdainful of others. Still, our goal is neither to champion nor dismiss technology, but rather to understand it and apply it in a manner more consistent with basic human values.

Below are some evolving basic principles that help explain technorealism.

Principles of Technorealism

1. Technologies are not neutral.

A great misconception of our time is the idea that technologies are completely free of bias — that because they are inanimate artifacts, they don't promote certain kinds of behaviors over others. In truth, technologies come loaded with both intended and unintended social, political, and economic leanings. Every tool provides its users with a particular manner of seeing the world and specific ways of interacting with others. It is important for each of us to consider the biases of various technologies and to seek out those that reflect our values and aspirations.

10 **2. The Internet is revolutionary, but not Utopian.**

The Net is an extraordinary communications tool that provides a range of new opportunities for people, communities, businesses, and government. Yet as cyberspace becomes more populated, it increasingly resembles society at large, in all its complexity. For every empowering or enlightening aspect of the wired life, there will also be dimensions that are malicious, perverse, or rather ordinary.

3. Government has an important role to play on the electronic frontier.

Contrary to some claims, cyberspace is not formally a place or jurisdiction separate from Earth. While governments should respect the rules and customs that have arisen in cyberspace, and should not stifle this new world with inefficient regulation or censorship, it is foolish to say that the public has no sovereignty over what an errant citizen or fraudulent corporation does online. As the representative of the people and the guardian of democratic values, the state has the right and responsibility to help integrate cyberspace and conventional society.

Technology standards and privacy issues, for example, are too important to be entrusted to the marketplace alone. Competing software firms have little interest in preserving the open standards that are essential to a fully functioning interactive network. Markets encourage innovation, but they do not necessarily insure the public interest.

15 **4. Information is not knowledge.**

All around us, information is moving faster and becoming cheaper to acquire, and the benefits are manifest. That said, the proliferation of data is also a serious challenge, requiring new measures of human discipline and skepticism. We must not confuse the thrill of acquiring or distributing information quickly with the more daunting task of converting it into knowledge and wisdom. Regardless of how advanced our computers become, we should never use them as a substitute for our own basic cognitive skills of awareness, perception, reasoning, and judgment.

5. **Wiring the schools will not save them.**

The problems with America's public schools—disparate funding, social pro-motion, bloated class size, crumbling infrastructure, lack of standards—have almost nothing to do with technology. Consequently, no amount of tech-nology will lead to the educational revolution prophesied by President Clin-ton and others. The art of teaching cannot be replicated by computers, the Net, or by "distance learning." These tools can, of course, augment an already high-quality educational experience. But to rely on them as any sort of panacea would be a costly mistake.

6. **Information wants to be protected.**

20   It's true that cyberspace and other recent developments are challenging our copyright laws and frameworks for protecting intellectual property. The answer, though, is not to scrap existing statutes and principles. Instead, we must update old laws and interpretations so that information receives roughly the same protection it did in the context of old media. The goal is the same: to give authors sufficient control over their work so that they have an incentive to create, while maintaining the right of the public to make fair use of that information. In neither context does information want "to be free." Rather, it needs to be protected.

7. **The public owns the airwaves; the public should benefit from their use.**

The recent digital spectrum giveaway to broadcasters underscores the corrupt and inefficient misuse of public resources in the arena of technology. The cit-izenry should benefit and profit from the use of public frequencies, and should retain a portion of the spectrum for educational, cultural, and public access uses. We should demand more for private use of public property.

8. **Understanding technology should be an essential component of global citizenship.**

In a world driven by the flow of information, the interfaces—and the under-lying code—that make information visible are becoming enormously pow-erful social forces. Understanding their strengths and limitations, and even participating in the creation of better tools, should be an important part of being an involved citizen. These tools affect our lives as much as laws do, and we should subject them to a similar democratic scrutiny.

Since March 12, 1998, over 2500 people have signed their names to these principles. [To see] the current list of names, . . . [to] add your own, [or to contact] the drafters of the document . . . , [visit] http://www.technorealism.org.

▓ QUESTIONS FOR INQUIRY AND ACTION ▓

1. The authors argue that we should neither praise nor criticize technology too much. Rather we should "understand it and apply it in a manner more consistent with basic human values." What are these basic human values for you? How does your use of technology relate to these values?

2. Technology influences our behavior by shaping how we learn about and interact within our communities. List all the technologies that influence your daily life. Using specific examples, discuss how they shape your views and behaviors. Are they enhancing your own potential as a human being?

3. "We must not confuse," the authors write, "the thrill of acquiring and distributing information quickly with the more daunting task of converting it into knowledge and wisdom." Plagiarism, particularly copying information from Internet sites without acknowledging the source, would seem just one example of this confusion. What can education communities do to discourage plagiarism and promote the development of knowledge and wisdom?

4. The authors argue that the Internet is complex. Spend one hour surfing the Internet. Keep a record of what you find that is "empowering or enlightening" and what is "malicious, perverse, or rather ordinary." Do you see a need for greater control over Internet content to protect citizens?

CASE STUDY

A Hitchhiker's Guide to the Blogosphere:
Blogs and the Standards of Professional Journalism

Lev Grossman

Meet Joe Blog: *Why are more and more people getting their news from amateur websites called blogs? Because they're fast, funny, and totally biased.*

Lev Grossman writes for Entertainment Weekly, Lingua Franca, *the* New York Times, Time Out New York, Salon, *and the* Village Voice. *He is also the author of the novels* Codex *(2004) and* Warp *(1997). The article "Meet Joe Blog" appeared in the June 21, 2004, edition of* Time *magazine.*

A few years ago, Mathew Gross, 32, was a free-lance writer living in tiny Moab, Utah. Rob Malda, 28, was an underperforming undergraduate at a small Christian college in Michigan. Denis Dutton, 60, was a professor of philosophy in faraway Christchurch, New Zealand. Today they are some of the most influential media personalities in the world. You can be one too.

Gross, Malda and Dutton aren't rich or famous or even conspicuously good-looking. What they have in common is that they all edit blogs: amateur websites that provide news, information and, above all, opinions to rapidly growing and devoted audiences drawn by nothing more than a shared interest or two and the sheer magnetism of the editor's personality. Over the past five years, blogs have gone from an obscure and, frankly, somewhat nerdy fad to a genuine alternative to mainstream news outlets, a shadow media empire that is rivaling networks and newspapers in power and influence. Which raises the question: Who are these folks anyway? And what exactly are they doing to the established pantheon of American media?

Not that long ago, blogs were one of those annoying buzz words that you could safely get away with ignoring. The word blog—it works as both noun and verb—is short for Web log. It was coined in 1997 to describe a website where you could post daily scribblings, journal-style, about whatever you like—mostly critiquing and linking to other articles online that may have sparked your thinking. Unlike a big media outlet, bloggers focus their efforts on narrow topics, often rising to become de facto watchdogs and self-proclaimed experts. Blogs can be about anything: politics, sex, baseball, haiku, car repair. There are blogs about blogs.

Big whoop, right? But it turns out some people actually have interesting thoughts on a regular basis, and a few of the better blogs began drawing sizable audiences. Blogs multiplied and evolved, slowly becoming conduits for legitimate news and serious thought. In 1999 a few companies began offering free make-your-own-blog software, which turbocharged the phenomenon. By 2002, Pyra Labs, which makes software for creating blogs, claimed 970,000 users.

5   Most of America couldn't have cared less. Until December 2002, that is, when bloggers staged a dramatic show of force. The occasion was Strom Thurmond's 100th birthday party, during which Trent Lott made what sounded like a nostalgic reference to Thurmond's past segregationist leanings. The mainstream press largely glossed over the incident, but when regular journalists bury the lead, bloggers dig it right back up. "That story got ignored for three, four, five days by big papers and the TV networks while blogs kept it alive," says Joshua Micah Marshall, creator of talkingpointsmemo.com, one of a handful of blogs that stuck with the Lott story.

Mainstream America wasn't listening, but Washington insiders and media honchos read blogs. Three days after the party, the story was on *Meet the Press*. Four days afterward, Lott made an official apology. After two weeks, Lott was out as Senate majority leader, and blogs had drawn their first blood. Web journalists like Matt Drudge (drudgereport.com) had already demonstrated a certain crude effectiveness—witness l'affaire Lewinsky—but this was something different: bloggers were offering reasoned, forceful arguments that carried weight with the powers that be.

Blogs act like a lens, focusing attention on an issue until it catches fire, but they can also break stories. On April 21, a 34-year-old blogger and writer from Arizona named Russ Kick posted photographs of coffins containing the bodies of soldiers killed in Iraq and Afghanistan and of Columbia astronauts. The military zealously guards images of service members in coffins, but Kick pried the photos free with a Freedom of Information Act (FOIA) request. "I read the news constantly," says Kick, "and when I see a story about the government refusing to release public documents, I automatically file an FOIA request for them." By April 23 the images had gone from Kick's blog, thememory hole.org, to the front page of newspapers across the country. Kick was soon getting upwards of 4 million hits a day.

What makes blogs so effective? They're free. They catch people at work, at their desks, when they're alert and thinking and making decisions. Blogs are fresh and often seem to be miles ahead of the mainstream news. Bloggers put up new stuff every day, all day, and there are thousands of them. How are you going to keep anything secret from a thousand Russ Kicks? Blogs have voice and personality. They're human. They come to us not from some mediagenic anchorbot on an air-conditioned sound stage, but from an individual. They represent—no, they are—the voice of the little guy.

And the little guy is a lot smarter than big media might have you think. Blogs showcase some of the smartest, sharpest writing being published. Bloggers are unconstrained by such journalistic conventions as good taste, accountability and objectivity—and that can be a good thing. Accusations of media bias are thick on the ground these days, and Americans are tired of it. Blogs don't pretend to be neutral: they're gleefully, unabashedly biased, and that makes them a lot more fun. "Because we're not trying to sell magazines or papers, we can afford to assail our readers," says Andrew Sullivan, a contributor to TIME and the editor of andrewsullivan.com. "I don't have the pressure of an advertising executive telling me to lay off. It's incredibly liberating."

10   Some bloggers earn their bias the hard way—in the trenches. Military bloggers, or milbloggers in Net patois, post vivid accounts of their tours of Baghdad, in prose covered in fresh flop sweat and powder burns, illustrated with digital photos. "Jason," a National Guardsman whose blog is called justanothersoldier.com, wrote about wandering through one of Saddam Hussein's empty palaces. And Iraqis have blogs: a Baghdad blogger who goes by Salam Pax (dear_raed.blogspot.com) has parlayed his blog into a book and a movie deal. Vietnam was the first war to be televised; blogs bring Iraq another scary step closer to our living rooms.

But blogs are about much more than war and politics. In 1997 Malda went looking for a "site that mixed the latest word about a new sci-fi movie with news about open-source software. I was looking for a site that didn't exist," Malda says, "so I built it." Malda and a handful of co-editors run slashdot.org full time, and he estimates that 300,000 to 500,000 people read the site daily. Six years ago, a philosophy professor in New Zealand named Denis Dutton started the blog Arts & Letters Daily (artsandlettersdaily.com) to create a website "where people could go daily for a dose of intellectual stimulation." Now the site draws more than 100,000 readers a month. Compare that with, say, the *New York Review of Books,* which has a circulation of 115,000. The tail is beginning to wag the blog.

Blogs are inverting the cozy media hierarchies of yore. Some bloggers are getting press credentials for this summer's Republican Convention. Three years ago, a 25-year-old Chicagoan named Jessa Crispin started a blog for serious readers called bookslut.com. "We give books a better chance," she says. "The *New York Times* Book Review is so boring. We take each book at face value. There's no politics behind it." Crispin's apartment is overflowing with free books from publishers desperate for a mention. As for the *Times,* it's scrutinizing the blogging phenomenon for its own purposes. In January the Gray Lady started up Times on the Trail, a campaign-news website with some decidedly bloglike features; it takes the bold step of linking to articles by competing newspapers, for example. "The *Times* cannot ignore this. I don't think any big media can ignore this," says Len Apcar, editor in chief of the New York Times on the Web.

In a way, blogs represent everything the Web was always supposed to be: a mass medium controlled by the masses, in which getting heard depends solely on having something to say and the moxie to say it.

Unfortunately, there's a downside to this populist sentiment—that is, innocent casualties bloodied by a medium that trades in rumor, gossip and speculation without accountability. Case in point: Alexandra Polier, better known as the Kerry intern. Rumors of Polier's alleged affair with presidential candidate Senator John

Kerry eventually spilled into the blogosphere earlier this year. After Drudge head-lined it in February, the blabbing bloggers soon had the attention of tabloid jour-nalists, radio talk-show hosts and cable news anchors. Trouble is, the case was exceedingly thin, and both Kerry and Polier vehemently deny it. Yet the Internet smolders with it to this day.

15   Some wonder if the backbiting tide won't recede as blogs grow up. The trend now is for more prominent sites to be commercialized. A Manhattan entrepre-neur named Nick Denton runs a small stable of bloggers as a business by selling advertising on their sites. So far they aren't showing detectible signs of editorial corruption by their corporate masters—two of Denton's blogs, gawker.com and wonkette.com, are among the most corrosively witty sites on the Web—but they've lost their amateur status forever.

We may be in the golden age of blogging, a quirky Camelot moment in Inter-net history when some guy in his underwear with too much free time can take down a Washington politician. It will be interesting to see what role blogs play in the upcoming election. Blogs can be a great way of communicating, but they can keep people apart too. If I read only those of my choice, precisely tuned to my political biases and you read only yours, we could end up a nation of political solipsists, vacuum sealed in our private feedback loops, never exposed to new argu-ments, never having to listen to a single word we disagree with.

Howard Dean's campaign blog, run by Mathew Gross, may be the perfect example of both the potential and the pitfalls of high-profile blogging. At its peak, blogforamerica.com drew 100,000 visitors a day, yet the candidate was beaten badly in the primaries. Still, the Dean model isn't going away. When another polit-ical blogger, who goes by the nom de blog Atrios, set up a fund-raising link on his site for Kerry, he raised $25,000 in five days.

You can't blog your way into the White House, at least not yet, but blogs are America thinking out loud, talking to itself, and heaven help the candidate who isn't listening.

—With reporting by Maryanne Murray Buechner/New York and Leslie Whitaker/Chicago

HOW TO FIND YOUR KIND OF BLOG

To navigate the blogosphere, you need the right tools. Here are five sites that make it easy to find, organize and keep tabs on your favorite bloggers:

—Kinja.com Launched April 1, this is one of the best ways to sample and auto-matically subscribe to a wide range of blogs. The site tracks more than 50,000 blogs, divided into 12 categories, from movies to politics to baseball. Click on a subject and up pops a listing of short excerpts from current postings, with the most recent ones listed first. See a blog you like? Simply click on the + button to have it added to your digest, which reads like a personalized online newspaper of new posts from your favorite blogs.

—*Bloglines.com* This site lets you organize your blogs in much the same way that your browser sorts its bookmarks. After creating a free account, you choose the blogs you want to track. There are more than 100,000 to pick from, including headlines from such mainstream sites as *NYTimes.com, Slate.com* and Yahoo. Each time you log in, the site notifies you how many new postings there are in your favorite blogs and lets you skim headlines. Click on a headline to read the full post.

—*Feedster.com* Regular search engines have trouble keeping pace with the constantly spewing bloggers. Enter Feedster, a search engine dedicated to indexing and finding the particular blogs you are after. Scanning more than 500,000 sources, it presents you with either the most recent posts or the most commented-on blogs (determined by analyzing how many other sites or blogs link to it), whichever you choose. Feedster also lets you save a customized search on, say, petunias and check back hourly or daily to see what the latest postings have to say about them.

—*Technorati.com* Because blogs tend to be updated more frequently than regular websites, they are a great way to find out what people are talking about online at any given moment. Technorati taps into this phenomenon by listing the top 10 current events, books and general news that people are blogging about. Last Friday afternoon those included Ronald Reagan's legacy, the new David Sedaris book and the prisoner abuse in Iraq at Abu Ghraib.

—*Blogdex.net* Created by the M.I.T. Media Laboratory, Blogdex presents the most contagious, or fastest spreading, ideas in the Web-log community. If bloggers are pointing en masse to your posting about, say, the situation in Iraq, chances are you'll come up high in the ranking. At press time, the most contagious information, according to Blogdex, was the death of singer Ray Charles and a list of "10 Super Foods You Should NEVER Eat!"

—*By Anita Hamilton*

WRITING STYLE

WRITING A NEWS ARTICLE

In Chapter 5, we learned that news articles inform the public of current events and issues affecting the community. Lev Grossman's "Meet Joe Blog" article for *Time* magazine offers a good example; it informs people about the growing number and influence of Web logs. As you read Grossman's piece, identify those features you would need to follow in writing your own news article. Here are some suggestions to get you started:

• *Write to match a newspaper's or magazine's needs.* Newspapers and magazines usually have set sections and assignments, so beginning news writers may have difficulty simply submitting something for publication. You should probably talk to the editor before writing a news article for publication to see if the subject would fit in their established sections and preferred subjects.

continued on next page

- *Write to represent your subject thoroughly and objectively.* News articles are often the first place readers learn of important issues so writers need to give them a thorough understanding of the journalist's basic questions: What is happening? Who is affected? When and where does it occur? How does it happen and why?

- *Write to complement the way newspapers or magazines are printed.* Newspapers and magazines are formatted in particular ways. For example, newspapers organize text into narrow columns, so you should keep your paragraphs short—only a few sentences each—to avoid creating thick blocks of text on the page. Also, you should avoid long, complex sentences. Long sentences are harder to follow when they are broken up across several lines.

- *Write to complement the way newspapers and magazines are read.* People often read newspapers and magazines in their spare moments—when eating breakfast, waiting in a doctor's office, or riding the bus. As a result, you should keep your writing active and direct, so readers can readily understand your points without having to work to decipher your prose. Using a few select details or descriptions also helps readers to see the events or issues for themselves.

- *Write to hook and keep readers' interest.* Because newspaper and magazine readers have many articles to choose from in any particular issue, you might try introductions that grab their attention (e.g., use visual details to put readers at the scene of a crisis). You might also include narratives, engaging quotes, shocking statistics, and so on in different places within the article to refuel readers' interest. For example, if background information bogs down your news article, you might provide that information through quotes from local experts, or you might move the information to a sidebar.

The Blogger Manifesto (Or, Do Weblogs Make the Internet Better or Worse?)

The following manifesto was posted by "Ryan C" to PeriodicDiversions.com *on September 16, 2003.* PeriodicDiversions *is a blog hosting several writers and maintained by Ulmo Stanton. The site hosts commentary on politics, society, technology, and other subjects, including reviews of new books.*

The promises of weblogging are manifest. As more Internet users become contributors to, as well as browsers of, the Internet, our sources of information become more diffuse and complete, and the experience of the Internet's casual reader becomes enhanced as the presence of weblogs makes it a more efficient place to gather information. The Internet and indeed media become democratized, and the community benefits.

The advent of the weblog, however, introduces the perilous prospect of a widening Internet wasteland as weblog authors produce unwitting editorial content without proper journalistic sensibility. Weblog authors' focus on themselves rather than on their readers threatens to undermine the reasons why they created sites in the first place and the rest of us indulged their vanity in doing so.

Weblogs represent journalism for the everyman, and in many respects, they open up unique and valuable resources for Internet readers searching for obscure content. Unencumbered by editorial restraint, shareholders to appease, and article subjects and interviewees to pacify, weblogs offer fresh glimpses into what the casual reader might not ever encounter. It was the powerful-constituency-less blogger Matt Drudge who broke the Monica Lewinsky scandal, not the *New York Times*. Bloggers ensure content gets published that would never otherwise see the light of day. An Internet searcher for information on installing a "courtyard satellite tripod," for instance, might rely upon the experiences another Internet user has had in installing one for help in doing so, provided that the latter user published the fruits of his toils. Blogs allow us to share our obscure experiences and travails so that others might benefit. . . .

The central problem with the weblog as a mechanism for delivery of information is that authors of weblogs think of them as journals, while readers conceive them as magazines. The disparity creates an Internet that becomes simultaneously more and less useful to its user. . . .

Nobody Gives a Shit about What You Had for Breakfast

Weblog authors are natural extroverts, mavens who "traffic in information."[1] They might rightly be described as people who care more about sharing information than they do about considering whether the information should ever be shared. And while the existence of blogger-mavens ensures that plenty of information gets made public that would otherwise be kept private, their proclivity for sharing *everything* makes for an information superhighway littered with the entrails of irrelevant roadkill and misleading signage. It is left to Internet readers and Google to sort it all out.

Unsophisticated weblog authors misunderstand how they bring value to the Internet community. They are enamored of the concept of writing a journal and opening it up for all their friends to see. They write about what interests them; they tell their friends to visit; they bask in the magnanimity of having contributed something to the Internet cosmos.

---

[1] *As described by Malcolm Gladwell, who wrote about mavens but not about their most public cadre, bloggers, in* The Tipping Point, *2000.*

This approach sabotages their content in several ways:

1. When you write a journal you know is going to be read by someone else, you tend to leave the most interesting details out.

10
2. Because of search engines, the authors' friends are not the only ones drawn to their weblogs.

3. Diary-minded authors write temporally specific articles (e.g., "Next week this will happen"), making them almost instantly obsolete and rendering a site's archives completely meaningless and irrelevant except as, well, an old diary.

4. Most of what people have to say is much less interesting than they think it is. By definition, a democratized Internet is going to be populated mostly with average authors writing about average things.

Thus potentially inspired content becomes eviscerated, leaving behind only the banal, stale, and trite.

Publish or Perish

Even with the best of intentions, weblog authors end up producing wastelands of sites, devoid of meaningful content. The typical home page of a weblog consists of a catchy title followed by a listing of postings in reverse chronological order (newest first). The software pushes these postings off the home page and into the archives after a defined period of time (usually a week or so), ensuring that the home page is a fresh, constantly changing repository of the weblog author's self-perceived wisdom.

15
Unfortunately, the constantly fresh home page forces authors, lest their home pages become embarrassingly empty, to churn out content at such a frantic pace that its quality invariably diminishes (weblogging, for most, is not a full-time job but rather an extracurricular exercise in vanity). Weblog authors become slaves to software that should serve them, their desires for pretty home pages compromising their sites' content and ultimately their viability.

Authors who conceive of their sites as "open diaries" and who capitulate to the pressures of the emptying home page do themselves and their readers a disservice by dumping filler content into their sites. For some, this takes the form of writing about the most uninteresting things imaginable; for others, it manifests itself in the inclusion of links to other sites, surrounded by some uninspired commentary on why the author found what's at the other end of the link interesting (incidentally, again, it usually is not). If weblog authors thought of their sites more as magazines and less as diaries, as content rather than narcissism, the allure of using links to create filler content would become less compelling. Do you ever see an article on the front page of the *New York Times* in which the journalist wrote nothing more than, "You should check out what the *San Diego Tribune* wrote about issue X this morning"? If you are still wondering why not, ponder the difference between the *Times* and most weblogs: people read the *New York Times*. Why? Because the *Times* conceives of itself as something for its readers to read, not as something for its authors to write.

Besides content people actually want to read, journals such as the *New York Times* offer something else almost no weblog does: editors. In the absence thereof, a vain weblog author who succumbs to the pressures of the emptying home page falls victim to bad journalistic habits that are only exacerbated by the immediacy of Internet publishing: writing too fast, without thinking; publishing without peer review, or indeed usually without spellchecking; writing self-important and irrelevant articles that fill up space but not readers' minds.

Beyond the Banal

A responsible critic might point out that not every weblog strives to be the *New York Times*. The promise of weblogs is to round out the variety of information available to an Internet reader — to fill in the nooks and crannies of information available, if you will, and to make the Internet a more efficient research tool by voting with their links for its best content (the votes are collected and arbited by sites like Google and Blogdex).

Weblogs hold a promise to contribute something unique to the Internet. But for every Matt Drudge, there are fifty Sapnas. If weblogs are to enhance the Internet itself — not just authors' misplaced vanities, weblog creators should recognize that their contributions to the Internet are important to a world of curious readers and take them — and, by implication, themselves — much more seriously than the exercises in vain banality their sites have become. There are, after all, only so many anonymous voyeurs out there who care about what you had for breakfast.

Bonnie A. Nardi, Diane J. Schiano,
Michelle Gumbrecht, Luke Swartz
Why We Blog

"Why We Blog" is the report of a collaborative research project among scholars and students from diverse technological backgrounds. Bonnie Nardi, coauthor of Information Ecologies: Using Technology with Heart *(1998), is a faculty member at the University of California, Irvine's School of Information & Computer Science. She is currently working with Victor Kaptelinin on the book* Acting with Technology: Activity Theory and Interaction Design. *Diane Schiano is a consultant in several technology-related areas including interface design, information architecture, user experience research, user profiling, and ethnographic interviewing and observing. Michelle Gumbrecht is pursuing a Ph.D. in cognitive psychology at Stanford University, and Luke Schwartz is a student at the U.S. Navy's Nuclear Power School in Charleston, S.C. Their essay appeared in* Communications of the ACM *(Association for Computing Machinery) in 2004.*

Blogging is sometimes viewed as a new, grassroots form of journalism and a way to shape democracy outside the mass media and conventional party politics[3]. Blog sites devoted to politics and punditry, as well as to sharing technical developments (such as www.slashdot.org), receive thousands of hits a day. But the vast majority of blogs are written by ordinary people for much smaller audiences. Here, we report the results of an ethnographic investigation of blogging in a sample of ordinary bloggers. We investigated blogging as a form of personal communication and expression, with a specific interest in uncovering the range of motivations driving individuals to create and maintain blogs.

Blogs combine the immediacy of up-to-the-minute posts, latest first, with a strong sense of the author's personality, passions, and point of view. We investigated blogging practice to help determine why people blog, finding that bloggers have many varied reasons for letting the world in on what they think.

We conducted in-depth interviews with bloggers primarily in and around Stanford University, audiotaping in-person and phone interviews from April to June 2003. The interviews were conversational in style but covered a fixed set of questions about the informants' blogs, blogging habits, thoughts on blogging, and use of other communication media as compared to blogs. We interviewed most of them at least twice, with follow-up sessions in person or by phone, email, or instant messaging. We read their blogs throughout the time we were writing this article. To identify motivations for blogging, we analyzed the content of the blogs and the interview data. Interview follow-ups helped us clarify puzzling questions and gain additional understanding of the reasons for blogging.

We interviewed 23 people altogether, 16 men and 7 women, aged 19 to 60. All lived in California or New York and were well-educated, middle-class adults in school or employed in knowledge work or artistic pursuits. We developed the sample by searching Google's Stanford portal www.google.com/univ/stanford/) for "blog" and for "Weblog," creating an initial list of Stanford-hosted blogs. We also contacted several bloggers we knew personally. We then snowballed the sample, asking informants for the names of other bloggers to contact. We used pseudonyms when discussing specific informants and obtained permission for all quotes and images.

Blogging Practices

5 The informants typically found blogs through other blogs they were reading, through friends or colleagues, and through inclusion of the blog link in an instant message profile or homepage. Most blog pages reserve space for linking to other blogs.

Some bloggers post multiple times a day, others as infrequently as once a month. Bloggers sometimes poured out their feelings or ideas and sometimes struggled to find something to say. One informant stopped blogging when he inadvertently hurt the feelings of a friend he had mentioned. He took down his blog and later put up another, this time without advertising the URL in his instant messenger profile. Other bloggers experienced blog burnout and stopped blogging from time to time.

We found tremendous diversity in blog content, even in our limited sample. On the serious side, Evan, a graduate student in genetics, posted commentaries on science and health, covering such topics as AIDS, heart disease, science education, and health care policy. On the other end of the scale—blog-as-personal-revelation—Lara, an undergraduate, wrote: "I've come to realize rather recently that I can't regret that I didn't form any romantic attachments [my phrases for such things are always overly formal to the point of stupidity, and I don't know why or what to use instead, but bear with me] because, at the end of the day, a boyfriend would have taken away from all the awesome things that happened with people in the dorm, and all the great friendships that I formed and that will hopefully continue after this year (if you're reading this blog, you're most likely one of those people). Thinking back to the last couple of years, it's pretty obvious that I was really stifled by my insular, extremely time-consuming group of friends, and part of my discontent stemmed from a relative dearth of fun, casual relationships with interesting people. My friends are great, but they are also tightly knit to the point of being incestuous, and when I hang out with them it is difficult to maintain the time and energy necessary to play with other people."

This post encouraged a future connection to friends while Lara worked through her emotional issues.

Most bloggers are acutely aware of their readers, even in confessional blogs, calibrating what they should and should not reveal. Although Lara's post appears highly personal, she also kept a separate paper diary. Many bloggers have personal codes of ethics dictating what goes into their blogs (such as never criticize friends or express political opinions that are openly inflammatory). Not that bloggers eschew controversy—quite the opposite—but they express themselves in light of their audience. One blogger of liberal political opinions sometimes wrote posts she knew would irritate her Republican uncle. She was tactful enough to keep lines of communication open. Another blogger kept his writing suitable for a family audience: "Yeah . . . My mom mentioned something that was in [my blog] . . . my grandma reads it, too; she just got the Internet . . . It means that I kind of have to censor—less cursing and stuff."

10   Bloggers sometimes poured out their feelings or ideas and sometimes struggled to find something to say.

Blogging thus provides scope for an enormous variety of expression within a simple, restricted format.

Motivations

Previous survey research[1, 6] examined some reasons people blog but without the rich data of in-depth interviews. In our sample, we discovered five major motivations for blogging: documenting one's life; providing commentary and opinions; expressing deeply felt emotions; articulating ideas through writing; and forming and maintaining community forums. This list is not exhaustive, covering all bloggers, but does describe our sample. These motivations are by no means mutually exclusive and might come into play simultaneously.

Blogs to "document my life". Many informants blogged to record activities and events. Harriet, a Stanford graduate student, blogged to "document my life" for her family and friends in Iceland, as well as for her fellow students. Blogs were used by many as a record to inform and update others of their activities and whereabouts, often including photos. Depending on the audience and content, a blog could be a public journal, a photo album, or a travelogue.

Don, a technology consultant, called blogs "belogs" because he felt blogging is used to "log your being." This took a serious turn for him when his wife became gravely ill. He took over her blog to document the progress of her illness and treatment through text and photos. Blogging was an important way for him to communicate during this time: "[Blogging is helpful] when people's lives are compromised in some way . . . when [my wife] was sick, [I] was going through [the] hospital with the lens of how can I share this with others?"

15　　　Keeping family and friends abreast of life events is a key use of blogging. Katie, a graduate student, said she blogged to relate her life to others by telling her own personal story in close to real time. Even Evan, whose blog was primarily about scientific subjects, let his friends know of his whereabouts and sometimes to report a cold or other minor disturbance in his life. Arthur, a Stanford professor, and several others, found blogging a superior alternative to mass email: "[I started blogging] to communicate with friends and family, as well as [for] professional connections. It's easier than sending lots of email. I'll just put it on my blog."

Why use blogs instead of just sending email? Arthur felt blogging involves less overhead (such as addressing) than email, with added scope for other communication, including "rants" and speculation. Several bloggers emphasized the broadcast nature of blogging; they put out information, and no one need respond unless they wished to. Blogs are not intrusive. No one is "forced to pay attention," observed Lara, as they are with email. Reading is voluntary, when convenient.

Why not Web pages? A blog is a kind of Web page. What drew writers and readers alike to blogs is the rhythm of frequent, usually brief posts, with the immediacy of reverse chronological order. Writers could put up something short and sweet, expecting their audience would check in regularly. Readers knew they would be likely to get fresh news of friends, family, and colleagues in the convenient format of the blog, with no work-related email or the distractions often found on a homepage. Several informants saw homepages as more "static" than blogs, more formal and carefully considered, and somewhat less authentic. Jack, a poet and avid blogger, said, "[With a Web page] you don't hear their voice in the same way."

Blogs as commentary. Our bloggers found their voices by using blogs to express their opinions. While blogs are often portrayed as a breakthrough form of democratic self-expression, the darker side of the stereotype casts blogs as indulgent chatter of little interest to anyone but the blogger. Many of our informants were sensitive about this characterization and emphasized they blogged to comment on topics they found pertinent and important. A blog, said one, can be "a point of view, not just chatter."

Journey into the swamp: where I end and you begin, an individually authored blog focusing on the author's daily life and her thoughts on literature and pop culture.

Sam, a technology consultant, was knowledgeable about information technology and politics in developing countries. He started blogging to comment on a conference he attended but then decided to devote his blog to technology in developing countries: "[My blog started as] . . . a critique on [a] . . . conference called World Summit on the Information Society, which was a project that began a few years ago by the International Telecommunications Union . . . I was kind of interested in the way people reacted to it, putting a lot of resources into this conference, so I started tracking that, and I got very discouraged with . . . what was going on. So I just switched to . . . information technology in developing countries as a theme [for my blog], so that's really about all I'll . . . write about, looking at it . . . from a critical standpoint."

20   Part of the allure of blogs is the easy way they move between the personal and the profound. Alan, a historian of science, started a post by documenting his life, describing an incident in which his daughter wanted to watch a *Sesame Street* video clip. He added commentary on how "DVDs make it very easy to treat movies not as whole works, but as collections of scenes." He ended the post with a discussion of John Locke's worries about the way numbering biblical verses would change people's perceptions of the Bible (with a link to further discussion on Locke). Alan's post integrated comments on popular trends, works by other authors, relevant links, and personal experience.

Arthur, a humanities professor, explained why he blogged, saying: "I guess I'm an amateur rock and cultural critic. I also comment on things that I'd be embarrassed to email to others. I mean [they would think], 'Why do I care?' On the blog, you can be an amateur rock critic."

Blogging provided an outlet for expressing a point of view on topics the authors considered much more than just chatter.

Blogs as catharsis. Several of our informants viewed blogging as an outlet for thoughts and feelings. Their content was sometimes patently emotional. Lara described hers as "me working out my own issues." Undercurrents of more subtle but deeply felt emotions fueled other blogs. Jack started blogging around the time of the start of the Iraq war in March 2003, because, despite attending demonstrations and supporting anti-war politicians, he felt "futile" and that "no one was listening." Vivian, an attorney, called her blog "Shout," writing about such topics as the misapplication of the death penalty in the U.S. justice system.

Blogs helped explore issues the authors felt "obsessive" or "passionate" about. Blogs gave people a place to "shout," or express themselves by writing to an audience of sometimes total strangers, sometimes their best friends and colleagues and family members.

25 The format of frequent posts, diary-style, was both outlet and stimulus for working through personal issues. A blog often serves as a relief valve, a place to "get closure out of writing," as Lara said of a post on the death of her grandfather. Another claimed, "I just needed to, like, get it out there." Others needed to "let off steam."

Blog as muse. Still others found they could "get it out there" in a more constructive manner through what previous research termed "thinking with computers"[7]. Evan liked blogging because for him it was "thinking by writing." He wanted to see if he really had anything to say about what he had been reading in the news and in scholarly journals. Blogging let him test his ideas by writing them down for an audience. Alan said, "I am one of those people for whom writing and thinking are basically synonymous." His blog "forced" him to keep writing, a discipline he deemed important for his work. Jack noted that as a graduate student, "nobody wants to hear from me yet." For the moment, blogging gave him a small audience and a chance to "prove to myself that I can do it," that is, write.

Jack, Evan, Alan, and Vivian observed that some of their posts might have a future life in magazine articles, scholarly research, or other conventional publications. Alan said scholars generate a tremendous amount of material that usually stays private but could actually be a public good if released and shared with a general-interest audience. Vivian saw her posts as "good fodder for . . . political arguments later on." Jack archived his posts himself because he wasn't sure how long they would last on the www.blogger.com Web site and felt that some of them would "continue to be interesting to me."

For those who think by writing, blogging provides two main benefits: an audience to shape the writing and an archive of potentially reusable posts. Most bloggers reported they had regular readers. They could direct their writing at them, solving the key problem of knowing for whom they were writing. Having readers helped keep the writing moving along, as bloggers knew their readers expected new posts.

Blogs as community forum. Some of our informants expressed their views to one another in community settings. One blog supported a community of poets.

Two supported educational communities. Another was devoted to a "collective" of people who exchanged political opinions. We also learned of workplace blogs supporting workgroups we could not investigate directly because they were proprietary. Workplace blogs are a form of communication we expect to see much more of soon, as people become more familiar with reading and writing blogs.

30   Rob, who taught a class called dorm.net/residential-rhetorics, focused the class blog on locating the "intersection of residence community and all electronic communication tools," noting: "We'll try to take advantage of the general nature of Weblogs as 'public journals' in using them for personal reflection, in the context of a learning community, on issues that arise in the course, both rhetorical and content-related."

He required students to conduct field studies, post weekly blogs on assigned topics, and read and comment on one another's posts. He hoped to "facilitate the building of the learning community by getting [students] in conversation with each other electronically." Students found that blogging created a sense of community that would be less likely to emerge in a conventional classroom setting.

Colleen, an academic technology specialist, created a blog for an undergraduate archaeology course. The professor posted periodic reports on a class project involving the cataloging of artifacts from a 19th century San Jose Chinatown site. This blog succeeded as a Web site but failed to generate a sense of community among the students. The professor and teaching assistants made most of the comments, the students almost none. The students were either not moved to comment or decided not to, given the lack of a course requirement. As with other electronic media, blogs in themselves are not sufficient for building a community.

The most authentic, grassroots blogging community we investigated was that of a group of poetry bloggers. Comments on blog posts flew back and forth on the blogs, in email, and in person. Jack belonged to a poetry community and kept a set of links to others' poetry blogs that "map[ped] a community," as he described it. The community generated "peer pressure" to post regularly because people regularly checked the blogs for new posts. Jack said there was "a kind of reciprocity expected because I read others' blogs, so I have to make my contribution."

This community changed over time. During the study, several poetry bloggers began to post original poems, although at first many considered it "egotistical." Jack changed his mind on the issue, and the community became his muse; his poems developed as a "conversation" between himself and other bloggers. Jack began posting poems about halfway through the study, though he had initially told us the blog was not a proper forum for poems. Later he said: "I . . . discovered that allowing myself to post poems was helping me write poems, since I could think of it as material for the blog to be immediately posted, as opposed to being stowed in a drawer somewhere."

35   Here, thinking by writing intersected with blogging as community forum.

Most bloggers are acutely aware of their readers, even in confessional blogs, calibrating what they should and should not reveal.

Part of the allure of blogs is the easy way they move between the personal and the profound.

Six Stanford students formed a political blog called "The Cardinal Collective." Its members were "selected to represent a political spectrum" by the students themselves. Only a few had met face-to-face; an invitation to participate depended on having interesting political opinions and writing skill, also as determined by the students themselves. The blog was also intended for a wider audience, since people were invited to subscribe. Some posts were linked to InstaPundit, a widely read political blog, opening a wider frame of public participation for the blog.

Various electronic media support communities[8], including chat[5], [11], group Web sites[2], listservs[9], and multi-user dimensions (MUDs) and MUD object-oriented technologies (MOOs)[10]. Chat, MUDs, and MOOs are forums for textual interaction but generally don't provide access to archives or photos. Web sites support rich information but are usually limited in terms of interactivity.

40   Listservs promote a higher level of interactivity than blogs. Blogs can be characterized as having limited interactivity[4], [6]. The modal number of comments in individually authored blogs has been found to be zero. Many of our informants liked the interaction-at-one-remove provided by blogs. Max said: "I feel like I can say something in the blog and then have it be sort of like my safety net. Whereas like in a more immediate and personal like form of impersonal digital communication . . . I would sort of have to face their reaction. Metaphorically speaking, anyway . . . two bad things that blogging does for me, anyway, endorses [are] laziness and cowardice."

10   Blogs combine information and modulated interactivity. Bloggers value that they can post and share their thoughts without the intensive feedback associated with other forms of communication.

Conclusion

In our sample, we found a range of motivations for blogging. Blog content was equally diverse, ranging from journals of daily activities to serious commentaries on important issues. Blogging is an unusually versatile medium, employed for everything from spontaneous release of emotion to archivable support of group collaboration and community. Our investigation is an early look at blogging as a mainstream use of the Internet. Much work must still be done in examining this flourishing phenomenon as it grows and changes.

References

[1]*Efimova, L. Blogs: The stickiness factor. Presented at Blog Talk: A European Conference on Weblogs (Vienna, May 23, 2003).*

[2]*Fischer, G. Communities of interest: Learning through the interaction of multiple knowledge systems. In* Proceedings of the 24th Annual Information Systems Research Seminar in Scandinavia *(Ulvik, Norway, 2001), 1–14.*

[3]*Gillmor, D. Making the news. E-Journal: News, Views, and a Silicon Valley Diary (Apr. 11, 2003); Weblog siliconvalley.com/column/dangillmor/archives/000924.shtml.*

[4]*Gumbrecht, M. Blogs as 'protected space.' Presented at the Workshop on the Weblogging Ecosystem: Aggregation, Analysis, and Dynamics (New York, May 17–22). ACM Press, New York, 2004.*
[5]*Handel, M. and Herbsleb, J. What is chat doing in the workplace?* In Proceedings of Computer Supported Cooperative Work 2002 *(New Orleans, Nov. 16–20). ACM Press, New York, 2002, 1–10.*
[6]*Herring, S., Scheidt, L., Bonus, S., and Wright, E. Bridging the gap: A genre analysis of Weblogs. In* Proceedings 37th Annual Hawaii International Conference on System Sciences *(Big Island, HI, Jan. 5–8, 2004).*
[7]*Mortensen, T. and Walker, J. Blogging thoughts: Personal publication as an online research tool. In* Researching ICTs in Context, A. Morrison, Ed. InterMedia Report, Oslo, Norway, 2002.
[8]*Nardi, B. Beyond bandwidth: Dimensions of connection in interpersonal communication. J. Comput.-Supp. Coop. Work (2005).*
[9]*Preece, J. Empathic communities: Balancing emotional and factual communication.* Interacting with Computers 12 *(1998), 63–77.*
[10]*Schiano, D. and White, S. The first noble truth of cyberspace: People are people (even when they MOO). In* Proceedings of CHI'98 Conference on Human Factors in Computing Systems *(Los Angeles, Apr. 18–23). ACM Press, New York, 1998, 352–359.*
[11]*Wellman, B. Designing the Internet for a networked society.* Commun. ACM 45, 5 (May 2002), 91–96.

▓ QUESTIONS FOR INQUIRY AND ACTION ▓

1. One argument in support of using technology like computers to store information, whether public or personal, is that it lasts. Unfortunately, advances in technology continually make current forms obsolete and inaccessible (consider the 5.25-inch floppy disk, the eight-track cassette tape, and laserdiscs). In addition, the increasing volume of information communities need to update makes it unlikely that we can ever deliver on the promise of a permanent archive. Write an essay in which you outline criteria by which we can decide what to preserve from the past and what to leave behind. Then, apply your criteria to some specific examples to show how these decisions would be made.

2. According to "The Blogger Manifesto," weblogs could diminish the Internet by producing "unwitting editorial content without proper journalistic sensibility." Create a list of journalistic standards for how things should be researched and presented to readers. Then, compare and contrast one or two examples of blogs and traditional news sources (e.g., a newspaper) to determine whether the manifesto's concerns are legitimate.

3. Bloggers are often drawn to obscure topics that traditional media sources ignore. Search through the blogs indexed at sites like Feedster.com, Bloglines.com, or Blogdex.net and report on whether this is true. Are there patterns to the subjects that interest bloggers?

4. Using the same index sites listed in question three, locate and explore sites where individuals present thoughts and experiences from their personal lives. Are these sites interesting, meaningful, or useful? Why do you think people have an interest in publicizing their personal lives, and why are so many people interested in reading about the lives of people they have never met?

5. Lev Grossman argues that bloggers are "unconstrained by such journalistic conventions as good taste, accountability, and objectivity—and that can be a good

thing." Write an essay in which you take a position on Grossman's argument. Use examples from existing blogs to support your points.

6. One quality of blogs, and Internet communities generally, is that they are self-selecting; you can choose where you want to go and with whom you want to interact. Critics of the Internet argue that these communities can encourage people to interact only with those who agree with them, skewing their sense of other communities, of news, and so on. Write an essay in which you take a position on this issue. Does the Internet encourage us to insulate ourselves from different people and viewpoints?

▦ CONTINUING THE CASE STUDY ▦
Can Blogs Uphold the Standards of Good Journalism, and Should They?

As Lev Grossman points out, bloggers have successfully introduced or focused attention on political issues, promoting further inquiry or action in other communities. You can continue exploring this case study by creating a blog of your own, either individually or as a class, to investigate a community issue. You can collect and annotate relevant books, articles, or Web sites; publish interviews with experts; deliver your own opinions on the issue; solicit discussion; link up to other blogs or sites also exploring the issue; and so on.

If you cannot access a blog provider, you might imitate the conventions of other blogs (e.g., daily or weekly postings organized in reverse chronological order) on your class's Web space or even in a text document (though knowing your comments are being publicly scrutinized should be part of the experience).

Keep the blog going for at least a week. Then, evaluate your coverage of this issue with the principles of responsible journalism listed under "A Statement of Shared Purpose" on the Journalism.org Web site (www.journalism.org). The site was created by the Project for Excellence in Journalism and the Committee of Concerned Journalists. You can access the Statement under "Professional Guidelines."

After you have evaluated your coverage, write an essay that reflects on the experience and answers the following questions:

1. Did the conventions of the technology affect how you inquired and communicated with others?

2. Did the blog format encourage you to be "fast, funny and totally biased" as Grossman suggests they can? Did your attitude undermine your ability to uphold the standards of good journalism?

3. Did you accomplish any social action through your blog? Did it positively or negatively impact conversations on this issue in other areas? Why or why not?

4. Will you maintain your blog or continue to participate in the class's blog? Why or why not? What does your decision say about the role of technology in your own life?

Credits

PHOTO CREDITS

Index